Paul Between
Damascus and Antioch

PAUL BETWEEN DAMASCUS AND ANTIOCH

The Unknown Years

Martin Hengel
and
Anna Maria Schwemer

Westminster John Knox Press
Louisville, Kentucky

Translated by John Bowden
from a so far unpublished text.

German text copyright © Martin Hengel
and Anna Maria Schwemer 1997

Translation © John Bowden 1997

Cover design by Alec Bartsch
Cover illustration: Saul before Samuel and the Prophets.
*Benjamin West, 1738–1820. American. The Huntington Library,
San Marino, California. Courtesy of SuperStock.*

First published 1997 by
SCM Press Ltd., London

First American Edition 1997
Published by Westminster John Knox Press
Louisville, Kentucky

This book is printed on acid-free paper that meets the
American National Standards Institute Z39.48 standard. ∞

PRINTED IN THE UNITED STATES OF AMERICA
97 98 99 00 01 02 03 04 05 06 — 10 9 8 7 6 5 4 3 2 1

Library of Congress Cataloging-in-Publication Data

Hengel, Martin.
 Paul between Damascus and Antioch : the unknown years / Martin
Hengel and Anna Maria Schwemer. — 1st American ed.
  p.   cm.
 "Translated by John Bowden from a so far unpublished text"—T.p.
verso.
 Includes bibliographical references and indexes.
 ISBN 0-664-25736-4 (alk. paper)
 1. Paul, the Apostle, Saint.   2. Christian saints—Turkey—Tarsus—
Biography.   3. Tarsus (Turkey)—Biography.   I. Schwemer, Anna
Maria.   II. Title.
BS2506.H46   1997
225.9′2—dc21
[B]   97-1386

Contents

Preface

This book is basically the continuation of a short study, *The Pre-Christian Paul*, translated by John Bowden and published by SCM Press and Trinity Press International, Philadelphia (1991, second impression 1996).

It covers those unknown years of the apostle between his conversion before Damascus and his activity in Antioch up to the so-called first missionary journey to Cyprus and south-eastern Asia Minor or up to the Apostolic Council, i.e. a period of around fourteen to sixteen years, roughly between 33 and 47 or 49 CE. The account goes back to a series of twenty-four lectures which I gave at the Pontifical Biblical Institute in Rome in February/ March 1996. A short summary appeared in *Paul and the Mosaic Law. The Third Durham–Tübingen Research Symposium on Earliest Christianity and Judaism (Durham, September 1994)*, ed. J.D.G. Dunn, WUNT 89, 25–51. In other words, the beginnings of the book lie in 1994. It attempts to describe the period which was decisive for the development of Paul's thought and his mission strategy against the historical background of Judaism and its pagan environment in Palestine and Syria; here in addition to the letters of Paul, above all Luke's much underestimated Acts of the Apostles hold a key position.

Almost a century ago, the greatest German theological historian, Adolf Harnack, complained about nineteenth-century research into Luke:

> Among other things, the thesis that the tradition (that Luke, who presents himself as a companion of Paul in the first-person-plural reports in Acts, is the author of the Acts of the Apostles) is untenable is thought to have been so clearly demonstrated that people nowadays hardly take the trouble

any longer to prove it, and simply note the arguments of those who oppose it. They no longer seem to want even to acknowledge that there are such arguments.[1]

This complain is still as justified today. The historical incompetence of large circles of New Testament scholarship is nowhere so evident as in connection with Luke-Acts. Only in recent years has this begun to change on the basis of a better knowledge of the ancient sources.

The price for this incompetence was sometimes completely uninhibited ahistorical speculation. The present volume offers a small selection of examples of this. But we cannot give Paul a meaningful historical context without taking seriously the accounts which Luke has handed down to us; here of course taking them seriously presupposes a critical examination. The philological-historical method of historical research is always at the same time a critical one, but today, particularly in the sphere of New Testament scholarship since the old Tübingen school, there is a radical form of criticism which in the end must be said to be uncritical, because it wants neither really to understand the sources nor to interpret them, but basically destroys them in order to make room for its own fantastic constructions. In his 'Introductory Investigation' Harnack once listed the names of the opponents he reprimanded. We have consigned this controversy above all to the notes. However, it deliberately also appears in the main body of the text, since often over-hasty conclusions about the development of Pauline theology have been drawn on ground which has not been thoroughly investigated historically, conclusions which cannot be sustained if one looks more closely at Paul's initial years. The principles of Paul's theology were already fixed at a relatively early age; the geographical framework of his missionary plans extended.

Our investigation is a joint work, even if the regular use of the first person singular shows the author first mentioned to be the leading light. But without the intensive co-operation of his fellow-author it could never have appeared in this form. She has written a series of sections: the skilful literary critics in our discipline may attempt to identify these parts.

Together with other articles and studies this is important preliminary work towards a comprehensive history of Christianity in the first and second centuries.

The authors are most grateful to John Bowden for his admirably readable translation and at the same time to SCM Press for the careful preparation of a book which is also a handsome one.

This volume is dedicated to Peter Schäfer as a sign of gratitude for a fertile and friendly collaboration which has now lasted for twenty-five years.

Tübingen, Advent 1996

Martin Hengel   Anna Maria Schwemer

Note

1. *Beiträge zur Einleitung in das Neue Testament I. Lukas der Arzt. Der Verfasser des dritten Evangeliums und der Apostelgeschichte*, Leipzig 1906, 5.

Chronological Table

Tiberius 14–37 CE	Crucifixion of Jesus, Passover 30 CE
Pilate 26–36, deposed by Vitellius end 36	
Caiaphas 18–37	Persecution of the 'Hellenists', execution of Stephen c.32/33
Aretas IV King of Nabataea 9 BCE–40 CE	Conversion of Paul c.33
Death of Philip the Tetrach 34 CE	Paul in Damascus and Arabia c.33–36
Tensions and finally war between Aretas IV and Herod Antipas over Philip's territory 34–36 (defeat of Herod c.36)	Flight of Paul from Damascus c.36
	Visit of Paul to Peter in Jerusalem and journey to Tarsus c.36
37 Campaign of Vitellius against the Nabataeans; in Passover 37 he deposes Caiaphas in Jerusalem and there receives news of the death of Tiberius (16 March 37); the campaign is broken off	Mission of Paul in Tarsus and Cilicia between c.36/37 and 39/40. Beginning of the mission of the 'Hellenists' in Antioch c.36/37
Caligula (18 March 37 to 24 January 41)	

9 April 37 Earthquake in Antioch

Agrippa I receives the territories of
Lysanias and Philip from Caligula
(37 CE)

Agrippa I in Alexandria, summer
38; in addition to anti-Jewish
disturbances in Alexandria, from
autumn there are also disturbances
in Palestine (an incident in
Jamnia). Simon Kantheras high
priest

Autumn 38–spring 41 'Caligula
crisis'

Herod Antipas banished; Agrippa I
is given his territory (39 CE)

Caligula's command in summer 39
to set up his status in the temple in
Jerusalem

From the second half of 39:   Journey of Barnabas to Antioch
disturbances in Palestine caused   c.38/39
by Caligula's instruction to
P. Petronius, governor of Syria, to
carry out his order

In the third year of Caligula,   Barnabas brings Paul from Tarsus
i.e. 39/40, under the governorship   to Antioch c.39/40
of Petronius, anti-Jewish
disturbances in Antioch

Claudius (25 January 41 to   c.41 to 46/47 Mission in Syria and
13 October 54); after his   Phoenicia
accession, the edicts of Claudius
for Alexandria and Antioch

Spring 41 Agrippa again in Jerusalem

Incident in Dor 41 CE	
41/42 sabbatical year	Paul's 'heavenly journey' (II Cor. 12.2f.) around 42
Persecution by Agrippa I, Passover 43	Death of James the son of Zebedee, Peter imprisoned and escapes from Jerusalem, Passover 43
Death of Agrippa I, spring 44	Agabus and the collection for Jerusalem 43/44 (?)
Fadus; beginning of inflation in Judaea 44–45	
	c.46/47 First journey of Paul and Barnabas to Cyprus, Cilicia and southern Galatia
48/49 sabbatical year	
Expulsion of the Jewish Christians from Rome under Claudius c.49	End 48/beginning 49 'Apostolic Council'
	Spring 49 Paul sets out for Asia Minor and the Aegean
	49/50 Paul in Thessalonica
Gallio proconsul of Achaea May 51 to April 52	Paul in Corinth 50–52
	52/53 Journey of Paul to Ephesus, from there to Caesarea, Jerusalem (?), Antioch; 'incident at Antioch'; Paul returns to Ephesus through Galatia
Nero 54–58	

Paul in Ephesus 53–55

54 from Ephesus, I Cor.; 54/55 Gal.

55/56 Paul in Macedonia, II Cor.

56/57 Paul in Corinth, Rom.

Felix procurator of Judaea 52–28(?)

57 Paul in Jerusalem

Festus procurator of Judaea 58 (?) – 62

Paul in prison in Caesarea 57–59, Philemon

Albinus procurator of Judaea 62–64

62 Martyrdom of James the brother of the Lord in Jerusalem; martyrdom of Paul in Rome (?)

62/63 Paul's journey to Spain (?)

Nero's persecution of Christians 64

64 Martyrdom of Peter and Paul in Rome (?)

1. Preliminary Considerations

1.1 The 'fragmentary' Paul

Of all the early Christian authors before the second half of the second century we know by far the most about Paul. This earliest New Testament and only 'apostolic' author is also the only one to bring to life in his original letters not only theological thought but a personality which is full of tension. If we were to compare him with anyone, it would have to be with Ignatius, who in some respects is a kindred spirit, and who refers to him;[1] however, we know far less about the martyr-bishop of Antioch. For Harnack, it was Tertullian who was 'the first Christian individual after Paul of whose inner life and character we can make a clearer picture'.[2] Furthermore, it is no chance that Paul was 'the apostle' not only for Marcion but for all the early fathers who refer to him, already for Athenagoras and above all for Irenaeus.[3] So historically the 'apostle to the Gentiles',[4] Luke's special 'thirteenth witness',[5] appears in a way as the real 'founder' of Christianity in the ancient world and at the same time as the first 'Christian theologian'.[6] Principally through him Christianity became something quite different from the Jewish messianic-apocalyptic 'sect' which it had been in its first beginnings. Yet these original Christian testimonies (and the references in Acts which expand them and set them in historical context) cover only a small section of Paul's activity, namely the period of his missionary work in Macedonia, Achaea and on the west coast of Asia Minor between around 50 and 56/7, i.e. those seven years in which he wrote most (if not all) of his letters.[7] Of no figure in early Christianity before Tertullian and Origen do we learn so many biographical details and are we given so clear a character sketch as of him, and yet the majority of his activity as an apostle, which extends from around 33 to 62 or 64, i.e. about thirty years, remains obscure. So basically we know relatively little even of him: when Christoph Burchard says in conclusion, 'it is no more possible to write a *consecutive account* even of the activity of Paul, let alone a history of earliest Christianity, on the basis of the Acts of the Apostles, than it is to write a life of Jesus on the basis of the Gospels – and that means that it is quite impossible',[8] we can agree, though with the proviso that by the standards of ancient history the little that we do know is relatively quite a lot, and fragmentary accounts are possible which despite their fragmentariness still deserve the name 'history'. This additional statement applies even more if we include Paul's letters.

What we do have are fragments from Paul's thirty years' work as the preacher of a new message, as a theological thinker, founder of churches and pastor, though – even compared with ancient literature generally – these fragments are in their way unique. Eduard Schwartz dared to say: 'It is Paul the writer, and not the apostle to the Gentiles, who is a factor in world history.'[9] In view of the tremendous influence of these earliest 'Christian' writings, that sounds plausible. Yet it is too simplistic. For the letters are unthinkable without the 'apostle to the Gentiles' (Rom. 11.13), or more precisely without the missionary and preacher, since they have grown entirely out of his preaching, his living teaching. And according to his own judgment, did he not 'work' harder as a successful preacher, i.e. here as a missionary, and more successfully than all his rivals?[10] And are not the letters basically simply the 'reflection' of his unimaginably rich apostolic preaching? In reality preaching and letters, missionary and author shape each other. Without this specially, indeed uniquely, successful missionary and his charismatic-apostolic 'authority' as preacher and pastor, the letters would not have been collected, and without the letters the missionary would ultimately have been forgotten and Paul would not have become the first teacher of the church. At any rate we should reflect here that the Acts of the Apostles was written without knowledge of or help from the letters.[11] So we cannot separate the founder of churches, the preacher, the teacher, the pastor, the organizer and the writer, even if in the end we owe our knowledge of him exclusively to the writer. For while Acts was written without presupposing the letters, it only came down to us because the letters were so influential. Conversely, Acts in turn perhaps helped to bring about the canonical collection of ultimately thirteen Pauline writings, which then became the basis of the New Testament collection of letters generally. Not only the Deutero-Paulines including the Pastoral Epistles but also the 'Catholic Epistles' in turn presuppose Paul the writer of letters. This is even, indeed particularly, true of the Epistle of James, whether it is authentic or not. It, too, is understandable only as a reaction to Romans and Galatians.[12] That makes it all the more striking that Acts says nothing of Paul the letter-writer. In my view this presupposes a relatively early date for Acts, when there was still a vivid memory of Paul the missionary, but the letter-writer was not yet generally known in the same way. Here we must remember that unique though his letters may be, his missionary activity motivated by the passion of his faith must also have been impressive. Which should amaze us more, the two letters to the Corinthians, or the real life of the apostle which stands behind the shattering description in II Cor. 11.22–12.6 and is continued seamlessly in Acts 21–26? The seven authentic letters do not just give us the contours of a religious itinerant missionary of a kind hitherto unknown to the ancient world, a picture which Acts 13–28 basically does nothing but confirm; in them at the same time we find the outlines of a unique and living message, the living voice of the gospel, which was first proclaimed orally and found only very qualified literary expression in the letters, but the power of which has been influential to the present day – precisely through the letters.

Here it is striking that in his letters the apostle 'retains all the vigour of the spoken word'.[13] The criticism of Paul's opponents in Corinth in II Cor. 10.10, 'His letters are weighty and strong, but his bodily presence is weak, and his speech of no account', related to his outward appearance and manner of speaking – in addition one might also think of the lack of 'guild rhetoric', since in 11.6 he describes himself ironically as 'naive in speaking'.[14] However, there is a basic contradiction in this criticism, since the theological content of his preaching must have been overwhelming; otherwise he could not have written such letters and have been successful as a missionary. It is precisely their lack of school rhetoric which gives them a freshness and immediacy which is striking by comparison with all comparable ancient literature. Here is the writing of an author who is driven by the glow of the Spirit in the same burning passion with which he also proclaimed his Lord in preaching. The same is true of his physical constitution, which in the judgment of his opponents in Corinth is said to have been 'weak' (ἀσθενής, II Cor. 10.10). Think of all that he has gone through – as he himself describes a few verses later – and what still awaited him – up to his martyrdom between six and eight years later. An unknown presbyter from Asia Minor describes him in the Acts of Paul and Thecla:[15]

> A man small of stature, with a bald head and crooked legs, in a good state of body, with eyebrows meeting and nose somewhat hooked …

Whether behind this we have only the shadow of II Cor. 10.10 combined with the imagination of the author of an early Christian romance or still vague memories can no longer be decided now. But it is striking that in contrast to ancient biography Luke was not interested in such details. He is concerned only with the spiritual effect, not with the outward form.

But even the letters give only a very fragmentary picture and leave countless questions open.

> Who even after a history of exegesis now going back over almost two thousand years would contradict the judgment of a great Greek scholar and expert in ancient religion like A.D. Nock that the 'exegesis' of the letters is 'extraordinary difficult'? 'His words sometimes tumble over one another: there are the brief, vivid violences which most men would, on later reflection, have removed. Above there is a constant allusiveness: and what is common ground between him or his adversaries, or between him and his forgetful or disloyal pupils, is taken for granted. That is not all. The Pauline Epistles give us no clue to the early shaping of Paul's thought.'[16]

His letters are anything but self-contained religious treatises, 'not written in a mood of rest and reflection' but rather – with the exception of Romans – 'all products of the emotions and the controversies of individual moments and situations' in which 'the written word served as a substitute for direct speech'.[17]

Only Romans, with which the apostle wants to introduce himself to the church in Rome, which is unknown to him, is to some degree an exception here. Although it, too, is connected with a particular historical situation,[18] it shows in a special way the systematic power of Pauline thought. This is all the more astonishing since here we have the writing of a former Pharisaic scribe, and the rabbis, as grandsons of the Pharisees one or two generations later, deliberately rejected precisely this systematic way of presenting theological thought.[19] It is all too understandable that given this fragmentary character of the relatively sparse amount of writing that has come down to us (112 pages in the Nestle edition of the New Testament containing 18,825 words, according to the 25th edition),[20] much remains disputed and sometimes contradictory; and it is relatively easy (and cheap) to accuse the apostle of alleged obscurities, contradictions in his thought or a lack of logic generally.[21] Here no account is taken either of the special character of the letter form and its tie to a situation, or of the very different conflicts out of which these letters arose. In argumentation and power of presentation, the apostle was certainly superior to the great majority of his critics, old and new.

Finally, too little attention is paid to the fact that it must seem a miracle that despite the expectation of an imminent end the apostle wrote letters which are so unusual for his milieu and his time; for since people were well aware that 'the night is far spent and the day is at hand' and therefore thought that it no longer made sense even to have a family,[22] one could really no longer have any literary ambitions. Today in particular, when 'readers' response' is so popular, we should reflect that for all his ambition – also a personal characteristic – the apostle was exclusively thinking of his contemporary readers (i.e. for us, those of his time), and not of any kind of theological or even literary reputation, which is often so important to great authors. The literary ambition which Horace expresses in his ode *Exegi monumentum aere perennius ... non omnis moriar ... usque ego postera | crescam laude recens* ('I have finished a monument more lasting than bronze ... I shall not altogether die ... On and on shall I grow, ever fresh with the glory of after time')[23] was alien to Paul. He sought and expected his 'fame' no longer in 'this age' but from the coming Christ.[24] A later 'history of influence' simply did not occur to him. We should not forget this when we interpret him. Just as great a miracle as the fact that these 'end-time' letters were written at all is that they have been preserved. In this way, contrary to their original intention, they could be the stimulus for and nucleus of a quite new form of theological writing in earliest Christianity which spread after 70 CE – and thus also for the New Testament canon.

1.2 What we owe to Luke

However, because the information about the apostle remains so fragmentary, all the details in the sources are worth examining with great care, to some degree putting them under the magnifying glass (of course, always critically), to see what they contribute to the 'overall picture' of the apostle (as far as it is still accessible to us). Here what the letters say is surely most important by comparison with the other sources, although since they were mostly written in critical situations they are far from being free from personal bias. As a rule Paul reports *cum ira et studio*. However, the information about Paul from Acts, and the references from the Deutero-Paulines and related texts, do not deserve to be condemned *a priori* as completely and utterly unreliable, as has been customary since the days of the Tübingen school. We know too little to be able to reject in advance what sources say, in a hypercritical attitude which is at the same time hostile to history, without examining them carefully. Today, after more than 200 years of historical-critical work on the New Testament, such an attitude must be termed uncritical and unhistorical. The real danger in the interpretation of Acts (and the Gospels) is no longer an uncritical apologetic but the hypercritical ignorance and arrogance which – often combined with unbridled fantasy – has lost any understanding of living historical reality.

Contrary to a widespread anti-Lukan scholasticism which is often relatively ignorant of ancient historiography, I regard Acts as a work that was composed soon after the Third Gospel by Luke 'the beloved physician' (Col. 4.14), who accompanied Paul on his travels from the journey with the collection to Jerusalem onwards. In other words, as at least in part an eye-witness account for the late period of the apostle, about which we no longer have any information from the letters, it is a first-hand source.[25] This is also true of Acts 16.11ff. up to Philippi and then again of 20.4ff. from Philippi. Here the detailed descriptions of journeys and the account of events in Jerusalem, Caesarea and on the voyage to Rome speak for themselves. They are essentially different from the 'prehistory' in chs. 1–15 and are the goal of Luke's narrative.[26] This source would be historically quite incomprehensible if with F. C. Baur and his pupils it were to be put around 120/130 CE. Baur and the radical critics of Luke after him were simply too unfamiliar with the ancient Judaism; with Josephus, who in some respects comes close to his contemporary Luke; and with the special historical milieu of the time of the Flavians. Were Luke–Acts a later pseudepigraphy, it would certainly have been named after another author than the relatively unknown and insignificant Luke, say after Silvanus/Silas, Timothy, Aristarchus, Titus or Tychicus. The number of 'better' authors' names to choose from would have been considerable.[27] In 150 years of 'critical' research into Luke, so far no meaningful reason has been advanced for a later transference of this name to the Gospel.[28] In our view it came into being in the period of the late Vespasian (68–79), the emperor Titus (79–81) or the early Domitian (81–96), i.e. between around 75 and 85 CE – probably there is an interval of time between the Gospel and Acts, though the subject matter of the two works belongs closely together. So Luke–Acts looks back on the destruction of Jerusalem, which is still relatively recent, and moreover is admirably well informed about Jewish circumstances in Palestine, in this respect comparable only to its contemporary Josephus. As Matthew and John attest, that was no longer the case around 15–25 years later; one need only compare the historical errors of the former Platonic philosopher Justin, from Neapolis in Samaria, who was born around 100 CE.[29] We must also assume that the 'non-apostolic' Gospels of Mark and Luke are earlier than those which were attributed to an apostle, like Matthew and John, Peter, Thomas and still later apocryphal Gospels.[30]

It is also important for the dating that Luke still believes that despite some difficulties a positive relationship between Christians and the authorities of the Roman empire is possible. He offers numerous concrete examples of this of a kind that we shall not find for a long time afterwards. Despite all the 'Christian apocalyptic realism' (Luke 4.6; Acts 14.22), there is still no hatred of Roman rule in Luke–Acts as there is in the Apocalypse of John or reports of direct persecutions as in I Peter, Hebrews, I Clement and Ignatius, or even accusations of unjust condemnations by the Romans as in the Apologists. As in Paul, the Jews are primarily the persecutors, but as in Paul here we have something like a painful inner-Jewish 'family conflict'. Where the Roman state intervenes, this is because of Jewish accusations, or protests from super-stitious Gentiles. That was already the case with Paul.[31] Hardly anything can be seen of the oppression, legal uncertainty or sporadic processes against Christians with fatal outcomes under the late Domitian and then under Trajan (98–117). Interference comes from local magistrates and is sometimes instigated by the synagogue communities. There is still relatively general talk of the suffering of Christians. In Matthew, written about ten to fifteen years later, and the Johannine corpus, written twenty years later, the situation over Jews and Romans has changed quite con-siderably. Had his work come into being later, Luke would certainly have used or been stimulated by further sources like Matthew with his great discourses, the collection of Paul's letters, which was not yet available to him, or the Johannine corpus. That is not the case. Rather, John presupposes the Gospel of Luke, and the most striking of the 'minor agreements' in Matthew could come from Luke. That the Jewish Christian scribe Matthew in Syria or Palestine ignored what to him was the suspect work of the Pauline Luke would be only too understandable.[32] Furthermore there is still no reference in the Gospels and Acts to the Gnostic danger,[33] nor do questions emerge connected with the rise of the monarchical episcopate at the beginning of the second century.[34] Finally, if Acts were late, it would be hard to understand why Luke only alludes to Paul's martyr death in hints. If this were to have lain fifty to sixty years in the past, he would have had to give a more detailed account, since for a Pauline romance in the style of the apostolic Acts this was the real climax. However, because Luke is narrating what he himself experienced from the last years of Paul and is writing for people who still themselves knew about these events, the allusions say 'all'.[35] For all these reasons it is most probable that Luke composed his 'second book' around twenty to twenty-five years after the time when he had been the apostle's travelling companion on the journey with the collection to Jerusalem and the journey to Rome two years later.[36] Josephus, as I have already remarked, is a contemporary, and in some respects a kindred spirit.[37] He similarly was writing in the Flavian period, but Luke does not yet know his work. While Luke certainly uses Mark and the Logia source, he equally certainly does not know either the letters of Paul or the works of Josephus.[38]

Given all this, the lack of an authentic 'Paulinism' in Luke is no counter-argument against the later travelling companion and eyewitness.[39] Not every one of Paul's travelling companions need have remained theologically an authentic 'Pauline' all his life. In the case of Luke, contact with the bearers of the specific Palestinian Jesus tradition which he worked into his Gospel will also have brought about a certain *theological* change of position, possibly already during the time of Paul's captivity in Caesarea. His love of Paul was not affected by this. Should not what in our century would be almost taken for granted by many theologians have been possible then in a moderated form? In other words, some present-day theologians began as supporters of dialectical or existentialist theology, then changed with the times to neo-Marxist liberation theology, and today seek their salvation in a return to Jewish or – in a quite 'progressive' way – to feminist thought. Compared with such metamorphoses, Luke remained more true to his teacher Paul.

Despite the utmost personal appreciation of the missionary to the Gentiles and his unique life's work, Luke's book sought to

mediate between him and the supporters of the earliest community. Such a mediation only made sense when it was still necessary, i.e. not too long after 70. At the time Luke wrote, it was still
well known who Peter, John, James, Stephen, Paul, Philip,
Barnabas or even Mark had really been. Around 110 or 120
this was no longer the case in the same way. Unlike the later
apocryphal Acts, Luke did not have to invent any figures.
However, he, the 'mediator', who moreover also wanted to fulfil a
catechetical aim towards a member of the upper class (and his
circle of friends)[40] *had to* harmonize, to 'tone down' conflicts and
pass over much that was unattractive. He did not want to put off
Theophilus, for whom he was writing, with references to constant
disputes. Anyone who could read between the lines could still
discover conflicts enough. So Luke's picture of the earliest community 'between Jesus and Paul' is substantially beautified, and
certainly leaves out much that the author knew but preferred to
keep quite about. Some things he only hints at, and even his
silence can sometimes be very eloquent.[41] On many things he had
false or one-sided information, or none at all.[42] Nor does he
present a continuous history, but links scenes together – in
accordance with biblical style and Jewish historiography – with
brief transitional scenes which are often given dramatic form.
And of course, he does not write(any more than Paul himself
does) in any way without a bias, *sine ira et studio*. No author and
historian, early Christian, Jewish or ancient, least of all Tacitus,
from whom this requirement stems,[43] does that. The Baur school,
which discovered this 'tendency', saw only half the truth here:
'Acts is indeed a *Tendenzschrift*, but not a *Tendenzroman*.'[44] Like
most of the ancient masters, Luke can also express his hatred,
though not so powerfully as Paul, John[45] or Matthew. But above
all he reveres one person, Paul. Josephus acts in a similar way in
books 12–20 of his *Antiquities*. However, despite these undeniable
tendencies, which often seem quite deep, Luke–Acts remains of
inestimable value. It was not until 200 years later that Eusebius
wrote another 'church history'.[46] That means that Luke was far
ahead of his time. No wonder that since Overbeck so many dis-
gruntled judgments have been passed on him![47] However, these
are not 'historical' in the strict sense but have an ideological

foundation. Already for the Tübingen school it was the 'tendentious writer' and 'mediating theologian' who caused offence; here a 'philosophical-romantic' or later a 'dogmatic-dialectical' picture of earliest Christianity was presupposed and the author of Luke–Acts was measured by the unique greatness of Paul. In addition there was the view that this or that, especially miracle stories, omissions in the narrative or even inconsistencies, could only come from an author writing two or three generations later and not from a – partial – contemporary or eyewitness. Here more thorough study of Hellenistic-Roman, Jewish and later Christian historiography and hagiographical biography was to teach us differently. Scholars should read more ancient texts and less hypercritical and scholastic secondary literature.[48]

Basically, we do not know what we owe to Luke. Not only our knowledge of Jesus' preaching and its historical order,[49] but also the dates of Paul's life largely go back to him. Together with Paul's letters, Acts forms the only through corridor to the first beginnings of the community – very narrow, certainly, but still to some degree passable. That is, it helps us to built a bridge, more of a narrow footbridge, 'between Jesus and Paul'. Twenty years ago, under this title I attempted to illuminate the problem of the 'Hellenists' posed to us in Acts 6 and 7, which forms a particularly important 'plank' in this 'footbridge'.[50] The problem of the 'pre-Christian Paul', which is much neglected by scholars, is directly connected with this theme, and in 1991 I discussed it in a short monograph; in my view this is another not unimportant presupposition for the understanding of the apostle.[51]

1.3 The problem of development in Paul

So the present study is intended as a continuation, and will investigate the dark period of thirteen to sixteen years after the apostle's 'Jewish prehistory' between his conversion and his 'first missionary journey' or the 'Apostolic Council' which follows it (*c.* 33–46 or 48/49 CE). We have relatively little information about this rather long time from Paul himself or even from Luke, in comparison to the seven subsequent years of the 'missionary and literary harvest', and this scant information concentrates above all on the beginning and end of this era, the conversion and the 'Apostolic Council'. This obscure period of time, which is twice as long as the 'seven years of harvest', is particularly worth thorough investigation, for it is precisely these unknown years between Damascus and the end of the Syrian-Antiochene period which must be regarded as the decisive era in which Paul gained that towering missionary (and theological) profile which we meet in the same way in his letters during the missionary work around the Aegean. He was well aware of its quality, by comparison with other rival missionaries, as is shown by I Cor. 15.10 and other texts. In other words, in these thirteen to sixteen 'apprentice years' his theological thought, his missionary strategy and his 'apostolic self-awareness' must have matured to such a degree that in the seven subsequent wide-ranging 'years of wandering' he was able to harvest rich fruits. For already in the presence of the three 'pillars' in Jerusalem, at the 'Apostolic Council' at the end of the mission in 'Syria and Cilicia' and in the clash with Peter which led to the final break with Antioch, in what to him was the central question of 'justification by faith alone' and the inability of the law to lead people to salvation, Paul quite consciously held such an unambiguously clear position that a later further development in these basic theological questions which affected his whole existence becomes extremely improbable. Let us listen to A. D. Nock again:

> The thirteen or fourteen years 'in the parts of Syria and Cilicia' must have been of supreme importance in Paul's development, evolution, for during them he was engaged in missionary activity to Gentiles and he had need and time to develop his personal theology and his technique of preaching and argument. Some development can be traced in his extant Epistles, but it is more a matter of self-adjustment to situations: the main personal evolution lies before the years to which they belong.[52]

The 'truth of the gospel' which Paul presented in Jerusalem to James, Cephas/Peter and John, and probably two and a half years later in Antioch to Peter, Barnabas and the Antiochene Jewish Christians,[53] and which he then defended bitterly in Galatians, was quite simply that which he developed around seven to eight years later in systematic form in his letter to the Romans.

Here I firmly differ from the view put forward today by some exegetes inside and outside Germany that the apostle did not develop essential elements of his theological thought, like his doctrine of the law, the complete fallenness of the 'natural man' which makes him wholly dependent on God's grace, and the justification of the sinner by faith alone without 'works of the law', until a 'late' phase, from the Letter to the Galatians onwards, on the basis of the unpleasant events in Galatia, whereas in the 'early phase' 'the Torah was treated more as a matter of indifference' by Paul.[54] If we take his Pharisaic background really seriously, as it is unanimously attested by Paul and Luke, i.e. his training as a Pharisaic scribe, which according to the testimony of the sources known to us cannot have taken place anywhere else than in Jerusalem, and also his 'zeal for the law' as the motive for his attempt to 'destroy' the Christian community of the Hellenists – probably in Jerusalem –, then the encounter with the risen Christ before Damascus must have brought about a radical shift in his life, particularly in the question of the Torah. Philippians 3.2–11 may have been written between twenty-three and twenty-eight years after this shift, but the retrospect indicates this decisive change aptly. The place of the significance of the Torah as the 'way to life', indeed as a divine source of life in itself,[55] embracing the world, existence and salvation, is replaced by the crucified and risen Christ, that is, the unity of christology and soteriology which formed the foundation of Paul's thought and life after Damascus – for how could it have been otherwise? – regardless of the individual aspects under which he later expressed this unity in his letters. From now on the dialectical tension between Torah and Christ or Torah and Gospel determines his career. 'In Christ' the Torah is done away with and integrated – in the twofold Hegelian sense of the German word *aufgehoben*. F.C. Baur already saw clearly that the decisive theological shift takes place at the beginning:

Given his individuality generally and the nature and manner of his conversion, which was so sudden and deep a transforma-

tion within, it has to be thought that he did not first go
through a series of intermediate stages, but as soon as he had
gathered himself together and fixed himself, all at once what
we have seen in him since then was there.[56]

Of course that did not mean that he had always to present his
doctrine of the law and justification at length in quite specific
terms where the question of the ongoing validity of the Torah
was not virulent, as in Thessalonica, or where enthusiastic anti-
nomians had fundamentally misunderstood his own preaching
of freedom and therefore in principle put any kind of ethic in
question, as in Corinth. Only a very bad preacher always presents
the same message without paying any heed to the situation of the
community being addressed or speaks constantly of his conversion. And Paul was quite certainly not as poor a preacher as
that. So we must not suggest that he was. The apostle talks about
the law and his conversion where that is necessary, for example in
a situation of conflict (but not only there). However, the very fact
that he very clearly refers to these when he must, shows how
important for him the question of the law or his conversion and
call were. So there is a deep intrinsic connection between the
theology of the apostle to the Gentiles and his biography. 'The
unity of biography and theology in the life of the apostle'[57] thus
proves itself not least in the opposition which is fundamental for
Paul, between the former days of his personal past in blameless
obedience to the law 'under the law',[58] and his present activity
as the 'called apostle for the Gentiles' who proclaims the
gospel to them out of liberating grace in Christ. The fact that this
offensively long period of around sixteen years (33–49 CE), which
is obscure to us, lies between the turning point in his life that
represents the break between the Torah as a way of salvation in
the previous sense and complete dedication to the crucified and
risen Son of God and Kyrios, and the climax of his apostolic
ministry of about seven years around the Aegean which we know
from the letters, does not alter this.

For a more thorough investigation in particular will show that
at least hints of certain basic elements of Pauline theology which
emerge in the letters are already to be presupposed much earlier,

and are what makes the activity and thought of the early Paul understandable at all. The investigation of the *historical* detail in the letters of the apostle himself and also in Acts, about which perhaps yet more can be said than is usually the case, would also lead to a better *theological* understanding of the apostle to the Gentiles and help to solve some questions which are disputed today. Here I can keep referring back to results of my investigation into the early Christian Paul. Great help is also given by the masterly investigation by Rainer Riesner, *Die Frühzeit des Apostels Paulus*, which has made a viable path through the dense undergrowth of hypotheses, above all in the sphere of chronology and the strategy of Paul's mission, using all available historical and epigraphical sources.[59] It should become a standard work of Pauline scholarship; yet I fear that given the spreading inability within our unhappy 'New Testament scholarship'[60] to study ancient sources and use them to argue historically, this learned work will not easily find recognition. In any case it is easier to keep hawking round scholastic clichés and old prejudices pseudo-critically and without closer examination, than to occupy oneself with the varied ancient sources which are often difficult to interpret and remote.

1.4 The sources: Paul, Luke and the subsidiary sources

As sources we have primarily Paul's known references to his past before and after the change in his life, and in addition numerous smaller indications in his letters which refer indirectly to the significance of his call and his apostolate.[61]

Mention should be made here first of Gal. 1.10–2.18, 34 verses which contain so to speak an 'acts of the apostle' in a nutshell. Together with Phil. 3.2–11 they are the most important 'biographical' source for Paul's early period. In addition there are other autobiographical or historical reports like I Cor. 9.1–23; 15.1–11; Rom. 1.1–17; 9.1–5; 15.14–33, etc. It is amazing to what degree Paul constantly presupposes as a matter of course that people in the communities in Corinth or 'Galatia' have knowledge of his own past and also of the earliest community in Jerusalem or Judaea and of leading men of earliest Christianity.

Cephas, the Twelve and the other apostles, James and the brothers of Jesus were not unknown figures there. In other words, the preaching with which the community was founded also included reports about the beginnings of the earliest community in Jerusalem and its most important representatives. A text like I Cor. 15.1–11 could not have been understood properly had it not been preceded by basic information about the persons and events cited in it in connection with the foundation of the community. It is precisely because of this that Paul poses such difficulties to our 'ignorance'. He had given the necessary 'commentary' on this orally when he founded the community. But this also included information about his own biography. He must also have informed the Galatians at that time about his own past as a zealous student of the law and a vigorous persecutor of the communities.[62] The same goes for Corinth, where he presupposes not only acquaintance with Cephas/Peter, to whom indeed a distinct group in the community appeals, but also with James and the brothers of the Lord and with Barnabas. In my view, representatives of the Cephas group and perhaps even Cephas/Peter himself visited Corinth.[63] The special relationship with Jerusalem and the difficulties associated with it become evident at the end of Romans. All this must be the more striking, since elsewhere Paul is very sparing with private or even political information. We do not learn anything about his origin from Tarsus and his family, his twofold Roman and Tarsian citizenship,[64] his Jewish (and his official tripartite Roman) name, the great significance of Antioch, and indeed of Syria and Cilicia generally, over many years, for his biography,[65] his mission in the interior of Asia Minor,[66] the foundation and fate of the community in Rome, and the reasons for the acute danger to his life or his imprisonment in Ephesus. The only political authority which he mentions is – purely by chance – Aretas IV, king of the Nabataeans, in a report the core of which corresponds with Acts.[67] The Roman empire, the emperor, the governors in the provinces, the high priest and the authorities in Jerusalem, the magistrates of the cities with which he had to deal, no name of a single Gentile except this Aretas – none of these things which are important for the life of Paul and the communities is mentioned.

Not only Luke but also the apostle in his letters is very silent, but again in another way. So what he does say is all the more striking. We can hardly avoid concluding that if Paul communicated so many details about the earliest community and his own break with the past to his churches, he must all the more have given them abundant information about the story and tradition of Jesus. For his hearers were at least as interested in that as in stories about figures in the earliest community or about his own fate, indeed even more so. After all, the foundation of their salvation was not Paul or Peter but the Messiah and Kyrios Jesus, his life and death as the Son of God incarnate, and his resurrection.[68] That also applies to the words of Jesus, but above all to the details of his passion.[69] The basic Pauline kerygmatic formulae 'Christ died for us' and 'God raised Jesus from the dead' were quite incomprehensible to the communities without an original narrative of the real events. Therefore the Jesus tradition was needed from the start. The scholar at the desk poring over fragmentary texts all too easily forgets the elementary importance of human curiosity, above all over the basic questions of our existence, when these are bound up with a living person. Nowhere does Paul say that such questions were forbidden. Such a prohibition was first announced by radical representatives of the Bultmann school like W. Schmithals.[70] Galatians 3.1 is an interesting example. If the κατ' ὀφθαλμούς ... προεγράφη ἐσταυρωμένος there is to be translated 'was publicly made known as one who had been crucified' and not 'depicted before your eyes', it presupposes information about the crucifixion of Jesus Christ, and how else could this have been conveyed in the founding of a new community than through an account of the passion story? The κατ' ὀφθαλμούς here suggests a vivid narrative.[71] Contrary to the popular fashion today, Paul *could not* have spoken in a completely vague and abstract way about the crucified Christ. The hearer *must* have been able to envisage this unspeakably offensive fact in a very concrete way.[72] Now this already applied to Paul's preaching of the 'crucified Messiah' in Damascus or in Arabia, as similarly later in 'Galatians'. The question here is only whether the 'preaching of the crucified Christ' – always also in narrative form – was determinative for Paul's mission preaching from the beginning, or whether it is a later 'development'. In my view the latter is impossible. On the contrary, the relative chronological proximity of a few years and the unprecedented novelty of this event made the concrete preaching of the 'crucified Messiah' particularly offensive for Paul's hearers and necessary for precisely that reason. Many people, all too many people, had seen Jesus dying wretchedly on the cross in torments which lasted for hours on that fatal passover in 30 CE. After all, it was a public execution when the Jewish population of Palestine had flocked to Jerusalem for the festival, and the delinquent had been executed *de jure* in a shameful way, i.e. as one 'accursed', on charges of blasphemy and rebellion. There is a brutal concrete background to Gal. 3.1 and 13.

In addition to these texts from Paul there is Acts 9–15. I have already said all that is necessary on the historical value of these chapters, which scholars since the Tübingen school have been fond of devaluing. Contrary to prevailing opinion, I would regard the *agreements* in them with the Pauline letters as quite amazing, given that they arose around a generation later, and have a different theological tendency, connected – as I have already remarked – with a personal shift in the author's position, and a quite different literary form. In my view the best explanation for this is that their author, Luke, was personally close to Paul at an earlier time. The differences several times show the essentially different perspectives of the two authors; here it is natural that where there are clear contradictions which cannot be explained from the aspect of the person concerned, preference is to be given to Paul's account, though of course he too writes with clear tendencies.[73] Given his temperament, he was anything but a cool, objective reporter but 'was zealous' for his communities 'with God's zeal'.[74] In other words, he could see events of the past in this way from his own subjective perspective, above all when he was attacked.

Something more about Luke's sources. Contrary to the Gospel,[75] where he could refer back to Mark, the Logia source, the extent of which cannot be clearly determined, and various special traditions, probably already in part in written form, in my view he had no extensive written basis for Acts. The so-called 'we' passages are based on his own written notes and in this way – as C. J. Thornton has shown – he wanted to refer to his own eyewitness, above all during the apostle's last years, but in a personally restrained way.[76] Furthermore, as he already indicates in the Gospel prologue in a conventional and somewhat exaggerated way, he will have researched and gathered tradition within the framework of what seemed to him necessary and what was at his disposal. Whether he could already inspect community archives to any great extent around 75 to 80 CE remains very uncertain.

Nor can any independent basis be demonstrated for the much-discussed 'Antiochene source'.[77] Probably it is based on notes collected by Luke, since if we put together the remains of it, for the most part there is no consecutive 'source'. How this information came to Luke we do not know. What counts most against such a pre-Lukan literary source in Acts is that Luke tells us so little about events in Antioch. Here the events between Paul's arrival in the city and the Apostolic Council must have been very important. It is not least this sparse information from Antioch which makes it improbable that Luke himself came from the Syrian metropolis, as is reported in later sources from the early church. Probably Luke composed a framework in the form of a memorandum before he wrote Acts, which he then developed.[78]

For a movement which expected the end of the world, initially archives with 'collections of documents' were of quite secondary importance.[79] Perhaps Luke got the lists of personal names which play some role in his work from there.[80] More important, however, was the direct oral tradition also in connection with individuals and information about places which he probably wrote down, collected and evaluated selectively in a 'critical' way in accordance with the aim of his work. He did a great service to Christian faith with this collection of information relating to the time after Easter, which at that time was still quite unfashionable. Since at the same time he is a skilled stylist – Jerome, the greatest philologist among the church fathers, described him as '*inter omnes euangelistas graeci sermonis eruditissimus*'[81] ('the most learned of all the evangelists in speaking Greek') – it is also useless to seek to separate 'redaction' and 'tradition' through statistics and so on in Acts, where we can presuppose no written sources outside his own notes.[82] In the case of this narrator and author who has such rhetorical skill, the term 'redaction' is in any case misleading. We can hardly separate 'redaction' and 'tradition' by word statistics and other stylistic observations, for in Acts all 'tradition' is melted down by Luke's own skilful style. The efforts to demonstrate a wealth of freely-inventive 'redaction' with as little 'tradition' as possible,[83] above all in the first part of the work, where the parallels to Paul's letters are still sparse, often seem naive, since we do not know what Luke left out of the 'tradition', i.e. out of his own notes. On the other hand, on closer inspection what is put aside sometimes almost scornfully by superficial critics as Lukan 'redaction', or shall we just say 'invention', often proves to have good historical foundations. Here critics of Luke have often made it too easy for themselves. To make the point once again, they often really do not know what concrete historical knowledge they owe to him about a time of which otherwise we know almost nothing.

In my view this false judgment has a typically German background: Baur, his pupils like Zeller and Schwegler and later followers (down to the present day), regarded the sources all too much from a higher standpoint, purely in the history of ideas, since as Fichte put it, 'only the metaphysical and in no way the historical, brings blessing'; at most the latter brings 'understanding'.[84] And people wanted 'blessing' at any price. As later with Bultmann, the real history of 'objective, brute facts[85] was readily dismissed with scorn as this-worldly information and therefore as uninteresting, since theologically it was largely irrelevant and at the same time almost 'inferior', because it was only relative, i.e. the events of a distant past which could only be grasped with considerable uncertainty. However, for Luke these very facts were important. He wanted to narrate them as 'the mighty acts of God' (Acts 2.11). Nor may we expect a historian like Baur, who remarked of Alexander of Abonuteichos, the founder of a cult, 'that in this deceiver Lucian did not want to depict a historical person but only to paint the morals of his time', to approach Luke's historical narrative with greater understanding.[86] Scholarship still suffers to the present day from this bias, which wrongly limits the possibilities of our knowledge. In Paul's case, too, it is often associated with questionable hypotheses, not least in the literary critical sphere,[87] and in the case of Luke with a scepticism which is remote from reality, often expressed in a malicious way. In the face of this bias, to clarify the contemporary background of the Pauline and Lukan texts and the historical milieu depicted in them we must attempt to use other sources, above all Josephus, but also Strabo's description of Syria and also individual references in Pliny Major and Minor, Tacitus, Dio Cassius, Eusebius and other church fathers, pseudepigraphical and rabbinic accounts of the Jewish diaspora in Arabia, Damascus, Antioch and the Roman province generally, along with archaeological indications, inscriptions (especially Jewish and Semitic) and coins, i.e. evidence for the political, religious and social situation in 'Arabia', Syria and Cilicia with its great cities of Damascus, Tarsus and Antioch, in which Paul worked.

1.5 Geography: the problem of Syria

It is remarkable that Syria plays such a prominent role in New Testament research. Most of the Gospels, Mark, Matthew and John, are said to have been written there, and also the Gospel of Thomas, the Didache and the Letter of James; and above all since the history-of-religions school it has been seen as the place where earliest Christianity was permeated with syncretistic elements, especially Gnosticism and the mystery religions. This 'Pan-Syrianism' is still very popular, although as far as the Gospels are concerned it cannot appeal to any evidence worth taking seriously apart from Matt. 4.24. Certainly earliest Christianity between 32 and 48 spread above all in Palestine and Syria. However, the 'Syrian' sources cited are all much later, and the mother country of earliest Christianity, Palestine itself, is decidedly underrated by the same scholars in comparison with Syria. A completely new investigation adopts the expedient of simply putting forward details of places in Palestine or immediately bordering on Galilee as Syrian.[88] This speculative interest is in strange contrast to the little that we really know about Christian Syria between Paul's report in Gal. 1.16–2.15 or Acts 9–15 and Ignatius of Antioch.

Here we need to make a careful distinction between the Roman province of Syria and the reports from Edessa in Osrhoene, east of the Euphrates, from the end of the second century.[89] It cannot be demonstrated that Edessa, which at that time did not form part of the Roman empire but was still a relatively independent state with Parthian leanings, had any significance for an earlier Christianity.[90] The predilection of New Testament scholars for this area does not stem from early sources but from a romantic *ex oriente lux*. In the face of this widespread speculation we can refer to the investigation by the ancient historian Fergus Millar, *The Roman Near East*, written with brilliant matter-of-factness and a masterly knowledge of the sources, to which we owe a great deal. In this context I want just to quote the impression of a reviewer:

> Among the many observations which impressed me was the quiet criticism of the standard notion of religious syncretism ... The bankruptcy of the 'syncretistic model' is thus neatly exposed.[91]

Another quite essential perspective is that in the first century Roman Syria was predominantly orientated westwards, both culturally and politically: the Euphrates formed a barrier as the frontier between Rome and the Parthian empire, and this situation changed only in the second century, when after the Parthian War of 161–165, Edessa was incorporated by Rome into the empire. It definitely came under full Roman rule only in 214, when Caracalla made it a *colonia Romana*. Christianity can be *demonstrated* there only from the end of the second century.[92] By contrast, until 72 CE Syria, together with Cilicia, which borders it in the north-west, was one double province.[93] The journeys of Paul and later of Peter confirm the 'one-sided' orientation on the west. It is no chance that in Gal. 1.21 Paul speaks of τὰ κλίματα τῆς Συρίας καὶ τῆς Κιλικίας, 'the region of Syria and Cilicia'.[94] So in what follows we shall have to be interested above all in sources which relate to geographical area bounded in the south by Palestine and Arabia, i.e. the Nabataean empire, in the east by the client kingdom of Commagene and the frontier of the empire on the Euphrates, in the north by the Taurus and Cappadocia, in the north-west by 'Rough Cilicia', and in the west by the Mediterranean and Cyprus. A look at the map shows that this area was far from being a geographical, political and ethnic unity. This is already clear from its turbulent history between the time of the Seleucids and the second century CE. At the same time the question arises: why were the first fifteen to seventeen years of the apostle's activity primarily limited to this area? We shall have to keep returning to this question. It is one of the basic questions for our investigation.

2. Damascus and the Turning Point in Paul's Life

2.1 The chronology of the 'pre-Pauline' period and the basic events in it

Remarkably, in many accounts of the growth of earliest Christianity, which must still have seemed to be a Jewish sect, quite new and special even for the conditions of antiquity and dominated by messianic utopias, the element of time, or more precisely chronology, plays a quite incidental role, if it is discussed at all. Some exegetes, above all those interested in dogma, seem almost to have forgotten that 'history' is played out only in time and space, i.e. in a constantly changing present, and that even 'theological truth' is only mediated historically.[95] The brevity of a time span and the limits of an area are of fundamental significance, particularly in a 'primal event' in which everything is in the making and yet the decisive direction has been set. Just think how much has lightly been written about 'pre-Pauline' traditions or developments, regardless of whether they relate to christology or soteriology, mission or even community structure![96] Thus a mission of the Christian 'Hellenists free from the law' in Damascus has been conjectured even before Paul, which Paul would then have sought to prevent as a persecutor; indeed, sometimes this mission is even put in Jerusalem; or there are conjectures of already massive syncretistic influxes, say of a Gnostic kind; or there is a 'movement of radical itinerants' ('*Wanderradikalen*') starting from Galilee,[97] which is said to have disseminated a quite distinctive unkerygmatic tradition of Jesus in southern Syria including Damascus. Here from the start the question arises when and how all this could have happened before the conversion of Paul. It follows from I Cor. 15.8, the ἔσχατον δὲ πάντων ὡσπερεὶ τῷ ἐκτρώματι ὤφθη κἀμοί ('Last of all, as to one untimely born, he appeared also to me'),[98] where Paul describes his own vision of Christ as the clear conclusion of all the appearances of the risen Christ which is already chrono-logically out of sequence, that the distance between the Passover at which Jesus died and Paul's conversion cannot have been too great. In keeping with this he clearly distinguishes later visions of Christ (ὀφθασίαι καὶ ἀποκαλύψεις κυρίου, II Cor. 12.1) from the quite special, unique 'seeing' of the risen Lord (I Cor. 9.1). He had to speak of this unique and once-for-all 'seeing' because the legitimacy of his apostolate had been challenged, but he pre-ferred to keep silent about the later visions and raptures.[99]

Luke presents the Jerusalem counter-position to this in Acts 1.3, which limits the appearances of the risen Christ to forty days after Easter; but even here the circle of 'witnesses to the resurrec-tion' has to extend essentially beyond the eleven disciples[100] whom he lists by name in Acts 1.13; otherwise Matthias could not have been chosen and have been present with Barsabbas Justus as a candidate for the decision to be made by lot. That means that he, too, indicates a wider circle of 'witnesses to the resurrection' which includes the 'around 120' of Acts 1.15, and to which indeed the two disciples on the road to Emmaus and the brothers of Jesus (1.14) already belong;[101] however, he does not give them the honorific title apostle, which he reserves for the Eleven (1.26; 2.14) or, after the choice of Matthias, for 'the Twelve', although he never again speaks of the 'twelve apostles' and speaks of the 'Twelve' only once again, in 6.2. Apart from Peter and, some way behind him, John, they seem like impersonal bystanders.[102] Luke contents himself with the stereotyped expression 'the apostles'; in ch. 15 they appear for the last time, now with 'the elders', and then in ch. 21 are displaced by the latter. Luke puts so much emphasis on the Eleven (or Twelve) because they were still 'chosen' by Jesus himself as his most intimate group – here he is historically accurate.[103] He also certainly did not invent[104] the round figure of forty days (Acts 1.3) before the ascension, any more than he invented the number twelve[105] for the apostles. Basically, in his abrupt limitation of the resurrection appearances to forty days after Easter and the reduction of the apostles to twelve former disciples of Jesus, he is putting forward the idealized position of the Jerusalem Christians, or more precisely of Peter's circle, since in the Synoptics and Acts Peter and the Twelve are very closely connected, and in Corinth, where Paul's status as apostle was disputed,[106] Paul's opponents evidently emphasized the authority of Peter.[107] In other words, at this point, as I have already said, Luke had been convinced by the Jerusalem position: that is why in Acts 13.31 he makes Paul himself in Pisidian Antioch emphasize the special eye-witness testimony of the disciples of Jesus from Galilee and puts his own in the background; and it is precisely for this reason that he can also write a Gospel as a historical account of Jesus and in both the Gospels and Acts give Jerusalem unique prominence. Jesus had to go there; he was crucified and raised from the dead there; there the Lord appeared to the disciples, and there they have to stay;[108] he will come again there,[109] and there the eschatological gift of the Spirit will be poured out (a clear contradiction with Mark and Matthew).[110] For Paul, on the other hand, the composition of an extended 'story of Jesus' in this biographical form would hardly have made sense. Even if he obviously had a varied Jesus tradition at his disposal in his mission preaching, for him the 'earthly' Jesus was not a person who could be clearly separated from the 'exalted' Christ by a biographical narrative. For him the focal points are different from those of the first Christian historian. On the other hand, even he was clear – apologetically in I Cor. 9.1f. and biographically in I Cor. 15.8ff. – about the relative difference between his apostolate and that of the Jerusalem disciples of Jesus. Even if one does not share Luke's position, it remains historically comprehensible and is not simply his own late construct, remote from history.

We can only conjecture how long the time-span between the Passover at which Jesus died and the conversion of Paul really was. Not only 1 Cor. 15.8f. but also the indications of time in Gal. 2.1 and 1.18 which are so valuable for us, of 14 + 3 years which possibly include years that had begun, so that we might think of between 15 and 16 years, tell against too long an interval. If, as is still most probable, we begin from 30 CE as the year in which Jesus died and put the date of the Apostolic Council at the end of 48 or beginning of 49, that brings us to around 33 CE.

In his careful investigation of Pauline chronology, R. Riesner goes into the traditions in the early church.[111] The Ascension of Isaiah 9.16 speaks of 545 days between resurrection and ascension, the Apocryphon of James mentions 550 days (NC I 2, 19–24) or 18 months (NC I 8, 3), as do the Ophites and Ptolemy according to Irenaeus.[112] As part of the the Ascension of Isaiah (chs. 6–11) was probably written at the end of the first century CE[113] and the Apocryphon of James in the first half of the second century, this tradition may still come from the first century; thus it need not be much younger than Luke's forty days and clearly contradicts it. Later traditions from the early church date Paul's conversion or baptism in the second year after the Ascension.[114] 'With due restraint given the sources', Riesner arrives at 'the years 31/32'. This is an extreme possibility, and is probably too short. But I also think that a longer interval than three years is improbable.[115]

The first beginnings of the Jesus community after Easter were not stamped, as Dibelius and Haenchen conjectured, with a sectarian quietistic calm and a corresponding missionary restraint, expecting only the parousia of the Son of Man,[116] but were more like an unexpected powerful explosion with successive pressure waves. Both so-called 'critical' scholarship and our domesticated church piety have lost the sense of the monstrous and – in the eyes of outside Jewish observers – terrifying offensiveness of those events which Paul has listed with the utmost brevity in I Cor. 15.2–8 and which were recounted in the Easter narratives of the Gospels in sometimes elaborated, one might even say legendary, form. The supreme religious and political authorities of Jerusalem had handed over to the Roman prefect a Galilean suspected of messianic ambitions and instigation to revolution, and he immediately had him crucified at Passover as a messianic pretender. We find such a 'pressure wave' when fifty days later, at the next pilgrimage feast, Shebuot/Pentecost, Galilean followers who had fled at the arrest of Jesus appeared again in public in Jerusalem for the first time and, with Peter as their spokesman and driven by the eschatological prophetic spirit, preached to the

people gathered there that God had raised their master from the
dead as Messiah, Lord and Son of Man and had elevated him to
his right hand on the *merkaba* throne. From there he would
soon come again like the 'son of man' in Dan. 7.13 as God's
plenipotentiary and judge, and would judge Israel and the whole
world. But there was still an interval for the people to repent and
turn in trust to the crucified and exalted Messiah-son of man;
indeed, they might expect forgiveness of their transgressions,
since this Messiah had died vicariously for the sins of all. Judgment threatened anyone who rejected this offer of salvation.[117]

The tradition which Luke worked over for the first great painting in his second book could have looked like this, or something
like it. There is a historical occasion behind the description of the
story of Pentecost in Acts and Peter's preaching, even if Luke has
depicted them with relative freedom. Here it does not matter
whether all the motives which appear, for example, in Peter's
sermons in Acts 2–4, reshaped by Luke, were present in detail at
the first public preaching in Jerusalem. We can no longer 'reconstruct' this in any adequate way. It remains striking that here
Luke is fond of using 'archaic'-sounding titles, motives and
formulae like 'servant of God', 'sitting at the right hand of God',
or the suffering of the Messiah.[118] However, I am convinced that
the development of christological ideas on the basis of the
encounters with the risen Christ was stormy and that the fundamental kergyma of the earliest community was formulated relatively soon.[119] This proclamation of the one who was crucified and
raised by God in Jerusalem was intensified after the Feast of
Weeks by the claim that the gift of the Spirit promised by the
prophet had been poured out on his followers – as a sign of the
end-time which was dawning in the present. Here the certainty of
the resurrection of Jesus proves to be the unique beginning of
the general resurrection of the dead 'from their tombs';[120] it
was thought that Jesus was the 'firstborn' or the 'firstfruit' from
the dead, with whom the kingdom of God and thus the end
of human history hitherto was dawning.[121] Here we meet an
eschatological-apocalyptic enthusiasm which as far as we know is
unprecedented in Jewish history between the return from exile
and the Talmudic period.[122] For in contrast to the widespread

apocalyptic expectation, the disciples of Jesus preached 1. that the Messiah had already come and was appointed in heavenly power and glory, 2. that the resurrection of the dead had already begun, and 3. that the promise of the outpouring of the Spirit according to Joel 3.1 had already been fulfilled. No wonder that for understandable reasons the high-priestly leaders of the people who had handed over the agitator Jesus to Pilate again felt under attack and – as they were accustomed to do in the interest of retaining power – proceeded in a relatively moderate way against these Galilean enthusiasts who were provoking the city population. Luke's ideal, stained-glass depiction in Acts 2–5 thus has a very real background, in which events followed one another rapidly and certainly were much more turbulent than Acts portrays them. Luke, who is describing the earliest Christian community for a member of the Graeco-Roman upper class, prefers moderate tones and orderly conditions. The strange event which he narrates in Acts 5.1–11 presupposes an enthusiastic milieu and must have taken place amidst great excitement. That the new messianic sect which seemed to the political and religious establishment in Jerusalem to be a provocation gained a wider circle of followers[123] despite a message which to outsiders seemed rather strange may be seen as an after-effect of the activity of Jesus: following that of the Baptist, it had sparked off a new popular messianic movement. There was still a lively remembrance of Jesus, and his old sympathizers (and those of the Baptist) inside and outside Jerusalem were alerted by the unexpected and unprecedented message of the disciples and formed the nucleus of the growing new community.

From now on the holy city came into the centre, since in order to reach all Israel the people had to be addressed there in the 'agora' of Israel, the outer temple court, above all when they assembled for worship in the temple and at the great festivals. Luke is referring back to memories in mentioning here the 'hall of Solomon' on the east side of the temple which drops sharply down to the Kidron valley.[124] From now on the threads of the communities in Jewish Palestine came together in Jerusalem, not least also because this was the city in which Jesus was crucified and raised.[125] Both negatively and positively Jerusalem was the city of the saving event and at the same time the place where the parousia was expected.[126] By contrast, Galilee strikingly falls into the background, so that we hear almost nothing more of its Jewish Christian communities. Acts mentions them only in 9.31, and for the whole of early Christian literature Galilee merely plays a role as the home of Jesus and the place of his first activity. No early Christian author mentions it apart from the evangelists.[127] This is all the more striking since Luke, Matthew and Mark give most space to the activity of Jesus in Galilee and are very well aware that the disciples are Galileans, and strangers in Jerusalem.[128] Instead, in Paul and later Christian authors Jerusalem alone stands at the centre,[129] although the city was destroyed only forty years after the Passover of 30 CE at which Jesus died, and the focal point of Palestinian Judaism then shifted increasingly to Galilee. Along with this, Paul speaks only of the 'communities in Judaea', by which he probably means the whole of Jewish Palestine with Jerusalem at its centre.[130] There is no basis in the sources for the special role of Galilean communities and their theologies which scholars like to emphasize today; it rests on a misinterpretation of the Gospel texts and on speculations built on them.[131]

How much in such conjectures about a special – theological – role of the Galileans, which are contrary to all that the sources say, the wish is father to the thought, is shown by the remarks of W. Schmithals[132] and other exegetes. It is a misuse of the form-critical approach on the basis of the Gospels to invent as the founders of the mission to the Gentiles post-Easter Galilean communities which were particularly active in mission after Easter. It is equally questionable to make the Galilean communities the authors of the Logia source, and claim that it was not infected by the christology of the earliest community in Jerusalem. Isolated rabbinic sources refer to Jewish Christians in Galilee in the second century;[133] the references by Julius Africanus are even later.[134] Of course there were Jewish Christian communities there, but as far as we know they did not become more influential during the first century; rather, their influence declined. It is methodologically illegitimate to relate the fact that the Gospels – with historical accuracy – report in detail the actions and the words of the Galilean Jesus in his homeland to a later missionary

activity of Galilean communities which went beyond the frontiers
of Galilee and to make these the inventors of large parts of the
Jesus tradition. The Gospels give us no right to engage in such
fantastic extrapolations; Matt. 10.5 is a direct contradiction of
this. But sociological considerations also tell against it: the
Galilean disciples, who by profession were above all farmers,
fishermen and small craftsman, and knew Greek very imperfectly,
if at all, would hardly have been equipped to engage in a mission
(to the Gentiles) in Hellenistic cities where a command of Greek
was necessary; at best they were suited to local propaganda in
nearby areas like Gaulanitis and Trachonitis, which had a strong
Jewish element in their populations.

The clash in the first appearances of the risen Christ to the
disciples between Galilee (Mark, Matthew, Gospel of Peter) and
Jerusalem (Luke and John, the latter holding a mediating
position) indicates an old controversy, but it is no indication that
the Galilean Jewish Christians played a special role in christology.
Cephas and the Twelve (Mark 16.7) and also James the brother of
the Lord had Jerusalem as the centre of their activity, i.e. they had
left 'home' in Galilee, but in Jerusalem were still regarded as
'Galileans',[135] and the Jesus communities in Eretz Israel were in
their care.[136] At first they were active only in Jewish Palestine.[137]
Conjectures that Jewish Galilee was specially 'Hellenized',
syncretistic or leaning towards the Gentiles are unfounded. In
their embattled frontier situation in the north the Galileans were
particularly nationalistic Jews, like the Idumaeans in the south.
No *demonstrable* impulses came from there for early Christianity.

There is still less reason to assume that already two or three
years after Golgotha and still before the conversion of Paul there
was a flourishing Gentile mission 'free of the law' and – as
scholars like to say – 'pre-Pauline', which some writers think at
that time already extended as far as Antioch. Indeed, this is
nonsensical. It is completely impossible on chronological
grounds alone, and fails to recognize the character of the earliest
Jesus movement in Galilee and Judaea. Hans Conzelmann writes
in his article 'Gentile Christianity':[138]

When Paul becomes a Christian he already finds a mixed

'Hellenistic' community consisting of Jewish and Gentile
Christians (Heitmüller, Bousset, Bultmann) whose life often
shows new and unique features by comparison with that of
the earliest community (Kyrios cult, role of the sacraments,
pneumatism) ... The problem which was soon to emerge as a
motive force, that of the Law, at first had still not emerged
openly, but with it arose the question of the attitude of the
church to its own historical origin, Judaism, and the question
of the inner unity of the church generally.

This ignores historical reality. The first tentative steps of the
'Hellenists' who were driven out of Jerusalem to gain uncircumcised 'godfearers' in neighbouring Gentile cities for the Messiah
Jesus who had been crucified and raised to God cannot be called
an independent 'mission to the Gentiles'. The separation from
Judaism was far more complicated and lasted essentially longer
than such a historical misrepresentation, stamped by anti-Jewish
prejudice, wants to believe. On the other hand, the question of
the law had already been quite virulent since the preaching of
Jesus and then among the 'Hellenists'. This is the only explanation for the stoning of Stephen and the ensuing persecution in
which Saul/Paul plays so pernicious a role – and indeed in
Jerusalem itself. However, its consequences were not thought
through to the end. That happened only with Paul after his conversion. Here we find the influence of the ultimately disastrous
schematism of F. C. Baur and his pupils and the romantic
historical picture of the history-of-religions school with its anti-
Jewish stamp. Moreover Conzelmann has to concede that we have
'no direct sources ... for Gentile Christianity before Paul'. Luke,
he claims, has 'preserved some events'. Here the counter-
question immediately arises: are they really from the pre-Pauline
period? He also wants to find other elements in Paul, e.g. 'old
formulae of faith (passim), cultic cries (I Cor. 12.3), the cult
formula of the eucharist (I Cor. 11.23ff., cf. the synoptic accounts
of the eucharist ...), interpretations of the sacrament (Rom.
6.1ff.), schematic summaries of the mission kerygma (I Thess.
1.9f.)'. But what is *pre*-Pauline about that and (quite apart from
I Thess. 1.9, where we have an expression of Pauline mission)

specifically *Gentile* Christian? Behind this lies a complete mis-understanding of the religious situation of the *Jewish* Christian community in Palestine and Syria. This question will have to occupy us constantly.[139]

It was not in Jesus' home province but in the metropolis, Jerusalem, that very soon after Easter Greek-speaking Jewish Christians who had little or no understanding of Aramaic or deliberately wanted to use their Greek mother tongue in worship, the so-called Hellenists,[140] formed an independent group out of a need to worship in their own language. Presumably they came from the various Diaspora synagogues, in which even in Jerusalem worship was in Greek. As a result of their criticism of temple worship and individual prescriptions of the law (these two cannot be separated), they came into vigorous conflict with other Greek-speaking Jews linked with particular synagogues, a conflict which ended with the stoning of Stephen. Recent years in this same country have shown us how easily stones become deadly weapons and how ready to hand they are. The young scribal scholar Shaul/Paulus had taken part in these events,[141] indeed he became the main instigator of a pogrom which now followed. This led to this Greek-speaking group being driven out of the Holy City.[142] Why should this development not have taken place during the stormy initial period of about two or at most three years, i.e. between 32 and 33? The growing process of groups can be particularly turbulent and sometimes painful, but as time goes on everything becomes calmer and those involved get used to the new conditions. It is all too understandable that 'more conserva-tive' Aramaic-speaking Jewish Christians, i.e. the 'Hebrews' of Acts 6.1, under the leadership of the disciples of Jesus who came from Galilee, in the first place Peter and the sons of Zebedee, mindful of the conflict with the priestly leaders of the people which, while resolved according to Acts 5, was still latent, held back from these controversies within the Greek-speaking syna-gogue communities. Any open dispute would have restricted their possibility of calling their own fellow-countrymen in Eretz Israel to conversion. By contrast, their expulsion at the end of the conflict in Jerusalem indicated to the Hellenists that they should turn to their Jewish fellow-countrymen in the Hellenistic cities on the frontiers of the Holy Land and beyond. Here the momentous step forward took place, from the open country of Judaea to the cities around and later to the great metropolises. Through the Hellenists, the young faith step by step became a '*city religion*', since Greek-speaking Jews in Palestine, Phoenicia and Syria lived in the cities. Jesus had already once crossed the borders of Galilee to the west, north and east when he was threatened by Herod Antipas, but he avoided the cities.[143] Here Luke paradigmatically selects the example of Philip in the 'city of Samaria', Sychar, which was the then capital of Samaria, and not Gentile Sebaste, and Ashdod and Caesarea of the cities on the coastal plain (Acts 8). However, Philip was certainly not the only missionary of the Hellenists;[144] some will also have gone to Damascus and others to the Phoenician cities until finally, after more lengthy 'wandering', Antioch will have been reached.[145]

Memory of Jesus' behaviour and authority was still immediately present in these months and few years after Easter. The historically unreal and abstract problem of continuity and discontinuity or the significance of the earthly Jesus for the earliest community, which is much discussed today, merely shows how unreal our ideas of earliest Christianity are, when Jesus' way to Jerusalem and his passion was quite unexpectedly followed by appearances of him risen and exalted to God. For the hearers and followers of Jesus the honorific designation *maran/mari* or *adonenu/'adoni* on the one hand indicated a recollection of the Master before the memorable Passover of 30 CE, but on the other at the same time the possibility of invoking the one who was exalted to the right hand of God: this was the very person whose appearance and activity in words and deeds, in short the impression of whose personality, was still directly familiar to most people.[146] What we find so difficult to imagine was then very much a matter of course, and at the time, what seems to us to be in opposition formed an inseparable unity: on the one hand the recollection of Jesus, the 'Master' or 'Lord' *(rabbun*, the rather weaker *rab* and *mareh* basically have the same meaning) was abundantly present; on the other hand the Spirit answered quite spontaneously, as the eschatological gift of the exalted Lord, the ever-new questions which kept changing as time went on in an often oppressive present. Therefore there simply *could* not be any real formation of a tradition of these post-Easter words of the Spirit in the community. They were abundantly present and available in ever new ways. Therefore they did not need to be collected.[147] The sayings of Jesus were quite a different matter. These were remembered because they represented authoritative, abiding instruction and reinforcement of faith, and there was a concern to remember them as the unique words of the Messiah Jesus, the only master, although the Spirit was always present. So they also had to be translated into Greek and handed on to third parties. This would explain why the 'Hellenists' in particular were more dependent on the formation of a fixed and firm tradition than the 'Hebrews', who drew on a wealth of memory; indeed among them were the members of Jesus' family, including his mother Mary (Acts 1.14). Among the latter there was certainly no lack of living oral tradition. However, as Palestinian Jewish Christianity was decimated and in part also driven out by the Jewish wars of 66–73 and 132–135, this tradition has almost entirely been lost. The Greek-speaking 'Hellenists' who left Jerusalem relatively rapidly after the persecution by the Pharisee Saul and his fellow believers will also have been the first to fix the Jesus tradition in writing in their own language, because of the break in the linguistic tradition. In my view the Logia source, which is open and very old in its beginnings, may – first perhaps in the form of a notebook[148] – go back to them.[149] In particular the rendering in a completely different language made such a fixation necessary, although at the same time these Christians were united with their exalted Lord through the Spirit. The one did not exclude the other; rather, each supplemented the other.

2.2 Paul and the city of Damascus

2.2.1 Damascus, the place of the persecution?

Numerous monographs on Paul, studies of the history of earliest Christianity and commentaries almost assume as a matter of course without further justification that Paul persecuted the Christian community in Damascus.[150] Writers who assert this evidently take the report to the contrary in Acts, which they often do not mention at all, as a free invention of Luke. Sometimes there is a sweeping denial that Paul had ever been in Jerusalem before; that he was a Pharisaic scribe is deliberately overlooked, or he is made into a 'Diaspora Pharisee' of a kind that is nowhere demonstrable in the sources. At best it is conjectured that at an earlier date he perhaps once visited the Pharisaic school in Jerusalem. Since T. Mommsen,[151] a Pauline persecution of Christians in Damascus has been indirectly inferred from a combination of Gal. 1.22f. and 1.17. Paul writes:

> But I remained personally unknown to the churches *of Judea* which are 'in Christ'. They only heard that 'the one who once persecuted us now preaches the faith he tried to destroy'; and they praised God because of me.[152]

H.D. Betz remarks quite rightly on 1.22: 'The result of Paul's departure for Syria and Cilicia[153] was that he remained personally unknown to the Jewish-Christian churches of Judea', i.e. on his fourteen-day stay in Jerusalem he 'could not have appeared in their meetings and received instruction from them'.[154] Here too scholars are prone to overlook the fact that with Ἰουδαία Paul does not just have the Jerusalem community in view, nor the part-province of Judaea, but the whole Roman province of this name, which also included Samaria, Peraea, Galilee and the coastal cities, and which after the death of Agrippa I in 44 CE had reverted to Rome. For him Judaea always forms a geographical unity; he never speaks of its parts even when he is primarily thinking of the area with a Jewish population, which of course could not always easily be demarcated.[155] The report mentioned in v.23 will ultimately have come from those who were being persecuted (ὁ καὶ διώκων ἡμᾶς). However, Paul does not say precisely who they were. That they were Christians from Damascus would only be possible on the basis of a double inference from καὶ πάλιν ὑπέστρεψα εἰς Δάμασκον in 1.17c. The first conclusion is that at the time of his conversion (or shortly afterwards) and before his stay in Arabia Paul was in Damascus. He returned there. That is clearly the case. The second conclusion, however, remains very questionable: that the 'boundless' persecution of the 'church of

God' and the attempt to destroy it, as depicted earlier in 1.13, must also have taken place in Damascus. This is anything from certain; indeed in my view it is very improbable. For the subsequent v.14 'and I advanced in Judaism beyond many of my own age among my people' (καὶ προέκοπτον ἐν τῷ Ἰουδαισμῷ ὑπὲρ πολλοὺς συνηλικιώτας ἐν τῷ γένει μου)[156] is parallel to what is said about the persecution in v.13. It refers to the ambitious young Pharisee's study of the law, and young Pharisees from the Greek-speaking Diaspora preferred to study the Torah in Jerusalem rather than in the Syrian oasis city, which had no tradition of Jewish learning. The 'many of my own age among my people' were Paul's fellow students in the Holy City, and not his colleagues in a school in Damascus, of which there is no evidence elsewhere. Contemporary Jewish sources say nothing of Damascus as a special place of Pharisaic or rabbinic study of the Torah;[157] according to them, before 70 Torah was studied above all in Jerusalem, because only in Eretz Israel could one really fulfil the whole law – and therefore one could only learn it there by daily practice. And how could the Jew from Tarsus come to remote Damascus and there – out of the blue – persecute the community harshly?[158] And what drove him further south to Arabia from there? So the geographical sequence of the early Pauline period, even taking Gal. 1 into account, runs: Jerusalem, Damascus, Arabia, Damascus and again, if only briefly, Jerusalem.

Those persecuted, who gave the information in 1.23 to the 'communities in Judaea', will then most likely have been the *Hellenists* driven out of Jerusalem;[159] only to those who had been driven out was Paul 'personally known' and not to the Aramaic-speaking communities in the Jewish mother country from Galilee to Idumaea. When this report was generally disseminated for the first time in 'Judaea' we also do not know. Presumably it will already have been relatively soon after his conversion during his stay in 'Arabia', probably already some time before his journey to Jerusalem (see below, 91). However, the 'being *personally* unknown' still also applies to the time of Paul's visit to Peter in Jerusalem about three years later. That, as scholars also like to conjecture, the Jewish Christians in the mother country from the beginning had fundamental and insuperable 'theological' objections to Paul is ruled out by 1.24: 'and they praised God because of me'. In other words, the Jewish Christians in Judaea praised God for the miracle of the conversion of the persecutor and his transformation into a preacher described in 1.14f., because this was felt to be a positive event. This does not exclude an ongoing underlying mistrust of the former persecutor (and of his new views which were critical of the law) among some in Jerusalem and Judaea.[160] So there is no reason at all to reject the main lines of Luke's later parallel narrative account of the conversion of Paul in principle as a purely Lukan composition and therefore as unhistorical, with reference to a very question-able interpretation of Gal. 1.22.[161] That also applies to further statements in Luke's conversion narratives.

2.2.2 The conversion before Damascus: a comparison[162]

If we put Paul and Luke side by side and attempt to listen to both of them, the 'seeing of the Lord' of which the apostle speaks in I Cor. 9.1 or 'the appearance of the Risen Christ' of which he speaks in I Cor. 15.8 takes place in Luke on the journey from Jerusalem to Damascus as Paul is approaching his destination.[163] There are no reasonable grounds for rejecting this as 'legendary'. That according to Paul this 'seeing of the Kyrios' is a special vision of Christ can hardly be doubted. The so notoriously untrustworthy Luke tells of precisely this in all three somewhat varying reports.[164] This threefold report shows how important he thought this narrative was, and that it is not mere fiction but rests on tradition – presumably ultimately coming orally from the apostle himself.

Common to all three Lukan reports is a bright light shining 'from heaven',[165] the way in which the persecutor falls to the ground,[166] an audition with a reproach to the persecutor and, when he asks a question back, the exalted Christ's identification of himself as the Kyrios speaking from the light. Whereas the last report before Agrippa II and Festus (26.16f.) has commissioning for the mission to the Gentiles (including Luke's interpretation) follow directly as a word of the Lord, in the first and second reports – not so clearly – this follows only after the arrival of the blinded Saul in Damascus through the help of Ananias;[167] i.e. in the last narration Luke brings together what he considers to be essential.

By contrast, we do not know in detail how Paul will have understood this visionary 'seeing of the Kyrios' in I Cor. 9.1. At all events – contrary to present-day tendencies – he regards it as a real, 'objective' seeing of a supernatural reality in divine splendour of light, which makes itself known as the 'Lord' and is recognized by him as such. Nowhere is there any thought that this could have been an illusion.[168] The Corinthians evidently already know this story of 'seeing the Lord' (I Cor. 15.8) and Paul simply impresses on them what they already know, namely that he, too, like the other eye-witnesses, is an apostle because he has 'seen the Lord' (and has been sent out by him). Presumably he did not see him in such a way that he could simply have identified him because earlier he had known him face to face – after all, Jesus' appearance in Jerusalem was only a few years in the past.[169] So in Luke, who is following the pattern of an Old Testament epiphany, the Kyrios himself says who he is: Jesus, whom Paul has previously persecuted. Here the key word ὁράω in the aorist passive is also important for him. In 26.16 the Kyrios says to Paul: εἰς τοῦτο γὰρ ὤφθην σοι ('for I have appeared to you for this purpose').[170] In analogy to Luke's description, on the basis of the christological statements in the letters of Paul we may assume that Paul saw him as the one who was risen and exalted to God[171] in his heavenly glory, i.e. as the 'Lord of Glory' (κύριος τῆς δόξης),[172] the one raised through the δόξα of the Father,[173] who has a 'body of glory' (σῶμα τῆς δόξης), in which believers are to have a part.[174] In other words, Luke's threefold account helps us to understand Paul's statements better. So in Paul the divine δόξα of the Exalted One corresponds to the blinding light of the vision. This indicates the contemporary Jewish apocalyptic notion of God stamped by the Old Testament: the hymn I Tim. 6.16 uses the phrase 'God, who dwells in an unapproachable light' (φῶς οἰκῶν ἀπρόσιτον) in good Jewish style.[175] And because of course in Luke the person affected cannot recognize the cause of the light and his blinding, in addition to the vision of light there is an audition with the self-revelation of the Exalted One. The Pauline pendant to that would be the revelation of Jesus Christ (ἀποκάλυψις Ἰησοῦ Χριστοῦ, Gal. 1.12), which is a 'word event', however one may want to imagine it. Here Paul and Luke are very close together.[176] On the other hand, Luke makes a deliberate distinction between the vision of the martyr Stephen at his death, who sees the Son of man 'standing at the right hand of God' in the opened heavens,[177] and that of the persecutor, to whom the heavens are not opened, but who is blinded by the divine glory of the Kyrios. So he needs an audition, which the martyr no longer does.

The contrast between the audition and vision of Paul before Damascus and the realistic description of the bodily resurrection appearances in Luke 24 and Acts 1 is also striking, though here too at first Jesus is not recognized and has to prove his identity. Luke shares this physical 'realism' with John 20/21 and Matt. 28; in other words, he refers to a much earlier, pre-Lukan tradition. In these differing depictions of epiphanies Luke goes back to very different traditions and does not simply harmonize them. In contrast to the martyr, the persecutor does not look into opened heavens and does not see the figure of Jesus, but only the blinding light which hurls him to the floor. It is only Ananias in the second account in Acts 22.14 who speaks directly of Paul having seen 'the righteous one', i.e. the heavenly Messiah,[178] but he immediately adds the hearing and thus the sending – which is vital for Luke (and Paul). This hearing of the word of the risen and exalted Jesus is decisive; mere seeing is not enough for the conversion of the persecutor. Certainly Luke 'plays' in a narrative way with individual elements of the audition and vision and in part rearranges them, but the basic elements of the blinding appearance of light and the two sayings of Jesus: the question to the persecutor, Saul's counter-question and the identification, remain the same. The question of the form of the appearances of the risen Christ will already have been a point of difference between Paul and the Jerusalem community, and of course will also have affected the dispute over Paul's apostolate. If the appearance before the 500 (I Cor. 15.6) were identical with Pentecost, it would come closer to Paul's understanding in terms of a vision of light or fire. Historically, it is no longer possible to clarify the details of these questions, least of all by psychological conjectures about the causes.[179] For all those whom Paul lists e.g. in I Cor. 15.4–8, however, this was a deeply shattering event, and in a quite earth-shaking way for the persecutor Saul himself. His own life was changed in a quite radical way.

If the audition and vision of the persecutor before Damascus was bound up with a deep, even physical, shattering and resulted in a temporary blindness, and must therefore be not just a mere literary theme,[180] the same is even more true of the role of Ananias as an intermediary, which Luke quite skilfully connects with a double vision that guides the event.[181] For him, the whole earliest history of the new community of salvation is under God's miraculous dispensation. Presumably the first communities of disciples understood their way thus as being 'full of wonders'. Their capacity for perception was contradictory to all our every-day experiences in an externally 'enlightened', apparently 'demythologized' world.

That decisive shifts in the earliest community were connected with revelations, visions, dreams and other 'prophetic-ecstatic' experiences was a consequence of its possession of the Spirit and was regarded as an eschatological fulfilment of Joel 3.1–5. Luke deliberately puts this text on the lips of Peter as an introduction to Peter's Pentecost speech, but already for Paul it plays a central role in respect of calling upon the Lord to be saved.[182] In Paul in particular we find references to the connection between the possession of the Spirit, very special revelation, and concrete missionary decisions.[183]

Since usually the differences between Paul's short notes about his conversion and the relatively extensive threefold Lukan narrative are emphasized, we should not overlook the striking theological *agreements* between the reporting, despite the funda-mentally different forms.[184] In Paul the unconditional nature of the counsel of God is expressed in a special way: 'when God was pleased' (ὅτε δὲ εὐδόκησεν).[185] Behind this stands the Hebrew *raṣah*, which denotes God's free, underivable decision.[186] But in all three accounts Luke, too, emphasizes in a stereotyped way the completely surprising nature of the event and the motif of *election*.[187] In strong contrast to the characterization of Cornelius and his pious works in Acts 10.2–4, with Paul everything depends on God's free, unfathomable concern. Here there is no room for a psychological preparation in either Luke's or Paul's accounts. For both, a miracle of God took place which turned the life of the zealous persecutor upside down, and it is no longer possible to look behind it. That for Paul in Gal. 1.16 God himself is the active subject while in Luke it is Christ is insignificant. Already in Paul the action of God and Christ is largely interchangeable, so in Gal. 1.12 he can speak of the 'revelation of Jesus Christ', in 1.15f. of that of God, and in I Cor. 9.1 of 'seeing the Lord'. The narratives of the special double visions of Ananias and Paul or of Cornelius and Peter are reinforced in Luke by the emphasis that the call of the 'elect instrument' for the Gentiles and the acceptance of the first clear non-Jew, Cornelius (see below, 153), into the community by Peter is not a matter of human self-deception, but is rather proved to be God's miraculous intervention by two independent 'revelations'.[188] This sets the decisive direction for the further course of the community.

In II Cor. 4.4–6 we find the motif of light brighter than any earthly light, on which Luke puts particular stress, related to the preaching of the apostle and the illumination in the Lord which it brings about, but in such a way that at the same time there is a reference to the original 'illumination' of the unbelieving Saul/Paul 'by the knowledge of the glory of God in the face of Jesus Christ'.[189] The 'when God was pleased to reveal his son to me' (εὐδόκησεν [ὁ θεὸς][190] ἀποκαλύψαι τὸν υἱὸν αὐτοῦ ἐν ἐμοί) in Gal. 1.15f. also implicitly contains the motif, already discussed, of the revelation of the glory of the Son of God who has been exalted to God[191] and the illumination of the darkened heart (ἐν ἐμοί) of the persecutor which is indirectly connected with this.[192] The vision of light which shines in Paul and radically changes his life is christological and consequently soteriological, and all further conclusions depend on it.

Here for Paul himself, as for Luke, the most important consequence was the call to be missionary to the Gentiles, i.e. for Paul to become an apostle; for Luke it was that Paul became the *unique* 'thirteenth' witness (μάρτυς, 22.15; 26.16) who first really fulfils the promise to the Eleven in 1.8.[193] Here Luke puts more emphasis on the external course of the revelation of the heavenly δόξα of Jesus which physically blinds Saul/Paul. In other words, for the narrator, by comparison with Paul theological reflection fades relatively into the background, although as the triple, varying report shows, this too is not absent. It develops in the course of the narrative with its three stages and shapes it. That Saul is made to see again by the laying on of Ananias' hands[194] is of course also an expression of the inner illumination which is sealed through baptism,[195] in which for the first time the saving 'calling upon the Lord' according to Joel 3.5 takes place.[196] Through the different narrative variations Luke emphasizes that he is not only concerned with simple-banal historical detail, but even more with the different theological aspects of the event.

2.2.3 The baptism of Saul/Paul in Damascus, his independence and link with the community

That Saul/Paul, as Luke reports, was baptized[197] in the name of Christ in Damascus is to be presupposed on the basis of his whole missionary practice and above all because of the use of the first person plural 'we had been baptized into Jesus Christ' (Rom. 6.3: ἐβαπτίσθημεν εἰς Χριστὸν Ἰησοῦν). Historically, Paul's baptism can hardly have place taken anywhere but in Damascus, to which indeed he 'returns' after his stay in Arabia.[198] Galatians 1.15f. compellingly presupposes that Paul came to faith through his vision of Christ (presumably with Luke before Damascus) understood as revelation, and also connected his apostolate to the nations with this event. Now he could not be an apostle of Jesus Christ and sometimes even baptize in the name of Christ as one who had not been baptized and was not a disciple like the Twelve, but was a former persecutor.[199] However, if he received baptism soon after his encounter with the risen Christ, he must have made some contact with the Jewish Christians in Damascus – who were probably not yet very numerous. Given its reference to the 'community' in Damascus, which was similarly in its very early days, the long, tremendously compressed temporal clause in Gal. 1.15–17, in which events fall over one another, must not be interpreted wrongly. The assertion in 1.16, 'immediately I did not confer[200] with flesh and blood' (εὐθέως οὐ προσανεθέμην σαρκὶ καὶ αἵματι) includes the following 'nor did I go up to Jerusalem to those who were apostles before me' (οὐδὲ ἀπῆλθεν εἰς Ἱεροσόλυμα πρὸς τοὺς πρὸ ἐμοῦ ἀποστόλους); indeed this assertion is primarily made with reference to the authorities in Jerusalem. It is directed against the view disseminated by the opponents in Galatia that Paul is dependent on them in his preaching. Damascus plays a subsidiary role in this dispute; Paul does not mention the Christians there at all. The issue here is that he is authorized to preach by Christ alone and that he received this authorization from Christ alone and not from the 'original apostles' in Jerusalem. He justifies this independence in Galatians by a minimal amount of contacts: apart from the fifteen-day visit to Cephas/Peter and James, he did not go there again in the approximately fifteen to seventeen years before the 'Apostolic Council',[201] and his independence from 'the apostles before him' is so important to him that he endorses it in 1.20 with an oath. However, even if he did not receive his gospel and his apostolate through human beings, but above all 'through a revelation of Jesus Christ', he does have important traditions which he received from others, like I Cor. 15.1–7, where in connection with the message that he proclaimed in Corinth he himself emphasizes what he had 'already received' (ὃ καὶ παρέλαβον), and despite the 'received from the Lord' (παρέλαβον ἀπὸ τοῦ κυρίου),[202] the report of Jesus' last night and the Lord's Supper which he instituted (I Cor. 11.23–25) of course presupposes concrete historical tradition which rests on the living memory of participants. Moreover, a statement like I Cor. 15.11 with its emphasis on the basic agreement in the preaching of the eyewitnesses to the resurrection mentioned earlier is only possible on the basis of a common tradition which was communicated to Paul by third parties; this is true even if we conjecture that the essential content of the new message had already been made known to him through disputes and interrogations before he, the Pharisaic student of the Law, became a Christian. For such a basic statement as I Cor. 15.11, which modern 'theologies of the New Testament' like to suppress,[203] presupposes real 'agreement'.

Nor should we assume that Paul was baptized without any instruction or commitment to the new faith. Certainly in this earliest period we should not yet presuppose any kind of institutionalized instruction along the lines of the later catechumenate, and according to Luke the baptism of the Ethiopian eunuch, the centurion Cornelius, and the prison warder in Philippi were performed quickly, without much fuss; still, they always presuppose instruction in the basic content of belief in Jesus. Paul, too, will have 'called upon the Lord'[204] in his baptism, i.e. confessed him, and to do this he must have known some basic facts about this Lord. Granted, F. Vouga decrees that 'Paul does not know Jesus through Christian tradition (Gal. 1.22–24), but through the tradition of Pharisaic, anti-Christian polemic' and therefore 'for Paul Jesus was' only 'the transgressor of the law and the authority by which one could behave in freedom from the law'.[205] Quite apart from the fact that we know of Jesus' criticism of the law only from the Synoptic sources, while Paul can speak of the law of Christ (νόμος τοῦ Χριστοῦ) and even describe himself as 'not being without law towards God but under the law of Christ' (μὴ ὢν ἄνομος θεοῦ ἀλλ' ἔννομος Χριστοῦ),[206] are we really to suppose that he gained his christology simply through a transformation of his Pharisaic views, which were hostile to Jesus?[207] In his letters, Paul speaks of Jesus as the son of David who lived as a Jew 'under the law', and who 'for the truth of God', i.e. to 'confirm the promises to the fathers', became a 'minister of the circumcision', i.e. 'served' the people of Israel in his earthly messianic activity.[208] All this does not have much to do with his former Pharisaic hostile 'picture of Jesus'. If at that time he had 'known Christ according to the flesh' (II Cor. 5.16), now this is done with. That does not exclude the possibility that decisive points *of his christology* developed as an antithesis to his former view of Jesus. We shall come back to that. Unfortunately the seven letters of Paul tell us almost nothing in detail of the way in which he preached when he founded a community.[209] Here without any doubt he depended on tradition. He was certainly a solitary, but Gal. 1.12 should not lead us to imagine him, even to begin with, as a theological solipsist. The 'immediately I did not confer with flesh and blood' means that directly after the turning point in his life he did not ask 'third parties' for advice, so that these could not have had any influence on his 'call' to proclaim the gospel to

the Gentiles and on the *special* content of his new message
which distinguished him from others – especially the Jerusalem
authorities. Moreover his decision now to go to 'Arabia' and not
to Jerusalem was completely and utterly his own.

Moreover Luke agrees with Gal. 1.12 and 16c in so far as he
does not set Ananias off against Paul as a vehicle of the tradition
and does not make Paul dependent on the community in
Damascus. According to Luke, Ananias – like Paul himself and (if
we follow Luke) the whole of the earliest community[210] – with
visionary gifts only does what the Kyrios has charged him to do:
'Ananias acts as the representative not of the church but of
God.'[211] At the end of his audition of Christ, Saul/Paul had only
been instructed to go to Damascus: there 'it will be told you what
you should do'. What follows is concerned with this action, not
with instruction. Even Ananias only executes the commission of
the Kyrios to lay hands on Saul/Paul and free him from his blindness.[212] There is no direct statement that *he* baptized Paul, even if
the simple passive ἐβαπτίσθη suggests this,[213] far less is there any
mention of baptismal instruction. The address 'brother' is striking in the execution of the command. The motif of the giving
of the Spirit is added (9.17). In other words, Ananias already
prophetically sees in Saul the future Christian. Healing, baptism
and the end of fasting follow. The bestowal of the Spirit before
baptism recalls Acts 10.44 in the story of Cornelius. In the second
account (22.16), where the greatest importance is attached to the
role of Ananias, he calls on Saul to be baptized for the forgiveness
of his sins, 'after he has called upon the name (of the Lord)'.
Here, too, we can only indirectly infer that Ananias baptized Paul.
Furthermore, in 9.19 Luke merely says that 'for several days he
was with the disciples at Damascus, and in the synagogues
immediately he proclaimed Jesus, saying that "he is the Son of
God".' Is it mere coincidence that in Acts 9.20, as in Gal. 1.16, the
messianic title 'Son of God' appears, a title which is not very
frequent in Luke and Paul – and which for Luke in Acts is very
pointed?[214] We shall return to this over the question of the christology of the newly-called apostle.[215] Neither in Damascus nor three
years later in Jerusalem[216] will Luke give even the remotest hint
that Paul received his gospel 'from men' and was extensively

instructed in it; rather, after the laying on of hands, commissioning (and baptism?) by Ananias, he makes contact on an equal footing both with the disciples in Damascus and later with the apostles in Jerusalem: the latter do not instruct him, but hear his miraculous narrative; in other words, they are instructed by him.[217] Contrary to a common view, the problem of dependence on tradition does not emerge so much in Luke as through numerous references in the letters of Paul himself. Moreover, there are also good reasons not only in the narrative but also in the subject-matter why first of all in Damascus and then in Jerusalem there should have been a certain fear of the former persecutor.[218] This problem is even hinted at in Gal. 1.22. That the persecutor became a preacher was a quite unexpected, indeed initially an irritating, experience. Could one really trust him? Luke only knows nothing of the three years in Gal. 1.18; for him the stay in Damascus is simply 'a long time'.[219] The account in Acts can also give the impression that Paul received his message only through a revelation of Jesus Christ (δι' ἀποκαλύψεως Ἰησοῦ Χριστοῦ, Gal. 1.12), and that this was granted to him directly and effectively as a power of God (δύναμις θεοῦ, Rom. 1.16), giving him the courage to preach salvation in Jesus Christ in public.[220] Here its content seems to be have been completely christological.[221] But who would doubt that Gal. 1.10, 16 in particular points to the christological centre of the apostle's message? Stamped by his *theologia crucis*, this may sound essentially different from Luke's relatively simple account, which nevertheless differs as it treats the individual heroes of his work.[222] That kind of account is what this primarily excellent narrator wants to give, rather than being primarily an argumentative theologian. We should not treat too lightly the light touch of the author 'To Theophilus'.

2.2.4 The mission to the Gentiles

Two further points in Luke's account have contacts with Paul's remarks. Paul connects the seeing of the Lord or the revelation of the Son of God directly with his apostolate, i.e. his mission to the Gentiles. He is called to be 'an apostle – not from men nor through man, but through Jesus Christ and God the Father, who raised him from the dead'. He says this quite pointedly in the prescript to Galatians; and in I and II Corinthians and Romans, written in a conflict, he similarly puts great stress on 'called to be an apostle'.[223] Luke also emphasizes the motif of sending to the Gentiles. In the third account, Acts 26.16–18, which is most strongly stamped by the author's theology, he makes the Kyrios say to Paul, who has fallen to the ground:

> I am Jesus whom you are persecuting. But rise and stand upon your feet; for I have appeared to you for this purpose,[224] to appoint you to serve and bear witness to the things in which you have seen me and those in which I will appear to you,[225] delivering you from the people and from the Gentiles – to whom I send you[226] to open their eyes, that they may turn from darkness to light and from the power of Satan to God ... [227]

Here the exalted Kyrios himself is calling the persecutor as a chosen witness in an unique way. His vision of the (crucified) Risen Lord[228] becomes the basis of his message for the Gentiles. Election, mission and revelation are clearly expressed; only the title of apostle, i.e. the one 'sent' by Christ, is withheld from him. The author of the Gospel could not give this title to Paul because for him the twelve apostles must have been followers of Jesus during his earthly life and must be witnesses to the forty-days communion after the resurrection. Therefore he expresses this with verbs. Theologically, Luke attaches the greatest importance to his third account of Paul's calling. It is not just the most extensive,[229] but also theologically the most significant and rhetorically the most carefully composed. The fact that the risen Christ himself says 'I send you' (ἀποστέλλω σε), distinguishes it from the previous ones. The new tone is unmistakable; nevertheless, this mission is only inserted in a subsidiary clause and is completely subordinated to its purpose, that through Paul the eyes of the Gentiles will be opened and they will be converted from darkness to light, freed from the power of Satan to receive the forgiveness of sins and the inheritance among the saints through faith in Christ (26.18).[230] This is certainly not a Pauline formulation, but

rather the language of early Christian mission, but as such it is
also not completely alien to the apostle.[231]

In the second account, Luke makes Ananias bring Paul this
call, in which he is to 'be a witness for him to all men of what you
have seen and heard' (22.15). This is probably to emphasize the
special character of the revelation to Paul. Here Paul is not
dependent on the apostles. In the first account the Lord merely
discloses to Ananias the future function of Saul/Paul as an 'elect
instrument' who is to bear his name before the nations and the
kings of Israel; the Lord himself will reveal to him his future
suffering.[232] Here this is merely information to Ananias; nothing
is said of handing it on, though this is presupposed in connection
with the laying on of hands and healing (see above, 46).

The different variants thus presumably show that the calling of
Paul was handed down or interpreted in different ways, as having
been with or without intermediaries. The version which is most
important for Luke (and is the last) comes closest to the apostle's
own report: 'to reveal his Son to me that I may proclaim him
among the Gentiles', whereas 22.16 could recall Gal. 1.11f. Is
Luke in this account – which has many levels, and is deliberately
varied – always as far as scholars so like to claim from the testimony of the apostle in his letters? On the contrary, I would argue
that the all too brief biographical notes of the apostle can be
understood far better historically through Luke's account, which
in no way presupposes knowledge of the letters, despite, indeed
precisely because of, its different form. Why should this last
description not go back to what the apostle himself told his
disciples, including Luke, around twenty-five years before Acts
was composed, possibly with different variants, whereas in the
first reports Luke uses tradition from Damascus or even
Jerusalem? By the nature of the case, as a dramatic Hellenistic
historian Luke effectively works on the rhetoric and narrative of
this event, which is decisive for him. But we shall have to discuss
in detail later the historical development of this 'mission to the
Gentiles', which both Paul and Luke combine so closely with the
conversion that we can virtually speak of a call.

In my view, the vision of Christ before Damascus, the blinding
of the persecutor, his healing through Ananias as intermediary,

his baptism and contact with the Christians and the beginnings of his messianic preaching in the synagogues of Damascus are historical. Bound up with this is the receiving of a revelation of Christ full of content, from which Paul later 'derives his gospel' and which the conversion of the persecutor at the same time makes a call to become 'apostle to the Gentiles'. However, before we investigate more closely the relationship of Paul to the Christians in Damascus, we must first look at the Jewish community and conditions in the Syrian metropolis itself.

2.3 The Jewish community in Damascus and its political significance

2.3.1 The synagogues of the city and their 'godfearers'

Another special feature which will be based on reliable tradition is the fact that Luke knows that in Damascus, as in Jerusalem,[233] there were several synagogues. This is anything but a matter of course. According to Acts 9.2, Saul asks the high priest for 'letters to the synagogues in Damascus' to authorize him to bring any supporters of the new sect to Jerusalem as prisoners. According to 22.5 he received these from the 'high priest and the whole council of elders'. Such letters from the highest Jewish authorities in the mother country to the Diaspora communities are attested by Luke in Acts 28.21 and also by the early rabbinic tradition.[234] However, with the motif of the arrest and extradition of prisoners he has overstepped the bounds of historical probability. The criminal legal arm of the Jerusalem high priest hardly reached as far as Damascus, and it is hard to imagine a Jewish prison transport over a distance of around 220 kilometres as the crow flies going through different areas of jurisdiction – Damascus, the territory of Philip, the Decapolis and Judaea – although the Jewish high priest was an important power within the territories of southern Syria and Palestine.[235] That was certainly true above all of a diplomat like Caiaphas, who was backed by the powerful clan of Annas and was in office for around eighteen years, though probably because he got on well with the prefect Pilate (26–36 CE).[236] Here we may have an exaggeration on the part of Luke, who in any case sometimes tends to depict Paul the persecutor in rather too glaring colours.[237] Rather, Saul will have been sent by one or more Greek-speaking synagogues in Jerusalem to Damascus to help its Jews to stem the pressure from the Jewish-Christian 'Hellenists' who had fled there. However, it makes good sense that he should have asked for a letter of commendation from the high priest to back him up. The high priest and other heads of the Jewish leading class must have been interested in the restoration of peace in this important Jewish community.[238]

That Luke knows of several synagogue communities is in any case striking. This fact emerges again in 9.20 and goes against his terminology elsewhere: with the exception of Jerusalem[239] and Salamis on Cyprus,[240] he speaks of only one synagogue in the places which Paul visits.[241] Elsewhere we know of more than one synagogue only through the church fathers and Malalas in Antioch (see below, 184, 189), in Alexandria[242] and Rome,[243] and in the rabbinic period also in Tiberias and Sepphoris.[244] We need not suppose that Luke thinks that 'the city (of Damascus is) entirely under Jewish influence'.[245] His Jewish opponents could not arrest Paul and stone him, like Stephen, but only pester him.[246] Luke is better informed than is generally assumed not only about Jerusalem but also about Damascus.[247] Josephus in particular attests that there was a very extensive and old Jewish Diaspora community in Damascus, probably going back to the pre-Hellenistic period, round which a considerable circle of sympathizers gathered:

'In the meantime, the people of Damascus, when they were informed of the destruction of the Romans,[248] set about the slaughter of those Jews that were among them; and as they had them already cooped up together in the place of public exercises, which they had done out of the suspicion they had of them, they thought they should meet with no difficulty in the attempt; yet did they distrust their own wives, which were almost all of them addicted to the Jewish religion; on which account it was that their greatest concern was how they might conceal these things from them; so they came upon the Jews,

and cut their throats, as being in a narrow place, in number
ten thousand, and all of them unarmed, and this in one hour's
time without anyone to disturb them.' The speech of the
Sicarius Eleazar in Masada even speaks of 18,000.[249]

In the rather earlier pogrom at Caesarea by the Sea Josephus
gives a figure of 20,000 victims, and these are said to have
numbered 13,000 in Scythopolis, 2,500 in Ashkelon and 2,000 in
Acco Ptolemais.[250] As further places with pogroms he mentions
Tyre, Hippo Gadara and then sweepingly 'the other cities of
Syria'.[251] According to Josephus, only the citizens of Antioch,
Sidon and Apamea (and Gerasa) spared their Jewish inhabitants;
one of the reasons Joseph gives is that 'they spared them because
their number was so great that they despised their attempts'.[252]
In the introduction to his report on these pogroms in 66 CE
Josephus refers to an additional phenomenon, which also
appears in a different way in the Damascus note:

> The disturbances in all Syria were terrible, and every city was
> divided into two armies encamped one against another, and
> the preservation of the one part was in anticipating the other;
> ... for when the Syrians thought they had ruined the Jews, they
> had the Judaizers in suspicion also (τοὺς Ἰουδαΐζοντες εἶχον ἐν
> ὑποψίᾳ); and as each side did not care to slay those whom they
> only suspected on the other (τὸ γὰρ κατ᾽ ἑκάστοις ἀμφίβολον),
> so did they greatly fear them when they were mingled
> (μεμιγμένον) with the other, as if they were certainly foreigners
> (ὡς βεβαίως ἀλλόφυλον). The whole province (ἐπαρχία) then
> was full of inexpressible calamities, while the dread of still
> more barbarous practices which were threatened, was every-
> where greater than what had already been perpetrated.[253]

These dramatic and certainly also somewhat exaggerated
descriptions shed some light on the numerically strong Jewish
Diaspora communities in Syria, above all in the southern part of
the province, where Damascus was particularly prominent. In this
territory bordering on the mother country, the proportion of
Jews in the population[254] was higher than in all the other
provinces of the Roman empire including Egypt. For example in

Caesarea by the Sea (including the Samaritans) they will have amounted to no less than half the population.[255] In these cities evidently sympathizers well disposed towards the Jewish *ethnos* and its religion were also especially numerous, so that the Hellenized Syrians saw the Jewish minorities as a political danger within their cities. Certainly the Jewish-Christian communities in non-Jewish Palestine and southern Syria will also have been threatened after 66 CE. It remains uncertain whether by Ἰουδαΐζοντες Josephus means Christians or pagan sympathizers or, most probably, both.[256] Here one did not need to differentiate so sharply just after 70. We come up against the same problem as with Titus Flavius Clemens, his wife Domitilla and her friends in Rome, where it is not clear whether she sympathized with the Jews or the Christians.[257] That in 69/70 CE Mark does not say a word about these shattering events, the mass murder of tens of thousands of Jews in Palestine and Syria, is a hint that he did not write in Syria itself but rather at some distance, in Rome. The Gospel of Matthew, by contrast, appeared 25–30 years after these pogroms in Syria, so it could still refer indirectly to them in 27.25.

Thus it is no wonder that the Jewish Christian 'Hellenists' who were driven out of Jerusalem turned above all to the 'Hellenistic' cities beyond the closed Jewish area of settlement where the Jews were in the minority, for there sympathizers who were not full Jews were tolerated in the synagogues. The more rigorous attitude to non-Jews which was the norm in Jerusalem did not predominate there. Particularly in the case of the 'Hellenists', the 'ambivalence towards both sides' (τὸ γὰρ κατ' ἑκάστοις ἀμφίβολον) could have aroused their interest in these 'sympathizers'. Had not Jesus turned to 'marginal groups' in the twilight zone, indeed had he not helped individual Gentiles in their distress?[258] Therefore Philip appears first in mixed Ashdod and eventually settles in Caesarea, where around twenty-five years later he receives Paul with friendship; and according to Luke, who depicts it in a novellistic way, the first conversion of a god-fearer by Peter takes place there.[259] By contrast, Peter first turns to the purely Jewish cities of Lydda and Joppa (Acts 9.32–43). It seems at least plausible that just as Philip came to Ashdod and Caesarea, so other 'Hellenists' should have come to Damascus,

· which was no less important. Here we may assume from the beginning that they also baptized uncircumcised godfearers. Luke himself gives a clear indication of this in Acts 8.36, 38. First of all they may have been the exception, and with women in any case there was no problem (see below, 66f.). Up to the middle of the thirties such baptism was probably a widespread practice outside Palestine, and it was then energetically encouraged by Paul (see above, 43ff.). In Jerusalem, this practice was evidently tolerated outside the Holy Land up to the persecution by Agrippa, indeed up to the middle of the forties – presumably because of the example of Jesus, for whom ritual commandments were not central. So it does not make sense, either, to assume that the Pharisee Saul must have persecuted Jewish Christians when he was living in Damascus because they regarded the circumcision of Gentiles as superfluous, since the extensive local Jewish community showed itself very open to pagan sympathizers. This fact itself makes a persecution in Damascus alone very improbable. Even if Josephus was writing his description with bitter irony, he certainly did not invent these 'open' conditions in the community there, and where there were so many women 'godfearers' who sympathized with the ethical monotheism of the synagogue despite or against their husbands, there must also have been a substantial number of male godfearers.[260] One motive of the zealous Pharisee Saul in Jerusalem will have been much more understandable: he went to Damascus to stop the shameless messianic sectarians who were corrupting the numerous sympathizers there who could easily be led astray. With a Jewish male population of around 10,000 (presumably we are not to include women and children),[261] the city must have had several synagogue buildings, as did Jerusalem, Alexandria, Antioch or Rome; the twofold plural in Acts 9.22, 20 thus has a basis in reality. We only get precise figures again about the Jewish community in Damascus in the early Middle Ages in the travel account of Benjamin of Tudela, who gives an extended description: according to him there were 3,000 Jews, 100 Karaites and 400 Cuthaeans (Samaritans) in the city.[262] Petachiah of Regensburg a little later mentions 'around 10,000 Jews' and at least three synagogues.[263] Here members of families could also be included.

2.3.2 The history of the city and its Jewish community

It is worth taking a further look at the Jewish community and the city itself.[264] Damascus had been to some extent bound up with the history of Israel 'since the days of Abraham', since Eliezer came from there.[265] According to Josephus, the city, together with Trachonitis, which belonged to the kingdom of Agrippa II, was founded by Uz (Οὔσης), a great-grandson of Shem, who is probably identical with Uz the firstborn of Nahor (and nephew of Abraham) according to Gen. 22.21. It lies 'between Palestine and Coele Syria', i.e. on the frontier of Eretz Israel; indeed it can be considered as still belonging to this in a wider sense. From Judaea – also for Luke – it can be seen as the 'nearest foreign land'.[266] According to Nicolaus of Damascus, Abraham ruled as king over the city before he went on to 'Canaan, which is now called Judaea'. 'His name' is said to be 'still praised in Damascus', and 'a village is shown which is called "abode of Abraham" after him'.[267] Pompeius Trogus even wanted to make the Jews generally originate from there, since Abraham and Israhel were said to have been kings there. He also connects Moses with Damascus.[268] Later it belonged to the empire of David,[269] which set the boundaries for the coming messianic kingdom. In the rabbinic *halakah*, relating to the application of the agrarian laws like those of the year of remission or the temple offerings, it had an intermediate position, since from of old it was assigned to the disputed frontier area of Eretz Israel.[270] The fertility of the oasis was praised,[271] and indeed in the third century CE Resh Laqish wondered whether the entrance to paradise was here. In general it had an eschatological importance in many respects.[272] Prophetic texts like Zech. 9.1[273] and Amos 5.26 interpreted in terms of the end-time could give the place an eschatological significance; thus in the Damascus Document it is the place of self-chosen exile: 'These are the converted (or exiles: *sabe/s^abi*) of Israel who departed from the land of Judah and dwell in the land of Damascus.'[274] Thus through tradition, history and eschatological expectation it was bound up with the Holy Land in many ways.

During the monarchy it was the main opponent of the

northern kingdom of Israel, and even later it was not without influence on Jewish history. In the Hellenistic Roman period, too, it had considerable significance for Palestinian Judaism as a neighbouring 'city state' rich in tradition, especially as there had been no direct military conflicts with Damascus, in contrast to the Hellenistic cities of Palestine. It was turned into a Greek-Macedonian polis at a very early stage, towards the end of the fourth century and possibly already under Antigonus Monophthalmus,[275] i.e. before the battle of Issus in 301; we do not know the precise date. The street plan in great rectangular grids corresponded to the typical Hellenistic Hippodamian lay-out.[276] In the third century the Seleucids and Ptolemaeans fought over Damascus, and the city finally came into the possession of the Seleucids as a result of Antiochus III's victory at Paneas in 200 BCE. After the division of the already markedly reduced Seleucid empire towards the end of the second century BCE, it became the temporary capital of the southern part with Coele Syria and Phoenicia.[277] In 85 BCE it came under the rule of the Nabataean king Aretas III, who had the epithet Philhellene and between 84 and 72 BCE minted bronze and silver coins in the manner of the Seleucid king whom he had defeated. He probably regarded himself as a successor of the Macedonian rulers.[278] From 72–69 BCE King Tigranes of Armenia ruled the city. When Ptolemy Mennaeus, the ruler of the Ituraeans, threatened Damascus around 70/69 BCE, the Jewish queen Alexandra sent her son Aristobulus with an army to Damascus, probably to protect it, but without much success.[279] It was only with Pompey's intervention in Syria, who in 66 BCE had it occupied by his commanders Lollius and Metellus,[280] that the Hellenistic city state was freed from the pressure of the various oriental rulers and the neighbouring Arab tribes. From now on it was a firm part of the province of Syria, newly established by the Roman generals, rather like the Decapolis, in a somewhat isolated situation and separated from the other Hellenistic cities in the north of Syria by Semitic client rulers.[281] In 63 Pompey arbitrated in a dispute between the brothers Hyrcanus and Aristobulus, and thus sealed the fate of Judaea. In this turbulent time Antipater, the father of Nicolaus of Damascus, the long-time adviser to Herod, did good service towards the independence of the threatened city as an orator and politician. The autobiography of the polymath Nicolaus, who for a long time acted as confidant of the king in Jerusalem, shows the pride of the citizens of Damascus: they felt themselves to be Greeks but nevertheless could refer to Abraham as their famous ruler in ancient times.[282] That Pompey already connected Damascus with the Decapolis is improbable, since from Augustus and Tiberius and then again from the later time of Nero it minted coins dated by the traditional Seleucid era, and not that of the liberator, Pompey.[283] On the other hand, some time before 59 CE Pliny the Elder lists it as the first city of the Decapolis.[284] However, this alliance did not comprise a fixed number, and by the middle of the second century CE it had increased to eighteen cities. Perhaps initially after 63 BCE there was only a Pentapolis.[285]

The city territory of Damascus must have been relatively extensive.[286] It had probably been enlarged by Augustus at the cost of the territory of Ituraea. In the west it had a common frontier with Abilene and further south on the ridge of the Anti-Lebanon or in the Biqa' with Sidon, so that in the time of Tiberius there was a frontier dispute with the Sidonians;[287] in the south it bordered on the territory of Paneas (the later Caesarea Philippi), Gaulanitis,[288] Batanaea, Trachonitis and Auranitis, territories which had been given to Herod by Augustus in 24 BCE and 20 BCE so that he could put an end to the abundant banditry in this area. Herod did this among other things by settling Jewish military colonists who came from Idumaea and Babylonia. Client kings and free cities were meant to supervise each other.[289] Damascus, which now had a long common frontier with Herod's territory,[290] was a main beneficiary of the subsequent safeguarding of the trade routes in the south.[291] Herod, who already as a young *strategos* of Galilee had fled to Damascus to escape condemnation by the Sanhedrin for the murder of the bandit leader Hezekiah, attached special importance to good relations with the most important neighbouring city in the north-east of his kingdom. With good reason, in the later years of his reign he was advised by Nicolas of Damascus, who came from the Damascene aristocracy.[292] So he founded a gymnasium and a theatre in the city; Tyre and Sidon were only given a theatre.[293]

There were political, economic and cultural reasons for the mutual good will which continued under Herod's sucessors:[294] 1. the most dangerous neighbours for both the Jewish king and the Damascenes at the beginning of the first century BCE were the Nabataeans, who had become powerful with the decay of the Seleucid empire. The long shared frontier and the threats to the trade routes from robber nomads made positive collaboration necessary. 2. The most important connecting routes from Judaea to Mesopotamia and therefore to the Babylonian Diaspora led through Damascus, and conversely the land routes from there led to the southern Decapolis, the Palestinian coast and to Egypt through Herod's realm. 3. The Damascenes, like the Herodian rulers, regarded themselves as firm supporters of Rome and protagonists of Hellenistic culture; in Syria Roman rule and Hellenism were inseparably connected. Rome alone guaranteed peace towards the Arab tribes and the Parthians. 4. The large Judaean Diaspora community in Damascus presumably – as elsewhere in Syria (see above, 52f.) – saw Herod and his descendants as their protectors. Of course none of this excluded a concern also to have an orderly relationship with the Nabataeans, who controlled the trade routes to the east and south and like the Jews had a quarter of their own in Damascus (see below, 61). But ultimately peace depended on Roman protection.

The Jewish community in Damascus was not only very extensive,[295] but also very old. I Kings 20.34 reports that in the time of Ahab and Benhadad the Israelites had established bazaars in Damascus and the Aramaeans in Samaria.[296] Thus probably there had been an Israelite settlement in Damascus since the pre-exilic period and then, in the post-exilic period, one of Jews (and Samaritans). This is suggested by the geographical situation and the political significance of the city. The number mentioned by Josephus and the attractiveness of the Jewish synagogues to pagan sympathizers presupposes a long history of Jewish settlement there. Josephus' ironic report about the fear of the Damascenes on the outbreak of the Jewish War attests the importance of the Jewish minority in the city.

The political, economic and cultural significance of the Jews in southern Syria-Phoenicia is confirmed by the fact that in the first

century CE not only the south but also large parts of the former
Ituraean territory west and north-west of the city was successively
put under the rule of Jewish descendants of Herod.[297] After the
collapse of the Seleucid empire the Arab Ituraeans had gained a
sphere of power with its centre in Lebanon and reaching southwards as far as Galilee and in the east to Trachonitis, with its
capital in Chalkis. Whereas they lost Galilee to the Hasmonaeans
Aristobulus and Alexander Jannaeus, they put Damascus under
pressure.[298] Under Roman rule their territory was gradually transformed into smaller territories. After Herod had been given
Trachonitis and a little later the territory of Paneas on the south
side of Hermon,[299] at a later date further Ituraean territory was
added to that of his son Philip.[300] Therefore Luke is historically
well informed in Luke 3.1, when he calls Philip tetrarch of
Trachonitis and Ituraea. In 37 CE, on the accession of Caligula,
Agrippa received the territory of Abilene in the Antilebanon, only
about 26 km north-west of Damascus,[301] which had previously
belonged to the dynast Lysanias (Luke 3.1), together with the
tetrarchy of his uncle Philip, who had died. In 41 CE, the emperor
Claudius then made Agrippa I king of all Judaea, as once Herod
had been, and added further imperial possessions in the region
of Lebanon.[302] At the same time the kingdom of Chalkis, between
Lebanon and Antilebanon, bordering on Abilene to the west, was
transferred to his brother Herod.[303] After the death of Agrippa I
in 44 CE Herod was entrusted with the oversight of the Jerusalem
temple, and after his death in 48 CE his nephew Agrippa II, the
son of Agrippa I, was made ruler of Chalkis, presumably only until
53 CE, when Agrippa II was promised the former tetrachies of
Philip, Abilene,[304] and the territory of a further dynast in the
Lebanon, Varus,[305] while Chalkis together with the temple city of
Heliopolis/Baalbek presumably fell to the powerful Roman
colony of Berytus. However, Nero transferred the kingdom of
Lesser Armenia to Aristobulus, the son of the guardian of the
Jerusalem temple, Herod of Chalkis.[306] The daughters of Agrippa
I married Eastern client rulers who went over to Judaism for the
sake of their marriages: Drusilla married Azizus, the ruler and
high priest of Emesa, and Berenice Polemon, the king of
Pontus.[307] It becomes clear from this extension of the sphere

ruled by Jewish dynasts of the family of Herod and thus also
their influence in Syria (and eastern Asia Minor), which certainly
also encouraged the Jewish minority in their area, according
to old Herodian practice, that Rome regarded the descendants
of Herod and Mariamne as particularly loyal and therefore
accorded them considerable political power in Syria.[308] This
Jewish ruling house seemed to them to be a stabilizing element,
in contrast to the Arab Nabataeans and Ituraeans.[309] Among
other things this may be connected with the especial extent and
influence of the Jewish 'Diaspora' in southern Syria, which at
least among the upper class with their Greek education led to
sympathy with the Herodians and Roman rule. Therefore
Josephus has even Eleazar, the leader of the Sicarii in Massada,
say that the Jews in the Syrian cities 'are more hostile to us (i.e.
the revolutionaries instigating rebellion) than to the Romans'.[310]
For the *Pax Romana* guaranteed them freedom of worship,
the security of the law and an undisturbed tie with the mother
country.[311] This relatively positive attitude towards Roman rule
which later emerges in Paul in Rom. 13.1–7 will already have
been powerfully endorsed by his missionary experiences in Syria.
In view of the numerous political territories, client kingdoms and
princedoms, city states and tribal areas in Syria, Cilicia and Asia
Minor, we can also see why in Rom. 13.1 Paul speaks of 'the
powers that be' (ἐξουσίαι ὑπερέχουσαι) and does not have in
view, say, the sole power of Roman rule. Usually he had to cope
with the local magistrates (including those of the synagogue communities). The emperor in Rome was a long way off. What Paul
benefitted from as a travelling missionary was the relative security
created by the *Pax Romana*. It was a necessary presupposition
of his missionary work from the beginning. Knowing people as
he did and being a political realist, Paul was aware that for the
state authorities who kept order, to renounce the sword would
open the gate to the rule of force, anarchy and thus all forms of
criminal violence. To renounce jurisdiction as in I Cor. 6.7 was
possible only within an existing legal order. Where there is no
legal protection, one cannot dispense with these other forces.[312]

The great city territory of Damascus also had a series of Jewish
villages, the best known of which is probably Kochaba, around

ten miles south-west of Damascus.[313] The large Jewish community in the metropolis of Coele Syria thus had an old tradition and a fixed organization, comparable with communities in Antioch and Alexandria. Earliest analogies from the Hellenistic period in Palestine itself are the colonies of the 'Sidonians' in Shechem, in Marisa and Jamnia,[314] and mention should also be made of the settlement of Nabataeans in Damascus under the leadership of an 'ethnarch' appointed by King Aretas IV.[315] Moreover the Jewish community will have been led by a president or a 'council of elders' represented by a spokesman.[316] This president or spokesman was as a rule a rich, prominent citizen, comparable to John the tax farmer, who in the crisis year of 66 CE represented the interests of Jews in Caesarea by the Sea.[317]

Since despite its Aramaic/Arab surroundings Damascus was self-consciously a Hellenistic polis with Macedonian/Greek citizens, who attached great importance to their Greek education – among other things this is shown by the building of a (new) gymnasium and theatre by Herod – we must assume that the normative part of the Jewish minority spoke Greek and sought to attain the social and cultural status of citizens. The inscriptions on the local sanctuaries in the territory of the city (from Damascus itself the number of inscriptions is fairly small because of the modern constructions that have been built over them) are all in Greek, in contrast to those in the city-state of Palmyra which borders it to the north-east.[318] This shows that public and religious life was predominantly carried on in this language. Here the situation was hardly essentially different from that in other cities with large Diaspora communities like Antioch, Alexandria, Caesarea, etc.

Excursus I: The problem of the 'sympathizers' and Jewish propaganda

1. Sympathizers, 'godfearers', mixed marriages and proselytes

The 'missionary' effect of Jewish synagogue worship, which had no sacrifices but rather with its prayer, hymn-singing, inter-pretation of scripture, and presentation of doctrine and ethical admonition in a sermon, was more like a philosophical assembly than the usual pagan worship involving a sacrifice, had an impact above all on members of the non-Jewish urban middle and upper classes (and not least the matrons). Among the various synagogues in the city there may have been a few with worship in Aramaic, but the majority will have worshipped in Greek. So in contrast to Jerusalem, here that part of Judaism which had Greek as its mother tongue set the tone.[319] The Jews who only or mainly spoke Aramaic and came from the villages of the interior had only marginal significance, also in their social status.

It is these pagan sympathizers, men and women, whom Luke calls 'godfearers' or 'pious' (towards God).[320] We must imagine these Gentiles with leanings towards the synagogue in the form of several concentric circles. Thus in the first century CE they were still not a firmly defined and conceptually clear group; they only emerge as such around 200 years later in the Aphrodisias inscription, but it would be quite perverse to follow A. T. Kraabel in saying that they did not exist.[321] Nor is the designation of them uniform.[322] The innermost circle consisted of real 'godfearers' in the truest sense of the word, former Gentiles who faithfully attended synagogue worship, observed the law as far as they could, and concerned themselves with good works, who believed in the one God who had chosen Israel and tried as far as possible to avoid acts of idolatry. They could also send money – for example in the form of the diadrachm tax – or other sacrifices and consecrated gifts to Jerusalem, although they were not obliged to do so by law (see below, 65f.). Nevertheless they were still regarded as 'Greeks' or 'pagans' (i.e. *goyim* = ἔθνη) because, not being circumcised, they still were not *de iure* Jews. Luke depicts such people in a very positive way in the person of the centurion of Capernaum, Cornelius, Lydia the purple trader in Philippi, Jason in Thessalonica or Titius Iustus in Corinth. These are pagans who 'really fear God and do works of justice'.[323] He probably describes these figures so lovingly partly because he himself came from this milieu. By contrast, Juvenal gives us a well-known description with the opposite tendency, which describes the transition from 'godfearer' to proselyte in a change of generation:

Some by a father revering the sabbath begotten
(*metuentem sabbata*[324] *patrem*)
pray but to clouds and divine power of heaven in worship,
holding the flesh of the pig to be like flesh of humans,
which their father forbids. The foreskin they circumcise early,
yet have no custom to scorn or despise the laws of the
    Romans.
Jewish law they learn, and observe all the precepts
(*Iudaicum ediscunt et servant ac metuunt ius*[325]),
just as Moses once taught them in their secret scriptures,
 ... But the father is guilty who was lazed on the seven day
    always,
and never bothered himself with even the slightest of busi-
    ness.[326]

That Jewish propaganda was particularly successful in Rome in
the first century CE follows from the report that 'when the Jews
streamed into Rome in large numbers and converted many
Romans to their way of life' (συχνοὺς τῶν ἐπιχωρίων ἐς τὰ
σφέτερα ἔθη μεθιστάντων), Tiberius banished a large number
from the city.[327] This attractiveness of the 'Jewish rites' affected
all social strata: 'The senatus consultum of 19 CE is important
evidence for the wide diffusion of Judaism among the various
strata of the Roman population ... ranging from freedmen (as
attested by Tacitus) to the upper classes (the case of Fulvia).'[328]
It continues down into the second century. This is shown by
the measures of Claudius, now under the influence of the
Christian mission, the case of Poppaea and Nero's persecution of
Christians, which were directed against the striking activities of
a 'messianic-Jewish sect', the proceedings against Titus Flavius
Clemens and circles close to him, the rigorous collection of the
Fiscus Judaicus under Domitian and its reversal under Nerva,[329]
and finally the Juvenal text I have just quoted. Here to some
degree the Christians entered into the heritage of the Jews. Up to
the end of the first century they were in fact regarded as a Jewish
sect, and anti-Jewish polemic was transferred to them. Seneca
is an impressive example here. As a young man he became a
vegetarian. He gave up this practice when under Tiberius it

aroused the suspicion of interest in the strange superstition which was then spreading. He did this on the wishes of his father. Evidently he did not want to be suspected of being a Judaizing sympathizer.[330] Perhaps those youthful experiences influenced the anxious and hate-filled statement handed down by Augustine:

> In the meantime the life-style of this criminal people has become so influential that it is now accepted by all lands: the conquered have imposed their laws on the conquerors.[331]

That this was not just a specifically Roman problem is shown by the much discussed example of the royal house of Adiabene in the Parthian kingdom east of the Tigris.[332] As it shows how complicated and varied the possibilities of gradual transition to Judaism were, the event is worth reporting briefly here, since in my view it also illuminates the prevailing atmosphere in Damascus.

Here a Jewish merchant, Ananias, had caused the wives of the king 'to worship God as is the Jewish custom',[333] and finally with the help of his wives had also convinced King Izates himself. His mother Helena had similarly been instructed by another Jew. When Izates learned this, he also wanted to take the last step, since 'he believed that he would not be a real Jew unless he were circumcised'.[334] However, because of the political consequences which were to be feared, his mother and Ananias dissuaded him until another Jewish traveller from Galilee, Eleazar, 'who observed the laws particularly strictly', i.e. presumably a Pharisee,[335] forced him to be circumcised. Eleazar argued that if Izates refused he would 'sin most severely against the laws and therefore against God',[336] whereupon Izates immediately had himself circumcised. However, with God's help the political consequences which were feared failed to materialize.

These real 'godfearers', although convinced of the truth of Jewish belief in God and the revelation to Moses, did not want for political, family, economic or even quite personal reasons to be circumcised, to go over to Judaism fully and become proselytes. The social consequences, which were difficult to envisage, seemed to them to be too grave.[337] Jews from Palestine who observed the law strictly would inevitably reject them as Gentiles who were disobedient to God's commandment and inconsistent pagans, whereas Jews with a 'more liberal' view, because of their experiences in the Diaspora, could see them as having almost equal rights, above all in the question of personal eschatological salvation.[338] There was no general and clear attitude here, even if Palestinian Judaism and later the rabbis adopted a detached position towards the 'godfearers'.[339] The more generous attitude applied above all to the synagogue communities outside the mother country which – as in Damascus – gathered around them a relatively large number of such 'sympathizers' of different degrees. Presumably there were quite a number of people of higher rank in the Diaspora between Adiabene and Rome who for social reasons did not take the last step of circumcision, or, if they were women, did not finally become Jews.[340] The question of circumcision was evidently decisive above all for Jews coming from Eretz Israel, who were at the same time concerned about the holiness of the land.[341] So during the military expansion in the Hasmonaean period, the forcible circumcision of Gentiles in the conquered territories of the Idumaeans, Ituraeans, and the Hellenistic cities became a problem; it then broke out again at the beginning of the Jewish War.[342] The Herodian family also had to take account of the population in Eretz Israel by seeing that their princesses did not marry any uncircumcised pagan rulers.[343] In the Diaspora people could, indeed had to, be more generous. Therefore the number of real proselytes was much smaller than the relatively wide and varied circle of godfearers and sympathizers. This different attitude towards the uncircumcised sympathizers in the Diaspora and in Jerusalem and the conflict connected with it is confirmed by a further text which is rarely noted. Josephus reports a great four-month pilgrimage of Gentile 'godfearers', who came to Jerusalem from the Parthian empire beyond the Euphrates, 'out of reverence for our temple, with great dangers and at great expense'. He says that the pilgrims had,

> offered sacrifices, but received no part of the sacrificial flesh, as Moses has forbidden this for all who, though not governed

by our customs, still participate in our ancestral customs. But although they had to go away – after some did not even sacrifice and others had to leave their sacrifices only half performed, while many could not even enter the sanctuary – they preferred to obey the commandments of Moses than fulfil their own wishes, and this not out of fear of the one who enlightened them on these things but solely out of respect for conscience (ἀλλὰ μόνον τὸ συνειδὸς ὑφορώμενοι).[344]

These pious pagan pilgrims had evidently not been told in their country by the Jews there about the strict attitude in Jerusalem towards the uncircumcised; they arrived in the holy city thinking that they would be as welcome with their gifts in the temple as in their synagogue at home, and were certainly bitterly disappointed. The Jerusalem priest Josephus masks the conflict which is indicated here by his edifying closing remark. One might almost assume that some of the disappointed pilgrims decided on circumcision as the final consequence. The other theoretical possibility – Josephus dates the event in the most recent past before the destruction of the temple – would have been for them to join a Christian mission community, where the sacrificial cult of the temple had become insignificant and equal rights were guaranteed.

Among women before 70, however, since there is as yet no evidence of proselyte baptism as a fixed custom of the Diaspora,[345] the distinction between the 'godfearer' and the 'proselyte' is difficult. Perhaps – apart from the greater interest in religion among women in antiquity generally – this is one of the reasons why women from the middle and upper classes who had relative independence went to the synagogue in particular.[346] It is striking that two novellas from different times and different cultural areas glorify women proselytes, the Book of Ruth and Joseph and Asenath.[347] Evidently such literature had been called for since the early Hellenistic period. Even Philo praises Tamar in *De virt.* 220ff., who

grew up in a polytheistic (πολυθέῳ) family and a city full of idols.

But when she could see the brief shining of the truth from

the depths of darkness, risking death she went over to piety and scorned life if this life could not be a 'good life' (καλῶς ζῆν). But 'good' meant the veneration and worship of the one author (of the world).

Philo could also have described the women godfearers in Damascus in the same way.

In the Testament of Joseph the wife of Potiphar approaches the chaste Joseph on the pretext of 'learning from him the word of the Lord', in order then to convince her husband to turn from the pagan gods and accept the Jewish law, if only Joseph will satisfy her desire.[348]

A particularly 'archaic' 'godfearer' after the flood was the Jewish Sibyl, who was regarded as Noah's daughter-in-law or rather even as his daughter.[349] With this 'prophetess', still obligated to the 'primal revelation', began the chain of pagan sibyls. This primal prophetess was a quite explicit promoter of the ideal of the 'godfearers' in the synagogue. She admonishes 'the Greeks' to turn from idolatry, paedophilia, adultery, etc., but not to be circumcised and ostentatiously to go over to Judaism: rather, she calls for and generally expects acceptance of the law which was given to Moses on Sinai by all nations without casuistically presenting this to them.[350] Twice the Sibyl describes the Torah of Sinai as great joy (χάρμα) for all men and women, in contrast to her terrible prophesies of disaster on the world of nations, which she is compelled to cast out because the nations have not recognized the only true God and his law.[351] Matthew 1.3, 5, 6 in the pedigree of Jesus beginning with the first proselyte Abraham also proudly introduce the woman 'proselytes' Tamar, Rahab, Ruth and the wife of Uriah the Hittite into the genealogy of Jesus. There is a manifest coincidence between these very different literary examples, Josephus' accounts of the women around King Izates in Adiabene, the Roman matron Fulvia, who was not an isolated instance, Luke's references, the evidence of inscriptions and rabbinic accounts.[352] Venturia Paula, *mater synagogarum Campi et Bolumni*, who died at the ripe old age of 86 years and six months, only became a proselyte at the age of 70 and took the name of Sarah.[353] She may well have been a 'godfearer' for a long time previously.[354] At the other end of this wide scale stands the superstitious Roman matron depicted by Juvenal, into whose ears are whispered secret doctrines by a Jewish beggar woman who appears as *interpres legum Solymarum, magna sacerdos* and *summi fida internuntia caelis.*[355] Luke, who in Acts often emphasizes the importance of prominent women in connection with the synagogue, gives a completely accurate picture of the situation. The importance of women in Paul's letters corresponds to this.[356]

These prominent women (and men), who were close to the synagogue communities, raised the social status of such communities, and in critical situations could also provide some degree of protection. It was always good in the Graeco-Roman world to have as many 'contacts' upwards as possible. Therefore Diaspora Judaism was generous to people in high office. The main thing was that these people should extend their sympathies towards the alien religious community and if necessary make their influence felt on its behalf. In this way the circle of sympathizers spread very widely. It even included Poppaea Sabina, the consort of Nero, who advocated the interest of the Jerusalem priesthood against Agrippa II and is called θεοσεβής by Josephus.[357] A little later, through the mediation of a young Jewish actor, Alityrus,[358] she received the young Josephus as the leader of a priestly delegation and saw that he had rich presents when he left.[359] After her unexpected death she was not cremated according to Roman custom, but 'embalmed with many spices according to the custom of foreign kings', i.e. she was buried according to oriental-Jewish custom.[360] Already because of her elevated position she could not show any 'exclusive sympathy' to the Jews, but one can still call her a sympathizer, and Josephus understood her as such.[361] Menahem Stern refers to Julia Severa in Acmonia in Phrygia as a contemporary parallel; she played a key part in the building of the synagogue there. We know from inscriptions and numismatic sources that she was the high priest of the imperial cult and a sponsor of games, and that her son L. Servenius Cornutus entered the senate under Nero only a short time after L. Sergius Paullus and in 73 CE became proconsul of Asia. Although Julia herself was not a Jew, she was a patron of the

Jewish community.[362] Sergius Paulus, the governor of Cyprus, who is first advised by a Jewish seer and miracle worker and then becomes interested in Barnabas and Paul, is a Lukan parallel. It is significant that while Luke reports that Sergius Paulus 'believed', impressed by a miraculous punishment of his former adviser, the Jewish magus, 'astonished at the teaching of the Lord', he does not say anything about baptism, which elsewhere in such contacts is important for him. There is probably a connection between the encounter with Sergius Paulus and the appearance of the two missionaries in Pisidian Antioch, where the family of Sergius Paulus had possessions.[363] Personal relations and commendations were an important help to the earliest Christian missionaries in their planning.

Another interesting case – like Poppaea, on the extreme periphery, but against a completely different background – was that of P. Petronius, governor of Syria, who persistently resisted the command of Caligula to erect his statue in the temple in Jerusalem. Philo attempts to give reasons for his bold and humane conduct:

> But he probably had a glimmer of Jewish philosophy and piety, which he may have learned earlier in his urge for culture either while he was governor in areas where Jews live in large numbers in every city, in Asia and Syria, or because of the tendency of his soul towards an independent sovereign behaviour with self-control, which is worthy of the striving of its nature. But God apparently instils good thoughts in the good.[364]

We should not forget that there were not only mixed marriages between Jewish men and pagan women, whose conversion to the religion of their husbands was taken for granted, at least in the case of the ancestral mother of the clan, but also mixed marriages between Jewish women and pagan men, in which the conversion of the pagan partner to Judaism was not always the *sine qua non*.[365] The later unions of the sisters of Agrippa II, Drusilla and Berenice,[366] which have already been mentioned, and which by no means met with the approval of Josephus, kept occurring in the Diaspora. The designation ἰουδαΐζοντες[367] which was applied to the mixed group (μεμιγμένον ἀλλόφυλον) that was despised and feared by the Syrians, could among other things perhaps indicate such mixed marriages between Jews and Gentiles.[368] The god-fearing women and their husbands, who were then often well disposed towards Judaism, could be regarded as the 'prelude' to mixed marriages. Testimony to such marriages is understandably rare, but is not completely absent from the Diaspora.[369] This helps to explain the circumcision of Timothy (Acts 16.1–3), who was born of the marriage of a Jewess who had 'become a believer', and above all Paul's admonition and argument in I Cor. 7.12–16 that Christian husbands and wives should not be divorced from their Gentile partner for religious reasons.[370] As the case of Timothy's mother shows, the early Christian mission was evidently particularly successful with such women who through marriage to Gentile husbands tended to be on the edge of Judaism.

The widest circle is formed by those Gentiles who – in a quite syncretistic way – were interested in the power of Jewish magic. Moses was regarded as the greatest magician in the ancient world, and the Jewish God, the God of heaven of the Persian period and the ὕψιστος or παντοκράτωρ of the LXX, particularly with his Hebrew names Iao, Adonaios, Sabaoth etc., was thought to be particularly effective. Such convictions could also make the synagogue attractive. Around a third of the magical papyri and amulets are based on Jewish elements,[371] and beyond them we find illuminating references in Luke and Josephus. Here we should not overlook the fact that Jesus and the earliest Christians were initially accused by their opponents of magic, whereas the Christian missionaries rejected magic as the work of demons.[372] Prominent Gentiles who were close to the synagogue were basically in the same kind of situation as that of Naaman the Syrian, described in II Kings 5.16–19, when faced with Elijah.[373] The god-fearers in Damascus could look upon him as their biblical proto-type. The higher their social status, the greater the freedom they were granted in the Diaspora synagogues, and the prouder these synagogues were of them.

2. The controversy over circumcision

Particularly over the question of circumcision, people had to be relatively generous; otherwise they would have lost a considerable number of the sympathizers who were important for their social status in a foreign environment. Certainly Josephus emphasizes in *Contra Apionem* 1, 210 that the legislator

> gladly welcomes all those who want to live under the same laws with us and to join us, as he believes that affinity comes into being not only through descent but also through decision on a common way of life. But he does not want those who have no serious intent to join our form of life.[374]

However, in saying this he is formulating an ideal aim, and the critical addition indicates that there were quite a few ἐκ παρέργου προσίοντες. Here we still have an echo of the rigorism of the Pharisaic priest from Jerusalem, which could be compared with that of the Galilean Eleazar towards Izates, and this typical Palestinian restraint must in no way be transferred to the Diaspora. Therefore the rabbinic material, which puts forward a one-sided standpoint, does not help us much.[375] Moreover it is striking that Josephus speaks only generally of 'the same laws' and does not put particular emphasis on circumcision as a shibboleth.

The situation among those born Jews was quite different, especially in the strict mother country. They might have been relatively generous towards sympathizers because of their particular situation, but circumcision was in no way a matter of indifference to them: to refuse it essentially meant apostasy from Judaism. This was even true for the family of Herod, among whom in marriages of Herodian women with non-Jewish rulers from neighbouring regions the latter's circumcision was called for and such politically important ties would be allowed to fail rather than renouncing this demand.[376] The Jew who refused to circumcise his children, who rejected this in principle or even attempted to reverse the operation on himself, was regarded as an apostate, above all after the Maccabaean period.[377] This is the reason why Paul, the former Pharisaic scribe, had Timothy, the son of a Jewish mother, circumcised. Otherwise he would have barred Timothy's way and his own, as an alleged apostate, to the 'godfearers' in the synagogue.[378] When Philo once speaks of radical Jewish allegorists for whom the literal meaning of the law becomes insignificant because they only want to see 'symbols of spiritual things' in it, he is talking of intellectual outsiders in Alexandria, whom he himself resolutely repudiates.[379] He also gives circumcision an extensive allegorical interpretation which focusses on the liberation of the soul from dangerous passions, but in his exegesis of Gen. 17.8–14 he unconditionally insists on real circumcision.[380] By contrast, with reference to the proselytes in Ex. 22.20b he can say that scripture makes it 'manifest that the proselyte is someone who is not circumcised in his foreskin but in respect of his lusts, desires and other passions'. 'The disposition of the proselyte' means no less than 'alienation from the appearance of polytheism and becoming familiar with the honour of the one and the nature of all'. Those who come in are those who have 'gone over to the truth'.[381] Here there is clearly some tension between external circumcision and its real 'spiritual' meaning. This knowledge of the truth of the revelation of the one God, the creator of the world and Lord of history, which has been given to Israel, forms the real basis of Jewish religious propaganda, for this one truth of the one God also applied ultimately to all non-Jews, who were also among his creatures. This is very clear in Philo (for example in his eschatological writing *de praemiis et poenis*) and also in Josephus. However, despite the manifest tension, it would be wrong to read out of this text, which has been so much discussed, that Philo knew the possibility of 'uncircumcised proselytes'. In accord with the LXX he takes it for granted that the proselyte has himself circumcised, but this external operation has a deeper spiritual sense and that with the external operation an inner conversion is to come about. However, in some circumstances the godfearer or sympathizer could be encouraged to dispense with such an operation – and the consequences associated with it – altogether and to appeal to the circumcision of the heart as being all that was necessary; this is then essential for Paul and Luke, and even more for the Letter of Barnabas.[382] The argument of Ananias to Izates lay along this 'liberal line'. The contrast between the Jewish merchant Ananias, who was presumably a Babylonian Diaspora Jew, and Eleazar, who was presumably a Galilean Pharisee, indicates a basic problem which already became acute right at the beginning of the mission of the Jewish-Christian Hellenists.[383]

3. Synagogue preaching as a means of religious propaganda

The worship in the synagogues of these cities was public and will have been so attractive to outsiders above all because of its sermons. Leaving aside the great commentaries of Philo of Alexandria, from which we can infer something about his preaching and teaching,[384] we have only small fragments of this Jewish genre of preaching, which basically also include the speeches composed by Luke in Acts, based on the 'historical situation'.[385] Here, however, we shall refer to an originally Jewish sermon.

The pseudo-Philonic sermon *De Jona*, which was probably composed in Alexandria, is a particularly fine example of this inviting preaching in the synagogue which was at the same time 'liberal'. In it we can still clearly recognize the cautiously welcoming tone with which the preacher 'commends the Mosaic religion'[386] to his pagan hearers and awakens understanding for the 'Gentiles' among his Jewish audience. The 'repentance' of the people of Nineveh is an example for both Jews and Gentiles:

> The Ninevites, too, were once without fruits of piety. They did not know the fruit of divine righteousness, and they showed to this world the honour that is due to its Creator. But now they no longer give thanks to nature for its fruits and no longer hold worship for the warming power of the elements; but they confess and honour the Giver of fruits for the fruits, and have committed themselves to worshipping the Architect of this world rather than this world itself.[387]

The Ninevites are moved to the 'conversion of their hearts'[388] because of God's 'love of man' (he is *mardaser* = φιλάνθρωπος[389]):

God sent the prophet with his message of judgment against the city, to announce its destruction, because of the sins of the people of Nineveh. But God changed his plan, 'to allow love to prevail'.[390] Accordingly God himself then expounds his own preaching of judgment to the prophet and shows him how it has nevertheless been fulfilled: the city has indeed not been 'destroyed', but hearts have been 'turned'.[391] God as the philanthropist brings men who are lacking in true human self-knowledge and dignity out of their animal state to the true knowledge of nature and its creator. 'God is like a man who has bought a slave for money,[392] and has bought him back from death to life ... The price consists ... in God's concern through the word of the prophet, and it lies in God's unmerited forbearance.'[393]

This sermon expresses the liberal attitude of a Jewish synagogue preacher who is open to his environment and to Stoic ideas, but nevertheless, while not 'watering down' the biblical story of Jonah, woos his pagan fellow-citizens so that they attain the knowledge of God's love for humankind. At the same time he wants to convince them of the need to accept a divine philanthropy and the ethical attitude which corresponds to it in gratitude to the creator, i.e. a life which is pleasing to God.[394] Elements of this demand – now radicalized as eschatological talk of judgment – appear in Rom. 1.18–3.20.

In his introduction to the Mosaic account of creation Josephus can emphasize the philosophical character of the biblical account, which is not mythological but rather corresponds 'to God's majesty and philanthropy':[395] it fully 'corresponds to the nature of the universe'. It is a 'very philosophical view' (θεωρία λίαν φιλόσοφος).[396] The liberal Judaism of the Diaspora invited its pagan fellow-citizens to take part in its worship and allow themselves to be convinced of the true philosophy,[397] i.e. the 'saving message' of Moses.[398] In other words, it was not rejected because it was aware of having exclusive possession of the revelation of the one God; this was understood as an act of benevolence for all human beings. That did not make Judaism a 'syncretistic religion'.[399] Often enough this 'invitation' came up against repudiation, not least because of political developments.[400] The reason why the key word 'philanthropy' appears only on the periphery of earliest Christianity is connected with its Palestinian origin and its eschatological character. In Christianity – on the basis of Old Testament texts – the talk was of the 'love of

God' for his community and for all human beings.[401] This gave
the message of earliest Christianity its distinctive impulse.

4. Not 'mission' but 'power of attraction'?

Nevertheless, it would be misleading to speak of a Jewish
'mission' in the real sense.[402] 'Sending' to proclaim a message of
salvation is a new – Jewish-Christian – phenomenon and is connected with the eschatological character of the proclamation of
the kingdom of God and Christ and the limited time before the
parousia. Here the beginnings of this 'mission' go back to Jesus
himself,[403] though it should not be overlooked that already in the
Old Testament God 'sent' the prophets, above all to his people
Israel, but sometimes also to the Gentiles, like Jonah to Nineveh
and Elijah to Damascus in Syria to anoint Hazael.[404] By contrast,
the Jewish 'ethnos', which in antiquity was primarily not a
'religion' in our sense but at least externally a political corpora-
tion, though with exclusive and striking religious traditions,[405] did
not know any such general 'sending' to non-Jews. Rather – in
complete contrast to the anxious restraint of Greek cities over
giving citizenship to foreigners – it was uniquely open to the
attachment of προσήλυτοι, i.e. of 'incomers' to Israel, 'the people
of God'. Here, simply because of its lack of political power –
something new in the ancient world – the religious components
stood right in the foreground. In other words, no active or even
aggressive propaganda was practised, but the concern was 'attraction' in the best sense of the word, i.e. the attraction of interested
non-Jews, of whom there was no lack. For what was put forward
was the claim to the one true God. It is this that made Judaism
(and then Christianity) so interesting amid the religious and
ethnic 'pluralism' of late antiquity.[406] With good reason, Josephus
describes the Jewish constitution, in contrast to the monarchy,
aristocracy and democracy of other peoples, as the only 'theo-
cracy'.[407] This openness of Jews to 'proselytes' and sympathizers
can only be compared with the relatively generous gift of Roman
citizenship, though in the latter the religious component which
was decisive for the Jews retreated right into the background in
favour of political status and was connected with the extension of
Roman power. It was precisely this 'power of attraction' and

strength of identity in first-century Judaism which led to the religious phobia about the Jews described by P. Schäfer, and which disturbed not only Syrians and Egyptians but also Greeks and Romans. Beyond any doubt this primarily religious openness and power of attraction for strangers shown by the synagogue in the Diaspora – not so much in the mother country – at the beginning of our era, i.e. the special interest it had in gaining these for its own ethnos and its only true, divinely-willed religion, prepared the way for the new *mission* of the Jewish Christians with its eschatological motivation.[408] The curiosity of the 'sympathizers' about the ethical monotheism of the synagogue was matched by the interest of the Jewish communities in winning over Gentiles interested in the Jewish faith. Both met in the question of *religious truth*. The new, earliest Christian mission with its eschatological motivation could build on this. Above all Philo keeps stressing that the Gentiles are attracted by the question of truth: 'They left blood relations, fatherland, customs, cults and divine images, honours and privileges and as good colonists strove to depart from mythical deceptions to the clear truth and the worship of the one God who truly is.'[409] The Pauline 'truth of the gospel' is ultimately the eschatological-universal focussing and concretization of the message of the one true God[410] and loving Father who at the end of times (Gal. 4.4) has revealed himself to all people, Jews and Gentiles, in his Son, the crucified messiah.[411]

2.4 The power of attraction of Jewish monotheism in Syria and the problem of syncretism

The religious situation was particularly favourable for the ethical monotheism of the Jews in Syria and Arabia because of the pagan tendency towards *theocrasia* which is visible there from the Persian period and which on the Jewish side presented itself above all as the 'absorption' of the pagan supreme deity by the one true God of Israel.[412] There was a tendency to transfer as many divine functions as possible to the one 'God of heaven' with solar features, whether he was called Hadad, Marnas, Baal-shamem, El, Dushara, Dionysus, Zeus, Roman Iuppiter or something else. At the end of this development stood the monotheizing or pantheizing cult of the *Sol invictus*. In the Roman period the old Syrian high gods had often 'given up their native names' and transformed themselves into the supreme heavenly-astral Zeus, Iuppiter or simply the nameless 'God'. Thus in inscriptions they take on designations like *Optimus Maximus Caelus aeternus Iuppiter* or, as in the case of the God of Heliopolis-Bambyke, *Iuppiter Optimus Maximus summus Superantissimus.*[413] The Jewish 'God of heaven' of the Persian period, whose official designation in the Hellenistic-Roman period was θεὸς ὕψιστος, and the supreme Semitic God of Heaven (and the one God) could move towards each other.[414] The Idumaeans, who were forcibly Judaized under John Hyrcanus, will have identified their God Qos with the Adonai-Kyrios of Zion and have become loyally faithful, nationalistic Jews.[415] What had still been a danger in the religious persecution under Antiochus IV before the Maccabean rebellion in the Roman period became more of a sign of strength: the pagan inclination towards *theocrasia* with a tendency towards the 'one Lord of heaven' and ruler of all,[416] which on the Jewish side expressed the power of this faith to 'absorb' alien 'high gods', attracted sympathizers to the synagogue communities of Syria, above all in the large cities like Damascus and Antioch. One could see a later analogy in the fact that Aurelian, the enemy of Christianity, prepared for the victory of the Christian God under Constantine by his massive promotion of the cult of *Sol invictus.*[417] This does not exclude the possibility that Jews also engaged in polemic against the Semitic 'God of Heaven'. This happens in the book of Daniel and probably also in the designation Beelzebul, the 'Lord of the (heavenly) dwelling' or (the fourth) heaven. The supreme God of the Phoenicians, Ituraeans and Arameans living around Galilee would then have been disparaged by the Galileans as the leader of all the demons and Jesus as an exorcist would have been said to be in alliance with him.[418] The alleged Syrian syncretistic influence on the earliest Christian communities which has been much discussed since the history-of-religions school should not, however, be connected with these monotheizing tendencies.[419] Of the Greek 'mysteries' at the beginning of the first century CE, only that of Dionysus was known. He was worshipped in Damascus,

Scythopolis and later as a Greek interpretation of Dusares in the Hauran, but the Dionysus cult in a city did not in any case amount to the existence of mystery associations. There were not yet 'Oriental mysteries' of Isis, Mithras, Attis, etc., around 30 CE.[420] Contrary to the view put forward by the history-of-religions school,[421] in the early period no influence from the mysteries can be determined on earliest Christianity and on Paul, and this is even more the case with a Gnosticism of which there is no evidence in the sources.[422]

Neither the Jewish nor the first Christian communities of Syria give rise to such conjectures of real pagan influence in the sense of a 'paganizing', for example in the sphere of christology. The trend was, rather, in the opposite direction. None of the conjectures about a 'syncretistic' Christianity in the first century CE (as opposed to the synagogue) find support in the sources; they are unfounded speculations, since *theocrasia* or absorption is one thing and real religious mixing, which is what is commonly meant by syncretism, is another. The Greek interpretation of Semitic deities, which often took place relatively superficially, is to be distinguished from this. El, Baal and Hadad became Zeus/Jupiter, Allat Athena, Astarte Artemis and Dusara Dionysus, but the basic forms of piety remained largely the same as they had been from of old.[423]

Whereas we have only scanty reports of mantic practices and oracles at the Jerusalem temple in this period, and the Jewish sources were above all concerned with when and why the Jerusalem priesthood lost its power of divinization,[424] the priests at the local sanctuaries of Syria and Phoenicia continued to perform the old rites and practices.[425] The fact that with earliest Christianity a movement suddenly appeared which in the context of eschatological revelation and salvation through one God in his 'Son' and 'Anointed' showed marked prophetic and enthusiastic traits, claimed authority for 'signs and wonders' and removed the barriers between Jews and non-Jews erected by the law, made this Jewish-messianic movement particularly attractive. The success of the earliest Christian mission was prepared for by the tendency towards one universal God of heaven, though in Judaism and Christianity he was a God who was the creator, powerful in history but also quite personal, and not only a philosophical principle. Basically 'syncretism' is a label which veils more than it explains, unless one gives an accurate description of the phenomena that one wants to subsume under it. A famous thesis of Hermann Gunkel has had a pernicious influence down to the present day:

> 'Our thesis is ... that Christianity, which was born out of syncretistic Judaism, displays marked syncretistic features. Earliest Christianity is like a river which has flowed together from two sources: one is specifically Israelite and derives from the Old Testament; the other flows through Judaism from alien oriental religions. In addition, in the West there is then the Greek factor ... ' This then led to the concluding thesis: 'It is not the gospel of Jesus as we know it predominantly from the Synoptics, but the early Christianity of Paul and John that is a syncretistic religion', and this statement is heightened to end with the succinct words, 'Christianity is a syncretistic religion'.[426]

This is totally misleading, as the alternative which is formulated is a false one. Today we would have to say that earliest Christianity, including that of Paul and John, stems from the one broad fruitful river of the Old Testament Jewish tradition. In a history of more than a thousand years, from the beginning this one river, which in no way can be divided between the Old Testament and Judaism since the former first comes from Judaism, which only took shape in the post-exilic period,[427] constantly had smaller and larger tributaries which it absorbed without losing its identity as the one river, although it also kept bringing change. These 'tributaries' are Assyrian, Neo-Babylonian, Egyptian, Phoenician, Persian and of course from the fourth century onwards also Greek, sometimes in a substantial and varied form. The extent and character of the tributaries differed in different times, places and groups: they were different in the Diaspora of Babylonia, Egypt or in the mother country; different again in Philo, Josephus, the Essenes, many kinds of 'apocalyptists', or in earliest Christianity. Of course one could call them all 'syncretistic', and if need be the river itself. But this label is not much help, nor does it lead to a better understanding. The important thing is always the identification and description of the individual tributaries. Here what is unique is the powerful religious identity, creativity and absorbent capacity of Judaism, to which Christianity is historically also indebted, since it first showed itself as a particularly effective part of the old – more effective because it was eschatologically more active and had a more universal orientation.

The Jewish synagogue communities in Damascus may not have been all that different from the other Jewish Diaspora communities in the great cities of the eastern Mediterranean; however, they will have had a stronger 'Palestinian Jewish' stamp because of their relative geographical proximity to the mother country. After them, Antioch is the closest parallel.

In connection with his report of the anti-Jewish pogrom there after the destruction of the temple, Josephus not only relates that the Jewish Diaspora in Syria was the largest in the Roman empire but also goes into the fate of the Jews in the Syrian metropolis.[428] Because of the size of the city they were particularly numerous. 'They always attracted a large number of Greeks to their worship and they (viz. the Jews) to some degree made these part of them.'[429] We will also have to presuppose similar circumstances, though to a lesser degree, in Damascus. We shall have to go on to consider these in detail.

2.5 The beginnings of the Christian community in Damascus and the earliest mission outside Palestine

I have gone into Damascus, its Jewish community, the question of sympathizers and Jewish 'propaganda' at such length since it is the first Hellenistic city outside Palestine in which according to Paul and Luke Christians appear, and these questions are of fundamental significance for the missionary activity of the Hellenists and of Paul in Syria which now begins. Without clarifying them, we shall understand neither Paul's mission nor the genesis of his theology. For the first time the frontiers of Eretz Israel had been crossed. The 'city of Samaria', i.e. probably the Samaritan capital Sychar, and the coastal cities of Ashdod and

Caesarea which Luke associates with the name of the evangelist Philip,[430] could still be counted as 'Judaea' in the wider sense, but something new begins in Damascus. Luke presupposes that there are already Jewish Christians there, and he mentions just one of them, Ananias, by name, additionally describing him as a pious Jew.[431] However, it seems improbable from the narrative that Saul's host, Jude, in the 'street called Straight',[432] is a Christian. How would the failed persecutor, blinded by his vision of Christ, come to stay with a Christian in particular? It seems that he is unknown to Ananias. Evidently here Luke has fragmentary earlier accounts which ultimately may come from Paul himself and which he elaborates on in his narrative.[433] It is striking that he avoids the term *ekklesia* in Damascus, having used it in 5.11 and 8.1, 3 for the community in Jerusalem[434] and in 9.31 for the Christians in Judaea generally. Only in 13.1 does he speak of a community outside Judaea, in Antioch, and then in isolated instances of communities in the area of Paul's mission.[435] Instead, in 9.2 he uses 'the way' (ἡ ὁδός) in the sense of *hairesis*, 'trend', or *didaskalia*, 'teaching'.[436] This could be an older designation of Jewish origin which was used by Christians and their opponents. As it has become a favourite Lukan term, it remains uncertain whether it played a specific role in Damascus or Syria in particular. If that is the case, it must have been an 'archaic' internal designation in the sense of 'our way',[437] which then disappeared quickly. 9.19 and 25[438] simply speak of 'the disciples', whom Saul joins and who help in his flight from this city. This absolute use of οἱ μαθηταί is also a favourite Lukan term; there is no parallel to its use after Easter in the letters. Its basis could really be the earliest way in which the followers of Jesus described themselves, as *talmidayya diyesu*ᵃ', a term which was probably already formed in the time before Easter. However, it, too, is not specific to a place. Perhaps Luke, who has a sense for such 'archaic' formulations, means it to indicate that the community had not been firmly consolidated and was still in no way an organization independent from the synagogue communities. Presumably it met in one or more private houses as a kind of 'messianic conventicle', but at the same time it presumably also attempted to exercise influence on those who went to the synagogues. That is precisely why Saul wanted to go to Damascus, in order to create order there, so that the followers of this 'tendency' could no longer confuse the Jewish synagogues there and lead their members astray.

Nor are we told that Saul teaches in the assembled Christian community; it is only said that without delay (εὐθέως) he preached Jesus in the synagogue communities as Son of God.[439] This statement is further intensified in 9.22: 'But Saul increased all the more in strength, and confounded the Jews who lived in Damascus by proving that Jesus was the Christ.'[440] In other words, for Luke, in a comparable way to Gal. 1.16, without delay the previous persecutor becomes the one who proclaims the new doctrine which has been revealed to him. He, the one who had threatened and perplexed the Christians in a manner which still has an effect in v.21, now perplexes those who go to the synagogue because he (one could add, the Pharisaic scribe and pupil of the famous Gamaliel)[441] argues in public with proofs from the scriptures that Jesus is the Messiah.

However, according to Gal. 1.16 the change in Paul's life takes place with the revelation of the Son of God, with the aim 'that I should preach him among the Gentiles', whereas according to Acts 9.20, 22 Paul preaches the Son of God and Messiah in the *synagogues* of Damascus. But were not these synagogues full of pagan sympathizers, as Josephus attests? Was not preaching to the Jews at the same time inevitably also addressed here to (god-fearing) Gentiles? Nowhere does Paul say that his message was primarily or even only directed to such Gentiles as had never heard anything of the prophetic writings of Israel, its God, the law and its promises. Rather, his letters give the impression that those to whom they were addressed must have known a good deal of the Greek Bible. And where and how would he address these Gentiles who were completely and utterly unfamiliar with the holy scriptures of Israel, their proclamation of God and their promises? On the streets of Damascus, Tarsus and Antioch or even in front of pagan temples? We hear of public 'street preaching' by the apostle – in the style of the soap box in Hyde Park – really only in Athens, and there he has very limited success.[442]

But that has again taken us too far ahead of ourselves. We are still in Damascus, and a basic question has not yet been answered. Which Christians did Paul meet there who baptized him and communicated some teachings to him?[443] For Luke, going by the example of Ananias, whom he calls 'a devout man according to the law, well spoken of by all the Jews who lived there (in Damascus)',[444] they were pious Jews, faithful to the law. That is in accord with Luke's apologetic tendency to make only the other side fundamentally responsible for the break with the synagogue. But in Damascus both groups still evidently live side by side, albeit with tensions. That is quite plausible, given the chronology of the birth of the young messianic sect. Why Saul wants to arrest these Jewish Christians in particular and bring them to Jerusalem and leave Christians living closer, in the coastal region or in Galilee, untouched, is not explained in Luke's triple account: one of his many inconsistencies. In this plain account which simplifies a complicated reality, he limits himself to an emotional reason: it was the boundless angry zeal of the persecutor who wants to destroy the new sect everywhere.[445]

Since we are only three years after the death of Jesus, we can hardly doubt that the still small group of Christians in Damascus were Jewish Christians; however, it must be added that these Christians (like the synagogues there) also attracted godfearers, indeed were perhaps particularly interested in them. It was already reported of Jesus that he healed individual Gentiles and did not reject them in principle. The young Christian community in Damascus had no reason to be stricter over the law than the synagogues in the city. It also seems to me to be probable that like the earliest community in Jerusalem, on the basis of the Old Testament they understood themselves to be the eschatological *qahal YHWH/ekklesia theou*, though for the reasons mentioned above Luke does not use this term in connection with Damascus, but only for Jerusalem and Judaea.[446] Paul later calls himself a persecutor of the ἐκκλησία τοῦ θεοῦ[447] in a stereotyped formula, by which he means the community in Jerusalem,[448] and it is hard to see how the Christians in Damascus would have had a different sense of themselves as a community.[449] They will also have given baptism in the name of Jesus – how else? – not only to Jews but probably also to uncircumcised godfearers. By contrast, the three-day fast of the blinded Saul is a penitential fast of the persecutor as a result of his being shaken by the audition and vision and is hardly a reference to the institutional fast before baptism, which is only attested at a much later date.[450] The laying on of hands by Ananias in 9.12, 17, too, must not be understood in terms of the baptism which follows, but could refer to a gesture of healing and blessing by Jesus which the disciples continued.[451] We might ask whether the connection with the outpouring of the Spirit in v.17 does not possibly give this the additional signifi- cance of 'ordination' conveyed by the Spirit, which is not a fixed church custom for Luke but can go back to the Jerusalem com- munity, since its last roots are to be sought in Deut. 34.9.[452] According to his letters, Paul himself does not seem to practise this custom. Here it becomes hard to distinguish between the original significance and Luke's interpretation, especially as there are about fifty years between his writing and the event.

We can hardly infer from Luke's account any details of what was already 'fixed' custom in this community in Damascus which was very young and hardly institutionalized. Unconditional historical fidelity to detail is not always Luke's concern, even if he often reports interesting details which could be original. We cannot presuppose that this community in the making as yet had many fixed customs. Luke cannot and does not want to paint a full picture of the special characteristics of the early period and the enthusiasm caused by the eschatological Spirit, any more than he does in his description of the events in Jerusalem in chs. 2–7. This enthusiasm is probably most visible in the 'prophetic' spirit of Ananias.

Luke leaves completely open the question how this community came into being. An unclear formulation in the *Epistula Apostolorum,* the only early apocryphal writing to mention Damascus apart from the Acts of Paul and the Pseudo- Clementines, gives the impression that the communities there were founded by the eleven apostles to whom the Risen Christ spoke. As the author of this unique writing around the middle of the second century perpetrates the worst kind of inconsistency, despite his considerable use of Acts, there will certainly not be a special tradition here.[453] The Jewish-Christian source of the

Pseudo-Clementines reports that Peter fled to Damascus and Paul wanted to persecute him there: this sounds almost like a parody of Acts.[454]

I have already indicated the improbability of the hypothesis which has recently become popular that the community of disciples in Damascus was founded – quite independently of events in Jerusalem – by 'itinerant radical' followers of Jesus from Galilee. There are no arguments in favour of this (let alone any proofs). The first disciples in Damascus could just as well have been followers of Jesus from Philip's realm (Gaulanitis, Caesarea Philippi) or the Decapolis; indeed, we cannot even rule out the possibility that Jews from in and around Damascus made their way to Lake Genessaret to see and hear the eschatological preacher and miracle-worker. John the Baptist had already created a widespread movement among the people, and Jesus continued it in his own way. When the Gospels speak of wide-ranging influence, we should not explain this in all too primitive a way in terms of what is alleged to be state of the community at a later date. Moreover, there is hardly more than three or four years between the activity of Jesus and events in Damascus. Nor should we forget that at that time Damascus was probably already part of the Decapolis.[455] However, a small troop of simple, Aramaic-speaking disciples of Jesus from elsewhere, without a christological kerygma and armed with only the pious wisdom sayings of the Logia source, could hardly have provoked the ambitious Jerusalem Pharisee and scribe to intervene by force.

All this makes it plausible that it was the Jewish Christian 'Hellenists' who had just fled from Jerusalem who were disturbing the synagogue communities in Damascus. It is all too understandable, as I have already said, that they should have gone there. After Caesarea, Tyre and Sidon, as the metropolis of southern Syria Damascus was the nearest large Hellenistic polis, supposedly founded by a near kinsman of Abraham, with a sizeable Jewish community and above all many godfearers, i.e. a group which belonged to the periphery of the synagogue and in whom – as the example of Philip shows – the 'Hellenists' were particularly interested. As a eunuch the Ethiopian finance minister will already have been such a 'godfearer', and we may

also regard the Samaritans as 'heretics' standing on the edge of
Judaism. 'Godfearers' were probably baptized just as they were.
Here Philip seems to have been treading in the footsteps of Jesus,
who felt that he had been sent to 'the lost sheep' of the house of
Israel, to sinners and those who were despised.[456] Given the
eschatological 'spirit of enthusiasm' that prevailed in the earliest
community, an intimation from the Spirit or a prophetic interpretation of, say, Amos 5.26f. in the style of CD 6.5 or even of
Zech. 9.1 may have played a role for the expelled 'Hellenists'.
Indeed Damascus was specially the subject of prophetic-messianic
prophecy.[457]

Nor is it insignificant that the city could be counted as part of
the frontier territory of Eretz Israel. According to the schematic
description in Acts 8.1, those who were driven out of Jerusalem
did not immediately seek out Gentile territory, but moved
'throughout the region of Judaea and Samaria' (κατὰ τὰς χώρας
τῆς Ἰουδαίας καὶ Σαμαρείας). Only in 11.19, i.e. at a substantially
later point in time, does Luke then have them advancing to
Phoenicia, Cyprus and ultimately to Antioch.[458] This extension is
certainly also intended to put the direct mission to the Gentiles in
Antioch in the narrative only after the baptism of the first Gentile
Christian Cornelius, but it probably rightly indicates that Antioch
was only reached after a lengthy interval: first an attempt was
made to found mission communities made up of Jews and godfearers in nearer cities around Eretz Israel. In my view Paul's
'from Jerusalem and around' (ἀπὸ Ἰηρουσαλὴμ καὶ κύκλῳ, Rom.
15.19), which has been much puzzled over, is to be understood in
this sense. For Paul, Damascus (and Arabia) belonged in first
place here.[459] The coming Lord was pressing, and the geographical framework was still limited, relatively narrowly, to the frontier
territories of Eretz Israel which in fact Jesus had already visited.
The expectation of an imminent end still ruled out more
ambitious geographical missionary plans.

In the description of Paul's journey to Jerusalem before the
Feast of Weeks in 57 CE, in which the 'we' report indicates
that Paul was accompanied by the author Luke, Paul and his companions spend seven days with the 'disciples' in Tyre and one day
with the 'brethren' in Ptolemais/Acco. In both places Paul is

warmly welcomed. In Caesarea, he is even taken by Philip to Philip's house, where he stays for several days.[460] On Paul's journey to Rome, probably in autumn 59, he is able to visit his friends in the faith in Sidon, and be supported by them before his imminent voyage.[461] Presumably all these communities, which are positively inclined to Paul despite all the tensions with Jerusalem, Peter and the circle around James, are communities founded by the Hellenists, near to the frontier with Jewish Palestine, in which the old devotion towards him since his time in Syria had been maintained. The question of the Gentile mission without any requirement of observance of the ritual law had evidently not been a basic problem here, nor did it become one again. It is significant that these coastal cities in the west border directly on Galilee, i.e. the northern outposts of the Jewish settlement in Palestine, just as the city territory of Damascus borders on that of Caesarea Philippi and Gaulanitis with its substantial Jewish population.

In my view we must imagine developments in the cities of Syria and Phoenicia – and these are our main concern since as a result of those engaged in mission the new 'sect' relatively rapidly became a 'city religion' – as involving a constant advance northwards by the active Hellenists, step by step, founding new communities, until they reached Antioch and also crossed over to Cyprus. Later the Pseudo-Clementine romance makes Peter travel northwards along the coast from city to city, preaching and discussing there and then travelling to Antioch.[462] Like Paul in Asia Minor, Macedonia and Achaea, people 'jumped' from one larger city to another and spent some time there. Here Damascus, as the most important polis in southern Syria, which geographically formed the gateway to the north-east and north,[463] was particularly important. A text like Matt. 10.5, 'Go nowhere among the Gentiles, and enter no town of the Samaritans', which directly contradicts what Philip does in Samaria and 'on the road to Gaza', shows that initially there was resistance to this development.[464] However, this resistance evidently lasted only a relatively short time. Later, as is shown by events in Antioch and Galatia, the question of mission outside Eretz Israel and indeed even the question of winning over 'Gentile Christians' was not intrinsically

controversial; the controversy was over the conduct of the
mission and whether former Gentiles were to be circumcised,
and observe the Jewish regulations relating to cleanness and the
dietary laws.

Initially the Hellenists still practised their mission as a matter of
course in the synagogues of the larger Hellenistic cities. Where
else could they have found people to address? The new message
of the Messiah who had been crucified, raised and would come
again must have been almost incomprehensible to a Gentile
who had no inkling of Jewish doctrine. The earliest Christian
'missionaries' thus formed small conventicles with their
followers; one might even call them 'special synagogues' with
offensive messianic doctrines. It was a matter of one's temperament and zeal for the faith whether one shook one's head over
them or fought against them directly. It would also be misleading
to describe their preaching simply as 'free from the law'.[465] There
was never any preaching in earliest Christianity which was really
'free from the law'. The earliest Christians were not 'anti-
nomians', nor was Paul. The keeping of the Ten Commandments, particularly the First Commandment, and also the double
commandment to love taught by Jesus, was called for in this new
Jewish messianic sect with the same emphasis as in the synagogue,
indeed sometimes with more. This is true for Paul himself. Here
I Cor. 9.20f. speaks for itself: 'To the Jews I became as a Jew, in
order to win Jews; to those under the law I became as one under
the law – though not being myself under the law – that I might
win those under the law. To those outside the law I became as one
outside the law – not being without law toward God but under the
law of Christ – that I might win those outside the law.'[466] The
young messianic community could not compromise with pagan
idolatry any more than pious Jews could. This is already indicated
by the grim statements which Paul makes to the Corinthians,[467]
indeed by his parenesis generally, and similarly by the later
behaviour of Christians before state courts and their rigorous
attitude towards the *lapsi*, or apostates. Initially, the criticism of
the Hellenists in Jerusalem which had aroused the wrath of Saul
was presumably limited to the temple cult that had been made
obsolete by the death of Jesus and excessive emphasis on the

ritual law.[468] Here, too, the recollection of Jesus' teaching and behaviour, which was still quite near, may have been an important impetus. The last motive for such criticism lay in christology and soteriology. Moreover this applies to Paul's much more radical, fundamental attitude to the question of the law, which in my view can be understood only as a direct consequence of his encounter with the risen Christ before Damascus.

The preaching of the Hellenists, which was felt provocative in Jerusalem because of its temple and the zeal for the law which was widespread there, and which had led to the martyrdom of Stephen and their expulsion from the city, need no longer have provoked any open acts of violence in the quite different milieu of a Greek polis with predominantly Greek-speaking synagogue communities. This activity was felt to be a provocation only by the zealots in Jerusalem. Their promoter, Saul, then set off for Damascus to restore order there. Such 'aid' was evidently necessary, as the Jews in Damascus were neither able or willing to do this themselves. There the adherents of a new messianic sect who claimed, with reference to their teacher who had been exalted to God, that a pagan 'godfearer' would have a share in the coming rule of God and eternal life if he believed in the one God and Creator and led an unexceptionable ethical life, putting his whole trust solely in Jesus Christ, the Messiah and son of God who had been crucified and now united with God, might at first have been dismissed as a deviant sectarian superstition. It need not necessarily have been regarded as a cause for violent intervention – as it would have been in Jerusalem – had these people advocated their superstition in personal conversation and not disturbed synagogue worship. A Diaspora Jew with a Greek education could even respond affirmatively to some of the questions: belief in the one God, the strict and at the same time open ethic, the gift of eternal life and its independence from circumcision. A 'godfearer' who believed in the one God, took the moral commandments seriously, and avoided idolatry, might hope to obtain God's good pleasure even without circumcision.[469] God in his *philanthropia* was gracious, and not a tyrant who asked the impossible.[470] Indeed at the same time these people were also a political body in an alien city, and internal and external peace was a high priority. Therefore relative tolerance was called for towards the 'godfearers' who were so useful and who had good reasons for not being circumcised, and towards eschatological sectarians from the mother country, as long as they did not disturb the synagogue community.[471] That is why we hear nothing of persecutions of Christians by Jews and Gentiles in the first century before Ignatius in Syria, but only in Judaea itself. According to I Thess. 2.15 'the churches of God in Judaea', not in Syria, were persecuted. The Judaism of the time in fact had many kinds of special doctrines, in the Diaspora probably even more than in the mother country. On this point one could be tolerant, above all if the real offence of the new message, which bound salvation, exclusively and contrary to the law, to the crucified and exalted Messiah Jesus, as he then becomes visible in Paul's preaching, was not publicly proclaimed. Thus no great obstacles stood in the way of a moderate mission by the 'Hellenists' in the Diaspora synagogues. Only an explicit messianic 'zealot' like Paul could come up against resistance.[472] In the mother country things had been quite different. There the Jewish Christians had at least outwardly to observe the whole of the Torah for the sake of the holiness of the land and their existence as a community.

3. Paul's New Awareness of Himself as an Apostle and the Foundation of His Theology

3.1 Paul's new awareness of himself as an apostle

Unfortunately we do not know any more about the content of this very early Jewish-Christian mission preaching in the synagogues of Damascus, about the disciples who were already in the city, or about the newly converted Paul. We can only attempt to make some inferences. Preceded by the reputation of having hated and persecuted the young enthusiastic-messianic community and of having wanted to continue his baneful work in Damascus, Paul comes into the metropolis of Syria a changed man. Through the mediation of a Jewish Christian Ananias who is otherwise unknown, he joins the community, is baptized and preaches in the synagogues there, to the amazement, indeed the terror, of all, the new 'faith which he wanted to destroy'.[473] In describing the reaction of those concerned Paul formulates the statement 'He who once persecuted us is now preaching the faith he once tried to destroy' (νῦν εὐαγγελίζεται τὴν πίστιν ἥν ποτε ἐπόρθει, Gal. 1.23) almost as a quotation. Here he uses terms which are of decisive significance for himself, but which in addition also appear in other early Christian authors. Above all εὐαγγελίζεται as an equivalent to *biśśar* is an important word for the preaching of salvation in Deutero- and Trito-Isaiah, in the Psalms and in Joel 3.5 LXX.[474] This last text, which is expanded in the LXX and fundamental for earliest Christianity, could be understood as an encouragement of the missionary proclamation of the apostles going out from Jerusalem. I would assume that εὐαγγελίζεσθαι, εὐαγγέλιον, and πίστις[475] as an absolute already played an essential role for the 'Hellenists'. In the translation and formulation of their earliest message, which in many respects was unconventional, their language was quite creative. The new message sought a new linguistic form – on the basis of the Old Testament-Jewish tradition which already existed.[476] Paul's summary of his message under the heading 'the gospel which was preached by me' (τὸ εὐαγγέλιον τὸ εὐηγγέλισθεν ὑπ' ἐμου)[477] has its basis here. Paul himself did not create this terminology. Underlying it is presumably the substantive of *biśśar: bᵉśora', taba'* (see n.479 below). By contrast, the derivation of εὐαγγέλιον from the Roman ruler cult, which is still popular today, does not make sense.[478] It is ruled out for this early period on chronological grounds alone and completely fails to understand the prophetic-apocalyptic milieu of the earliest Christianity of the first years, its Jewish Palestinian origin and in addition the special character of Paul's preaching, which from its first beginnings must have had a distinctive stamp, shaped by the language of the psalms and prophets.[479]

We can infer this personal – Pauline – stamp from Paul's remarkable behaviour. After a brief and understandable hesitation he is accepted by the community in Damascus, which itself was still very young and was probably only just consolidating itself, and in the synagogues he proclaims with arguments, i.e. with the aid of scriptural proof, that Jesus is Messiah and Son of God, in a way which causes astonishment, indeed offence there. Presumably he preached in a more aggressive form than his new Jewish-Christian brothers, probably from the start showing very much more interest than they did in the numerous Gentile sympathizers in the synagogue in Damascus. Therefore in his later retrospect in Gal. 1.16 the 'that I might preach him among the Gentiles' (ἵνα εὐαγγελίζωμαι αὐτὸν ἐν τοῖς ἔθνεσιν) may already have applied to his first beginnings as a 'called apostle of Jesus Christ'.[480] In other words we need not have fundamental doubts about this information in Luke any more than in that of Paul.

However, now, according to Gal. 1.16f., Paul must have left the community relatively quickly, without allowing his radically changed theological thinking, which was beginning to take shape, to be essentially influenced by the Jewish Christians there. This *could* indicate differences. Perhaps his preaching to the synagogue audience was too revolutionary for them, so that they feared new conflicts; perhaps his one-sided approach to the god-fearers led some to mistrust him; or perhaps it was also only the personal danger to the newly converted through radical members of the synagogue communities which drove him from Damascus. They could easily have felt the unexpected change of mind in the young Pharisaic scribe from whom they had hoped for powerful support against the machinations of the new messianic sect to be intolerable provocation (Acts 9.23). Indeed we may probably assume that when Saul the persecutor made the decision in Jerusalem to set out for Damascus he had already made contact with influential members of the synagogue in Damascus, since he must have had news from there. We can understand only too well that his contacts were deeply disappointed after the arrival of someone who had been so completely changed. So it would be conceivable that Paul already received the first of the five synagogue beatings which he mentions in II Cor. 11.24 in Damascus, and that he left the city primarily because of this threat.

The fact that he returned after his stay in Arabia tells against the assumption of deeper differences with the Christians in Damascus. Moreover the fact that he did not 'go up to Jerusalem to those who were apostles before me', in order to make their acquaintance, was hardly because of any theological differences, since as yet he knew little or nothing of their views, which were certainly not completely in harmony among themselves. For that reason he later wants to meet Peter.

The information about Jerusalem and the apostles there before him is interesting because it, too, shows that soon after the original event, Jerusalem, the Zion of salvation history, had become the recognized centre of the new messianic community. The 'apostles' were to be found there and not in Galilee, the province of Judaea or somewhere in Syria, and the rule was that one orientated oneself on Jerusalem as the centre of the new messianic community. Paul's behaviour seemed so unusual that he later had to justify it to his Galatian opponents. 'The apostles before me' are identical with 'all the apostles' of I Cor. 15.6, including Cephas/Peter and the Twelve; perhaps Paul is also including the brothers of the Lord whom in I Cor. 9.5 he distinguishes from 'the rest of the apostles'. We do not know whether there was unanimous agreement over who bore the title 'apostle' or whether Paul always used the word uniformly of third parties. We can conclude from I Cor. 15.11 that all these 'apostles' proclaimed the one gospel of the death of the Messiah for our sins and his resurrection and exaltation to God in their basic preaching.

There are several reasons why Paul did not travel to Jerusalem.

1. There is the fact that he, the former persecutor, now wanted to preach the new message with the same zeal, indeed with greater zeal, and without delay to the 'Gentiles', i.e. specifically to the 'godfearers', in an area which like Damascus bordered on Eretz Israel and whose inhabitants were kinsfolk to Israel, namely Arabia. There were hardly completely new 'mission objects' as such in Jerusalem.

2. The imminent expectation of the Lord necessitated missionary goals which could be realized in a short time. The time was too short. Guided by the Spirit, one had to choose carefully missionary spheres which were limited by the short interval.[481]

3. But above all, a rapid return to the Holy City would have been an undertaking that put Paul's life at risk, since his previous friends, who were inspired by the same zeal for the law as he once was, must now have seen him as an 'apostate' who had allowed himself to be led astray and who now deserved the most serious punishment. An immediate return to Jerusalem could have meant his death, but he had to proclaim the Son of God to the Gentiles! Even after two to three years he does not seem to have been safe there. However, he does not mention this reason in Gal. 1.17f. It would not fit in with his apologia.

In any case, Paul understands the sudden change in his life as call and mission: like the authorities in the Holy City, he too is 'called to be an apostle of Jesus Christ'.[482] Through Jesus he received 'grace (χάριν) and apostleship (ἀποστολὴν) to bring about the obedience of faith among all the nations'.[483] We may see the 'gift of grace' as the gospel revealed to him by Christ and entrusted to him for preaching, since before this, at the beginning of the prescript to the letter to the Romans, he describes himself as 'called to be an apostle, set apart for the gospel of God';[484] here 'set apart' emphasizes the radical nature of the change for those who know. The *paruš* had once 'set himself apart' for the sake of the Torah; now he has done so for the sake of the gospel.[485] In Romans 15.15f. he defines the grace given to him by God, 'to be a minister of Christ Jesus to the Gentiles in the priestly service of the gospel of God'.[486] By contrast, in Gal. 1.16f. we have the motif of the prophetic calling: like the prophet Jeremiah and the servant of God he has been called by God to be a preacher to the Gentiles from his mother's womb.[487] Here we have earlier motifs.

The Hellenists and even more Paul himself give the terms ἀπόστολος, εὐαγγελίζεσθαι, εὐαγγέλιον, κήρυγμα, χάρις, πίστις, ἀγάπη, ἐλπίς and δικαιοσύνη θεοῦ a new content and a special emphasis;[488] for Paul the eschatological 'apostolic' sending by God or Christ is orientated on the sending of the prophets of the Old Covenant,[489] indeed it surpasses these. Now the sending relates to the eschatological final salvation and therefore to decision; the time which has dawned is the time of salvation: God has decided for the salvation of all men and women in the person and work of Jesus Christ: those who hear are to give a decisive answer to this in faith: 'Behold, now is the acceptable time, now is the day of salvation.' In other words, with the Christ event and Paul's present apostolic ministry the prophetic promise is being fulfilled.[490] For Paul, who like Jeremiah remained unmarried,[491] entering into this service for the sake of this salvation is from the beginning like a compulsion which he cannot avoid without putting his existence at risk:[492] 'For if I preach the gospel, that gives me no ground for boasting. For necessity is laid upon me. Woe to me if I do not preach the gospel! For if I do this of my own free will, I have a reward; but if not of my own free will, I am (only) entrusted with a commission.'[493] The former persecutor does not understand himself as a free worker who has a claim to wages and can give up his work if it no longer pleases him, but he is the slave of his Lord,[494] who, whether he wants to or not, is obliged to carry out the *oikonomia*, the service of the proclamation of the gospel among the nations which has been entrusted to him, in the face of all resistance. Reliable slaves were often entrusted with administrative tasks, say in connection with estates, imperial or city resources, and so on. Unconditional fidelity was required of them, and they regularly had to give account of their stewardship. 'This is how one should regard us, as servants of Christ and stewards of the mysteries of God. Moreover it is required of stewards that they be found trustworthy.'[495] For Paul, his calling was at the same time a change of master and of service. This firebrand[496] will not have dreamed of hesitating and weighing up the pros and cons for any length of time. As a persecutor he had known (wrongly) Jesus 'after the flesh', since the 'God of this age' had 'blinded his senses' and he had acted accordingly.[497] Once the 'glory of Christ' as the 'Lord' exalted to the Father had shone on him before Damascus, he felt himself to be free from the lordship of darkness and sin and to have been put in the service of his new Lord and of that Lord's kingdom, present and to come. He had experienced the truth of his message in his own person. Moreover the eschatological awareness of the nearness of the Lord must have been even more urgent in the early period than in the fifties, when he could still write sentences like Rom. 13.11 or I Cor. 7.29, 31. From now on he must have regarded himself as one of the 'godless justified by God through Christ', as a former 'enemy of God', but now reconciled through Christ's death.[498] One could read off him the nature of the justification of the unrighteous. His past as a persecutor will have weighed heavy on him all his life. It will also have been held against him by Christians and may be why he could not claim the title apostle for himself.[499] It may also be that from the beginning, among other things he also understood the 'compulsion' to preach the gospel which has already been mentioned and the refusal of support from the communities for which he was criticized in Corinth as an act of 'reparation' for having once 'destroyed' the community of God.[500] This new awareness, this completely changed 'self-understanding', is also expressed in the contrast between 'once' and 'now' which pervades his letters.[501] It is expressed most sharply in his autobiographical confession in Phil. 3.4b–11, where more than twenty, perhaps even thirty, years after the change in his life he still – or better once again – takes stock of his past: 'But what to me was gain I counted loss for Christ's sake ... '

We cannot simply separate all these considerations, insights and decisions chronologically from the radical turning point in Paul's life and distribute them between very much later stages of his development. This would be to falsify the unity of his biography and theology. The certainty of having been sent in a special way to the Gentiles as an apostle and slave of Jesus Christ by the Risen Christ is the basis of the whole of his later activity, and the same is true of his new understanding of himself as a 'justified godless' person. Just as he himself had surprisingly and overwhelming experienced the unconditional grace of God in Christ without any preliminary action of his own, indeed in abrupt opposition to his previous convictions and behaviour, so now he was to proclaim to the Gentiles the message revealed to him through Christ of salvation received as pure gift and the new life 'in Christ'. The one who had been freed by Christ from now on becomes a debtor to all men and women in this service; indeed, he has now made himself 'a slave to all' in order to win over as many as possible.[502] It did not take him many years to arrive at these insights. He certainly did not first make the claim to have seen the Lord and to be an apostle of Jesus Christ at the Apostolic Council, and according to his own judgment in Gal. 1.15f. his mission to the 'Gentiles' appears as a direct consequence of the 'revelation of Jesus Christ' before Damascus and the commission to preach the gospel which he was given then. Could it have been otherwise in such fundamental questions as the meaning of the law for salvation and the 'justification of the godless' by grace alone? Therefore Paul could, indeed had to, testify immediately afterwards to Jesus as messiah and eschatological redeemer in the synagogues of Damascus, and then quickly set off for pagan 'Arabia'. However, 'the Gentiles' were no general abstract factor for him; they were very concrete. The mission to them always manifested itself in one people with a quite distinct geographical location, in the first place the inhabitants of 'Arabia'.[503]

I would think that on the basis of his newly-gained missionary experience Paul was already in a position on his visit to Jerusalem after around three years to explain his gospel and the commisssion associated with it quite clearly to Cephas/Peter (and James), and also to sum it up conceptually.

3.2 The foundation of Paul's theology

3.2.1 The justification of the sinner by grace alone

At the centre is not immediately and directly the question of the law – or even the phantom of a preaching 'free of the law' – but the basic question of Christian faith down to the present day: who is Christ, and what did he do for us? The starting point could only be the person of the exalted Christ who had encountered Paul before Damascus and his saving work. At the beginning stands a personal encounter, a being overwhelmed by the crucified and exalted Christ. The question of the function of the Torah is then the necessary and immediate consequence which always must also be taken into account. But in my view the basic features of christology (and the soteriology which is indissolubly bond up with it) were fully developed in the earliest Christian community on the day when Paul saw the risen Christ before Damascus; otherwise the turning point which he describes could not have assumed the radical form that it did. It was the revelation of Christ and nothing else – if we can believe Paul's own words (and if we do not want to, we can only be silent) – which gave a clear direction to his further career. At most a development can be seen in the geographical conception of his mission: Damascus, Arabia, Cilicia and Syria (together with adjacent Cyprus, Pisidia and Lycaonia) and then in the last third of his activity Asia Minor, Macedonia, Greece and the prospect of Rome and indeed Spain, the end of the inhabited world. We shall have to reflect later on this initially restrained shift of Paul's geographical perspectives; here it is striking that in Rom. 15.19 Jerusalem is mentioned as a starting point and Damascus, Arabia and Syria are contained in the enigmatic καὶ κύκλῳ.[504]

We find the pre-Pauline – in the full sense of the word –

christological basis of Paul's new thought above all in the many christological formulae and motifs which resound in his letters. We cannot go on here to develop Paul's christology, but must limit ourselves to some points which were 'fundamental' for him. The most important starting point is that confession-like text which he himself described as 'the gospel preached by me', the substance of which he possibly received already in Damascus, from a tradition which was still quite young, and which he handed on to the Corinthians in a shaped form 'among the first things' which he told them when he founded the community. This is a confession which is not only the basis for their salvation, but also binds all 'apostolic preachers' in the young church. In form and content it points back to the earliest church in Jerusalem and is not just a product of the community in Antioch.[505] The decisive line for us is the first one: Χριστὸς ἀπέθανεν ὑπὲρ τῶν ἁμαρτιῶν ἡμῶν κατὰ τὰς γραφάς.

Here the original significance of Χριστὸς as a title still glimmers in the name,[506] and first gives the whole formula its deeper sense: the sinless messiah died for our sins and did so, moreover, as Paul himself often emphasizes in formulae, by crucifixion on the wood of curse and shame.[507] Behind this there stands historically the knowledge that a short time earlier Jesus had been crucified on a charge of making messianic claims and that he had been exalted by God to himself through the resurrection, thus endorsing his claim. The 'died for our sins' ultimately goes back to the symbolic action and its interpretation at the last meal Jesus had with his disciples.[508] The 'according to the scriptures' refers to the earliest Christian proof from scripture, made in the Spirit; here from the beginning Isaiah 53 must have played a decisive role in the soteriological interpretation of the death of Jesus.[509]

As I have already remarked, the atoning death of the Messiah interpreted in universal terms made the sacrificial practice in the temple obsolete for the first Christians and led to open criticism of the temple and the ritual law – at least among the Hellenists, represented, say, by Stephen.[510] Whereas presumably from the start the Jewish Christians who proclaimed the crucified and risen Jesus as the Messiah of Israel were presented with a text like

Deut. 21.23 to show the absurdity of their argument, they
could have turned the argument round – as Paul certainly did –
and emphasized that on the cross the Messiah Jesus had representatively borne the curse which according to Deut. 27.26 is
threatened against all those who transgress the law. In other
words, they could have claimed that through his death Jesus
reconciled disobedient Israel, indeed all sinners, with God. It was
probably above all this soteriological interpretation of the death
of Jesus on the accursed tree,[511] which put in question the atoning
effect of temple worship and thus essential parts of the Torah,
that embittered the young Pharisaic scribe and made him a
persecutor. Could the promised Messiah and redeemer of Israel
be the one who misled the people and according to the law was
accursed[512] by his shameful death? Was he to put in question clear
statements of the Torah? Had this not to be seen as blasphemy?[513]
Paul, the zealot for the holiness of the law and God's honour,[514]
drew the consequences of this and became an active persecutor
of those followers of Jesus who publicly put forward these
blasphemous views, i.e. the Hellenists. His experience before
Damascus shattered the young scholar's proud zeal for the
law. He himself, the one who believed he was only fulfilling
the demands of the law, recognized that he was the real
blasphemer,[515] who in persecuting the community of God was
also persecuting its exalted Lord and thus God's eschatological
plenipotentiary,[516] and in so doing – given the imminent divine
judgment – had incurred the most serious guilt conceivable. He
had become a fighter against God (θεομάχος),[517] who sought to
oppose God's eschatological salvation. So the change in his life
first of all meant the recognition of abysmal guilt. This motif runs
through his biographical retrospects.[518] At the same time his
previous system of orientation, focussed on the Torah, had been
shattered, since his zeal for it and the consequences he drew from
it had made him a persecutor. The description in Acts[519] of the
collapse of his whole person, which even affected him physically,
thus has a very real background. As a rule, modern psychological
considerations here lead only to almost intolerable banalities. At
the same time the 'revelation of Jesus Christ', 'who was put to
death for our transgressions and raised for our justification',[520]

opened up the possibility of a complete new beginning through certainty of the forgiveness of all guilt in the death of Christ, which had happened once for all. Jesus had representatively for all taken upon himself the curse uttered in the law against the transgressor and thus brought about universal atonement.[521] This certainty, in the form of obedient, unconditional trust in the salvation brought about through Christ alone, in short what Paul in his letters calls 'faith', πίστις, no longer rested, like conversion (*t^ešuba*) in the Pharisaic tradition, on one's own decision,[522] nor could it any longer be understood as a 'work'; it was pure gift, χάρις, the gift or effect of the revelation of Christ, i.e. the words of the exalted Christ; it was not that Paul had 'converted', but that the grace of God had overcome him and called him.[523]

I shall not attempt here to put back to the time of Paul's conversion his doctrine of salvation wholly by grace or the justification of the sinner by faith alone as he developed it conceptually, fully and in so many aspects. We can only guess when and how he developed individual formulas. Here he may already have used at a very early stage those concepts and ideas which we find similarly in Qumran or rabbinic texts, like the revelation of the righteousness of God, the inability of the sinner to do God's will and his dependence on justification from God and the working of the spirit, the formula 'works of the law' and much more. These may have been familiar to the Pharisaic scribe from Jerusalem.[524] We might also ask whether the use of ἐν Χριστῷ as a formula is not formed in analogy to ἐν νόμῳ: through the Damascus event the Pharisaic scribe had been transposed from the previous 'realm of salvation' provided by the law, which for him now had suddenly become a place of the divine judgment which kills, into the sphere of salvation 'in Christ' created by Christ's dying for us.

3.2.2 *Christological presuppositions*

At the same time this already presupposes a relatively developed christology. The most important honorific titles were already given to Jesus at that time. First of all he was called Messiah,[525] which in the Greek-speaking world became a proper name with amazing rapidity. This designated Jesus the one who fulfilled the promises of the Old Testament. Closely associated with *mᵉšiḥa/ christos* is 'Son of God', which expresses Jesus' unique relationship to God, his 'Father'. It is probably not by chance that it appears at decisive points in Gal. 1.16 and 9.20, and indeed plays a central role in Galatians as compared with the other letters of Paul. For Paul, the Son is pre-existent and is sent by the Father as a human being into the world in order through his death to 'ransom' human beings who have fallen victim to judgment and death as a result of the inexorable demand of the law.[526] That this title was transferred to Jesus at a very early stage follows, for example, from the old formula Rom. 1.3f., which should not be interpreted all too simply in an adoptionist way; it merely expresses the exaltation of the Messiah and Son of David to divine power and glory. Jesus' divine sonship has its origin in the mystery of his person, expressed in his unique relationship with his Father, behind which investigations cannot reach.[527] As has been emphasized, Jesus as the risen Davidic Messiah already appears as the Son of God exalted to God in this old confession in Rom. 1.3f. The ordinary man Jesus does not first become Son of God through the resurrection, but the crucified Messiah Jesus of the family of David has been appointed by God Son of God in power and a transfigured spiritual figure since the resurrection.[528]

The designation and invocation of the Risen Christ as 'Lord' is also already to be presupposed. This is indicated not only by the Aramaic cry of prayer 'Maranatha',[529] but also by the christological interpretation of Ps. 110.1 as a consequence of the resurrection appearances: the Kyrios raised by God has not been transported to just any place in the heavenly world, but to some degree is enthroned at its highest point, 'at the right hand of God' on the throne above the heavenly *merkabah*.[530]

Paul himself emphasizes that because he has seen the Kyrios, he is his apostle.[531] The invocation of Kyrios Jesus for salvation in accordance with Joel 3.5 is already to be presupposed for the time of Paul's conversion.[532] By contrast, the formula ὁ υἱὸς τοῦ ἀνθρώπου seems to have become insignificant for confessional-type formulations; for Greeks it was completely incomprehensible, in contrast to the Aramaic equivalent *bar'ᵉnaša*, 'the man', among Palestinian Jews. It lived on in the Jesus tradition, since he had spoken of himself and the one who was to come as *bar 'enaša*. The ὁ υἱὸς τοῦ ἀνθρώπου, which always has the article, as opposed to the LXX υἱὸς ἀνθρώπου[533] of Ps. 8.5; 80.16 and Dan. 7.13, which does not, indicates a uniform and very early translation of this formula in the circle of the 'Hellenists' when they gave the language of the tradition and preaching of the new movement its first Greek form.[534]

The question whether and when the earliest community made definite statements about pre-existence can remain open. In Paul, despite occasional arguments to the contrary, these are clear and many-sided.[535] Now the Son of Man of Dan. 7.13 appears in his interpretation as messiah in the Similitudes of Ethiopian Enoch and in IV Ezra 13 as a pre-existent figure, and the Q tradition connects Jesus with the pre-existent divine Wisdom.[536] There is nothing to tell against Jesus himself having spoken such words of wisdom as a messianic bearer of the spirit and teacher of wisdom (Isa. 11.1ff.). Furthermore, the pre-existence of the Messiah is spoken of in a series of 'messianic' texts,[537] and in particular in Ps. 110 (109).3 LXX.[538] Even if this text is first quoted by Justin (though after that it is quoted frequently), it does not mean that in analogy to v.1 it was not noted relatively early. However, it did not have the same central significance as the first verse, but merely expressed a 'secondary' consequence.[539] The christological development in particular must have been particularly stormy in the first two or three years of the church, driven forward by what in the eyes of contemporaries was the monstrous message (or, in the eyes of opponents, assertion) of the resurrection and exaltation of the crucified Jesus of Nazareth, together with the eschatological gift of the Spirit and the enthusiasm which it caused. As I have already said, Luke does not exaggerate here, but tones things down and 'domesticates' them.

Paul's encounter with the risen Christ showed him that his previous form of existence was a 'being under the law';[540] in other words, so far he had lived in that 'sphere of power' in which through his 'holy, righteous and good commandment'[541] God inexorably judges human beings as sinners, even if they regard themselves as completely righteous, and delivers them over to death.[542] His view of the law hitherto had made the young scribe who was scrupulous and zealous in his obedience to the law the persecutor of Christ and thus – as he later understood things – a manifest sinner.[543] However, as a result of his call he had been transposed into the sphere of the righteousness of God, i.e. 'in Christ'. Now since according to a widespread Jewish view the law, as the wisdom of God 'made scripture', was present with God before all time,[544] the predicate of pre-temporal being also had to be transferred to the Son. Therefore it is quite imaginable that this notion, too, in analogy to the pre-existence of Wisdom/ Torah, and 'driven by the Spirit' for the sake of soteriology, was interpreted relatively quickly in different forms. However, we cannot say precisely when the first beginnings of pre-existence christology emerge. Still, this too could have happened relatively early in the circles of the 'Hellenists'.[545] Here the medium will have been the christological hymns inspired by the Spirit, beginning with the 'messianic psalms' 2; 8; 16; 22; 45; 69; 80; 89 ; 110; 118, etc., which were very quickly sung as hymns to Christ and gave the impetus to the composition of hymns with a distinctive christological stamp.[546] The earliest early Christian messianic hymns which we have are the Magnificat and the Benedictus, which celebrate the birth of the Messiah Jesus in conjunction with texts from the Psalms and Isa. 7.12.[547]

If salvation 'in Christ' thus took the place of the form of existence 'under' or even 'in the law', then Christ really was 'the end of the law for righteousness for all who believe'; given the context of Rom. 10.4, however, this can only be seen as an incidental aspect, not as indicating that Christ is the 'goal of the law'. This is the case not only because ὁ νόμος as scripture also contains the promise, but because precisely through its commandments the Torah 'became a tutor to Christ',[548] which kept Israel as it were imprisoned and prevented it from losing, or forgetting by assimilation to the nations of the world, the word of God which had been entrusted to it alone, together with the promise contained in it,[549] 'until the future faith was revealed'.[550] In other words, the law was given with a view to the revelation of the gospel, in its double form of promise and commandment, for without the preceding commandment the saving power of the gospel

(Rom. 1.16) cannot be effective and be recognized. 'Knowledge of sin comes (only) through the law (in the light of the gospel).' For God does not justify anyone who is righteous by nature, since there cannot be such people by comparison with God's holiness, but only the sinners who recognize themselves as such in the mirror of the law which is illuminated by the light of Christ.[551]

Paul thought over the radical break with his previous past which had been brought about by the Damascus experience in a way unique in the history of religion in antiquity. We do not know how long this thought-process lasted before it took on in individual points that clarity which we later find in the letters to the Galatians and the Romans. We should not doubt that the process of rethinking began the moment Paul's life changed, and that for this highly-gifted Jewish scribe its course was very intense. The question of the saving significance of the Torah and the work of Christ which justifies the sinner must have occupied him intensively from the beginning; in my view, particularly intensively at the beginning. Here we have neither a mere 'subsidiary crater' as A. Schweitzer thought, nor 'an unnatural fruit of thought'.[552] Far less can this have been a late, secondary development. On the contrary, the change in Paul's life before Damascus culminates in the experience of the 'justification of the godless' – Saul from Tarsus – and to the last, until Galatians, Philippians and Romans, it remains the centre of his theology – the first Christian theology that we know of.

4. Arabia and Aretas IV, King of the Nabataeans (9 BCE–40 CE)

4.1 The theological occasion and the political circumstances

According to Gal. 1.17 Paul leaves Damascus quickly and goes to Arabia,[553] but returns to Damascus in order to visit Jerusalem from there. By contrast, Luke knows nothing of the visit to Arabia. Such gaps do not prove his general unreliability but are quite normal for a biographical narrator who is dependent wholly on what he himself has heard and on the oral reports of third parties. Anyone who has already done any work in the sphere of oral history can confirm that from experience. How full of gaps a biography of my father would be if I wanted to tell it only from memory up to 1930, i.e. the time when my own recollection of him begins! Although he said much about his youth, I would have to pass over important stages of his life out of ignorance.[554] Luke is writing between twenty and thirty years after his encounter with Paul, the turning point in whose life goes back at this point almost the same time. Large gaps were quite inevitable here. Had Luke been the first author of an apostolic romance in the style of the Acts of Paul around 100 years later, who like such authors was merely writing out of love of Paul,[555] he could easily have filled the gaps with edifying fiction. The Pseudo-Clementine romance offers a good example here for Palestine and Syria. All the events follow on in it without a gap. As a narrator who, while fully orientated on Paul, is nevertheless a responsible historian of mission and a biographer,[556] Luke does not write like this. We cannot exclude the possibility that he knew of the visit to Arabia, but passed over it because it was not essential to his plan and remained an episode. On grounds of space alone he had to limit the extent of the 'second account', which comprised no more than one papyrus scroll. Here select scenes shaped rhetorically were most important for him; a good deal else had to be left out.

The duration and the purpose of his stay also remain open. Earlier, I had assumed a relatively short period, but here I must correct myself. Paul's activity in Damascus will not have lasted all that long after his return, since we may assume that the action of the Nabataean ethnarch against him was somehow connected with his stay in Arabia, i.e. in the Nabataean kingdom. That would mean that if the 'three years' up until the journey to Jerusalem, which are not to be dated from his return from Arabia but from the turning point in his life,[557] are interpreted in accordance with the ancient practice in reckoning time as being between two and two and a half years, Paul could have been active there for up to two years.[558]

Both Gal. 1.16, 'that I might preach him among the Gentiles', and Luke's account in Acts 9.18b–22 par make it very probable that Paul became the preacher of the new message without delay, with the one difference that by his own account, Paul had primarily the 'non-Jews' outside the mother country[559] in view from the start, whereas Luke speaks of preaching in the synagogues of Damascus to Jews; although in his threefold narration about Paul's calling he himself increasingly emphasizes the mission to the Gentiles.[560] Here, too, we have only an apparent contradiction. As I have already remarked, the ἔθνη are primarily the 'godfearers' in the synagogues. That means that Paul always also addressed Jews at the same time. He says this himself in Rom. 1.6 with his Ἰουδαίῳ πρῶτον καὶ Ἕλληνι; here the πρῶτον is to be taken quite literally and seriously. This programmatic statement in defining the theme of Romans is matched by I Cor. 9.20, where he also mentions the Jews first, and above all Rom. 11.13, where he praises his ministry as apostle to the Gentiles because through it he can make his own people 'jealous', gain them for Christ and thus 'save' them.[561] Paradoxically, in places where he attempted to carry on his mission, as a rule the way to the 'Gentiles' led through the synagogue. Probably he preferred larger cities not least because they had synagogues in them. Nowhere else could he find so many Gentiles ready to listen, with some basic presuppositions with enabled them to understand his preaching. From Damascus to Corinth and Ephesus, Paul seems to have remained faithful to this 'mission strategy' which Luke depicts on the great journeys, and which no longer in any way corresponds to the situation in his day, i.e. after 70 CE, despite the dangers associated with it. Only when he had been driven out of the synagogues and had brought with him from there at least a small group of pagan 'sympathizers' and individual Jews, did a separate, predominantly 'Gentile Christian' community with a Pauline stamp come into being, which then gathered in some private house. The message which he addressed to pagan 'sympathizers', and here not least to women in the synagogue, can be summed up in the one sentence in Gal. 3.26–38:

> For in Christ Jesus you are all sons of God, through faith. For as many of you as were baptized into Christ have put on Christ. There is neither Jew nor Greek, there is neither slave nor free, there is neither male nor female; for you are all one in Christ Jesus.

While the apostle may have coined phrases like 'put on Christ in baptism' or 'one in Christ Jesus' later, there is no doubt about the basic insight that through the revelation of the Son of God all become sons of God. In other words, all belong without distinction to the true eschatological Israel,[562] and through Christ's work of salvation, in the sphere of salvation which he has created, the limits drawn by the law in the old era have been done away with, limits which the persecutor wanted to defend. Otherwise the turning point in the life of the newly-called apostle would only be an apparent one. But in this way he is proclaiming to his Gentile sympathizers, to wives and slaves, full equal rights 'in Christ' in contrast to being 'in' or 'under the law'. Part of the secret of his missionary success may lie here. This insight of the former Pharisaic scribe was stamped on the one hand by the eschatological-pneumatic enthusiasm of the earliest community and on the other by the fruits of a first fundamental theological reflection on the consequences of fulfilling the Old Testament promises in the 'revelation of Jesus Christ' with which the end-time has dawned.

A further striking feature is that the newly-converted Paul evidently goes to 'Arabia' as a 'solitary missionary', although it was the custom in Judaism, with Jesus and the earliest community, and also later, to send people out in pairs.[563] Luke also knows that Saul/Paul first emerged as a lone champion. It accorded with the character of his call, in which he was addressed and sent by the Kyrios as a sole individual, like the Old Testament prophets,[564] and probably also with his inner temperament. He loved independence, yet if he had to, he could fit into a community, though he rapidly took a leading role in it because of his paramount gifts.[565]

He wanted to proclaim the message which he had received from Christ, as a sole individual, in Arabia. This excludes the possibility that – as E. Meyer puts it – 'he withdrew into the solitude of Arabia to master the effects of the powerful upheaval he had experienced and to gain inner clarity'. He could also have achieved this in the semi-wilderness of the great city territory immediately bordering on the city of Damascus. However the text does not say εἰς τὴν ἔρημον,[566] as it does with John the Baptist and the temptation of Jesus, but εἰς Ἀραβίαν. So I would agree more with the following statement: 'Here he will have struggled towards his later teaching, at least in fundamentals; to this degree he is justified in having nothing to do with a conversion through human beings: the view which he arrived at is in fact his very own, and so by his way of thinking stems directly from the Lord himself.'[567] However, I would have to add that this was not one-sidedly through meditation in solitude, but even more – already beginning in Damascus – through the living proclamation of the crucified messiah, closely associated with the interpretation of scripture.

But why to 'Arabia' in particular and not to Palmyra, Emesa, the Phoenician cities and the Decapolis? We can assume that individual Christian missionaries, say from the ranks of the expelled 'Hellenists', were already at work in southern Phoenicia and in the cities of the coastal region and the Decapolis bordering on Eretz Israel. Later, in Romans, Paul emphasizes that he attached importance to not preaching 'the gospel where Christ has already been named, lest I build on another man's foundations'.[568] That is how Ambrosiaster[569] on Gal. 1.17 already understands it: 'Therefore he set out from Damascus to Arabia to preach where there was no apostle and so that he himself might found churches here.' Among other things, that is to be understood as an expression of his concern for independence. He was and remained an outsider.[570] But precisely in this capacity he could develop an activity which was so far unique in the ancient world. Here his daring spirit, the readiness for suffering and sacrifice which we now find almost unimaginable, and in which he put himself wholly at the service of his Lord, and his charisma, helped him to make an impact on people by word and example. A theological thought which worked with strict arguments, an enthusiasm inspired by the Spirit, missionary energy and thoughtful planning, combined into a single activity which also remained a model for the later history of the church.

So the fact that Paul went to 'Arabia', or more precisely to the territory of the Nabataeans,[571] and attempted to work there for some time, does not just indicate a short insignificant episode which he mentions only because he did not go to Jerusalem,[572] nor were there merely personal and pragmatic reasons for it. The fact that from the perspective of Damascus and Eretz Israel it was 'on the doorstep' and had a long common frontier with both, and probably had so far been overlooked by the other 'missionaries' in the short interval of around three years since the crucifixion of Jesus,[573] is in my view not enough to explain Paul's step. There were also *theological* reasons for it.

The Jews regarded the 'Arabs', embodied by what was then politically the most powerful Arab people in the immediate environment of Eretz Israel, the Nabataeans, as descendants of Ishmael the son of Abraham, i.e. as kindred tribes. Another more closely related people, the Idumaeans and 'descendants of Esau', had been converted to Judaism by John Hyrcanus I (135/4–104 BCE). So the Arab Nabataeans appeared to be the closest 'kinsfolk' of the Jews who were still Gentiles.[574] According to Deut. 23.4, the Ammonites and Moabites, who were descended from Lot, had been excluded from joining Israel[575] or no longer existed. So the Nabataean Arabs remained not only the closest kinsfolk but also geographically the nearest and most important 'neighbours' of Israel, to whom the threat and promise in Jer. 12.14–17 to 'my neighbours' applied, namely that they were 'to learn the ways of my people'. Josephus describes this geographical proximity vividly when he depicts how from the tower of Psephinus in the north-west corner of Jerusalem, seventy ells high, at dawn one could see to Arabia, i.e. to the mountains on the east shore of the Dead Sea.[576] In addition there is the prophetic promise: according to Isa. 60.7, the first things to be consecrated to the service of YHWH in the sanctuary on the pilgrimage of the nations are the treasures of Midian and Ephah, and as sacrificial animals the herds of Qedar and Nabaioth, the Arab tribes in the south. Targum Isa. 60.6 speaks in general terms of the Arabs, 60.7 in synonymous parallelism with the Nabataeans.[577] In MT there follow the ships of Tarshish (LXX Θαρσις), in the Targum the islands which are waiting for God's *memra*; the MT has 'strangers' (LXX ἀλλογενεῖς), in the Targum 'the sons of the Gentiles' will build the walls of Jerusalem. Now in Josephus and sometimes in the Targum Tarshish/Θαρσις is identified with Tarsus, to which Paul goes after his visit to Jerusalem. Later Justin, who comes from Neapolis in Samaria, constantly speaks of the μάγοι ἀπὸ Ἀραβίας in accordance with Matt. 2, who fulfil the prophetic promise with respect to the coming of the Messiah.[578]

Above all after the Maccabean period, the Jews lived in a constant close economic and political-cultural exchange with the Nabataeans, though this was interrupted by vigorous fighting.

According to Josephus, the last military conflict was caused by the adultery of Herod Antipas. When his consort, a daughter of Aretas IV, heard that Antipas had promised marriage to his niece Herodias, she fled back to her father. However, this was only the external reason, especially as this affront lay years in the past. The concrete occasion was, rather, a dispute over the territory of Philip, who died in 34 CE. Thus the clashes seem to have taken place somewhere between 34 and 36, i.e. still during the time of Paul's missionary attempts in 'Arabia'. They ended with a defeat of Antipas, who successfully complained to Tiberius. The

emperor sent Vitellius, governor of Syria, with an army against
the Nabataeans, and he appeared with this army in Judaea
around Passover 37. On visiting Jerusalem on 11 March 37 he was
given news of the death of Tiberius, whereupon he broke off the
campaign.[579] Since as a result of the death of Philip his tetrarchy,
stretching far eastwards towards the western part of the Hauran,
had fallen to the province of Syria, and its eastern area had been
settled by Nabataeans, it is probable that Aretas was attempting to
extend his influence to this notoriously unruly region, which was
difficult to administer, since it was far from the provincial capital
Antioch. Here there were frontier disputes in Gaulanitis in the
territory of Gamala, which led to war between the two client
rulers.[580] We may conjecture that Paul's 'mission' in Nabataean
Arabia was hindered and perhaps even ended by political
tensions between Aretas and Antipas as the only Jewish ruler still
ruling, and that therefore the apostle returned to Damascus,
where he had brothers in the faith whom he knew and who
trusted him.[581]

In the first four decades of the almost fifty-year reign of Aretas
relations between Jews and Nabataeans had been peaceful.[582] The
king, whose epithet was 'who loves his people', encouraged
Hellenization and urbanization, trade and culture. Petra became
'a cosmopolitan place'.[583] Strabo reports that 'in the time of the
emperor Augustus', his teacher of philosophy, Athenodorus of
Tarsus, a Stoic, had visited Petra and been amazed at the
numerous visitors, Romans and other foreigners. In contrast
to the peace-loving Nabataeans, he said, it was above all the
foreigners who got entangled in legal proceedings, among themselves and with the natives.[584]

Because of the close affinity, there can be no doubt that Jews
were also settled in the Nabataean cities.[585] We find a vivid
example of the life-style of a Jewish family at the beginning of the
second century CE in the former Nabataean region of the Roman
province of Arabia from the time before the Bar Kochba revolt in
the archive of Babatha,[586] which is striking not least because it is
trilingual, in Aramaic, Greek and Nabataean. In addition we now
have the archive of another lady, Salome Komaise from Mahoza,
a Nabataean place on the south-east corner of the Dead Sea.

There numerous Jews, and perhaps even Jewish mercenaries, were living. Of the six documents, five are in Greek and one in Aramaic, but Arabic and Nabataean appear in the signatures in a Greek document.[587] Paul must have been in a position to move confidently in this bi- (or tri-)lingual milieu.[588]

4.2 Petra, Hegra, Hagar, Sinai and Abraham

Presumably Paul, as on his later missionary journeys, visited the synagogues in the larger cities during his stay of about two years, above all in the capital Petra.[589]

He will have earned his living – as he did persistently during his later long travels – by his own craft of 'tentmaker', which involved working in coarse material but also leather.[590] This was a craft with many aspects, which was employed everywhere, but particularly also in Arabia, and formed an essential basis for his missionary success. In a new and still unknown missionary area it made him totally independent of the help of third parties, even if he gladly made use of them when the occasion arose. In this point he will have differed right from the beginning from the original Jerusalem apostles. He was independent not only in respect of his 'gospel' but also in respect of his support. Therefore he could always remain a solitary whenever he wanted to.

Galatians 4.25, where he identifies Hagar with Mount Sinai in Arabia, could perhaps indicate that he penetrated even further south in Nabataean Arabia.[591] We should not doubt that this is a geographical identification. H. Gese is probably right in recognizing an Old Testament-geographical word-play here. Hagar, the slave and concubine of Abraham, the mother of Ishmael, points towards the Sinai covenant which leads into slavery, because Paul and numerous Jewish contemporaries located Sinai on the east side of the Dead Sea in 'Arabia', to the south of the Nabataean kingdom in Hagra (Hegra). To quote Gese:

> It is natural here to think of Εγρα ἐν τῇ Ἀραβίᾳ. Εγρα (Ptolemy VI 7, 29; Stephen of Byzantium I 260), *H(a)egra* (Pliny, *Natural History* VI, 157), Nabataean *hgr'* (*CIS* II 2112, 6) = Arabic *el-hegr*

... was the most important place in the Nabataean kingdom after Petra, which it also resembled in location. As is shown by the inscriptions mentioning Aretas IV (9 BCE – 40 CE), which represent by far the majority in Hegra, in the time of Paul (cf. II Cor. 11.32) the city was having a particular heyday. It is well known that there was a Jewish population in the northern Hejaz. Jews are attested relatively frequently in Hegra itself.[592]

This identification of Hagar with Hegra is confirmed by the Targums Onkelos and Yerushalmi I and the Arabic Hagar-Ishmael legend, which draws on Jewish sources.[593] So it 'does not come from Paul, but must go back to the local Jewish legend. We can best derive Paul's knowledge of the Jewish Hagar tradition rooted in Hegra from his lengthy stay in Arabia (Gal. 1.17), i.e. in the region of the Nabataeans. Paul must have known that Sinai was to be located near Hegra.'[594]

The location of Sinai on the Arabian side in the southern kingdom of the Nabataeans and the identification of Hagar and Hegra heightened the reputation of Jews throughout this region. Targum Onkelos and Jerushalmi I on Gen. 20.1 report that Abraham had already settled in the south (*darom*), between Petra[595] and Hegra,[596] i.e. in what was later the region of the Nabataeans and near Sinai. In the LXX appendix to the book of Job, too, an exemplary 'godfearer', is said to have settled in this area as the fifth king after Abraham 'over the territories of Idumaea and Arabia', and to have been visited by the kings of Teman and southern Arabia.[597]

We might perhaps infer an earlier reference to a Jewish Diaspora in 'Arabia' from 4QOrNab.[598] Here Nabonidus stays in the oasis of Teman for seven years, 'smitten with an evil sore', and is saved from his severe illness when on the instructions of a Jewish seer he bids farewell to his gods of 'silver, gold' and so on and gives 'honour and greatness to the name of Go[d most High]'. The God of the Jews forgives him his sins.[599] No full predicates of the Jewish God have been preserved. Cross and K. Koch think in terms of 'Most High', while R. Meyer assumed that 4QOrNab goes back to a Jewish tradition from Teman, and from this inferred that there were

Jewish military settlers in Teman in the Persian period.[600] However, the 'Daniel' tradition contained in 4QOrNab may also come from the Babylonian Diaspora.[601]

We are given a further geographical reference in the Genesis Apocryphon. There Abraham makes a circuit of the 'promised land' after he has surveyed it from Hazor, a mountain near Bethel:

> And I, Abram, departed to travel about and see the land. I began my journey at the river Gihon (the Nile) and travelled along the coast of the Sea (the Mediterranean) until I came to the Mountain of the Bull (Taurus). Then I travelled from the coast of the Great Salt Sea and journeyed eastwards by the Mountain of the Bull, across the breadth of the land, until I came to the river Euphrates. I journeyed along the Euphrates until I came to the Red Sea (Persian Gulf) in the east, and travelled along the coast of the Red Sea until I came to the tongue of the Sea of Reeds which flows out of the Red Sea. Then I pursued my way in the south until I came to the river Gihon, and returning, I came to my house in peace and found all things prosperous there.[602]

The land promised to Abraham which he inspected on his circuit and indeed solemnly took into his possession corresponds to the description of Arphaxad's heritage in Jub. 8–9. 1QGenAp is dependent on Jub. in literary terms. Thus the whole of Arabia is also traversed in a great sweep, though this need not be mentioned in so many words. In the south, Abraham evidently travelled along the incense route. Probably the idea that this whole area, including the area of settlement of the eastern 'Diaspora'[603] directly bordering on Eretz Israel, was promised to Abraham, corresponds to this. It basically comprises those territories which Paul mentions in Gal. 1: Syria and Cilicia, which extend to the Taurus and the Euphrates and (the whole of) Arabia. There must be 'eschatological, salvation-historical' reasons for the limitation to this area over many years; in my view this applies to the Pauline 'mission geography' generally.

With an anachronism, the life of Elijah in the *Vitae Prophetarum* (21.1) makes the prophet come 'from the land of the Arabs'.[604] For Paul, Elijah is the 'type' of his so far rather unsuccessful mission to Jews; like Paul, Elijah sought 'Arabia', i.e. Sinai, in a crisis.[605] In retrospect (Rom. 11.1ff.) the apostle sees the promise in I Kings 19.18 confirmed in an exemplary way in his call, which transformed him from the persecutor to the one who was persecuted.[606]

According to Josephus, the Nabataeans took their name from Nabaioth, the oldest son of Ishmael, so the whole area from the Euphrates to the Red Sea was called 'Nabatene'. The twelve sons of Ishmael gave the 'people of the Arabs' their name 'because of their *are*te and the fame of *Ab*ramos'.[607] This 'supranational' Abraham tradition gave 'Ishmael and his descendants the land of the Arabs, the descendants of Keturah the land of the Troglo-dytes in Arabia Felix and Eritrea, and Isaac Canaan'.[608] These neighbours, from the north-east to the Red Sea, thus had close ties of kindred[609] through Abraham, the first proselyte, primal sage and 'father of many nations', in contrast to the Phoenicians, Canaanites and Egyptians, who were descended from Ham. As in the synagogues of Damascus, people in the synagogues of Nabataean Arabia will have revered Abraham specially and will have attempted to introduce his authority to their godfearing Gentile 'kinsfolk'.

In this milieu will not Paul – at least to begin with – have reflected on the new salvation-historical significance of 'our fore-father after the flesh'[610] under the sign of the 'revelation of Jesus Christ' which overturned all his previous pre-judgments? Did not the one whom God had already pronounced righteous before his circumcision on the basis of his faith in God's word of promise[611] have to become the 'father of believers'[612] and all those who believed in the new message, whether Jews, Arabs or other 'Gentiles', his 'spiritual sons'?[613] Indeed, in the light of the preaching of John the Baptist the question of being sons of Abraham seems to have been a vigorously discussed controversial question in Jewish Palestine, and it also played a not unimportant role in the preaching of Jesus.[614]

Circumcision was a further point of contact: according to Josephus,[615] Isaac was circumcised on the eighth day, but in the Jewish view Arabs were circumcised only at the age of thirteen; here they followed Ishmael, on whom, according to Gen. 17.23ff. (P) Abraham performed circumcision at this age. According to ancient views, as a rule this rite could be presupposed among the Arabs.[616] In other words, this question was not oppressive among them as in the Jewish mother country, where there was unconditional insistence on it, or in a Greek polis, where it was resolutely repudiated. At all events, proselytes were easier to win here. Perhaps this was a reason why the 'compulsory Judaizing' of the Idumaeans after the conquest of Idumaea under John Hyrcanus took place relatively quickly. The Arabs and kindred tribes may have regarded circumcision as a matter of indifference, so that dispensing with it was more a matter of judgment.[617] Conversely, for Paul the fact that Gentiles too practised the custom of circumcision without believing in the true God and his revelation could be understood as an indication that – as the example of Abraham shows – in contrast to faith it lost all significance for salvation and was only an outward sign. Thus one of the reasons why Paul could mention the key word 'Arabia' in Gal. 1.17 and 4.25 was because he gained fundamental insights there. Given the authority of Abraham in Nabataean Arabia, it is quite conceivable that already at that time the young scribe had used the argument that the circumcision of Abraham at ninety-nine and of his son Ishmael at thirteen took place very late, and that the justification of Abraham by faith predated this by a long way,[618] so that already in the case of Abraham circumcision became a mere 'seal for the righteousness of faith' (Rom. 4.11). Granted, Romans is Paul's last letter; however, in it he does not present his most recent insights, but basic ideas of his theology which are ultimately rooted in the 'revelation of Jesus Christ' at his call, which governs his whole 'gospel'. In my view, Paul also developed the basic features of the relationship between the promise to Abraham, justification and the giving of the Torah on Sinai[619] at a very early stage, namely where 'Abraham' and 'Sinai' were there before his eyes. Must he not have grappled with these basic questions in his stay in 'Arabia'? It is more than improbable that he still 'preached circumcision' there. Behind the brief comments in Rom. 4 and Gal. 3 and 4 in this outstanding first Jewish Christian theologian there is an abundance of oral exegetical teaching or lively discussion in dispute with his Jewish and pagan audience. Paul was no 'Hellenistic' thinker and writer in the style of Philo, versed in philosophy and educated in rhetoric, though he was a master of logical argumentative exegesis like that of the midrash and the haggadah, with a practical sense and a concrete reference to life.

In addition there is a further argument: probably Paul hardly had his own 'memory of Jesus'. He had the traditions about Jesus, which he could not dispense with as a missionary, only at second hand. On the other hand, he was a scriptural scholar, the first Christian biblical scholar known to us and at the same time the most significant before Origen. In other words, he had to provide exegetical grounds for his mission preaching to Jews and Gentile sympathizers. Was not the Abraham tradition particularly natural for the scholar with his Pharisaic training here? Did he really discover this much later, somewhere between Ephesus and Corinth?

The two to three years of the 'apostle of Jesus Christ' between his conversion and first visit to Jerusalem somewhere between 33 and 36, with his first missionary preaching in Damascus and in Nabataean Arabia, should not simply be dropped in favour of 'Hellenistic' Antioch, which German New Testament scholars since the history-of-religions school have so loved.

Thus Paul's motive for beginning his first missionary activity among the 'Gentiles' in Arabia, i.e. in the Nabataean kingdom, seems to me to be clear. First there was the geographical proximity to Damascus and Eretz Israel, and secondly the fact that the 'Arabs' were also real sons of Abraham. In addition there was the prophetic promise and the nearness to the exodus and journey through the wilderness, and to Sinai. This first missionary activity already gave him abundant occasion to reflect on Abraham, being a child of Abraham, circumcision and the law.

In conclusion, I must draw attention to one last point. In Damascus, very probably the language in the synagogues was predominantly Greek, though Hebrew as the language of the readings and the liturgy and Aramaic as the vernacular of the country population may have played some role. According to the testimony of the inscriptions, in Nabataean Arabia the language was predominantly Aramaic. Nabataean was only a dialect of Aramaic. In other words, if Paul engaged in mission there he must have spoken fluent Aramaic. The fact that his mother tongue was Greek does not rule this out. Rather, he will have had mastery of all three languages, Greek, Aramaic and Hebrew, and perhaps as a Roman citizen also Latin, which was necessary in Spain, his last missionary goal.[620]

The conjectures by R. A. Martin, that the strict Pharisee Paul learned Greek and became open to Greek culture only after his conversion to the new faith,[621] merely confirm that the superstition of many New Testament scholars that one can only develop a picture of Paul which is in any way historically adequate on the basis of Paul's letters, without Luke and contrary to him (though basically even then he is not dispensed with), leads to absurdities. For a long time the 'exclusive Paulinists' wanted to depict the apostle as an unimpeachable 'Hellenistic' Diaspora Jew who had never been to Jerusalem before his conversion; now on the same basis he is made a rigorous Shammaite Palestine Jew.[622] There was often a touch of 'anti-Judaism' in the case of the 'Hellenist' Paul: today fashions have changed. Conversely, the 'Christophobe' Chaim Maccoby wants to see Paul as a former pagan and (notorious) liar.[623] Everything seems possible in the game that our New Testament discipline has now become. Were Paul originally a real Palestinian Jew who did not know Greek, his career would have looked quite different, and as an 'apostle to the Gentiles' would have taken him from Damascus through 'Arabia' to Palmyra, Edessa, and Hatra to Babylonian and Iran, i.e. to those areas which were assigned to the apostle Thomas. Between Asia Minor, the Indian Ocean and the Caspian Sea more people spoke Aramaic than spoke Greek. According to Josephus, the Diaspora in the East was more numerous, since at the time of Ezra ten tribes had remained beyond the Euphrates. Therefore now only 'two tribes in Asia and Europe' were subject to the Romans. By contrast, in the East there remained 'myriads, whose number no one can know'.[624] Paul's move westwards, which was decided later, is connected with his origin in Tarsus, his Greek mother tongue, his Roman citizenship and also his scriptural 'missionary geography'.[625]

Excursus II: The religious situation in Arabia and Syria

The religious situation in Nabataean Arabia will not have been fundamentally different from that in Damascus, except that the milieu was more Semitic or 'Arabic' than the south Syrian metropolis, which was proud of its status as a Greek city and where the *interpretatio Graeca* of the traditional Semitic gods predominated. Thus what was said above about Damascus is even more clearly the case with the Nabataeans.

There will also have been a subliminal tendency towards an undoctrinaire, non-exclusive 'practical monotheism' among the Arabian tribes, who worshipped their anonymous 'tribal gods' or 'gods of the fathers'[626] under numerous changing personal names. Often a 'most high' God is invoked as God of heaven in inscriptions; he towers in might above all other gods, so that they could be regarded as his messengers or active plenipotentiaries.[627] Thus we find the divine designation 'Lord of the world (age)' in Hegra (Madain Salih), in Palmyra for Bel Shamin, in the Genesis Apocryphon and in the Aramaic Enoch fragments of Qumran and then almost stereotypically in Jewish prayers.[628] In contrast to the Greek world, divine designations with *mr', mrn mrn'* or κύριος and κύρια are relatively frequent,[629] and in addition 'Lord' was also a form of address to someone held in respect.[630] In Gaza, Marnas was the designation of the city god, who was identified with Zeus; it probably simply meant 'our lord'.[631] In the Nabataean temple in Si'/Seeia near Kanatha already mentioned we find a dedicatory inscription from the year 29/30 which mentions Philip as lord of the land: 'our lord Philip' *(maranā Philippos)*.[632] This recalls that the Alexandrians mocked Agrippa I in 38 CE as *marin*.[633] The title 'lord' for Agrippa appears on a dedicatory inscription in El Mushennef in the Auranitis: 'For the welfare of the Lord Agrippa' (ὑπὲρ σωτηρίας κυρίου βασιλέως Ἀγρίππα). It gives thanks for the ruler's return from Rome and reports the erection of a temple for Zeus – because of a vow – and the ancestral God Apollo, i.e. for the supreme God and his son, who represents a Hellenized tribal deity.[634] The same title was also given to Agrippa II: an inscription from 37 or 32 has been preserved in Es-Sanathen (Aire) in Trachonitis, βασιλέως Ἀγρίππα κυρί[ου], in connection with the consecration of a temple gate for Zeus Kyrios decorated with a small Nike and figures of lions. Does this not remind us of the twofold significance of Kyrios in Paul's terminology?[635]

A Nabataean in nearby Siaʿ in the Hauran had already dedicated a statue to Agrippa's great-grandfather Herod: Ἡρώδει κυρίῳ Ὀβαίσατος Σαόδου ἔθηκα τὸν ἀνδριάντα ταῖς ἐμαῖς δαπάναι[ς.[636] In Hegra inscriptions call Dusares the 'God of our Lord Aretas', i.e. Aretas IV.[637] By contrast, a bilingual ossuary inscription from Jerusalem before 70 designates the brothers Matthias and Simeon 'lords (i.e. proprietors) of the tomb'.[638] Thus the range of meaning for *'adon/mareh/rab/rabbun/kyrios* was very great. It extended from the owner of a tomb, through persons who were respected, teachers and rulers, to the deity.[639] Against this Semitic linguistic background, which was at the same time Palestinian-Jewish, we can understand how from the beginning the exalted Lord could be invoked as 'our Lord', but that at the same time one could speak of the 'brothers' of the Lord and by this mean the physical brothers of Jesus.[640] The designation Lord for Jesus could refer both to the exalted Christ and the man Jesus, and expressed a relationship to both. In the Lord's Supper it was used in a request for his presence in the Spirit and with a view to his imminent coming in the parousia. The proclamation 'Jesus Christ, our Lord' similarly corresponded to current linguistic sensibility in Jewish Palestine and the directly adjacent territories, both in Aramaic and in Greek. The same is also true of the formula which we find almost as a stereotype in the salutation of Paul's letters: 'from God the Father of our Lord Jesus Christ'.[641]

The peculiarities of the religion of Arabia and Syria which could lead to the monotheizing tendency described above also include an anonymous way of speaking of God.[642] In an inscription protecting a tomb in Hegra the curse is threatened of the 'one who divides night from day'.[643] In and around Palmyra we

find on around 300 altar inscriptions an anonymous god with the
designation 'whose name be praised for ever' (*lbryk smh l'lm'*);
with few exceptions there is no pictorial representation of him
in the period between 103 and 268 CE.[644] The invocations are
supplemented by predicates like 'one, only, merciful',[645] good,
generous, whom one called and he heard,[646] 'whom one called in
tribulation and he heard us by bringing us relief', 'whom one
invokes in every place',[647] 'whom one invokes on the dry land
and on the sea and he hears, saves and brings to life',[648] whose
good deeds one 'confesses publicly every day',[649] who performs
healings and other 'mighty acts'.[650] This is probably a religious
development of the originally essentially different cult of the
supreme God Baal Shamim, who in isolation is given partially
similar predicates and whose worship was suppressed by this cult
with its more individual colourings. This anonymous God of
whom on the whole there were no images can in circumstances
be invoked, like the God of heaven, as Ζεὺς ὕψιστος καὶ ἐπήκοος.[651]
Inscriptions for the θεὸς ὕψιστος or also Ζεὺς ὕψιστος are not so
frequent in Syria and Arabia (and in Asia Minor, see below, 163)
but are also attested, and could be used both for the local deities
and for the 'highest God'.[652] The official designation of the Jewish
God was also θεὸς ὕψιστος, the Greek version of the old 'God of
Heaven' of the Persian period. Non-Jews preferred to give the
Jewish God this name.[653] Just as pagan authors from the time
of Hecataeus of Abdera (*c.*300 BCE) asserted that the Jews
worshipped heaven,[654] so in the second century CE Arrian could
say of the Arabs that they worshipped Οὐρανός.[655] There is a
striking verse inscription from Philadelphia-Amman *c.*140, which
after invoking Ἀγαθὴ τύχη affirms θεὸς ἡγεῖται and repeats this in
abbreviated form Ζ(ευς) ἡ(γεῖται) before the second part; it then
goes on at the end to praise Demeter (i.e. the earth) as the giver
of fruits and Zeus (i.e. heaven) as the giver of rain. Does not the
emphasis on the lordship of the deity, i.e. Zeus, here seek
to express a repudiation of the claim to rule of another god,
the God of Judaism or Christianity?[656] The tendency towards
enlightened mono- or pantheism, orientated on nature, is also
unmistakable in this inscription.

With some justification, the anonymous god of Palmyra has

been compared with the Jewish conception of God. The formula 'whose name be praised for ever' recalls the most important formula in the Jerusalem cult, 'Praised be the glorious name of his kingdom for ever', and there are also Old Testament and Jewish parallels to the other predicates.[657] So in the anonymous God in Palmyra one may see a sign of that 'monotheizing and individualistic' tendency in the Syrian Arabian belief in gods, already mentioned, which favoured both Jewish religious propaganda and the earliest Christian mission in this area. O. Eissfeldt saw in the anonymous God 'a conception of God of astonishing purity and depth', indeed the 'climax of the history of Palmyrene religion', behind which stood the 'wish derived from monotheistic sensibility to replace the gods hitherto worshipped in Palmyra with the one and only God, who was therefore necessarily nameless'.[658] In the most recent investigation, M. Gawlikowski speaks of a tendency to worship the divine presence more in transcendent form: 'this tendency was to culminate in the personal cult of the anonymous God, in part detached from ancient ritual practices'.[659] The Jewish liturgy of the word in the synagogue in honour of the 'most high God' and the 'Lord of the world' was such a more 'spiritual' form of religion, related to the piety of the individual. The same is true of the Jewish Christian missionary communities which were taking shape, in which the eschatological impulse and the hope of eternal life with Christ provided an additional power of attraction.[660] Both were therefore particularly successful in West Syria and Arabia, where the young messianic movement was not 'more syncretistic' than the institutionalized synagogue communities. The two groups, still linked together, responded to the basic religious questions which were alive in the early empire.

Pagan listeners could also understand the sending of the Son by the Father and the trinity of Father, Son and Spirit, since triads of gods with a supreme God,[661] a mother goddess and a son were widespread in Syria and Arabia.[662] In the triad of Heliopolis Baalbek, which was also worshipped as an anonymous deity on Carmel, the Son, who was identified in a Romanized form with Hermes/Mercury, was at the same time the messenger of the gods.[663] Triads also appear in other local cults in Coele Syria.[664]

The saying from the Gospel of the Hebrews, 'Even so did my mother, the Holy Spirit, take me by one of my hairs and carry me away on to the great mountain Tabor', which is quoted several times by Origen and Jerome, is probably dependent on this Semitic notion of the triad.[665] Here the spirit appears, like the Aramaic *ruha'*, as feminine. One could perhaps read the function of the Spirit as a second maternal-feminine primal principle out of Gen. 1.2.

This notion also appears in the account of the baptism in the Gospel of the Hebrews:

And it came to pass when the Lord was come up out of the water, the whole fount of the Holy Spirit descended upon him and rested on him and said to him: 'My Son, in all the prophets I was waiting for you, so that you should come and I might rest in you. For you are my rest; you are my first-begotten Son, who reigns for ever.'[666]

However, it is significant that no comparable statement about the Spirit as 'mother' of Jesus occurs anywhere in the New Testament. A second feminine primal principle appears only in the Gnostic systems. We find more of a parallel in Jewish Wisdom, which appears in Prov. 8 as a mediator and child at creation and in the Wisdom of Solomon as the *parhedros* and throne consort of God.[667] The nearest pagan Jewish analogy would be the 'Lady Prayer House' (κυρία προσευχή) and the 'Holy (place of) Refuge', (ἁγία καταφυγή) as the *parhedros* of God in pagan inscriptions from Asia Minor (see below, 163ff.). It is the pagan Athenians who according to Luke misunderstand Paul's preaching of the risen Christ and think that he is proclaiming 'strange gods', Jesus and the Anastasis.[668] In some sayings of Jesus in Q, 'maternal features' of Wisdom are indicated, thus in Luke 7.33, which speaks of the 'children of Wisdom', a phrase which Matt. 11.19 turns into 'works of Wisdom', or also in Luke 13.34 = Matt. 23.27, where she is compared with a solicitous mother bird. But this is not developed further. Rather, in I Cor. 1.30 Christ draws the predicate of Wisdom wholly to himself. Here in particular we cannot speak of a special earliest Christian 'syncretism', since the cult of the divine Mother which was so alive in Syria did not influence earliest Christianity, despite its intensive mission in Syria.[669]

If we want to speak of an 'influence' of a Semitic Hellenistic 'goddess' on Paul or earliest Christianity, then perhaps this is most likely in the comparison of the two covenants and 'cities' in Gal. 4.24–26, the 'present' Jerusalem which is 'in slavery' and the Jerusalem 'above', i.e. the heavenly free Jerusalem, the latter corresponding to Hagar/Hegra in Arabia. The city goddess appears countless times on the coins of Syrian and Phoenician cities from the Decapolis to Antioch, quite often in the form of Tyche, the bringer of luck, with a mural crown on her head, and of course the cities, above all the more significant ones, loved to call themselves 'free' and even 'metropolis', as 'mothers' of whole regions and peoples.[670] The 'free', 'heavenly Jerusalem' which 'is our mother' (Gal. 4.26) derives from this political-religious metaphorical language. When κυρία[671] appears in II John 1, she is addressed as 'the chosen lady and her children' (ἐκλεκτὴ κυρία), and denotes the community which is being addressed.[672] In II John 13 the greeting names as the sender 'the children of the chosen sister' (ἡ ἐκλεκτὴ ἀδελφή), the sister community. Nor should we forget that '*ekklesia*' in the ears of the pagan citizen unfamiliar with the Septuagint meant the assembly of the free citizens of a city state, and that this political connotation was always suggested by the term the earliest Christians chose to describe themselves: the '*ekklesia*' was the assembly of the citizens of the heavenly Jerusalem. When in Ephesians this then becomes a pre-existent, more than earthly body,[673] it takes on almost a divine character, but this in particular is still not an authentic Pauline notion. The apocalyptic notion of the city of Jerusalem standing ready in heaven for the end time may also be influenced by the Hellenistic transfiguration of a city through its citizens.[674] The '*ekklesia*' as a heavenly aeon in the divine pleroma then appears first in Valentinus, in the fourth syzygy as the consort of Anthropos.[675] But such speculation, which objectivizes and connects male and female entities in the divine consciousness, is still alien to earliest Christianity. We find the first beginnings of this applied only to Christ and the *ekklesia* in the relatively late letter to the Ephesians. As the Wisdom of Solomon and Philo show, Hellenistic Judaism was more open to such attempts of a 'philosophical' kind than earliest Christianity. Here church Gnosticism took further the beginnings made by Hellenistic Judaism.

5. The Return to Damascus and the Flight from the City

5.1 Return and further stay

I have already remarked that Paul's stay in 'Arabia', i.e. in the Nabataean kingdom, was quite a long one, lasting eighteen months or even two years. Moreover, as later, he will have carried on his missionary activity only in the larger cities, since only in them will there have been synagogues with a circle of Gentile sympathizers.[676] We should also remember that his activity in the Nabataean kingdom fell in the period of the tensions between Aretas IV and Herod Antipas, after the death of Philip (34–36 CE), when there was a dispute over who had the influence in Philip's former sphere of rule on the southern frontier of the territory of the city of Damascus, ending in a military conflict which forced Rome to intervene. A war was avoided only because Tiberius died on 16 March 37. At all events the situation was very tense for a long time. Understandably the open proclamation of a crucified Jewish Messiah whom God had exalted to himself as Kyrios and who would soon return as redeemer will also have disturbed the synagogue communities and their Gentile clientèle in the cities of 'Arabia' . That can be inferred from the turmoil which Paul later caused in Jewish communities, and also from II Cor. 11.24 and the note in Suetonius.[677] Presumably the cautious Aretas will have come to hear of the machinations of the Jewish sectarian missionary. In a critical political situation between Nabataeans and Jews his preaching could well have seemed political. We do not know whether and how far this first attempt at mission was really successful and whether lasting

communities were created. However, that is quite possible.[678]
So Paul left his Nabataean mission area – which had become
threatening – and returned to Damascus, which was to some
degree familiar to him, to the Christian brothers there; this is
probably a sign that the small community which was coming into
being, presumably led by expelled 'Hellenists', on the whole had
quite a positive attitude towards him. This return also tells against
supposing that he had been a persecutor in Damascus itself.
Where else could he have gone? There was hardly a Christian
community outside Judaea which would have trusted him – the
former persecutor of the 'Hellenists' – and where he could have
turned predominantly to pagan 'sympathizers'. A little later –
again under threat – he went from Jerusalem to Tarsus in the
north, also familiar to him, but quite remote.[679]

5.2 Flight

However, he could not stay very long in Damascus either. We
have two independent reports of his adventurous flight from the
city, one from himself, the other from Luke:

> II Cor. 11.32f.: At Damascus, the governor under King Aretas
> guarded the city of Damascus in order to seize me, but I was let
> down in a basket through a window in the wall, and escaped
> his hands.

> Acts 9.23–25: When many days had passed, the Jews plotted to
> kill him, but their plot became known to Saul. They were
> watching the gates day and night, to kill him, but his disciples
> took him by night and let him down over the wall, lowering
> him in a basket.

Here again Paul's account is to be preferred. That the Jews
launch attacks on Paul seems almost to be something like a fixed
theme in Luke, though it was historically well grounded in Paul's
life[680] and would also have been understandable in Damascus;
however, Paul's remarkable reference to the ethnarch of King
Aretas gives the whole scene a more concrete background. The
ethnarch's intervention would make sense if he had had a hint

from his royal lord that he should seize the agitator who had caused offence in his missionary activity in the Nabataean kingdom. πιάζειν means seize, arrest, and not simply kill: that would have been simpler. Thus this event can also be dated. In all probability it marks the second phase of the stay in Damascus. It would not be understandable either why Paul should have escaped from the ethnarch of Aretas straight into the king's territory or why he should have returned when he had already been in acute risk of his life there. But it would be plausible that after his life had also been endangered in the metropolis of southern Syria he should have spontaneously decided to catch up on developments by a visit to the leading men of the new movement in Jerusalem which had so far been postponed because of the threat there. In both places his life was in danger and was in the hand of his new Lord.[681]

Both accounts agree that Paul had friends and helpers in Damascus. Paul himself expresses this in II Cor. 11 by a mere mention in the aorist passive, 'I was lowered' (ἐχαλάσθην). In Luke we find an interesting variant reading: the good manuscripts of the Alexandrian text read '*his* disciples took him' (λαβόντες δε οἱ μαθηταὶ αὐτοῦ, P[74] sin ABC 81[c] pc), but the majority text has only '*the* disciples' (οἱ μαθηταί).[682] This first reading, which is unique in Acts because elsewhere the absolute μαθηταί, used frequently, means disciples (of Jesus), i.e. Christians,[683] seems to me to be more original. According to Luke they are 'disciples' of Paul, i.e. men whom he has won over through his preaching. This un-Lukan terminology probably comes from pre-Lukan tradition. Luke keeps it in order to indicate the first missionary success of the new convert by this little reference. The un-Lukan text would then have already been altered at a very early stage. That 'disciples' of Paul appear here should perhaps also be taken as an indication that Luke did not regard the stay of the former persecutor in Damascus as being so short as the 'critical' commentaries claim, and perhaps also that there was a certain distance between Paul and the Christians in Damascus. But with such considerations the danger of over-interpretation immediately arises.

Scholars also argue over the position of the ethnarch of Aretas in the city. As we have no city coins from Damascus between 33/4 and 62/3, it is conjectured on the basis of II Cor. 11.32f. that Damascus was handed over to Aretas IV by Caligula in 37 CE on the latter's reorganization of the East. Since in my view Paul's flight from Damascus took place as early as around 36 CE, this old disputed question is not of basic importance for us. Moreover it can be answered simply: Aretas III had already ruled Damascus *c.* 85–72/1 BCE and had also minted coins there, while we have no such indications of Aretas IV.[684] Had the city been handed over to Aretas IV, the ethnarch would have been the royal governor in the city. However, in that case one would have expected the titles *strategos* or *epitropos* and not *ethnarches*. We find Nabataean *strategoi* in various significant cities in the kingdom, including Hegra. It is also very improbable that Caligula would have handed over a famous Hellenistic *polis* rich in tradition to a client king who was a 'barbarian' and therefore wilful, and against whom his predecessor Tiberius had wanted to wage war. This conjecture is also geographically improbable, since at the same time Caligula gave the territory of Philip, which extended a long way eastwards as far as the Hauran, to his friend Agrippa I, and made him king. Damascus would have largely been cut off from Nabataean territory by the kingdom of Agrippa I, and on the other hand such a gift would have represented a political threat to Agrippa, as the Nabataeans had almost encircled his territory from the south, east and north. Zahn already remarked that the Pauline formulation πόλις Δαμασκηνῶν indicates a free *polis* and its citizens; even if Paul (Gal. 1.17) says that he 'returned' from 'Arabia' to Damascus, he does not presuppose that the city was part of the Nabataean kingdom.[685] The question of coins must not be overestimated, since the minting in Damascus is extraordinarily full of gaps, and coins were minted for a lengthy period, to some degree for stock. Finally, we do not have any kind of references in the sources to such an unusual event. On the other hand, it is probable that after the death of Philip (34 CE), and even more after the defeat of Antipas, the pressure of the ambitious king on the city and thus also his influence had grown for the moment.

E. A. Knauf offered a convincing solution to the problem, by proposing that the ethnarch had been the 'leader of the Nabataean trade colony in Damascus', who 'represented the interests of the Nabataean state as a kind of consul'.[686] The Jews with their synagogues probably also formed a separate colony in Damascus, as in Antioch (see below, 186f.), and in Alexandria to the time of Augustus under an 'ethnarch' or 'genarch'.[687] We find Nabataean trading colonies in the Decapolis, but also in Sidon and even in Puteoli.[688] Certainly the Nabataean colony and its head were particularly important in Damascus, which was an important link in international trade. That is indicated by the fact that according to Arab sources there was a quarter in the north-east of the city the name of which, *en Naibatun*, is to be derived from the genitive Ναβαταίων; in Roman times it was inhabited by Nabataeans. Presumably it had originally been outside the city wall and was then later brought within it. Starcky and Riesner point out that the Ananias chapel, the local tradition of which goes back to Byzantine times, lay in the Nabataean quarter; indeed, Riesner conjectures that 'the house of Ananias may have been situated ... directly on the wall'.[689] Possibly the Nabataean and Jewish quarters were originally side by side. We do not know how large the Nabataean 'colony' in Damascus was. It may have been substantially smaller than the Jewish colony, but because of the power of the Nabataean king over the caravan routes, its influence was hardly smaller. What moved the ethnarch to take this step, whether it was an instruction from Petra, an intervention from the Jewish community or even both together, can be left open. At all events, we may assume that the apostle's preaching caused serious offence in Nabataea, 'Arabia', which was entangled in political dealings with the Jewish tetrarch Herod Antipas, and in Damascus, i.e. among 'Arabs' and the synagogue communities. Would that not have been connected with his public preaching of the Messiah of Israel who had been crucified and was to come again, and the questioning of the Torah as a way of salvation? Can we give another, better, reason for this act of persecution? 'But if I, brethren, still preach circumcision, why am I still persecuted? In that case the stumbling block of the cross has been removed!'[690] Did that apply only to a later time, after the machinations of the 'Judaizers' in Galatia, or was not Paul,

preaching the 'scandal of the cross', i.e.the crucified messiah as
heavenly Kyrios and eschatological saviour, threatened from the
beginning? As a young scribe he had 'preached circumcision' in
the Greek-speaking synagogues of Jerusalem, and at that time he
became the sharpest persecutor because of this scandal of the
cross. By contrast, the flight from Damascus is the first act of
violence against Paul about which we know from the apostle himself.

Now, after the radical change in his life, he himself became the
victim, but because of his new offensive messianic message, which
already at that time must have seemed 'to the Jews a stumbling
block' and to the Nabataean ruler and his minions the dangerous
political agitation of a Jewish enthusiast. Here we cannot exclude
the possibility that Paul *and* Acts are right, namely that the Jewish
community authority and the Nabataean 'consul' collaborated in
an attempt to do away with this sinister person.

6. The Visit to Peter in Jerusalem

6.1 The two reports in Gal. 1.18–20 and Acts 9.26–30

Only now, after two or three years, during which he had accumulated missionary experiences in Damascus, for some time in Arabia, and then again in Damascus, does Paul travel to Jerusalem.

> Then after three years I went up to Jerusalem to visit Cephas, and remained with him fifteen days. But I saw none of the other apostles except James the Lord's brother. (In what I am writing to you, before God, I do not lie!)[691]

The 'missionary loner' now wanted to make contact with the head of the group of the Twelve and the spokesman of the young Jesus community in the Holy City. Paul's autobiographical account gives a clear and precise impression, but at the same time it raises questions. The few facts that he reports are so important to him that he confirms their truth with an oath.[692] In so doing he rejects the false view that he met a number of apostles in Jerusalem, just as later, too, he emphasizes that he remained unknown to the 'churches of Judaea which are in Christ' (1.22). It had probably been spread around by the Judaizers in Galatia that he had initially had close connections with the community in Jerusalem and its leading body and was dependent on them. In other words, here his report has a certain apologetic tendency. Luke reports this visit at rather greater length (Acts 9.26–29), putting the adventurous flight from Damascus immediately before it (9.23–25). We can conclude from II Cor. 11.32f. that this last point accords with historical reality.[693]

2. The Lukan version seems on the one hand to supplement

the few pieces of information given by Paul, but on the other to contradict him on the decisive point. There is no doubt that Paul's account is certainly to be given the preference here, and even the attempt at an over-hasty harmonization is to be rejected, but that does not mean that Luke's contribution is from the start historically worthless as a whole.[694] After all, although it is completely independent, it again agrees in an amazing way with Gal. 1.18f. If we want to compare Luke with Paul, we must listen to him carefully.[695]

> And when he came to Jerusalem, he attempted to join the disciples,[696] and they were all[697] afraid of him, for they did not believe that he was a disciple. But Barnabas took him, and brought[698] him to the apostles, and he (Paul) declared to them[699] how on the road he had seen the Lord, and he (the Lord)[700] spoke to him, and how at Damascus he had preached boldly in the name of Jesus.

6.2 Common presuppositions

1. The common starting point of Gal. 1.18f. and Acts 9.26–30 is that Paul comes to Jerusalem from Damascus, from which he has been driven by the danger to his life depicted in II Cor. 11 and Acts 9.23–25. We are also to presuppose from Gal. 1.18f. that the flight from Damascus narrated in II Cor. 11.32f. preceded the ἀνῆλθον. Thus it emerges indirectly from both reports that the apostle was not in a hurry to get to Jerusalem. The immediate external occasion was the need for sudden flight. This makes it improbable that Paul had any possibility of planning the journey from Damascus or even of preparing for his visit by informing Cephas/Peter beforehand. Nor is there any mention of an invitation from Peter. In Luke and Gal. 1 the initiative is solely Paul's. This already is an amazing agreement. I have already referred to the different indications of time. In contrast to the second half of Acts, to which Luke is closer as an eye-witness, in the first half he can hardly give exact details of time. The ἡμέραι ἱκαναί simply indicates an undefined but *lengthy* period.[701]

According to Acts, too, Paul did not hasten to get to Jerusalem

in order to make that 'connection with the twelve apostles which
… is indispensable for the legality of his ministry'.[702] On the contrary, in both Acts and Galatians the date of the visit arises out of
the circumstances. Now if we assume on the basis of Gal. 1.22f.
that the turning point in the life of the persecutor was known in
Jerusalem, then we should also surmise that Paul still had to fear
the vengeance of his former friends and fellow persecutors, the
Jewish 'Hellenists', that his life was also in danger in Jerusalem,
and that he attempted to remain unknown as far as possible on
his visit there. Since according to Acts 23.16–22 he had a nephew
there who even twenty years later remained loyal to his Christian
uncle and thus saved his life, we can assume that he initially
stayed with his relatives without attracting attention. At least that
could have happened. For Gal. 1.18f. in particular makes it seem
plausible, on the basis of the known fact that Paul met only with
Peter (and James) and otherwise saw none of the men who were
'apostles' in Jerusalem 'before him' (Gal. 1.17), that this visit was
quite deliberately meant to take place without attracting great
attention. It is improbable that all the other apostles – we do not
know how many there were, but there were probably more than
twelve[703] – happened by chance to be on missionary journeys.
Rather, we should assume that Paul did not meet with them
because – for reasons of secrecy – they were not meant to see him,
or because they did not want to see him, the former persecutor
and preacher of a special gospel. The converse possibility, conjectured by H. Wendt, 'that he deliberately limited his dealings to
Peter and James and therefore did not see the rest of the apostles
because he did not want develop relations with the real community in Jerusalem',[704] fails to recognize the situation in
Jerusalem, where Paul could not present demands or make
regulations. The limitation – at least for the length of the stay –
probably arose on the side of the Jerusalem people. He comes
there as a guest, not as a master.

That James the brother of the Lord also appears alongside
Cephas/Peter may be connected with the fact that he was the
leading man of the other wing – which observed the law more
strictly – who after Peter's flight, as a result of Agrippa's persecution around seven years later (probably in 43 CE), took over the

leadership in Jerusalem and therefore at the 'Apostolic Council' in around 49 CE had first place among the pillars and relegated Peter/Cephas to second place.[705]

2. The most plausible explanation why Paul (as far as the apostles were concerned) met only with Cephas/Peter and James is thus the motif of secrecy. Here we must remember the tense and always threatening situation of the Jerusalem community between the martyrdom of Stephen and the ensuing expulsion of the Jewish-Christian Hellenists and the persecution under Agrippa I. In between will lie around ten years in which despite the assurance of Luke in Acts 9.31 there may have constantly been smaller attacks. The threat remained, as is also indicated by I Thess. 2.14; Gal. 4.29 and numerous Gospel texts.[706]

Around two to three years after the expulsion of the Hellenists, the Jerusalem community will have consisted quite predominantly of 'Hebrews', i.e. Aramaic-speaking Jewish Christians,[707] though there may also have been individual disciples who were connected with those who had been driven out and had some sympathy for them.[708] The appearance in Jerusalem of the former persecutor and zealot for the law, whose attitude towards the law was now even more critical than that of the expelled 'Hellenists', could have been felt to be dangerous, and that would explain the limitation of his conversation partners to the two key men in the community and his acceptance as Peter's guest. There was a concern that as little as possible about his stay should get out. News of the visit of the persecutor who had been 'turned round' could have been dangerous for Paul himself, but the community could also have put itself in a bad light with the 'zealots for the law' in Jerusalem.[709] This problem persisted down to Paul's arrest in the temple around twenty years later.[710] In other words, Paul's report of his first visit to Peter in Jerusalem indicates just as serious problems as Luke's narrative – which is certainly secondary – does. Paul does not say that he went to Jerusalem with the definitive wish simply and solely to get to know Cephas/Peter and that he rejected all other contacts. But that will have been his main reason and indicates the absolutely leading role of Cephas/Peter at that point in the early period, which is thus impressively confirmed to us by Luke as well. Other possible wishes had to come behind this one. Still, he also had to meet James – probably only for a while. The limitation to these two 'prominent' conversation-partners and the fact that he could stay two weeks with Cephas/Peter at the same time shows the importance attached to his visit in Jerusalem also.

But how did Paul find his way to Peter and only to him? Did he take Peter's address with him from Damascus and go straight to his home, saying 'Here I am!'? Or did he only begin to make enquiries about Peter after he had arrived in Jerusalem? And is it not likely that a third party arranged the visit and the stay with Peter?

So it is by no means as certain as radical critics claim that Luke knew only of the fact of Paul's visit to Jerusalem and shaped everything else freely in accordance with his theological bias. We have already referred to some amazing agreements; but they are harder to recognize than the contradictions, which are blatant.

1. They begin with the fact that in Jerusalem Paul again finds 'disciples', after according to 8.1 'all'[711] but the apostles had been driven out of Jerusalem to Judaea and Samaria. This is one of Luke's pieces of carelessness or exaggerations. Historically, presumably only the Jewish-Christian 'Hellenists' were driven out,[712] while the tribulation passed by the 'Hebrews' and the group of their leaders. We may assume that they too felt the shaking caused by the martyrdom of Stephen and the subsequent shock waves. Presumably Luke would have replied to the critical objection in amazement: of course the disciples had returned in the lengthy interval. Already in 8.2. he has pious men burying and mourning Stephen; immediately afterwards follows Saul's raging against the *ekklesia* (with the exception of the apostles there), which had by no means already been scattered.[713] The contradictions are manifest. This may be connected with the fact that Luke put together different pieces of tradition in the wrong order and that the whole narrative structure suffers from the fact that he extended the persecution and expulsion to the whole community,

2. 9.26 gives the impression that the Jerusalem 'disciples' had not been informed of Paul's conversion and that his concern to make contact with them put them 'all' in fear and trembling, as

they still saw him as a persecutor. That would then be in line with
9.13 and 21 and would contradict Gal. 1.21f. However, we must at
least reckon with the possibility that the tradition before Luke
spoke of fear and mistrust of the sudden new arrival, but perhaps
on the basis of other motives, for example that his appearance
could lead to a new threat and unrest, or that people had heard
from Arabia or Damascus and elsewhere of his radical theological
tendencies, which for many people in Jerusalem went too
far. After all, the 'expulsion of the Hellenists' was still clearly
remembered and to have the former persecutor next door was
something different from hearing from afar of the change in his
life and his preaching of a new faith.

3. At all events the scene in which Luke has Paul appearing
'before the apostles' is unhistorical: he applies the term οἱ
ἀπόστολοι formally to the leading group in Jerusalem, consisting
of the twelve disciples of Jesus, which goes back to their institution through Jesus and is supplemented by the choice of
Matthias. Certainly Luke speaks only once of the Twelve,[714] but as
a rule he presupposes them as a normative entity and mentions
'the apostles' eighteen times between 1.2 and 11.1 with this fixed
meaning. We find exceptions only in 8.18, where Peter and John
are given this title, and 14.4, 14, where it is given to Paul and
Barnabas. After 15.2 we similarly have the stereotyped formula
'the apostles *and the elders*'[715] as a sign of the new form of community leadership in the Holy City; 21.18 mentions only James
and 'all the elders', showing the completely different situation in
Jerusalem. This fixed talk of 'the apostles' as a closed unit is part
of Luke's stained-glass-window style which applies to the ideal
early period. It cannot be explained, as happened in the earlier
conservative commentaries,[716] by pointing out that 'the apostles'
means Peter and James. By this term Luke understood the
whole group of leaders in Jerusalem. We can only guess what
conversation-partners Luke really found in the tradition which
came down to him (see above, 18ff. and 6.6 below). However, it
is striking that he has Paul[717] presenting to the apostles only his
vision of Christ and his preaching of the name of Jesus in
Damascus; he does not say anything about an answer from the
apostles or even a legitimation of the new missionary. On this

point Luke corresponds completely with Paul's brief account in Gal. 1.18f. Here in Gal. 1.24 we even hear more about the reaction of the 'churches in Judaea': 'and they glorified God in me (καὶ ἐδόξαζον ἐν ἐμοὶ τὸν θεόν)'.[718] Certainly we can conclude with Barrett, 'It is clearly implied that Saul was accepted by the apostles', but in connection with v.28 he adds: 'The wording suggests that Saul was not only with the apostles but shared their activities, and there is nothing to suggest that he did not do so on equal terms.'[719] C. Burchard also stresses that 'there is no indication of approval by the apostles',[720] indeed, contrary to E. Haenchen and G. Klein he comes to the conclusion 'that Paul's status and activity are as directly related to Christ as the status and activity of the Twelve'.[721] Luke may withhold the title apostle (as a rule) from Paul on historical and theological grounds – it is hard to separate the two in his writing – but there is no more sign of any dependence of his preaching on the Jerusalem authorities or an approval of it by them than there is in Paul himself.

4. The difference between Gal. 1.18f. and Acts 9.27–29 becomes even less given the situation after 70 in Luke's time and later, when the great names of Peter and James, who had meanwhile become martyrs, denoted a greater authority than the anonymous 'apostles'. Paul's own report also corresponds with that of Luke to the degree that both emphasize the towering significance of Cephas/Peter for the earliest community in Jerusalem and the church generally. Indeed, in Paul this is even more the case when we note the difference between the letters and Acts, since for him the influence of Cephas/Peter continues even more after the Apostolic Council, and extends to Galatia and Corinth, whereas Luke makes it break off abruptly with the speech in Acts 15.7–11. Peter subsequently has to disappear from Acts. One might almost say with Schiller's Fiesco, 'The Moor has done his duty, the Moor can go.' From now on Luke is interested only in the fate of Paul. Conversely, it is striking how much Paul adopts a position over against Peter. Peter is later in a special way his 'counterpart'.[722] Nor can he suppress the importance of James, whom Luke does not love and therefore puts into the background as a person:[723] James says the concluding word at the

Apostolic Council which resolves the conflict, and Paul must go to him shortly before his tribulations begin and follow his advice.[724] He mentions him only three times, but Peter fifty-seven times (all but one in the first half of Acts!). So perhaps the silence of the apostles in 9.27, despite the equal rights indicated in v.28 by the complete freedom of preaching, is eloquent in its own way because despite a fundamental agreement[725] it could refer indirectly to a certain distance.[726] Luke is not the thoughtless harmonizer that people want to make him. But he wants to write in pastoral responsibility, and modern radical-critical exegetes fail to understand this because they do not consider his historical situation.

5. The function of the person of Barnabas, whose significance is sometimes heavily exaggerated, also caused offence. It is plausible that Paul needed someone to introduce him – to Peter –, and Luke will have taken the name of Barnabas from tradition.[727] Perhaps as a Levite from Cyprus in Jerusalem he was a point of contact there for the 'Hellenists' who had fled to Damascus. This would explain his later role between Jerusalem and Antioch, not an easy task, which also contained the possibility of conflict. That is indicated by his later defection in Antioch in Gal. 2.11, and also by Luke's reference to the dispute with Paul over John Mark in Acts 15.37–39. I think it improbable that Luke simply made him up completely in 9.27. Luke is relatively restrained in dealing with names and persons – in contrast to the later apocryphal acts of apostles.[728]

One could object to this that Paul says nothing of Barnabas and emphasizes that he 'saw none of the apostles'. But did he include Barnabas, his missionary companion of many years, among the *Jerusalem* apostles? In I Cor. 9.6 he sets himself and Barnabas over against the 'other apostles'. Be this as it may, Luke will not simply have invented the role of Barnabas in Jerusalem freely on the basis of his later collaboration with Paul, but will have taken it over, and we cannot exclude the possiblity that Barnabas at that time really showed Paul the way to Peter or himself played a role in the conversations, although we can no longer reconstruct events in detail.[729]

6. It is clear that in Gal. 1.15–24 Paul is defending himself

against a different account which was already circulating in
Galatia at that time. This could include the report that Paul made
contact with the whole group of the Twelve, was dependent on
them in his preaching, and changed his convictions in order to
please people.[730] Luke presumably took over from the tradition
the fact of the visit to the 'apostles', but rejects any anti-Pauline
consequences which go further, just as much as Paul himself
does. There could be another reason why he thinks the plural
'the apostles' important. Galatians 1.18–20 gives the impression
that the visit to Peter took place in some secrecy because Paul's
life was threatened in Jerusalem. Paul himself is silent about what
happened directly after the two weeks had elapsed, and in 1.21
immediately goes over – with an ἔπειτα, 'then' – to his stay 'in the
regions of Syria and Cilicia'. In this sequence there is again a
fundamental agreement with Luke, but Luke introduces more
detailed information which it is hard to check out. Could it not
be that Paul's opponents later also spread the report that Paul
had kept hidden in Jerusalem out of anxiety, did not dare to
appear publicly and present his message there, and finally fled
from there in a cowardly way?

By contrast, Luke would then have emphasized the convincing
appearance of the former persecutor of the apostles, his fellowship with them,[731] and his free and untroubled stay in Jerusalem,
which led to heated disputes[732] with his former friends, the Jewish
'Hellenists' from the Greek-speaking synagogues of Jerusalem. At
the end of this comes another attack on his life. It comes not
simply from 'the Jews' generally, but from these 'Hellenists' who
had now become embittered at the complete change in their
former ally and inevitably saw him as a traitor. So this scene is not
to be understood as an echo of the story of Stephen, nor simply
as part of Luke's schematic persecutions.[733] Luke may have
presented it in an effective style – as he does throughout his work
– but here too he is relating earlier tradition about Paul. That
such a conflict was natural emerges indirectly from the rigorous
limitation of contacts in Gal. 1.18f. Paul and Luke also agree that
the stay in Jerusalem was not too long, but not all that short
either. However, the reasons for the brevity of this stay are not
mentioned in Gal. 1. By contrast, Luke gives the attempt of the

Jewish Hellenists to kill Paul (οἱ δε ἐπεχείρουν ἀνελεῖν αὐτόν) as a reason. He then repeats in a different form the motive which he gave in v.23 for the flight from Damascus, the decision of the Jews there to kill him (συνεβουλεύσαντο οἱ ᾽Ιουδαῖοι ἀνελεῖν αὐτόν). Did Luke transfer to Jerusalem what he had schematically already related as a cause for the flight from Damascus (where we know 'better' because of II Cor. 11.32)? Here, if we are to conjecture anything, it should rather be the opposite, that the motif of persecution by Jews was transposed from Jerusalem to Damascus; however, that is not necessary (see 2.2.1 above). The 'zeal for the law' which was not afraid to use violence in God's cause was essentially more at home in Jerusalem and in Eretz Israel than in the Diaspora synagogues. Moreover, it would be understandable for Paul to be interested in explaining the radical change in his life to his former companions and thus in bearing witness to Jesus as Messiah, and for this wish to be ultimately stronger than the alleged caution of the one who had returned secretly. Possibly the attempt to make contact happened after he had left Peter's house, or it was the reason for breaking off the two weeks' hospitality. Perhaps the unique ἀπὸ ῾Ιερουσαλήμ in Rom. 15.19 refers to this very brief and failed 'missionary contact'. In that case the sudden threat which he had to attribute to his own missionary zeal caused the abrupt ending to his stay in the Holy City. Such a violent end to his visit is also supported by the fact that he did not visit Jerusalem again for around thirteen years. It is equally in keeping with what happened that in view of the danger which threatened, 'the brothers'[734] without delay escorted him to Caesarea and sent him to his home city of Tarsus.[735] The deadly danger to Paul because of his incautious behaviour at the same time represented a threat to the community. People there did not want to provoke any acts of violence through his further stay in Jerusalem. That is how this interlude in Jerusalem *could* have happened, and such an understanding of Luke's text, which not only identifies opposition to Paul but also shared views and meaningful connections, seems to me to be more plausible than the postulate that Luke was fundamentally only the author of an apostolic romance with certain theological tendencies.

6.3 Acts 22.17–21, an alternative Lukan account

C. Burchard[736] pointed out that the mere fact 'that 22.17–21 seems to report the reason, nature and time of Paul's departure differently from 9.29f., and in a form which Luke could have used here, suggests that vv.29f. also rest on tradition'. Acts 22.17–21 is a remarkable description of a vision which Luke makes his hero present as the conclusion of the speech about his conversion to the crowd after his arrest in the temple court. According to this, on his visit to Jerusalem Paul saw the Kyrios (22.19 κύριε) in the temple in an additional vision and was ordered by him to leave the city without delay, because its inhabitants were not accepting his testimony to Christ. When Paul objected that this was because people there knew of his fury as a persecutor, the Lord persisted in his instructions: 'Depart; for I will send you far away to the Gentiles.'[737] The account of this vision stands in clear contrast to 9.29–30.[738] Now follows the command to leave Jerusalem without delay, contrary to the wishes of Paul, who explains the ineffectiveness of his preaching by his lack of credibility as a persecutor. This command is given by the same Lord who appeared to him before Damascus and already had his mission to 'all men' (22.15) reported to him by Ananias. Paul's testimony to Christ, which the people of Jerusalem will not accept, is the really momentous thing, despite the 'myriads' of Jewish Christians in the Holy City mentioned by James in 21.20. Here there is no mention at all of a threat; rather, the motive for departure is the unbelief of the inhabitants, who here stand for the Jews generally,[739] and Christ's will for the salvation of the Gentiles. Paul is being sent far away (9.30 and 22.21 ἐξαποστέλλειν); no longer, however, by the Jewish Christian brethren, but by the Lord himself. Perhaps Luke saw in this vision the direct invitation to the mission to the Gentiles, after the preliminary announcement at Paul's calling;[740] it would then have begun to some degree in silence, through Paul in distant Tarsus (see below, 156f.) – even before the baptism of Cornelius by Peter and the activity of the Hellenists in Antioch. Without eliminating the contradictions, Luke would then have presented in 22.18–21 a further interpretation of the external events of 9.28–30. In any case the conversion of Cornelius is a

unique episode and the exiled 'Hellenists' are at work only as far
as Antioch.[741] The decisive development – also in Luke's view –
has already taken place before, at Paul's calling (see above, 38f.).

Here the tradition underlying the account of the vision in
22.18–21 deviates from 9.28–30 and does not correspond to the
Pauline tradition of Gal. 1.16ff. either. One could at most refer
again to Rom. 15.19, ἀπὸ Ἰερουσαλήμ, but the μακράν there seems
to contradict the καὶ κύκλῳ, which refers to Damascus and Arabia
(see above, 86). The vision itself would have a parallel in
II Cor. 12.1ff. However, this cannot be made to agree in time,
geography or content with Luke's account. So the origin of the
tradition remains a riddle. We should not doubt that during his
long activity as an ecstatic bearer of the Spirit Paul had several
such visions.[742] However, he regarded them as quite personal
experiences which were not part of his message. Perhaps the
elaboration of this narrative of a vision comes from disciples of
Paul who were particularly critical of Jerusalem (including the
Jewish Christianity there). The fact that Luke does not insert
this – edifying – narrative in 9.28ff. shows that as a historian he
preferred the brief account there, even if he expressed his own
theological view more clearly in the account of the vision.[743] At all
events, Acts 22.17–21 makes it clear that for Luke, too, the sending of Paul to the Gentiles chronologically precedes the conversion of Cornelius and the activities of the Hellenists in Antioch.
For Luke, too, Paul is the real missionary to the Gentiles.

6.4 Paul as Peter's guest

Of the most interesting event during this short visit to Jerusalem
we learn only the fact that for two weeks Paul was a guest of
Cephas/Peter. The 'and remained with him fifteen days' (καὶ
ἐπέμεινα πρὸς αὐτὸν ἡμέρας δεκαπέντε) is best understood to indicate that he spent the whole of this time as a guest in Peter's
house.[744]

Hospitality was an important virtue in earliest Christianity, and
from the beginning was one of the basic presuppositions for the
coherence of various Jesus communities and for the successful
work of their itinerant missionaires.[745] But it was by no means a

matter of course that Cephas/Peter should have entertained in his house for two weeks a guest previously unknown to him who was still problematical in a number of respects. When around twenty years later Paul comes to Jerusalem with the collection of money for 'the poor' in Jerusalem, now as a known missionary, he does not live with James or one of the elders of the community, but with a 'long-time disciple', Mnason, who, like Barnabas, comes from Cyprus and was probably close to the 'Hellenists'. The 'brothers' in Jerusalem who received the travellers 'gladly' are not described more closely. It is striking that Luke has to emphasize this fact.[746] That James gave him an audience at all already appears as a concession.[747]

According to the later Didache, Christian travellers could not stay more than two or three days; if they wanted to stay longer, they had to contribute to their support by working. An exception was made only for real prophets. If a prophet asked for money and gifts with a reference to the Spirit, he was not to be listened to.[748] False teachers even more had to be shown the door.[749]

In the first years of the messianic community, in which the word of Jesus was still vivid in the memory and the direct instruction of the Spirit was still very much alive, of course these problems of a church in the process of becoming an institution were not envisaged. Peter's presumably spontaneous hospitality[750] must also have been connected with a personal interest in this special visitor who suddenly turned up in Jerusalem. In Paul's case this interest was even clearer; otherwise he would not have come to Jerusalem at all. As he reports it, the two-week stay seems almost like a retreat, in which there was ample occasion for exchanges. In Paul's retrospective description, the contrast between his around three years absence in his previous activity in Arabia and Damascus and the mere two weeks with Peter is meant to emphasize his complete independence from the apostles in his apostolate; however, this does not exclude the possibility that during these memorable 'fifteen days' both figures not only got to know each other properly, but also learned from each other. The significance of each for the other was already known previously to both of them, since we may take it for granted that the former persecutor had already heard something about Peter when he was proceeding against the 'Hellenists' in Jerusalem and then again in Damascus. Otherwise he would not have looked him out at all. And that Peter, too, knew something about Paul follows not only from Gal. 1.22 but also from the expulsion of the Hellenists, which certainly did not leave the 'Hebrews' and their leaders uninvolved. These two weeks were thus a good occasion for demolishing prejudices on both sides and building up a relative basis of trust.

One thing is certain, that this was not just a 'courtesy visit',[751] for which even in the Orient half a day would have sufficed, but a real encounter which was important for the further development of earliest Christianity. Conzelmann, too, speaks of a 'short visit' and adds: 'He passes over the content of the conversations because it was apparently not of substance for his own theology.'[752] For without these fourteen days together, the encounter at the 'Apostolic Council' roughly thirteen years later would hardly have been so positive, especially as the other key person among the pillars, James, who at the second meeting occupied first place in the enumeration of the pillars and banished Cephas/Peter to second place, was involved – possibly only sporadically, because as a representative of the wing which was particularly faithful to the law, he too wanted to get to know (and probably also form a judgment on) this special guest. Perhaps here James was meant to play the role of the additional 'witness'. In the earliest community, too, Deut. 19.15 had a special significance.[753] It is very probable that Peter later reported this unique visit to the community.

So in Paul's case this process of acquaintance will certainly not have been limited to 'getting information from Cephas' nor will it have been limited to 'information about Jesus' teaching and ministry'.[754] There was more to it than that.[755] On the other hand there is no personal acquaintance which does not include obtaining information, above all if it is spread over two weeks, and we may assume that Paul was less concerned with personal information about Peter and his character than with his theological thought, more precisely christology and soteriology or – less abstractly – the content of his preaching, which certainly also included a narrative of Jesus' words and actions.

In other words, Jesus above all will have stood at the centre of the conversations – around six years after the Passover at which he died – the earthly and crucified, risen and exalted Jesus, who was now preached and was to come. For both Peter and Paul, his person and the salvation which he had achieved had become the centre of their lives. Here Peter's interest in getting to know Paul and his message thoroughly was probably no less, otherwise he would not have had him as a guest for around fourteen days. In other words, Paul certainly reported his call by the Risen Christ and his missionary preaching, as Luke makes him do before 'the apostles', and at the same time spoke – as a former Pharisaic scribe – of his understanding of the prophetic promise and the Torah[756] and – inseparably connected with this – of his gospel, which he had received personally from the risen Christ. If all this had not been discussed, they could have parted earlier. Since time was pressing,[757] it would have been a pity to talk only about the weather. The duration of the hospitality indicates the intensity of the exchange. In both cases there will have been a charismatic curiosity brought about by the Spirit.

Scholars have argued indefatigably over the last forty years whether the often-discussed account in I Cor. 15.2–8, half confession and catechesis and half history, comes from Jerusalem, Damascus or Antioch: but why not should its content (its formulation may have been later) at least in part have been discussed at this memorable visit, on which the only three individual witnesses listed there by name, Cephas, James and Paul, met for the first time? And where could there be a better basis for Paul's final summary remark, 'Whether then it was I or they, so we preach and so you believed',[758] which banishes the view so popular today that there were many contradictory 'kerygmata' and disputatious groups at the beginning of earliest Christianity to the realm of modern mythologizing?

One other thing needs to be added. As a rule exegetes ask what traditions Paul could have received in these two weeks. The opposite question, whether Paul, who had trained as a scribe in Jerusalem, who at the same time also knew 'Hellenistic' Judaism, and who soon became the most successful missionary and founder of communities, did not in turn have an effect on Peter, is hardly ever asked. According to Gal. 2.15, in Antioch Paul reprimands Peter because he is abandoning their common basis: '*We* ourselves, who are Jews by birth and not Gentile sinners, yet who know that a man is not justified by works of the law but through faith in Jesus Christ ... ' Here Paul includes Peter in this knowledge grounded in the saving action of Christ, and in so doing takes it for granted that Peter shares it with him. This also suggests that initially Peter unreservedly had table fellowship with the Gentile Christians in Antioch, i.e. celebrated the eucharist with them. Paul expresses this abundantly clearly: because Peter knew all this, he 'lived like a Gentile'.[759]

We can go on to conclude that because Peter knew all this, along with the two other 'pillars' he could already acknowledge Paul's gospel at the previous 'Apostolic Council' in Jerusalem. Here I ask myself whether he was not the real motive force among the three, who ultimately – after negotiations which were certainly not at all easy but which hardly lasted longer than the first fourteen-day visit to Peter – carried through the recognition of the mission of Paul and Barnabas to the Gentiles at the 'Apostolic Council'. In the same context it is said that the εὐαγγέλιον or ἀποστολή for the 'circumcision' was entrusted to Peter.[760] Granted, in Acts 10 he does not appear as the real founder of the Gentile mission; the 'mission to the Gentiles according to Luke denotes something which is solely Paul's concern'. However, his initiative, directed by a special revelation, leads to 'the Jerusalem community hearing news of this (11.18)'.[761] That is no small thing – in the framework of Luke's 'biographical mission history' which is completely orientated on Paul. According to I Corinthians and the later Petrine tradition from Mark and I Peter through I Clement up to the Acts of Peter and the Pseudo-Clementines, Peter himself had practised a mission to the Gentiles afterwards, without calling for circumcision. Indeed it is striking that in the Synoptic tradition, which to a large degree goes back to Petrine tradition, circumcision plays hardly any role if we leave aside the birth narrative in Luke 1.59 and 2.21, which comes from another Jewish-Christian milieu.[762]

Accordingly, Luke in Acts 15.8–11, referring back to 10.44–48, makes Peter, as the first speaker, say in his plea for the Gentile mission without circumcision and strict observance of the law that God, 'who knows the heart', makes no distinction between Jews and Gentiles in the gift of the Spirit, since he 'cleansed their hearts by faith'. Therefore the yoke of the law is not to be imposed on the Gentile Christians 'which neither our fathers nor we have been able to bear. But we (Jewish Christians) believe that we shall be saved through the grace of the Lord Jesus, just as they will.' Given the view of the law, this is certainly no flawless 'Paulinism', but in some respects it does correspond to what Paul already presupposes in the clash in Antioch.

So the question is whether the scribally trained missionary to the Gentiles did not make an impression on the leading disciples in Jerusalem particularly at that time during his two-week stay with Peter, their only meeting before the 'Apostolic Council', which took place much later, especially as Paul's gospel corresponded to a tendency in the preaching of Jesus himself, that God accepts and justifies sinners, a statement verified by Peter himself in the Synoptics, which goes back to Petrine tradition.[763] And could not this influence also have affected the decision at the Apostolic Council and the freer attitude of Peter which preceded it? This assumption would also explain the 'Paulinisms' in the Gospel of Mark and I Peter, which stand in the Petrine tradition.[764]

In any case, these intensive fourteen days in Jerusalem, the brevity of which should not constantly be emphasized – fourteen days' hospitality is no short time, as all hosts know[765] – were not unimportant for the further fortunes of the young movement. Peter seems also to have learned from Paul, and Paul could admonish Peter later. Conversely, it is improbable that in the disputed question of the law Paul should have essentially changed his view during the thirteen years up to the 'Apostolic Council' which now followed. Such a move from a former, less clear position, for example that at an earlier stage the circumcision of non-Jews was only a matter of indifference for him,[766] or that the Torah had originally had partial significance for salvation for him along the lines of the Pharisaic and early-Christian 'synergism' between God and human beings, would certainly have been held against him by his opponents. There is no trace of this. One could not accuse Paul of theological inconsistency and a readiness to compromise on the question of truth. It may be modern, but it is not Pauline. The steadfastness of the 'truth of the gospel' is not a late discovery for him. With his attitude, which is unbending on this decisive point, he may have already impressed Peter and James on his first visit to Jerusalem, around three years after the radical turning point in his life.

Paul does not say in Gal. 1.18–20 how and why this memorable visit came to an end after two weeks, any more than he says whether he left Peter's home and the Holy City on the same day. Certainly he was not a man who was fond of hiding or being hid. Perhaps his stay ultimately became known, or after he had been with Peter he attempted with his distinctive courage and zeal for conversion to make contact with his former fellow fighters, in order to witness his new faith to them; indeed he may have had one or more arguments with them (see above, 146). Certainly he could hardly be accused of 'cowardice in the face of the enemy'. So it is not all that improbable that at the end, as Luke tells us, his life was in danger and so he was quickly taken by the 'brethren' to Caesarea. His host will certainly have continued to feel responsible for the safety of his endangered (and dangerous) guest. If we do not always utterly mistrust Luke (and why should we?), we could concede that he still gives the most illuminating explanation of the end of this surprising stay in Jerusalem – which was evidently abrupt.

On his visit to Switzerland, between 7 and 15 September 1779 Goethe visited Tübingen and stayed in a 'cheerful room' with his publisher Cotta. He 'visited gardens and collections, marvelled at the windows of the choir of the Stiftskirche, was interested in the Ammer canal and made discoveries in the university library at the castle'. In addition, these eight days led to a 'lasting relationship with his publisher Cotta'.[767] Would Paul's fifteen days with Peter in Jerusalem have been less full of experiences – and consequences?

7. The New Mission Territory in the North: Tarsus and Cilicia

7.1 Why did Paul go to Tarsus, and did he engage in mission there?

We know that Paul comes from Tarsus in Cilicia only through Luke. This fact is hardly doubted, even in so-called critical scholarship – it made it possible to keep Paul from Jewish Palestine and turn him into a pure 'Hellenistic Diaspora Jew'.[768] Therefore in the commentaries his stay in Tarsus after the visit to Jerusalem is only relatively rarely denied; however, offence is taken that Luke says nothing about his activity in Tarsus.

This suggests to Overbeck

> that Acts casts a veil over these journeys,[769] by bringing them together into a mere journey by Paul to his ancestral city without a definite character, and making the apostle disappear in Tarsus until the moment when after the actions of Peter (ch.10) and the Hellenists (11.19f.) and under the patronage of Barnabas he too may finally appear among Gentiles (11.25f.).[770]

Here Overbeck refers to E. Zeller,

> Anyone who knew just this work could only believe that in the meantime he had been completely silent, all the more so since there is mention of a Gentile Christian community first in Antioch; by contrast, if we listen to Gal. 1.6, 21 it is highly improbable that the fieriest of men, who went not only to Tarsus but to the regions of Syria and Cilicia, should not have engaged in the most zealous activity.[771]

Here false conclusions are drawn from observations which are partly correct, with the aim of proving Luke fundamentally wrong once again. It is correct that Luke, despite his emphasis on Paul's calling as missionary to the Gentiles from the beginning,[772] waits a surprising amount of time until he has Paul preaching to those specificially identified as Gentiles. That does not even happen in the one year while he is working in Antioch with Barnabas, who has brought him there. Here we read only the succinct:

> For a whole year they met with the church, and taught a large company of people.[773]

That means that they appeared in the assembled community and taught a great crowd of people there – i.e. probably in worship and not in independent preaching in the streets, specifically addressed to non-Jews.[774]

That there were now only non-Jews among the many hearers can only be indirectly concluded from 11.20f., the successful preaching to the 'Greeks'[775] of those who had been driven out of Jerusalem. Paul and Barnabas also preach on the so-called 'first journey' 'in the synagogues' of Salamis to Jews; in Luke's narrative, the first[776] Gentile that they meet is Sergius Paulus, the high-placed 'sympathizer' and governor of Cyprus, who has been 'attended on' by the Jew Barjesus/Elymas. According to the narrator, the clear, decisive turn to the 'Gentiles' then finally takes place in a dramatic scene following the preaching in the synagogue in Pisidian Antioch.[777] In other words, Luke turns Paul into the 'missionary to the Gentiles' in the full sense on the first journey; from then on, the missionary behaviour which is becoming visible here is repeated several times, basically until Paul's last word before the heads of the Jewish community in Rome (28.28). Thus Luke describes schematically and in the form of a gradual development a basic conflict which in reality has governed Paul's attitude from the beginning of his preaching.

There are various reasons why Luke is so hesitant to make Paul the missionary to the Gentiles in the full sense. First, he wants to make the programmatic baptism of Cornelius and his house, brought about by the special intervention of God, an example involving the Jerusalem Christians, and to give pre-eminence, at least outwardly (but see above, 46), to Peter as the spokesman of the apostles[778] and the first disciples. Presumably on this point, too, he is following the Petrine or the Jerusalem version. Luke has hardly any chronological points of reference for the first two decades of the earliest community up to, say, the Apostolic Council, so he can arrange his material with relative chronological freedom, but historically speaking he is quite skilful in doing this.[779] The conversion and baptism of Cornelius, a socially prominent godfearer from the upper classes, was certainly a significant event for the communities in Palestine. It was a point of honour that the leader of the messianic movement, Peter, should be personally involved with a prominent centurion in Caesarea, who on the basis of his military position could become a 'godfearer', but not a proselyte.[780] Cornelius's conversion is chronologically to be put between the visit of Paul in Jerusalem (*c.*36 CE) and the accession of Agrippa (41 CE), i.e. presumably not too far from the deliberate move of the Jewish Christian 'Hellenists' in Antioch to the 'Greeks'. At the Apostolic Council in 48/49 CE Luke makes Peter say that God has already 'in the early days' (ἀφ' ἡμερῶν ἀρχαίων) chosen Gentiles through him 'that they should hear the word of the gospel and believe'.[781] Basically, the new element in this action is that the baptism of the 'godfearer' Cornelius, a member of the upper class, takes place in the presence and with the explicit consent of the head of the new 'messianic sect',[782] and that he not only rejects the protest of the Jewish Christians in Jerusalem and Judaea, but even convinces them.[783] For in reality Philip had already long been baptizing non-Jews on occasion in Caesarea, and we may assume that the same thing was happening in the community in Damascus. The tenor of Luke's narrative suggests that the author knew this and probably even presupposed that the attentive reader could infer it. For after carrying on a successful mission and baptizing in Samaria, i.e. among 'heretics', and here (for the moment) convincing even the arch-heretic Simon and converting the Ethiopian eunuch and finance minister,[784] who to the reader (like Cornelius) must have seemed to be a godfearer, what would Philip have done in Azotus/Ashdod and in Caesarea, both cities with mixed Gentile-Jewish populations, if not carry on a

mixed mission and baptize there, too?[785] The reader could then
infer from the depiction of Philip's hospitality in Acts 21.8–14
that Philip was taking the same line as Paul. Nor does Luke say
anywhere in so many words that in Damascus or the Palestinian
coastal region *no* Gentiles at all (i.e. godfearers) became
Christians before Acts 10. The proselyte Nicolaus from Antioch at
the end of the list of Seven is already a pointer as to where the
development is going.[786] Indeed Luke could even have left out
the striking designation προσήλυτος. The paradigmatically broad
depiction of the conversion of the pious Gentile Cornelius
merely gives Peter the priority in the narrative, since he alone can
teach the Jerusalem apostles and brothers better. The confession
of fidelity to the law after the vision, the answer to the heavenly
voice in 10.14f., applies to the special situation of the Palestine
Jew Peter.[787] As a result of Luke's silence over Philip's missionary
activity in Caesarea, which probably also involved founding and
leading a community – and which in my view Luke takes for
granted – the priority of the 'leading disciple', Peter, in the conversion of the first Gentile clearly addressed as such is preserved.
In addition, Peter also has to do the first basic work of convincing
people in Jerusalem; in other words, in the narrative everything
takes place in good order according to the sequence of 'salvation
history', although Luke himself (in my view quite deliberately)
leaves room for the well-founded conjecture that the sequence
could really have developed otherwise. 'Officially', the leading
apostle in Jerusalem, who was prompted to this by God's intervention, must give the green light to the Gentile mission.[788]
Probably here, too, Luke is using Jerusalem tradition which
attributed to the apostle Peter the first conversion of an important pagan godfearer in Eretz Israel. The reference in 11.19 looking back to 8.4 that the 'Hellenists', who had been driven out of
Jerusalem and who were gradually advancing through Phoenicia
to Antioch, had proclaimed the new message only to Jews before
they arrived in the Syrian capital, is along the same lines.[789] This is
a typical Lukan exaggeration, which underlines the priority (of
honour) of the 'prince of the apostles' in Jerusalem. It would
have been substantially correct to say 'especially to Jews' (μάλιστα
Ἰουδαίοις) instead of 'only to Jews' (εἰ μὴ μόνον). In other words,

Luke puts the fundamental 'to the Jew first and also to the Greek' ('Ιουδαίῳ πρῶτον καὶ "Ελληνι)[790] in a historically inappropriate chronological scheme, though he himself does not take this completely seriously. Here the 'order of salvation history and church politics' weighs more heavily than historical reality. Theophilus certainly gets his account prepared 'in good order', indeed in too good a one. The new development in Antioch was that the Hellenists, probably in a lengthy process in the capital (see below 200), because of their rejection in the synagogues, deliberately and in a focussed way turned to the Greeks, who also still for the most part belonged to the many layers of the circle of 'sympathizers'. Here too the argument still holds good that a Gentile completely untouched by Jewish tradition could hardly have understood this new messianic-enthusiastic message (see above, 88, and below, 277–86).

This step-by-step approach of Luke explains why at first he is silent about Paul's missionary activity in Tarsus and Cilicia. It may be that he had almost no information about it, but why did he not fluently insert a few edifying scenes, since in the view of his critics invention came to him so easily? On the contrary, I would think that he so took it for granted that Paul worked there as a missionary (to the Gentiles) that (as in the case of Philip) he did not feel it necessary to mention the fact. Such gaps and inconsistencies are frequent above all in the first part. Luke deliberately does not want to give a continuous report, but merely to report some focal points with individual transitions, omitting what does not fit into the main line of his narrative; indeed he even makes some 'corrections', contrary to historical reality. That he tacitly makes Peter depart from the scene after the 'Apostolic Council' does not mean either that he did not know any more about him or that subsequently Peter kept quiet. In the vision of Christ in the temple during Paul's first visit to Jerusalem which has already been described, the Kyrios takes leave of Paul with the words, 'Depart, for I shall send you far away to the Gentiles.'[791] In the historical account the sending far away to the Gentiles is matched by the fact that the 'brethren' sent him from Caesarea to Tarsus.[792]

By the use of ἐξαποστέλλειν in these two apparently contradictory events – though for him in substance they belong together[793] – Luke indicates that the sending 'far away to the Gentiles' began with the journey to Tarsus, which at any rate is around 500 kilometres from Caesarea as the crow flies. Since for Luke, too, there is an indefinite lengthy interval between 9.30 and 11.25, Barnabas's visit to Tarsus, and the depiction of the peaceful growth in 9.31, has the 'character of a *fermata*',[794] while on the other hand Paul has already proclaimed his new faith in the synagogues in Damascus and before the Jewish 'Hellenists' in Jerusalem powerfully and freely,[795] Luke unmistakably indicates to the reader that Paul did the same thing in Tarsus and Cilicia and did not devote himself to a life of ease there. Romans 15.19 ('so that from Jerusalem [cf. Gal. 1.18] and in a circle [i.e. in Arabia and Damascus] I have fully preached the gospel of Christ' (ὥστε με ἀπὸ Ἰερουσαλὴμ καὶ κύκλῳ πεπληρωκέναι τὸ εὐαγγέλιον τοῦ Χριστοῦ), in conjunction with Gal. 1.12, the regions of Syria and Cilicia (τὰ κλίματα τῆς Συρίας καὶ τῆς Κιλικίας), contradicts the supposition that Paul had a lengthy 'pause from preaching' in Tarsus.[796] He was also active in his home city as a missionary. One does not have to state the obvious. Paul, too, does not say in so many words that he preached in Arabia or in 'the regions of Syria and Cilicia'. However, this follows from Gal. 1.16b and – in respect of Damascus – from 1.23.[797] Luke later refers indirectly – but still clearly enough – to this preaching, as he is fond of doing: after the 'Apostolic Council' Paul (with Silas) goes through 'Syria *and Cilicia*' and strengthens the brothers, i.e. probably in the communities which he himself founded earlier.[798] Here Tarsus was on the way, immediately before the Cilician gates to Asia Minor. Accordingly, the letter formulated by Luke from the 'apostles and elders and the whole community' (in Jerusalem) which contains the 'Apostolic Decree' is addressed to 'the brothers from the Gentiles', not only in Antioch, but also in Syria and Cilicia; in other words, he presupposes a mission to the Gentiles everywhere there.[799] According to Luke, the only person who can be responsible for this is Paul, since only he had spent any length of time earlier in Cilicia. He wanted to have readers who sometimes could also read between the lines.

Tarsus then vanishes from Christian missionary history for

around 200 years. This is a period in which we have relatively few and quite fortuitous pieces of geographical information about the existence of Christian communities. But then around 250 Dionysius of Alexandria suddenly reports to Stephen of Rome that he has been invited to a synod in Antioch 'by Helenus, the bishop of Tarsus in Cilicia, and the bishops of Firmilian in Cappadocia and Theoctistus in Palestine who are associated with him'.[800] The suddenly frequent mention of its bishop shows the importance of the community of Tarsus and its leading role in Cilicia. We may assume that after the founding of the community by Paul there were always Christians in this famous and busy city.

Critics also sometimes contrast the geographical information in Gal. 1.21, 'then I went into the regions of Syria and Cilicia', with the journey from Caesarea to Tarsus by sea.[801] However, here Paul is certainly not indicating an itinerary,[802] but the whole territory of his activity in subsequent years, hence first the generalized 'the regions' (τὰ κλίματα),[803] which cannot strictly be fixed to precise provincial frontiers; here the stereotyped Syria and Cilicia (τῆς Συρίας καὶ [τῆς] Κιλικίας) refers to the double province which remained united until 72 CE.[804]

'Syria and Cilicia' (in the reverse order) thus become the most important sphere of activity for the apostle for the next roughly thirteen years, until his second visit to Jerusalem for the 'Apostolic Council'. That does not exclude the possibility that he could not sometimes also have gone beyond the frontiers of this area, especially as these frontiers were not always completely clear – above all in the period of early Roman rule.[805] If we follow the threads of Luke's narrative – and we have no alternative which is at all probable –[806] then the so-called first journey into neighbouring territories, to the island of Cyprus, Pisidia and Lycaonia (i.e. the southern part of the province of Galatia) falls into this period.[807] R. Riesner envisages as a further field of activity Cappadocia beyond the Taurus, which borders the whole length of Cilicia on its northern side;[808] the LXX identified it with Caphtor, and like Syria, Cilicia or Cyprus, it had a considerable Jewish population. Its south-west corner with its main port Tyana, the home of the itinerant philosopher and miracle-worker Apollonius, was easy to reach through the Gate of Cilicia. But this remains just as much a conjecture as the suggestion of J. Weiss that Paul may already at that time have made a voyage westwards, say to Cyrene, which is enigmatically mentioned alongside Syria in the Coptic Acts of Paul. We hear nothing from Luke of the three shipwrecks which Paul himself reports in II Cor. 11.25; only in Acts 27 does he narrate the third and probably the last.[809] But Gal. 1.21f. in conjunction with 2.1 tells against major voyages into quite different provinces.

7.2 Tarsus and its Jewish community

But why did Paul go from Jerusalem to Tarsus in particular? Why did he shift his sphere of activity so far north, having worked for around three years in the East? Now he evidently could not go back to Damascus and Arabia, and Tarsus in Cilicia was his birthplace and the home of his family. On the other hand, the fact that in contrast to Damascus, Antioch or even Jerusalem he does not mention it again later in his letters perhaps indicates a certain distance; moreover this distance also becomes evident towards Antioch, which he has to mention – the one time in all his letters – in Gal. 2.11. Had Paul not had to defend and justify his early history as a Christian and missionary to the Galatians, we would learn nothing at all about it from him, and Rom. 15.19b would remain an incomprehensible cipher. At the same time one could have accused Luke of even more massive tendentious falsification on the basis of the argument from silence. It is strange, anyway, that apart from Gal. 1 and 2 he does not mention the approximately thirteen years activity 'in the regions of Syria and Cilicia' again, even if a considerable number of the dangers and sufferings which according to II Cor. 11 he experienced may have already happened to him during this period. That is true especially of the synagogue punishment meted out to him five times, according to the regulation in Deut. 25.3. The Jews in this area between the mother country and the Taurus mountains were not only particularly numerous, as Josephus attests, but also very powerful and aware of themselves.[810] The Syrians' fear of the Jewish minority in their cities after 66 CE was not wholly unfounded (see below, 8.1.3).

This silence may not least be a result of the interlude in Antioch reported in Gal. 2.11–21, which must have deeply wounded Paul and at least for the moment have led to the break not only with Barnabas but also with the Jewish Christians in Antioch, who had the say there. Relations with Peter also became difficult and probably also permanently burdened. Moreover, presumably this had an effect on the mission communities in Cilicia and Syria generally, where the proportion of Jewish Christians was greater than in the later mission communities in the West. Luke also indicates such a break in Acts 15.39 by the very pointed 'and there arose a sharp contention (καὶ ἐγένετο δὲ παροξυσμός) between Paul and Barnabas'; however, he is getting ahead of himself, since the interlude in Antioch probably happened only after the end of the so-called second missionary journey around 51/52 CE.[811] First of all there was simply a separation of tasks, because of John Mark, whose failure on the 'first journey' Paul could not forget:[812] Barnabas visited the communities in Cyprus gained on the first journey, Paul those in the interior of Asia Minor. Since Paul reports his activity in Syria and Cilicia so scantily, we should not be surprised that Luke, too, does not have very much to say about it – although he informs us a little better. Perhaps Paul was later as unwilling to speak of these severe disappointments as emigrants from Germany were to speak of the years after 1933.

However, there may have been other reasons than the mere family relationship, which does not play a further role in the letters, for Paul having chosen Tarsus in Cilicia or, as Luke puts it, having let himself be 'sent' there. The city was not only the 'metropolis' of Cilicia but in the first century politically, culturally and economically the second most important centre after Antioch in the double province between 'Rough Cilicia' in the west,[813] the Taurus as the frontier with Cappadocia in the north, the imperial boundary on the Euphrates in the east and the Syrian desert in the south-east. It hardly falls short of its politically more important Syrian rival in the praise of contemporaries about its flourishing life and as the home of famous men, philosophers, orators and also other scholars. This praise extends from Xenophon to Ammianus Marcellinus, the church father

Basil the Great, and Zonaras.[814] Promoted in particular by Augustus, since his teacher, the Stoic Athenodorus, came from there, the city flourished throughout the first century, and as the provincial capital of Cilicia Pedias was at the same time the centre and seat of the provincial assembly, the κοινὸν Κιλικίας,[815] with a great city territory extending from the Gate of Cilicia, the most important pass through the Taurus which led through Western Cappadocia to Lycaonia and into the interior of Asia Minor, down to the sea a few kilometres to the south. To some degree it was the 'springboard' to Asia Minor. In contrast to Antioch, the city itself also had a seaport, since it was linked by the Cydnus with the sea nearby. So in it the most important roads from the north to Asia Minor met up with the difficult coastal road from Cilicia Tracheia coming from the West. The road in an eastward direction led through Adana and Mopsuestia and divided at the Portae Amanicae. The main route went southwards, reached the sea at Issos and led on to Alexandreia, crossed the Amanus mountains at the Portae Syriae and led to Antioch. Paul will often have travelled this road. Another road led directly eastwards and met the Euphrates at Zeugma, the great legionary camp.[816]

In keeping with its political and economic significance, Tarsus had a Jewish community, traces of which are to be found above all outside the city.[817] Philo has Agrippa I in his letter to Caligula listing Cilicia among the provinces in which Jews live.[818] Acts 6.9 mentions in Jerusalem alongside the synagogue communities of the Libertines, Cyreneans and Alexandrians also representatives of those 'of Cilicia and Asia',[819] with whom Stephen is said to have discussed. Here is a first indirect indication for him.

The later rabbinic tradition often speaks of synagogues of the Tarsians, thus in Jerusalem, where the parallel tradition mentions a synagogue of the Alexandrians.[820] Two epitaphs in which Tarsus is mentioned were found in Jaffa: the first relates to a Judas son of Joses and Ταρσεύς, i.e. a citizen of Tarsus, like Paul in Acts 9.11 and 21.39.[821] The other inscription runs: 'Here lies Isaac, elder (of the community) of the Cappadocians, linen merchant from Tarsus.'[822]

The analogy of these later texts to Paul is striking: here are two Jews from Tarsus who settled in Eretz Israel, including one whose work, like that of Paul, was in textiles. There is also a geographical parallel: Paul travels by ship from Caesarea to Tarsus; Joppa is the nearest Jewish port.[823] The linen merchant may have chosen his home among other things because of the good communications with his source of supply.

Excursus III: Jewish-pagan 'syncretism' in Rough Cilicia and the adjacent territories of Asia Minor

Unfortunately, so far we have few Jewish inscriptions from Tarsus itself and from Cilicia Pedias.[824] One reason for this is the difficulty of excavating in the modern city and the densely populated plain. But the fact that an amazing amount of Jewish or Judaizing epigraphic evidence has been preserved in the politically and economically much less significant 'Rough Cilicia' and the adjacent areas allows us to assume that the Jewish population of Tarsus and other Cilician cities must have been considerable.[825] An epitaph – much later – of the ducenarius Aurelius Eusambatios Menandros with the surname Photios, citizen of Corycus, around 80 kilometres east of Tarsus, and his wife Matrona, which comes from the necropolis of Corycus, is particularly interesting. It ends with the consolation:

> Do [not despai]r, for no one is immortal but one who has commanded that this should happen, and [who has also put us in the ci]rcle of the planets.[826]

The dead person must have been a well-to-do councillor of the city of Corycus, and the name Eusambatios and the closing formula indicate that he was a Jew. A Jewish presbyter and perfume manufacturer from the same necropolis also bears this name.[827] By contrast the simple form Sabbataios/Sabbatis is frequent.[828] M. H. Williams refers to two other Jewish inscriptions; Φιλονόμιος appears on one of them as a proper name.[829] Immediately adjacent to this in Korasion we find a Mennandros Sanbatios. On the other hand we find the markedly Jewish name Sabbatios on five sarcophagi marked with a cross. These may have been 'Judaizing' Christians or Jews who went over to

Christianity.[830] Lietzmann refers to the much-discussed essentially earlier inscriptions in Elaeusa Sebaste, the frontier city of Rough Cilicia, also on the sea around 7 kilometres north-east, which attest a cultic association – much earlier – of the Sabbatistai from the time of Augustus;[831] these 'gathered on the basis of the good providence of the god Sabbatistes'.[832] They consist of 'Hetairoi', i.e. probably sympathizers in the wider sense, and 'Sabbatistai' proper under the leadership of a 'synagogeus' with the Semitic name Aithibelios;[833] a 'hiereus' is also mentioned, and dedicated gifts which are kept in 'naoi'. A second inscription, of which only the beginning has been preserved, dedicates the 'association of the Sabbatistai to the god Aithibel'.[834] This is a pagan cult which was presumably influenced by the Jewish celebration of the sabbath.[835] In Asia Minor (and Egypt) we find still further traces of the worship of a 'sabbath god', e.g. in Philadelphia a dedication to the 'great, holy god Sabathikos', in Lydia the vow of a women to the same god without an additional name, and in Egypt a σύνοδος Σαμβαθική and on an ostrakon the name Σαμβαθις among a list of goddesses.[836] Milik refers to the name Βαρσαββαθας from a papyrus from Dura Europos and sees in it, against the background of the name Sabbation or Sabbatis (or similar) which was widespread not only in Asia Minor but also in Egypt, Rome and Syria, 'the first witness to the cult of the sabbatical god in Syria'.[837] By contrast, a 'Sambatheion' in Thyatira is in all probability a synagogue.[838] So we can hardly doubt that like the 'anonymous' god in the region of Palmyra, this pagan cult of the θεὸς Σαββατιστής in the time of Augustus, not too far from Tarsus, is connected indirectly or directly with the Jewish God and the attractive forms of his cult. Moreover for Gentiles, too, it was attractive regularly not to work on one day of the week. This particular pagan interest in the sabbath (and sometimes also in other Jewish festivals) in Asia Minor in particular explains the polemic in Col. 2.16f. By contrast, for earliest Christianity this Jewish custom, like circumcision, had – relatively speaking – lost its significance. Even Plutarch angrily quotes the verse from Euripides, 'you Greeks who discover your barbarous abomination', and refers it to the forms of barbarian superstition practised by them, which also include σαββατισμοί.[839]

The polemics of such different authors as Plutarch and Juvenal, and the proud reference of Josephus and Philo to the interest in the sabbath, show how widespread pagan interest in, indeed veneration of, this day was.

As the Jewish Diaspora in Asia Minor (like that of Syria) was already very old[840] and also numerous, for a long time it exercised an influence on its pagan surroundings. Because of certain features akin to the indigenous forms of piety, this Jewish element was also particularly persistent in wide areas of the country, not least in the south and the interior. In addition to the Theos Hypsistos,[841] who was widespread here, these included the worship of angels,[842] the sabbath cult which has already been mentioned, memories of Noah and the flood in Apamea Kibotos[843] and the Enoch-Annakos tradition[844] which was probably connected with it. The origin of the Jewish Sibylline poetry, which really reaches its heyday in the Egyptian Diaspora, can probably be derived from the Jewish Diaspora in Asia Minor.[845] Noah's daughters, the Jewish Sibyls, bore the name Sabbe, Sambethe.[846]

From Sibidoudna in neighbouring Pisidia we have the inscription of a 'godfearer' with altar and column, Ἀρτιμας υἱὸς Ἀρτιμου Μομμίου καὶ Μαρκίας, which is dedicated to Θεῷ Ὑψίστῳ καὶ Ἁγείᾳ Καταφυγῇ. From its external form it seems to be dedicated to the 'highest God' and his female partner 'Refuge'. Its Jewish character has long been recognized, since this inscription takes up Ex. 17.15.[847] But in addition it must be emphasized that it really can only come from a pagan sympathizer.[848] We have something analogous from Amastris in Pontus in a thanksgiving inscription which is dedicated 'to the invincible God Asbamaios and the Lady Proseuche' (τῇ κυρίᾳ προσευχῇ). Asbamaios is probably another name of Zeus which comes from a source in Tyana in Lycaonia; in other words, this is originally an anonymous local god on the frontier of Cilicia. By contrast, as L. Robert again has shown, the 'Lady Proseuche' is to be derived from the Jewish synagogue.[849] This inscription from the third century also indicates a Judaizing pagan cult association.

This *pagan* syncretism in Asia Minor, which also involved the Jewish God and identified him with the highest God, is also attested by the oracle of Klaros near Colophon on the west coast of Asia Minor which Cornelius Labeo (second or third century) attempted to interpret and which was quoted by Macrobius.[850] The Apollo of Klaros is said to have given the following answer to the question which of the gods was to be identified with the one who is called Ἰαώ:

> Those who have learned the secret religious teaching (ὄργια) should keep silent about the unutterable, I but anyone who has a slight insight and weak understanding may say that the highest God of all is Ἰαώ.[851] In winter he is Hades, I but Zeus at the beginning of spring, Helios in summer and the tender Iao in autumn.[852]

The concluding verse gives the Jewish God, whose name was disseminated widely by the magical texts, as already in Plutarch and Tacitus, the features of Dionysus, who however is already at the same time understood as the universal God.[853] Here one could finally refer to the numerous oracles attributed above all to Apollo, but also to Hermes, etc., which are contained in Tübingen theosophy and which centre on the question of the true and only God. Jewish influence is unmistakable in some of them. They may be predominantly late and in part influenced by Neoplatonism or Christianity, but they do show what interest there was in late antiquity in the question of the one true God, his creation and revelation, which also includes the soul, its origin and destiny, and true worship, and they have points of contact with the earlier genuinely Jewish texts of the Sibyls.[854]

No wonder that in Asia Minor in particular – perhaps even more than in Syria – apart from the worshippers of the sabbath god and related testimonies elsewhere, we also find many kinds of references to 'sympathizers' of all kinds who see in the Jewish God the one true God.[855] The great inscription of Aphrodisias from the third century CE offers an impressive example of the 'godfearers' in the synagogue itself. Despite all the unresolved historical questions, at all events we may regard these indications as the fruit of this Jewish (and moreover Christian) influence on the pagan environment.[856] It is typical of this milieu of 'sympathizers' or pagans influenced by

Judaism that nowhere so much as in Asia Minor[857] do inscriptions attest in so many different ways that it is often difficult to distinguish between Jews or proselytes influenced by syncretism, real 'godfearers' who are close to the synagogue, and pagans who sympathize with Judaism only in a more or less loose way, and who take over only a few elements of Jewish (and from the second century also Christian) worship of God. In the majority of cases, membership of the last group seems likely. One example of this difficulty is an inscription on a small altar published in 1988, to which P. W. van der Horst has drawn attention: θεῷ ἀψευ[δεῖ καὶ]/ἀχειροποιήτῳ εὐχήν. It comes from Pamphylia, the province bordering on Cilicia Tracheia to the west, and is to be dated to the first or second century CE. In the LXX and early Jewish literature, the same word χειροποίητος is frequently a periphrasis for the 'idols'. Both predicates, ἀψευδής and ἀχειροποίητος, are best understood as references to the one true God, otherwise an altar would hardly come from a Jew. So we may best conjecture that this one stems from a 'sympathizer'; a worshipper of Sarapis cannot be completely ruled out, but is less probable. Perhaps the pious worshipper had sympathies with both gods, since they were the same God for him. However, Sarapis is almost always given his name in the inscriptions, and there were also countless pictorial depictions of him.[858]

Since Tarsus, as the metropolis on the frontier between Syria and Asia Minor,[859] was influenced from both regions, one might conjecture that the interest there of pagan 'sympathizers' of the most varied kinds on the Jewish cult and its individual elements there was even greater than in Damascus or in Arabia, where the more marked political tensions between the Jews and their neighbours again limited the religious attraction of the ethical monotheism of the Jews. At all events, there were at least as many points of contact for Paul's missionary work in his old home city as in southern Syria or the region of Nabataea.

Given the pagan interest in Judaism in Cilicia and in southern Asia Minor generally, another perspective might have played a role, one which as far as I know has yet to be noted. According to Josephus (or Nicolaus of Damascus), the Hasmoneans had recruited numerous mercenaries from Cilicia and Pisidia, but no Syrians because of their 'innate hatred against the (Jewish) people'.[860] This recruitment of pagan mercenaries probably already began under Jannai's father, John Hyrcanus, soon after the Seleucid kingdom had attained complete independence on the death of Antiochus VII Sidetes (129 BCE), and may have lasted until the conquest of Judaea by Pompey (63 BCE). It continued again under Herod (40–4 BCE).[861] As the Syrian mercenaries[862] were ruled out, Hellenized Cilicia Tracheia and Pisidia were geographically the most obvious possibility. When mercenaries from there returned home after a lengthy period of military service, they brought not only knowledge of Jewish religious customs but also a positive interest in Judaism with them. So the mixed forms which are particularly frequent in Cilicia and Asia Minor need not go back to the Jews from Babylonia settled by Antiochus III, but could also come from Cilicia and Pisidia and later also Galatian mercenaries in the service of the Hasmonaeans and Herod.[863]

But it would be one-sided to take seriously in Cilicia only those mixed Jewish-pagan forms and pagans interested in Jewish customs. Particularly in Tarsus, there was certainly a firmly-structured Jewish community which had many links with the mother country. We have already drawn attention to Jews from Cilicia in Eretz Israel.[864] Paul and his family are also an example of this link. He himself describes himself as a Pharisee and '*Hebraios*', i.e. an Aramaic-speaking Palestinian Jew, and Luke puts on to his lips the sentence, 'I am a Pharisee, son of Pharisees.'[865] There is no reason to doubt this information, or the report that he was sent by his parents relatively early to Jerusalem to receive a genuine Jewish education in the law. His sister was married there.[866] Fortuitus' later reports also confirm this connection. In the third century CE the Palestinian Amoraean Nahum b. Simlai is said to have presented an interpretation of Ex. 12.3 in Tarsus,[867] and Epiphanius reports from the fourth century that the Jewish patriarch in Tiberias sent a delegation to Cilicia under the leadership of the ἀπόστολος Joseph, to collect offerings and give rulings in the synagogue communities. Because of alleged Christian tendencies – the gospel was found on him – he was thrown into the Cydnus by his opponents.[868]

However, in the first century the link with the authorities in Jerusalem may not yet have been so close. Finally, towards the end of the fourth century Palladius attests Jewish and Samaritan synagogues in Tarsus.[869]

7.3 Pagan and philosophical-rhetorical influences on Paul?

In general, religious life in Tarsus, the Hellenistic metropolis near to the frontier between Asia Minor and Syria/Cilicia, was presumably richer, more lively and more confusing than in the oasis of Damascus. Unfortunately we do not know a great deal about it. Hans Böhlig has attempted to develop individual pieces of evidence into an imaginative painting and has spent 120 pages describing 'the religion of Tarsus'.[870] Sandon (Sandau, Sandos, etc.), the old Cilician god of war and the weather, who was identified with Heracles in Hellenistic times and appears on coins of Tarsus up to the middle of the third century CE, since together with Perseus he was regarded as founder of the city, should no longer be connected with Paul. He neither impressed the young Jew, as Böhlig conjectured, nor influenced his christological thought. According to H. Seyrig, the images on the coins with the alleged pyre which were thought to show that he was a dying and rising vegetation god indicate an architectural structure widespread in this area.[871] Far less was Heracles Sandon a 'mystery god'. Böhlig makes the quite misleading suggestion that 'with this Sandon-Heracles of Tarsus we have in the Augustinian era the same deity who otherwise is designated Adonis in Syria, Attis in Phrygia, Osiris in Egypt, and Tammuz in Babylon', thus claiming that the celebration of the burning of his effigy and his ensuing resurrection in Tarsus is, like that of Adonis in Hierapolis, 'a preliminary stage to a mystery religion'.[872] Such conjectures remain a sheer unprovable construction, typical of the speculations of the history-of-religions school. There were no Heracles mysteries in antiquity, and it is still questionable whether oriental gods already had any kind of 'mystery' character in the first half of the first century. Rather, we need to make a strict distinction between 'the language of mysteries', which spread very widely from Eleusis between the time of the pre-Socratics and above all from Plato, and any real influence of the mystery *cults*. There is isolated mystery language already in the LXX, more massively in the Wisdom of Solomon and above all in Philo. In the New Testament, by contrast, it fades right into the background.[873]

Böhlig went one stage further and also wanted to identify Sandon of Tarsus with the Iranian Anatolian Mithras, whose cult he similarly presupposes in Tarsus. Here he can refer to the well-known account of Plutarch[874] that the Cilician pirates 'celebrated secret rites (τελετάς τινας ἀπορρήτους ἐτέλουν), of which those of Mithras continue to the present day, after they had first been made known by them'. On this an expert like R. Merkelbach[875] observes: 'We cannot make any direct connection between the Mithras ceremonies of the pirates and the later mysteries; there are 150 years between the Mithras ceremonies and the later Roman mysteries. There was Mithras worship in all Iranian countries or regions ruled by the Iranian nobility; it is mere chance that the ceremonies of the pirates were to become known more closely by the Greeks.' The Mithras mysteries from the second and third centuries CE are 'a new religion'.[876] Paul cannot have known anything about them at all. In Tarsus the cult of Mithras is first attested by coins from the time of Gordian III (238–44).[877]

So we can doubt whether – apart from the traditional, long-established Dionysus and perhaps Isis – real mystery gods were worshipped at all in Tarsus in the time of Paul, i.e. in the first decades of the first century. Nor was Sarapis, relatively wide-spread from the time of the Ptolemies, but only flourishing again after Vespasian's stay in Alexandria in 69 CE, a mystery god.[878] There should be no more talk of a demonstrable influence of the mysteries on the apostle and the earliest Christian communities. We shall have to discuss the problem of 'dying' in baptism later (see below, 299f.). Moreover, what has been said of Tarsus also applies to Antioch. Like all Jews up to Philo or the author of Wisdom, Paul sharply rejected the pagan cults and the leading astray towards idols that they caused: Paul too 'abhorred idols' (βδελυσσόμενος τὰ εἴδωλα).[879] In this respect, like all real Jews he continued obligated to the first commandment and knew no compromises. Idolatry and the fear of idols (if only in the form of a troubled conscience) was quite incompatible with the message of the gospel; here Paul contrasted with the lax attitude of the Corinthians, whom he opposed most sharply on this point.[880]

By contrast, synagogue preaching and thus Paul himself may have been influenced by the Stoic philosophy and rhetoric which flourished in Tarsus. Strabo praises its inhabitants' zeal for education in the highest tones; he says that it relates not only to philosophy but to 'the whole ἐγκύκλιος παιδεία', so that they surpassed even Athens and Alexandria. Among others, he lists four Stoic philosophers: Antipater, Archedemus and two contemporaries both called Athenodorus, one a friend of Marcus Cato and the other a tutor of Augustus and later reformer of city ordinances in his home city.[881] His successor in city government was the academic Nestor, the teacher of Augustus' nephew Marcellus; the Epicurean Lysias then played a questionable political role under Tiberius. Strabo also mentions grammarians and poets, but adds that most of them emigrated to Rome. Rome was 'full of Tarsians and Alexandrians' – not Antiochenes! In complete contrast to Strabo, Philostratus, presumably referring to an earlier source of Maximus of Aigai, later reports that the young Apollonius of Tyana was to have been entrusted by his father to a Phoenician orator Euthydemus in Tarsus, but soon retreated to nearby Aigai because of the hostile climate to philosophy in the city.[882]

A rhetorical training was the foundation for all disciplines. At least in the larger cities, the leading members of the synagogue were also interested in both rhetoric and philosophy. In the competition between the various cults and spiritual tendencies there was a desire to attract members of the (more or less) educated middle class to the synagogue by artistic religious preaching with a philosophical colouring – something new in the sphere of ancient religion – and also to convince those who had risen in society and were inclined towards emancipation that one could live as a Jew in fidelity to the ancestral laws and at the same time also be 'progressive'.

As Jewish apologists, Philo and Josephus as a matter of course presuppose discussions with educated pagans. This was possible only on a basis of education which to some degree was shared.[883] Conversely, there are hints of discussions with Jews in pagan philosophers and scholars. We find this, for example, with the most famous Peripatetic of his time, Nicolaus of Damascus, who among other things had intensive conversations on philosophical questions with Herod: during his long stay at Herod's court in Jerusalem he certainly had contact with other Jews, for example leading Pharisees.[884] The unknown author of *De sublimitate,* with his praise of Moses and writers like Numenius, Galen and Celsus, will certainly have discussed with Jews.[885]

We must also assume this to be the case with Paul, on the basis of Acts 17.18 and the speech on the Areopagus which follows (17.22–32). For Luke this has paradigmatic significance. Paul could also speak in this style when he wanted to. On the other hand, I Cor. 1.22 (cf. 1.19f.) and 1.26 indicate negative experiences when dealing with Greek sages.[886] H. Böhlig investigates thoroughly the question of the possibility of the influence of Athenodorus son of Sandon, a pupil of Poseidonius and main representative of the Middle Stoa, on the young Jew with his thirst for learning, but has to concede that 'it cannot be proved that Athenodorus had a direct influence on Paul'.[887] He thinks, rather, that Paul read Athenodorus' writings, but this cannot be proved either. In a note he has to agree with P. Wendland, whose verdict should be taken to heart again today, when scholars are so fond of depicting Paul as an author with a high degree of oratorical training: 'How far the Jew and pupil of the rabbis who can still be recognized in the letters took part in Greek education is hard to know. He regarded worldly wisdom and oratorical skill as trinkets. It is quite improbable that he shaped his speeches anywhere in accordance with the precepts of oratorical theory, nor can this be proved', even if his letters contain 'some artistic forms of Greek speech' which occasionally may have resounded in his ears; 'this is probably to be explained from such influence'.[888] In reality, Paul's language and 'elements of education' do not go beyond what he could have learned within the Greek-speaking synagogues and in conversation with learned non-Jews, whom he did not avoid. His letters are much less stamped by the 'jargon' of the orators or philosophers than e.g. II–IV Maccabees, Aristeas, the Wisdom of Solomon, Aristobulus, Josephus or even Philo. Here Tarsus need not stand at the centre, as the place where he was educated; Jerusalem, where Greek synagogue preaching was similarly at home and which was sought by pagan sympathizers and proselytes from all over the Roman empire and even the Parthian East, would have been enough.[889] The ideas of Greek popular philosophy were also at home in Jerusalem from the third century BCE, as Koheleth and Ben Sira show.[890] Above all from the time of Herod, we can presuppose Greek education in the Holy City, with its countless visitors from all over the world, on a wider scale, even if its level was in no way comparable to that in Tarsus and Antioch. But the striking thing about Paul and the whole of earliest Christianity is that we do not find a deeper philosophical-oratorical education and a style corresponding to what we meet in Philo, Justus of Tiberias or Josephus. Luke and the author of Hebrews are exceptions here. The wave of philosophical education first broke with the earliest Christian Gnostics, Basilides, Carpocrates and Valentinus, and then with the Apologists after Justin. This also applies basically to higher oratorical training.[891] The significance of the rhetoric of the schools on Paul is much exaggerated today, following a fashionable trend.

7.4 Chronology and geography

To conclude our consideration of the complex Tarsus and Cilicia, which externally looks so unyielding but which must have been essential for Paul in the years after his visit to Peter, and may not simply be suppressed in favour of the key word Antioch, which is not all that more productive, we need to look further at the problem of chronology and geography. Paul carried on mission and founded communities in his home city (and probably also in the neighbouring cities of Cilicia Pedias). It is hardly credible that he first became a successful missionary only later, in Galatia, Macedonia and Achaea. He had already long since accumulated his fundamental experiences. The 'I worked more than all of them' (I Cor. 15.10) applies from the beginning. This is the most meaningful explanation of the existence of the Christian communities in Cilicia of which we hear in Acts 15.23, 41.

How long Paul stayed in Tarsus (or in other larger cities of Cilicia Pedias, which similarly had synagogue communities),[892] remains relatively uncertain. Certainly it was not a very short time. Luke presupposes a lengthy period between Acts 9.30, Paul's 'being sent' to Tarsus, and 11.25, his being 'brought back' from there to Antioch by Barnabas. To this period – with only limited historical accuracy – he transfers the decisive missionary step towards the 'Gentile mission', which for him must be duly ordered in 'salvation-historical terms'. As I have already remarked (see above, 154), the 'Hellenists' who were driven out of Jerusalem advanced only slowly northwards along the Phoenician coast with its world-famous cities rich in tradition,[893] to some degree step by step, but always engaged in active mission and concerned to found communities. Some crossed to Cyprus; in other words, when Barnabas, Paul and John Mark visited the island around eight to ten years later there will already have been some communities there.[894] Here it seems to me to be questionable whether Luke is thinking of a single closed group which visited Cyprus after travelling through southern Phoenicia, and then returned to the mainland from the island, continuing until they finally reached Antioch. The 'travelled as far as Phoenicia, Cyprus and Antioch' (διῆλθον ἕως Φοινίκης καὶ Κύπρου καὶ Ἀντιοχείας) seems more to indicate that those who were 'dispersed' worked in different very small groups and that from Judaea some only got as far as the Phoenician cities, others took ship to Cyprus, while the most active reached the capital of the province of Syria. This alternating process of travel, missionary preaching and the attempt to found communities on the periphery of the synagogues communities – how else are we to imagine this? – *must* have taken some time. We have an example in the activity of Philip in Samaria and the coastal plain, which ultimately led to the settlement in Caesarea. Thus the arrival of a first small group of 'Hellenists' in Antioch will hardly have happened much earlier than that of Paul in Tarsus, i.e.

around 36 CE. A year earlier or later is neither here nor there.[895] Luke's circumstantial account which in 11.19 refers back to 8.4 indicates a not inconsiderable stretch of time; here 'preaching the word' (εὐαγγελιζόμενοι τὸν λόγον, 8.4) and 'speaking the word' (λαλοῦντες τὸν λόγον, 11.19) indicates continued missionary activity at the individual stages, which of course presupposes lengthy stays. The certainty of the imminence of the coming Lord was initially stronger than a missionary impetus aimed at winning over geographically widespread lands and provinces. Neither the 'Hellenists' with their mission in Syria and Phoenicia nor Paul rushed 'through the country as headlong reporters of the imminent end'.[896] During these years there was as yet no thought of a preaching to 'all nations' or 'to the ends of the earth'.[897] According to the prophetic promise, it was expected, rather, that the Jewish Diaspora and the Gentiles would stream to the 'pilgrimage of the nations on Zion' and would gather in Eretz Israel in expectation of the return of the 'Lord'.[898] In Syria, too, people were still in the forecourt of the Holy Land. That those who were 'scattered' were a relatively small group[899] follows from the qualification in 11.20, 'But there were some of them' (ἦσαν δὲ τινες ἐξ αὐτῶν). Even the 'Hellenists' were not a closed unit: at the beginning only a small group of them formed a new focal point of preaching in Antioch because of the special situation and after a certain lapse of time deliberately and successfully won over 'Gentiles', i.e. above all sympathizers, and in so doing left the synagogue communities because of the special circumstances. But here we have again got ahead of ourselves. We shall be returning to this special development (see below, 8.1).

Initially we are concerned only with the chronology: this specifically Antiochene development – according to Luke's scheme – also needed time. A year or two previously the news of this new successful form of preaching and the formation of a community to which it led will hardly have reached Jerusalem and led to Barnabas' journey (11.22). Verses 22 and 23 again presuppose a certain interval of time between his arrival in the Syrian metropolis and his visit to Paul in Tarsus, as a result of which he brought Paul back from Tarsus to Antioch. During this stay, of course, he also got to know the community there. *In other words,*

*Paul's stay in his home city and province may have lasted at least three
and perhaps even four years, i.e. until 39/40.* So we should not fix
Paul's early period one-sidedly in Antioch, and we should also
note that already in the first six or seven years of his missionary
activity he was primarily addressing Gentiles who were more
or less sympathetic to Judaism in addition to the obligatory
'Jews first' (᾽Ιουδαίῳ πρῶτον). In other words, we must be very
restrained in reconstructing a developed pre- or extra-Pauline
theology which, itself already with a 'Gentile Christian' stamp, is
said to have influenced the apostle. Could not Paul have been the
decisive theological pioneer of the Greek-speaking, missionary
Jewish Christianity in Syria, which as such around 39/40 CE also
exercised a decisive influence on the first predominantly 'Gentile
Christian' community known to us in more detail in Antioch,
which was gradually consolidating itself, since he had already
put his stamp on the communities he founded in Cilicia? The
influence and originality of Paul, the first Christian *theologian*,
like that of John later,[900] has been underestimated in favour of
anonymous, speculative sources of tradition and 'trajectories'. He
can no more be 'dissolved' into 'traditions' than Socrates or
Plato. His influence was all the greater. Emanations of his mission
preaching in 'Syria and Cilicia' can be traced to Ignatius, 'John
the Elder' in Ephesus and Polycarp of Smyrna. Jülicher already
commented rightly that 'the theologian John stands on Paul's
shoulders'.[901]

But back once again to the question we have already asked
twice: why did Paul go to Tarsus?[902] A reference to his home
city and the probably considerable number of the 'pagan sympathizers' interested in Judaism is hardly enough. Here – as
already in Damascus and even more in Arabia – salvation-
historical geography, and at the same time missionary eschatology, may have provided reasons.

Here again we should be struck by the points of contact with
1QGenAp 21.15–19, the description of Abraham's circular
journey which goes round the inheritance promised to him and
his descendants. In so doing it follows the coast of Palestine,
Phoenicia and Syria northwards to the Taurus, changes direction
there and goes along the Taurus eastwards to the Euphrates, and

then travels round the Arabian peninsula until Abraham gets back to the Holy Land .[903] The western Taurus extends from the deep cut of the Tekir Gap, over which the pass northwards leads through the Cilician Gate, beginning in the northern hinterland of Taurus, eastwards as far as the upper Euphrates. If Abraham walked along the Taurus eastwards on foot, a glance at the map will show that he chose the route from Tarsus to Zeugma.[904] Thus the Genesis Apocryphon presupposes that Abraham roughly takes the road eastwards from Tarsus at the foot of the Taurus as far as the Euphrates, i.e. along the northern border of Cilicia and Syria.[905] It sees the 'promised land', in connection with Jubilees 8–9, in the inheritance of Shem and his sons, 'the kingdom of the centre' (Jub. 8.12). In this view of the world, Tarsus is the north-western frontier point where Japhet and Shem meet. Paul then later – certainly deliberately – crossed this frontier into the terri-tory of Japhet.

There is another interesting geographical indication in Josephus. According to him, Jonah was commanded by God to travel into the kingdom of Ninos and proclaim the end of his rule in the capital Nineveh.[906] However, Jonah was afraid of this com-mission, fled to Joppa, got into a ship, 'and attempted to sail to Tarsus in Cilicia'.[907] In three days the whale brings Jonah to the Black Sea (213): evidently Josephus conjectured that this was nearest to Nineveh.[908] *ṭarsōs*, i.e. Tarsus, also appears in individual Targums on Gen. 10.4 as an interpretation of *taršiš*, thus in the Fragment Targum, Neofiti 1 and a manuscript of the Targum Pseudo-Jonathan.[909] Josephus' interpretation of Gen. 10.4 corresponds to this. According to him, Tharsos the son of Jawan and grandson of Japhet gave the Tarsians (Θαρσεῖς) their name: 'for thus was Cilicia once called. A proof of this is that the most famous of its cities, the metropolis, is called Tarsus, the Θ having been turned into a T.'[910] As the old Tartessus in Spain was no longer known and the Semitic element had been completely suppressed by the far-reaching Hellenization of Cilicia, in con-trast to the earlier tradition of the book of Jubilees and the Genesis Apocryphon, for Josephus Cilicia, with its capital Tarsus, was already included in the territory of Japhet. Here, in contrast to the Genesis Apocryphon, the Taurus no longer forms the frontier between Shem and Japhet, the two sons of Noah. However, the saying in Gen. 9.27, 'God enlarge Japhet, and let him dwell in the tents of Shem', could be referred to the Cilician metropolis. Targum Pseudo-Jonathan[911] interprets this statement in 'missionary' terms: 'May Yahweh beautify the borders of Japhet! May his sons become proselytes and dwell in the school of Shem.' Irenaeus is the first Christian author to quote this saying in a missionary sense.[912] It will already have played an important role for Paul in his missionary activity in Tarsus and then even more in the founding of the mission in the territory of Japhet in Asia Minor.

The apostle makes a similar voyage to that of Jonah according to Josephus,[913] but for quite the opposite motives. Whereas Jonah wants to escape his commission to preach, Paul remains true to his, since with the compulsion upon him (as it was upon Jonah) he knows that he cannot escape it: 'for woe is me if I do not preach'.[914] That was certainly not a later insight won after some years, but is clearly connected with the shift in his life and there-fore also applies to his stay in Tarsus and Cilicia. So the choice of place was no mere chance, governed by pragmatic considera-tions, any more than it was in 'Arabia'. At the same time it was a decision of Paul the scriptural scholar, who understood himself to be an instrument of the eschatological fulfilment of the prophetic promises.

The view, one might almost call it a superstition, dominating German exegesis since Bultmann that 'eschatology' and 'salva-tion history', which always has a geographical component, are opposites would have been incomprehensible to Paul. Not only is 'Old Testament history' of eminent importance for Paul as prophetic prediction of the 'eschatological history of the present',[915] but his missionary activity, guided by the Spirit, is itself a living 'eschatological saving event' which becomes salvation history in concrete terms through the progression of time.[916] This is shown by his varied reflections on the missionary tasks before him which are governed by geography,[917] and also by the earliest Christian 'church and missionary strategy' lying behind him, on which he sometimes looks back.[918] Here too I am certain that he associated chiliastic notions with the *parousia*; this is indicated by texts like I Cor. 15.23–28; I Cor. 6.2ff.; Rom. 11.12, 25–27. Paul's thought and his ideas were far richer than our modern theological reasoning, reduced by the Enlightenment and interpreting him in moral, idealistic or existentialist terms, will concede. In Paul, among other things (though to mention this is already offensive to theologians), we find references to a densely filled, mythical-eschatological drama, and at the same time a no less 'dramatic' biography utterly determined by christology, bound up with a fascinating way of thinking which argues clearly in a way which is amazing for its Jewish and Jewish-pagan environment. Where mission is carried on with such theological passion in a fashion which is completely new in world history, fundamental geographical considerations must be present. There is no history without geography, and that is also true of an 'eschatological-missionary history of salvation'.

8. Antioch

8.1 The beginnings of the community in Antioch and its relation to Jerusalem

8.1.1 Paul's move from Tarsus to Antioch

In Tarsus (and in Cilicia) Paul did not work in complete isolation. Even if he himself did not visit Jerusalem again for thirteen to fourteen years – in my view because his life was in danger there[919] – he did have a loose link with the mother community of the church. That follows not only from his later efforts, which had not been made easier by the clash with Peter in Antioch and the developments in Jerusalem around 50 CE, but also from the concession in Gal. 2.2 that he presented his gospel, which he 'preached among the Gentiles', separately to the leaders of the community there 'lest somehow I should be running or had run in vain'. Mission work as a 'separatist' was inconceivable for him. Although a 'lone champion' of a particular kind, he remained bound up in the unity of the community as the body of Christ.[920] That must also already have been the case before the time of the Apostolic Council.

Moreover Barnabas would hardly have looked for Paul in Tarsus had he not known that he could be found there. That suggests that there was also some contact between Paul and the predominantly 'Gentile Christian' community in Antioch which was just forming, especially as the new communities taking shape in Tarsus and Antioch were linked by their special interest in the 'Gentile Christian' mission. The Lucan formulation of Acts 11.25f., 'So he went to Tarsus to look for Saul; and when he had found him, he brought him to Antioch' (ἐξῆλθεν δὲ εἰς Ταρσὸν ἀναζητῆσαι Σαῦλον, καὶ εὑρὼν ἤγαγεν εἰς Ἀντιόχειαν), may indicate that it was not all that easy for Barnabas to find Paul,[921] since it was in the nature of the case that an active missionary constantly travelling into the province could not always be found immediately. By this formulation Luke hardly wanted to indicate that Paul had gone underground in Tarsus and Barnabas found him only by chance. The Western text sees this difficulty and reports that Barnabas heard in Antioch that Saul was in Tarsus and thereupon sought him out there. So it avoids the misunderstanding of a 'speculative journey',[922] and also replaces the harsh 'when he had found him, he brought him' (καὶ εὑρὼν ἤγαγεν εἰς) with a more elegant 'and on meeting him asked him to come ... ' (καὶ ὡς συντυχὼν παρεκάλεσεν ἐλθεῖν εἰς ...),[923] i.e. Barnabas does not simply take Paul to Antioch, but asks him to come there with him.

The momentous stay in Antioch in which Paul gave up his independent missionary work, joined a community which, while certainly still being young, had not been founded by him, and associated with an older disciple for the earliest Christian beginnings in Jerusalem, may have lasted about eight or nine years, if we put the move around 39 or 40 CE. It was certainly an important phase in the apostle's development, but it is over-valued by scholars, as at this point Paul could look back on between six and seven years of independent missionary work which was certainly not without success. An unsuccessful missionary would not have been much help to Barnabas in building up the church in Antioch. Moreover the powerful self-awareness that we find in the letters will already have been established at the time of this move. Furthermore, we should not overlook the fact that the lengthy collaboration which now began was unexpectedly ended with a deep disappointment which had a *theological* foundation.

The motives for this move remain unclear. Perhaps the apostle's activity in Cilicia, as later in Corinth and Ephesus or then in the eastern Mediterranean generally,[924] had come to a certain conclusion. Presumably the communities which he had founded had to some degree become independent. On the other hand, Barnabas, who must have regarded Paul as a missionary authority 'with equal rights', must have convinced him, with the theological agreements which were fundamental to him, that he was *urgently needed* in Antioch at that very moment. In other words, the apostle, who hitherto had worked on the frontier between 'Japhet' and 'Shem', called off 'Japhet', i.e. did not cross the Taurus and advance into Asia Minor, and first returned to 'Shem' – a decision which at that time, in view of the imminent coming of the Lord, he perhaps regarded as final. Contrary to his expectations, this way took him for a long period not towards the north-west but again towards the south-east.

8.1.2 The crisis sparked off under Caligula, autumn 38 to spring 41 CE

In ancient history, the period of ten to twenty years in the development of a cultural, philosophical or even religious community does not amount to much. Our sources are much too fragmentary for that. We know almost nothing about how e.g. Gnostic thought developed in and on the periphery of the church in the decisive years, say, between 110 and 130. Moreover, apart from the somewhat isolated references in Acts 1–11; Gal. 1.1; I Thess. 2.14 and I Cor. 9.1ff., we have hardly any information about the concrete events during the first ten years of the church after the Passover of 30 CE at which Jesus died. Yet by the standards of antiquity that is an amazing amount, because the isolated accounts can be fitted approximately into an overall picture of the development. By contrast, it is very hard to relate the Gospel narratives to events in the first beginnings of the church, i.e. to the time immediately after Jesus, however popular this attempt is today. Here we can certainly speak of some kind of 'community formations', but little is at all probable. Sayings like Matt. 10.5, 23 or 17.24 may indicate an aversion in Palestinian Jewish Christianity to the Gentile mission outside Jewish Palestine, and of course 'post-Easter' christology found a record in many ways in all the Gospels, so that in the end with John it has almost completely suppressed the historical account; however, it is difficult to read concrete events during the first – decisive – years even out of the Fourth Gospel.[925] Here there must have been a stormy development which at the same time took place under difficult circumstances. This includes sporadic measures of persecution from the side of the synagogue,[926] but also internal tension and controversies which Luke, in keeping with his harmonizing tendency, only hints at in Acts 5.1–11; 6.1ff. and 11.1–18. We must assume this stormy development for the development of doctrine, especially christology and soteriology, and also for the development of the community itself.

Here it is striking that the external, political course of history plays hardly any role, although it was far from being unproblematical. Thus we hear nothing in our earliest Christian sources of the defeat of Herod Antipas in the war against Aretas IV, *c.*35–36 (see above, 111f.), which people regarded as a just punishment for the murder of John the Baptist, a sign how the violent death of John was vividly remembered years later.[927] Nor do we hear anything of the recall of Pilate by the Syrian governor Vitellius because of the massacre among the followers of the Samaritan prophet on Gerizim,[928] nor of the deposition of Caiaphas on Vitellius's visit to Jerusalem at Passover 37 CE.[929] The same is true of the appointment of Agrippa I as king and successor to Philip by Caligula,[930] or of the banishment of Herod Antipas to Gaul in 39 CE, which was caused by a denunciation of his nephew and brother-in-law Agrippa I.[931] The power-plays of the 'rulers of this age'[932] had become unimportant for the new messianic movement, which had already experienced the dawn of the kingdom of God in the present and was constantly experiencing it anew: they were no longer 'worth talking about'. Agrippa is mentioned under his popular titular name Herod[933] by Luke only when, having been appointed king of all Judaea by Claudius in Rome as a reward for helping Claudius to power,[934] presumably at the Passover of 43 he persecuted the community in Jerusalem and had James the son of Zebedee and other Jewish Christians executed and Peter put in jail. This violent intervention marks the beginning of a new period in the history of the earliest church.[935]

Even an event which deeply shook the whole of Jewish Palestine and Syria and brought them to the verge of war, Caligula's attempt to erect his statue in the temple in Jerusalem, does not find any direct mention in the early Christian texts.[936] It may have been regarded – like the destruction of Jerusalem in the Synoptic apocalypses later – as a symptom of the intensifying messianic woes, but even the fate of the temple had lost its fundamental significance for the new messianic movement, since Jesus himself had been executed as a messianic pretender (guilty of crimes against the holy place) and his representative death on the cross had made the bloody sacrificial cult in the sanctuary obsolete.[937] Stephen, too, had been stoned for his criticism of law and temple. Precisely because the temple had lost its soteriological significance as a place of atonement, even its destruction in the year 70 emerges relatively little in the earliest Christian writings. It was noticed far more in Roman historiography. A text like Mark 13.14–20 is certainly not to be interpreted as an apocalyptic flysheet from that time of terror, when the demand of the megalomaniac[938] emperor Caligula put the land in an uproar, but is to be understood as a reference to the imminent Antichrist in the form of Nero redivivus about 70.[939] The same is true of II Thess. 2.3–12.[940] The text is difficult to date, since its authenticity is questionable.[941] The image of the enemy of God who has himself worshipped as God and usurps the temple goes back to Antiochus IV and his actions against the sanctuary and the Jews loyal to the law in 167–164 BCE, and already has a model in Isa. 14. It was reactivated in a new form by Caligula, say, between 38 and 41 CE. This was recorded only a generation later in (Jewish-) Christian sources, in which Nero's persecution also played a role.[942] It is all the more striking that these events under Caligula, which intensified the apocalyptic fever especially in Eretz Israel and in Syria, were not worth mentioning in the letters of Paul, in Luke or in the Gospels. For not only were Alexandria and a little later the mother country affected by them, but the whole Diaspora, especially in the eastern part of the empire, was shaken.

The unrest began in Alexandria in summer 38 CE in connection with the return of Agrippa, who had been nominated king by Caligula, from Rome to his new territory, the former tetrarchy of Philip. Here the new Jewish king was mocked by the Alexandrian mob during an interim stay. The desecration of synagogues in Alexandria by the introduction of images of the emperor followed, and when the Jews tried to defend themselves against it, a bloody pogrom followed.[943] The conflict was intensified by the Jewish repudiation of the emperor cult, which in Palestinian Jamnia led to the destruction of an imperial altar by the Jewish part of the population.[944] When the news of this incident reached him, probably in the summer of 39, Caligula gave the disastrous order[945] which brought Judaea to the verge of armed rebellion.[946] The incident in Jamnia shows that the pogrom against the Jews in Alexandria also spread in late summer and autumn 38 to the Gentile cities of Palestine, where the hatred against the Jews was no less than in Alexandria. The anti-Jewish wave which emerged from this under the aegis of the emperor cult and the tensions associated with it continued in Syria until the pacifying intervention of the new emperor Claudius in spring 41; this will have calmed most of the larger cities, though we do not hear many details. The tensions intensified in the second half of 39 CE because of Caligula's instruction to P. Petronius, governor of Syria, to erect his statue in the temple in Jerusalem. According to Philo, the statue was to have a sanctuary of its own in honour of the Διός 'Επιφανοῦς Νέου Γαίου.[947] The reign of terror of Antiochus IV seemed to have broken out again, and in Palestine and Syria there was an acute danger of war. The situation was as tense as before the outbreak of the Jewish war in 66. Had P. Petronius not acted essentially more wisely than the procurator Florus and Cestius Gallius, governor of Syria, did later, there would have been a catastrophe as early as 39/40.

That means that the trend towards a deliberate preaching 'to the Greeks also' by the movement sparked off by the 'Hellenists' engaged in mission there,[948] which Luke describes all too briefly, and the general development of a predominantly Gentile community which resulted from that, took place at a time when the anti-Jewish attitude of the city population in Antioch was also hardening, and it reached its climax around the time when Barnabas brought Paul from Tarsus to Antioch in 39/40.

8.1.3 The anti-Jewish unrest in Antioch

In contrast to Ptolemaean and Roman Alexandria, we have only relatively isolated, chance reports about Antioch.[949] That makes it all the more striking that in his major monograph on the city Downey can say that 'the history of Antioch during Gaius' short reign was eventful'.[950] Here particular emphasis is put on the four short years between 18 March 37 and 24 January 41. Caius Caligula was the son of Germanicus, who died in Antioch on 10 October 19 CE, and whom the population there treasured highly.[951] They transferred this high esteem to his son.

In general, their attitude towards Roman rule was essentially more positive than that of the citizens of Alexandria, who were proud of their Macedonian background and their past, since only Rome could protect Syria and its capital against the covetousness of Eastern kings and peoples like the Armenians, the Parthians and the Arab tribes; as a powerful people the Jews, too, were feared in Syria. Soon after the beginning of his reign Caligula was able to show his favour towards the capital of the province of Syria by remedying the consequences of the earthquake of 9 April 37.

An account from the Chronicle of Malalas which is obscure in detail but ultimately historical in its basic content makes it clear that the unrest against the Jews which broke out from summer 38 in Alexandria and in which the divine worship of Caligula played an essential role was carried over not only to Palestine but also to Antioch.[952]

According to it, in the third year of Caligula, i.e. 39/40, under the governorship of Petronius, there was unrest in Antioch which started with a dispute among the circus parties; this degenerated into a pogrom of the 'Gentiles' against the Jews, in which many Jews were killed and their synagogues[953] were burnt down. What now follows sounds quite strange: in a counter-action the Jewish high priest Phinehas (Pinhas) sent 30,000 men to Antioch and killed many inhabitants of the city. Thereupon the emperor intervened; his representative Pontius (Petronius?) and Varius were punished because they had not stopped these events. Phineas was beheaded as the instigator, and the emperor gave money to restore the fire damage in the city.

The report is certainly confused in its present form, above all over the military intervention of the Jewish high priest Phinehas in favour of the persecuted Jews. The narrative in I Macc.

11.43–51 about the successful intervention of powerful Jewish auxiliaries 3,000 strong to support the Seleucid Demetrius II may have influenced the narrative here. Evidently two quite different accounts have been fused.[954] On the other hand, this unique narrative is not sheer invention.[955] The event in Jamnia in 39 CE which set the ball rolling, and the later event in Dor at the end of 41,[956] when pagan fanatics set up a bust of the emperor in the synagogue there, show how the Alexandrian anti-Judaism found a breeding ground in Palestine and Syria. King Agrippa I thought the attack in Dor so serious that he immediately travelled to Antioch and secured a sharp letter from Petronius to the magistrates of Dor.[957] This not only called for the guilty ones to be severely punished, but also emphasized the special interest of the governor and Agrippa, 'that the Jewish ethnos does not have any occasion under the pretext of self-defence to conspire to commit acts of desperation'.[958] At the beginning of the same year the Jews had taken up weapons in Alexandria after the murder of Gaius to exact vengeance for the persecution that they had suffered. Claudius ordered the prefect to put down this revolt, but at the same time, at the request of Agrippa and his brother Herod of Chalcis, he drafted an edict for Alexandria *and Syria* which commanded that the old rights of the Jews should be respected and at the same time warned Greeks and Jews against any form of unrest. Evidently there had also been unrest in Syria; here we are to think primarily of Antioch.[959] Perhaps events could be reconstructed *hypothetically* as follows. The disputes between the two circus parties, the Greens and the Blues, also had an ethnic background, as the Jews who took part as spectators in the public games[960] supported one of the two parties. These latent quarrels intensified after Caligula's letter and the departure of Petronius and his army in the direction of Judaea for a pogrom against the Jews. After the surprising murder of the emperor, as in Alexandria the Jewish minority embarked on acts of vengeance which, as in Alexandria, were suppressed on the orders of Claudius. Petronius, however, who was recalled soon afterwards, continued to enjoy the emperor's favour.[961] That Josephus does not report these events may be because he wanted to avoid any reference to an armed rebellion by the Jews. For Philo,

the Alexandrian Jew, the events in Antioch were just not worth
mentioning.

Against this background the development in the young community in Antioch around 36/37 will not have been as peaceful
and straightforward as Luke describes it in his brief summary. We
have already demonstrated several times[962] that the new messianic
message of the 'Hellenists' who had reached Antioch was not
being preached for the first time to the 'Greeks' – contrary to
Luke's one-sided account. Those who had been expelled from
Jerusalem had long had pagan sympathizers in view.

The new development is connected, rather, with the special
situation of the metropolis. Antioch was the third largest city in
the empire, and in the time of Augustus only fell a little short of
Alexandria in the size of its population.[963] However, towards the
end of the republic Alexandria is said to have had more than
300,000 free inhabitants.[964] Estimates for Antioch in the time of
the empire fluctuate between 180,000 and 600,000. 300,000 may
be a more realistic estimate. For the first time the new messianic
movement had gained a footing in a real metropolis, a city with a
large Jewish minority[965] and – as Malalas shows – a considerable
number of synagogues. As in Alexandria, this does not exclude a
main synagogue.[966] A Jewish element will have lived in the city
since its foundation by Seleucus I Nicator around 300 BCE.[967]
According to Josephus, they received special privileges from the
'kings of Asia' for their mercenary services.[968] As one example he
mentions Seleucus I, who in the cities of Asia and northern Syria
which he founded, and 'in the metropolis of Antioch himself', is
said to have accorded Jews citizenship (πολιτεία) and the 'same
political rights as the Macedonians and Greeks'.[969] These equal
rights were maintained in the Roman period despite all the
protests and denunciations from the Greek citizens, even in the
critical period during and immediately after the Jewish War. As
proof of this, Josephus mentions the old privilege of Jewish
citizens of Antioch to be given a sum of money instead of the
obligatory distribution of oil by the gymnasiarch, as they did not
want to use pagan, i.e. impure, oil. C. Licinius Mucianius, the
governor of Syria in the Jewish War, did not abolish this privilege
despite the urging of the popular assembly.[970] Even Titus opposed

not only the frequent and urgent requests of the Antiochenes that the Jews should be driven out of the city but also their second wish to remove the bronze tablets on which the privileges (δικαιώματα) of the Jews were publicly displayed; indeed he left their legal status completely unchanged.[971]

We need not go here into the much-discussed question whether the Jews had full citizenship in the cities of the East, as Josephus often reports.[972] In Alexandria, where the Romans were very restrictive in granting urban citizenship, as it was the presupposition for gaining Roman *civitas*, the letter of Claudius and other papyri show that Josephus' information is apologetic exaggeration. In Antioch, as perhaps also in Tarsus, citizenship may have been limited to a small number of old-established prominent Jewish families, while the large Jewish community as such had corporate privileges, above all the right 'to live according to its own ancestral laws'. Here the legal situation differed from place to place. The dispute over Jews having equal political rights with the 'Greeks' or Macedonians also concerned other cities in Syria and Palestine. In Caesarea the disputes over this question really sparked off the Jewish War.[973]

From the various reports of Josephus, our most important source, about the old and large Jewish community in Antioch, we can conclude an ambivalent situation. It is evident that, as in Alexandria, its members were largely Hellenized and spoke Greek as their mother tongue, which is why they attached such importance to their old-established privileges and claimed an equal legal standing with the Greek citizens. The privilege over oil shows on the one hand that at least their upper class took part in gymnasium training, and on the other that more than other provinces of the empire they strictly adhered to the demands from the mother country for purity, a tendency which also makes the fearful and vacillating attitude of the Antiochene Jewish Christians in Gal. 2.11–13 easier to understand. The urgent striving for ἰσοπολιτεία[974] has points of contact with Paul's metaphor in Phil. 3.20 with its sovereign reference to the 'citizenship in heaven' (πολίτευμα ἐν οὐρανίοις) of those who expect the Kyrios as redeemer from there. Thus behind Paul's metaphor is more than just an allusion to the Latin citizenship rights of the

Colonia Iulia Augusta Philippensium. Here was a basic question for the Jewish communities in the metropolises of the eastern Mediterranean, which time and again could lead to vigorous conflicts. For the members of the new messianic movement – expecting the imminent return of their Lord and his kingly rule[975] – this old point of dispute had lost all significance. Precisely for that reason Paul – expecting the imminent end – can call for loyalty to the state magistrates in Rom. 13.1–7, since he knows (contrary to all later 'theologies of the state') that their end is near.[976]

At the same time, as in the Alexandrian Letter of Aristeas or in Philo's work, we can see the self-awareness of the Jewish community in Antioch, which maintains its old rights despite all oppression, indeed persecutions: the successor of Antiochus IV, the enemy of God, presumably his nephew Demetrius I, who was hostile to his uncle, had given the main synagogue there the dedicatory gifts of bronze which Antiochus had plundered from the temple in Jerusalem. They remained there and were not handed back to Jerusalem. After that the Jewish community in the city flourished again:

> As the later kings treated the Jews in the same way, their number increased; they adorned their sanctuary (τὸ ἱερόν)[977] with artistic and splendid gifts.[978]

It is possible that the Seleucids were concerned to emphasize the main synagogue in Antioch as a place where the Jews held religious assemblies because of the Maccabaean efforts to gain political independence for Jerusalem and Judaea, but this never became a rival sanctuary like the temple in Leontopolis in Egypt, which as a result was closed by Vespasian and destroyed.[979] By contrast, immediately after 70 Titus had a theatre erected in Daphne, at the place where a synagogue had formerly stood, with the inscription *ex praeda Iudaea*, and had bronze figures recalling the victory over the Jews attached to the city gate which led to Daphne. In other words, he met the anti-Jewish wishes of the population in another way.[980] According to a Jewish-Arab source,[981] the synagogue of the 'Hasmonaean Woman', named after the mother of the seven sons in II Macc. 7 and IV Macc., was the first to be built after the destruction of the second temple, on the tombs of the martyrs of the time of the Macabbees. In building this were the Jews of Antioch not thinking at the same time of the victims of the pogroms under Caligula and in the year 70 and the prisoners of war killed in the circus games?[982] This synagogue was then turned into a Christian church around 380 CE. Here the Jewish commemoration of the Maccabaean martyrs precedes that of the Christians.[983] At around the same time John Chrystostom also mentions a number of synagogues in the suburbs which were also visited by Christians, not least by prominent women.[984]

Josephus also confirms the power of attraction of the Antiochene synagogue(s) on non-Jews around 300 years earlier when immediately after the adornment of the Jewish 'sanctuary' he continues: 'and through their worship they (the Jews) attracted a large number of Greeks and in a way made them part of themselves'.[985] Here, too, the synagogue services had a considerable power of attraction as a result of the monotheism with a slight philosophical colouring which was preached there, combined with the great antiquity of the Jewish religion, which could claim to be the true primal religion. One of those who belonged to these προσαγόμενοι moved – probably for religious reasons – to Jerusalem; we meet him in Acts 6.5 as the last of the 'Seven', Nicolaus the proselyte from Antioch.[986] The qualification, namely that 'this large mass of Greeks' had been made part of the Jewish community only 'in a way', probably indicates that these, too, were quite predominantly 'sympathizers' who attended synagogue worship, but did not go over to Judaism completely. So circumstances were very like those in Damascus and other Syrian cities (see above, 58ff.); however, the number of these sympathizers of all shades was larger, and they were much more varied because of the substantially larger number of inhabitants and the much greater number of Jews and synagogues. H. Kraeling estimated the number of the Jewish population of Antioch in the Roman empire at between 45,000 and 60,000; perhaps we should extend the range to 30–50,000.[987]

Part of the ambivalence of Jewish community life in the capital of the province of Syria was the anti-Judaism of the majority of the city population, although no mass killings are reported from Antioch during the Jewish War – this was not the case under

Caligula – in contrast to southern Syria.[988] Nevertheless, here too
there was almost a pogrom. Thus Josephus relates that shortly
after the outbreak of war and after the arrival of Vespasian in
Syria 'hatred against the Jews reached its climax among all'.[989] At
that time a Jewish apostate, who as the son of an archon of the
Antiochene Jews enjoyed great respect, had denounced the Jews
to the popular assembly in the theatre for planning arson, 'in
order to show his hatred of the laws of the Jews'.[990] He sacrificed
in Greek fashion and called on the Gentile population to require
the other Jews to do the same in order to show their innocence. A
few of the Jews who had been denounced yielded to the pressure,
and the majority, who refused, were executed. This apostate is
said also to have compelled his fellow-Jews in Antioch and other
Syrian cities for a short time to stop observing the sabbath.[991]
In other words, during the Jewish War the Jews again lived in
constant fear of threats that could mean death, and only the level-
headedness of the legate Gnaeus Collega and later the moderate
attitude of Titus prevented greater catastrophes, like those in the
cities of southern Syria.[992] The catchword 'hatred against the
Jews' keeps cropping up in Josephus' accounts.[993] During the first
century CE this 'hatred' had an influence throughout Syria and
Arabia, where the Jewish element in the population was greatest
because of the geographical proximity.[994] It was there in a latent
form, even if it was not expressed directly in denunciations,
pogroms and warlike clashes, and thus formed the negative background to the form of Jewish worship and the self-conscious
religious identity of the people of God which was attractive to
non-Jews.

When Paul refers in his earliest letter, written on the so-called
second journey some time after 50 CE, to the Jews who 'have
persecuted the churches of God in Judaea' and 'also us', who
'hinder us from speaking to the Gentiles that they may be saved',
who 'displease God and oppose all men',[995] he is resorting, in a
bitterness against Jewish enmity which is historically understandable but hardly justified,[996] to a basically pagan anti-Jewish
formula which was familiar to him above all through his long
years of missionary activity in Syria. I Thessalonians 2.14 and
Luke's parallel account in Acts 17.5–9 show that the new move-

ment was exposed to pressure from both sides, though here in Syria at first the Jewish pressure was predominant.[997] When the Marcan apocalypse in Mark 13.13 prophesies, in view of the messianic pangs which are imminent, 'and you will be hated by all for my name's sake', it is at the same time expressing the missionary experience of a generation. The Christians were not more popular for attempting to stand between the front lines.[998]

Excursus IV: Antioch, IV Maccabees and Paul

We have a Jewish Hellenistic writing which on the one hand employs refined rhetoric and an artistic philosophical style, i.e. wants to be up with Greek education, and on the other inexorably maintains the iron validity of the law given by God and subjects everything else, not least human life, to loyalty to him. It has the literary form of a eulogy given in honour of the martyrs of the Maccabaean period[999] reported to us in II Macc. 6 and 7, probably in Antioch,[1000] in the period between Tiberius and Nero: so-called IV Maccabees.[1001] Here it is striking that despite the philosophical rhetorical form with which the unknown author seeks to present a φιλοσοφώτατος λόγος and prove that the εὐσεβὴς λογισμός has sovereign control of the passions,[1002] the piety underlying the speech has a more marked Palestinian Jewish stamp than, say, the work of Philo, in which quite a few linguistic points of contact with Paul can be seen.

The law as God's decree is consistently spoken of in the singular almost forty times, while the commandments (ἐντολαί) appear alongside this only three times, twice as the 'command-ments of God'.[1003] Because the martyrs believe (πιστεύεντες) that God has appointed the law, they know that naturally the Creator of the world who has given the law suffers with them (συμπαθεῖ). By contrast, the formula πάτρια ἔθη, popular in Hellenistic Judaism, appears only once, in a passage the text of which is critically uncertain.[1004] The father of the house himself taught the children 'the law and the prophets'.[1005] Alongside the Torah, the Psalms and Proverbs – in contrast to Alexandria[1006] – and here above all Daniel, play an important role. The idea of the vicarious suffering of the martyrs also points to Palestine and the martyr tradition there.[1007] Also striking is the constant reference to Abraham[1008] and descent from him, and in second place also to the other patriarchs: the martyrs entered into communion with them.[1009] That Paul, too, despite the imminent expectation of the parousia, has similar ideas, follows from Phil. 1.23.[1010] Although the bodily resurrection[1011] fades into the background because of the philosophical style, the influence of Dan. 12.2f. can still be traced. The metaphor of astral immortality in 17.5 is primarily dependent on that passage. The statement in 7.20 that 'those who believe in God do not die ... but live for God' – like the patriarchs,[1012] accords with widespread Jewish and Pauline, early Christian belief.[1013] In general we also find the essential eschato-logical terms like ἀθανασία, ἀφθαρσία or ζωὴ αἰώνιος in Paul. 9.22, which says that the martyr gave the appearance of 'being transformed by fire into incorruption', also corresponds to his language.[1014]

IV Maccabees 2.4–6 takes from the Decalogue the basic commandment 'not to covet'.[1015] This commandment also appears in Paul, though with the opposite intention: human beings fail because sin can now arouse deadly desire. The heroic-optimistic understanding of the law in IV Maccabees is radically opposed to that of the apostle. It is very Palestinian to regard the small and the important commands as being of equal worth in obedience to the law. Paul also requires the observance of the whole Torah of those who take the law upon themselves.[1016]

In IV Macc. 5.33 the law itself is called a 'tutor'.[1017] By contrast, in Gal. 3.24 Paul speaks in the context of salvation history, in a more derogatory though not completely negative way, of the law as παιδαγωγὸς . . . εἰς Χριστόν, which 'kept' Israel until the final revelation,[1018] so that it was not really a 'tutor' but an external supervisor (cf. I Cor. 4.15) of the people of God, protecting them for the time of 'future faith'. However, παιδαγωγός can also mean 'disciplinarian': ὁ μὴ δαρεὶς ἄνθρωπος οὐ παιδεύεται,[1019] nor is it a coincidence that in this connection Paul does not speak of the law as a 'warder' (δεσμοφύλαξ).

Immediately before 5.33 the scribe Eleazar emphasizes that he does not want the law of the fathers to be destroyed by him.[1020] By contrast, in Gal. 2.16–18 Paul objects to Peter that through his life-style hitherto, which has been critical of the law, he has – rightly – 'destroyed' the significance of the law for salvation.[1021] In now establishing it again by his separation from the Gentile Christians at the table (of the Lord), he is proving to be a law-breaker and making Christ the 'servant of sin'. Here, too, despite the same terminology, we can see the contrast in the view of the law among the earliest Christian missionaries to the Gentiles, above all Paul, which even Peter has evidently adopted – though still in a vacillating way.

If Paul writes in I Thess. 4.13 that the community should not lament the dead like the others who have no hope, the mother does not mourn her sons as though they were dead.[1022] Rather, with her unshakeable faith she gives the impression that she wants 'to bear the full number of her sons again to immortality'.[1023]

We also find the formula ὑπομονὴ τῆς ἐλπίδος (I Thess. 1.3) similarly with the mother of the heroes in IV Macc. 17.4: τὴν ἐλπίδα τῆς ὑπομονῆς βεβαίαν ἔχουσα πρὸς τὸν θεὸν,[1024] and whereas Paul previously speaks of ἔργον τῆς πίστεως, she speaks of γενναιότης τῆς πίστεως (17.2).

We find the verb ἀπολαμβάνειν for receiving the eschatological gift of God in IV Macc. 18.23, where the martyrs receive holy and immortal souls. In Gal. 4.5 it is the divine sonship which believers receive, in Col. 3.24 the heavenly inheritance, and in Rom. 1.27 the divine judgment that they deserve.[1025]

The list of points of contact can be prolonged further. IV Maccabees 18.6 alludes to the fact that the serpent led Eve astray; in Paul this motif appears in II Cor. 11.13 and probably also in I Cor. 11.10. We find the use of the term Ἰουδαϊσμός in the sense of (strict) obedience to the law in IV Macc. 4.26 and Gal. 1.13f. In both cases it denotes more than mere 'Jewish way of life'. The catalogue of vices which concludes Rom. 1.29–31 has a parallel in the list of comparable and sometimes identical failings and sins in IV Macc. 1.25–27 and 2.15, and whereas in Rom. 1.24, 26, 27 Paul says that God has delivered those who have fallen away from him to the 'lusts of their hearts' (ἐπιθυμίαις τῶν καρδίων), 'dishonourable passions' (πάθη ἀτιμίας) and a 'base mind' (ἀδόκιμον νοῦν),[1026] IV Macc. fights against the dominance of the ἐπιθυμία over the human reason governed by the law,[1027] and in good Stoic fashion inveighs bitterly against πάθη as the root of all evil. Together with its opposites λογισμός and λόγος, the negative πάθος/πάθη pervades the whole work like a scarlet thread.[1028] Instead of these central Stoic concepts, Paul has the typical Palestinian antithesis of flesh/sin (σάρξ/ἁμαρτία) and spirit (πνεῦμα). Here too, however, at the same time the contrast is evident: a text like Rom. 7.7–25 resolutely contradicts the idealization of the εὐσεβὴς λογισμός in IV Macc.

However, the most marked parallel – despite the fundamental soteriological and anthropological contrast – consists in the language related to martyrdom and contests.[1029] Thus the heroic readiness for martyrdom in I Cor. 13.3 broadly attested with the reading καυθήσομαι, which I regard as at least worth considering, given the context,[1030] receives some support from the several occurrences in IV Macc.

In Phil. 2.17 Paul, facing the possibility of imminent martyrdom and his service in preaching the faith, uses terms from the sacrificial cult.[1031] In the well-known passage IV Macc. 17.20–23 (and 6.28ff.), the death of the martyrs is interpreted as a sacrifice which atones for the sins of the people.[1032]

Immediately before this text, the clash of the martyrs with the tyrant is depicted as a contest. Through them an ἀγὼν θεῖος takes place. Paul and the Deutero-Paulines use ἀγών five times both for proving faith in tribulation and for mission work.[1033] Arete itself, δι᾽ ὑπομονῆς δοκιμάζουσα, expresses the prize to be won, and the victory represents ἀφθαρσία ἐν ζωῇ πολυχρονίῳ; by contrast, Paul speaks in Rom. 5.3f., of 'boasting about suffering' because it brings about ὑπομονή, and this brings about δοκιμή, which in turn leads to unshakeable hope. However, the victory which achieves ἀφθαρσία and ἀθανασία is not understood as a reward for the martyrs, but is given by Christ (I Cor. 15.54–57). In the 'divine contest' of IV Macc.,

> Eleazar entered the arena (προηγωνίζετο) as champion, and the mother of the seven sons came in as a fighter (ἐνήλθει); the brothers continued to fight the battle (ἠγωνίζοντο). The tyrant was the enemy (ἀντηγωνίζετο). The world and

humankind looked on (ἐθεώρει). But the fear of God proved victorious and crowned its contestants.

In the same way, in I Cor. 4.9 Paul can describe the apostles as 'those who have been condemned to death' (ὡς ἐπιθανατίους), i.e. as *morituri*.[1034] Tertullian translates this when quoting it with *uelut bestiarios*, i.e. criminals who have been condemned to death by fighting with animals in the arena.[1035] Paul then continues, 'for we have become a spectacle (θέατρον) for the world, for angels and men'. In other words, the apostle compares the messengers of Christ with 'gladiators doomed to death' who 'offer a spectacle' in the 'arena of the world' for men and angels.[1036]

However, there is an essential difference. In IV Macc. 17 the emphasis is on the brilliant victory of the martyrs; by contrast, Paul has in view the present lowliness and threat. But he too knows the image of the demanding contest at the end of which the ascetic contestant receives the crown of victory.[1037] In I Thess. 2.19 and Phil. 4.1 the communities founded by Paul appear as his crown of victory. The success of his missionary work takes on significance for the former persecutor's own eschatological fulfilment.

This variety of points of contact between the letters of Paul and IV Maccabees is striking, because in style, conceptuality and even more in intention and theology, Paul's letters are miles away from this mannered triumphal speech. We can hardly assume that the apostle knew this special work – as distinct from the Wisdom of Solomon, which in some ways is akin to it. What links the two is the common Jewish-Hellenistic milieu of Antioch or the double province administered from there. Here, as also with other examples, it becomes clear that the apostle's language has been shaped by the synagogue preaching within the triangle formed by Jerusalem, Tarsus and Antioch.

Furthermore this work, even more than its model, IV Maccabees, makes clear the ambivalence, which has already been mentioned, of the Jews in Syria and Palestine (in contrast to Egypt; geographically it is hard to separate the two), who, while faithful to the law, have had a Greek education. A highly rhetorical and popular philosophical form of language, stylized with some art – not to say artificiality – is combined with a self-conscious rigorous observance of the law revealed by God, which is put above all else. Here we can see a religious and ethnic identity which is probably unique in the period of the early empire. To the Greeks it could seem either repulsive – in the majority of cases – or ethically convincing among seekers who could find no inner support in the confusing multiplicity of cults. This helps us to understand the note about the 'great crowd of Greeks' who according to Josephus[1038] 'attended worship in the synagogues', particularly in Antioch.

8.1.4 The origin of the Christian community in Antioch

Against this historical background we can also get a better understanding of those brief statements of Luke about the particular development of the community in Antioch.

The view suggested by his account that the preaching of the gospel to 'Greeks', i.e. Greek-speaking non-Jews, first took place in Antioch is historically inaccurate. This took place to a smaller degree from the moment when Jewish-Christian 'Hellenists' left Jewish Palestine in the narrower sense, for example in the case of Philip in Samaria and Caesarea, and also of Paul himself in Damascus, Arabia and Tarsus. By contrast, Luke is following a 'salvation-historical scheme' which was probably put forward for the first time from Jerusalem.

The new development which Antioch brought was that for the first time the gospel was preached in a real metropolis, with numerous synagogues, not least on the periphery of the city and in the suburbs.[1039] If we begin from a Jewish population of between 30,000 and 50,000,[1040] which did not live so much in a relatively enclosed quarter, as in Alexandria or in early Rome,[1041] but scattered over different parts of the city, it becomes understandable why the small group of Hellenists in the foreign city did not seek to make contact with one synagogue community, but developed their activity on the periphery of several synagogues. They addressed above all interested sympathizers there and gathered these together first, probably soon, in various house communities along with Jewish Christians, who similarly joined the missionaries.[1042] This was presumably the same thing as happened in Rome. In other words, there was no longer that natural lengthier contact with synagogues which we must presuppose for the mother country of Palestine and also the smaller cities of Phoenicia and southern Syria. From the beginning 'messianic conventicles' were formed, and whether or not in addition links were maintained with a synagogue may have been left to the judgment of individual members of the community. In the case of Jewish Christians the bonds were presumably stronger than in the case of sympathizers. These quickly found their 'spiritual home' in the new eschatological community of salvation with its relatively free worship, inspired by the Spirit, the broad outlines of which we can imagine on the basis of Acts 2.42, 45 and I Cor. 11; 14. The prophetic-ecstatic element of an eschatological character with predictions, prophetic paraclesis, hymn-singing, glossolalia and its charismatic interpretation may have proved at least as attractive as later in Corinth, since in the indigenous Syrian religion, from of old numerous local cult places had given oracles, and religious ecstasy had always already played an important role.[1043]

The question of circumcision and the observance of the ritual commandments thus lost its significance among the former 'sympathizers'; in any case they had become meaningless to the Greek newcomers, while the Jewish Christians and 'liberal Jews' had relative freedom. They will at first have circumcised their own children, simply to avoid the charge of apostasy, as Paul did with Timothy.[1044] However, in common with Gentile Christians they will have dispensed with the observance of ritual regulations, while following them in dealing with Jews who observed the law strictly. At any rate the ritual law was not a further presupposition of salvation. The rise of such a small community was possible only given great personal freedom and respect. Paul himself in I Cor. 9.19–23 gives instructions on this, derived from practice. The respect for the 'conscience' or the 'faith' of the weak in I Cor. 8–10 and Rom. 14 also presupposes concrete experiences in the community. Here the imminent eschatological expectation and the presence of the Spirit was decisive. Paul will also already have given his instructions and reasons as contained in I Cor. 7.17–31 in Antioch and in the communities of Cilicia and Syria. The two principles formulated in I Cor. 7.19 and Gal. 6.15, 'For neither circumcision counts for anything nor uncircumcision, but (only) keeping the commandments of God', or, 'For neither circumcision counts for anything, nor uncircumcision, but (only) a new creation', express the same thing from different perspectives and describe in the tersest form the new modes of behaviour of the messianic community, made up of a mixture of Jews and Greeks. Someone who has been newly created 'in Christ' by the Spirit also keeps God's ethical commandments, which can be summed up in the commandment to love.[1045] This basic attitude again goes back to the preaching of Jesus, for whom the commandment to love pushed the ritual law into the background, and who knew that only the 'good tree can bring forth good fruits'.[1046] According to a scholion on Gal. 6.15 which appears in Euthalios, Synkellos and Photios, the formula in that verse goes back to an apocryphon of Moses. However, it will be Christian and presumably dependent on Gal. 6.15 or I Cor. 7.19, since in Judaism circumcision was regarded as a 'basic commandment of God'. Both formulas, by contrast, express the conviction of the 'Hellenistic' missionaries and Paul, which had a christological (eschatological) foundation.[1047] Moreover both texts, I Cor. 7.19 and Gal. 6.15, show that one cannot speak of a preaching 'free from the law' in the real sense in Paul, far less with the 'Hellenists'. Only the term 'critical of the law' is appropriate. The question was how far this criticism went in particular instances. Its ultimate roots lie in Jesus himself.

That here there were tensions with individual synagogues is suggested not only by the analogous reports of Luke about the difficulties of the Pauline mission from Damascus through Pisidian Antioch to Corinth and Ephesus, but also by the note in Suetonius.[1048] However, the size of the city, in which one could even withdraw and remain unnoticed in the short term, may have blunted these conflicts in Antioch.

Presumably this detachment was also favoured by the growing tensions between 'Greeks' and Jews after the pogrom in Alexandria in summer 38 and the subsequent demands by the megalomaniac Caligula. As 'the form of this world' was passing away and the kingdom of God and its eschatological plenipotentiary was coming ever nearer, the community of his anointed no longer wanted to be drawn into the business of 'this age',[1049] especially as the threatened temple in Jerusalem had already been 'desecrated' since the crucifixion of Jesus in Jerusalem and its cult had become obsolete.[1050] Neither the 'rulers of this world' in Jerusalem nor those in Rome had recognized the 'Lord of glory' (I Cor. 2.8). What were now breaking out were the messianic woes, caused by the 'enemy of God' on the model of Antiochus IV. God would preserve his community from the final trial in these times. For this reason, too, it was important to be restrained, not to allow oneself to be provoked, and to keep a distance from the disputes which were beginning.

This tendency was supported by the fact that as sympathizers, the majority of the new members of the community were legally 'Greeks', even if the Jewish Christian part of the community was by no means small and exercised spiritual leadership. The five 'prophets' and 'teachers' in Antioch in Acts 13.1, who represented something like a governing body of the community, were all Jews.[1051] Titus is the only Gentile Christian from Antioch from the time of Paul that we know of. Whether Luke came from there remains quite uncertain; if he did he would probably give more information about what had gone on. In Acts Luke appears first in Troas and then in Philippi.[1052] Gal. 2.11–13 and Paul's reaction to it show that the authority of the Jewish Christians continued to be decisive. Here we may not assume, as Bousset, Heitmüller, Bultmann and other representatives of the history-of-religions school did, that now a massive pagan syncretistic influence began which deeply influenced the simple messianic message of the earliest Christians from Judaea and changed it completely, as it also did the preaching of Paul.[1053] The building material of the structures of earliest Christian christology, soteriology and anthropology continued to be Jewish, even if they had a 'Hellenistic' veneer. Such material had already long been used in Jerusalem as well, and texts like the Wisdom of Solomon, Joseph and Asenath, II and even more IV Maccabees had a much stronger 'Hellenistic' colouring than the letters of Paul and the Gospels.

The new message could not deny its Palestinian Jewish origin even in Syria and Cilicia, but the gradually increasing 'Gentile Christian' majority favoured an inner detachment from the synagogue communities. The small group of founders who had been driven out of Jerusalem in any case no longer had a tie to particular synagogues in Antioch; for them their environment was above all a favourable mission opportunity. Should there be a conflict, it was better to retreat into one's small house community than to bring the conflict to a head. Similarly, the 'sympathizers' who had been won over to the new message will not have had such a strong personal tie to particular communities as old-established Jewish families; certainly sympathy and curiosity had driven them into the synagogue, but legally they never had the opportunity there really to gain completely equal rights. Even proselytes were initially always still second-class Jews[1054] by comparison with those who appealed proudly to their 'circumcision on the eighth day', their origin 'from the people of Israel, the tribe of Benjamin, as a Hebrew of the Hebrews', or even to their origin from 'the descendants of Abraham'.[1055] In the new, small and therefore narrow community, which together awaited the imminent coming of the Lord and in possession of the eschatological spirit celebrated its prophetically inspired and sometimes also rather chaotic worship, all these differences fell aside, like national, sociological and biological differences.[1056] Through the risen Kyrios, whose coming they longingly awaited, they had all equally become 'God's children' by means of the gift of the Spirit.[1057]

Thus this new, enthusiastic message in the long run formally compelled the separation from the synagogue communities, since such eschatological communities were difficult to accept for a fixed religious association which also exercised social and political functions, not least in a tense situation which was getting increasingly worse and therefore politically uncertain.

In addition (from the perspective of the synagogues), there was the fact that these people – enthusiasts driven out of Jerusalem with good reason – turned like parasites to the unsettled 'sympathizers' and confused them. It was a cause for rejoicing if they left the well-ordered synagogue committees in peace, or only bothered them on the periphery. 'Theologically', in any case, they could only be regarded as 'sectarians', not only because of their crazy, indeed blasphemous, message of the crucified and risen Jesus who was now said to be enthroned at the right hand of God and was to come as judge of the world, but also because in their eschatological enthusiasm they no longer took the law seriously, and neglected important parts of it. The highly-esteemed martyrs of the Maccabean period had given their lives for this law. Now suddenly circumcision was to be of little importance, indeed of no importance at all, among those who were really radical, and the traditional and well-considered distinction between full Jews, proselytes and godfearers was to be dropped. Finally, this novel worship of a messianic agitator executed by the prefect Pontius Pilate could cause additional offence to the Roman authorities, on whose understanding and protection Jews were particularly dependent because of the growing hostility of the urban masses. The best thing was to show them the door as quickly as possible. Thus in the metropolis, where people were not sitting painfully side by side and where the tense political situation suggested that the two sides should move apart, separation was unavoidable. So what Luke depicts in Acts 11.20 as the first successful preaching to the Greeks was probably the origin of a first larger 'Gentile Christian community' in which after some time Gentile Christians predominated, at least numerically.

From now on missionary expansion needed no longer to take place through direct disturbances in the synagogues, nor did it need to resort to public preaching in the streets; it could come about through the personal invitation of relatives, friends and others who showed interest to worship in the house communities. Here from the beginning an important motive was 'religious curiosity'. How this could attract a Gentile is shown by Paul in I Cor. 14.24: 'But if all prophesy, and an unbeliever or outsider enters, he is convicted by all, he is called to account by all; the secrets of his heart are disclosed; and so, falling on his face, he will worship God and declare that God is really among you.' This kind of pneumatic worship with not only an ethical but above all a soteriological orientation was something new in the ancient world, and must either have impressed or repelled pagan visitors. There can hardly have been a neutral attitude. The religious milieu of Syria will have been particularly receptive to such an enthusiastic-prophetic and eschatological-soteriological message. Here the worship in Antioch cannot have taken a very different course from that in Thessalonica and Corinth between eight and ten years later. Thus the formula which appears in I Thess. 5.19f., 'Do not quench the Spirit, do not despise prophesying, but test everything; hold fast to what is good', indirectly already characterizes the worship in Antioch. What Macedonian sobriety shrank from was highly prized on Syrian soil. The form of worship indicated by Paul – which was almost too free – was not his invention but part of the new message. By contrast, the form of worship first presupposed by Justin around 100 years later in Rome, with prayer, reading from scripture, sermon, prayer and celebration of the eucharist, which comes much closer to synagogue worship,[1058] will be a special development of the Roman community. Here, as I Clement shows, in accordance with Latin tradition good order was prized more highly than the working of the Spirit, and a direct Palestinian influence was also involved.[1059]

As well as the different form of worship, we also find other indications of separation. Already in the case of the 'Hellenists' in Jerusalem the eschatological self-designation ἐκκλησία θεοῦ indicated a distinction from the current term συναγωγή. Now baptism in the name of Jesus Christ came to be regarded outwardly as an eschatological religious 'rite of initiation' in contrast to circumcision, which also represented political acceptance into the Jewish alliance of peoples. Proselyte baptism was presumably not yet an institutional custom in the synagogue at that time (see above, 66). The celebration of the eucharist with the re-enactment of the last supper of Jesus and the saving significance of his death also had no parallel in Jewish worship. We do not know when the liturgical celebration on the first day of the week as the day of the resurrection was introduced. It is probably already to be presupposed with Paul.[1060] There is nothing to suggest that it did not already happen in Antioch. The Lord's Prayer and the christological acclamations also gave a distinctive stamp to worship. In these two forms of worship it was decisive that no longer 'the law' but the person of Christ as the redeemer sent by God stood at the centre. This gave worship a quite new personal reference. Christ's teaching could not be detached from his person. The word of God and the word of the Lord or Christ fundamentally became one and could be understood as both subjective and objective genitives.[1061] Finally, the cheaper and more practical form of the codex may first already have been used in this early period for individual important 'Holy Scriptures' like Isaiah and the Psalms, in contrast to the expensive and luxurious Torah scroll; moreover the use of the *nomina sacra*, the special writing of sacred names in place of the Hebrew tetragrammaton will have been introduced in the Holy Scriptures. The Greek Qere 'Kyrios' for YHWH was now to take on a quite new significance with a christological colouring in quotations from scripture.[1062]

In the capital of the frontier province of Syria, where the Roman authorities were probably already keeping an eye on the large Jewish community, this growing independence of a messianic group from Judaea which showed a special interest in winning over non-Jews could not remain hidden. This is all the more the case since the separation took place at a time of relative tension, indeed bloody controversy, between the different ethical and religious groups. So it is not surprising that this new community was given a name which derived from the name *Christos* which dominated everything in it and orientated itself on a nomenclature current among both Greeks and Romans. The designation Χριστιανοί (Acts 11.26) was to some degree in the air, and it was 'invented' where it was needed for the first time, in Antioch. The Roman authorities thus had their attention drawn to the Jewish missionary sect in the provincial capital, but we hear nothing of violent measures against it. At least outside Rome, people were tolerant of foreign superstition as long as it was not politically dangerous. But we shall have to discuss all this at more length later (see below, 225–30).

However, all this did not happen in a few months, but needed time to mature, i.e. some years. Moreover, Luke's indications of success are highly exaggerated – as numbers often are in ancient historians. The number of occasional listeners may, however, have been substantially greater. If there were around one hundred baptized Christians in Antioch after three or four years, that was already quite a lot. There is great uncertainty about the numerical success of the earliest Christian missionaries precisely because of Luke's exaggerated figure,[1063] so it is also difficult for us to imagine the reality of these first Gentile Christian communities, which are so alien to us. Gregory of Nyssa reports in his life of Gregory Thaumaturgus that when around 250 as a young man he became bishop of the church in his not insignificant ancestral city of Amasia in Pontus, it consisted of seventeen Christians. Under Licinius, around sixty-five years later, the city then had several churches, not least as a result of the missionary effectiveness of this great teacher.[1064] And the small group of around twelve disciples of John in Ephesus before Paul should also make us think.[1065]

8.2 Antioch and Jerusalem

The development in the first predominantly 'Gentile Christian' community in Antioch can never be completely separated from what happened in Jerusalem. In particular, the authentic letters of Paul, as the earliest literary evidence, show that no real separatism can be demonstrated in the early period of the new messianic sect. There may have been tensions and parties; in an enthusiastic movement like earliest Christianity these can never be avoided, but there is no evidence of definitive divisions or splits in the earliest period. They would have made the new message unbelievable from the start. The one Lord,[1066] the one Spirit[1067] and the community as the 'one body of Christ'[1068] made cohesion, not least with the 'mother community' in Jerusalem, an obligation. If this is true for the Paul of the letters during his mission in Macedonia, Achaea and the province of Asia despite all the disappointment and deeper theological differences,[1069] it is even more true for Antioch and the other communities in Syria. Barnabas was without doubt a guarantor of this connection between Jerusalem and Antioch. It is striking that this man in particular, who by virtue of his origin had a special link with the Jerusalem community, now for a long time became Paul's missionary partner, and after the break between him and Paul, he was replaced by Seila-Silvanus from Jerusalem, though only for a journey of around two and a half years. Paul took this bond, which linked him to Jerusalem and was probably obligatory for all Christian communities up to the execution of James around 62 CE or until the flight to Pella,[1070] very seriously right up to his arrest in the Jerusalem temple (Acts 21.27–33), although the more time went on, the more trouble it caused him.

8.2.1 Paul and Barnabas

At between eight and nine years (*c.*39/40 to 48 or 49), the period of Paul and Barnabas's joint work in Antioch, the double province of Syria and Cilicia and later, as Acts 13 and 14 show, in the adjacent regions of Cyprus, Pamphylia, Pisidia and Lycaonia, lasted longer than the apostle's seven- to eight-year activity in the Aegean which is illuminated by the letters. If anyone influenced Paul theologically, then Barnabas must have done so more than any other person. However, given the strong personality and spiritual power of the former scribe, the reverse will have been even more the case, namely that Paul had an influence on Barnabas and that Barnabas in turn became the mediator of Pauline ideas. But we know practically nothing of Barnabas's theological thought. With his failure in Gal. 2.13 or his vigorous dispute with Paul in Acts 15.36–39 he vanishes from 'church history'. The letter which was subsequently attributed to him has nothing to do with him; at best it is interesting that the unknown author of the letter named after him, writing at least two but more likely three generations later, attributes to Barnabas a rigid criticism of the ritual law, especially circumcision[1071] – that is, presupposing that the title of the letter is original.[1072] In general, the observation by R. A. Lipsius that 'the earlier church tradition is quite silent about Barnabas',[1073] is correct. As a rule he was merely seen as the travelling companion of the apostle Paul. 'He is called an apostle in the real sense only in the fourth century.'[1074]

At best it was conceded that he was one of the seventy disciples of Luke 10.1.[1075] Be this as it may, right at the beginning of the work the Pseudo-Clementine Recognitions have him still appearing as an individual missionary under the emperor Tiberius in Rome; he impresses Clement so much that Clement travels to Palestine after him and is introduced by him to Peter in Caesarea.[1076] In the *Actus Petri Vercellenses*, by contrast, he is sent as a companion of Paul's along with Timothy from Rome to Macedonia.[1077] He does not appear at all in the Nag Hammadi texts. Although Barnabas is the most important figure – apart from Paul – in Paul's letters and in Acts after Peter and James, in a later period up to the fourth/fifth century he retreats right into the background as compared with the real apostles. When he is mentioned at all, he stands in the shadow of the two great apostles.

Paul and Luke are strikingly in agreement in attesting that this was originally not the case. The 'missionary collaboration' of the two in the 'mission to the Gentiles' is described by Luke in Acts 13 and 14. In connection with this, according to Luke both together present the basis of this mission, the dropping of the circumcision of Gentile Christians, in Jerusalem to the apostles and elders.[1078] They are supported here by Peter and James with two speeches, the points of which are strikingly different. The Jerusalem authorities, apostles and elders, agree to the compromise proposal of James with the so-called Apostolic Decree, which dispenses with the requirement of circumcision. The two delegates return successfully to Antioch: circumcision and the observation of the ritual law (with the exception of the two dietary regulations in the decree) are no longer to apply to Gentile Christians. We need not go further here into the considerable differences between Acts 15 and Gal. 2.1–10. Since F.C. Baur an enormous amount has been written about them. For us the basic agreement between Gal. 2.1–10 and Acts 15 over the *dramatis personae* is enough. On the one side were Barnabas and Paul, as representatives of Antioch (and the mission communities in Syria and Cilicia), accompanied by further delegates who were probably subordinate to them. In 15.2 Luke speaks of 'and some of the others' (καὶ τινας ἄλλους ἐξ αὐτῶν). Paul, who in retrospect puts his own role right in the foreground – modern 'modesty' was not his style – mentions only the 'Gentile Christian' Titus, who is close to him.[1079] The predominance of the first person singular in his account, though at decisive points it is replaced by the first person plural, on the one hand shows its 'one-sidedness', but at the same time indicates that despite the painful break which took place afterwards, Barnabas cannot simply be passed over.[1080] Even after the break with Antioch, he remains an important person for Paul; indeed basically, after Cephas and James, he is the only one of the leading authorities originally in Jerusalem whom Paul mentions by name.[1081] Although in Gal. 2.1–10 Paul, who for a long time had been an independent missionary again,[1082] puts himself so completely in the foreground, he does concede that as his partner in mission on an equal footing, Barnabas was in full agreement with him in the negotiations and that the opening up of the Gentile mission without circumcision and the ritual law applied to them both.[1083] On the other hand, the parenthesis in 2.6b, 'those who were of repute added nothing to me', suggests that either then or later, say after the clash in Antioch, Barnabas did accept the obligation to have something 'added'. As 2.13 shows, he tended to be ready to compromise. The 'addition' could be the instructions of the 'Apostolic Decree' relating to eating together.[1084] Nevertheless, there is some reason for the emphasis on the first person singular. When Paul emphasizes in 2.7 that after the presentation of his 'gospel which I preach among the Gentiles' (2.2), 'those of repute' arrived at the insight (ἰδόντες) 'that I had been entrusted with the gospel to the uncircumcised,[1085] just as Peter had been entrusted with the gospel to the circumcised', and that herein lay the special 'grace entrusted' to him by God,[1086] he is emphasizing the fact that the Risen Christ had called him from the beginning, 'that he might preach him among the Gentiles' (Gal. 1.16), and that he did not simply go to Jerusalem as a mere delegate of the Antiochenes, as the other side probably claimed. He understood himself to be as much a 'called apostle of Jesus Christ' as the Jerusalem authorities. The comparison with the charge of the risen Christ to Peter to proclaim the message of salvation to the Jews shows the tremendous eschatological, salvation-historical self-consciousness of the apostle to the Gentiles.[1087] Here he was making the claim to be the first messenger of Christ, whom the Lord had sent to the non-Jews with a message which had been specially revealed to him. The message which he explains to the Jerusalem authorities can only be his gospel critical of the law, which he himself received from the risen Christ (Gal. 1.10ff., see above, 100f.). Paul's report about the memorable council in Jerusalem also resolutely contradicts the claim that his gospel as he develops it in Galatians, Romans and also I and II Corinthians is only the product of a later development. This unique comparison with the 'apostolate' of Peter not only indicates that he claimed the primacy for the mission to the Gentiles – critical of the law (no other mission is conceivable for him) – but also suggests that the period between Easter and his call had not been all that great.[1088] This makes it improbable that before his call there had already been a deliberate mission to the Gentiles, 'free of the law', which was worthy of the name, whether by 'Galileans' or by 'Hellenists', as is constantly asserted.[1089] An intensive 'pre-Pauline' mission to the Gentiles is impossible on chronological grounds alone. However, there will have been isolated baptisms of godfearers.[1090] This again explains the striking reason given, 'lest somehow I should be running or have run in vain'(2.2). If the community in Jerusalem now – contrary to an earlier attitude – called for the circumcision of the 'Gentiles', Paul's whole proclamation of the gospel to the 'Gentiles' since his call, i.e. since Damascus, would have been in vain,[1091] as his message and the faith brought about by it would be 'nothing' if Christ had not risen from the dead (I Cor. 15.14). For Paul, a separated Gentile Christian church which alone was 'orthodox', i.e. a divided body of Christ, was an impossible idea.

In the extended conversation with Peter (and James) about thirteen or fourteen years before, this point had not yet been controversial, certainly not because at that time Paul had only been a missionary to the Jews but because – say since Agrippa I (41–44) – the situation in Jerusalem had gradually become more acute.[1092] Presumably Barnabas, who by then already had a hand in the game, and Paul himself had reminded the Jerusalem authorities of the visit at that time, and, as Luke's carefully stylized speech in Acts 15.7–11 shows, Peter will have mediated between the Antiochene delegates and the other Jerusalem people. So Paul can refer to the comparison with Peter (Gal. 2.7f.), with which he had indeed agreed; for that reason Peter later visited Antioch and lived in full table-fellowship with the

Gentile Christians. As a result, after Peter's yielding for fear of the delegates from James, Paul can talk to him about salvation by faith alone, which appears as the climax in Peter's short speech in Acts.[1093] Here, too, the problem of the theological influence of Paul (or indeed of Barnabas) on Peter reappears – in conjunction with the – intensive – moulding of him by the preaching of Jesus, a moulding which found expression in Mark and in the Deutero-Petrine I Peter.

Although in Gal. 2.1–10 Paul thus puts himself in the foreground as the first and real 'apostle to the Gentiles',[1094] the facts as reported also apply to Barnabas, and in his quite tendentious account Paul cannot pass over Barnabas's role if he is to be truthful. At that time Barnabas was a conversation-partner with equal rights; the two of them together fought for the good cause of the 'Gentile Christians' in Antioch and the other communities of Syria and Cilicia, and convinced the 'pillars' in Jerusalem. Much as the scriptural scholar Paul may have been the spokesman in the theological argument – for good reason Luke makes Paul the speaker in Acts 13 and 14[1095] – Barnabas, who was familiar with conditions in Jerusalem and was esteemed there, will have played at least an equal part in the success. This was the case even if in retrospect – with some justification – Paul regarded himself as the first and most successful 'missionary to the Gentiles'.

The opinion which Paul had of himself, and which after the break with Peter, Barnabas and the community in Antioch would have been offensive to many Christians in Syria and even more in Judaea, may have been a reason why the Jerusalem Christians saw the beginnings of the Gentile mission in a different way from Paul, and here gave preference to Hellenists like Philip or then even Peter himself, with the baptism of Cornelius. One could also cite Barnabas in this connection. No wonder that Luke the mediator here prefers the Jerusalem picture, at least partially, even if he also indicates between the lines that it was all rather more complicated. This could be all the easier for him, since Paul did not report very much at a later date about those long sixteen years between Damascus and Antioch which came to such a bitter end – we do not hear a word about them in Romans apart from the enigmatic 15.19. Even in Gal. 1 and 2 he does so only under

pressure, and makes it clear that for him this long period ends
with a very severe disappointment. Only in this connection does
Antioch appear once in his letters, in Gal. 2.11. If we did not have
Luke, we could not put Gal. 1 and 2 in any kind of meaningful
historical order. The questionable chronological reconstructions
by G. Lüdemann are the best indication that here we cannot get
further without Luke.[1096]

For this reason this long, close collaboration between the two
men on an equal footing, which then ended in such an unhappy
way, must prove all the more striking. In contrast to the later
church tradition and also to some modern monographs,
Barnabas was not basically a subordinate 'fellow worker' among
others.[1097] He was an old disciple who was respected in the earliest
community in Jerusalem and who also had personal roots there.
In I Cor. 9.6 Paul emphasizes that only he and Barnabas earned
their living by their own craft during their missionary journeys, in
contrast to the other missionaries; whether they had the same or
a similar profession[1098] must remain open. So must the question
whether Barnabas, like Paul, was unmarried (or a widower); however, on the basis of the double 'we' in I Cor. 9.4f., I would
assume that in that case Paul would have expressed himself somewhat unclearly.[1099] Presumably Barnabas will have been treated,
like Paul, as an 'apostle' in Antioch; however, it is improbable
that he was regarded as such in Jerusalem.[1100] For nowhere is it
evident that like Paul he could refer to 'seeing' the Lord (I Cor.
9.1) and could therefore be counted among the very limited
number of 'all the apostles' (ἀπόστολοι πάντες) or the 'apostles
before me' (πρὸ ἐμοῦ ἀπόστολοι).[1101] Paul nevertheless puts
Barnabas alongside himself – albeit in a somewhat obscure
formulation – in I Cor. 9.5 when contrasting them with 'the other
apostle and brothers of the Lord'; the reference is to their long
missionary experience in Syria and adjacent areas. This indication in no way means that the break in Antioch was healed again.
In the later Gal. 2.13 the former indignation still resounds in the
'even he was carried away by their insincerity' (συναπήχθη αὐτῶν
τῇ ὑποκρίσει). 'No precise historical evidence ... can be produced that he was in fact counted among the apostles'.[1102]
The solution to the problem is that the extent of the apostolic

circle was not clearly defined and that there was dispute over it between Antioch and Jerusalem, indeed perhaps even in Jerusalem itself.[1103]

On the basis of Acts 4.36, scholars still sometimes doubt whether Barnabas joined the community in Jerusalem at a very early stage. But all the details are disputed. His real name was the very frequent name Joseph, and Barnabas was only a surname given to him by the apostles. Luke's interpretation of the name, 'son of consolation' (υἱὸς παρακλήσεως), is remarkable, but the origin of the name itself is enigmatic.[1104] Taking account of the fact that in Acts 13.1 Barnabas is mentioned first among the 'prophets' in Antioch, is given his surname by 'the apostles', and that this, as in the case of Cephas/Peter, becomes the name under which he is constantly referred to in the Christian community, the interpretation '*filius prophetiae*', going back to Hugo Grotius, which is put forward in the old commentaries, still seems to be most plausible. In a Greek-speaking environment, the *bar nabiyya* (or similar) was then smoothed down to become *bar naba* and had the meaning 'the one with prophetic gifts'. In that case, Luke's translation would be a periphrasis for the 'man of the (prophetically inspired) admonition' or 'the one gifted with inspired speech'.[1105]

Now the Barnabas of Acts has had to suffer a great deal in anti-Lukan criticism. Here are a few examples. According to G. Schille, Barnabas the Cypriot probably had nothing to do with Jerusalem; Luke merely transferred him there to introduce him effectively to readers. That he visited Jerusalem before Acts 15 or Gal. 2.1ff. remains uncertain; moreover (also according to Haenchen), the 'field' which he bought could have been on Cyprus; in that case the apostles, i.e. for Schille the earliest Christian itinerant missionaries, need not have received the proceeds in Jerusalem. The giving of the name by the apostles is of course a Lukan invention, and possibly also his levitical origin, although Schille will not allow Haenchen's argument, 'As the bearer of the name of a pagan divinity, however, Barnabas could not have been a Levite', 'since the Hellenistic period with its sometimes bizarre syncretism did not even stop short at Judaism'.[1106] Already according to Loisy, Luke introduces

Barnabas here only in order to offer the reader at least one example of the sale of property for the common purse and at the same time to connect one of the most important figures in earliest Christianity in this way with the earliest community in Jerusalem, thus confirming his own picture of it. This is a 'reflected, thin and artificial anticipation'. The introduction of Barnabas prepares him for his future role in 11.22. The very question of the name points to a deliberate manipulation on the part of the 'redactor'. In reality Barnabas belongs to the Hellenists in Antioch, and the 'redactor' has deliberately transplanted 'Joseph surnamed Barnabas, (a Levite?), a Cypriot' into his description of the earliest community.[1107]

For Schmithals, too, Barnabas is merely 'a leading missionary of Syrian Christianity' and was 'presumably never a member of the Jerusalem community'. It was Luke who first 'transposed him (like Paul ...) to Jerusalem in 4.36'.[1108] Contrary to all historical reality, he argues that Luke wants 'to derive all Christian activity and preaching from the Twelve Apostles as the original witnesses and authentic bearers of tradition. In this way any other origin of the gospel independent of the circle of the Twelve Apostles is to be excluded.'[1109] But in I Cor. 15.5 does not Paul himself put Peter and after him the Twelve at the head of the witnesses to the resurrection, and does he not emphasize expressly in 15.11 that all the witnesses cited, including himself, proclaim the one gospel claimed in 15.1? Isn't his attention (along with his travelling plans) directed in an amazing way to Jerusalem, which he mentions ten times – far more than all the other cities, thus also informing his communities about events and people there, while he mentions Antioch only once? Isn't this completely unrestrained criticism of Luke just a pretext for developing one's own creative imagination as freely as possible?

But even where writers do not aim so high, and do not completely deny a stay of Barnabas in Jerusalem, they make him a leading 'Hellenist' who comes to Antioch with those who were driven out of Jerusalem, although he is not mentioned in Acts 6. They relegate reports like Acts 9.27, the introduction of Saul through Barnabas in Jerusalem or 11.22–24, the sending of Barnabas by 'the community' in Jerusalem (not by the apostles) to Antioch, similarly to the sphere of Lukan invention in the same way as they do his detour to Tarsus, to get Paul (11.25). Luke is said to have produced the early relationship to Paul from the later collaboration between the two men.[1110] But perhaps scholars are making things too easy for themselves with all these hypotheses. First of all there is the name, 'Joseph who is called Barnabas' ('Ἰωσὴφ δὲ ὁ ἐπικληθεὶς Βαρναβᾶς). This is clearly a surname, not a patronym. This enigmatic additional name must in all probability have been given by Aramaic speakers. Not only the fact that pagan theophoric names for Jews hardly occur in a Semitic language tells against a patronym. Conversely, Semitic names with the first syllable Bar = son are relatively rare in Greek-speaking Judaism outside Palestine, but more frequent in the mother country. And besides that, his name is Barnabas and not Barnabou, which is quite different.[1111] Thus in the case of a Jew the name points towards Palestine, and it is hard to see why this name, meaning 'the one gifted with inspired speech', should not have been given to him in the early period of the Jerusalem community as a recognition of his gift.[1112] That he was not one of the 'Hellenists' who celebrated their worship in Greek is suggested, despite his origin in Cyprus, by his special family link with the Holy City, attested in the person of his nephew (or cousin) John Mark, the son of a well-to-do Mary, in whose house Peter stayed.[1113] The property (certainly not on Cyprus) and the levitical origin are also indications of this link.[1114] It is dishonest to accuse Luke of simply having added 'Levite' in 4.36 because it looks better; in that case it would have been far more effective had he made Barnabas a priest.[1115] The argument of Preuschen and Haenchen that as a Levite he would not have been allowed to bear a pagan theophoric name[1116] is quite foolish, quite apart from the fact that it is highly improbable that this surname was understood in those terms.

In reality, as an Aramaic-speaking Jew who had a command of Greek, in a way comparable to men like John Mark, Silas/Silvanus, Judas Barsabbas or the Cypriot Mnason, 'an old disciple',[1117] Barnabas belonged among the 'Hebrews' who took part in worship in Aramaic, which they could understand. He can be counted a member of the circle of the 'Graeco-Palestinians' who belonged to both cultural and linguistic areas and whose predominant importance for earliest Christianity is too readily suppressed in favour of the 'pure Hellenists', who knew no Aramaic. So there is no real reason to count Barnabas among the 'Hellenists' – defined by their liturgical assembly held in Greek – who were driven out in connection with the persecution of Stephen.[1118] On the other hand, the Western text goes too far when it turns Joseph who is named Barsabbas and bears the surname Justus, the candidate at the election of a new member of the Twelve, into Barnabas. How easily Luke could have replaced an S with a N and omitted a B to bring his important hero even nearer to the group of Twelve![1119] However, we should take seriously the form Ἰωσῆς in Acts 4.36, clearly the more difficult reading, since it is typically Palestinian and does not occur again in Luke.[1120] Ἰωσήφ would then have entered the text very early as a biblicistic correction.

The questionable separation of Barnabas from Jerusalem, in analogy to that of Paul, is caused by the ahistorical tendency, in the footsteps of F. C. Baur, to make the gulf between Jerusalem and Antioch as wide as possible from the beginning. Behind this lies a latent aversion to the Judaism of the mother country.

The fact that the Antiochenes sent Barnabas and Paul as negotiators to Jerusalem also tells against all these attempts. Barnabas was sent because he enjoyed great respect in Jerusalem, and Paul as a Christian 'scribe' because – as we see from his letters – he could argue so well. Here the stakes were highest – theologically as well – for Paul. In Gal. 2.1 he therefore uses the singular ἀνέβην, especially since in the meantime he has broken with Antioch. By contrast, the κατ' ἀποκάλυψιν has its closest parallel in Acts 13.1–3.

Here we can only assume from Acts 15.2, the report which Gal. 2.1 here illuminates in an interesting way, that both together are sent from Antioch to Jerusalem. Nor is it correct to assume that Luke makes both appear only as marginal 'extras'. In 15.4 they report their mission success at length. There is a heated discussion among the assembled 'apostles and elders' about their narrative, which prompts Peter to speak. After he has finished speaking, Barnabas and Paul once again report 'the signs and wonders which God has done through them among the Gentiles' (15.12); this is followed by James's speech, at the end of which is the compromise proposal of the 'Apostolic Decree'. In other words, the two delegates finally make their case, and their request for the recognition of this 'apostolate' critical of the law is approved by the first men in Jerusalem, James and Peter/Cephas. Both in Gal. 2.9, where James is mentioned as the first and Cephas as the second of the three pillars, and the John who is well known from Acts 3–4 and 8 appears as the third authority, but also in Acts 15, where the speech of James brings the positive division, the situation among the leaders in Jerusalem also becomes visible. However, we know only through Luke why there was a shift here and why James suppressed Peter from the first place which he occupied in Acts 1–10. It was a consequence of the persecution by Herod Agrippa I (see below, 252–7).

Finally, this relatively strong tie of Barnabas to Jerusalem also becomes visible in Gal. 2.13, where Barnabas, like the other Jewish Christians in Antioch, allows himself to be 'carried along', through Cephas/Peter's fear of James's delegates, to break off eucharistic table-fellowship with the Gentile Christians. Paul's form of expression suggests that this 'defection' took place after some hesitation,[1121] but evidently the tie to Jerusalem and the solidarity with the other Jewish Christians in Antioch were stronger than the mission shared with Paul over long years which also had a theological basis. Probably this – final – break only took place some time later than the great success in Jerusalem, i.e. around 51/52, after the so-called second journey, where Luke enigmatically gives all too brief reports about Paul's visit to Caesarea, Jerusalem (?) and Antioch.[1122] Presumably at that time Silas/Silvanus also returned to Jerusalem. After the explosion of Gal. 2.11ff., Silas probably could not accompany Paul again as a missionary 'companion', and subsequently the apostle would not have spent any more time in Antioch.[1123] That the community there, with which he was associated for around eight or nine years, completely disappears from Paul's letters except for the account of the catastrophe in Gal. 2.11, shows a deep hurt which was not fully healed even years afterwards. This follows from Galatians and from the restraint towards Peter in the two letters to the Corinthians. Only in the imprisonment in Caesarea or in Rome, where Mark evidently meets him again and proves useful, does the resentment seem to have been stilled.[1124]

Presumably it was the first vigorous argument between Barnabas and Paul over John Mark in Antioch after the 'Council' that led to their separation as missionaries. Barnabas went back with Mark to his home province of Cyprus, and Paul went with Silas/Silvanus, whom he had got to know more closely since Jerusalem, to Cilicia and over the Taurus to Lycaonia, then to cross Asia Minor. Evidently he now attached importance – particularly after the 'Council' – to having a companion from Jerusalem instead of Barnabas. Around two and a half years later he met Barnabas again and also – probably surprisingly – Peter in Antioch; this was followed by the real break: perhaps the deepest rupture in his life between his conversion and his arrest. Luke may have known of these events, but they were decidedly too unedifying for Theophilus. Therefore he contents himself with the reference to the 'vigorous dispute' (παροξυσμός) over Mark in 15.39, which led to the separation of the missionary ways, but not yet to the final theological break.

I believe that Paul's sparse but at the same time illuminating information about Barnabas will be understood better if we trust Luke's accounts rather more than is usual today. Barnabas was a disciple of the very early period in Jerusalem who won esteem in the earliest community and among its leaders through the gift of a substantial piece of land[1125] and who, although born in Cyprus, as a Levite speaking Greek and Aramaic and with family ties to the Holy City, belonged to the 'Hebrews', but was a 'link man' with the Hellenists. Therefore he was not one of those who left Jerusalem because of the persecution. It would be quite conceivable that the Hellenists who had fled to Damascus drew Paul's attention to Barnabas as a 'link man' after his return from Arabia, when he was considering the visit to Jerusalem. Like much else, this too of course remains an unprovable conjecture. It should not surprise us that the Jerusalem community had a burning interest in the special development in Antioch, the populous provincial capital and alongside Alexandria the most important metropolis in the Roman East. So, just as Paul visited Jerusalem to discover about Peter, it is only too understandable that the 'link man' Barnabas, who was particularly interested in these events on behalf of the community in Jerusalem, should have travelled to Antioch to inform himself about them personally. The extension of earliest Christianity cannot be imagined at all without constantly renewed contacts between the old communities and those which were coming into being. In outward appearance Jesus himself had already been a 'itinerant teacher' with support in various places and families; he had already sent out his disciples, and after Easter things were hardly otherwise.

However, there were certain geographical and religious limits. In Antioch such a boundary had been crossed by the formation of a community independent of the synagogue in which circumcision and the ritual law no longer played an essential role, where eucharistic table-fellowship between Jewish Christians and 'Gentile Christians' was possible without problems, and the Gentile Christians soon predominated. Therefore this was a cause for concern, and no one was more suited to taking up such contacts than Barnabas, who certainly also knew normative 'Hellenists', say his fellow-countrymen from Cyprus (Acts 11.20). Personal acquaintance through visits and the trust based on it played a fundamental role in this oriental milieu, which had no post or forms of telecommunication. Letters had to be sent by messengers (and could also be elucidated by questioning them).[1126] The danger of being led astray by 'false brethren' and deceivers was great, so letters of commendation were also important. This problem exists throughout the first century and far into the second.[1127] In Acts 11.22 also, Luke does not say anything about a legitimation by the apostles, any more than he does in Acts 9.26–30. What is decisive for him is the inner cohesion of the communities, and this is also attested by texts like I Cor. 15.1–11; 9.1–6; I Thess. 2.14; Rom. 15.43; Gal. 1.2, indeed by the authentic letters of Paul generally – despite all the difficulties.

If Barnabas remains in Antioch, according to 11.2ff. he does so because he is needed more in this new growing but still unconsolidated community than in Jerusalem and the surrounding areas; he may well have enjoyed the open milieu and the broad mission field more than the narrow situation in Jerusalem. It is also clear – although Luke depicts this differently – that the earliest Jerusalem community tolerated the gaining of 'god-fearers' and other Gentiles, and did not just look with suspicion on their baptism by the Hellenists outside Jewish Palestine, despite a lack of circumcision, and their acceptance into the community, but in part welcomed it. This initial tolerance seems to me to be connected with the open attitude of Jesus to sinners and marginal settlers in Israel, and also with individual Gentiles. The recollection of Jesus' conduct must still have been particularly powerful during these first ten to twenty years. How could his model and his activity have been forgotten so quickly?

That Barnabas can then seek out Paul in Tarsus some three or four years after the meeting between Peter and Paul around 39/40 CE and can bring him to the provincial capital is connected with the fact that the Cilician communities had become relatively independent,[1128] whereas the situation in the Syrian metropolis became more critical, so that a theologian with Paul's competence in the scriptures, capacity to argue strongly, resolution and capacity for organization was urgently needed. It could be that the apostle's family favoured the rapid formation of a stable core community in Tarsus, though we do not hear of it elsewhere.[1129]

The partnership in teaching and mission lasting almost ten years which now begins was possible only because despite all the differences, there was a fundamental theological agreement between the two people involved. Barnabas, who was presumably the older, may externally have had the greater authority, since he had also been respected as a disciple in Jerusalem from earliest times. Around 40 CE, about ten years after the Passover at which Jesus died, there may have still been many Jews – not just in Galilee – who had known Jesus or at least had heard him in person and had been impressed by him. Barnabas *could* have been one of them, and *to this degree* even the legend in Clement of Alexandria and later, which includes him among the seventy of Luke 10.1, would not be completely remote from historical reality (see above, n. 1075). It is striking that Luke, who attaches importance to the sequence in which names are given, initially puts Barnabas first,[1130] but then has Paul in first place after his great speech in Pisidian Antioch;[1131] after that, the order of names

changes again.[1132] Presumably Luke wants to indicate that both
have the same status; in 14.4, 14 – as a typical Lukan 'exception',
by which, contrary to his usual account, he leaves a back door
open – he calls both of them apostles and in so doing perhaps
gives the Antiochene view. But in the last mention of the pair[1133] in
15.35, Paul comes first, and four verses later, with their departure
to Cyprus, Barnabas and Mark take their leave of Acts. Shortly
beforehand, with his speech in Jerusalem and the mention of his
biblical name Simeon[1134] by James, Luke has done the same thing
with Peter. Peter, too, must leave the stage. Luke makes the
figures which he no longer needs as a narrator disappear merci-
lessly, though this certainly does not mean that he did not know
substantially more of them. So we should not suppose that Luke
had no information whatever about Barnabas and the early Paul
either, and was therefore compelled to invent details. Rather, he
leaves out everything which disrupts his narrative thread or which
he does not want to report – because it is offensive.

As a theological thinker and probably also as a preacher, the
former scribe Paul was superior to the older Barnabas. Therefore
in Luke, too, he is the spokesman, as he is already in the dispute
with Elymas Barjesus.[1135] We may assume that, as was probably
also the case to a much lesser degree in the encounter between
Peter and Paul, during their long work together Paul above all
influenced Barnabas and that they were of one opinion on basic
theological and christological questions, for example that salvation is brought about through Christ alone and appropriated in
faith in him, so that the law has lost its significance for salvation.
Such a shared mission preaching was possible only on such a
clear basis; the same thing is true of their joint representation of
the Antiochene concern that the requirement of circumcision
and observance of the law would not just hinder the 'Gentile
mission', but indeed make it impossible.

Now as Barnabas stands first in the 'list of prophets' of 13.1,
followed by Simeon called Niger, Lucius of Cyrene, Manaen the
confidant of the tetrarch Herod (Antipas) and Paul, he must
have played a role, indeed the leading role in Antioch, on the
basis of his education and his gifts, and the respect he enjoyed
in Jerusalem. Paul's position at the end recalls the list in I Cor.

15.2–10 and does not exclude the possibility that he was a more successful missionary and preacher than the others. This could express a lack in the outsider and former persecutor, who in addition could not appeal to a special relationship of trust with the leading figures in the community in Jerusalem. It is striking that all five names relate back to the Palestinian community: Simeon through the form of his name, which is quite rare in the Diaspora.[1136] Lucius of Cyrene may be one of the Cyrenaicans expelled from Jerusalem;[1137] Manaen/Menahem is not only Jewish-Palestinian in the form of his name, but the indication that he was a friend of Herod Antipas marks him out as a member of the Jewish-Palestinian aristocracy.[1138] So all five come either from the mother country or, like Lucius and Paul, evidently spent a long time there. The five names listed by Luke presumably form something like the leading group in the first ten to fifteen years of the community, comparable to the Twelve in Jerusalem and the Seven among the 'Hellenists'. Here it is striking that of the last five of the Seven, only one appears again among the five 'prophets' in Antioch as someone who has been expelled from Jerusalem: the enigmatic Nicolaus, a proselyte from Antioch, about whom there are special legendary reports in Irenaeus and above all Clement of Alexandria, and traces of whom we find again – perhaps – in the Apocalypse.[1139]

These numerous names, of the 'Twelve', the 'Seven' and the 'Five', and then again in the lists of greetings in Paul's letters, for example in Romans 16, only show us how little we know about earliest Christianity. At the same time it becomes clear that this was not an anonymous movement in which 'collective creativity' predominated, but that everything depended on the authority of the individual teachers and prophets. Indeed, on any occasion only the individual could become a Christian. Rather, we must reckon with a plurality of individualities. Here it is amazing that this expansive enthusiastic-messianic movement did not rapidly fall apart into many sectarian groups. Working against this was the fact that the really normative missionaries of the early period were aware of having been sent out by the one Lord as 'apostles of Jesus' Christ and did not simply preach their private religious experiences, but the message which had been entrusted to them.

This tie to the 'one truth of the gospel', i.e. ultimately to the one Lord, remained the bond which united the church in the 'apostolic age' which is so dark for us, despite all the disputes over opinions and all the sometimes bitter controversies, on top of which came external pressure. When Paul speaks impressively of 'the apostles of Jesus Christ', he does not have in view his own individuality, which was certainly difficult, but the whole of this circle of the ἀπόστολοι πάντες, i.e. all those who 'had seen the Lord', that circle which is largely unknown to us. But that was not yet enough. A few towering personalities countered the danger of sectarian splintering; we do at least know something about them, though in very different degrees, thanks to Paul and Luke. They were the three 'pillars' James, Peter and John; men like Philip, and last but not least Barnabas and (more than all the others) Paul.

8.2.2 The year together in Antioch

Luke makes Paul's activity with Barnabas in Antioch begin with a stay of one year. Here he expresses himself very briefly and somewhat unskilfully, so that the Western text 'corrects' him: 'Now it happened that they came together for a whole year in the community and taught a considerable crowd of people.'[1140] Luke has the reference to the year from tradition. His line of thought is that after a large number of Greeks had already come to the faith through the preaching of the 'Hellenists' who had been driven out (11.21), and a 'considerable crowd' had been won over by the spirit-filled preaching of Barnabas (11.24, 26: ὄχλος ἱκανός), the process was continued by the joint appearance of Barnabas and Paul. Their teaching together happens in the assembled community, i.e. probably in the new house churches, and not, say, on the street: in other words, the members of the community who have already been won over are strengthened, and new ones are gained by the preaching of the pair. The final result of this is that people in Antioch are made aware of this new movement and are given the new, unusual designation *Christianoi*. Lake and Cadbury freely translate συνάγεσθαι 'were entertained in the church for a whole year'.[1141] But as Luke often uses the verb in the sense of 'assemble',[1142] what is meant here is certainly 'assembling' for worship. This also corresponds with reality. The real place of the earliest Christian 'mission' was the liturgical assembly. After the community had been founded – and that had already happened in Antioch some years back – interested parties and acquaintances were invited to it. However, the missionary success, as almost always, may have been heavily exaggerated by Luke. In Gal. 2.11f. Paul does not presuppose any tremendously large community. Thus for Luke 'assembling in the community' and 'teaching' belong inseparably together. In the case of Paul, appearing in the synagogue was always only a preliminary stage towards building up a community. In Antioch this separation had already taken place soon after the community was founded, before his arrival. We may infer from Acts 15.3, 23, 41 but also Gal. 2.2 that over time a similar development took place in most of the early mission communities in Syria and Cilicia.

The emphasis on the *one year* of shared teaching activity in Antioch which comes from the tradition remains enigmatic. One could conjecture that this year was to indicate the interval before the visit of Agabus and the subsequent visit to Jerusalem, but in that case the very general note of time 'in those days' (ἐν ταύταις δὲ ταῖς ἡμέραις) seems a disruption; one would expect a simple μετὰ ταῦτα or a similar formulation.[1143] It is enough, therefore, to suppose that by the phrase Luke wanted to emphasize the special significance of the visit of the prophet from Jerusalem. Here he is concerned to give a further example of the link between the mother community and the 'young community', with the initiative now going over to the latter: 'It now as an adult child was able and willing to care for its mother in her need. This proved both its independence and a continuing relationship.'[1144]

On the other hand, the apparently exact note of time has only later parallels in the information about Paul's missionary stay in other metropolises, e.g. Corinth and Ephesus.[1145] In Damascus Luke gave only an indefinite indication of a lengthy activity, while in 11.26a for the first time a specific period of time is mentioned. The remark probably indicates that Barnabas and Paul worked together for a whole year as teachers (and therefore at the same time as missionaries) in the provincial capital of Syria and did not set off to visit or to found other communities after a short time. Northern Syria was densely populated. First there were the four main cities which even in the time of the Seleucid empire gave the region the name ὁ τετράπολις (μέρις): in addition to Antiocheia Seleucia Pieria, mention should also be made of Apameia and Laodicea. In addition there were many other places like Rhosos, Alexandreia, Nikopolis, Cyrrhus, Berrhoea, Zeugma, Chalcis on the Belos, Epiphaneia, Hierapolis, Bambyce and so on.[1146] Indirectly, this information probably indicates that it is to be understood in the same way as the later references to a lengthy stay in Corinth and Ephesus, and that after this whole year had elapsed the two missionaries also visited other cities of (north) Syria and founded communities there. Previously, around 39/40, at best there will probably have been a few smaller communities on the Phoenician coast,[1147] a situation which then gradually changed in the course of the next ten years, not least through the activity of Barnabas and Paul.

First of all, however, the two were needed for a year in Antioch. That confirms our conjecture that in the crisis of 38–41 the young, still unconsolidated, community in Antioch, which had made itself 'independent' of the traditional synagogue communities, needed internal consolidation, and that the two partners saw this initially as their primary task. Here we can assume that it was above all Antiochene 'godfearers' who did not want to be dragged into the often long-drawn-out controversies between the militant anti-Judaism of the 'Greeks' and the Jewish minority embittered at the wickedness of Caligula, among which the spokesmen for nationalistic religious zeal were gaining influence, and who therefore turned to the new messianic community with its two outstanding teachers, helpful, open on the question of the law and filled with eschatological enthusiasm. Not only the living preaching of the person of Jesus as heavenly redeemer and judge[1148] – a contemporary who had lived around ten years previously and was now expected again soon as the Lord of the community and of the world and the one who had been exalted to God – but also the man Jesus must have played a key role here. Paul and Barnabas could certainly not have preached the new and amazing message without telling of this man, his death on the cross and his resurrection, but also his actions and his life. At that time they did not just recite kergymatic formulae which only initiates could understood. That already follows from the fact that alongside Paul there was now the old Jerusalem disciple, who – only ten years after Easter – certainly had a rich Jesus tradition at his disposal. A further critical problem, precisely when the community was growing, was the building up to some degree of a firm structure for the community, which nevertheless had charismatic worship, baptism and Lord's Supper, all features by which it Idiffered from the synagogue. However, for both 'Antiochene apostles', teaching remained decisive. Here they certainly provided the greatest and most abiding stimuli. The letters of Paul, written between ten and sixteen years later, do not so much stand at the beginning of the formation of communities as presuppose the formation of communities as the ripe fruit of a missionary work of between one and two decades, bound up with intensive theological reflection. So time and again the apostle can refer to other, older communities. That even includes the communities in Judaea.[1149] He sums up his own missionary communities in Rom. 16.4 in an exaggerated way as 'all the churches of the Gentiles' (πᾶσαι ἐκκλησίαι ἐθνῶν).They all, like Paul himself, owe Priscilla and Aquila a debt of gratitude, because they once staked their lives for him in Ephesus. The circle of these communities may also include those in Syria and go back to Arabia and Damascus.

Paul's relationship to the other prophets and teachers, who were all Jews – the spiritual predominance of Jewish Christianity governs the whole of the first century – was one of mutual giving and taking as in the case of Barnabas, for despite all his self-will, Paul was also co-operative. This is indicated by his later attitude to people like Priscilla and Aquila, to Apollos – who presumably had a very different nature – but also to Silas/Silvanus from Jerusalem and to his numerous companions like Timothy or Titus. Nevertheless, probably he will soon have gained a role of spiritual leadership already in Antioch. From the beginning he could not deny the outstanding theologian and scriptural scholar, even if he apparently involved himself in, or in some circumstances subordinated himself to, a collective.[1150]

8.2.3 The name 'Christians' (Acts 11.26b)

As has already been said, the development in Antioch in this tense period led to the Gentile public for the first time being made aware of the special Jewish-messianic sect which differed considerably from the traditional Jewish synagogue communities and accorded the non-Jewish 'sympathizers' the right of full membership without circumcision. This interest was aroused not least by its missionary activity and its success among non-Jews. In other words, in this way the new sect no longer appeared simply as an internal, 'purely Jewish' movement. It is also understandable that this first acquaintance with it should have come about in the capital of the eastern frontier province of Syria. Certainly people in the Roman administration of the small province of Judaea, where around ten years previously the prefect had had the 'founder of the sect' executed as a political agitator, had already been made aware of the revival of the messianic movement, but they saw it as politically innocuous eschatological enthusiasm, since what it had particularly inscribed on its banner was opposition to external force. This contrasted with the fanatical zeal of the physical and spiritual descendants of Judas of Galilee or the followers of Eleazar ben Dinai, who were waiting in their hiding places in the wilderness of Judaea for the next opportunity to strike.[1151] Indeed, it may have seemed only right to the prefect Pilate, who towards the end of 36 CE was deposed by Vitellius, and his succcessor Marcellus (or Marullus),[1152] that in a Judaea stirred up by chiliastic hopes a messianic group should already be interpreting the present as the beginning of the time of salvation and therefore advocating political non-violence, loyalty and the payment of taxes to the Roman authorities. It is striking that in the first century we do not hear of a Roman persecution of the Jewish Christians in Palestine. On the contrary. In 62 the Roman procurator threatened to put the Sadducean high priest Annas II on trial for his execution of James the brother of the Lord and other Jewish Christians, and his predecessors Felix and Festus deal with the accused Jewish Christian Paul in a very humane way. Since he has only just arrived in the province, Festus asks Agrippa II for advice about this special prisoner, as he understands nothing of 'religious disputes within Judaism' (Acts 25.19), and sends the prisoner for the imperial judgment in Rome. Luke experienced this part of Paul's trial as an eyewitness and reports it objectively within the limits of his possibilities.

The attitude of the pagan authorities seems to have been similar in the provincial capital of Syria. Perhaps there was even a certain agreement over this question between Caesarea and Antioch, since this Jewish messianic movement had been noted there too – albeit in a new, more 'universalistic' form. It would be understandable that this 'perception' took place at a time when because of Caligula's crazy command, the attention of the Syrian public had been directed in a special way to the Jewish minority in their cities. Just as on the basis of the Nabataean Jewish conflict in 34–36 CE the eschatological preaching of the Jew Paul in Arabia must have struck King Aretas,[1153] now everything that was taking place in the great Jewish communities in Antioch (but also elsewhere in Syria) was of interest to the civic and Roman authorities. Thus it is improbable that the designation *'Christianoi'* emerged in Antioch purely as a way in which Christians designated themselves, since the term appears elsewhere in the New Testament texts outside Acts 11.26 only in 26.28, on the lips of a non-Christian, Agrippa II, and I Peter 4.16, around 100 CE, which refers to the first trials of Christians by Roman authorities for the 'name itself'.[1154] In the Apostolic Fathers, too, it occurs only in the letters of Ignatius, i.e. the 'bishop of Syria',[1155] who after a persecution of his community in Antioch around 110–113 was transported to Rome for sentencing. Here it occurs relatively frequently, now for the first time deliberately as a term used by Christians of themselves with the meaning 'true Christians'. This may again be connected with accusation 'because of the name', i.e. the specific situation of persecution.[1156] In addition, the designation appears just once more in Didache 12.4. Perhaps it is no coincidence that apart from the Apologists after Aristides,[1157] who then understandably use it often, the term appears predominantly in texts which either refer like Acts 11.26 or 26.8 to Syria (and Palestine) or come from there.[1158] According to the legend handed down by Malalas, based

on Acts 11.26, Evodius, the first bishop of Antioch, appointed by
Peter around 41, is said to have introduced this name into an
address instead of the older designations Nazoraeans and
Galileans, designations which were used from the Jewish side.[1159]
This note, which goes back to an older local source, certainly has
no historical value, but it does show the pride of the Antiochene
community in the first use of the name Christian in their city.
It is even less likely that the designation comes from the Jews,
since they largely used the geographically based designation
naṣrayya/Ναζωραῖοι, Hebrew *noṣrim*,[1160] derived from the place
Nazareth, and alongside that perhaps also 'Galilean'.[1161] Yet other
authorities are mentioned by the church fathers who are said
to have given the Christians this name.[1162] Thus Chrysostom
attributed the giving of the name to Paul,[1163] Virgilius of Thapsus
(fifth century) to the apostles who met in Antioch: they had given
all disciples the new name 'Christians'.[1164] Epiphanius also presupposes this when he emphasizes that the apostles did not
denote any community or group with their name, since they did
not proclaim themselves, but Christ Jesus; rather, they had given
the church one name. Therefore 'in Antioch they were called
Christians for the first time'.[1165] Others explained the term by
the 'new name' of the servants of God according to Isa. 65.15 or
by the Spirit which inspired the disciples in Antioch.[1166] However,
we may not follow Bickerman and Spicq in concluding that
Christians gave themselves this name, especially as χρηματίσαι
need not be translated one-sidedly as a reflexive, 'they named
themselves'. However, it is correct that the verb means a public
designation: 'and the disciples were first called Christians (in
public) in Antioch'.[1167] Of course we can no longer say who
invented this designation, but it does seem certain that it played
hardly any role within the community, but was disseminated outside it. Bickerman points out that it is striking that the new movement was not named after its 'founder', Jesus, as were the
Pharisaic schools of Beth Hillel or Shammai and the Greek philosophical schools. This is all the more striking since the title Kyrios
which predominates in Paul is never linked with Christ alone, but
only with the name 'Jesus' or 'Jesus Christ'. It is Epiphanius who
reports that all the Christians were originally called 'Nazoraeans'

and then for a short time Ἰησσαῖοι (a designation which the Jewish Christians in the time of the author derived either from Jesse 'or from the name of Jesus our Lord'), before they adopted the name Christians (Χριστιανοί). This late report is of no significance for the early period.[1168] The fact that the designation is derived from the most common honorific title of the 'founder' and 'hero' of the new movement casts some light on the development of christology in the young Antiochene community. Evidently the movement was characterized with 'Christ' because this title, which was in process of becoming a name, had a central place in it. Probably those in the movement already used the formula ἐν Χριστῷ (Ἰησοῦ) to describe their own state of salvation, and therefore the Antiochene Christians could correspondingly call themselves οἱ ἐν Χριστῷ Ἰησοῦ and understand themselves as δοῦλοι Χριστοῦ Ἰησοῦ or διάκονοι Χριστοῦ.[1169] Belonging to *Christ* was the special feature which distinguished them from all other religious groups, in Judaism and also among non-Jews. It is in keeping with this that already in the authentic letters of Paul, 'Christ' (Χριστός) with 270 occurrences comes in second place after 'God' (θεός), and more than half of the 531 examples of Χριστός in the New Testament already occur in Paul.[1170] Here he already uses Χριστός almost as a proper name, except that in individual places and through the possibility of the inverted usage Χριστός Ἰησοῦς, which is very rare in cognomens, it becomes clear that this was originally a title, like κύριος Ἰησοῦς. In contrast to Caesar and to some degree also Herod, where a name becomes the appellative, here an appellative becomes the name; this expressed the uniqueness of the saving person with his eschatological, God-given authority.

The Latinizing form of the name with the ending -ιανός/-ιανοί = *ianus/iani* indicates a linguistic creation coming from outside rather than a typically Christian one; originally an adjective, in surnames it expressed a family relationship, a geographical origin, a client relationship or in general a political or spiritual adherence.[1171] Military or political designations like *Caesariani* (Καισαριανοί), *Pompeiani, Augustiani*[1172] or even *Ciceronianus*[1173] were formed on this basis. The most interesting parallel, to which E. Peterson in particular referred, is familiar to us from the New

Testament: the Herodians ('Ηρωδιανοί),[1174] i.e. partisans, clients or even members of the extensive Herodian house, including slaves, freemen or officials.[1175] There were such 'Herodians' not only in Judaea but also among the Jews of Rome, especially as members of this clan were constantly living in Rome,[1176] and also in Antioch.[1177] Herod I and his descendants were by far the most influential family of client kings and princes in Syria and Asia Minor, and their influence in the province was an important political support for the Jews in the capital.[1178] Herod Antipas, and from 37 also Herod Agrippa I, certainly had people representing their interests at the seat of the Roman governor in Antioch. There is something to be said for the conjecture by E. Peterson[1179] that *Christianoi* was formed as a direct parallel to the *Herodianoi* who were already known in Antioch. This is a form which is unusual in the Greek-speaking world, and indeed was unique for a religious sect, since the later names like Μαρκιανοί, Οὐαλεντινιανοί, Βασιλειδιανοί and Σατορνιλιανοί[1180] are modelled on the earlier Christian form.[1181] Its early influence developed above all in the *political* sphere over against the pagan, i.e. primarily the Roman, authorities. Accordingly the word appears from the beginning among Roman writers, among whom in this case is also to be included the earliest, Josephus, who writes in Rome and uses the name in a political context in a slightly derogatory way.[1182] He is followed by Pliny, Tacitus and Suetonius.[1183] The two names link what are of course the extremely different 'claims to power' of two Jewish groups 'open' to non-Jews: one group was politically open towards Roman rule and the Gentile client princes of the East,[1184] the other was open in religious and missionary terms, particularly in Antioch, to the Gentiles, and recognized them as members of the community with equal rights. The claim to political power associated with the name Herod was clear, but political associations could also be evoked particularly from the Roman side[1185] by the title 'Christ', as is shown by the account of the trial of Jesus in the Gospels.[1186]

We do not know how this name first came about. It *could* be the consequence of contacts between the new sect and the civic authorities, who in the tense situation of 39–41 also handed on their information to the Roman provincial administration. The magistrates of Antioch, proud of their good relations with Rome since the days of Germanicus and even having Roman citizens among their leaders, had a positive attitude to the Roman provincial administration, unlike their counterparts in Alexandria. It is striking that at first Christians were tolerated by the Romans. Serious state measures were taken against them only in Rome in connection with the expulsion of the Jewish Christians under Claudius in 49 and in the persecution by Nero in 64 CE, evidently because – in keeping with the great Roman tolerance in religious matters – the new movement was thought to be relatively harmless in the first decades, despite its missionary activities.

Against this historical background, texts like Romans 13, but also Mark 12.13–17, take on greater significance than is often given them. That is true of Paul and of all the communities which were founded by the new missionary work of the 'Hellenists'. Antioch in the crisis years of 38–41, i.e. at the very time when Barnabas brought Paul into the Syrian capital, was in some respects the first test case. By then Paul was no 'clean sheet' but an acute theological thinker, a careful community organizer and a 'missionary to the Gentiles' with six or seven years experience of independent preaching. As we have already remarked, the one year in Antioch with which their relatively long shared work began will have been a time of consolidation for the young community. It is quite understandable that at this time the community will also have been seen by the civic and state authorities in the perspective of the name '*Christianoi*' with its political overtones; this was first a sign of their growing missionary success, despite all the tensions between Jews and Greeks, and secondly an expression of their exclusive allegiance to the crucified and risen Messiah Jesus of Nazareth. By making the title 'Christ' a proper name, at the same time they confessed indirectly that the one bearer of this (honorific) name was the only true anointed of God.[1187] Even the Jew Josephus hesitates to give him this title (*Antt.* 20,200). The non-Jews, for whom Χριστός was incomprehensible in connection with a person,[1188] soon itacistically replaced the name '*Christos*', which they could not understand, with the slave name '*Chrestos*' and, as Tacitus already shows, turned '*Christianoi*' into '*Chrestianoi/Chrestiani*'.[1189]

8.2.4 The visit of the prophets

Luke has the report of the one year's joint activity by Barnabas and Paul in Antioch and the designation '*Christianoi*' for the 'disciples' followed by the visit of prophets from Jerusalem to the Syrian capital; the prophecy by one of them, Agabus, of the famine under Claudius; and the sending of 'Barnabas and Saul' with support to Jerusalem. Thus in a very compressed space he reports very different things. First we need to investigate the purpose of his narrative and then the historical background of what is reported.

Luke introduces the new section with an indeterminate 'transitional formula' which he likes to use, with slight variations, to introduce new things.[1190] Here for the first time in Luke's work Christian prophets appear, after in Peter's speech at Pentecost in Acts 2.17 he has used a quotation from Joel 3.1 (LXX) as a basis for the claim of the earliest Christian community to possess to a rich degree the spirit of God given to them as an eschatological gift and the charisma of prophecy.[1191] However, it is strange that Luke is then silent in Acts about the earliest Christian prophets until 11.27, and mentions them only four times in all in the work.[1192] By contrast, he speaks of Old Testament prophets twenty-six times. We can conclude from this that in his time the significance of 'prophets' in the larger communities had declined markedly in favour of the more strongly institutionalized office of elders, indeed that as a 'man of order' he was relatively critical of them. But of course he was aware of their significance and activity, which for him is concentrated above all in Judaea and Syria. Evidently they no longer play an important role for him in the sphere of the Pauline mission.[1193] But even in Paul, those who have a prophetic charisma emerge only because of the abuses in Corinth (I Cor. 11–14), where at the same time we are given a vivid picture of the enthusiasm of earliest Christian worship. Paul's admonition to the community in Thessalonica, 'Do not despise the gift of prophecy, do not quench the Spirit', shows that this charismatically enthusiastic understanding of the Spirit was an element in the foundation of Pauline communities which was quite taken for granted, but was a novelty to the newly-won Jewish and Gentile Christians; it probably goes back to the custom of the older communities in Syria and Cilicia.[1194] In the Deutero-Pauline letter to the Ephesians, roughly contemporaneous with Luke, the prophets appear inserted into the series of offices as a fixed institution: 'apostles, prophets, evangelists, pastors and teachers'.[1195] Presumably this is an extension of the lists of charismas in I Cor. 12.28f., where no fixed 'offices' are yet described apart from 'apostles'. Around ten to twenty years after Luke we find an explicitly 'anti-charismatic' tendency in Matthew and I Clement.[1196]

By contrast, with its 'itinerant prophets who are, however, in the process of becoming settled (13.1)',[1197] the Didache has retained the old charismatic form of prophecy. This text probably comes from southern Syria or Palestine, not from the metropolis of Antioch, since there, as the letters of Ignatius show, at the beginning of the second century the monarchical episcopate with elders and deacons had become established.[1198]

This description in the Didache of 'apostles and prophets' who are almost interchangeable,[1199] and of itinerant prophets and prophets settled in a place, who were regarded as special authorities and closely associated with 'the teachers',[1200] since they are both given the agricultural firstfruits (ἀπαρχή) reserved in Judaism for the priests, and can even be called 'high priests' of the community, is unique. Like the eucharistic prayers, it in part points back to an essentially earlier time. Prophets and teachers are also mentioned together in worship. However, those chosen as 'bishops and deacons'[1201] serve in worship along with the 'prophets and teachers', and like them are 'honoured (by God)'.[1202] Here in the latest stratum we can see that revolution which fundamentally changed the church after the last decades of the first century. All in all, in its 'lagging behind the development of church law',[1203] the Didache points to a rural milieu formerly with a Jewish Christian stamp where old charismatic forms were preserved more easily than in the larger urban communities. There the fixed offices of (deacons,) priests and bishops became established earlier.

We find the description of a prophetic-ecstatic spirit-filled

service in another Christian text from Syria from the early second
century, the Ascension of Isaiah. Chapter 6 relates that the
prophet Isaiah was with King Hezekiah. Although he was offered
a seat, he wanted to speak standing, and all the princes, eunuchs
and counsellors of the king gathered to hear the 'words of faith
and truth' that he spoke. Forty prophets from the surrounding
regions had heard of this and had come not only to hear his
words but so that he would lay his hand on them[1204] and they
themselves could prophesy, and Isaiah could hear (and test[1205])
their prophecy.

> 6 And when Isaiah spoke with Hezekiah the words of truth
> and faith, they all heard a door[1206] 7 being opened and the
> voice of the Spirit. 8 And the king summoned all the prophets
> and all the people who were to be found there, and they
> came ... 9 And when they all heard the voice of the Holy
> Spirit, they all worshipped on their knees, and they praised
> the God of righteousness, the Most High, the One who
> (dwells) in the upper world and who sits on high, the Holy
> One, the one who rests among the holy ones.[1207] 10 And they
> ascribed glory to the One who had thus graciously given
> a door in an alien world, had graciously given it to a man.
> 11 And while he was speaking with the Holy Spirit in the
> hearing of them all, he became silent, and his mind was
> taken up from him, and he did not see the men who were
> standing before him. 12 His eyes indeed were open, but his
> mouth was silent, and the mind in his body was taken up from
> him. 13 But his breath was (still) in him, for he was seeing a
> vision ... 14 And the people standing by, apart from the circle
> of prophets, did think that the holy Isaiah had been taken
> up.[1208]

Revived from his trance, depicted in this realistic way, the
prophet then relates his journey into heaven. The Christian conclusion to the *Paralipomena Jeremiae* in ch. 9 anachronistically
relates in a similar way the transportation of Jeremiah in a vision.
The difference is that this takes place during temple worship,
while the prophet is saying the Trishagion. Both the Ascension of
Isaiah and the *Paralipomena Jeremiae* depict visions (of Christ) by

Old Testament prophets in the light of the experience of
Christian worship with a prophetic-ecstatic stamp.

In II Cor. 12.2f., Paul himself reports such an ecstatic journey
into heaven which he must have experienced fourteen years
before he wrote the letter, say around 42 CE, in other words
during his activity in Syria. Here he does not know whether he
was 'in the body or outside it'.[1209] We may also presuppose similar
experiences among his opponents in Corinth, who probably
come from Palestine or Syria. They may well have been representatives of Peter's mission. Peter himself is also depicted as a
visionary.[1210]

The significance of the early Christian bearers of the Spirit for
the first decades of the new movement, which was spreading relatively rapidly, is greater than the somewhat fortuitous testimony
to them in the New Testament and later texts suggests. The
roots are completely Jewish. They grow from the certainty of the
earliest community that the spirit of the prophets has been given
to it again as the true Israel of the end-time. There is no evidence
of any dependence on pagan oracles or on ecstatic-orgiastic cults;
at best one can assume that Gentile Christians misunderstood the
phenomena of the Spirit, say in Corinth, in this way, especially as
these missionaries in particular were active there. The problem
can be traced as far as Montanism, to Tertullian, the Acts of
Perpetua and Felicitas, the Egyptian martyrs who understand
themselves as successors to Elijah, and indeed as far as Cyprian.
In other words, it dies out only in the third century and is
replaced a few generations later by monasticism.[1211] Luke sometimes pushes it into the background because in his idealizing
description of the beginnings according to Acts 2.17f. (= Joel 3.1)
initially all Christians were to share in the gift of the prophetic
spirit. This is true of Peter,[1212] Stephen,[1213] Philip,[1214] but also of
Paul and Barnabas; in other words, as later still in the Didache,
the boundaries between 'apostle' and 'prophet', or even
'teacher' and 'prophet', are blurred – if we leave aside the unique
'dogmatic' function of the twelve apostles in Luke, Matthew and
the Apocalypse of John. In 13.1f. five 'prophets and teachers'[1215]
are enumerated in the community in Antioch, who after prayer
and fasting receive a missionary instruction from the Holy Spirit.

Fasting was a preparation for the revelations and visions of the Spirit and 'intensified' prayer.[1216] Barnabas, 'the one gifted with the prophetic admonition inspired by the Spirit',[1217] is mentioned first, and Saul/Paul last. No distinction is made between who is a prophet and who is a teacher; evidently all five are to be both prophets and teachers,[1218] although later in 14.4 and 14 the first and the last are also given the title apostle.

In 15.32, Judas Barsabbas[1219] and Silas/Silvanus, Paul's partner on the so-called second journey, are emphasized as prophets in a striking way.[1220] In other words, in Luke's account the 'office' of prophet is not clearly demarcated and defined; the same is also true of Paul in I Cor. 12 and 14: he would like as many people as possible, indeed all, to have the gift of 'prophetic speech'.[1221] This is dependent more on the free working of the Spirit: those who had proved themselves by the gift of the spiritual knowledge and speech of revelation, which took many forms, could be called prophet; again I Cor. 12.29; 14.29–32, 37 show that the number of such charismatics in the communities was quite considerable. On the other hand, there were a few individual prophets who stood out for their extraordinary 'parapsychological' gifts, like impressive visions, prophesying the future, 'reading thoughts' or 'gifts of healing'. Luke paradigmatically makes Agabus appear as one such figure in his work.

This form of charismatic prophecy, which appears in the Pauline communities, has its origin in the earliest worship of the communities in Palestine and a little later in Syria. Whereas itinerant prophets were active in the small scattered rural communities of Galilee and Judaea, the large cities of Syria called for longer stays and greater stability. Much as Paul and Luke differentiate between apostles and prophets for theological reasons, they will have not been very different in their charismatic activity in missionary and admonitory preaching combined with exorcisms and the gift of healing.

However, the office to which the future belonged was not that of the prophets or 'itinerant charismatics'[1222] of any kind, the significance of which tends to be exaggerated in the social romanticism which is widespread today, but that of the local presbyter. Luke shows this very well. The home of the presbyter,

like that of the prophet, is to be sought in Palestine and more precisely in Jerusalem.[1223] By having 'prophets come down from
Jerusalem to Antioch' in 11.27, while in 11.29 a collection is sent
from Antioch 'through Barnabas and Saul' as messengers 'to the
elders' in Jerusalem, Luke for the first time indicates a shift in
perspectives and in the development of the church: according to
his narrative the focal point of events will move first to the north
and then to the west. The persecution by 'King Herod' (Agrippa
I) in Jerusalem in ch.12 then represents just a momentous interlude (see below, 244ff.).

It is impossible to overestimate the importance of earliest
Christian prophecy, as the most important phenomenon of the
charismata given by the Spirit, for the extension of the new
Jewish-eschatological movement. To the Jews who were addressed
it was the striking 'proof' of the fulfilment of the prophetic
promises, for the dawning of the last time, indeed for the anticipation of the messianic time of salvation, and at the same time a
demonstration of the power of the Messiah Jesus exalted to the
right hand of God. The gift of the Spirit is due solely to his work
of salvation, even if God himself is named as the giver.[1224] No
wonder that the visible and tangible manifestations of the Spirit
were particularly treasured in Corinth. Here both Jewish and
Gentile visitors to worship could be compelled to confess: 'God
(i.e. the one true God, the God of Israel) is truly in you!'[1225] For
Jews, the argument that here the widespread scribal view that
inspiration had ended with Ezra had lost its validity was important.[1226] The Spirit of God at work among the *nosrim* could surpass
the old prophecies; it opened hearts to the message of the
gospel[1227] and gave reality to quite new revelations of God.[1228]
Other manifestations of the eschatological Spirit were the healings of the sick, exorcisms and the occurrence of 'wonderful
experiences' of all kinds. In other words, the fullness of the salvation already present in faith was revealed in the Spirit, and precisely for that reason it had so many aspects and produced
numerous charismata. Here, for Paul, 'faith, love and hope'
stood at the centre,[1229] as he was concerned not so much with
ecstatic and miraculous features as with the power of the Spirit
which was the basis for existence in faith.

Basically, men like Paul and Barnabas are apostles, prophets and teachers in one; in other words they combine in one person those three charismatic offices which Paul lists separately and in gradation because of the special problem of the challenge to his apostolate and the false understanding of charismata in Corinth. The 'prophetic gift' of Barnabas is already evident from his name, and as a missionary he must also have been a teacher sent out by Christ. Numerous prophetic traits can also be recognized in Paul.[1230] That he nevertheless terms himself an apostle but never a prophet (though see the slightly ironical observation in I Cor. 7.40b) is connected with the unique gift of the gospel which he has been given 'by a revelation of Jesus Christ' (δι' ἀποκαλύψεως Ἰησοῦ Χριστοῦ). This makes him 'apostle to the Gentiles' (ἐθνῶν ἀπόστολος),[1231] and gives him a commission and an authority which transcends all prophetic analogies. In retrospect the Deutero-Pauline letter to the Ephesians can rightly say that the church is 'built on the foundation of the apostles and prophets'.[1232]

The emergence of this new movement with its pneumatically ecstatic worship was particularly impressive for sympathizers who on the one hand inclined towards the synagogue but on the other did not want to be separated from their local and family Semitic cults. It was not only that here they were accorded equal rights and fellowship, but Syrians and Arabs could find the gift of prophecy, of speaking with tongues (i.e. in the language of the angels) and its 'translation', exorcisms, healings, visions and so on particularly attractive, since individual local cults in Syria had always been associated with the gift of oracles and often also with other ecstatic phenomena. Lucian's depiction of the cult of the *Dea Syria* in Hierapolis/Bambyce gives a vivid impression of this.[1233]

By comparison with this old and widespread Syrian oracular religion, the earliest Christian enthusiasm in the Spirit with its prophetic gifts as a revelation of the one true God and his Son, exalted to his right hand, could prove something quite new and superior. Here heaven had opened as an anticipation of imminent salvation,[1234] since the workings of the Spirit in worship were constant and present in ever new forms, no longer tied to holy places, times and sacrificial rites. When compared with this, the ecstatic-parapsychological phenomena of the pagan cults were dismissed, as they were later by the Apologists, as the deception and imitation of the demons.

This earliest Christian 'enthusiasm', which also expressed itself in cries of acclamation and prayer like 'Kyrios Jesus', 'Maran atha' or in the liberated cry 'Abba',[1235] did not first arise in Antioch.[1236] That is immediately evident from the Aramaic cries of prayer. Rather, it is a 'primal phenomenon' of the earliest community which at a later date caused a degree of perplexity, even for Luke. People still remembered it, but attempted to domesticate it.

Although it goes against Luke's basic tendency, he indicates this enthusiasm in the idealized image of the earliest Jerusalem community with its sharing of possessions inspired by the Spirit. It appears in the 'rejoicing' (ἀγαλλίασις) at the meal, which, however, Luke immediately corrects by adding 'with a generous heart' (ἀφελότης καρδίας);[1237] in the depiction of the first outpouring of the Spirit, with its tongues of fire and 'glossolalia' in foreign languages, in which different elements are fused;[1238] or even in the prayer which causes an earthquake (4.31). The story of Ananias and Sapphira, which seems so offensive to us, also belongs in this context.[1239]

Codex D, which corrects Luke because it believes that it understands him better than he understands himself, therefore supplements the news of the arrival of the prophets from Jerusalem in Antioch by a reference back to 2.42: 'and there was much rejoicing' (ἦν δὲ πολλὴ ἀγαλλίασις).[1240] For the scribe, prophets and jubilation caused by the Spirit belong together.

As Conzelmann rightly remarks, these visitors from the Holy City are not 'delegates from Jerusalem' but 'free charismatics'. However, it should not be denied that they come from Judaea. Here again many commentators know too much. According to Schillle, 'Luke has again sweepingly generalized, in making the one Agabus into a number of Jerusalem prophets. In the background here is probably no more than an awareness that communities in Judaea had "prophets" ... The concrete narrative begins in the middle of the action and knows only one prophet.'[1241] Haenchen objects that the prophets of the Didache 'appeared as individuals, and not here in the plural' and also that Luke does not 'describe them as itinerant prophets'; they are 'at home in Jerusalem'. Moreover, he argues, 'Antioch did not actually need such visitation; the community had its own prophets.' Thus there is no reason at all for 'their journeying to the sink of iniquity that Antioch was at the time'.[1242] Here criticism of Luke becomes utterly pedantic.

Zinzendorf basically gave the reason for such visits with his well-known saying, 'I cannot imagine any Christianity without community'. The newly-founded mission communities could only exist only if they constantly remained in touch with the other earlier communities, above all those of the capital cities. In other words, real *koinonia* had to be brought to life not only in individual communities but also between them. This notion also stands behind the collection for Jerusalem in Paul. Therefore the whole of the first and second centuries is full of journeys and visits to communities which are made by individuals or in twos and threes – the latter is the case with Barnabas, Paul and Mark and then in the case of Paul, Silas and Timothy; here, as we saw, the boundaries between apostle, prophet and teacher were fluid. The unity of the *ekklesia* which soon extended beyond provinces and in the time of Mark and Luke already claimed the whole ecumene could only be maintained by constant exchanges. This exchange as a realization of *koinonia* was vitally necessary for the new movement. It applies to the whole of the early church.

8.2.5 The prophecy of Agabus, the famine and the visit to Jerusalem

There is thus no adequate reason for mistrusting in principle the account of the visit of the prophets from Jerusalem. Rather, we can conjecture that Luke has paradigmatically combined a number of visits into this one.

He makes it follow Barnabas and Paul's year in Antioch because he wants to use it to direct attention back to Jerusalem again and provide a motive for the visit of Barnabas and Paul to Jerusalem with the collection, which is historically controversial.

Here the key event is the prophecy of Agabus. We need not doubt that individual prophets in earliest Christianity were given the visionary gift of clairvoyance; indeed in this respect they should not be ranked behind the Old Testament prophets.[1243] This phenomenon is part of the earliest Christian 'wonder-working' caused by the Spirit, which in the last resort again goes back to Jesus himself and thus to the foundations of the Jesus movement. It made a vital contribution to the missionary success of the new 'messianic sect'.[1244] That today 'miracle' is no longer, as for Goethe's Faust, 'the favourite child of faith' but rather 'the greatest scandal of faith' for the 'enlightened' theologian should not distort our perspective on the reality of life in earliest Christianity, which in many respects was quite different from our own. People had a different, finer capacity for perception.

Behind the unusual name Ἄγαβος there probably stands the Hebrew *ḥagab*, locust.[1245] In Ezra 2.45, *bᵉne hᵃagabah* and in 2.46 *bᵉne ḥagab* appear among the 'members of the temple' who returned.[1246] Presumably this was one of the numerous surnames which often replaced the all too widespread proper names.[1247] The same prophet appears in Caesarea, in connection with Paul's last visit to Jerusalem, as 'coming from Judaea', and with the help of a prophetic symbolic action predicts Paul's arrest and his being handed over to the Romans in Jerusalem. Luke reports this last event relatively precisely as an eye-witness.[1248]

By contrast, the content of the first prophecy and the dating of the prophet's visit remain uncertain. The 'great famine' which affected 'the whole world' did not take place under Claudius or later. Commentaries do not weary of pointing this out. However, we need not spend much time on the fact, since R. Riesner has given a model account of the whole complex.[1249] First of all, λιμός is better translated 'price increase'; here we should reflect that the sporadic famines in antiquity were not least a problem of food distribution and social strata, and the 'price increase' primarily hit the poor hard.[1250] Secondly, throughout the reign of Claudius (15 January 41 to 13 October 54), from the beginning a series of severe crises over food production arose, which affected above all the east of the empire, but also Rome itself.

According to Suetonius, *Claudius* 18.2, 'frequent crop failures' (*assiduae sterilitates*) in the granaries and disruption in the provisioning of Rome led to a direct threat against the emperor from the angry population.[1251] In Palestine, Josephus attests a famine while the procurators Cuspius Fadius and Tiberius Alexander were in office (44–48 CE),[1252] but it probably lasted beyond that time,[1253] since it was accentuated by a sabbatical year (presumably 48/49).[1254] The previous sabbatical year would then fall in 41/42, the first year of Claudius, immediately after the crisis year of 40 CE, when the Jews refused to sow seed in the autumn because of Caligula's threat.[1255] This refusal, together with the following sabbatical year, could have produced a local price increase in Judaea. It would be understandable that the Jerusalem community, in its enthusiastic 'having things in common' in expectation of the imminent end, had failed to make any reasonable economic provisions.[1256] This also explains the instruction given to Paul and Barnabas around seven or eight years later at the 'Apostolic Council' to 'remember the poor'.[1257] The number of the poor must in any case have been so large that the community itself found difficulty in coping with them.

Thus it would be plausible if Agabus had prophesied a coming world famine in apocalyptic terms because of the price increase in Judaea (and also in Rome) from, say, 41 CE, with the situation in the mother country being understood as the 'beginning of the woes'. Here the world catastrophe began from the Holy Land as the 'centre of the world' – as the Caligula episode also shows.[1258] The argument which keeps appearing in the commentaries, that this distress will also have affected the Antiochenes, gets nowhere, since their decision to help now where there was a specific need would simply have corresponded to Jesus' saying in Matt. 6.36, 'take no thought for the morrow'. The Christians in Antioch will have been following Jesus' simple command here. In the time of Luke, who was writing around forty years later, this apocalyptic prophecy of the world famine would have been interpreted as referring to the *assiduae sterilitates* under Claudius.

The description of the collection in the community is also striking. It is fundamentally different from what is reported about the earliest Jerusalem community in Acts 4 and 5, but corresponds to the way in which Paul commends the collection to the community in Corinth in I Cor. 16.1–4 and II Cor. 8 and 9. Each gives voluntarily as he can afford (καθὼς εὐπορεῖτο); here it is presupposed that the young community was not wholly poor.[1259]

The date of the prophet's visit and the journey with the collection to Jerusalem which it prompted remains unclear. There is argument as to whether the latter took place at all, since from Paul's own information in Gal. 2.1 we should assume that he was not in Jerusalem between his visit to Paul and the journey to the Apostolic Council for fourteen years – thirteen if we count the beginning of years. This would put it between around 36 and 49 CE.

Even if we leave out a possibility which cannot be completely excluded, but is improbable, namely that in Gal. 2.1 Paul simply passes over the collection visit of Acts 11.30 in silence,[1260] we can still make a number of conjectures. I regard as even more improbable the hypothesis that 11.30 is identical with the journey to the 'Apostolic Council' in Gal. 2.1–10 and that Acts 15 reports a second series of negotiations in Jerusalem at which the 'Apostolic Decree' was resolved, about which Paul persistently keeps silent. Nor is the suggestion illuminating that Luke simply duplicated the visits to the Holy City in 11.30 and 15.2ff., for whatever reasons. There is a great difference between a visit of support because of the threat of famine and a visit for negotiations over circumcision and the observance of the law. It would remain inexplicable why Paul, who in Gal. 2.10 mentions in detail the obligation to support the poor imposed on him at Jerusalem, should have kept quiet about aid to the Jerusalem poor which had been given earlier. An error on Luke's part would be quite understandable. He could have made a mistake over the names of the delegates or at least one of them, Paul. But the possibility would also remain that Paul travelled with the delegation but kept out of Jerusalem himself because there his life was still in danger, or because the people there did not want to see him.[1261]

· Here we can make all kinds of assumptions, but we can no longer clarify what actually happened. I see no occasion to dismiss the whole report simply as a Lukan invention. The supportive journey will have taken place. It seems natural that it was led by Barnabas, who came from Jerusalem; this is also supported by the fact that he takes his nephew John Mark with him on the return journey to Antioch (12.25). By contrast, Paul's role remains obscure, but he does not seem to have been in Jerusalem in person.

There are two possibilities over the date: if we begin by assuming that 'the whole year' in Acts 11.26 falls in the crisis year of 40/41 CE and that for the reasons given above, the refusal of seed and the subsequent sabbatical year, an increase in price in Jerusalem prompted the prophecy of Agabus, the aid to the community of Jerusalem would have taken place around 42 CE. In other words, it would have come chronologically close to the persecution by Agrippa I, which is presumably to be put around Passover 43. In that case, the Lukan chronology, which moves within a rough framework of episodic historiography, would be relatively correct.

However, the other possibility is more probable, namely that this support came only after the inflation which according to Josephus began after the death of Agrippa I,[1262] under the first procurator Cuspius Fadus, i.e. in 44/45. In support of this is the fact that Barnabas took his nephew John Mark along, and Paul and Barnabas then – presumably not too long afterwards – set out on the so-called first journey to Cyprus. The Jerusalem community will also have been in special need of help after the persecution by King Agrippa, which must have deeply shaken it. But above all the fact that according to 11.29 the collection was brought to the elders, whereas the gifts had once, in Acts 4.37 and 5.2, been laid 'at the feet of the apostles', indicates a basic change in the community (see below, 244, 254f.). All this supports the later date.

Here it is important that the link between the young community in Jerusalem and the starting point of the earliest Christian movement, Jerusalem, was never broken off. In particular the later development immediately before the 'Apostolic Council' and the years after it show that there was a constant mutual exchange between the two communities, and thus a reciprocal influence. On this point Paul and Luke are in complete agreement. If this was the case in the later decades –

from the clash in Antioch in which Paul came off worst – we must assume such an exchange even more for the 'founding years', especially as the development in Judaea under and after Agrippa made such an open exchange more difficult.

8.2.6 The persecution under Agrippa I and the change in the situation in Jerusalem

Luke inserts into the account of the bringing of the Antiochene collection to Jerusalem (11.30) and the return journey to Antioch of the messengers, Barnabas and Paul together with John Mark (12.25), his narrative of the persecution of the earliest Jerusalem community by 'King Herod', Agrippa I. Agrippa was king of all Judaea from spring 41 to the beginning of 44, and ruled a territory which approximated to that of his grandfather Herod. Claudius, who owed the fact that he had been made emperor not least to Agrippa's diplomatic skill, sought by appointing Agrippa to bring calm again to a Judaea which had been deeply shaken by Caligula's megalomaniac plans. As Agrippa had personally committed himself to keeping the temple intact and had dared to go against Caligula, he also had the advantage of enjoying trust in Jerusalem. His aim must have been to restore peace to the province. Luke has been censured for his placing of the journey, on the grounds that from the lofty stand-point of a later age he should not have mixed up these events which were so different.[1263]

However, this account makes sense here. First, with 11.29 it brings its brief account of the foundation of the community in Antioch and the events which followed to a meaningful con-clusion. There is a quite new beginning in 12.24, namely the description of a mission journey by Barnabas and Paul with John Mark, introduced by 12.24a, 'The word of God grew and increased', which may be taken as the title of chs. 13 and 14. In addition, in 11.30 Luke mentions for the first time the new governing body, the Christian 'elders'[1264] in Jerusalem. Hitherto in Acts there has been mention of πρεσβύτεροι only as the *Jewish* governing body in the Holy City;[1265] later in the course of the narrative a clear distinction has been made where necessary to indicate whether the 'elders' spoken of in Jerusalem are Christian or Jewish.[1266] In 12.17 Peter instructs those who are assembled in Mary's house to report his deliverance to 'James and the brothers', which at this point probably means 'James and all the other Christians' in Jerusalem. This probably indicates a special Petrine source. By contrast, Paul does not mention these presbyters when he describes the situation at the 'Apostolic Council' around seven or eight years later; he speaks generally, with clear reserve, about 'those of note' (οἱ δοκοῦντες), whom he does not want to list by name (Gal. 2.2, 6). By contrast, he emphatically mentions by name the three leading figures, James, Peter and John, with whom Paul comes to an agreement over the future missionary aims. They are 'reputed to be pillars' (οἱ δοκοῦντες στύλοι, Gal. 2.9), and their decision is authoritative. By contrast, the anonymous 'people of note' (δοκοῦντες) could refer to the new circle of 'elders'. Paul, however, says no more about 'those who were apostles before me'.[1267] Probably the 'certain men from James' (τινες ἀπὸ ᾽Ιακώβου Gal. 2.12) are also identical with such 'elders', who were sent by James to Antioch.[1268] In other words, the account of the basic changes in personnel after Agrippa's persecution in Luke corresponds clearly to what is to be inferred from Paul in Gal. 1 and 2. We shall have to examine these presbyters in more detail later.[1269]

With the narrative in Acts 12.1–23 which immediately follows, among other things Luke gives a reason for the change of leading body in Jerusalem indicated in 11.30, by adding an explanatory 'recapitulation'[1270] of what had happened there in the meantime and had essentially changed the situation. We must not understand this as meaning that he wants to report that Paul and Barnabas had stayed undisturbed in Jerusalem throughout the persecution.[1271] Rather, he has to explain why Peter, the head of the group of Twelve (and other apostles), was no longer in this city to receive the gifts from Antioch, but rather these 'elders'. According to Luke, Paul had stayed before with the 'apostles' on his first visit to Jerusalem, and Barnabas had introduced him to them.[1272] That Paul can hardly have taken part in this new visit – according to his own testimony in Gal. 2.1 – but appears in Luke as the second of the delegates from Antioch is one of those inaccuracies which often creep into Luke's account – as into the accounts of any historian, ancient or modern.[1273]

If we understand Acts 12.1–23 in this way as a 'recapitulation', Luke's account becomes clear.[1274] Luke does not describe the miraculous deliverance of Peter at such length just because he had a special tradition at his disposal which reported in detail about Peter shortly before the martyrdom of James the son of Zebedee, and gave more details about Agrippa I.[1275] In addition to this, he has to explain why Peter was no longer in Jerusalem, and why the delegates from Antioch handed the collection over to a body of presbyters. We also find similar chronological overlaps elsewhere in his work.[1276]

If we follow his account, 'at that time'[1277] Agrippa I had seized some members of the earliest community (τινες τῶν ἀπὸ τῆς ἐκκλησίας) and maltreated them, and had had James the son of Zebedee[1278] killed with the sword. When he saw that this pleased the 'Jews', he also had Peter arrested. However, Agrippa postponed Peter's (public) execution[1279] until the cycle of spring festivals – Passover and the next week, 'the days of unleavened bread' – and during this time kept him in prison under strict guard.

Why Agrippa had 'James the brother of John' and some others seized, and James in particular executed 'by the sword', seems enigmatic, because Luke gives no reason for it and simply adds 'because it pleased the Jews' (ὅτι ἀρεστόν ἐστιν τοῖς ᾽Ιουδαίοις) as an explanation for the extension of the persecution to Peter. In the earliest list of disciples in Mark 3.17 (cf. Matt. 10.2; Luke 6.24), James the son of Zebedee comes even before his brother John and immediately after Peter, i.e. as the second man in the group of disciples, a sign of the age of this tradition.[1280] He is also mentioned before his brother in the Gospel of Luke in 5.10; 6.14; 9.54; in Luke 8.51; 9.28 the textual tradition is divided.[1281] In Acts James is behind John in rank, which again indicates the later development which becomes visible in Gal. 2.9. After the execution of James, his brother John had to fill the gap. Elsewhere James is mentioned only in Acts 1.13, where he comes after his brother, who in the opening chapters always appears together with Peter.[1282] On the other hand, in Acts only the notice of his martyrdom indicates his importance in the earliest community in Jerusalem. Agrippa could not have made an example of an unimportant member of the messianic sect to 'test' public opinion. Possibly he released the less important persons after interrogation and flogging as 'not worthy of notice'.[1283] So there is no reason to accept on the basis of the saying of Jesus in Mark 10.39, understood as a *vaticinium ex eventu,* and the report of Papias that both sons of Zebedee were killed by the Jews, that John was also executed at that time. This false hypothesis then compels us because of Gal. 2.9 to put the 'Apostolic Council' before the persecution by Agrippa, i.e. before the Passover of 43 CE. Nowhere is it indicated that both sons of Zebedee were killed at the same time, nor would Luke, who emphasizes John alongside Peter to such a degree in Acts 3–4; 8, and describes James in 12.2 as 'brother of John', have kept silent about his execution. He may have been killed at a later date, say, by Annas II in 62 CE, in the confusions of the Jewish War or even outside Judaea.[1284]

That his execution was by the sword indicates that Agrippa I made use of the royal *ius gladii,* hardly that James died as one who 'led the city astray'.[1285] Moreover the arrest and planned execution of Peter indicates that the authorities were to be done away with. D. R. Schwartz assumes that Agrippa persecuted the earliest community in Jerusalem for political reasons. The two sons of Zebedee, the 'sons of thunder', had been close to the Zealots, and Peter after all had been the one who had seized a sword at Jesus' arrest.[1286] But even if there were former Zealots among the disciples, these no longer pursued their aim of a violent revolution after 'Easter',[1287] but waited for the kingdom of God from heaven with the return of the risen Lord.[1288] Moreover, the Roman prefects and procurators, who took vigorous action against eschatological prophets like Theudas and 'the Egyptian' posing as Moses redivivus, never spontaneously undertook any action against the Christians at this early time in Palestine.[1289] They evidently regarded them as politically innocuous. So why should Agrippa have persecuted them for political reasons?

By contrast, R. Riesner refers once again to the earlier proposal that the occasion had been the move of the Christian mission towards the Gentiles.[1290] But here Agrippa would have had more reason for violent intervention in the port of Caesarea. This motive could at best explain a growing aversion to Christians 'critical of the law' in Jerusalem. This becomes increasingly visible in the later years before the arrest of Paul in the courtyard of the temple in 57 CE, but it was hardly the predominant motive for the king. Riesner considers as a further reason that Agrippa himself had messianic ambitions.[1291] But none of these explanations is satisfying.

In contrast to his mention of the martyrdom of James the brother of the Lord in 62 CE, when he himself was staying in Jerusalem,[1292] Josephus has no corresponding account of the persecution of the earliest community in Jerusalem by Agrippa. Nevertheless, his description of the character and the conduct of the king also sheds some light on Luke's account and its historical background. Josephus writes – probably in dependence on a biographical source[1293] – of the king's intention to make himself popular with all the population groups in his empire through the mildness of his attitude, saying that he attached importance to being respected by both Jews and Gentiles. Indeed he says that in contrast to his grandfather, Agrippa preferred his own people.[1294] The Jews had been agitated by the events of 38–41, and had become even more mistrustful of Roman rule. Here Agrippa had to come to an arrangement with the upper class, the first families of the priestly aristocracy, who set the tone. In his concern for recognition he was helped by the fact that he was descended from the Hasmonaean ruling house through his grandmother Mariamne. This tendency is matched by the information in Acts 12.3 that Agrippa first waited for the reaction of the 'Jews' to the maltreatment of some Christians and the execution of James the son of Zebedee, and only after that had Peter seized. The source friendly to Agrippa which Josephus writes out emphasizes with a considerable degree of exaggeration that the king liked to go regularly to the great festivals in Jerusalem.[1295] This agrees with the information in Acts 12.3 that the persecution took place during Passover. Josephus also mentions Agrippa's extraordinary generosity towards a scribe, Simon, who had publicly doubted in Jerusalem the cultic purity or the legitimate descent of the king. This Simon must have been a man of

influence, since he summoned an assembly (ἐκκλησία) at which
he called for Agrippa to be excluded from the temple area.
Agrippa reacted with royal mildness to this affront, summoned
Simon to see him in Caesarea, received him during a visit to the
theatre, and put him to shame with the question what he saw here
that 'offended against the law' (παράνομον[1296]). Simon kept silent.
This suggests that Simon was not a Pharisaic scribe but was
descended from the priestly nobility.[1297]

In other words, Agrippa I sought above all to secure and keep
the good will of the Sadducean priestly party of the nobility who
were the political leaders. Thus he restored the high-priestly
office to the family of Annas by taking it back again from Simon
Kantheras, whom he himself had appointed at the beginning of
his rule in 38 CE.[1298] Simon Kantheras belonged to the family
of Boethus (Josephus, *Antt.* 19, 297). Under Herod I, the family
of Simon son of Boethus, who himself came from the Egyptian
Diaspora, was a father-in-law of Herod and held office between 23
and 5 BCE, appointed the high priests. With the appointment of
Simon Kantheras as the successor to Theophilus son of Annas,[1299]
Agrippa I was demonstrating that he regarded himself as a legitimate heir of his grandfather Herod and wanted to adopt his
policy towards the Jerusalem temple.[1300] Presumably there was
some tension between the Alexandrian Herodian clan of the
Boethusians and the family of Annas, which was protected by the
procurator.[1301] After Agrippa had been rewarded by Claudius
with rule over Judaea and Samaria for support in his becoming
emperor in the difficult situation after the murder of Caligula,[1302]
he offered the high priestly office again to Jonathan, the first of
Annas' five sons[1303] who held office as high priests between 36 and
62 CE. Agrippa received a proud refusal from Jonathan, with the
indication that he should give Jonathan's brother Matthias the
office.[1304] The fact that Agrippa did so shows that he needed to be
in the good books of the most powerful high-priestly clan; at
the same time it indicates the unique position occupied by the
family of Annas. Perhaps Agrippa was making a concession to
Claudius with this nomination, since the members of Annas'
family had had good relations with Rome since the time of the
procurators.[1305] The families of Boethus and Annas were possibly

also related, as competing 'high-priestly families'; Caiaphas, the
son-in-law of Annas, who held office for an exceptionally long
time, perhaps came from the Boethus family.[1306] After Matthias,
Elionaios Kantheras, the brother of Simon Kantheras, again
secured the high-priestly office.[1307] Probably Agrippa wanted in
this way to strike a balance between the house of Annas and
the Boethusians. In his seven-year reign (37–44, from 41–44 over
all Judaea), Agrippa did not change the high priests more
frequently than was usual before 70 CE, if we date his appointment of Simon Kantheras to 38 and not as late as 41. In other
words, he wanted to avoid any break with the two leading families
of the priestly nobility because in principle he had to be concerned for continuity, harmony and stability in relations. Here
the high priests regarded themselves as high priests for ever, even
if they had held office only for a short time. This did not limit the
influence of the first families.[1308]

The followers of the crucified messiah Jesus were a thorn in the
flesh of these inter-related Sadducean high-priestly 'clans'. The
high priest Annas (6–15 CE) and Caiaphas, his son-in law (18–36
CE), led the investigation before the supreme council in the trial
of Jesus and handed him over to Pilate for execution. The trial
of Jesus was clearly remembered not only by the community in
Jerusalem but also by the leading figures of the priestly nobility
who had been involved in it. A short time afterwards, Peter and
John were interrogated by the high-priestly group of the family of
Annas (Acts 4.6; cf. 5.17f.).[1309] That this family continued to hate
the Christians is also indicated by the action of Annas's son of the
same name, who immediately exploited a vacancy after the death
of the procurator Festus. Before the arrival of Albinus and in
62 CE he had James the brother of the Lord 'and some others'
stoned 'as law-breakers' (ὡς παρανομησάντων).[1310] Agrippa had
good reason to show a favour to this powerful priestly clan and its
supporters which cost him nothing. The fact that after Peter
escaped, Agrippa had the soldiers who were meant to be guarding
him executed, but that the matter went no further than this,
suggests that the persecution was not his personal concern but
was meant to further good relations with the highest priestly
nobility. Moreover the sudden breaking off of the persecution

suggests that it cannot have taken place on the first Passover after Agrippa's return from Rome, i.e. in 42, but is to be put in the last year of the reign of Agrippa, at Passover 43.[1311] This would also confirm the Lukan order, which reports the death of Agrippa immediately after Peter's escape.[1312] The precise date of Agrippa's death is not certain. He died three years after being given rule over all Judaea.[1313] That brings us to January/February 44. That he had a fatal illness when he was arranging games for the *soteria* of the emperor in Caesarea does not provide any certain point of reference, since Josephus does not give the name of the emperor. So it is unclear whether these games were in honour of Claudius or Augustus.[1314] In other words, the journey of Barnabas (and according to Luke also of Paul) with the collection can be dated to the time after the persecution or the death of Agrippa. In that case, leaving aside the impossibility of Paul's participation, we could assume that the motive for the collection was not only the price increase (see above, 241), but also the support of a community which had been very much impoverished by the failure of the sharing of goods, the persecution and partial boycott. That it was basically dependent on support from the 40s on follows from Gal. 2.10.

The lively and detailed account of the liberation of Peter from prison seems only partly legendary; in other parts it is realistic. The appearance of the angel, which is quite naturally explained as Peter's subjective impression, is 'legendary'.[1315] When the commentators find typical legendary motives here like the 'miracle of the opening of the doors'[1316] or the typological parallel to the liberation from Egypt on Passover night, they do not reflect that the 'miracle' did not take place on Passover night itself but at the last possible point before the execution, and at the end of the seven days of festival which lasted to 21 Nisan. Because the miraculous release did not take place on Passover night in Luke, the *Epistula Apostolorum* (c.15) around the middle of the second century introduces it. Here Peter is released by the angel during Passover night so that he can take part in the celebration of the Passover, the commemoration of the death of Jesus. After the cock crows he returns to prison until his release – as reported in Acts 12 – which takes place so that he can preach the gospel.[1317]

Above all, we should take seriously historically the information at the end of the narrative about the circumstances in the visit to the house of Mary the mother of John. Luke merely makes mention of Peter's instructions to communicate his deliverance 'to James and the brothers' and reports that Peter went 'to another place' (Acts 12.17). Peter had to reach safety and left the area over which Agrippa ruled. That may also have applied to his family, since his wife accompanied him on his later mission journeys.[1318] That 'the other place' is a cipher for Rome (with a learned allusion to Ezek. 12.13 LXX) and that Peter now immediately went there and founded the Roman community certainly rests on early church tradition, and scholars still like to put it forward today, but there is no adequate historical evidence for it.[1319] We meet Peter again in Acts 15 in 48/49 as a solid member of the Jerusalem community at the 'Apostolic Council' and some time afterwards in Antioch. Here we have not only Luke's report but Paul's account in Gal. 2. That only the three pillars, and the anonymous δοκοῦντες, are mentioned in Gal. 2.1–10 suggests that other 'apostles' also fled Jerusalem as a consequence of the execution of James and the arrest of Peter.

According to Gal. 2.9, James the brother of the Lord is at the head of the Jerusalem community; then follows Peter, with John in third place. That means that at this time Peter no longer had the leading place in the Jerusalem 'hierarchy'. He had probably been absent long enough for people in Jerusalem to have had to choose a new community order, after the persecution, without him. However, he was not away so long that he was regarded as an outsider – like Barnabas and Paul. That he then came after the brother of the Lord in authority and was in some way now subordinate to him helped towards peace in the community.[1320]

We can only guess why Paul went to Mary's house after his escape, and not directly to James. This may indicate some distance, but we need not draw the further conclusion that there was a tense relationship between the two.[1321]

After the betrayal and death of Judas Iscariot, a twelfth member of the circle of disciples had been chosen in the earliest period. After the death of James the son of Zebedee and the flight of Peter, however, there is no longer a simple choice of a replacement.[1322] It could be that the result of the persecution, the withdrawal of the 'Twelve', i.e. in Luke the 'apostles', into the background as a leading group,[1323] had been one of the aims of those responsible for it. By removing or driving away the leading disciples of Jesus, they sought to strike at the core of this enthusiastic movement. Now the leadership of the earliest Jerusalem community passed to James the brother of the Lord and his body of elders, which is mentioned for the first time in Acts 11.30. The Lord's brother was one of the earliest witnesses to the resurrection (I Cor. 15.7), but not one of the Twelve. Luke mentions him here for the first time (12.17), and in so doing suppresses the fact that he was the brother of the Lord. He only mentions the brothers of Jesus in general terms, along with Jesus' mother in Acts 1.14f.: after the Eleven, and among the 120. James must already have played a role in Jerusalem in the earlier years as an impressive personality. Therefore he is the only one to be involved in Paul's secret first visit to Peter.[1324] However, it is going too far to suppose that with his 'request' to communicate his deliverance and flight, Peter himself to some degree handed over the leadership to James.[1325] Luke's mention of James corresponds more with his significance in Gal. 1.19; 2.9, 12 and Acts 15.19. The brother of the Lord helped the communities which had been disturbed after the persecution to a firm new self-awareness.[1326] However, this involved a certain theological reorientation, not least over the question of the law.

Luke's next extensive report of events in Jerusalem, in Acts 15, mentions Peter and James as the speakers; here the latter makes the decisive proposal for resolving the conflict. Alongside them 'the apostles and the elders' appear together as a stereotyped leading group, the former for the last time.[1327] In this way Luke makes them take their leave (together with Peter, who is their spokesman), elegantly and almost without conflict. This creates a transition which causes the first reader, 'Theophilus', and his circle no offence. For Paul in Galatians, the situation was more difficult. Later, in Acts 21.18, in the first-person plural account by Luke on Paul's visit to James in Jerusalem, only 'all the presbyters' are present, a sign that for Luke the 'apostolic age' of the community is coming to an end. Around seven years later the great figures of the earliest community are all dead.

As has already been emphasized above (244f.), the Christian office of elder probably goes back to these first presbyters in Jerusalem. The reverse is not the case, since Luke does not introduce any later 'Diaspora presbyters' from the situation of his own community into his narrative.[1328] Πρεσβύτεροι are already mentioned as founders of a synagogue in the Theodotus inscription from Jerusalem.[1329] This synagogue was built before 66 CE, and Theodotus, its builder, refers to the fact that in the time of Herod the foundation stone of the synagogue had been laid three generations earlier by his father and his grandfather, together with the elders of the community and a further patron called Simonides. In Palestine, the elders were the leaders of the local civil and religious communities; in places where the inhabitants were wholly or predominantly Jews, the two offices were not separated.[1330] Whereas in the synagogue inscriptions from this period the corresponding officials in the Diaspora are called ἄρχοντες, these πρεσβύτεροι seem to be a typical phenomenon in the synagogues of Palestine.[1331] This form of constitution for the synagogue and the community was probably the model for the second group chosen by James and the Jerusalem community alongside the 'apostles' who were becoming fewer, after flight and death, in order to return to stable conditions after the persecution. However, the 'apostles' were not suddenly just removed or replaced during their lifetimes. So there will have been a transitional phase. The presupposition for the choice of the elders was that they were settled locally. We do not know how many members this council of elders had. An election had already solved a problem in Jerusalem, once before, when the 'Seven' were appointed from the 'Hellenists'. Presumably James's council of elders was larger, corresponding to the growth of the community – which Luke exaggerates (Acts 21.20).[1332]

The elders of the Jewish community probably also above all had the task of deciding on disputes and on the exclusion of members from the community.[1333] The Christian elders in Jerusalem, too, will have seen their main task as supervising the acceptance of new members of the community and the exclusion

of those members who proved unworthy.[1334] Similarly, the acceptance of the collection from Antioch and its distribution fell
within their competence. According to Acts 4.36f.; 5.1–11, 'the
apostles' performed this task, but according to Luke's account in
Acts 6.1–6 they delegated it to the 'Seven'. This could be a feature
which idealizes the earliest community and refers to later conditions, when the office of deacon was introduced. On the other
hand, in Rom. 15.31 Paul fears that his collection (διακονία) will
not be accepted in Jerusalem. Presumably he was right here. That
Luke knew of the collection is clear from his account of Paul's
defence before Felix in 24.17: 'After some years I came to bring
my nation alms and offerings.' Probably James and the elders –
note the plural in 21.20 – proposed to use this money to release
the four Jewish-Christian Nazirites from their obligations (21.24)
and thus prove Paul's faithfulness to the law. Where else could
Paul himself have found the considerable financial contribution
that was necessary?

It is only consistent with this that the later tradition of the
second century should have made James the first 'bishop' of
Jerusalem, appointed by the apostles, and thus have legitimated
the church constitution which became established in the first half
of the second century with the example of the earliest community
in Jerusalem. The historical truth of this tradition is that later
James took on the character of a monarchical community
leader.[1335]

The persecution of the Christians by Agrippa I in Jerusalem
was a 'momentous interlude' for the earliest community there.
After the persecution, for around twenty years it was able to
recover and consolidate itself under the leadership of James the
brother of the Lord, but from now on it had to take special heed
of the changed situation in the Holy City under the new unhappy
rule of the procurators, a situation which was becoming more
radical. The shock caused by Caligula's order continued, the
antipathy to non-Jews intensified, and zeal for the law and the
readiness to use violence associated with it increased. Now the
charge of belonging to the 'lawbreakers' (Josephus, *Antt.* 20, 200)
could quickly be made when different views clashed, especially as
the high-priestly families, still powerful but feeling very insecure,

continued to be hostile to the Christians. The cautious attitude of James, who wanted to avoid causing any offence in Jerusalem on the question of the law, and the zeal of his supporters, who wanted to extend this attitude outside Judaea as well, along with the intensified view of some – perhaps in Jerusalem most – Jewish Christians that all Gentile Christians should be circumcised, is probably connected with the effect of this persecution. It would also be understandable if James had attempted to make closer links with that opposition in Jerusalem to which Peter perhaps owed his life, i.e. the Pharisaic circles faithful to the law, by his own strict personal obedience to the law. That this tendency was successful is shown by the Pharisaic protest against the execution of James and other Jewish Christians through the high priest Annas II in 62 CE. Nevertheless, the development could no longer be reversed, especially as the 'opposition party', which essentially was led by Paul, was more convincing – despite the disappointment that Paul had to experience in Antioch. The flight of the earliest Jerusalem community to Gentile Pella, the outbreak of the Jewish War, and the destruction of Jerusalem sealed this development.

The execution of James the son of Zebedee, Peter's flight from the territory ruled over by Agrippa I, and the transfer of the leadership of the Jerusalem community from Peter and the apostles to James and the elders, is matched by an account which we find for the first time in the *Kerygma Petri*, which comes from the beginning of the second century. According to this, the Lord commanded repentance to be preached to Israel so that through his name Israel could come to believe in God. 'But after twelve years, go out into the world, so that no one can say, "We did not hear."'[1336] The anti-Montanist Apollonius, around 197, gives a similar report from earlier tradition (ἐκ παραδώσεως): 'the Redeemer commanded his apostles not to leave Jerusalem for twelve years'.[1337] According to the *Actus Petri cum Simone*, on the basis of a command from the Lord, Peter stayed twelve years in Jerusalem before going to Rome, because of a vision of Christ.[1338] This relatively long interval of twelve years is in some contrast to the command to go forth in Matt. 29.19, which in later apostolic literature was understood as an immediate mission with which the division of the various missionary territories was connected. Here we should reflect whether the tradition of leaving Jerusalem after twelve years does not represent a schematic reminiscence of the expulsion of Peter and other leading disciples because of the persecution by Agrippa I in 43 (or less probably 42).[1339] The persecution and the flight introduced on the one hand a basic change in the community in Jerusalem, and on the other close contact between the Christians who had escaped from Jerusalem and the young mixed or predominantly Gentile Christian communities outside the Holy Land. Perhaps the prophetic embassy in Acts 11.27f. was also already a consequence of this revolution.

As in the case of the apostle's early journey to Rome, so, contrary to later reports after Eusebius, it is also questionable whether Peter already visited Antioch at this time. The early Christian reports after Eusebius here rest on a false interpretation of Gal. 2.11ff. and an inference that Asia Minor was his mission territory, on the basis of I Peter, so that his journey there had to go through Antioch.[1340] The 'other place' (ἕτερος τόπος) in Acts 12.17 probably lay outside the sphere of power of Agrippa I, but remains unknown to us.

8.2.7 *The beginnings of the community in Rome and the silence over Egypt*

The beginnings of Roman Christianity may go back to the reign of Caligula. According to Augustine, pagans, referring to Porphyry's work against the Christians, claimed that after the Jewish law had only been disseminated in the narrow area of Syria, it had come to Italy, 'after the emperor Gaius (Caligula) or at least in his reign'.[1341] These pagan opponents, or the version of the Porphyry text which they had, had presumably misunderstood what Porphyry was saying and applied it to the Jews instead of the Christians. We cannot attribute so nonsensical a statement that the Jews only came to Rome under Claudius to the learned and precise Neoplatonist. Presumably his statement referred to the *lex nova* of the Christians.[1342]

The famous note of Suetonius about the expulsion of the Jews, i.e. presumably the Jewish Christians, from Rome, which according to Orosius took place in the ninth year of Claudius, i.e. *c.*48/49, and Paul's long-conceived plans to visit the young community in Rome, which he indicates at the beginning of Romans[1343] and which he had probably been nurturing since the 'Apostolic Council', suggest that the beginnings of Roman Christianity go back to the time before the accession of Claudius on 25 January 41 CE. Probably the community was not founded from Antioch, where at this time the community there had first to consolidate itself, but from Jerusalem, where a close link had been established with the capital through the numerous Jewish prisoners of war from the years 63, 37 and 4 BCE who had been carried off to Rome and the many who had returned to the Holy Land.[1344] In Jerusalem the synagogue of the 'Libertinoi', i.e. the Jewish freemen from Rome, which is first mentioned in Acts 6.9, and the Theodotus inscription (because Theodotus' father probably bears the Roman gentilic name Vett[i]enus) attest this link with Rome.[1345] It is matched in Rome by the largest and oldest synagogue community of the 'Hebrews', i.e. the Jews who originally spoke Aramaic, in Trastevere.[1346] Given the constant close exchange between Jerusalem and Rome, we may assume that Greek-speaking Christians also came to Rome towards the end of the 30s, i.e. not too long after the foundation of the community of Antioch.[1347] Here it is remarkable that in the prescript in Rom. 1.7 Paul avoids the term *ekklesia* and speaks only of the beloved of God and those 'called to be saints', 'who are in Rome'. Only in 16.5 does the 'house church' of Prisca and Aquila appear. Presumably at the time of the writing of Romans in winter 56/57 there was not yet a coherent overall community, but only several 'house churches' loosely linked together.[1348]

Given the enthusiastic apocalyptic expectation of an imminent end, the capital of the empire must have exercised a particular attraction. To some degree it was the antipodes to Jerusalem – hostile to God – and the 'lion's den'. Did not the good news of the victory of the crucified Christ and his claim to rule over all creatures have to be proclaimed there in particular?[1349] Therefore for a long time Paul, too, is anxious to go there – contrary to his principle only to work in places where the gospel had not been preached before him. For that reason the apocalyptist John also looks, full of anger and contempt, on the 'whore Babylon' which sits on seven hills (Rev. 17.9), and Luke ends his second work with Paul's arrival in Rome, since there, as far as the author is concerned, the 'to the ends of the earth' (ἕως ἐσχάτου τῆς γῆς) of Acts 1.8 has been fulfilled. One could cite all this as an argument for a visit by Peter to Rome after his expulsion from Jerusalem,[1350] but it is not enough to make such a visit probable. That remains 'not proven'.

By contrast, the silence of Luke, and indeed of all early Christian literature up to the great Gnostics, beginning with Basilides, about Alexandria and Egypt is striking. We have only two – scanty – exceptions: the Ethiopian eunuch and finance minister who has to return through Egypt to Meroe in his kingdom and thus is the first to bring the gospel in the deep south 'to the end of the (inhabited) world', and the Jewish Christian Apollos, versed in rhetoric, whom Luke in Acts 18.24 calls an Ἀλεξανδρεὺς τῷ γένει, i.e. a citizen of Alexandria by descent. However, the Ethiopian does not come to faith in Egypt but on the road to Gaza, and in the case of Apollos, too, one could ask whether he did not gain his new faith in Judaea, since he is alleged to know only the baptism of John (Acts 18.25). Elsewhere we have no evidence of a particular influence of John the Baptist from Egypt. Only the later Western text is concerned to fill this gap, and adds, 'who had been instructed in the word of the Lord in his home city'.[1351] This silence is probably an indication that the gospel came to Alexandria later than to Antioch and Rome. According to the later church tradition Mark, the disciple of Peter, was the first to come to preach the gospel in Alexandria – a rather questionable piece of information.[1352] This distance is also suggested by the fact that while already in the Old Testament period Egypt is the typical land of the exile and the Diaspora,[1353] on the other hand a return to Egypt, to the 'house of slavery', was tabu, indeed was sometimes explicitly forbidden.[1354] As indeed Paul and Luke show clearly that plans for travelling and mission were connected with 'instructions by the Spirit' and sometimes also with the exegesis of particular scriptural texts, we can assume that these Old Testament prohibitions were for a long time combined with warnings from early Christian prophets and at first prevented any plans of extending mission to Egypt. During the twelve or thirteen years between the death of Jesus and the persecution of Agrippa missionary interest was concentrated on the area between Arabia and Cilicia; here the area of northern Syria was still treated in a relatively superficial way. The growth of the community outside Palestine should not be imagined as having happened all that quickly. Earliest Christianity brought an offensively new and unusual message, and the expectation of the imminent coming of the Lord was initially greater than the wider geographical prospect of mission. It was the grandson of Herod who here introduced a certain reorientation through his violent intervention. Like the stoning of Stephen earlier, a persecution led to wider missionary activity. The advance of Christians to Rome seems here at first to be the exception which proves the rule. Basically, for the first twenty years of earliest Christian history the biblical motto was: Shem, then – cautiously – Japhet, but not Ham.

8.2.8 The collegial mission in Syria and Cilicia

According to Gal. 1.21, Paul stayed 'in the regions of Syria and Cilicia' in the roughly fourteen years between his visit to Peter in Jerusalem and the 'Apostolic Council'. That this was – we must add, above all – Tarsus and Antioch we learn only through Luke, who is so often censured as being unreliable. Even the fact that the apostle sets out on the journey to the 'Council' from Antioch, on behalf of the Antiochenes, is something that we know only through him. That Luke is telling the truth follows, despite the pronounced use of the first person singular in Gal. 2.1–10, from the fact that not only did Paul (and Barnabas) have a burning interest in a mission 'critical of the law' but the whole community in Antioch had already been engaged in this kind of mission for more than ten years. We must also read Paul's own auto-biographical information with understandably critical eyes – in his self-defence in Gal. 1. and 2 he does not put his apostolic light under a bushel. But from the days of the history-of-religions school Antioch has been ardently loved by many New Testament scholars, since it appears – under its Gentile Christian aegis – as the place of the radical 'Hellenization' and syncretistic alteration of earliest Christianity, which then shines out almost like a 'new religion', in contrast to its beginnings in Jerusalem, since here the 'Jewish leaven' was cast out.[1355] If we take Paul's information about the 'whole region of Syria and Cilicia'[1356] seriously in every respect, as compared with the one-sided preference for the Lukan Antioch, that would mean that the apostle (and Barnabas) probably spent only a fairly short part of that time between the end of the one year in Antioch and the 'Council', i.e. say between 40/41 and the end of 48 and beginning of 49, in Antioch itself, and more frequently was travelling (as a rule with Barnabas). As is his custom, Luke gives a paradigmatic description of two such journeys. First, very briefly, there is the historically obscure journey to Jerusalem with the collection, on which Paul himself did not go as far as Jerusalem, and secondly Paul's so-called first missionary journey with Barnabas to Cyprus and south-east as far as central Asia Minor, more precisely to Pamphylia, Pisidia and Lycaonia, which bordered on Cilicia. With geographical generosity Paul can evidently still include these areas under the term κλίματα in the information that he gives in Gal. 1.21. In Corinthians he speaks, like Luke, only of Achaea and Macedonia, and in Rom. 15.19 he surprisingly says 'as far as Illyricum',[1357] a province which only borders Macedonia to the north for about 100 km from Dyrrachium. But presumably he simply means Illyris Graeca, which comprised western Macedonia and extended as far as Epirus to the south.[1358] By Galatia, conversely, he means southern Galatia, i.e. the area of the first journey.[1359] If we allow around one or two years for this – a whole series of communities was founded, and this does not take place in a few days – that still leaves between five and six years of missionary activity, predominantly in Syria. Paul had already founded a basic core of communities in Cilicia between 36/37 and 39/40, so that, following Barnabas' invitation, he could move to Antioch. Unfortunately both Paul himself and Luke are silent about these years. Now it would be completely perverse to want to fill this gap, as Gerd Lüdemann persistently attempts to do, with an advance by Paul into the Aegean.[1360] That would hopelessly confuse not only the clear sequence of statements in Gal. 1 and 2 but also large

interconnected complexes of texts in Luke.[1361] The missionary
extension of the new messianic movement did not yet take a
geographically stormy course in the first two decades. Here
Luke tends to exaggerate, not in geography – where he is relatively realistic – but in numbers and in his plerophoric mode of
expression. This tendency to exaggerate can still be found in the
letter of Pliny the Younger to Trajan in 110 CE, in which Pliny
wanted to emphasize to the emperor the magnitude of the
danger threatened by the Christians and the success of his harsh
penal measures. There is also the *multitudo ingens* of the
Christians who according to Tacitus were condemned in Nero's
persecution in 64 CE because of their 'hatred towards the human
race'. This is simply an imitation of the description of the
Bacchanalia scandal of 186 BCE by Livy.[1362]

After their expulsion from Jerusalem the 'Hellenists' had first
extended into the bordering territories, say, of the Decapolis and
southern Syria, and then along the coast northwards. Thus on the
accession of Claudius at the beginning of 41, with the exception
of the coast and Antioch, central and northern Syria had hardly
been opened up to active mission. This mission was and
remained a mission to the cities, which was orientated on the
synagogues of the larger cities with their circle of Greek-speaking
sympathizers. The much-discussed itinerant Syrian charismatics,
whom scholars seek to reconstruct on the basis of the sending out
of disciples in the Synoptics and the Didache,[1363] hardly fit into
this picture. The tradition about their sending out, with its
radical quality which could hardly have been practised over a
lengthy period, goes back to an initiative of Jesus himself, and at
best could have had an influence on Jewish Palestine, where from
the beginning there were points of support for the Jesus movement in the villages. The Didache, which is between two and
three generations later and which in many respects stands
close to the Gospel of Matthew, again (or still) presupposes the
existence of such village Christian communities, presumably
on the borders of Syria and Palestine. However, it no longer
speaks of mission, but only of the edification of already existing
communities.

By contrast, the mission of the Greek-speaking 'Hellenists' will hardly have found much of an echo in the villages among the Syrian fellahin. The building up of urban communities had to be done more systematically and took time. This was the same in Syria as in Macedonia, Achaea or Asia Minor. Despite the silence of Luke, who in his narrative only elaborates the major episodes and presses westwards, where he himself later becomes an eye-witness, and even of Paul, where one gets the impression that he wants to forget the long years in Syria, we do have some isolated traces. According to Acts 15.3 Paul and Barnabas walked through 'Phoenicia and Samaria' on their journey to Jerusalem for the 'Apostolic Council' and 'to the great joy' of the brethren relate the 'conversion of the Gentiles', i.e. probably for Luke the success of the journey to Cyprus and to the interior of Asia Minor. So he presupposes that this mission was not only allowed but also practised there. Acts 21.3–9 reports the friendly reception of Paul by the Christians in Tyre, Ptolemais and Caesarea, and Acts 27.3 the support of the prisoner by friends from Sidon. Paul will have got to know these communities on the coast during his journeys in Syria and Phoenicia and have gained friends there. Unfortunately such indications of place have only been preserved quite by chance, even in Luke, and this applies generally to the pre-Christian sources before the Council in Nicaea. The most extensive catalogue of places of apostolic preaching in Phoenicia and Syria is given us by the romance-like Pseudo-Clementines, the oldest version of which is to be put only towards the end of the second century.

In Acts 15.23, Luke calls those addressed in the letter of the 'apostles and elders' of Jerusalem the 'brothers in Antioch, Syria and Cilicia'. According to this, Paul and Barnabas appeared in Jerusalem as representatives not only of the community in Antioch but of all the communities in Syria and Cilicia, i.e. probably of all those communities in which they had worked and which shared their view over the question of circumcision and the ritual law. When Paul emphasizes here (Gal. 2.2), 'lest some-how I should be running or had run in vain', the ἔδραμον refers to his own quite vital share in this missionary work 'critical of the law'. Above all its theological establishment and implementation in these communities may not least go back to his influence.

I Corinthians 9.5f., in which Paul is probably referring to experiences of missionary work he shared with Barnabas, the way they worked to earn their living, and their unmarried state, also presupposes shared journeys. Their complete independence pre-destined them to that and also explains why it was 'the Spirit' which sent them out on a shared collegial mission in Acts 13.17.

Later, Luke says that Paul and Silas strengthen 'the churches in Syria and Cilicia' on their journey to Lycaonia (15.46). The first station he mentions after crossing the Taurus is Derbe; in other words, both could have travelled the road through rough Cilicia through Corycus, Claudiopolis and Laranda. In that case the 'Syrian' part of this journey would have been brief, and these would have been communities which were founded above all by Paul himself in Cilicia (see above, 156ff.).

Harnack has collected the scanty information about communities in Syria before the time of Constantine in his history of Christian mission.[1364] Ignatius speaks of communities near Antioch which have sent bishops or presbyters and deacons to Antioch.[1365] However, here the provincial capital had a pre-eminence, so that in the letter to the Romans Ignatius can call himself 'bishop of Syria' and call for prayer for the persecuted 'church in Syria which has God for its shepherd in place of me'.[1366] Are we to see behind this ultimately the model of Jerusalem before 62 CE as the centre of Judaea with James at its head, so that Antioch took over the monarchical episcopate – in substance, not in title – from there?[1367]

The pre-eminence of the bishop of Antioch and his responsibility for the communities of (northern) Syria is also evident from the correspondence of Bishop Serapion around 200 with the community in Rhossus over the Gospel of Peter, which was suspected of heresy.[1368] In the list of those taking part at Nicaea, from north Syria alone more than twenty dioceses between the Euphrates and the sea (and nine from Cilicia) are listed, including the majority of important cities. On this Harnack observes: 'The distribution suggests that Christianity was to be found quite consistently and quite strongly in Syria around the year 325.'[1369] A first basic root will have been established in the five or six years, say, between 41 and 46/47, by the activity of Barnabas and Paul and other missionaries unknown to us. Here, however, these travels seem to have extended far to the south, since Sidon, Tyre, Ptolemais and Caesarea, where Paul was welcomed with such hospitality, lie outside this area. Paul could also have visited Damascus and perhaps even 'Arabia' again, where he had ventured his first missionary attempts after the death of Aretas IV in 40 CE.

The sending out of the two missionary partners to Cyprus and Asia Minor described in Acts 13.1ff. indicates a belief that the mission territory of Phoenicia, Syria and Cilicia had been 'worked' sufficiently and that now finally a move had to be made from Shem to Japhet. Perhaps the man from Tarsus had had this move in view for some time. Paul's thought may have then already been similar to that in Rom. 15.23, 'since I no longer have any room for work in these regions' (νυνὶ δὲ μηκέτι τόπον ἔχων ἐν τοῖς κλίμασι τούτοις), except that at this time he was thinking of leaving 'Syria and Cilicia' and now going to Macedonia, Achaea and Asia. In both cases he was pressing further westwards. Precisely for that reason, as a preparation for the mission in Achaea and for the difficult way to Rome, Luke's report with its paradigmatic account of this mission in 13.1ff. and the journey associated with it is important information. The sending itself serves as an example. It is not Paul's own decision or a 'democratic' vote of the community, but the instruction of 'the Holy Spirit' which after preparatory 'prayer' and fasting (λειτουργούντων δὲ αὐτῶν τῷ κυρίῳ καὶ νηστευόντων) speaks through one or more of the five prophets mentioned – presumably the charismatic 'governing body' in Antioch: 'Set apart for me Barnabas and Saul for the work to which I have called them.' There προσκαλεῖν calls the κλητὸς ἀπόστολος of the prescripts to Paul's letters,[1370] and the ἀφορίζειν εἰς ἔργον the ἀφωρισμένος εἰς εὐαγγέλιον θεοῦ which follows in Rom. 1.1. The impulse to missionary work and major journeys often frequently came from 'instructions' of the Spirit or 'revelations'.[1371] In other words, we may assume that the process described in 13.1ff. took place in a similar way in forming the mission in Syria.

Unfortunately we do not know how far after the persecution by Agrippa, i.e. after 43 CE, emissaries from Jerusalem also engaged

in mission in Syria and whether and how far there were conflicts
here with the earlier mission of the 'Hellenists'. If these emissaries penetrated as far as (southern) Galatia in the 50s, however,
they must previously have also worked in Syria. The visit of the
prophet Agabus (and his fellow prophets) in 11.27f. was to make
contact with a community which was already existing, and did not
aim at founding new communities. The appearance of delegates
from Jerusalem reported in Acts 15.1ff. and Paul's reference to
'brothers secretly brought in, who slipped in to spy out our freedom which we have in Christ Jesus, that they might bring us into
bondage' (Gal. 2.4) are such visits to communities, and are
probably connected with them; they indicate events, say, in
Antioch in 48 which then made the 'Apostolic Council' necessary. The deep resentment expressed by the apostle's sharp
formulations suggests that the controversy that he reports in Gal.
2.4f. was not the first. Probably the conflict depicted here in the
forties after the persecution of Agrippa, which was becoming
more critical, developed gradually and came to a climax with the
controversy preceding Gal. 2.1 which Luke mentions briefly in
Acts 15.1f. This climax necessitated a solution for a problem
which had become intolerable. The strange thing is that it had
not already emerged ten or fifteen years later, in the thirties,
when Gentile 'godfearers' were also already being baptized. This
can be explained by the sharpening of the former more 'liberal'
position in Jerusalem and the growth of Zealotism there, which
has already been touched on several times. At the same time, the
terseness of Paul's account of events in Jerusalem and later in
Antioch shows that the basic theological problem of righteousness by faith or works of the law, 'merit' or 'grace', Christ or the
Torah, did not first break out with the offence felt at the Galatian
communities, but had already become virulent during the
missionary work in Syria in this critical time. For Paul (and
Barnabas) at that point everything was at risk, not just his
previous missionary work but in fact the truth of his gospel, 'that
the truth of the gospel might be preserved for you'.[1372]

So there may perhaps already have been similar controversies
in the other Syrian communities for some time. Therefore the
later apostolic decree is addressed not only to Antioch but at the

same time also to the churches in Syria and Cilicia. By contrast, the attitude of many Palestinian Christians could be expressed in statements like Luke 16.17Q or in the three verses in the Sermon on the Mount, 5.17–19, which already sound contradictory within the universal framework of the Gospel of Matthew.

On the other hand the three leading men in the community in Jerusalem and thus the communities in Judaea, the three 'pillars' James, Peter and John, were ultimately largely positive towards the mission to the Gentile 'critical of the law', despite all their reservations; above all Peter. Otherwise the positive result at the 'Apostolic Council' described in Gal. 2.6–10 would not have been arrived at. It was a green light for Paul on the way to Japhet, i.e. to the west, and the Aegean coast of Asia Minor, to Macedonia, Achaea, Rome and indeed – as he hoped – to Spain.[1373]

It therefore seems to me to be probable that already in these roughly five or six years between 41 and 46/47 the conditions of missionary work in Syria critical of the law slowly got worse, above all in the south bordering on Palestine, where the Jewish Diaspora was strongest, and that these circumstances, quite apart from the later interlude in Antioch, so darkened Paul's memory of his time in Syria that later he is silent about it in his letters, with the exception of Gal. 1 and 2. His own action in respect of salvation through Christ alone, through grace and faith alone, 'without the works of the law', did not basically change, otherwise it would have been easier for him to yield to Jerusalem, to circumcise Titus and later to join Peter and Barnabas in Antioch. But here we have again gone beyond the framework of the 'unknown years'. Basically they end with Acts 13.1ff. From then on Luke has his uninterrupted story of Paul and the founding of those communities which are then also addressed in the letters – first of all in 'southern Galatia'.[1374]

Therefore we must return to Antioch and ask the last question: how did the apostle's theological thought develop there?

8.3 Antioch and Pauline theology

8.3.1 The religious situation in the city: Syrian 'syncretism'?

We have already gone into the significance of the Jewish Diaspora community, its synagogues and the sympathizers visiting its worship, and also the tense and oppressed situation of the Jewish inhabitants of Antioch during the Caligula crisis. According to figures from antiquity, the Jewish element in the city and the suburbs which formed part of Greater Antioch may have amounted to around ten or fifteen per cent of the population.[1375] We know relatively very little about the religious milieu of the city as a whole for the first century CE. Antioch remained predominantly pagan until well into the period after Constantine.[1376] Until late antiquity (East) Syrians regarded it as 'the fair city of the Greeks'.[1377] The most extensive report for the first century CE is in Josephus, but he is interested only in the Jewish element in the population. As further ancient sources for pagan Antioch we really have only the few notes in ancient authors,[1378] the later writings of Libanius and Malalas, and the archaeological discoveries.

The excavations in the years 1932–1939 could only cover the city area inadequately. In Antioch itself they were limited by the modern building over the former Syrian quarter mentioned by Strabo, which it was not possible to excavate,[1379] and were further made very difficult by the deep layers of rubble and earth which cover the ancient city by up to 10 metres. The excavations concentrated on parts of the ceremonial street, its colonnades and the nympheum. After the discovery of numerous interesting mosaics in the suburbs, above all in the villa suburb of Daphne, it was decided to safeguard these first. The picture produced by these excavations of the city confirmed what was known from the ancient sources: Antioch was a typical Hellenistic Roman metropolis.[1380] The Syrian character of the city does not emerge clearly and stands more in the background.[1381]

In 37 CE an earthquake shook the city so severely that even Daphne was also affected.[1382] As has already been mentioned, Caligula was able to show his concern for the city by giving support in rebuilding. When Paul came to the city and lived – according to local tradition – in the street by the pantheon,[1383] Antioch was a major 'building site', flourishing in a sudden boom.

Caligula had already shown himself a generous benefactor to the city, and since the early Hellenistic period such men had 'the honour of altars',[1384] before the turbulence over the erection of his statue in the Jerusalem temple broke out, involving the Jews and the inhabitants of Antioch who sympathized with them in the same feelings of indignation. Since the foundation of the city, the Antiochenes had been accustomed to the erection of statutes of rulers in the city, in the temple precincts and above all the ruler cult.

Seleucus I is said to have inaugurated the foundation of Seleucia Pierias, as of Antioch, by sacrifices to the earlier Semitic indigenous gods and to have determined the location of the cities by their instructions;[1385] the old Semitic cults on the city mountains remained, and each was given its *interpretatio graeca*. But the new foundations themselves were to have a purely Hellenistic character and were dedicated to the founders and guardians of the Seleucid dynasty. Antioch was dedicated to Zeus by the erection of a temple – probably in the Agora[1386] – and Zeus was always the predominant god in the city itself. In Daphne, the sanctuary of Apollos (and Artemis) was founded;[1387] this was a place for asylum and oracles.[1388] The Jewish high priest Onias III, who had taken refuge in the pagan temple, although he is later depicted as a model of piety, was persuaded to leave his asylum and subsequently murdered.[1389] The statue of Apollos in Daphne was made by Bryaxis, by whom Seleucus I similarly had a portrait of himself made. In the first century CE, alongside the temple precincts in Daphne there was a luxurious villa suburb, since Germanicus died here. However, the great private houses with their splendid mosaics, which were discovered in the investigations, are of a much later date. As a synagogue has been found here, Jews also belonged to the well-to-do circles.[1390] The early minting of coins by the Seleucids indicates a preference for Apollo.[1391] These sanctuaries were probably connected with the ruler cult from the start, since the Seleucids traced their descent from Zeus and Apollo.[1392]

The 'Tyche' of the state protected the ruler and his foundation, and her statue at the same time symbolized the state. A
famous bronze statue of her was made by Eutyches of Sicyon, a
pupil of Lysippus. The goddess is enthroned – the mural crown
on her head, a swimming youth at her feet representing the river
(god) Orontes – in a flowing robe, her right leg over her left, resting on Mount Silpion; in her right hand she is holding a bundle
of ears of corn, and she is resting her left hand on the mountain.
The whole statue is Hellenistic in a surprisingly elegant way, but
combines the oriental side in its emphasis on Mount Silpion. No
wonder that it became the model for the depiction of the city
goddesses of many Hellenistic cities in the East.[1393] In addition,
initially on coins, a second image, that of a standing Tyche of
Antioch, became established.[1394]

Since the foundation of the city, the other main gods of the
Greek pantheon had also been represented in the city, with Zeus
always at their head. Seleucus stationed his troops here, and in a
synoecism the inhabitants of the earlier Greek settlements (above
all Antigoneia) and Syrian settlements in the area; these also
brought their private house cults and gods with them alongside
the official cults.[1395] However, the official state and ruler cult was
artificial and constructed, and took little account of the older
cults.

On his *pompe*, the ceremonial procession from Antioch to
Daphne, Antiochus IV took with him in triumph 'all the gods
named or worshipped by men'.[1396] The images of the gods were
impossible to count. In the encomium on his home city (around
360 CE), i.e. more than 500 years later, Libanius still emphasizes:

> Our city was the abode of the gods, so that if we wanted to, we
> could compete with Olympus. For there the stories of the gods
> depend on words, but here the proof is before people's
> eyes.[1397]

The comparison with Olympus and the tense are significant: it
was the city of an *extended Greek pantheon*, and that was still visible
in the temples in the form of statues. The orator does not want
this heritage to be barbarically destroyed by the Christians, but to
be preserved.[1398] Libanius is giving his report in the context of the

introduction of the cult of Isis into the city by Seleucus III (second half of the third century). As the city was under Ptolemaic rule from 245 to 240, Isis was perhaps introduced into Antioch by Ptolemy III,[1399] whereas the local tradition which Libanius cites relates this to Seleucus. Libanius further recalls that once the gods had become indigenous, they could no longer be transplanted, but alien gods liked to become Antiochene.[1400] Understandably, one Olympian did not stand very high in the veneration of the Antiochenes, Poseidon, the shaker of the earth.[1401] What seems to us to be a confusing multiplicity of cults served Libanius in praising the beauty of his city.

However, already from the beginning of the first millennium there had been trade relations between Greece and northern Syria; there is archaeological confirmation of an old Minoan-Greek trade settlement in the Orontes valley. The variant legends about the foundation of Antioch also reflect these earlier traditions and links.[1402]

The narratives about the foundation of a city also betray something of the religious self-understanding of its inhabitants. The foundation legends of Antioch derive its origin from mythical times. In contrast to Alexandria, where the founder of the city, Alexander, dominates all the legends, here Seleucus I is not praised as the first founder. Nor do we have any Jewish version of the foundation legend as we do in Alexandria.[1403] The Jewish population here probably never identified itself as strongly with the city as it did there. What is chronologically the earliest account, in Strabo, derives the foundation of the city from Triptolemus, the hero of the classical mysteries of Eleusis. Indeed he was regarded as the one who brought Demeter's gifts all over the world to all Greeks:

> Triptolemus was sent out by the Argives to seek Io,[1404] who had disappeared in Tyre. After Triptolemus and his companions had searched throughout Cilicia, they gave up the search on the Orontes and remained there. Seleucus I settled the descendants of Triptolemus in Antioch. Therefore the 'Athenians' of Antioch to this day worship Triptolemus as a hero and celebrate his feast on Mount Casius in Seleucia.[1405]

The link between Cilicia and Antioch which appears in Strabo is
striking. Perhaps the Persians already settled Greek mercenaries
in Cilicia, where Soloi and perhaps Anchiale had been founded
as Greek colonies, and in north Syria. 30,000 Greeks are said to
have fought on Darius's side at the battle of Issus.[1406] In any case,
already long before Alexander there were many sometimes close
ties between the north Syrian coastal area and Cilicia, and the
Aegean and Greece, as in the case of the Phoenician cities.

Libanius differs somewhat from Strabo.[1407] Triptolemus and his
companions come to Silpion, ask the inhabitants about Io and
remain there because they are struck by the fertility of the area.
In his eulogy Libanius could 'quote' the foundation legend
briefly, since his hearers knew the tradition.

Malalas gives the most illuminating account:

> Io's brother and other Argive relatives, together with
> Triptolemus, had sought on the local mountain of Antioch,
> Mons Silpion, Io, who had fled for shame at her child con-
> ceived, out of wedlock, by Zeus; she having previously been
> in Egypt and from there out of fear of Hermes (i.e. Thoth)
> having fled further. They had discovered that she had died
> there and was buried on Silpion. She had appeared to them in
> a dream in the form of a cow and said, 'Here am I, I, Io.'[1408]
> The Argives had then resolved to remain in this place and had
> built a temple on the mountain to Io and Kronos.

The divergence in detail between Strabo and Libanius can
suggest that here myths about Isis-Io and Demeter[1409] have been
adopted. Kronos and Triptolemus are also linked in the Demeter
mysteries. Here the cutting off of the ears is called 'Kronos's
harvest'.[1410] Even if there were as yet no mysteries of Isis
(Demeter) in Antioch at the time of Strabo, they could have
found their way into the foundation legend later, in the course of
the first or second centuries CE. Moreover we must reckon with
the effects of earlier worship of local Semitic deities on Silpion.
What is most striking is the mention of a temple building for
Kronos, who is not otherwise bound up with the Io saga. Kronos is
the *interpretatio graeca* of El and Bel.[1411] Triptolemus corresponds
to the fertility god Baal or Dagon, whom the Old Testament and

Phylo of Byblos describe as the 'Philistines'' god of grain.[1412] They may have formed a triad[1413] with Io, who was originally a moon goddess. However, so far there is no trace of Semitic sanctuaries on Silpion, because there have been no excavations.[1414] It is significant that such Syrian Semitic traditions in Malalas and in the Syrian Lucian, who comes from Samosata, appear only in their *interpretatio graeca*.[1415]

One custom of the Syrian population which Malalas reports perhaps points to Semitic tradition in Greek garb: every year the Syrians, who up to his time called the precinct on Silpion, Ionitai, went into the houses of the Greeks in the city with the question ψυχὴ ᾿Ιοῦς σωζέσθω, 'Should Io's life be saved?', which once the Argives had put in their search for Io.[1416] This may have been an old begging custom, but what it was about is hard to say.

The Charonion, a colossal bust hewn out of the rock of Silpion, is also enigmatic testimony to Syrian oriental deities in the city. It can be defined iconographically as Dea Syria, the goddess of Hierapolis.[1417] Antiochus IV is said to have erected the statue when there was a plague in the city. A 'prophet' of the goddess named Leïos had prompted this measure.[1418] However, the apotropaic image was never finished. The reasons for this are obscure, and it will hardly have attracted an official cultic practice. Moreover the 'Macedonian-Athenian' citizens tended to be somewhat distanced from the 'Syrian goddess'. After the earthquake under Caligula, another miracle worker with the Syrian name Debborios, 'Bee(man)',[1419] is said to have erected a column with an apotropaic bust and inscription.[1420] The pedestal of a statue which has on it small reliefs of the triad of Heliopolis-Baalbek ('Jupiter Heliopolis', 'Venus Heliopolis' and 'Mercury Heliopolis') perhaps suggests a Romanized Syrian cult in the city, but these gods were omnipresent in the later period after the second century CE. A narrative by Libanius about Semiramis, who is said to have built the temple of Artemis in the part of the city called Meroe, may indicate a Semitic background. But the legendary Semiramis also played a varied role elsewhere in Greek narratives about the Orient.[1421] These few quite fortuitous pieces of evidence for the ancient gods of the area show how strongly Seleucus I's new foundation was stamped by the Greek-

Hellenistic population and its religious ideas.[1422] The official cult was orientated on the Olympian pantheon and Greek mythology which – as (later) mosaics in the villas of the rich show – also dominated the private sphere.[1423] That Isis and Sarapis were worshipped in the city does not tell against this. Their cult was accepted by the Greeks from the beginning.[1424] The Syrian population, like the Jewish population, will have made pilgrimages on festivals to the ancestral sanctuaries of, say, Hierapolis-Bambyke.[1425]

The best known of the feasts is the Maiuma, a spring festival celebrated every three years with water and fertility rites, which is seen as being typically Syrian. It was reorganized under Commodus (180–192) as ὄργια for Aphrodite and Dionysus, whose nocturnal festivals are already mentioned by Virgil – as also by Malalas.[1426] In addition Malalas mentions horse races and animal baiting, etc.

According to Malalas, the Jewish inhabitants of the city had a dispute with their pagan neighbours during circus games in the reign of Caligula;[1427] they probably went to the theatre,[1428] and perhaps also took part in the Olympic Games, founded by Sosibius, a well-to-do citizen, under Augustus, which were revived under Claudius and Commodus.[1429] The athletic metaphors in IV Maccabees could have been prompted by this new upsurge in gymnastics and musical and literary contests. As is shown by the right of the Jews of Antioch to receive as a monetary payment the gift of oil made to the ephebes mentioned above, so that it could be exchanged for pure oil , they took part in the training of ephebes in the gymnasium, which was under the patronage of Hermes and Heracles.[1430]

The Romans rebuilt the city, which had suffered greatly at the time of the collapse of the Seleucid empire, and adorned it as the residence of the governor and then of the emperor. Caesar renewed the *libertas* of the city with a close link to Rome and began a new building programme.[1431] As well as an amphitheatre, baths, etc., he built the basilica, the Kaisarion, in which the statues of Caesar and the Tyche of Rome stood, and which since Augustus served the Divus Julius and Dea Roma cult. Roman techniques guaranteed water supplies and offered protection against inundations.[1432] Tiberius renewed the temple of Juppiter Capitolinus which Antiochus IV had erected,[1433] and founded a cult of the Dioscuri in honour of himself and his brother Drusus. The ceremonial street was laid out by Herod I and Tiberius along the wall of the Seleucid city.[1434] Herod attempted in this way to extend his influence to Antioch, in the same way as in Damascus and the Phoenician cities. When the first Jewish Christian 'Hellenists' entered the city, the street formed the 'modern' centre of business life. It was extended further east, and on its 'kink' there was a circular place as the 'omphalos', at which the statue of Tiberius dominated the axes of the city. At the north-east end Tiberius erected a gate, crowned with the she-wolf and the twins. Rome was constantly present in Antioch as a political and a *religious* power, from the smallest coins to the colossal new buildings, and was treasured by the population – in contrast to Alexandria – as protector of the population and provider of 'development aid'. After the collapse of the Seleucid empire it had been possible to restore and preserve the social status and Greek culture only with Roman help. So the 'Hellenists' came into a city in a revolution, which was developing into a Roman residence.[1435]

W. Bousset described 'the atmosphere' 'in which Antiochene Christianity and the rest of the earliest Christian Hellenistic communities came into being and grew'[1436] as a religious milieu which had come into being in the 'area of Syrian religious syncretism' (97). In it the deities were called on as 'Lord' or 'Lady' in the mystery cults and Gnostic circles in a way which was a 'model' and a 'mould' for earliest Christianity.[1437] This view, which was taken over by Bultmann and propagated by his disciples, was long dominant in Germany – indeed it is today.[1438] It has still influenced, for example, a remark by Feldtkeller:

> Thus the title Kyrios in Christianity free from the Torah has not been taken over from the Hellenistic world; its precise use is more Hellenistic than traditionally Jewish.[1439]

Here the old and well-known false alternative between Judaism and Hellenism is being handed on. For what does 'Hellenistic' mean here? In the *shema* the Jews prayed in Greek: κύριος ὁ θεὸς

ἡμῶν κύριος εἷς ἐστιν (Deut. 6.4). The corresponding Christian
'formula' takes up this prayer and changes it. The strict
'Semitizing' parallelism of the formula in I Cor. 8.6[1440] speaks for
its antiquity. There is no proof that it came into being in Antioch.
Paul introduced it to the Corinthians between 50 and 51. The
formula may be 'old'; the 'Hellenists' could already have brought
it to Antioch, or Paul himself could have created it himself at a
very early stage. The earliest Christian mission came up against
the common Semitic use of the title Kyrios from the beginning,
but found it quite incompatible with its own 'Maran'-Kyrios, the
crucified and exalted Lord, just as earlier Hellenistic Judaism
knew in the confession of Deut. 6.4 that 'many gods and lords'
who are worshipped as idols are in reality 'nothing', or are
demons.[1441] Does that not presuppose a completely unbroken
continuity with the Jewish tradition? Nowhere were there more
gods with the titles *ba'al, bel, mareh, 'adon* or Kyrios than in
Palestine and Syria. The Jewish and Christian use of 'Lord' in its
various linguistic forms represents the absolute, unbridgeable
opposition to all indigenous pagan cults. Basically that has little
to do with 'Hellenism', since Kyrios was never an authentic Greek
divine epithet.

The postulate that the mystery cults have to be brought in to
illustrate the 'atmosphere' for the first Antiochene Christians has
also completely lost its force.[1442] Moreover for Antioch we have
no evidence of a Jewish (or Christian) controversy with pagan
mysteries, as we do from Alexandria in the case of the mysteries of
Dionysus.[1443] Dionysus and personal names derived from him are
attested quite sparsely in the Syrian capital,[1444] though of course
this is connected with the unsatisfactory situation over sources
generally. Perhaps 'Kyrios' occurs in Antioch as a normal proper
name, but more probably it is an honorific form of address.[1445]
The unique elaboration of the legend of the birth of the prophet
Elijah, the 'prophet like fire', in the VP with a motif of the
Demeter myth points not to Syria but to Palestine.[1446] If IV Macc.
18.10–19 accurately indicates the 'atmosphere' of the Jewish
population in Antioch in the first century BCE, the families
attached great importance to the domestic instruction of their
children in the law and the prophets and taught them to sing the

psalms before they came into contact with the pagan environment. The early Christian missionaries will also have taken up this
domestic 'teaching' in an intensified form in Antioch, if access to
the synagogue was denied them there.[1447]

According to Gal. 2.11–14, the dispute in Antioch was over
table-fellowship between Jewish and Gentile Christians, i.e. over
a problem of the ritual law, and not over the problems which
emerged in Corinth, say that some Gentile Christians continued
to take part in private (?) cultic meals in the temples and in so
doing ate meat offered to idols and drank wine poured as
libations, after lighting an incense stick in honour of the god.[1448]
From the second half of the third century, Isis was established in
Antioch (thus Libanius, above 271). There is no clear evidence
that a mystery cult was associated with the temple of Isis
in Antioch in the course of the first century CE, but this is
conceivable.[1449] However, the Eleusinian mysteries and their
Dionysian rivals in the (original) Greek homeland were probably
more attractive to the proud Greeks of Antioch, who in part still
regarded themselves as 'Athenians'.[1450] According to Libanius,
Artemis was called Eleusinia in Antioch. The temple of Dionysus
in Antioch was a Roman podium temple, but this does not
exclude the possibility that there were Dionysian cultic associations, and that private initiations involving intoxication were celebrated as a mystery of the god.[1451] Gnosis appeared in Antioch
with the Samaritan Menander around 100, and even more
clearly, rather later, with his pupil Satornilus, but was already
influenced in the case of the latter by Christianity. We find real
'Gnostics' here only from the beginning of the second century
CE.[1452]

Remarkably, Antioch itself does not play any great role in
A. Feldtkeller's most recent history-of-religions investigation.[1453]
Paying homage to pan-Syrianism, he comes to the somewhat
ambiguous and enigmatic conclusion:

To have developed the idea of a world-wide mission is Syrian
Christianity's own contribution, which was at best prepared
for in Judaism, but not in the pagan religions of Syria. But
the successful implementation of this idea was also certainly

helped by the competence in dealing with inter-religious situations which the first Gentile Christians brought with them from their Syrian home culture.[1454]

Even if, like Feldtkeller, we subsume all that has any status and name in the New Testament under 'Syria', we can hardly agree with him.[1455] The assertion that Syrian Christianity as a whole developed the 'idea of a world-wide mission' as its 'own contribution' is nonsensical. Is 'Syrian Christianity' to denote, say Paul, Barnabas and the authorities mentioned in Acts 13.2, or even Philip, Silas, Mark and other earliest Christian missionaries? Or is Feldtkeller thinking of the mission charge in Matt. 28.18ff., which – as he writes in the 'Result'[1456] in his first book – gave the real impetus to his investigations? But does this mission charge go back to Syrian 'Gentile Christians'? The author of the first Gospel was a Jewish Christian, but whether he lived in Syria, and if so where, remains open. Here Palestine or its border regions in the north would be most probable. Nor was the controversy in Antioch about whether the Gentile Christians had a competence which made them engage in world-wide mission, but about whether they first had to become Jews in order to be able to be full Christians. Moreover the Jewish-Christian 'Hellenists' in Antioch addressed their mission preaching less to authentic Syrians than to the 'Greeks', a term which at this time does not, as later, simply mean 'Gentiles', but the Greek-speaking middle and upper class on which the Jews of the city had already orientated themselves. There is no description whatsoever in Feldtkeller of the religious situation in Gentile Antioch. Galatians 2.11f. and the – initially abrupt – break with Antioch show clearly that 'Gentile Christianity' was not dominant in Antioch and in Syria generally up to 70 (and sometimes even later), but that open Jewish Christianity had the spiritual leadership (not without difficulties) in the mission to the Gentiles. The original Christian mission to the Gentiles is a *Jewish-Christian* achievement.

Finally, there are yet other witnesses to lively pagan superstition in Antioch which did not first emerge in the third century:[1457] apotropaic mosaics against snakes and the evil eye and magical gems. Apollonius of Tyana is said to have protected the city with talismen. The many forms of superstition which Lucian enumerates in the *Philopseudes* were certainly also present in the Syrian metropolis. His 'Syrians from Palestine' who healed sick people who were possessed is a parody of Jews or Christians.[1458] But the Christians did not want to be included in the circles of philosophers who had come down in the world, mocked by Lucian, nor did they regard their 'Lord' as a newcomer in the Antiochene pantheon, whom they wanted to make at home like other 'ladies' and 'lords' in the Antiochene pantheon – even if Paul is said to have lived in the street next to the pantheon.

8.3.2 Is Antioch the place where Christian theology began?

This last section on the question of the 'unknown years of the apostle' will particularly interest the theological reader who comes from a background of the theories of the history-of-religions school, which seemed revolutionary in their time and were then made common property by R. Bultmann and some of his disciples. For almost all the accounts of a history of earliest Christianity, and New Testament theologies with a historical tendency, pay quite special attention to the theological development in Antioch. Here the letters of Paul are the main source as our earliest evidence and alongside them – willy-nilly – in a free and often varied selection the Acts of the Apostles.

Particularly in most recent times, a variety of works which have come in almost a flood have emphasized the unique significance of Antioch as the place where Christian theology really developed. Thus J. Becker emphasizes in his major monograph on Paul: 'In the first twenty years after Easter, there was no place after Jerusalem which was as important for Christianity as Antioch.' Antioch 'entered church history because this community detached itself from the synagogue and formed a community free of the law which based itself only on Christ; in other words, it gave up the view of Christian faith as that of a group within Judaism, which hitherto was undisputed and had been taken for granted, and understood Christianity as a phenomenon with a new quality which was to be defined only in its own terms.'[1459] In addition Antioch has a 'second merit, namely that

Paul was able to work in this community for around twelve years, matured to become the greatest theologian of the first generation of earliest Christianity, and certainly played an energetic part in shaping the Antiochene situation and determining its future.'[1460]

We would gladly agree with the last statement about the apostle's energetic collaboration in shaping the new doctrine in the metropolis of north Syria, but with the best will in the world one cannot speak of Paul having worked in Antioch for twelve years. Here one should take Paul himself more seriously: he speaks of a long – probably missionary – stay in 'Syria and Cilicia'. If we subtract the time in Tarsus (and Cilicia), the roughly twelve years condense to around eight or nine at most (c. 40–48/49), and Paul spent at least half of these with Barnabas on missionary journeys to the adjoining regions (Acts 13 and 14) or – as we must assume – by himself in Syria (and Cilicia). If we leave aside the so-called 'first' and 'second' journeys, what he depicts in II Cor. 11.23–29 did not all take place in Antioch. That is true above all of the fivefold synagogue punishment of thirty-nine strokes, which shows that even in Syria, after his conversion before Damascus, the detachment from the synagogue did not take place quite so simply and unproblematically as the schematizing account by J. H. Becker would have it.

W. Bousset, from whom one might almost say the 'phantom' of a 'Gentile Christian earliest community' started, begins Chapter 3, which is decisive for his overall account, with the careful statement: 'Between Paul and the earliest Palestinian community stand the Hellenistic communities in Antioch, Damascus and Tarsus. That is not always noticed sufficiently.'[1461]

In other words, Bousset sees that the theological development of Paul cannot be fixed only to Antioch in the time before the Apostolic Council, but is also connected with his activity in Damascus and Tarsus, i.e. in 'Syria and Cilicia', However, his judgment is too one-sided when he states that 'the apostle Paul's relations with Jerusalem were of a very scanty nature'.[1462] This is contradicted not only by the significance of Jerusalem in the letters of Paul, in which above all the Jerusalem authorities are mentioned – with Peter at the head – but also by the fact that in his early period up to the end of the second journey, Paul collaborated above all with people from Jerusalem. Of the four leading teachers in Antioch mentioned alongside Paul in Acts 13.1, three come from Jerusalem, and the exchange between the two metropolises, which is often attested by Luke – and sometimes also by Paul – shows how dependent Antioch was and remained on Jerusalem. That Paul himself had to avoid Jerusalem for a long time because there his life was threatened by 'zealots' is quite a different matter. Ultimately the so-called 'Hellenism' of the earliest community goes back to Jerusalem itself, which was far more 'Hellenistic' than the history-of-religions school and its uncritical followers want to believe even now.[1463] However, there should be no more talk of the 'Gentile Christian' or 'Hellenistic' earliest community, but rather of a Greek-speaking Jewish Christian community, since the term 'Hellenistic' is far too general and indefinite – as meaningless as, say, the term 'syncretistic'. Moreover, such a simple distinction between 'Palestinian' and 'Hellenistic' Christianity is misleading, since here not only do we have a contrast between a geographical and a 'linguistic-cultural' term, but we also we need to note that Palestinian Jewish Christianity was very varied in itself; moreover in Palestine and adjacent regions there are numerous significant 'Hellenistic' cities with a mixed population. In his introduction to the fifth edition of Bousset's work in 1964, Bultmann could still write: 'A distinction needs to be made between the earliest Palestinian community and the Hellenistic Christianity within which Paul and John first become understandable. Bousset made it clear that it is important to construct a picture of pre-Pauline Hellenistic Christianity. We may say that this view has meanwhile become commonplace in historical research into the New Testament.'[1464]

Thank God, the thesis of a '*pre*-Pauline Hellenistic' earliest Christianity which is separated by a gulf from 'Palestinian' earliest Christianity has not become a 'commonplace of historical research into the New Testament'; it comes to grief on chronological grounds alone. In the few years up to the conversion of the apostle, no quite different 'Hellenistic' community, or even one already shaped by Gentile Christianity, was forming. Even the 'universal religious community of Antioch, made up of Jews and Hellenists', which 'came into being without Paul', is not really 'Gentile Christian' in the real sense, as both Luke's account in Acts 11.19ff.; 13.1ff.; 15.1ff. and that of Paul in Gal. 2.11ff. show. A community with a really Gentile Christian stamp would probably have got on with things, with Paul, and thrown out the 'Jewish Christian separatists'. The opposite happened. This must apply all the more if – as Bousset and his imitators through Bultmann to Schmithals conjecture – massive pagan influence, say, from the Hellenistic oriental mysteries or an 'oriental Gnosticism', had shaped christology as the heart of the new teaching, the view of the spirit and its cult with the sacraments. Here, too, what has already been said in connection with Tarsus and its city god Sandon/Heracles, and the religious situation in Antioch, applies – indeed even more so.

Bultmann's basic remarks on the syncretistic form of the early christology of the 'Hellenistic' community can in no way be verified from the historical religious sources for the first half of the first century in Syria. Among other things, he refers to the 'idea of son deities, upon whom cultic worship was bestowed and who were regarded as saviours', who as 'divinities worshipped in mysteries ... had suffered the human fate of death but had risen again from death', and whose 'fate ... establishes a basis for salvation after the death of their worshippers', if these 'experience with the deity his death and resurrection in the rites of the mysteries'. The 'Redeemer figure is akin' to these 'divine figures whose origin lies in ancient vegetation gods ... to the extent that in that figure the paradox that a divine being should become man and suffer a human fate is most emphatically expressed'.[1465]

But nothing of the kind is the case. No pagan alienation of the new faith took place immediately after Easter – where and when is not asked about in this kind of 'historical-critical' work – nor did Paul, the former Pharisee who observed the law strictly, throw himself unrestrainedly into its arms.

By contrast, it must be asserted emphatically that all the elements of Pauline theology, in so far as they have not been shaped by the apostle himself – and their proportion should not be over-estimated – come from the abundantly rich Jewish tradition of his time. In so far as they are of Greek or 'oriental' origin, they are mediated by Judaism (which was many-sided). Basically speaking, this is also true of the whole of earliest Christianity.

The attempt to stress the role of a very early 'Gentile Christian' community, which has been constantly made afresh for around a century, is a wrong way, which often has anti-Jewish overtones. One can no longer simply repeat Bousset when he claims that 'where the apostle appeals to tradition, it is not the tradition of Jerusalem but primarily that of the Gentile Christian community of Antioch', and 'only indirectly that of the Jerusalem community'.[1466] For at the time when Paul was working in Antioch, i.e. (with substantial interruptions) between 40 and 48/49 CE, the community there was not really 'Gentile Christian' – that term can definitely be used for it after 100 CE under the first of its bishops who is known to us, Ignatius[1467] – nor did Paul first receive the traditions which were essential to him in Antioch. As we have seen, his way led him from Jerusalem, where he made his first – unpleasant – acquaintance with the new messianic sect, by way of a long period of travelling of between seven and eight years through Damascus, Arabia, Damascus again and then (quite briefly) Jerusalem, Tarsus and Cilicia to the Syrian capital. He brought there the essential foundations of his faith, and in subsequent years certainly helped to shape the 'Antiochene creed' (of which we know nothing) more firmly than he allowed himself to be shaped by it.

At this point we should really put more trust in the Paul who received his gospel by 'a revelation of Jesus Christ', started from Jerusalem and worked all over Syria and Cilicia, than in the false conclusions which are drawn this time above all from Luke, because here he fits in especially well with the wishes of the 'critical' New Testament scholars.

In contrast to Bultmann, who despised such 'brute facts', Bousset at least saw the chronological problem: 'It is a remarkable scene of a quite rapid development. Coverings and garments which had first been woven around the figure of Jesus were taken off again, and new coverings and garments were woven.'[1468]

That is true and false at the same time. At the beginning there

was not a 'quite rapid development', but an 'explosion'. To it
we owe the christology which is a consequence of the messianic
claim of Jesus and the appearances of the risen Christ. The one
who had been exalted to the right hand of God on his Merkaba
throne could also be called on as 'Lord' in the 'cult', say, in the
eucharist, on the basis of Ps. 110.1. A few years previously he had
been 'host' at a supper as the earthly lord and master. This invocation was as possible in Jerusalem as in Damascus, Caesarea,
Antioch or Rome – in Hebrew, Aramaic or Greek. I cannot
understand how Bousset could assert against the well-justified
criticism of Wernle that in Ps. 110.1, 'the title Adoni ... still has a
marked profane and not a religious character':[1469] God's throne
consort is no longer an areligious, profane figure. Moreover the
generally widespread Qere Kyrios for the Tetragrammaton used
in reading the LXX aloud shows that *'adonai* was already read for
YHWH in Hebrew.[1470]

The special feature of the title Kyrios was that it could be
applied *both* to the one who was exalted to the right hand of God
and would come to judge the world *and* to the earthly Lord who
was still quite directly and intensively present in the memory. But
in the case of the one who had proclaimed God's eschatological
revelation in judgment and salvation in the very immediate past,
indeed almost in the present, who had sealed it by death and
resurrection and would consummate it in the imminent future,
the question had to be put whether he was not associated with
God from the very beginning like God's Wisdom, the Torah, his
throne or the name of the Messiah. With inner consistency the
exaltation christology entailed the question of the pre-existence
of the son.[1471] There was intensive reflection on all this in the first
years after the Passover at which Jesus died, in enthusiasm
inspired by the Spirit; the scriptures were searched and there
were discussions when the community assembled – but also with
opponents from among the Jews, and these were in the majority.
In other words, when Paul came to Tarsus in 36 CE and the
Hellenists probably a little later to Antioch, the basic notions of
christology had already been formulated, as well as part of the
preaching – also as a foundation of Paul's gospel.

If the title 'Lord' already refers back to Jerusalem, the same may also be the case with the idea of pre-existence and mediation at creation which Paul already takes for granted.[1472]

A further point to which Becker refers is also worth thinking about. Becker sees the unique significance of Antioch in the fact that 'this community detached itself from the synagogue and formed a community free of the law, based on Christ alone' because it 'abandoned the hitherto undisputed ... view of Christian faith as a group within Judaism and understood Christianity as something qualitatively new'.[1473] One might perhaps make this judgment retrospectively in a large-scale framework, from a lofty standpoint, on an event which took place almost 2000 years ago, but even then it would be wrong, because it does not correspond to historical reality. The community in Antioch at that time certainly did not understand itself in this way. 'Christianity' was not yet thought of as a wholly new (world) religion, nor did people speak of a 'third race' or 'people'; we find that only with the apologists of the second and third centuries.[1474] Here the fundamental eschatological-messianic character of what was (still) a Jewish group is being overlooked: this group understood itself as the real, spiritual 'Israel of God',[1475] the true messianic people of God in which the promises to the patriarchs and the prophets were being fulfilled. The term ἐκκλησία θεοῦ as a designation for this eschatological community of salvation here takes up the *qahal YHWH* of the Pentateuch. Nor did people simply 'detach' themselves from the synagogue; rather, they were forced out, as was attested by the scars of the five times thirty-nine strokes on Paul's back. Because he represented the true eschatological Israel made up of Jews and Gentiles, the latter above all recruited from the 'godfearers', Paul kept visiting the synagogues time and again despite constant failure. Furthermore, the 'synagogue' was not a firmly organized association which one 'left'; it was always possible to found relatively independent 'special synagogues'. Finally, this gradual process of becoming independent, step by step, achieved with some pain, was a wearisome one which took on a stamp of its own in Antioch because of the special position of Christians in a metropolis, but it had already been long in process when the 'Hellenists' began to work in Antioch around 36/37. For not only Paul after his conversion but also Peter and John will have based their salvation 'on Christ alone', and we do better to say 'critical of the law' rather than 'free of the law', for the whole of earliest Christianity was anything but antinomian. The Ten Commandments and the commandment to love remained valid without interruption, indeed they were heightened, and Paul himself could act very fiercely against those who broke these basic laws. It was all more complicated than we imagine in a good, critical Protestant way, in the footsteps of F. C. Baur.

So there is no occasion for that 'pan-Antiochenism' which keeps haunting the literature again (or still?) today. The decisive christological developments in particular already took place before the time when the new Jewish-messianic sect gained a firm footing in Antioch *c.*36/37 (?) and gradually formed an independent community there, a community which after some time consisted of more erstwhile Gentile godfearers and sympathizers, and sometimes real 'Greeks', than Jewish Christians. This last development probably first took place – not without powerful help from Paul – in the forties.

So we have no reason to regard the community in Antioch in the first roughly ten years of its existence as having been theologically far more creative than the other communities in Jerusalem, Syria or Cilicia. What were 'creative' beyond all measure were the 'explosive' effects of the primal event at the beginning. Individual representatives were also theologically 'creative', above all Paul himself, but also Barnabas and others; however, they were already creative before they came to Antioch.[1476]

8.3.2.1 *Antiochene traditions in Paul?*

At the end of his section on 'The Significance of the Antiochene Community for Christianity', J. Becker rightly emphasizes that only 'reasoned conjectures, no more' are possible 'for describing Antiochene theology'.[1477] I would want to go one step further: what we believe we know about 'Antiochene theology' is completely 'Pauline theology', which of course may have taken up and worked over earlier traditions that Paul received from third parties. We can only conjecture that Paul first adopted certain theologoumena in Antioch, and should give reasons for our conjectures. Where Paul himself (or others) shaped the much-discussed formula-like pieces of tradition which appear in his letters must be examined instance by instance.

The problem becomes particularly clear with the relatively numerous 'pre-Pauline' phrases in Romans, which are in part essentially different from those of other letters; so here we can also assume that Paul knew that they would be treasured or at least understood in Rome. The letter presupposes that Paul was accurately informed about conditions in Rome and about the reservations people had about him there. We can infer from Rom. 16.3 that he was given information by the couple Prisca and Aquila, who had returned to Rome, especially as he had long wanted to travel there.[1478] The conjecture by A. Suhl and R. Riesner that Paul had already planned to go to Rome by land through Macedonia on the so-called second journey in 49 CE but was deterred from doing so by the edict of Claudius[1479] is worth considering. So his meeting in Corinth with Prisca and Aquila, who were close collaborators and friends, was a quite special piece of providence. But as the Roman community was probably founded from Jerusalem and not from Antioch (Paul does not mention Antioch once in Romans, while he mentions Jerusalem four times in Rom. 15!), we can probably hardly regard the formula which Paul uses in an attempt to link up with the faith and preaching of the Roman Christians as typically Antiochene. The common basis points rather to the 'Hellenists' in Jerusalem and the communities which they founded in the Hellenistic cities of Palestine and Phoenicia: for example Caesarea, as the main port for the link with Rome. We hear nothing of a connection between Antioch and Rome independent of Paul. That applies to the basic formula in Rom. 1.3; to 4.38; 8.34,[1480] and also Rom. 3.25; 4.17; to baptism in Rom. 6.3f.; to the 'sending of the Son' formula 8.3 and many other examples. Paul wanted not only to be understood in Rome but also to be approved of, so he had to refer to an undisputed shared basis of faith. Furthermore, the whole letter shows how 'negative' the information was in Rome about his person (probably also from Jerusalem); therefore the theological testament in which he develops his gospel at the same

time becomes an impressive theological apologia. There is no
reason here to read typical 'Antiochene' theology into it. On the
contrary, Rom. 15.14–31 emphasizes both Paul's link with
Jerusalem and his fears about it, and asks the Romans to understand this and 'fight with' it in prayers, so that all goes well there.
The Romans were evidently well informed.

The same goes for the most important statements of tradition
in I Corinthians. The last memorable meal of Jesus with the
disciples 'on the night that he was delivered up' took place in the
Holy City, and the memory of this was burning in the disciples'
hearts, above all in Peter's heart. Paul may already have heard
of this tradition, which goes back to the 'Lord' himself, as a
persecutor in Jerusalem between two and three years after the
Passover at which Jesus died. That here in terms of the history of
the tradition we reach 'bedrock' follows from the fact that the
Gospel of Mark (which is Petrine) basically reports everything in
a very similar way, even if (despite the impressive attempt made
by Jeremias)[1481] we can no longer reconstruct the event and the
wording precisely. The 'do this . . . in remembrance of me'
(τοῦτο ποιεῖτε . . . εἰς τὴν ἐμὴν ἀνάμνησιν, I Cor. 11.24) has
nothing to do with the ancient meals in memory of the dead, far
less with a mystery rite; it corresponds to the Hebrew *lezikkaron*,
and must be understood in terms of the Old Testament Jewish
concept of liturgical remembrance. This is the 'proclamation in
praise of the mighty acts of God' which we already find in the
Psalms, in which the 'remembering' is closely connected with
the 'proclaiming' (cf. I Cor. 11.26: 'you proclaim the death of the
Lord until he comes', τὸν θάνατον τοῦ κυρίου καταγγέλλετε ἄχρις
οὗ ἔλθη).[1482] This proclaiming 'the death of the Lord' includes –
as the title Kyrios indicates – resurrection and exaltation; the two
form a unity. It happens above all and *eo ipso*[1483] in prayer and
praise, i.e. in the 'blessing' (εὐλογεῖν) over bread and wine.[1484]
Here the salvation achieved once for all on Golgotha is confessed
and praised in a presence which is efficacious for all. Luke indicates this 'remember' in terms of praise – indeed, it relates
primarily to an event which is still immediately obvious to all and
determines their lives quite directly – by the words 'partook of
food with rejoicing and a generous heart' (μετελάμβανον τροφῆς

ἐν ἀγαλλιάσει καί ἐν ἀφελότητι καρδίας). This follows the 'break-ing of bread in the houses', as he describes the earliest celebra-tion of the meal in Jerusalem in Acts 2.46. The Lord's Supper here, as in I Cor. 11.21, 25 (after supper, μετὰ τὸ δειπνῆσαι), is a real meal in which people eat their fill; it opens with the rite over the bread and is concluded with the 'blessing over the cup'. The rejoicing (ἀγαλλίασις) also directly takes up the praise of God's saving acts in the Psalms.[1485] There can be no question that the petition for the presence of the Lord in the meal in the form of bread and wine and the prospect of his imminent coming 'in glory' were very closely connected; it would be quite perverse to want to read a contrast between a Hellenistic Kyrios cult and an apocalyptic parousia Kyrios into the texts. The cry of prayer, Maran atha, which is directly connected with 'proclaiming the Lord's death until he comes', knows only the one Lord who is exalted to the right hand of God, who gives himself in the meal and will come in glory. Thus Paul's eucharistic practice points back to the celebration of the meal by the earliest community in Jerusalem, which there was already held in Greek by the Hellenists. It is interesting that the unity of the eschatological community of Christ is manifested even beyond the barriers of language in the Aramaic prayer formulas 'Maran atha' or even 'Abba' which Paul handed on to his Gentile Christian communi-ties. Of course there was a particular form of the Lord's Supper in Antioch, and Paul could have handed on the form customary there between 40 and 48 CE to his Gentile Christian mission com-munities around the Aegean, but we do not know whether this form was essentially different from the one that he previously celebrated in Tarsus, in Damascus or even with Peter (and his family) in Jerusalem, nor whether he differed from it in individual points in his later mission communities around the Aegean. The apostolic 'freedom of the Spirit' may always also have been at work here – in particular in the shaping of worship. At the beginning of the new faith there was no liturgical compul-sion, but the grateful acceptance of certain proven elements of tradition which refer back to the person of Jesus as the now exalted Lord: these included the cry of prayer Abba, the Lord's Prayer, and the actions and words of Jesus at the Last Supper which look forward to the future. Freedom and a link with tradition are bound together in Paul in a unique way. Those decisive points in which the accounts of Mark 14.22–25 and Paul in I Cor. 11.23–26 agree are in any case already to be presupposed in the celebration of the earliest community; here Paul has in part taken over earlier features – after all, his partners in mission did come from Jerusalem: first Barnabas, then Silas/Silvanus, the latter still even at the foundation of the community in Corinth, when Paul introduced the celebration of the eucharist there.

The conjectures of Bultmann, who wants to identify the later version of Justin's Apology[1486] after 150 CE, which is completely formalized, as the earliest, are completely erroneous, although this mixed form is dependent both on Mark 1.22–24 (= Matt. 26.26–28) and on Paul (I Cor. 11.25) and in its theological interpretation on John 6.53–58 and John 1.14.[1487]

We find the other formula which scholars like to connect with Antioch, though in terms of content it is again utterly Palestinian and from Jerusalem with the exception of the last person mentioned, in I Cor. 15.1–8. In content it has nothing at all to do with Antioch. It is entirely about events in Jerusalem or in Galilee or at least Judaea. As the last one – by some distance – who clearly stands apart from 'all the apostles' (!) as a special case, Paul is the only one who also falls outside this framework geographically. He was already confronted with the content of most of the statements in this formula in Jerusalem. In Damascus or during the fourteen days with Peter he will have received further supplementary information. The 'of whom most are still alive' (ἐξ ὧν οἱ πλείονες μένουσιν ἕως ἄρτι, 15.6) shows that he has more recent information from Jerusalem, i.e. that despite all the tensions he is indirectly or directly in contact. And finally I Cor. 15.11, a text which scholars are persistently fond of suppressing, is a pillar for the – last – unit of the earliest Christian message at least during the first generation, i.e. the real 'apostolic' age, Despite Gal. 1.10ff., for Paul in particular there was only one saving event and therefore only one gospel, i.e. one message of salvation, because in Christ there can only be one salvation and correspondingly only one eschatological community of salvation as the one body of Christ.[1488] Into this one body of Christ men and

women are baptized by one baptism.[1489] Precisely because Paul
was such a contentious theologian, I Cor. 15.11 is a tremendous
statement to come from his pen, and we should reflect on it again
today, when so much is being dissolved into vain subjectivity and
confused pluralism (the two are connected). We do not know
where and how the basic formula in I Cor. 15.3–5 was first
formed. When Paul brought it to the Corinthians 'first', around
50 CE, his partner was Silas/Silvanus from Jerusalem. He too will
have put himself completely and utterly behind it.

8.3.2.2 The problem of Paul's theology of baptism

Are there any better reasons for deriving the special formulation
of the baptism tradition which Paul introduces in Gal. 3.26–28
from his stay in Antioch, and is Paul citing a 'pre-Pauline
Antiochene baptismal formula' here?[1490] Paul describes the situation of all believers, not only of the community in Antioch but
in the other communities which he founded on his missionary
journeys in Arabia, Cilicia and Syria. This situation was a matter
of course for him before conflict sparked off by the 'false
brethren' who 'slipped in', which was then resolved at the
'Apostolic Council' in Jerusalem, as 'freedom which we have in
Christ Jesus' (Gal. 2.4). Specifically, this freedom consists in the
fact that Gentile Christians must not be forced to accept circumcision, or indeed to observe the ritual law generally (Gal. 2.3),
though nevertheless Jewish Christians and Gentile Christians eat
together without restrictions. Paul emphasizes in Gal. 2.11–14
that this table-fellowship must not be given up – even temporarily
– out of respect for the Jewish Christians who come from James
and who observe the commandments of cleanness and the
dietary laws; indeed it concerns the one shared Lord's Supper
which Jesus himself founded on his last night and which brings all
together as the 'community of the body of Christ', for 'we who
are many are one bread, one body, for we all share in the one
bread'.[1491] A break in the sharing of the eucharistic meal splits the
one body of Christ. Ultimately Christ's work of salvation is put in
question here by requiring observance of the law. For Peter's
behaviour would ultimately have led to pressure on Gentiles to

have themselves circumcised so that the community was not split, and that goes against the 'truth of the gospel'. However, if salvation does not come from Christ alone, but in addition the law still seems to be in some way necessary for salvation, e.g. for the sake of the unity of the community at the eucharist, then 'Christ has died in vain, i.e. meaninglessly' (Gal. 2.21). But justification by God does not come 'from works of the law'; only from the faith in Christ given by God (Gal. 2.16).[1492] Although Paul is not speaking explicitly of baptism here, in vv.19f. he uses terms like 'being crucified with' Christ and the new life in faith which, as Rom. 6.6 suggests, are traditionally also connected with baptism. But we shall be returning to that later.

Thus Paul formulates his doctrine of justification for the first time in principle, in the letters we have, in Gal. 2, but he emphatically states that he had put this forward at the time in Antioch in the face of Peter and the assembled community as the 'truth of the gospel'.[1493] That does not exclude the possibility that in his very brief retrospect, he is focussing his argument on the one decisive point and that the original controversy was more complicated and more wearisome. The fact that Paul definitively parted company even with Barnabas after this dispute shows that what was being discussed was not Antiochene community tradition, but exclusively the theological question of truth as the apostle understood it. Here he had all the Antiochene Jewish Christians, i.e. the leading men in the community, against him. We certainly also find this 'Antiochene' freedom as interpreted by Paul in Gal. 3.26ff. The 'formula', with its circular structure and forming a sequence in a triad with antithetical diction, seems to the unprejudiced eye to be typically Pauline.[1494]

We have already pointed out (4.2 above) that the core of these statements, that 'in Christ' the Gentiles become sons of God and therefore are also the seed of Abraham, will have been part of Paul's message to the Gentile godfearers already in Damascus (and Arabia) and later in Cilicia and Syria, and that the insight that Gentiles, slaves and women 'in Christ' have full, equal rights, and that the barriers drawn by the law which determined being 'in the law' have been removed in this new sphere of salvation. The problem whether the godfearing sympathizers, women and

men, had equal rights in the community and full fellowship with
Jewish Christians (also at the table) without first going over to
Judaism completely must already have emerged in Damascus
and have been resolved there. For since his 'conversion' Paul
had known that he had been called to be a missionary to the
Gentiles. The question of the position of Gentiles who had
become believers and the circumcision of men cannot first have
emerged in Antioch, when this freedom was suddenly mistrust-
fully suspected and disputed by Jewish Christians.[1495] The reasons
given for Gal. 3.26f. containing a liturgical baptismal formula
which Paul took over slightly changed are in no way tenable: he is
said to have kept the second person plural of the direct address
to those being baptized, so that he changes from the first to the
second person plural. But the same thing also happens in Rom.
8.12f., in quite a different context. Such a change in person is
typical of Paul's lively, urgent parenesis. The form critics want to
define the verse as a 'baptismal cry which defines the new situation of the baptized person before God',[1496] and which is said to
have been used in Antioch liturgically during baptism. Certainly
we know that believers called on the Lord in baptism and that
they were baptized 'in the name of the Lord', but the assumption
of fixed liturgical 'baptismal cries' as a definition of the new state
of being a Christian remains completely uncertain. There is no
reference to such a baptismal formula in either the early or the
later sources.[1497] Was the newly baptized person congratulated
with such a 'baptismal cry'? If we follow the thread of the argumentation of the letter, Paul is now addressing the Galatians
directly and reminding them of the preaching or instruction with
which he, along with Barnabas, had once explained the meaning
of baptism to the newly-won Christians in particular when he was
founding the communities in Galatia; he is 'quoting' this in
Gal. 3.26f. We can just as well also see this common principle of
the 'Hellenistic' Gentile missionaries, with which the Jerusalem
authorities must also have agreed at one time (Gal. 2.3), in
the formulation in I Cor. 7.19, that neither circumcision nor
uncircumcision have soteriological significance, but that
Christians – whether born Jews or Gentiles – still have to keep
God's commandments.[1498] That is focussed by Paul more sharply

in the polemical discussion, with deliberate intent, on the mention of the 'commandments' in Gal. 5.6 (the 'faith active through love'). In Gal. 6.15, in the conclusion in his own 'big letters' at the end of the epistle, the motif is taken up once again and deepened in the direction of eschatology and the theology of creation: for Paul (and for any Christian), the old world with its distinction between circumcision and uncircumcision died on the cross; the one who is justified by God's grace is a 'new creation'.[1499] Within Galatians this conclusion refers back not only to the beginning of the letter but also to Gal. 3.26ff.

The phrase that in baptism the faithful 'clothe themselves with Christ' is taken as a further argument for the Antiochene origin of the 'baptismal cry' of Gal. 3.26f. J. Becker again argues for the origin of the 'clothing symbolism' from the language of the Hellenistic mysteries. Given the mixed composition of the Antiochene community, he claims that its baptismal formula is 'syncretistic'.[1500] Both these statements are misleading.

Various suggestions have been made about the origin of the 'metaphor' that the faithful have put on Christ as a garment in baptism or have been clothed with him.[1501] There is a dispute as to whether ἐνδύεσθαι here, as in Rom. 13.14, is to be understood ethically[1502] or whether this notion is 'ontological'.[1503] As Paul can evidently express both these with the metaphor 'put on Christ' – aorist indicative middle in Gal. 3.27 and imperative in Rom. 13.14 – the alternative is a typically false one. Both in Paul and in the Deutero-Paulines, both the 'ontological' and the 'ethical' aspects of the metaphor – quite apart from the eschatological 'trans- formation' in I Cor. 15.53f. – are mentioned in a parenetic context.[1504] For Pauline thought 'ethics' and 'ontology' cannot be separated. We should not constantly read our modern categories into the texts.

The metaphorical use of ἐνδύεσθαι was widespread in antiquity.[1505] In Judaism the Greek linguistic form goes back to the LXX translation which uses the phrases ἐνδύ(ν)εσθαι σωτηρίαν or δικαιοσύνην, but also speaks, in a negative sense, of being clothed with 'shame'.[1506] The expression being 'clothed' with 'sadness' or 'joy' comes nearer to the image of the garment. The metaphorical usage is preserved in early Judaism. In the *Vita*

Adae et Evae (Greek), Eve depicts her sorrow at the loss of the innocence of paradise with the words:

> my eyes were opened, and I saw that I was naked, without the righteousness with which I had been clothed, that I had been changed from the glory with which I had previously been clothed.[1507]

It is interesting here that an (allegedly) 'ethical' concept (δικαιοσύνη) and an 'ontological' concept (δόξα) can stand directly side by side. It can probably also be inferred from this writing that the meaning of ἐνδύω, 'immerse', was not completely alien to ancient Judaism. Adam commands Eve to stand in the Tigris for thirty-four days in penitence:

> take a stone and put it under your feet; remain standing immersed in water up to the neck.[1508]

In the Latin *Vita Adae*, Satan complains that he has been stripped of his heavenly glory.[1509] The motif is elaborated in the early Jewish and Christian exegesis of Gen. 3.21: after the 'fall', God clothed Adam and Eve in 'garments of skin', i.e. human bodies. Meeks sees 'paradisal motives' also taken up in the Pauline and Deutero-Pauline passages about baptism in the 'image of clothing', and combines them with the baptismal garment.[1510]

There is Old Testament evidence for the view that the Spirit (of God) 'clothes' the prophets.[1511] Did Paul take up and transform this idea? If we understand ἐνεδύσεσθε in the passive sense, this connection is likely, but not compelling. The old conjecture that the symbolism of clothing represents direct borrowing from the 'language of the mysteries' or even from 'Gnosticism' does not hold – as was already emphasized somewhat one-sidedly by Wagner and more cautiously by Wedderburn.[1512] The ritual of initiation into the mysteries of Isis – as described by Apuleius – contains the elements of the bath of purification and the garments of deity, but does not correspond to the early forms of Christian baptism. Between ritual purification and being clothed with the garments of the deity, which belong to her and are preserved in her temple, is a ten-day fasting and the decisive night of initiation in which the mystic is initiated into her mysteries. In

this night he reaches the 'frontier of death', goes through all the
elements and at midnight sees the sun in a bright blinding light.
The morning after, 'the people' may see him in the miraculous
twelve-fold garment with a radiant crown, so that he resembles
the sun god. After that he celebrates his birthday as an initiate
with joyful eating and drinking.[1513] Long before his initiation, the
goddess had promised him her protection in this life and in the
beyond.[1514] We can see more in common here with the later form
of baptismal celebration from the third century on than with the
baptism which becomes visible in early Christian sources.

Throughout the ancient world the garments of deities were
'worn' – above all in processions – by priests, priestesses and
worshippers, not only in the mystery cult of Isis but also particularly in the public cult. To this degree there is perhaps already
an indirect connection in the early Christian period. Because
these garments were worn by people in the cult (but also in the
triumphal procession, in the theatre or by the emperors[1515]), the
metaphor 'be clothed with Christ' could be understood in an
analogous way by the former pagans.[1516] The (high-) priestly
garments in the Jerusalem cult also had a special holiness, and
had already long been associated with the concept of 'righteousness'.[1517] By contrast, the Christian baptismal garment will hardly
have stood behind the metaphor 'be clothed with Christ'. It only
came later.[1518] Putting off the 'old man' was part of baptismal
parenesis before the baptismal garment itself played a role.[1519]
But Paul takes the 'horizon of understanding' of his communities
into account and trusts in reliable communication and explanation by the fellow-workers who bring his letter. For that reason he
could also resort to the abbreviation 'be clothed with Christ' in
Gal. 3.27, which is probably meant to express several aspects at
the same time. Those who are baptized are associated with Christ
in their baptism as with a garment;[1520] they do not wear the
garments of pagan lords and ladies, but have even – according to
Rom. 6.5 – grown together with Jesus Christ's own 'baptism',[1521] so
that they are taken up into the 'body of Christ', a sphere in which
all previous ethnic, social and creaturely limitations do not count
where salvation is concerned. Therefore they should behave as
'free sons of God', thanks to the sending of the Son and his death

on the cross. Then they are 'one in Christ', i.e. not only one in Christ but also the one body of Christ which corresponds to the oneness of God the Father and of his Son, 'through whom are all things and we through him'.[1522] Paul gave theological reasons why believers must be united and not divided into communities, one with rites for the circumcised and one with rites for the uncircumcised, in Antioch, in Corinth (I Cor. 12.12f.) and in Galatians. He already developed this conviction in Syria and similarly put it forward there. It is rather improbable that he took over the metaphor of the garment from Antiochene community tradition, because he does not quote any Antiochene baptismal formula, but it cannot be proved either that Paul *used* the metaphor of the garment for the first time in Antioch. At any rate it was common in his letters. In I Thess. 5.8 and Rom. 13.13,14 he uses it in a more understandable way in a parenetic context.[1523] But for baptism itself he adopts much stronger metaphors in Romans.

Origen[1524] already referred to I Cor. 1.30 in explaining the metaphor of the garment in Gal. 3.27: 'Christ, who has become the wisdom from God for us, who has become righteousness, sanctification and redemption.' In I Cor. 1.30 Paul remains closer to the metaphorical language of the LXX than in Gal. 3.27. Here Paul expresses with three abstract nouns what he can apply even more clearly to baptism with three verbs in I Cor. 6.11: 'You were washed, sanctified and justified in the name of the Lord Jesus Christ and in the Spirit of our God.'[1525] I Cor. 1.30 forms the conclusion to the first section of the letter which Paul had begun in a very brusque way with a harsh reprimand over the partisan dispute in Corinth. No 'party' has the right to appeal to its own 'apostle'. Paul takes these disputes to the point of absurdity with three rhetorical questions: 'Is Christ divided? Was Paul crucified for you? Were you baptized in the name of Paul?' This argument must also be directed against the Corinthians' understanding of baptism. For Paul continues with a 'thank God, I baptized none of you'. Still, he remembers Crispus, Gaius and the 'house of Stephanas', certainly not insignificant members of the Corinthian community.[1526] It is not the one who baptizes who is decisive, but only Christ and faith, which is given by the Spirit

from God in hearing the gospel.[1527] Before all else, the special
ministry and charisma of the apostle is the preaching of the
gospel which arouses faith and founds the community. Paul
regards this apostolic office as more important than the ritual
action of the 'baptizer', since it is the word proclaimed as the
'word of the cross' and not baptism which really lays the foundation for the eschatological ἐκκλησία θεοῦ. Others can perform the
ritual of baptism.[1528] It is his burning anxiety that the present divisions in Corinth will have their effect in the last judgment that
makes Paul strike such a sharp tone right at the beginning of the
letter and describe his former activity of baptizing in Corinth with
great restraint. The subjective baptism of the individual, even if
in individual cases the person baptizing was Paul himself, is no
guarantee of eschatological justification before the judgment seat
of Christ, if the unity of Christ's body has been abandoned. It is a
sign of the shift in ages, the coming of the new aeon, but does not
'automatically' protect from sin and apostasy or a lapse into
paganism; that is why we find 'baptismal parenesis' (in the widest
sense) so often in Paul and in the New Testament writings.
Presumably a good deal of preaching in worship could seem to a
young community to be 'baptismal parenesis', because it was an
admonition to live in accordance with the gift of salvation.[1529]
By contrast there is no description of the rite; this was taken
for granted and probably was not clearly fixed liturgically. The
recollection of baptism is meant to make the members of the
community aware that they are no longer irredeemably delivered
over to their former habits, which were under God's wrath (Rom.
1.18ff.), as they once were. In other words now, since the
resurrection of Jesus, the new age has dawned and they are in the
sphere of Christ's salvation and inseparably bound up with him.
With baptism, as I Cor. 6.11 recalls, 'washed, sanctified and
justified', they at one time began their 'official' life in Christ,
which was visible to all. The 'baptism in Moses', the journey
through the Red Sea and the wandering in the cloud, but also
the rejection of many Israelites in the wilderness, took place
in that long-distant past as an example and a warning for the
believers of the end-time. Not only those very few, like Joshua and
Caleb, who were saved at that time drank from the spiritual

rock that was Christ, but also the multitude in whom God had no pleasure and who died in the desert.[1530] In Antioch the dispute was not over the value of baptism as opposed to circumcision. Correspondingly, Paul does not cite baptism when he recalls the dispute in Antioch, but justification by faith alone. 'Justification' traditionally takes place through the forgiveness of sins in baptism.[1531] But Paul, equally, does not see the gift of the Spirit as given to believers only in baptism or even first in the performance of baptism;[1532] he cannot also limit the 'justification of the godless' to the ritual sacramental act of baptism. Because his theological reflections on 'justification' are deeper and more fundamental, he arrives at a more restrained, indeed 'ambivalent' attitude to the rite of baptism. This may go back to a natural 'magical' misunderstanding of baptism in individual 'Gentile Christians', i.e. experiences which he could already have in Syria and Cilicia. But he takes no offence at what for modern eyes is the strange 'vicarious' baptism of the Corinthians, though he himself certainly did not join in it.[1533]

Paul speaks in the greatest detail about baptism in Rom. 6, but it is not his main theme even there. He chooses the eschatological rite of initiation to bring to life the change of rule from the reign (βασιλεύειν) of sin to life in the grace and righteousness given by God. Here he takes up the baptismal tradition which is familiar to the Roman community – independent of Antioch (see above, 8.2.7).[1534] With abundant clarity, he expresses this with the question 'Do you not know?' Paul does not elsewhere connect the vicarious atoning death of Jesus on Golgotha and his resurrection directly with statements about baptism. In Rom. 6.3ff., by contrast, he calls 'baptism in (the name of) Christ Jesus' 'baptism in his death' and in turn explains this as 'being buried with him through baptism in (his) death'. The confession in I Cor. 15.4 already mentioned 'Christ's being buried', and this again presupposes the tomb tradition of the Gospels. As in I Cor. 15.3f., Paul connects the death, burial and resurrection of Christ and concludes that all those who are baptized have a share in the death and burial of Christ, so that like Christ they will be raised from the dead and should therefore 'walk in newness of life'.

The deviations from the normal imagery of Paul's statements

about baptism originally go back to the earliest community in Jerusalem. Here soon after Easter the baptism of John the Baptist, which Jesus and a large number of his disciples had received, was taken up again in altered form. The baptism of John was already an eschatologically sacramental rite. John baptized 'beyond Jordan' at the place where Joshua went through the Jordan as Moses once went through the Reed Sea. 'The waters of Jordan have their eschatological-protological sense ... As the "water of the Reed Sea" and the water of chaos they are less water of purification than water of death. All that is hostile to God sinks into them.'[1535] Here Elijah and Elisha repeated the miracle of the Reed Sea, and here Elijah was transported to heaven in the fiery chariot. John the Baptist expected the return of Elijah in the 'judgment of fire'. Immersion (βαπτίζειν) in the Jordan after the confession of sins was a symbolic dying, and rising from it again 'a rite of rebirth from death'.[1536]

The new Christian interpretation of baptism not only adopted the rite of John as a single baptism in water, but alongside the forgiveness of sins also took over the symbolism of death[1537] and new birth given by the words of Jesus. It understood this as a baptism into the death and resurrection of Jesus which gave the person baptized a ritual share in the event of atonement and salvation. Because Christ died 'for us', we are incorporated into his death and 'there is baptism as fellowship in his fate'.[1538] Here the baptism of fire already announced earlier by John the Baptist was no longer seen as judgment but understood as the eschatological outpouring of the Spirit.[1539]

In Rom. 6 Paul takes up a baptismal tradition which he does not use elsewhere, or gives only hints that he knows (Gal. 2.19). We can establish the place of origin of this baptismal tradition with very much greater certainty than in the case of the phrases in Gal. 3.27; I Cor. 1.30; 6.11. It points to Rome and from there again to Jerusalem. Paul's ambivalence towards baptism is probably not least connected with the fact that for him a person is not first 'justified' in baptism (sacramentally),[1540] but rather in the 'coming to faith' brought about by the word, which precedes baptism.

8.3.2.3 *The letters of Paul as a source for the Pauline theology of the early period: I Thessalonians as an example*

Around the year 50 CE, about eighteen months after the Apostolic Council, Paul wrote the first letter of his that has come down to us, to the community in Thessalonica. It is the earliest literary evidence of Christianity that we possess. The time of his stay in the capital of Macedonia had been relatively brief. Luke tells us that the apostle preached and discussed in the synagogue during three sabbaths and as a result gained a large following among 'the godfearing Greeks' and 'prominent women', i.e. Gentile Christians. However, it becomes clear from I Thessalonians, which Paul writes a brief year later, that the small new community was not yet established and had suffered to some degree from its fellow citizens. So Luke will be right in reporting that the missionaries had to flee the city rapidly.[1541] It is striking that in I Thess. 2.14 Paul makes a connection between the suffering of the community and the persecution of 'the community of God' in Judaea 'in Christ Jesus', i.e. that he had in mind the Jewish Christians in Judaea, and that of course means primarily in Jerusalem. Evidently the communities in Syria had not so far been persecuted in this way, even in Antioch: II Cor. 11.24 relates quite personally to Paul. By contrast, he does not keep silent about the maltreatment which he and Silas had previously suffered in Philippi.[1542] Thus he is writing a letter of consolation and admonition which goes into the quite specific questions and needs of the community, in the way that a good and skilled letter-writer does. By contrast, he omits any explanation of his theology; the community in Thessalonica knew the essential points of it. In Romans, a letter addressed to a community personally unknown to him which had already developed its own self-awareness, he introduces himself as a theological thinker, not with his newest 'developments' and 'bright ideas', but above all with those key points which had already been more or less a matter of contro-versy between him and those in Jerusalem, and had led to polemic and calumniation against him in Rome. In other words, he is writing as the Paul who is 'well-known' (one could almost say notorious) for his missionary work in Antioch and Syria, who energetically and argumentatively presented and defended his gospel to the Jerusalem authorities at the Apostolic Council, and some years later – after the foundation of the communities in Thessalonica and Corinth – had put it forward in sharp polemic against a vacillating Peter, Barnabas and the other Jewish Christians. Therefore we read at the beginning of Romans that 'I have often intended to come to you, but thus far have been prevented'.[1543] In other words, experiences from the six- to seven-year mission round the Aegean may certainly also have found their way into Romans, certainly in the 'ethical' chapters 12 and 14, where he sometimes takes up the problems there were at Corinth, albeit in sometimes changed form. The differences from I and II Corinthians generally are striking, although he is writing to the Romans from Corinth, and he had had difficulty enough in resolving the problems there. Here in particular the fronts in the community which he had founded had been quite different, and in his letters Paul was always deliberately concerned to address quite specific problems in the community. They are far removed from the abstract theological treatises which we encounter, say, from the time of the Apologists. So we have no reason to read 'developments' towards a quite different 'theology' which were quite decisive for him out of the letters of those six years. This may be a favourite occupation and theme for many Pauline scholars, but in my view it is a vain labour of love. Might this interest in the theological changes in Paul be connected with the fact that for many theologians today it is the done thing to change one's views in accordance with rapidly changing fashions, or adapt oneself to them?

What has just been said applies even more to Galatians. The communities in south Galatia were founded by Paul along with Barnabas on the so-called first journey around 46/47 CE, i.e. during his 'Antiochene-Syrian' period. In my view he wrote the letter towards the end of his stay in Ephesus after I Corinthians, where he refers to the collection for Jerusalem which he has arranged,[1544] and before II Corinthians, where Galatia is no longer mentioned. All the numerous schemes for dividing up I and II Corinthians seem to me to be very hypothetical and there is no really reliable basis for them.[1545] The abrupt change of situation in Galatia relegated the collection there to third place. Perhaps the sum of money which had been collected was taken directly by the messengers from Jerusalem,[1546] who are perhaps connected with the 'certain men from James' (τίνες ἀπὸ Ἰακώβου) in 2.12. That meant that Paul had to be all the more concerned to arrange an orderly collection around the Aegean, not even knowing whether this would be accepted in Jerusalem.[1547]

In founding the communities he had proclaimed the one gospel critical of the law which he received from Christ himself. The content of his 'proclamation of faith' (ἀκοὴ πίστεως) is the crucified Christ. Only the message of Christ in the power of the Spirit brings about faith, and in this communicates the gift of the Spirit. This faith brought about by the Spirit which then manifests itself in powers (δυνάμεις) can therefore have nothing at all to do with the ἔργα νόμου, the works required by the law.[1548] Thus the requirement that circumcision is necessary for salvation also fundamentally contradicts that message with which the apostle once founded the communities of (south) Galatia. Paul could not have argued with such incisive sharpness in Gal. 1.10–12; 3.1–5; 4.8–19 and 5.12 and kept recalling the beginnings of the community if at that time he had presented quite different views, more ready for compromise, about circumcision and literal observance of the Torah. In the apostle's defence there is no sign of a repudiation of the – fatal – charge that his preaching had been different earlier, and that on the decisive point, the question of the law, he had formerly been much more generous. Thus despite all the sharpness of the controversy, Galatians is above all a precise *recollection* of the gospel which the apostle preached at a much earlier time. That here he does not mention Barnabas, his colleague (and helper) on the mission, or Silas or Timothy, is not just connected with the fact that after the break with Antioch he must now carry on this dispute alone,[1549] but also with the fact that in the past days of the collegial mission the christological and soteriological content of the message had been stamped by the gospel which *he* had received. He was really the towering theologian and missionary of Greek-speaking Jewish Christianity outside Palestine, between Damascus and Rome.

Now it is readily objected that Paul's earliest letter to the community in Thessalonica, which still wholly bears the stamp of 'Antiochene theology', knows nothing of this whole theology of justification by faith alone, works of the law, the fallenness of the human *sarx* into sin, the incapacity of human beings for salvation, and predestination. Precisely for that reason, F. C. Baur and the critics of the time had declared it untypical of Pauline theology and therefore un-Pauline. This view can hardly still be put forward today. Rather, it is seen as a paradigm of the simpler theology of Paul's earlier period, with its marked sacramental stamp, which basically only continued to hand on the views of the 'Hellenistic community' of Antioch. However, it is dangerous to put such a burden of proof on a short letter of 1475 words, no longer than an average sermon. I already said at the beginning that a good preacher, and Paul was certainly that, does not pack all his theology into every sermon, above all when he wants to address quite concrete pastoral problems in the community. And these problems were present to excess in this community, which was still very young. They included the pressure of suffering, the right way of living in the faith, and the fate of the dead in view of the coming of the Kyrios which was expected in the imminent future. The apostle had to give an answer to these questions, not to basic 'dogmatic' problems. Everything else could, indeed had to, be left on one side. This is the real difference from the great letter to the Romans.

Nevertheless, it is worth taking a look at the letter. Here first of all the relationship between the gospel or the word of God and faith is striking – almost more so than in other Pauline letters. Paul thus has a good 'Lutheran Reformation' stamp: his main characteristic is a solid 'word of God theology'. By contrast, there is little trace of a real 'sacramental theology'.

The starting point is the proclamation of the gospel[1550] by Paul and his companions, Silas and Timothy. This proved to be not only a word of man, but worked 'in power and in the Holy Spirit and with full conviction' (1.5f.). Rarely does the unity of the proclamation of the gospel and the power of the Spirit in Paul's letters become as clear as it does here.[1551] Precisely for that reason, the listeners in Thessalonica could accept[1552] the gospel

boldly proclaimed[1553] by the apostles[1554] despite the preceding
suffering in Philippi, not as a human word but as the word of God
which proves to be effective in believers.[1555] The decisive term
πίστις, faith, appears eight times, more frequently than in I and
II Corinthians (seven times each) or in Philippians (five times).
Paul does not need to explain the word here. He wrote into the
heart of the community what faith is and what it is based on
during the brief stay when he brought it into being; indeed he
can praise its faith as a model for other communities.[1556] This
faith is not human work; it is based upon God's free election by
his grace and love, which Paul already mentions at the beginning
of the letter.[1557] The key word ἐκλογή here must be interpreted in
terms of the usage in Romans (especially the κατ' ἐκλογὴν
χάριτος of Rom. 11.5).[1558] In keeping with this, Paul three times
says that God has *called* the members of the new community,[1559]
and moreover – as he remarks at the end of the letter – has called
them as the God who remains true to himself, i.e. his election in
grace and promise of salvation in Christ: 'He who calls you is
faithful, and he will do it' (πιστὸς ὁ καλῶν ὑμᾶς, ὃς καί ποιήσει):
he will quite certainly bring about the salvation promised in the
preaching of the gospel, 'sanctify' the community and preserve
it for the imminent parousia of Christ. Can one express the
typically Pauline (and then Reformation) certainty of salvation
more strongly?[1560] In other words, salvation is founded solely on
God's faithfulness. One might almost see in this Pauline formula
of the faithful God who stands by his election in grace a theological principle of the apostle which has grown out of his
encounter with the risen Christ before Damascus. At that time he
himself, the persecutor and blasphemer of Christ, experienced
God's unmerited election in grace and call, and the faithfulness
of the one who called him accompanied him all his life.
Presumably this formula belongs to the language of prayer which
is typical of him.[1561] Both God's faithfulness and his election in
grace are revealed in the death and resurrection of Jesus, which
in its saving significance as the foundation of faith and hope is
addressed briefly in I Thess. 4.14[1562] and at greater length in 5.8
and 10. The believers are equipped with the 'breastplate of faith
and love and the helmet of the hope of salvation'; here for Paul

hope is none other than the faith directed towards God's future, 'for God has not destined us for wrath, but to obtain salvation through our Lord Jesus Christ, who died for us[1563] so that whether we wake or sleep we might live with him'.

In both passages the apostle reminds the recipients of the letter of the preaching with which he founded the community, and presupposes that they really understand these basic statements of his message, which must have initially seemed to a hearer of antiquity, just as much as a modern neo-pagan, to be confused talk. Here, however, we may always assume that the messenger who delivered the letter could explain details in answer to questions. That through Christ's vicarious atoning death (τοῦ ἀποθανόντος ὑπὲρ ἡμῶν, 5.10) and his resurrection by God (ὃν ἤγειρεν ἐκ τῶν νεκρῶν, 1.10) – the two cannot be separated, but rather one statement entails the other – deliverance in the coming judgment is certain (τὸν ῥυόμενον ἡμᾶς ἐκ τῆς ὀργῆς τῆς ἐρχομένης) is said by Paul not only at the end of his letter, but also right at the beginning in 1.10, there with an eschatological missionary formula. It can hardly be denied that this formula originated in the original preaching of the Jerusalem community.[1564] Paul also speaks of the Christ who will return as ὁ ῥυόμενος in the quotation from Isa. 59.20 in Rom. 11.26,[1565] in view of the deliverance of Israel through the coming Lord who brings this forgiveness of sins. In this, the election of the people of God is fulfilled as an act of God's free grace. But what is the deliverance of the former pagan idolaters (1.9) in Thessalonica and that of Israel through the coming Christ in the light of the last judgment in which God's righteous anger is made manifest (Rom. 1.18ff.), if not the 'justification of the godless'? The forensic language used in Romans and Galatians takes its starting point in judgment as a manifestation of the wrath of God. It must seem striking that only in the late Romans (winter 17) and in his earliest writing does Paul speak so massively of God's eschatological 'judgment of wrath' and contrast Christ as saviour with this.[1566] Christ is the one who alone, as the one 'who delivers us from the wrath to come' (1.10), turns away God's wrath by his death 'for us' (ὑπὲρ ἡμῶν) and makes the young Christians certain of salvation (5.10), and as the saviour brings forgiveness for sin (Rom. 11.26). In other words, through him God has reconciled with himself his creatures who have become enemies; Christ's death on the cross has made 'justification by faith' and 'peace with God' real.[1567] We should not read out of Paul different, indeed opposed, 'soteriologies' because of the abundant wealth of language with which he can describe the saving event in its different aspects. In the preaching with which he founded the community in Thessalonica Paul addressed both the predestinarian election of grace and the forensic 'justification of the sinner' in the judgment. So I do not believe that his christology and soteriology were essentially different during his stay in Thessalonica (and then in Corinth) from what they were in the letter to the Romans, which was written seven years later: the striking terminology of election in grace, call and deliverance from the wrath of God, and also the emphasis on the connection between word and faith, tell against this.

The whole letter shows that the faith which expects the parousia imminently did not lead in Paul to a passive attitude of 'wait and see', but in I Thessalonians can only be understood as 'faith working through love' (πίστις δι᾽ ἀγάπης ἐνεργουμένη, Gal. 5.9). Paul wants to strengthen the life by faith beginning in this young community, which is being attacked and is under considerable external pressure, and not present some theological theories remote from life. Indeed Paul is never only a theologian, but always at the same time a successful founder of a community, the missionary *par excellence*, and an experienced pastor. Therefore he already speaks in the preliminaries of 'active faith',[1568] and at the beginning and the end of this letter makes love and hope[1569] follow the mention of faith. Here too we have an old and customary triad from the apostle which he has probably already been using for some time.[1570]

The new life in faith which Paul describes in Gal. 6.15 and II Cor. 5.17 as a 'new creation' (καινὴ κτίσις), in Gal. 5.22 as 'the fruit of the Spirit', and in Rom. 8.12 as 'being driven by the Spirit' which 'kills the works of the flesh', is described above all in I Thessalonians with the key word 'sanctification' (ἁγιασμός;[1571] once ἁγιωσύνη also appears[1572]). The term is not to be understood in a moralizing way, but as an effect of the gospel in the power of the Spirit and at the same time as a consequence of faith in the salvation brought about by Christ.

Thus the theology of the first extant letter of the apostle is not fundamentally different from his other letters; it is important to reflect that in all the letters Paul always goes into the special questions and needs of those whom he is addressing. He is anything but a rigid 'dogmatic' theologian, and therefore he can present the same message, the gospel entrusted to him,[1573] with rich and varied metaphors and from different aspects, depending on the situation. So I think it over-hasty to want to conclude that he often essentially changed his theological views. That is also true of the much-discussed question of the allegedly very different eschatology in I Thess. 4.13–18 and I Cor. 15.35–38. The questions of the community in Thessalonica were different from those of the Corinthians. The bodily resurrection was not denied there. Rather, people were asking about the fate of those who had died before the parousia. It is even more nonsensical to conjecture that the question of those who had died in Christ became a problem only through the aporia in Thessalonica around seventeen years after Paul's conversion.

We must not forget that Paul's letters represent a tiny selection of the unimaginable wealth of an oral missionary practice and preaching lasting over seventeen to twenty years. What they contain is to a large degree conditioned by the situation and is therefore in a way fortuitous. That makes the richness and depth of these few fragments all the more amazing. It should make us more cautious about the attempt to read out of the little that we possess deep developments in the apostle in his late period, which go against his earlier period in Syria and in Antioch. The way in which Paul talks of the gospel which has been entrusted to him and his successful fight for the recognition of this gospel at the 'Apostolic Council', after showing that this really was the 'power of God for salvation to all who believe' in a successful 'mission to the Gentiles', i.e. predominantly among the sympathizers on the margin of the synagogue communities, should make us more cautious here.

The theological and pastoral experience which we meet in every sentence in I Thessalonians suggest that when the apostle set out for Asia Minor and the Aegean after the first break with Barnabas, presumably in 49, his message had a clear christological and soteriological centre and firm outlines. A disordered, vacillating thinker could never have written such letters. That would mean that the basic theological ideas which appear in his letters already in his time in Syria and Antioch, i.e. between 40 and 48, were part of his own spiritual property, and it cannot be claimed that they were typically 'Hellenistic' Antiochene developments. At the latest in Gal. 2.11ff., but perhaps already in the break with Barnabas in Acts 15.36, it proved that Antioch and Paul may not simply be identified. As a theological thinker Paul towered above his fellow missionaries, so he must have exercised decisive influence – where and when he was influenced by outside traditions which he certainly also accepted abundantly, is more difficult to say. At the precise point where we must necessarily accept the strongest outside influence, in the Jesus tradition, which he needed for the preaching with which he founded communities, he unfortunately remains very taciturn in the letters. Here he often has something else controversial to say. I would doubt J. Becker's belief that 'well-founded conjectures are possible for describing Antiochene theology, but no more'.[1574] Rather, well founded conjectures are possible for the *theology of Paul* in those years between 33 and 49 CE which were decisive for him. One can sum them up in a sentence: his theology which we find in the letters between 50 and 56/7 (or 60) was already shaped in this previous period. The decisive developments in his thought stood much more at the beginning than at the end of his activity. And this had unforeseeable historical effects: without him the mission to the Gentiles critical of the law would not really have become fully established, first in 'Syria and Cilicia' and then in Asia Minor, Greece and even in Rome; nor would the conflict with Jerusalem have come about (a necessary one, because it brought clarification). Christianity would rather have remained a messianic sect on the periphery of Judaism and gradually have disappeared from history like other Jewish sects of antiquity. The old history-of-religions school was right on this point. From a historical perspective, Paul is the 'second founder of Christianity'. As a theologian and missionary he put it on the way by which it became a world religion – the first. The basis of this was laid in those unknown years of the apostle between Damascus and Antioch.

Conclusion: A Chronological Comparison – Paul and Luther

Inferences by analogy are misleading and – if made too hastily – can easily result in error in the sphere of history. But here, to conclude with, I hope I may be allowed to compare Paul's development with that of one of his greatest interpreters. We can follow the development of Luther's theological insights very much better than those of Paul. The 'young Luther' is already essentially closer and more familiar to us than Paul 'between Damascus and Antioch'.[1575] His decisive insights matured between 1513 and 1515/16, i.e. between his first lectures on Psalms and the lectures on Romans. The developments concluded at the latest in the lectures on Galatians in 1515/17. He was probably a bit older than Paul, since the corresponding period lies between the thirtieth and thirty-fifth years of his life.[1576] But like the Pharisee and scribe, at the beginning of his activity as a monk and 'doctor of holy scripture' Luther arrived at the decisive insights which he retained right down to his late writings, and which determined his activity after the 'turning point'. There are no later insights of advanced age which could have led to a renewed upheaval with essential changes to his thoughts.[1577] In other words, we may not simply divide Luther's way towards becoming the Reformer into two stages, first the 'doubting monk' and then the 'Reformer sure of his aims'.[1578] The 'Reformer sure of his aims' was basically already present in the 'doubting monk'. In the case of Paul, too, one cannot divide the radical theologian from the purposive missionary. The unity of biography and theology applies to both.

Unlike what we know of Paul, the most important writings after the turning point in Luther's life appear in quick succession: the first work given to the printer by Luther himself belongs to the year 1517.[1579] The writings on the dispute over indulgences (1518)[1580] and on the sacraments, and above all his Galatians commentary (1519), were followed in 1520 by others, the most important of which were the 'Sermon on Good Works',[1581] 'To the Nobility', *De captivitate ecclesiae* and 'On the Freedom of a Christian Man'.[1582] The *Operationes in psalmos* appeared in 1521. However, the works of the years between 1521 and 1524 show particularly clearly that Luther – like Paul – always writes with reference to a special situation.[1583] In 1525 he composed his most mature work, *De servo arbitrio* – an answer to Erasmus – which at the same time marked the conclusion of this theological revolution extending over twelve years (1513–1525). With a pinch of salt Paul's 'unknown' period of around fourteen years, between 33 and 49, could be taken to correspond to this early period of time. In terms of external evidence, it is just 'chance' that we have no writings of Paul from this period. In the case of Luther everything is more 'complicated' because we have many more writings. If we had Luther's works only from 1527, we would in no way be justified in concluding that in the previous 'unknown years' he had not yet developed his doctrine of law and gospel and the justification of the sinner by grace alone. He, too, by no means presented these 'basic' doctrines in all his works, which as a rule were related to situations. Would everything have been quite different with Paul, the turning point in whose life and whose theological upheaval had been even more radical?

In the next twenty years, in the case of Luther further publications follow with breathtaking speed: in addition to his lectures, his activity in preaching and pastoral care, political and church disputes, care of his family and serious illnesses.

In retrospect, Luther often depicts the 'decisive shift towards the basic insight of the Reformation', as he does in 1545, shortly before his death: 'A strange burning desire had seized me to understand Paul in the Epistle to the Romans ... "For in it the righteousness of God is revealed" (Rom. 1.17). For I hated this phrase, "the righteousness of God" ... until I remembered the context in which the words occur, namely, "In it the righteousness of God is revealed" … that is, passive righteousness, through which the merciful God makes us righteous through faith, as it is written: "The righteous shall live by faith." Then I had the feeling that straightway I was born again, and had entered through opened doors into paradise itself. The whole scripture revealed a different countenance to me. I then went through the whole scripture in my memory and compared analogies in other expressions … As I had hated the phrase "the righteousness of God" before, I now valued it with equal love, as the word that was sweetest to me. Thus in truth this passage in Paul was the gate of paradise for me.'[1584] In his retrospects Luther does not conceal the tormentingly long time of searching. But after the decisive breakthrough he remained faithful to this insight. One could compare this late confession with an equally late passage from Paul, Phil. 3.4–11, above all if Paul had written the letter in Rome during his last captivity a few years before his death.

There is a crass disproportion between Luther's written word – not to mention the testimonies of contemporaries about him – and the extremely narrow range of the extant letters of Paul. What we have from Paul is a shadow of the fullness of what he preached. So arguments from silence are extremely deceptive, particularly in the exegesis of Paul. 'Justification of the godless by grace alone' is not an insight from the apostle's late period, but shaped his proclamation from his earliest period as the cause of his theology of the cross.

Abbreviations

AASF	Annales Academiae Scientiarum Fennicae
ADPV	Abhandlungen des Deutschen Palästina-Vereins
AGJU	Arbeiten zur Geschichte des antiken Judentums und des Urchristentums
AGWG.PH	Abhandlungen der (K.) Gesellschaft der Wissen schaften zu Göttingen Philosophisch-Historische Klasse
AJP	*American Journal of Philology*
ALLG	Archiv für lateinische Lexikographie und Grammatik
AnBib	Analecta biblica
ANET	*Ancient Near Eastern Texts relating to the Old Testament*
ANRW	*Aufstieg und Niedergang der römischen Welt*
ARW	Archiv für Religionswissenschaft
AThANT	Abhandlungen zur Theologie des Alten und Neuen Testaments
BAR	British Archaeological Reports (International Series, Oxford)
BASOR	*Bulletin of the American Schools of Oriental Research*
BBB	Bonner biblische Beiträge
BEFAR	Bibliothèque des écoles françaises d'Athènes et de Rome
BEThL	Bibliotheca Ephemeridum theologicarum Lovaniensium
BEvTh	Beiträge zur Evangelischen Theologie
BGBE	Beiträge zur Geschichte der biblischen Exegese
BGU	Berliner griechische Urkunden
BHHW	*Biblisch-historisches Handwörterbuch*

BHTh	Beiträge zur historischen Theologie
Bib	*Biblica*, Rome
Bill.	P. Billerbeck, *Kommentar zum Neuen Testament aus Talmud und Midrasch*
BJSt	Brown Judaic Studies
BRGA	Beiträge zur Religionsgeschichte des Altertums, Halle
BSELK	*Die Bekenntnisschriften der evangelisch-lutherischen Kirche*, edited under the auspices of the Deutscher evangelischer Kirchenausschuss, Göttingen ⁵1963
BSGRT	Bibliotheca scriptorum Graecorum et Romanorum Teubneriana
BTAVO	Beihefte zum Tübinger Atlas zum Vorderen Orient
BThZ	*Berliner theologische Zeitschrift*
BWANT	Beiträge zur Wissenschaft vom Alten und Neuen Testament
BZ (NF)	*Biblische Zeitschrift* (Neue Folge)
BZAW	Beihefte zur Zeitschrift für die alttestamentliche Wissenschaft
BZNW	Beihefte zur Zeitschrift für die neutestamentliche Wissenschaft
CAH	*Cambridge Ancient History*
CBQ	*Catholic Biblical Quarterly*
CCSA	Corpus Christianorum Series apocryphorum
CCSL	Corpus Christianorum Series Latina
CIJ	*Corpus inscriptionum Judaicarum*, ed. Frey
CIS	*Corpus inscriptionum semiticarum*
CorpAp	Corpus apologetarum
CPJ	*Corpus papyrorum Judaicorum*, ed. Tcherikover and Fuks
CSEL	Corpus scriptorum ecclesiasticorum Latinorum
DAWW.PH	Denkschriften der (K.) Akademie der Wissenschaften in Wien Philosophisch-Historische Klasse
DBS	*Dictionnaire de la bible. Supplément*
DDD	*Dictionary of Deities and Demons in the Bible*, ed. K. van der Toorn, Leiden 1995

DJD	*Discoveries in the Judean Desert*
DUJ	*Durham University Journal*
EHPhR	Études d'histoire et de philosophie religieuses
EJ	*Encyclopaedia Judaica*
EKK	Evangelisch-katholischer Kommentar zum Neuen Testament
EPRO	Études préliminaires aux religions orientales dans l'empire romain
ErIs	*Eretz Israel,* Jerusalem
ExpT	*Expository Times*
EvTh	*Evangelische Theologie*
EWNT	*Exegetisches Wörterbuch zum Neuen Testament*
FAT	Forschungen zum Alten Testament
FEUC	Forschungen zur Entstehung des Urchristentums, des Neuen Testaments und der Kirche
FGNK	T. Zahn, *Forschungen zur Geschichte des neutestamentlichen Kanons und der altchristlichen Literatur*
FGRH	*Die Fragmente der griechischen Historiker*
FKDG	Forschungen zur Kirchen- und Dogmengeschichte
FRLANT	Forschungen zur Religion und Literatur des Alten und Neuen Testaments
FS	Festschrift
GBL	*Das grosse Bibellexikon, Wuppertal*
GCS	Die griechischen christlichen Schriftsteller der ersten drei Jahrhunderte
GGA	Göttingische gelehrte Anzeigen
GLAJ	M. Stern, *Greek and Latin Authors on Jews and Judaism*
GNT	Grundrisse zum Neuen Testament
Grammatik	Blass/Debrunner/Rehkopf, *Grammatik des Neutestamentlichen Griechisch*
GTA	Göttinger theologische Arbeiten
HABES	Heidelberger althistorische Beiträge und epigraphische Studien

HNT	Handbuch zum Neuen Testament
HThK	Herders theologischer Kommentar zum Neuen Testament
HTR	*Harvard Theological Review*
HUCA	*Hebrew Union College Annual*
ICC	International Critical Commentary
IEJ	*Israel Exploration Journal*
IG	*Inscriptiones Graecae*
IGLS	*Inscriptions grecques et latines de la Syrie*
IGR	*Inscriptiones Graecae ad res Romanas pertinentes*
JANES	*Journal of the Ancient Near Eastern Society*
JAOS	*Journal of the American Oriental Society*
JBL	*Journal of Biblical Literature*
JBTh	*Jahrbuch für biblische Theologie*
JJS	*Journal of Jewish Studies*
JQR	*Jewish Quarterly Review*
JR	*Journal of Religion*
JRS	*Journal of Roman Studies*
JS	*Journal des savants*
JSHRZ	Jüdische Schriften aus hellenistisch-römischer Zeit
JSOT.S	Journal for the Study of the Old Testament Supplement series
JSS	*Journal of Semitic Studies*
JTS	*Journal of Theological Studies*
KEK	Kritisch-exegetischer Kommentar über das Neue Testament. Founded by Heinrich August Wilhelm Meyer
KIT	Kleine Texte
KNT	Kommentar zum Neuen Testament
KP	*Der kleine Pauly*
LectDiv	*Lectio divina*
LIMC	*Lexicon Iconographicum Mythologiae Classicae*
LJ	*Liturgisches Jahrbuch*
LSJ	Liddell/Scott/Jones, *A Greek-English Lexicon*

MAMA	Monumenta Asiae Minoris Antiqua
MBTh	Münsterische Beiträge zur Theologie
MGWJ	*Monatsschrift für Geschichte und Wissenschaft des Judentums*
MUSJ	*Mélanges de l'Université Saint-Joseph*

PatMS	Patristic Monograph Series, Macon

NBL	*Neues Bibel-Lexikon*
NewDoc	G. H. R. Horsley, *New Documents Illustrating Early Christianity. A Review of the Greek Inscriptions and Papyri*, Macquarie University, 1981ff.
NGWG.PH	Nachrichten (von) der Gesellschaft der Wissenschaften (zu) in Göttingen Philologisch-Historische Klasse
NIGTC	New International Greek Testament Commentary
NKZ	*Neue kirchliche Zeitschrift*
NT	*Novum Testamentum*, Leiden
NT.S	– Supplements
NTA NF	Neutestamentliche Abhandlungen, Münster (Neue Folge)
NTApoc	*New Testament Apocrypha*, edited by W. Schneemelcher and R. McL. Wilson
NTD	Das Neues Testament Deutsch
NTF	Neutestamentliche Forschung
NTG	Neue theologische Grundrisse
NTOA	Novum testamentum et orbis antiquus
NTS	*New Testament Studies*

OBO	Orbis biblicus et orientalis
OECT	Oxford Early Christian Texts
OGIS	*Orientis Graeci inscriptiones selectae*
OTP	*Old Testament Pseudepigrapha*, ed. J. H. Charlesworth

PG	Migne, *Patrologia Graeca*
PGL	*A Patristic Greek Lexicon*, ed. G. W. H. Lampe
PhilSuppl	Philologus Supplementband

PL	Migne, *Patrologia Latina*
POxy	Oxyrhynchus Papyri, ed. Grenfell/Hunt
PW	*Paulys Real-Enzyclopädie der classischen Altertums-wissenschaften*

RAC	*Reallexikon für Antike und Christentum*
RB	*Revue biblique*
rde	rowohlts deutsche enzyklopädie
RE	*Realencyklopädie für protestantische Theologie und Kirche*
RÉS	*Répertoire d'épigraphie sémitique* I–VII (1900–1950)
RGG	*Die Religion in Geschichte und Gegenwart*
RGRW	Religions in the Graeco-Roman World
RHR	*Revue de l'histoire des religions*
RIDA	*Revue internationale des droits de l'antiquité*
RivAC	*Rivista di archeologia christiana*
RM	Religionen der Menschheit
RV	Religionsgeschichtliche Volksbücher

SBS	Stuttgarter Bibelstudien
SC	Sources chrétiennes
Schürer	Emil Schürer, *The History of the Jewish People in the Age of Jesus Christ*, I–III/1, rev. and ed. by G. Vermes, F. Millar et al., Edinburgh 1979ff.
SDAWB	Sitzungsberichte der Deutschen Akademie der Wissenschaften zu Berlin
SEG	*Supplementum epigraphicum Graecum*
SGUÄ	*Sammelbuch griechischer Urkunden aus Ägypten*
SHAW	Sitzungsberichte der Heidelberger Akademie der Wissenschaften
SHAW.PH	– Philosophisch-Historische Klasse
SJ	Studia Judaica
SJLA	Studies in Judaism in Late Antiquity
SNTS.MS	Society of New Testament Studies Monograph Series
StANT	Studien zum Alten und Neuen Testament
StEv	Studia evangelica
StTh	Studia theologica, Lund, etc.

TDNT	*Theological Dictionary of the New Testament*
ThB	Theologische Blätter
ThNT	Theologischer Handkommentar zum Neuen Testament
ThLZ	*Theologische Literaturzeitung*
ThWAT	*Theologisches Wörterbuch zum Alten Testament*
ThZ	*Theologische Zeitschrift*, Basel
TLS	*The Times Literary Supplement*
TRE	*Theologische Realenzyklopädie*
TSAJ	Texte und Studien zum antiken Judentum
TU	Texte und Untersuchungen zur Geschichte der altchristlichen Literatur
UALG	Untersuchungen zur antiken Literatur und Geschichte, Berlin
UCPH	University of California Publications in Semitic Philology
UTB	Uni-Taschenbücher
VigChr	*Vigiliae Christianae*
WB	*Wörterbuch*
WdF	Wege der Forschung
WMANT	Wissenschaftliche Monographien zum Alten und Neuen Testament
WUNT	Wissenschaftliche Untersuchungen zum Neuen Testament
ZBK	Zürcher Bibelkommentare
ZDPV	*Zeitschrift des Deutschen Palästina-Vereins*
ZNW	*Zeitschrift für die neutestamentliche Wissenschaft*
ZPE	*Zeitschrift für Papyrologie und Epigraphik*
ZThK	*Zeitschrift für Theologie und Kirche*

Notes

1. Ignatius, Eph. 12.2; Rom. 4.3.
2. *Lehrbuch der Dogmengeschichte*, Tübingen ⁴1909, 1, 556 n.1. His italics.
3. Athenagoras, *Resurr.* 18; Apollonius in Eusebius, *HE* 5, 18, 3; Irenaeus, *Haer.* 4, 21, 1f.; 24, 1; 27, 3f.; 29, 1; 33, 10, etc. See also Lampe, *PGL*, 212 III G. The fact that he is also called *haereticorum apostolus* is another question (Tertullian, *Adv. Marc.* 3, 6, 4). For Irenaeus see now R. Noormann, *Irenaeus als Paulusinterpret*, WUNT II/66, Tübingen 1994. Irenaeus' terminology is striking, because he is the first author after the *Epistula Apostolorum* to make extensive use of Acts, in which Paul is denied the title of apostle. See 47–52: 'The letters are not subordinated to Acts, but are fully illuminated by it.' Acts is 'mediated by Luke – legitimated by Paul'.
4. Rom. 11.13, cf. Irenaeus, *Haer.* 4, 24, 1.
5. For this see C. Burchard, *Der dreizehnte Zeuge. Traditions- und kompositionsgeschichtliche Untersuchungen zu Lukas' Darstellung der Frühzeit des Paulus*, FRLANT 103, Göttingen 1970, esp. 173ff., which is still fundamental. It made a substantial contribution to the gradual change of the picture of Luke in Germany, which of course is not completed even yet. E. Haenchen, *The Acts of the Apostles*, Oxford 1974, 327f., fails to understand this specific function of Paul as the thirteenth – and special – witness and thus to recognize his role in Acts. As this quite special witness, Paul is the focal point of the whole work, in which everything culminates. Quite recently a doctoral student heard a young German professor remarking that Acts is 'not a source but secondary literature'. It would be a good thing for New Testament scholars, too, to read Droysen's *Historik* (n.95). See now the justifiable sharp criticism by the ancient historian H. Botermann, *Das Judenedikt des Kaisers Claudius*, Hermes Einzelschriften 71, Stuttgart 1996, 14–43: while New Testament scholars 'work in accordance with the "historical-critical" method, if we consider their treatment of the earliest Christian sources, this is

evidently a different "historical" method from the one used by ancient historians' (21); cf. 24 n.39: 'If ancient historians used their sources as "critically" as most theologians, they would have to close the files on Herodotus and Tacitus.' Thus already J. B. Lightfoot; see M. Hengel, 'Bishop Lightfoot and the Tübingen School on the Gospel of John and the Second Century', in *The Lightfoot Centenary Lectures*, ed. J. D. G. Dunn, *DUJ* (Complementary Number for Subscribers), January 1992, 23–51: 30f.; vgl. A. von Harnack, *Geschichte der altchristlichen Litteratur bis Eusebius. Die Chronologie* I, 1897, IX, quoted by Botermann, 25 n.42.

6. G. Ebeling, 'Theologie', *RGG*³ VI, 1962, col. 760: 'Theology in the sense which is now being discussed clearly begins with Paul'; cf. W. Wrede, 'Paulus', *RV* I, 5/6, Halle 1904, 102. This does not exclude the possibility that well before him there were highly impressive *Old Testament and Jewish theological outlines*: the Deuteronomistic and Chronistic histories, Deutero-Isaiah, the Priestly Writing, Ben Sira, the Essenes of Qumran, Philo, etc.

7. We may ask whether Philemon and Philippians (which we still regard as a unity) were written in Rome or in Caesarea; cf. C. J. Thornton, *Der Zeuge des Zeugen. Lukas als Historiker der Paulusreisen*, WUNT 56, Tübingen 1991, 202–7, 212. In that case the period of time would be extended by around two to six years, depending on how one dates the two letters and whether Paul's death is put as early as 62 (cf. Acts 28.30) or in the Neronian persecution in 64 CE.

8. Burchard, *Zeuge* (n.5), 173. Emphasis ours. By contrast, one could refer here to B. G. Niebuhr, the founder of modern historical criticism: 'I am a historian because I can create a complete historical picture from the details which have been preserved'; quoted by Botermann, *Judenedikt* (n.5), 24 n.39. A 'picture' might perhaps be too much, but clear outlines are evident from the fragments.

9. *Charakterköpfe aus der Antike*, ed. I. Stroux, Leipzig ²1943, 219.

10. I Cor. 15.10; cf. 9.1ff.; II Cor. 11.5, 23; Rom. 15.16–21.

11. Despite many assertions to the contrary, since F. C. Baur and his pupils there has been no evidence that knowledge of Paul's letters by Luke can be demonstrated. The same can also be said of Luke's knowledge of Josephus, which is claimed by some scholars. The reason for parallels lie in the history of the tradition. When Luke was writing, Paul's letters may have been in the archives of one community or another. The use of them begins only with I Clem. or shortly after 100 CE (I Clem. 47.1–3; cf. 37.3; Phil. 4.15. But cf. the incorrect information in Ignatius, Eph. 12.2). They will have been collected and edited around this time. However, Luke was writing around twenty years earlier, without any

access to the letters.

12. M. Hengel, 'Der Jakobusbrief als antipaulinische Polemik', in *Tradition and Interpretation, FS E. Earle Ellis*, ed. G. F. Hawthorne and O. Betz, Michigan and Tübingen 1987, 248–78.

13. A. D. Nock, *Paul*, London 1938, 146.

14. U. Heckel, *Kraft in Schwachheit*, WUNT II.56, Tübingen 1993, 14ff., 122ff, see also the index. For the question of Paul's education in rhetoric – which is discussed almost excessively today – see the balanced and generally positive view of C. J. Classen, *Philologische Bemerkungen zur Sprache des Apostels Paulus*, Wiener Studien 107/8, 1994/95, *Festschrift H. Schwabl*, 321–35 (with bibliography). Here we should note that ancient epistolography did not know the same strict rules as oratory proper and high prose literature.

15. *Acta Apostolorum Apocrypha* (Lipsius/Bonnet) I, 237 = *NTApoc* 2, ²1992, 239. For the author see Tertullian, *De bapt.* 17, 5 (CCSL 1, 291f., ed. Barleffs).

16. Nock, *Paul* (n.13), 14, our emphasis.

17. Ibid. So New Testament scholarship is on the wrong track if it believes that it can really understand Paul philologically without having read as many comparative Greek texts as possible from the LXX through Philo to Plutarch and Plotinus. We must attempt more than ever today to put Paul in his historical and linguistic environment'; see M. Hengel, 'Aufgaben der neutestamentlichen Wissenschaft', *NTS* 40, 1994, 321–57: 345f.

18. See A. J. M. Wedderburn, *The Reasons for Romans*, Edinburgh 1988, 140ff.

19. F. Avemarie, *Tora und Leben. Untersuchungen zur Heilsbedeutung der Tora in der frühen rabbinischen Literatur*, TSAJ 55, Tübingen 1996.

20. This is the content of three one-hour lectures!

21. Today this has partly become the fashion. See e.g. H. Räisänen, *Paul and the Law*, WUNT I/ 29, Tübingen ²1987 (1983), 199ff., 264ff.

22. Rom. 13.12; I Cor. 7.8.29–35; cf. I Thess. 5.1–11; Phil. 4.5.

23. *Odes*, 3, 30, 1.

24. I Cor. 1.31; II Cor. 10.17, cf. Heckel, *Kraft* (n.14), 14f., 172–85; S. Vollenweider, 'Die Waagschalen von Leben und Tod. Zum antiken Hintergrund von Phil 1, 21–26', *ZNW* 85, 1994, 114 n.91, on the eschatological aspect of 'boasting'.

25. Philemon 24; Col. 4.14; cf. M. Hengel, *Earliest Christianity*, London 1986, 66f.; E. Meyer, *Ursprung und Anfänge des Christentums III: Die Apostelgeschichte und die Anfänge des Christentums*, Stuttgart etc. 1923 (reprinted Darmstadt 1962), 17ff.; Thornton, *Zeuge* (n.7), 67–70, 227ff. etc.; Boter-

mann, *Judenedikt* (n.5), 35.

26. Meyer, *Ursprung* (n.25), 17–23; Thornton, *Zeuge* (n.7), 313ff., 341–67; Botermann, *Judenedikt* (n.5), 29–47. For a pertinent account of the voyage which is completely misunderstood by theologians who are remote from reality see H. Hellenkemper, in *Das Wrack. Der antike Schiffsfund von Mahdia,* ed. G. Hellenkemper et al., *Kataloge des Rheinischen Landesmuseums Bonn,* I, 1, Cologne 1994, 158ff.: 'The most accurate and extensive account of a catastrophic shipwreck' to be 'depicted by an … ancient author' (159).

27. See the index of names in W.-H. Ollrog, *Paulus und seine Mitarbeiter,* WMANT 50, Neukirchen 1979, 272ff. Luke is decidedly a marginal figure.

28. There is a skilful attempt in R. Pesch, *Die Apostelgeschichte.* 1. Teilband (1–12), EKK V/1, Zürich 1986, 26; but see Thornton, *Zeuge* (n.7), 7f., 145–8 etc.: see index 426 s.v. 'Lukas' (as author of Acts, as author of the Third Gospel).

29. Cf.. *Apol.* 31.2ff.; 35.9; 40.6; 48.3; 103.3f.: Herod the Great is a contemporary of king Ptolemy (II) and Herod Antipas, king of Judaea, and successor of Archelaos. The Acts of Pilate could still be inspected, *Dial.* 80.4: Sadducees, Pharisees, Galileans, etc. are no more authentic Jews than the Gnostic heretics are Christians!

30. See M. Hengel, 'The Titles of the Gospels and the Gospel of Mark', in *Studies in the Gospel of Mark,* London 1985, 64–83: 66f.; Thornton, *Zeuge* (n.7), 69–81.

31. II Cor. 11.24f.; cf. Acts 18.12ff.; 21.27–26; 17.1–10.

32. For the Semitisms in Matthew see S.T. Lachs, 'Studies in the Semitic Background of the Gospel of Matthew', *JQR* 67, 1976, 195–217; also M. Hengel, 'Zur matthäischen Bergpredigt und ihrem jüdischen Hintergrund', *ThR* 52, 1987, 327–400.

33. Despite the warning against false teachers in Acts 20.29f. – who were omnipresent even in Paul's time – there is absolutely no evidence that the Lukan church is engaged in an acute defensive struggle against the gnostic movement which has sprung from its midst: against G. Klein, *Die zwölf Apostel,* FRLANT 77, 1961, 214. There was no 'orthodox church' as early as the time of the author, nor are 'gnostic complaints' against Paul evident. In the meantime this whole unhistorical pan-gnosticism emanating from Marburg has collapsed. See M. Hengel, *Die johanneische Frage,* WUNT 67, Tübingen 1993 [this is a substantially expanded version of *The Johannine Question,* London and Philadelphia 1989; references will be given to it, and also, in square brackets, to the English version where a parallel passage exists], 39 n.85, and id., 'Gnosis und Neues Testament'

(*Festschrift P. Stuhlmacher zum 65. Geburtstag* 1997, forthcoming).

34. However, these problems are discussed in the Pastoral Epistles, which with H. von Campenhausen I put around 110–120, though a direct connection with Polycarp himself cannot be demonstrated. See H. von Campenhausen, *Aus der Frühzeit des Christentums*, 1963, 195–252. They already presuppose Acts, to some degree from a later perspective – see the 'martyrs' confession' in II Tim. and H. W. Tajra, *The Martyrdom of St Paul*, WUNT II/67, Tübingen 1994, 84–98. Cf. II Tim. 3.11 = Acts 13 and 14. The Lukan sequence Antioch, Iconium, Lystra is striking and rests on tradition. Cf. also e.g. Acts 20.24 and II Tim. 4.7. For gnosis cf. I Tim. 6.20; for the episcopate see also the letters of Ignatius.

35. Cf. Acts 9.16; 20.24f.; 25.23ff. I Clem. 5.1–7; 6.1ff. (after 96 CE), too, can only be understood by comparison with the account in Tacitus, *Ann.* 15.44. Clement still includes himself in the generation of those who have personal experience of the Neronian persecution.

36. See M. Hengel, 'The Historian Luke and the Geography of Palestine in the Acts of the Apostles', in *The Book of Acts in Its First Century Setting 4. The Palestinian Setting*, ed. R. Bauckham, 1995, 27–78.

37. Cf. C. J. Hemer, *The Book of Acts in the Setting of Hellenistic History*, WUNT 49, 1989, 94–100; G. E. Sterling, *Historiography and Selfdefinition. Josephus, Luke-Acts and Apologetic Historiography*, NT.S 64, Leiden, etc. 1992, esp. 365–9; cf. also D. W. Palmer, 'Acts and the Ancient Historical Monograph', in *The Book of Acts in Its First Century Setting 1, The Book of Acts in Its Ancient Literary Setting*, ed. B. W. Winter and A. D. Clarke, 1993, 1–29: 15–18; cf. the index of this composite work. The *War* was begun shortly before the death of Vespasian in 79 CE; the *Antiquities* were written around fifteen years later in 93/95 CE, see Schürer I, 47f.

38. M. Krenkel, *Josephus und Lukas. Der Einfluss des jüdischen Schriftstellers auf den christlichen*, Leipzig 1894, among others, attempted to prove dependence. From Krenkel's remarks it can be seen that this proof can be offered only with very powerful mental contortions. See Hemer, *Acts* (n.37), 95: 'the theory of Lukan dependence on Josephus has had in its day a certain vogue, and has been used as a major argument for the late dating of Luke-Acts'; cf. also Sterling, *Historiography* (n.37), 365f. n.281.

39. Against P. Vielhauer, 'Zum "Paulinismus" der Apostelgeschichte', *EvTh* 10, 1950/51, 1–15; Klein, *Apostel* (n.33), 1961.

40. Luke 1.1–4; Acts 1.1f.

41. See above, 159.

42. See below, nn.49, 1273.

43. *Ann.* 1, 1, 3; cf. Josephus, *BJ* 1.2f., 7 , 9.

44. W. Gasque, *A History of the Criticism of the Acts of the Apostles*, BGBE 17, 1975, 37.

45. Hengel, *Johanneische Frage* (n.33), 148f., 164f., 202 [44f., 53f., 73].

46. It seems to us questionable whether Hegesippus' *Hypomnemata* can be regarded as such.

47. See the strict verdict of F. Overbeck, *Christentum und Kultur. Aus dem Nachlass herausgegeben von C. A. Bernouilli*, 1919, reprinted Darmstadt 1963, 78, often repeated: the fact that he 'gives the Gospel an Acts of the Apostles as a continuation', is 'a piece of tactlessness of world-historical dimensions, the greatest excess of the false position in which Luke puts his subject'. Acts stands alongside the Gospels 'as one of the poorest and most miserable books'. Here we have an expression of Overbeck's hatred of Harnack, who venerates Luke. Basically, Overbeck understood neither Luke nor Paul. As an enlightened contemporary he saw only what for him was ultimately the absurd and utterly *alien* character of primitive Christianity – for all the romantic transfigurations of the first beginnings.

48. See Thornton, *Zeuge* (n.7), index s.v. 'Historiker', 'Historiographie', 'Lukas', and the examples given in M. Hengel, 'Literary, Theological and Historical Problems in the Gospel of Mark', 47–50, on Papias' note and 'The Gospel of Mark: Time of Origin and Situation', 11, on the Alexander and Augustus tradition and on miracle with contemporary eye-witnesses in Christian historiography, both in id., *Studies in the Gospel of Mark*, London 1985. The examples could be multiplied. See also O. Betz, 'Das Problem des Wunders bei Flavius Josephus ...', in id., *Jesus. Der Messias Israels, Aufsätze zur biblischen Theologie*, WUNT 42, 1987, 398–419; id., 'Miracles in the Writings of Flavius Josephus', in L. H. Feldman and G. Hata, *Josephus, Judaism and Christianity*, Leiden 1987, 212–35; Morton Smith, 'The Occult in Josephus', ibid., 236–54: 'For him ... the occult was more than a decorative element. It was a constituent part of the Graeco-Roman world, a part made particularly important by the conflict between that world and his inherited Israelite monotheism.' He too often writes a tendentious *Zeitgeschichte* which sometimes corrects historical reality (e.g. in *BJ* as opposed to the account in the *Life*). Why may that not also be the case in Luke?

49. Luke 2.1; 3.1ff. That Luke has not realized that a 'census' by the Roman governor of Syria was simply impossible in the kingdom of Herod I is one of his mistakes which is understandable in view of the historical situation. See Schürer I, 399–427; R. Riesner, *Die Frühzeit des Apostels Paulus. Studien zur Chronologie, Missionsstrategie und Theologie*, WUNT 71, Tübingen 1994, 293f. (more recent literature). Probably

here he was dependent on a Jewish-Christian source, oral or (more likely) written, which gave legendary reasons for the birth of Jesus in Bethlehem.

50. Hengel, 'Between Jesus and Paul. The "Hellenists", the Seven and Stephen (Acts 6.1–5; 5.54–8.3)', in id., *Between Jesus and Paul*, London 1983, 1–29.

51. M. Hengel, 'Der vorchristliche Paulus', in *Paulus und das antike Judentum*, ed. M. Hengel and U. Heckel, WUNT 58, Tübingen 1991, 177–291 [this is a revised and expanded German version of id., *The Pre-Christian Paul*, London and Philadelphia 1991 (in collaboration with Roland Deines)]. References will be given to both the German and the English texts, the latter in square brackets.

52. Nock, *Paul* (n.13), 85.

53. Gal. 2.5, 14. See above, 291f. and below, n.1080.

54. Thus G. Strecker, 'Befreiung und Rechtfertigung', in: *Rechtfertigung. Festschrift für E. Käsemann*, ed. J. Friedrich, etc., Tübingen and Göttingen 1976, 479–508: 480 = id., *Eschaton und Historie, Aufsätze*, Göttingen 1979, 227–59: 230. See above all his pupil U. Schnelle, *Gerechtigkeit und Christusgegenwart. Vorpaulinische und paulinische Tauftheologie*, GTA 24, Göttingen 1983, 100ff. etc.; id., *Wandlungen im paulinischen Denken*, SBS 137, 1989, with bibliography. Cf. also H. H. Schade, *Apokalyptische Christologie bei Paulus*, GTA 18, Göttingen ²1984 (1981), 49f.; F. H. Horn, '1 Korinther 15, 56 – ein exegetischer Stachel', *ZNW* 82, 1991, 88–105, who wants to demonstrate that I Cor. 15.56 is an interpolation by a disciple of Paul, because such a statement about law and sin is not yet possible 'within Pauline theology at the time of I Cor.' (101); it is possible only in Rom. 7, but see T. Söding, 'Der erste Thessalonicherbrief und die frühpaulinische Evangeliumsverkündigung. Zur Frage einer Entwicklung der paulinischen Theologie', *BZ* 35, 1991, 180–203; Riesner, *Frühzeit* (n.49), 349–58; D. Sänger, *Die Verkündigung des Gekreuzigten in Israel*, WUNT I/75, Tübingen 1994, 236–44. See already the verdict of A. Schweitzer, *The Mysticism of Paul the Apostle*, London ²1953, 225, cf. n.552 below.

55. See Avemarie, *Tora* (n.19).

56. F. C. Baur, *Paulus, der Apostel Jesu Christi*, Stuttgart 1845, 90. Cf. n.68 below.

57. Sänger, *Verkündigung* (n.54), 222.

58. Phil. 3.6; cf. C. Dietzfelbinger, *Die Berufung des Paulus als Ursprung seiner Theologie*, WMANT 58, Neukirchen-Vluyn 1985, 84, 88 etc.

59. Riesner, *Frühzeit* (n.49).

60. See Hengel, 'Aufgaben' (n.17), 321–57.

61. Cf. J. Becker, *Paulus. Der Apostel der Völker*, Tübingen ²1992, 34ff., 73ff., though caught up in the old prejudices he notoriously underestimates the significance of Acts, although he could certainly not have written so long a book on Paul without it.

62. Gal. 1.13; cf. I Cor. 15.9; Phil. 3.6, see also M. Hengel and R. Deines, review of Sanders, *JTS* 46, 1995, 1–70.

63. See H. Lietzmann, *Kleine Schriften* II, TU 68, 1958, 288ff.: 'Peter really was in Corinth and had a pernicious effect there.' T. Zahn, *Apostel und Apostelschüler in der Provinz Asien*, FGNK VI, 1900, 7, conjectured that 'Peter's people ... introduced themselves into Corinth as apostles', and originated from the 'mother community' of Jerusalem. See also Meyer, *Ursprung* (n.25), 441 n.2; Schwartz, *Charakterköpfe* (n.9), 218f.; see also Dionysius of Corinth, *HE* 2, 58, 8. More recent literature is given in M. Karrer, 'Petrus im paulinischen Gemeindekreis', *ZNW* 80, 1989, 210–31, who arrives at nonsensical results because of his misleading use of the argument from silence. After the interlude in Antioch there was an understandable tension between Paul and Peter, which caused Paul difficulties in the communites. The 'absence of any mention in the Deutero-Pauline literature in the second half of the first century' (213) is insignificant. Here the difficulties are either kept quiet about or harmonized, as already happens with Luke and later with I Clement, Ignatius and Polycarp.

64. Hengel, 'Vorchristlicher Paulus' (n.51), 193–208 [6–14].

65. He speaks of a fourteen-year stay in the double province, but he says nothing about his experiences other than in II Cor. 11.32 (cf. Acts 9.24f.).

66. Hence the dispute over the North and South Galatian hypotheses; see Hemer, *Acts* (n.37), 277–307; Riesner, *Frühzeit* (n.49), 257, 350ff.

67. II Cor. 11.32; for Aretas IV cf. Riesner, *Frühzeit* (n.49), 66–74 (bibliography); for the ethnarch see 74–9.

68. See already Baur, *Paulus* (n.56), 90: 'All that is certain is that, much as he based his whole apostolic activity on the immediacy of his apostolic calling and wanted to say all that he was only through the Christ who had appeared to him, he did not fail to incorporate information about the life of Jesus. Anyone who can speak so definitely and specifically about the Gospel history as the apostle does in I Cor. 11.23f.; 15.8f. cannot have been unfamiliar with the rest of the main contents of this life.'

69. I Cor. 11.23ff.; 15.3f.

70. *Jesus Christus in der Verkündigung der Kirche*, Neukirchen 1972, 75f.: 'Though the question of the historical Jesus may be historically possible

and permissible, theologically it is forbidden. The church has never been interested in the how and what of the life of Jesus; for it this life has stood under the sign of kenosis, the emptying out of the divinity of Christ (Phil. 2.6ff.).' I do not understand this mistaken argument. Indeed the Philippians hymn itself requires us to ask about the incarnate son of God's 'form of a slave' and 'existence as a man', i.e. his concrete activity and suffering, his obedience 'to death, even the death of the cross', and the temporal μέχρι θανάτου points to the man Jesus in space and time, in which the 'presence of God' is to be presumed.

71. Lightfoot, *Galatians* ad loc., 134, translated 'placarded', see also Moulton and Milligan, 538, and Schrenk, *TDNT* 1, 771f.

72. See M. Hengel, 'Crucifixion. In the Ancient World and the Folly of the Message of the Cross', in *The Cross of the Son of God*, London 1986, 93–182, arguing against H. W. Kuhn.

73. We have from antiquity a number of first-hand reports (letters, etc.) by persons involved and historical accounts of the same events. In them we can note divergences which are always at least similar to those between the letters of Paul and Acts. Thus Sallust merely mentions in one sentence that at the time of the Catiline conspiracy Cicero was (only) a significant consul. Although Sallust was in a much better position than Luke over written sources, and knew Cicero's speeches (though these, unlike the letters of Paul, had undergone subsequent literary revision by Cicero), together with other written evidence about the year 63 BCE, he preferred to give a general description of the events. There are further, later, examples in T. Hillard, A. Nobbs and B. Winter, 'Acts and the Pauline Corpus I: Ancient Literary Parallels', in *The Book of Acts in its First Century Setting* 1, ed. B. W. Winter et al. (n.37), 183–213. Josephus felt it necessary as a result of Justus of Tiberias's criticism of his account of the Jewish War to compose his *Life* as an appendix to his *Antiquities*, to remove contradictions and misunderstandings and to emphasize his status as an eye-witness and the reliability of his report. In this he often deviates considerably from his account in Book 2 of the *Jewish War*. There are also numerous discrepancies between Book 1 of *BJ* and *Antiquities* 18–20. Thus there is no lack of contradictions in Josephus; they can be attributed to various tendencies and to the sources which he writes out, but they also document his own intellectual development.

74. II Cor. 11.2, cf. Gal. 4.18 and, by contrast, I Cor. 13.4 and II Cor. 11.29.

75. Luke 1.1–4.

76. Meyer, *Ursprung* (n.25), 3ff.; Thornton, *Zeuge* (n.7), 192ff., 361–6;

see also U. Schnelle, *Einleitung in das Neue Testament*, UTB 1830, Göttingen 1994, 313–17.

77. Against J. Jeremias, 'Untersuchungen zum Quellenproblem der Apostelgeschichte', *ZNW* 36, 1937, 205–21 (= id., *Abba. Studien zur neutestamentlichen Theologie und Zeitgeschichte*, Göttingen 1964, 238–55); R. Bultmann, 'Zur Frage nach den Quellen der Apostelgeschichte', in id., *Exegetica*, Tübingen 1967, 412–23; see J. Dupont, *The Sources of Acts*, London 1964, 62–72, 166f.; Hengel, 'Jesus and Paul' (n.50), 3f.; id., *Earliest Christianity* (n.25), 37ff. (I have changed my mind on this point); cf. the bibliographical survey in Schneider, *Apostelgeschichte*, HThK V/1, 84–9; C. K. Barrett, *The Acts of the Apostles*, ICC, I, 1994, 53–6.

78. Cf. G. Lüdemann, *Earliest Christianity according to the Traditions in the Acts of the Apostles*, London 1989, who discusses the individual sections of Acts in terms of 'redaction', 'traditions' and 'historical'; for the source of the legend of Luke's origins in Antioch cf. n.1052 below.

79. For the later community archives see Hengel, *Evangelienüberschriften* (n.30), 37–40.

80. Acts 1.13f., cf. Luke 6.13–16; Acts 6.5; 13.1, cf. 20.4.

81. *Ep. ad Damasum* 20, 4.

82. Among other things this is also shown by a stylistic comparison of the 'we source' with the rest of Acts, see Thornton, *Zeuge* (n.7), 275–8.

83. See above, 134ff. for the visit to Jerusalem and 206ff. for Barnabas.

84. *Anweisung zum seligen Leben*, 1806, lecture 6.

85. On the lips of theologians shaped by Marburg this sounds almost like a taunt.

86. Baur, *Paulus* (n.56), 94; cf. 470ff. on Clement, Phil. 4.3. He identifies Clement with the Roman Titus Flavius Clemens in Suetonius and Dio Cassius and sees this as one of the indications of the inauthenticity of the letter to the Philippians. For J. B. Lightfoot's protest against this and numerous other violations of the Tübingen School see Hengel, 'Bishop Lightfoot' (n.5), 23–51 (31f.). For Alexander of Abonuteichos see W. Sontheimer, *KP* 1, 254 No. 22. German historical theology has not realized that research into the earliest Christian history was stimulated above all by a school which despised concrete historical details and the individual and began from the overarching movement of the spirit – or what it regarded as such. This was repeated in the twentieth century under the catchwords 'existence' and 'self-understanding'.

87. The most recent 'consistent' weed of this kind is the Schmithals pupil H. Detering, *Der gefälschte Paulus*, Düsseldorf 1994, who disputes the authenticity of all Paul's letters, seeking to explain them as the fabrication of Marcion. But cf. also W. Schmithals, *Der Römerbrief als historisches*

Problem, Gütersloh 1975, 152–211, on the cutting up of Romans and W. Schenk, 'Korintherbriefe', *TRE* 19, 1970, 620–32, who divides the two letters into 28 parts and a few glosses. For the naive confidence in the possibilities of literary criticism see Hengel, 'Aufgaben' (n.17).

88. Thus in the remarks by A. Feldtkeller, *Identitätssuche des syrischen Urchristentums. Mission, Inkulturation und Pluralität im ältesten Heiden-christentum*, NTOA 25, Freiburg and Göttingen 1993, 16ff.; id., *Im Reich der syrischen Göttin. Eine religiös plurale Kultur als Umwelt des frühen Christentums*, Studien zum Verstehen fremder Religionen 8, Gütersloh 1994. The real Syria of the first century had previously been much neglected in New Testament scholarship. In these two monographs Feldtkeller has made a rich collection of sometimes very interesting material; however, his evaluation of it is historically most unsatisfying. A typical feature of the bias in the 'quest for identity' is that the author pays virtually no attention to the central role of the Jewish Diaspora communities in Syria with their numerous synagogues and their relationship to the pagan environment. The term 'Gentile Christian' is not clarified; the political and social situation in the Roman province is hardly discussed. It is precisely at this point that one might really have expected more information. The author falls victim to a 'pan-Syrianism' comparable to the old 'pan-Gnosticism' and postulates unprovable early Christian movements, completely sweeping away the differences between Palestine and Syria and between Jesus and what in our view are the completely hypothetical 'itinerant radicals', taking no account of chronological and geographical questions and the fact that earliest Christianity was an acutely eschatological movement. No account at all is taken of so fundamental a statement as I Cor. 15.11 or of the fact that the 'invocation of the Kyrios Jesus' presupposes the confession of the resurrection and exaltation of Jesus. The book is a very assiduous and learned product of fashionable modern sociologizing exegesis, but it is also full of mistakes.

89. J. Weiss, *Earliest Christianity. A History of the Period AD 30–150*, 1937 reissued New York 1959, II, 740, begins his chapter 'Syria' with this distinction, which is often ignored today: 'Under this head, we are to consider the beginnings of the later Syriac national church of Edessa; by this title we mean instead the Roman province of Syria with its capital, Antioch.'

90. Against H. Koester in id. and J. M. Robinson, *Trajectories through the World of Early Christianity*, Philadelphia 1971, 119–43, who discusses Palestine and West Syria in 7 pages but devotes 16 pages to Edessa and the Osrhoëne (and Thomas Christianity), spinning out Walter Bauer's

fragile thread. See id., *Einführung in das Neue Testament*, Berlin and New York 1980, 434f., 527, 587ff., 601ff; id., *Ancient Christian Gospels*, Philadelphia and London 1990, 79f., 165, 205, 245, 290. Koester also wants to put the Gospel of Peter, the *Kerygma Petri* and the Apocalypse of Peter in Syria. He argues that Mark was written there by an unknown Gentile Christian. Here 'facts' are freely invented, contrary to the whole tradition of the early church. One further example among many is given by F. Vouga, *Geschichte des frühen Christentums*, UTB 1733, Tübingen 1994, 91–4, who derives the Thomas tradition in Edessa from an independent development of '*early* Easter movements' (93, our italics). Against this see J. Tubach, *Im Schatten des Sonnengottes. Der Sonnenkult in Edessa, Harran und Hatra am Vorabend der christlichen Mission*, Wiesbaden 1986 and also the survey by H. J. W. Drijvers, *TRE* 9, 277ff.

91. Seth Schwartz, *TLS*, 18 April 1994, 13. For the problem of syncretism see above, 268–76.

92. F. Millar, *The Roman Near East 31 BC–AD 337*, Cambridge, Mass. and London 1993, 460–6. Tubach, *Sonnengott* (n.90), 49, reckons the beginning of the second century, without giving examples.

93. 44 BCE, see below, n.805.

94. Cf. also Acts 15.23. For the double province see E. Bickerman, *Studies in Jewish and Christian History* I, AGJU IX, Leiden 1976, 279 (= Louis Ginzberg Jubilee Volume 1945); id., 'Syria and Cilicia', *AJP* 68, 1947, 353–62; E. M. B. Green, 'Syria and Cilicia – A Note', *ExpT* 71, 1959/60, 52f.; Hemer, *Acts* (n.37), 172, 179; R. Riesner, *Frühzeit* (n.49), 236. The two provinces were first separated by Vespasian in 72 CE; he combined *Cilicia campestris* with the mountain province of *Cilicia tracheia* after deposing the client king of Commagene, Antiochus IV, who had previously been its ruler.

95. Cf. J. G. Droysen, 'Vorwort zur *Geschichte des Hellenismus* II, 1843 (Theologie der Geschichte)', in *Historik*, ed. R. Hübner, Darmstadt 1972 (1937), 385: 'Even what is true, right and noble is not above space and time but has its measure and its energy in the fact that it appears so to speak projected on to a here and now' (reference from Tobias Jerzak).

96. For the problem see Hengel, 'Christology and New Testament Chronology', in id., *Between Jesus and Paul*, London 1983, 30–47.

97. W. Schmithals, *Theologiegeschichte des Urchristentums. Eine problemgeschichtliche Darstellung*, Stuttgart 1994, see the index s.v. 'Damaskus; damaszenische Theologie' (331) and s.v. 'Stephanus' (332). For the 'itinerant radikals' see Vouga, *Geschichte* (n.90), 30ff., 88f., who takes up the thesis of Downing and Mack that these Galilean itinerant preachers are 'sociologically' comparable to the fourth-century Cynic preachers in

Greece. Among other things he wants to connect even Peter with them, though he cannot deny that Peter, who was married and had a family, is said 'initially to have settled in Jerusalem'. H. D. Betz, 'Jesus and the Cynics: Survey and Analysis of a Hypothesis', *JR* 74, 1994, 453–75, is rightly critical of the thesis of itinerant Christian preachers with a Cynic style.

98. In the LXX ἔκτρωμα is the translation for a child dead in its mother's womb, whose birth does not take place at the expected time and can in some circumstances endanger the mother, see Num. 12.12; cf. Job 3.16; Koh. 6.3. M. Goguel, 'ΚΑΤΑ ΔΙΚΑΙΟΣΥΝΗΝ ΤΗΝ ΕΝ ΝΟΜΩΙ ΓΕΝΟΜΕΝΟΣ ΑΜΕΜΠΤΟΣ (Phil. 3.6). Remarques sur un aspect de la conversion', *JBL* 53, 1934, 259, understood ἔκτρωμα as a child torn violently from its mother's womb, which normally is not viable, arguing that this was a taunt of Paul's opponents, used by Paul as '*un titre de gloire*'. Cf. further Fridrichsen, *Paulus abortivus*, 1932, reprinted in id., *Exegetical Writings*, WUNT 76, 1994, 211–16.

99. II Cor 12., 1–4, see Heckel, *Kraft* (n.14), 54–66. The same is true of a fundamental ἀποκάλυψις 'Ιησοῦ Χριστοῦ, to which he owes his gospel (Gal. 1.12), in relation to the later ἀποκαλύψεις, cf. also Gal. 2.2.

100. Cf. Luke 24.9, 33.

101. See already the sending out of the seventy-two disciples in Luke 10.1, 'the crowd of *disciples*' in 19.37 and 24.9, 10, 33, where 'the eleven' have been replaced by 'the rest'.

102. But cf. the designation of Paul and Barnabas as apostles in 14.4, 14. This divergent terminology may perhaps go back to a 'source'. In my view Luke uses it quite deliberately to indicate the problem, which is familiar to him. The retention of the title ἀπόστολοι in the first description of a major missionary journey is meant to indicate that the view was also current in the church that Paul and Barnabas (and others) were likewise called 'apostles'. It is also striking that he uses 'the Twelve' only in 6.2 as a counterpart to the 'Seven' (6.3, 5; cf. 21.8: ὄντος ἐκ τῶν ἑπτά, where it becomes clear that this is also a fixed group). Here too the figures and names could indicate a 'source'. For these texts see Barrett, *Acts* (n.77), 305f., 310–15, 666f., 671f., 678f. Luke knows far more than he writes. He merely hints at delicate questions: *Sapienti sat.*

103. Luke 6.13: ἐκλεξάμενος; 9.1, 12; 18.31; 22.3, 30; cf. the Markan original 3.14, 16, etc.

104. Against G. Lohfink, *Die Himmelfahrt Jesu*, StANT 26, Munich 1971. Probably forty as a round number for the period of revelation has already been introduced into the pre-Lukan tradition: Moses' time on the mountain was the model (Ex. 24.18; 34.28; Deut. 9.9; 18.25; 10.10, cf.

IV Ezra 14.23, 36, 42, 44; SyrBar 76.2–4). Luke 24.36–51 directly contradicts Acts 1.3ff. Here too Luke points to the existence of different traditions (cf. also 13.31: πλείους). Moreover there could be an interval of several years between the composition of the Gospel and that of Acts. Normally the ancient historian explained away such divergent traditions with the comment 'some said that ..., others said this', cf. e.g. Dionysius of Halicarnassus, *Ant Rom* 1, 64, 4 (Aeneas); 2, 56, 2 (Romulus); Livy 1, 16, 1–8 (exaltation of Romulus) or the Jewish historian Artapanus (F 3, 35). Josephus, too, is similarly cautious, as for example in the cases of the death of Moses (*Antt.* 4, 326f.) and the translation of Elijah (*Antt.* 9, 28). Luke, who wants to report about the reliability of the tradition ἀκριβῶς καὶ καθεξῆς, cannot and will not make use of this profane secular attitude. We do not find it in the 'sacred history' of the LXX. He prefers to leave smaller contradictions as they stand.

105. Klein, *Apostel* (n.33), quite nonsensically claims this. His exegesis of Rev. 21.14 (pp.76ff.) and the way in which he practically passes over Matt. 10.2 are indications of the nature of his method. It is also striking that in the Gospel Luke speaks of the twelve apostles (like Matt. 10.2; cf. Mark 3.14 v.l.) and in Acts once of the eleven apostles, and also Acts 6.2 once of 'the twelve'. We do not know whether in the 32 instances of 'apostle' up to 16.4 (apart from 14.4, 14) he always only has the names of Acts 1.13, 26 in mind. According to 12.2 James the son of Zebedee is executed. In such questions Luke is perhaps less 'dogmatic' than dogmatizing exegetes want to make him.

106. I Cor. 9.1; II Cor. 11.5; 12.11.

107. I Cor. 1.12; 3.22; 9.3. Cephas and the twelve also follow one another directly in I Cor. 15.5.

108. Luke 24.49; Acts 1.2ff.; but cf. Mark 14.28; 16.7 par. The conflict cannot be resolved historically. Here one statement stands over against another and that indicates a conflict in the tradition.

109. Acts 1.11; cf. Rom. 11, 26; Luke 21.24, 27.

110. Probably Luke had personal knowledge of Jerusalem, see Hengel, 'The Historian Luke' (n.36), 152–62, 82.

111. Riesner, *Frühzeit* (n.49), 56–65.

112. *Adv. Haer.* 1, 30, 14, 1, 3, 2; see Riesner, *Frühzeit* (n.49), 56–60.

113. For the dating and origin cf. A. Acerbi, *Serra lignea. Studi sulla fortuna della Ascensione di Isaia*, Rome 1984; id., *L'Ascensione di Isaia. Cristologia e profetismo in Siria nei primi decenni del II secolo*, Studia Patristica Mediolanensia 17, Milan ²1989; this is taken further by the investigations of E. Norelli, *Ascension d'Isaïe, traduction, introduction et notes*, Apocryphes. Collection de poche de l'AELAC, Turnhout 1993, 87–99; id., *Ascensio*

Iesaiae. Commentarius, CCSA 8, Turnhout 1995, 53–66, who dates AscIsa 6–11 to the end of the first century and AscIsa 1–5 to the beginning of the second century and argues that they were composed in Syrian Antioch.

114. Riesner, *Frühzeit* (n.49), 61–3. This report could perhaps go back to the lost beginning of the Acts of Paul and link up with the earlier one of one and a half years. Around 130/140, Valentinus claimed that he still stood above Theodas in the oral teaching tradition of Paul, see Clement of Alexandria, *Strom.* 7, 106, 4.

115. In Hengel, 'Christology' (n.96), 42, I had conjectured *c.*32/34; see also Hengel, *Earliest Christianity* (n.25), 8. Today I would be inclined to reduce this interval further, on the basis of the clear statement in I Cor. 15.8f.

116. M. Dibelius, 'The First Christian Historian', in id., *Studies in the Acts of the Apostles*, ed. F. Greeven, London 1956, 124; Haenchen, *Acts* (n.5), 234f., etc. Against this Hengel, 'The Origins of the Christian Mission', in id., *Between Jesus and Paul*, London 1983, 48–64.

117. See M. Hengel, 'The Son of God', in *The Cross of the Son of God*, London 1986, 55–64; id., '"Sit at My Right Hand!"', in *Studies in Early Christology*, Edinburgh 1995, 119–225: 172–5, 214–25.

118. For example παῖς θεοῦ, Acts 3.13, 26; 4.27, 30; exaltation to the right hand of God: 2, 33f.; 5.31; formulae which sound adoptionist: 2.36; suffering of the Messiah, 3.15, cf. 2.23; sending of the Messiah and 'apokatastasis', 3.20f.

119. This is suggested e.g. by I Cor. 15.11, a text of which so far too little notice has been taken. However, that does not mean that the high christology of Hebrews or the Gospel of John can simply be attributed to the first witnesses of the resurrection. The historical communication of christological ideas in space and time may not be suppressed in favour of the dogmatic postulate. That makes no difference to the 'stormy development'.

120. Cf. Matt. 27.53; John 5.28; 11.38ff.; 12.17; cf. Isa. 26.19; Isa. 37.12; Dan. 12.2. For this reason the empty tomb must have played an essential role in the earliest community from the beginning, cf. I Cor. 15.4; Mark 16.1–8 par. A purely spiritual 'notion of the resurrection' in which the body decays cannot be demonstrated in Palestinian Judaism, which has a predominantly Pharisaic stamp. Moreover it would be indistinguishable from the immortality of the soul. Therefore this is not what the resurrection message is about. Cf. Hengel and Deines, review of Sanders (n.62), 1–70. Nor would it have been possible in Jerusalem to preach a crucified man as 'risen' who had been devoured upon the cross

by birds or was resting in the grave in a way which was demonstrable to everyone.

121. I Cor. 15.20, 23; Col. 1.18; Rev. 1.5; Acts 26.23, cf. 3.15, 26; Heb. 2, 10. For the resurrection of the patriarchs first in the endtime cf. TestJud 25.1; TestBen 10.6ff.; the Life of Jeremiah in the *Vitae Prophetarum (VP* 2, 12) speaks of the first resurrection of the 'ark of the law'.

122. At best one could point to Daniel's prophecy of the imminent divine judgment on Antiochus IV and the redemption of the true Israel (Dan. 11.45–12.3), the desperate expectation of an imminent end to the world towards the end of the siege of Jerusalem by Titus, and the activity of Zealot prophets when deliverance was expected in the temple on 9 Ab (Josephus, *BJ* 6, 283–286). Here the deadly danger of destruction gave decisive impetus to an extremely intensive – but still future – expectation. The Messiah had not yet come here and the resurrection of the dead had not yet begun; see M. Hengel, *The Zealots. Investigations into the Jewish Freedom Movement in the Period from Herod I until 70 AD*, Edinburgh 1989, 243.

123. This is indicated by what are the exaggerated numbers in Luke: Acts 1.15; 2.41; 4.4; 21.20; cf. more realistically I Cor. 15.6.

124. Acts 3.11; 5.12. Perhaps people gathered there recalling Jesus' sermon: John 10, 23. Tertullian contrasts this original location of Christian preaching in Jerusalem with Athens and its philosophical schools (*Praescr.haer.* 7, 9ff).

125. Mark 10.32 par. Luke 13.33f. par.; Acts 2.22–36; Rev. 11.8, etc.

126. Acts 1.11; cf. Rom. 11.26.

127. We do not find it as a place where Christians live in the epistolary literature; in the Apostolic Fathers; in Justin, who comes from Neapolis in Samaria; or in the other Apologists.

128. Acts 1.11; 2.7; 5.37; Matt. 26.69; cf. Mark 14.70. Matt. 26.73 even knows that they speak a distinctive dialect. Cf. also Justin, *Dial.* 80, 4, where they appear in a catalogue of Jewish sects, and 108.1, where Jewish emissaries call Jesus a Galilean deceiver. Here we are reminded of Judas the Galilean, see Hengel, *Zealots* (n.122), 76–9. Epictetus, *Diss.* 4, 7, 6 reports the crazy readiness of the 'Galileans' for martyrdom, meaning by this Christians generally. See also S. Freyne, *Galilee from Alexander the Great to Hadrian. 323 BCE to 135 CE*, Notre Dame 1980, 208–11.

129. Cf. even Q, Matt. 23.37 = Luke 13.34, or Matt. 5.35 and Rev. 11.1–13 (8). For Paul and Jerusalem see P. Stuhlmacher, 'Die Stellung Jesu und des Paulus zu Jerusalem', *ZThK* 86, 1989, 140–56, against K. Berger.

130. Gal. 1.22; I Thess. 2.14; cf. Rom. 15.31; II Cor. 1.16.

131. E. Lohmeyer, *Galiläa und Jerusalem*, Göttingen 1936; W. Marxsen, *Mark the Evangelist*, Nashville 1969; W. Grundmann, 'Das Problem des hellenistischen Christentums innerhalb der Jerusalemer Urgemeinde', *ZNW* 38, 1939; Feldtkeller, *Identitätssuche* (n.88), 26, 152–5, cf. n.88 above; Vouga, *Geschichte* (n.90), 30–7; also M. Sato, *Q und Prophetie*, WUNT II/29, 1986, 382–8 etc. Against this already M. Goguel, *La Naissance du Christianisme*, Paris 1946, 198f.

132. W. Schmithals, *Paulus und Jakobus*, FRLANT 85, 1963, 25f.: 'The home of Christianity is not Jerusalem but Galilee ... Of course an earliest community remained alive in Galilee, emanations from which reached Jerusalem not only through Samaria but also through Syria, Damascus and Antioch, in all of which places Acts presupposes early communities of Christians. The religious and political relations of "Galilee of the Gentiles" were at least as strong to the north as to the south.' For him, too, 'Galilee steeped in syncretism' (26 n.0) is the starting point of 'Christianity without the law' which was first persecuted by Paul. Cf. already Grundmann, 'Das Problem' (n.131), 45–73; id., *Jesus der Galiläer und das Judentum*, [2]1941, 82–90. Like Schmithals he refers to Lohmeyer and W. Bauer, and as a German Christian conjectured a partly non-Jewish 'Aryan' milieu in Galilee. This suppressed the fact that the Galileans were nationalistically minded Jews who were faithful to the law, see Hengel, *Zealots* (n.122), 56–9, 74, 293, 316ff. The works of S. Freyne have shown how misleading these conjectures of Bauer, Schmithals and others about a Galilean syncretism are. Such a syncretism cannot in any way be demonstrated from the sources or from archaeology.

133. Bill. I, 36ff.: tHul 2, 22f. (Zuckermandel 503); jAZ 2, 2 (40d–41a); QohR 1, 8 (4d), etc.: the story of Eleazar ben Dama and the Jewish Christian Jacob from Kefar-Sema(i); also the 'event' told next in tHul 2, 24 (par.: bAZ 17a. 27b; QohR 1, 8 [4a–b]) involving R. Eliezer, to whom Jacob of Kefar-Sakhnin had told a 'heresy' which pleased him.

134. *Ep. ad Aristidem* (in Eusebius, HE 1, 7, 14). Judaism remained prominent in Galilee until the fifth and sixth centuries, see Epiphanius, *Haer.* 30.11f. on Joseph of Tiberias (see n.868 below on his activity in Cilicia). One (!) bishop from 'Zebulon' took part in the Council of Nicaea in 325 who perhaps came from Kabul in Galilee; cf. Riesner, 'Galiläa', *GBL* I, 406f. In Sepphoris inscriptions twice bear witness to an otherwise unknown bishop in the fifth and sixth centuries (?) (We are grateful to Prof. Dr Ehud Netzer for this reference). Cf. M. Goodman, *State and Society in Roman Galilee, AD 132–312*, Oxford Centre for Postgraduate Hebrew Studies, Totowa 1983, 32, 106, who rightly refers to the

note in Epiphanius (*Haer.* 30, 11) that at the beginning of the third there were no Christians in the larger Jewish cities in Galilee; see also A. M. Schwemer, *Studien zu den frühjüdischen Prophetenlegenden. Vitae Prophetarum II*, TSAJ 50, Tübingen 1996, 34f., 179 n.15 on the transfer of the Jewish prophetic traditions to Galilee, which after the Bar Kochba revolt became the real Jewish heartland. In the *Onomastikon* (22, 9; 26, 9; 78, 6; 86, 18.21; 88, 17; 92, 21; 98, 26; 108, 9; 136, 2.25) Eusebius explicitly notes as exceptions villages in the south of Palestine which had Jewish inhabitants in his time, but not in Galilee: there this was a matter of course. The Jewish Christian influence in Galilee remained limited to a few villages. In other words, early Christian knowledge of the real Galilee – apart from the Gospels – was very restricted. So we should not want to know more!

135. Mark 14.70 par.; Acts 1.11; 2.7; cf. 10.37.

136. I Cor. 9.4ff., 14; cf. Luke 10.7; Matt. 10.10.

137. Matt. 10.5; 10.33; Acts 9.32–43: Peter visits only the Jewish places on the coastal plain, but cf. Philip in Acts 8.

138. *RGG*[3], III, 129.

138. Conzelmann, *RGG*[3], III, 130; cf. Hengel, 'Christology' (n.96), 30–47.

140. Hengel, 'Between Jesus and Paul' (n.50); id., 'Vorchristlicher Paulus' (n.51), 257–60 [54–7], 292f.; K. Haacker, 'Der Werdegang des Apostels Paulus. Biographische Daten und ihre theologische Relevanz', *ANRW* II 26, 2, 849, contrary to H. Conzelmann and A. Lindemann, *Arbeitsbuch zum Neuen Testament*, UTB 52, [9]1988, 428, who consider as a second possibility that this is 'simply about Greeks', the whole context in Jerusalem allows *only* the meaning 'Greek-speaking Jews'. At best one could think of other 'Greek-speaking' non-Jews, but there were hardly any of these in Jerusalem and they were certainly not the goal of the missionary efforts from the beginning. The word is clearly to be derived from ἑλληνίζειν = speak Greek. Alongside Ἕλλην, Greek, a Ἑλληνιστής with the same meaning would be senseless.

141. Acts 7.58; 8.1a; on this see Burchard, *Zeuge* (n.5), 26–31; Riesner, *Frühzeit* (n.49), 53ff.

142. Acts 8.1b–4; 9.1f.; 11.19.

143. Mark reports here with striking precision: 7.24 τὰ ὅρια Τύρου καὶ Σιδῶνος; cf. 31; 8.27, εἰς τὰς κώμας Καισαρείας τῆς Φιλίππου. This is still only the territory of the city and not the city itself.

144. Hengel, 'Between Jesus and Paul' (n.50), 26; id., 'The Historian Luke' (n.36), 164–82; id., *Earliest Christianity* (n.25), 71–4; id., 'Vorchristlicher Paulus' (n.51), 279ff. [73ff.]; Hemer, *Acts* (n.37), 175f.

145. See above, 7.1.

146. For the title 'Lord' in Aramaic and West Semitic languages see above, 120ff.

147. Such a tradition only reappears in the unique Montanist women prophetesses Maximilla, Priscilla and Quintilla and their master Montanus, see R. E. Heine, *The Montanist Oracles and Testimonia*, PatMS 14, Macon 1989.

148. Cf. Sato, *Q* (n.131), 62ff.

148. It also follows from this that Jerusalem is the most likely place for the fixing of the Q collection. Perhaps the earliest version was connected with the name of Matthew and this name was then given *a parte potiori* to the First Gospel. There is hardly any area in which over the last twenty years 'analytic fantasy' has blossomed so much as in research into Q. H. Räisänen, 'Die "Hellenisten" der Urgemeinde', *ANRW* II, 26.2, 1995, 1507f., also only gets into difficulties when he transfers the Jesus tradition to Galilee.

150. Thus e.g. J. Knox, *Chapters in a Life of Paul*, Nashville 1950, 35f.; R. Bultmann, *RGG*² IV, 1021; Haenchen, *Acts* (n.5), 328: 'there, in or near Damascus, Paul persecuted "the community"'; Becker, *Paulus* (n.61), 70ff.; Dietzfelbinger, *Berufung* (n.58), 21f. Sänger, *Verkündigung* (n.54), 237f., leaves the question unresolved. But cf. already W. Bousset, *Kyrios Christos. Geschichte des Christusglaubens von den Anfängen des Christentums bis Irenaeus*, Göttingen (1913) ²1921 (quoted from the fifth edition, the third impression of the second revised edition of 1921, ed. R. Bultmann, Darmstadt 1965), 75 n.2: 'In the first edition here I doubted that Paul had appeared as a persecutor of the earliest Palestinian community at all, and attempted to make him begin as an opponent of the Christian movement in Damascus. I no longer believe that Gal. 1.22 gives us the right to engage in such radical criticism.' See also A. J. Hultgren, 'Paul's Pre-Christian Persecutions of the Church: Their Purpose, Locale, and Nature', *JBL* 95, 1976, 97–111; Burchard, *Zeuge* (Anm. 5), 26–31; Hengel, 'Vorchristlicher Paulus' (n.51), 218f., 276–83; K. Haacker, 'Werdegang' (n.140), 882.

151. *ZNW* 2, 1901, 85f., who thought in terms of Tarsus; see Hengel, 'Vorchristlicher Paulus' (n.51), 218, cf. 208 [23f., cf.15].

152. Gal. 1.22–24; translation follows H. D. Betz, *Galatians*, Hermeneia, Philadelphia 1980, 56, see 80f.

153. Gal. 1.21; cf. Acts 9.29f.

154. Betz, *Galatians* (n.152), 80.

155. Against Betz, *Galatians* (n.152), 80f., see Hengel, 'The Historian Luke' (n.36), 151 nn.20–25: the terminology in Luke is not uniform. For

the province of Judaea see e.g. Luke 1.5; 4.44; 7.17; 23.5; Acts 10.37; 26.20. In Paul cf. I Thess. 2.14 and Rom. 15.31: here too the province or *a parte potiori* the area settled by the Jews is meant; large parts of the population of the Hellenistic cities were also Jewish. The previous mention of the double province of Syria and Cilicia also suggests the *province* of Judaea in Gal. 1.22 etc. See also Bauer and Aland, *Lexicon*, 768, 2. According to Josephus, *Antt.* 1, 160, Nicolaus of Damascus identified 'Judaea' with 'Canaan' in his World History; Strabo 16, 2, 21 calls the whole area between Gaza and the Antilebanon 'Judaea'. According to Stern, *GLAJ* I, 234, 263 this extension belongs 'to the results of the Hasmonaean conquests'; one might also add 'and to the results of the extension of Herod's kingdom'.

156. προκόπτειν here clearly means 'make progress', see Bauer and Aland, *Lexicon*, 1417f.; cf. Luke 2.52; II Clem 17.3: ἐν ταῖς ἐντολαῖς; TestJud 21, 8; Ps. 44 (45), 5 Symmachus; Josephus says of himself at fourteen: 'I made great progress in my education, gaining a reputation for an excellent memory and understanding' (*Vita* 8). For Ἰουδαϊσμός in the sense of Jewish custom or the teaching of the law see Bauer and Aland, *Lexicon*: 'the Jewish way of believing and living'. The translation by Betz, *Galatians* (n.152), 57, 'and advanced in Judaism ...', is misleading. See Hengel, 'Vorchristlicher Paulus' (n.51), 240f. [41f.].

157. A. Astor, ' Damascus', *EJ* 5, 1971, 1239: 'there were no institutes of learning ... in the city of Damascus'.

158. See Hengel, 'Vorchristlicher Paulus' (n.51), 239–65 [40–53].

159. In the – exaggerated – depiction of his persecution in his last personal account before Festus and Agrippa II in Acts 26.11, Luke makes his hero confess: 'I tried to persecute them even to the cities outside (Judaea and the surrounding regions)'. Here too, for Luke those involved are the ones who have fled from Jerusalem (8.1, 4; 11.19), i.e. in reality the 'Hellenists'. These cities also include Damascus. See C. Burchard, *Zeuge* (n.5), 47, cf. 44: 'Luke can only have thought of the message having carried further from Jerusalem. The term μαθητής which appears again in 9.10, 20 occurs previously only in Jerusalem, 6.1f., 7.'

160. Cf. Acts 9.26.

161. For the earlier history of research cf. E. Pfaff, *Die Bekehrung des H. Paulus in der Exegese des 20. Jahrhunderts*, Rome 1942, 107–39.

162. For the parallels within Luke, 9.1–21; 22.6–21; 26.12–18, see Barrett, *Acts I* (n.77), 439–45: 'The agreements are much more important than the disagreements'. Here the agreements relate to typical features of the theophany. He rightly describes the much-cited Heliodorus parallel in II Macc 3 and those from JosAs as 'superficial'.

Despite the typical feature, the account has an unmistakable stamp of its own. Cf. n.166 below.

163. Acts 9.3; 22.6. Schmithals, *Paulus* (n.132), 24, conjectures with reference to Gal. 1.22, that 'Paul was active in Syria and Cilicia ... at the time of the beginnings of the community'. Three pages later he is more specific: 'Nor could Luke ignore the fact that Paul was active as a persecutor in the neighbourhood of Damascus' (27). Has the author ever looked at a good map of 'Syria and Cilicia'? Similarly Conzelmann, *History of Primitive Christianity*, London 1973, 80: Paul as a persecutor 'must rather have travelled through the country from (Cilicia-)Syria' (that is first reported by the *Epistula Apostolorum*, evidently a particularly trustworthy witness from the middle of the second century, see below n.453). No wonder that the same author succinctly decrees: 'The three-fold account in Acts ... is no use as a source, as it is legendary' (*An Outline of the Theology of the New Testament*, London 1969, 163). Is not the 'formation of legends' more the work of the modern, O so 'critical', New Testament scholars? According to Vouga, *Geschichte* (n.90), 42f., 'Paul's activity as a persecutor ... was not carried on in Judaea ... but probably in the area of the first Hellenistic centres (Damascus, Gal. 1.17).' This list of 'historical-critical' (false) judgments could be extended a long way further.

164. Acts 9.1–19; 22.3–21; 26.9–20.

165. Acts 9.3 in a narrative context: 'and suddenly a light from heaven flashed about him', Paul's own account in 22.6: 'a great light from heaven suddenly shone round about me', a more developed account by Paul himself in 26.13: 'I saw ... a light from heaven, brighter than the sun, shining around me', see Burchard, *Zeuge* (n.5), 88–136; K. Löning, *Die Saulustradition in der Apostelgeschichte*, NTA NF 9, 1973, 106ff.; Dietzfelbinger, *Paulus* (n.58), 78–87. The 'from heaven' presupposes the exaltation 'to the right hand of God' according to Ps. 110, see Acts 2.25, 33f.; 5.31; 7.55f.; cf. Rom. 8.34, and on it Hengel, '"Sit at my Right Hand!"' (n.117); cf. John 20.17. A. Segal, *Paul the Convert*, New Haven and London 1990, 34–71, imagines the vision of Christ before Damascus in the context of Jewish visionary experience from Ezekiel to Merkaba mysticism. However, that applies more to II Cor. 12.1ff. than to the vision at the call, which has a stamp of its own. Here in particular there is no talk of a journey to heaven. Luke also avoides the ἐν ἐκστάσει (but cf. the vision in the temple in 22.17; Peter, 10.10 and 11.5; and Paul himself, II Cor. 5.13).

166. Here there is a narrative variant: 9.4 and 22.7 relate this only to Paul, 26.14 also to his companions. According to 9.7 the latter share only

in the hearing; according to 22.9 they share only in the vision of light. By means of these – contradictory – distinctions Luke wants to indicate that different versions were in circulation. 26.12ff. includes his own interpretation. The dependence on accounts of visions and conversions (II Macc. 3; Joseph and Asenath; Apuleius, *Met.* 11) should not be over-emphasized, though they are partial analogies; the account has its quite distinctive peculiarities, which derive from Pauline tradition.

167. Cf. 9.15f., where no direct commissioning yet takes place, but see 22.17–21. Cf. already 22.14f.

168. But cf. Luke 24.37ff.; Matt. 14.26; Ignatius, Smyrn. 3.2; John 20.20, 27.

169. That he saw him briefly at that time cannot completely be excluded, but it remains completely uncertain. II Cor. 5.16 refers to the 'fleshly' knowledge of unbelief.

170. Cf. 9, 17. On this see I Cor. 15.5–8, but also 13.31 on the appearances of the Risen Christ to the disciples and Acts 7.2, 30, 35 on the Old Testament epiphanies. For the seeing see also Acts 22.15, ὧν ἑώρακας and 26.16b; cf. I Cor. 9.1.

171. See Hengel, '"Sit at My Right Hand!"' (n.117), 137–45, 151–68, 174.

172. Cf. I Cor. 2.8; Phil. 3.21.

173. Rom. 6.4.

174. Phil. 3.10f.; cf. Rom. 8.18–30.

175. See M. Weinfeld, כבוד, *TWAT* 4, 1984, 27ff., 38: 'The *kabod YHWH* has ... a concrete significance: a fiery phenomenon from which the radiance and splendour proceed.' See also the designation of God as a 'consuming fire', Deut. 4.24; 9.3; Isa. 33.14; cf. Isa. 10.17 the *kabod* of the divine chariot in Ezekiel and Dan. 7.9f.; 4QShirShabb, see C. C. Newman, *Paul's Glory-Christology*, NT.S 69, Leiden 1992, 79–153, 223f.

176. Newman, *Paul* (n.175), 223 n.24: 'Could it be that Luke is here reflecting good Pauline tradition?'

177. Acts 7.55f., see Hengel, '"Sit at My Right Hand!"' (n.117), 141, 143ff., 152, etc.

178. 9.17 formulates it even more cautiously, see n.167.

179. G. Lüdemann, *The Resurrection of Jesus*, London and Minneapolis 1995, 16–19, 102–7, 119–21, 172f., etc., does not recognize these limits on the historian. Here he gets into the realm of psychological speculations, for which no verification is really possible, and in the end this quite extraordinary event appears to be everyday banality (the working out of guilt complexes). Moreover the sources are far too limited for such psychologizing analyses. See the warning against the psycho-

logizing explanation of religious phenomena given by E. Bickerman in his review of M. G. van der Leeuw, *Phänomenologie der Religion*, in *Studies in Jewish and Christian History* III, AGJU, Leiden 1986, 224: 'the pernicious belief in the omnipotence of psychological divination'. One could transfer to Lüdemann's book Bickerman's praise of van der Leeuw's book: 'It is good … that it has been proved to us that psychology is not the right way to grasp the order and relations of things.'

180. Cf. Gal. 4.15 and U. Heckel, 'Der Dorn im Fleisch. Die Krankheit des Apostels Paulus in 2 Kor. 12, 7 and Gal. 4, 13b', *ZNW* 84, 1993, 84–92.

181. Barrett, *Acts* I (n.77), 444: 'It is most improbable that Ananias is a fictitious character.'

182. Acts 2.17–21; cf. Rom. 10.12–14; I Cor. 1.2; I Cor. 12.1–3 should probably also be understood against the background of Joel 3.1–5. In the case of Luke one could also refer to Acts 9.14, 21; 22.16. The christological interpretation and its reference to the present time of the community goes back to the earliest period.

183. For Luke cf. also Acts 10.3ff., 11ff.; 13.2; 16.6, 10; 20.23; 21.13f.; 22.17ff.; for Paul see Gal. 2.2; II Cor. 12.1, 7; cf. 14.6, 26 and 7.40; for travel plans 'if God wills' see Rom. 1.10; 15.32. Luke schematizes this phenomenon in his cut-and-dried account; it may probably have played an essential role in the earliest period in the development of the community. He knows many other forms of decision in addition to this: the lot, Acts 1.26; information conveyed by the Spirit, Acts 15.22, 28.

184. Here first of all mention should be made of the suddenness and at the same time the unconditional character of the event, which is twice emphasized by Luke: ἐξαίφνης, Acts 9.3; 22.6.

185. Gal. 1.15.

186. See H. M. Barstadt, רצה , *TWAT* 7, 1993, 640–52. Parallel terms are 'elect', 'find pleasure in', 'love'; M. Jastrow, *Dictionary* II, 1493f.; M. Hengel, 'Bergpredigt' (n.32), 361 n.59, 386f. on *rāṣōn* and θέλημα (θεοῦ); cf. Hatch and Redpath, *A Concordance to the Septuagint* I, 569, s. v. εὐδοκεῖν, εὐδοκία. Cf. also Luke 2.14 and 10.21. Both terms, *rāṣāh* and *rāṣōn*, also occur frequently in Qumran.

187. Acts 9.15: σκεῦος ἐκλογῆς ἐστίν μοι οὗτος; 22.14: ὁ θεὸς τῶν πατέρων ἡμῶν προεχειρίσατό σε; 26.16f.: εἰς τοῦτο γὰρ ὤφθην σοι, προχειρίσασθαί σε ὑπηρέτην καὶ μάρτυρα.

188. K. Berger, *Theologiegeschichte des Urchristentums*, Tübingen and Basel 1994, 60, 195, 202, 212, 253, 434f., often draws attention to the correspondence between Matt. 16.16f. and Gal. 1.15: here we have the revelation of the Son of God only through God himself and the rejection of mediation through flesh and blood, i.e. the unique revelation of God

which is the foundation of the apostolate. Could Paul have known a saying like Matt. 16.16–19? Cf. also the reference in I Cor. 13.11 to the 'corner stone', which in my view is an indirect allusion to the name 'Cephas'.

189. Cf. also II Cor. 3.18.

190. The ὁ θεός which is lacking in the early Alexandrian text, p⁴⁶ B and in Western witnesses, Lat Iren[lat], cf. F G Epiph syrP, must either have found its way into the text at a very early stage as a gloss or correction, or dropped out when the eye of the copyist skipped from the article of ὁ θεός to ὁ ἀφορίσας; cf. I Cor. 1.21; 10.5.

191. Rom. 1.3f.; cf. also 8.34, see Hengel, 'Son of God' (n.117), 57–74; id., '"Sit at My Right Hand!"' (n.117), 137–63, 172f.

192. II Cor. 4.4, 6; cf. I Cor. 4.5; Eph. 5.8.

193. Acts 22.15; 26.16, but cf. 13.31. See also 19.21; 25.11f., 21, 26: one of the basic themes of Acts is that the promise of Acts 1.8 is fulfilled in Paul despite all the difficulties of his journey to Rome.

194. Acts 9.12, 17. As a gesture of healing see also 28.8; Luke 4.40; 5.13. In 22.13 the regaining of sight comes about through a healing command without the laying on of hands. Baptism for the forgiveness of sins and invocation of the Lord follow. From Luke to John the New Testament healings of the blind often have a deeper significance.

195. Acts 9.12, 17f.; cf. 22.13,16. For this see C. Weizsäcker, *Das Apostolische Zeitalter der christlicher Kirche*, Tübingen and Leipzig 1902, 76: 'The blinding ... and its healing by Ananias is a narrative of penetrating symbolism. At any rate we need to reflect that according to Gal. 4.15 at least later Paul seems to have had a severe problem with his eyes.'

196. Acts 22.16; cf. 9.14, 21; Rom. 10.12–14, see above n.182: the one who calls on the name of the Lord in baptism is baptized in the name of this Lord; indeed the name of the Lord is 'named' over him. In both cases the verb ἐπικαλεῖσθαι (*qara*') found in the LXX is used.

197. Acts 9.8: καὶ ἀναστὰς ἐβαπτίσθη. It is not said directly who baptized him, 9.19 (see above, 46, on Ananias): καὶ λαβὼν τροφὴν ἐνίσχυσεν need not only indicate the end of the baptismal fast, but could also indicate participation in the Lord's Supper, cf. 22.6.

198. J. Weiss, *Earliest Christianity* (n.89), 169 n.12, who wants to introduce baptism in earliest Christianity only at a later stage, wonders whether Paul was baptized only years afterwards, 'perhaps in Antioch'. That seems to us to be impossible. J. Gnilka, *Paulus von Tarsus. Zeuge und Apostel*, HThK.Suppl. VI, Freiburg etc. 1996, 47 thinks it generally improbable that Paul was baptized, and does not note the contradiction with Rom. 6.3.

199. I Cor. 1.14–16. The baptism in the name of Jesus is a basic pre-supposition of the formation of the eschatological community of salvation in Jerusalem as a consequence of the event of Pentecost. It takes up the baptism of John and brings together the Jesus community as the eschatological ἐκκλησία/*qāhāl*. Possibly those who had received the baptism of John were not, according to Luke, baptized again, thus the 120 in Acts 1.15. That could also explain the enigmatic texts Acts 18.25 and 19.1ff.

200. For προσανατίθημι see Bauer and Aland, *Lexicon*, 1425: 'take counsel', *TDNT 1*, 353; 10, 979f; F. Mussner, *Der Galaterbrief*, HThK IX, ⁴1989, 78, 90 n.59.

201. Weiss, *Earliest Christianity* (n.89).

202. Here this means that the action and words of institution go back to the Kyrios himself, see above, 288ff.

203. See below, nn.758, 1093, 1534 and above, n.88.

204. Acts 22.16.

205. Vouga, *Geschichte* (n.90), 100.

206. Gal. 6.2; I Cor. 9.21. The curse of the law on the Crucified in Gal. 3.3f. means something different from 'transgression of the law'.

207. Later we find such anti-Christian polemic in Celsus's Jewish confidant, in Trypho (in Justin's *Dialogue*), in the Talmud and then in the *Toledot Jeshu*. There is no trace of anything of this kind in Paul.

208. Rom. 1.3; Gal. 4.4f.; Rom. 15.8f.

209. See above, 301–3.

210. Acts 2.1ff.; cf. 4.31, but also I Cor. 15.6.

211. Barrett, *Acts* I (n.77), 444, following S. G. Wilson, *The Gentiles and the Gentile Mission in Luke-Acts*, SNTS.MS 23, 1973, 165: 'God is the subject of Paul's election and sending' – as for Paul himself in Gal. 1.15f.

212. Acts 9.12.

213. But cf. Acts 8.38; 10.48. See also Barrett, *Acts* I (n.77), 458.

214. In Acts only 13.33 the quotation from Ps. 2.7; more frequently in Luke 1.32, 35; 3.22; 8.28; 9.35; 10.22; 22.70: in Luke 'Son of God' seems above all to be a Jewish messianic title. It fades right into the background in the mission to the Gentiles. See Hengel, 'Son of God' (n.117), 18–31; id., *Earliest Christianity* (n.25), 104ff.

215. See above, 3.2.

216. Acts 9.19–30.

217. Acts 9.27.

218. 9.13f.: Ananias' counter-question; 9.26: the disciples' reserve.

219. Acts 9.23 ἡμέραι ἱκαναί, cf. 9.19 ἡμέρας τινάς. ἱκανός with a temporal meaning is a favourite word of Luke's and indicates a lengthy

period of time: Luke 8.27; 20.9; 23.8; Acts 8.11; 14.3; 18.18; 27.7.

220. Acts 9.22: μᾶλλον δὲ ἐνεδυναμοῦτο καὶ συνέχυννεν τοὺς Ἰουδαίους; 9.28: παρρησιαζόμενος.

221. Acts 9.20: υἱὸς τοῦ θεοῦ; 9.22: ὁ χριστός; 9.28: ἐν ὀνόματι τοῦ κυρίου (θεοῦ).

222. It is significant, for example, that he makes only Peter and the disciples in Jerusalem use the title παῖς: Acts 3.13, 26; 4.25, 27, 30, whereas 'Paulinizing' phrases can appear with Paul: 13.38; 20.21, 24, 28, 31f.

223. Gal. 1.1; cf. I Cor. 1.1; II Cor. 1.1; Rom. 1.1; cf. I Cor. 9.2.

224. εἰς τοῦτο γὰρ ὤφθην σοι cf. I Cor. 15.8 ὤφθη κἀμοί.

225. προχειρίσασθαί σε ὑπηρέτην καὶ μάρτυρα ὧν τε εἶδές [με] ὧν τε ὀφθήσομαί σοι. For ὑπηρέτης the closest parallel is the prologue Luke 1.2; for election as a witness cf. 22.14f.; προχειρίζεσθαι appears in the NT only three times, in Acts, cf. also 3.20, there referring to Jesus as the Messiah who will come again.

226. εἰς οὓς ἐγὼ ἀποστέλλω σε.

227. Cf. Col.1.13; II Cor. 4.3f.

228. Acts 2.36; 4.10; cf. 5.30; 10.39; 13.29.

229. In ch. 9 the actual process of the call is described rather more briefly.

230. Here we should not primarily read out of Luke 'pious Christian language with a biblical touch', thus H. Conzelmann, *Acts*, Hermeneia, Philadelphia 1987, ad loc., 211, quoted with approval by Schneider, *Apostelgeschichte* (n.77), 374f. The catchword 'edifying' is used by modern exegetes of Luke all too easily with the disparaging connotations of 'unreflective pious talk'. In Luke – contrary to the tenets of modern critical Lukan scholarship – hardly anything is 'unreflected', and what he writes is not edifying in the church tone of the nineteenth and twentieth centuries but – something to which we are unaccustomed – a reality which is full of life. The fulfilment of Isa. 42.7, 16 is already an eschatological event for Paul (I Thess. 5.4f.; II Cor. 4.6) the grateful praise for this salvation which has been given is never silent (Col. 1.12–14; Eph.5.8; I Peter 2.9) and leads to rejoicing in a hymn to Christ (Col. 1.15–18); but cf. above all Luke 1.76–79; 2.32. The originally messianic hymn describes the task of John the Baptist in its Lukan context: see U. Mittmann-Richert, *Magnifikat und Benediktus (Lk 1, 46–55 und 1, 68–79)*, Tübingen theological dissertation 1994 (WUNT II/90, 1996).

231. Cf. e.g. ἀνοίγω, I Cor. 16.9; II Cor. 2.12; 6.11; ὀφθαλμός, Rom. 11.8, 10; Gal. 3.1; ἐπιστρέφω, I Thess. 1.9; II Cor. 3.16; cf. Gal. 4, 9; the opposition of σκότος and φῶς, Rom. 2.19; 13.12; I Cor. 4.5; II Cor. 4.6; I Thess. 5.4f.; in I Thess. 2.18 Paul sees his missionary work hindered by

Satan. Instead of the stereotyped formulas ἄφεσις ἁμαρτιῶν and κλῆρος ἁγίων, in Paul we find long well-thought-out theological passages, especially in Rom. 5–8 and Gal. 3–4 on liberation from the power of sin and on Christians being sons and (joint-)heirs. Luke abbreviates in his very much simpler, cut-and-dried way.

232. ὑποδείξω αὐτῷ Acts 9.15. The reader for whom Acts was written recognized that this was at the same time pointing forward to the apostle's violent death.

233. Acts 6.9; cf. Hengel, 'Between Jesus and Paul' (n.50), 16–18.

234. See I. Taatz, *Frühjüdische Briefe*, NTOA 16, 1991, 18ff., 82ff., 89ff.

235. For the relatively looser political order in southern Syria and in Palestine see Millar, *Roman Near East* (n.92), 34–43.

236. See Schürer II, 230 (no. 14): 18–36 CE.

237. Acts 22.4f.; see Hengel, 'Vorchristlicher Paulus' (n.51), 269, 272–81 [66, 69–71]; Burchard, *Zeuge* (n.5), 43f. esp. n.10.

238. H. Lietzmann, *History of the Early Church*, 1, *The Beginnings of the Christian Church*, London ³1953, 105 assumes 'a commission ... to encourage the Jews to repel the new danger in the name of the sanhedrin'.

239. For the Jewish synagogues in Jerusalem see Hengel, 'Between Jesus and Paul' (n.50), 16–18 and id., 'Vorchristlicher Paulus' (n.51), 56 with n.264 (bibliography).

240. Acts 13.5; 24.12; 26.11. Salamis: according to Dio Cassius 68, 32, 2, see Stern, *GLAJ* II, 385 no. 437, in the Jewish rebellion 240,000 people were killed on Cyprus. The Armenian translation of Eusebius's *Chronicle* reports on the revolt in the nineteenth year of Trajan: 'The Jews fell upon Salamis, the city of the island of Cyprus, massacred the Greeks and razed the city to the ground', GCS 20, ed. J. Karst 219, cf. the *Chronicle of Jerome*, GCS 47, ed. R. Helm, 196, 116 CE: *Salaminam, urbem Cypri, interfectis in ea gentilibus subuertere Iudaei*. Salamis must have had a large and very old Jewish community. In the revolt of 115–117 the Jews captured the city, killed the non-Jews and then presumably retreated into the interior after destroying the city, on the approach of a Roman fleet; cf. Georgios Synkellos, *Chronographia*, ed. Mosshammer, Leipzig 1984, 657, 10f. The confessional war in Bosnia is a living illustration of these events in ancient Cyprus, Cyrenaica and Egypt.

241. Cf. 13.14 in Pisidian Antioch; 14, 1: Iconium; 17.1: Thessalonica; 17.10: Beroea; 17.17: Athens; 18.4, 7: Corinth; 18.19: Ephesus. No synagogues are mentioned in Syrian Antioch and Tarsus, though there were certainly a number of synagogues in these provincial metropolises.

242. Philo, *Flacc* 48; *Legatio* 132; tSukk 4, 6 (Zuckermandel 273);

Schürer III, 43, 104, etc.

243. Philo, *Legatio* 155–158; cf. H.J. Leon, *The Jews in Ancient Rome*, Philadelphia 1960, 140ff.; Schürer III, 1, 96ff., 142. D. Noy, *Jewish Inscriptions of Western Europe II, The City of Rome*, Cambridge 1995, 539f., index s.v. 'Names of Synagogues', cites for Rome from catacomb inscriptions 11 or 12 different synagogues mentioned by name for the third and fourth centuries CE. Juvenal 3, 296 already presupposes a number of synagogues.

244. S. Krauss, *Synagogale Altertümer*, 1922 (reprinted Hildesheim 1966), 205–10; for Sepphoris, where a new synagogue has now been discovered, see E. Netzer and L. Weiss, *Zippori*, Jerusalem 1994, 56ff., 69ff.; according to jKil 9, 4 §32a/b there were eighteen synagogues, according to GenR 33.3 and 52.4 one 'of the Babylonians'.

245. Burchard, *Zeuge* (n.5), 45 n.0.

246. Luke reports a similar 'conspiracy' in Corinth, Acts 20.3.

247. See Hengel, 'The Historian Luke' (n.36), 101–9.

248. Under the leadership of the governor Cestius Gallus at the ascent of Beth-Horon in October 66 CE, Josephus, *BJ* 2, 546ff.

249. *BJ* 2, 560f.; 7, 368; *Vita* 27; for a criticism of Josephus' account see A. Kasher, *Jews and Hellenistic Cities in Eretz-Israel*, TSAJ 21, Tübingen 1990, 285f. (and on this n.295 below). For the size of the gymnasium see T. Weber, 'DAMASKINA. Landwirtschaftliche Produkte aus der Oase von Damaskus im Spiegel griechischer und lateinischer Schriftquellen', *ZDPV* 105, 1989, 162ff.

250. *BJ* 2, 468, 477; cf. also on Caesarea 2, 266–270; *Antt.* 20, 173–178, 184. For 10,500 Jewish men one would have to assume a community of 30–40,000 members, but the number may be slightly exaggerated (cf. below, n.295). The mother of R. Jose b. Dormaskit (c.80–130) was probably a Damascene proselyte. Her son interpreted the eschatological significance of Damascus in a unique way (see below, n.272). He still visited the house of study in Jamnia (mJd 4, 3). For his person see W. Bacher, *Die Aggada der Tannaiten*, I, ²1903, 389f.

251. *BJ* 2, 478, cf. 461 and Eleazar's speech in 7, 367, which exaggerates: 'Among the cities of Syria there is none that has not killed the Jews living in it, although these had been more hostile towards us (the Sicarii) than to the Romans.' I.e. these first victims of the revolt did not want the rebellion against Rome at all – in contrast to the radicals in the mother country. See also above, 189f. Perhaps Pella was also an exception; according to Eusebius, *HE* 3, 5, 3, it had welcomed Jewish Christians from Jerusalem before the outbreak of the Jewish war. In connection with Caligula's command that his image should be set up in

the temple, Philo, *Legatio* 226, shows that the πολυανθρωπία of the Jews
in the frontier areas – in this case Phoenicia – could cause anxiety; cf.
Josephus, *Antt.* 18, 263ff., 269, 273f.
    252. *BJ* 2, 479. As an exception in immediate proximity to Eretz Israel
Josephus mentions only Gerasa in Transjordan (480). For Antioch see
above, 190.
    253. *BJ.* 2, 462f., 465. For the last word in 465 we should follow
Eusebius, *HE* 2, 26, 2 and read ἀνάτασιν instead of ἀνάστασιν. For the
size of the Syrian Diaspora see also Philo, *Legatio* 245: in large numbers
in every city of Syria (and Asia); cf. 281.
    254. The discovery in Hirbet Umm ed-Dananir between Philadelphia
and Gerasa in Transjordan of a workshop in which stone vessels corresponding to the Pharisaic regulations for cleanness were made shows not
only that the Jewish element in the population must have been significant, but also that there was Pharisaic influence. Cf. R. Deines, *Jüdische
Steingefässe und pharisäische Frömmigkeit*, WUNT II/52, Tübingen 1993,
154f.
    255. *BJ* 2, 266; I. L. Levine, *Caesarea under Roman Rule*, Leiden 1975;
id., *Roman Caesarea: An Archaeological-Topographical Study*, Qedem 2,
Jerusalem 1975; Kasher, *Hellenistic Cities* (n.249), 198, 201, 205f.; Herod
had refounded Caesarea, the former Tower of Strato, as a Hellenistic
city with an imposing harbour and a strong fortress for his own security,
along with Sebaste/Samaria. However, for fear of the communal anger
of the Jewish population he did not dare to have his sons by Mariamne
executed in Caesarea but transferred the execution to Sebaste, which
was hostile to the Jews. The Jewish element of the population at that time
must already have been considerable, Josephus, *Antt.* 16, 394; *BJ* 1, 551;
cf. *Antt.* 15, 292ff.
    256. For the question whether μεμιγμένον in Josephus, *BJ* 2, 463 etc.
also denotes Gentiles married to Jews see below, n.368.
    257. Dio Cassius 67, 14, 2; Suetonius, *Domitian* 15, 1; Eusebius, *HE* 3,
18, 4; Stern, *GLAJ* II, 379ff. no. 435; M. Hengel, 'Der alte und der neue
Schürer, review of *The History of the Jewish People in the Age of Jesus Christ
(175 BC – AD 135) by Emil Schürer. A New English Version*', revised and
edited by Geza Vermes, Fergus Millar and Martin Goodman, Vol. III/1,
1986; III/2, 1987', *JSS* 35, 1990, 19–64: 39f.
    258. Matt. 8.5–13 = Luke 7.1–10. As Luke 13.28f. shows, Matt. 8.11 was
not yet in the Q version of the narrative: Mark 7.24–30 = Matt. 15.21–28.
Neither narrative yet contains any reference to the later intensive
'Gentile mission'; they are not formulated to justify it but in each
instance deal with striking exceptions. The command for the Gentile

mission only appears in Mark 13.10 par. and 14.9, both Marcan redaction, cf. Matt. 28.19f. Here the Synoptic Gospels do *not* correspond to the 'needs' of the community.

259. Acts 8.40; 21.8; 10.2: it is understandable that a prominent godfearer like Cornelius should seek to meet the head of a special Jewish group which interests him. Philip emigrates – presumably because of the anti-Jewish unrest in Caesarea at the beginning of the 60s – to Hierapolis in Asia Minor which lies within Pauline mission territory, see Hengel, *Johannische Frage* (n.33), 82, cf. index s. v. Philip; cf. also id., 'The Historian Luke' (n.36), 110–16 (on Philip); 116–19 (Cornelius).

260. For the problem see Excursus I (61–76).

261. See n.250 above.

262. P. 48, see H. P. Rüger, *Syrien und Palästina nach dem Reisebericht des Benjamin von Tudela*, ADPV 12, Wiesbaden 1990, 61.

263. See the translation by S. Schreiner, *Jüdische Reisen im Mittelalter*, Sammlung Dieterich 416, Leipzig 1991, 155f.

264. For a bibliography see C. Watzinger and K. Wulzinger, *Damaskus. Die antike Stadt*, 1921; Benzinger, 'Damaskos', *PW* IV, 2, 1901, 2042–8; Schürer II, 1979, 125–30; Kasher, *Hellenistic Cities* (n.249), see index s.v.; Riesner, *Frühzeit* (n.49), 66–79; cf. J.-P. Rey-Coquais, 'Des montagnes au désert: Baetocécé, le Pagus Augustus de Niha, la Ghouta à l'est de Damas', in *Sociétés urbaines, sociétés rurales dans l'Asie Mineure et la Syrie hellénistiques et romaines, Actes du colloque de Strasbourg (novembre 1985)*, ed.E. Frézouls, Université des Sciences humaines de Strasbourg. Contributions et travaux de l'Institut d'Histoire Romaine IV, Strasbourg 1987, 191–216: 213: 'Paradoxically, the great Syrian metropolis is not well known to us. The inscriptions are rare by comparison with the importance of the city.'

265. Gen. 15.2; Jub. 14.2; GenR 59.9; 60.2; ExR 17.5; the later Haggada no longer evaluates his origin positively, cf. L. Ginzberg, *The Legends of the Jews*, I, 293; V, 260 n.282.

266. *Antt.* 1, 145, cf. 153: Οὔξος; LXX Ὡς or Ὡξ MT I עוּץ: Gen. 10.23; I Chron. 1.17: son of Aram and grandson of Seir; Gen. 22.21: firstborn of Nahor. The Damascenes belonged to the 'wider kinsfolk' of Israel. Quotation from Burchard, *Zeuge* (n.5), 45 n.0.

267. *Antt.* 1, 159f. Cf. also the *Chronicle of Jerachmeel*, 35.3, trans. M. Gaster, 1899 (reprinted New York 1971), 77.

268. See Justin's epitome of Pompeius Trogus (end of the first century BCE), 3, 2, 1, (quoted from) Stern, *GLAJ* I, 335: *Namque Iudaeis origo Damascena, Syriae nobilissima civitas. After the founder Damascus, Azelus, mox Adores (Hasael=Hadad) et Abrahames et Israhel reges fuere* (3, 2,

14): *Itaque Moyses Damascena, antiqua patria, repetita montem Sinam occupat, in quo ... per deserta Arabiae ... venisset.* Here Pompeius Trogus muddles some things up. However, his account shows how closely together Damascus, Judaea and Arabia belonged for the ancient observer. In the Middle Ages Benjamin of Tudela (pp. 47f.; trans. Rüger, 61) saw in Damascus the relics of the giant king Abanes (see GenR 14.6), who 'ruled over the whole world' from Damascus. This is a clumsy depiction of Abramos. Cf. Gen. 14.15 and Josephus, *Antt.* 1, 178. According to the anonymous Samaritan (F 1 = Eusebius, *Praep.ev.* 17, 3), at God's command Abraham came to Phoenicia, which in Hellenistic times sounded better than Canaan (cf. Mark 7.26 and by contrast the parallel Matt. 15.22). There he learned astronomy and helped in the war against the king of Armenia (cf. Josephus, *Antt.* 13, 419–429).

269. II Sam. 8.5ff.; I Kings 11.24f.; Josephus, *Antt.* 7, 100–104: David defeats King Hadad of Damascus, who according to Nicolaus was excessively powerful, by the Euphrates and subdues 'Damascus and the rest of Syria'.

270. G. Stemberger, 'Die Bedeutung des "Landes Israel" in der rabbinischen Tradition', *Kairos* 25, 1983, 176–99; Hengel, 'Vorchristlicher Paulus' (n.51), 279f. n.318 [76 and n.318]; cf. Josephus, *Antt.* 5, 85: the tribal territory of Naphthali (against MT Josh. 8.32f.) comprises Upper Galilee and the land 'eastwards to the city of Damascus'.

271. Weber, 'DAMASKINA' (n.249), 151–65; Bill. II, 689f. For the fertility and irrigation cf. also E. Wirth, *Syrien. Eine geographische Landeskunde*, Wissenschaftliche Länderkunde 4/5, Darmstadt 1971, 153, 403.

272. bEr 19a, Bill. 2, 689d. According to SifDev 1 on Deut. 1.1 (Horowitz/Finkelstein 7f.) not only does Damascus belong to the messianic kingdom (Zech. 9.1), but the 'gates of Jerusalem (or the Temple) will reach to Damascus'. Similarly also the Targum on Zech. 9.1: 'and Damascus will again belong to the land of the house of the Shekinah.' In PesK 20, 7 (Mandelbaum, 316f.) Isa. 4.2 is also expounded in this sense; cf. CantR 7, 5 §3; Yalkut Sh II, 574 ad loc. For the numerous later parallels cf. L. Ginzberg, *The Legends of the Jews*, VI, 73; see also G. Vermes, *Scripture and Tradition*, SPB 4, Leiden ²1973, 43–9. According to GenR 44, 23 (Theodor/Albeck 2, 446) only seven of the ten promised peoples were subjected under Joshua. Three were still to be conquered. According to R. Shimeon b. Jochai, *c.* 100–150, these were the *Damascene*, Apamea (i.e. northern Syria and Asia Minor); according to Jehuda han-Nasi (rabbi): *Arabia*, Shalamiyya, Nabatiyya; Eliezer b. Jakob: Asia Minor, Thrace, Carthage. This roughly corresponds to the course of the Pauline mission; cf. also jQidd 1, 9 61d lines 13ff., in a partially different

sequence. On the other hand Damascus can appear as the citadel of idolatry, with 365 temples to idols in which a different deity is worshipped every day and all are worshipped together only on one day in the year. By contrast, in Israel the One God was worshipped every day: R. Jochanan, middle of the third century according to LamR proem 10; EstR 3, 4. Cf. Hengel, 'Vorchristlicher Paulus' (n.51), 279f. n.318 [76 and n.318].

273. See above, n.272.

274. CD 6.5f., cf. 7.13: 'Those who held fast escaped to the land of the north'; there follows the quotation from Amos 5.26, cf. also their settling there, 6.19; 7.19; 8.21; 20.12. We need not discuss the disputed question of the interpretation of these passages here. However, 'the land of Damascus' does seem to me to have offered at least temporary exile in the early period of the Essene movement. It is also attested elsewhere as a place to flee to (to some degree as a counterpart to Egypt). For the flight of Herod I to Damascus see Josephus, *Antt.* 14, 178.

275. For the cities he founded see V. Tcherikover, *Die hellenistischen Städtegründungen von Alexander d. Gr. bis auf die Römerzeit*, PhilSuppl 19, 1, 1927, 154ff.

276. D. Sack, *Damaskus*, Mainz 1989, 7–14; cf. T. Weber, '"*Damaskòs Pólis Epísemos*", Hellenistische, römische und byzantinische Bauwerke in Damaskus aus der Sicht griechischer und lateinischer Schriftquellen', *Damaszener Mitteilungen* 7, 1993, 135–76; for the history of the region south of Damascus see also J.-M. Dentzer, 'Développement et culture de la Syrie du Sud dans la période préprovinciale', in id. (ed.), *Hauran* I, 2, Paris 1986, Institute française d'archéologie du proche Orient, Bibl. archeol. et hist. 124, 387–420 (chronological table, 390f.).

277. Antiochus IV Cyzicenus made it the capital of Phoenicia and Coele Syria in 111 BCE after the division of Syria, see Benzinger, 'Damaskus' (n.264), 2045f.; cf. W. Schottroff, Die 'Ituräer', ZDPV 98, 1982, 133f.

278. See Schürer I, 578f. For the history of Damascus and the Nabataeans see also Schottroff, 'Ituräer' (n.277), 134; J. D. Grainger, *Hellenistic Phoenicia*, Oxford 1991, 150f.; Millar, *Roman Near East* (n.92), 310ff. For the coins see E. T. Newell, 'Late Seleucid Mints in Ake-Ptolemais and Damascus', *Numismatic Notes and Monographs* 84, 1939, 92–4. For Damascus and the Nabataeans see R. Wenning, *Die Nabatäer – Geschichte und Denkmäler*, NTOA 3, 1987, 24f.; id., 'Die Dekapolis und die Nabataeans', ZDPV 110, 1994, 1–35: 4f., 15–17; Dentzer, 'Développement' (n.276), 412, 417f.

279. *BJ* 1, 115 = *Antt.* 13, 448, cf. already Jonathan's journey.

280. *BJ* 1, 103 = *Antt.* 13, 392.

281. Millar, *Roman Near East* (n.92), 37f.

282. Jacoby, FGrH 90 F 131; Ben Zion Wacholder, *Nicolaus of Damascus*, UCPH, LXXV, Berkeley 1962, 54f.

283. For the Decapolis see H. Bietenhard, 'Die syrische Dekapolis von Pompeius bis Trajan', *ANRW* II, 8, 1977, 220–61; Schürer II, 125–27, 157: 127–30 on Damascus. There is an indication there that Damascene cohorts were to be found even in Germania in the second century along with Ituraean archers. For the latter cf. Schottroff, 'Ituräer' (n.277), 125, 152. For relations between the Decapolis and Damascus see now also Wenning, 'Dekapolis' (n.278), 15ff., though he puts the origin of the Decapolis much too late, dating it 'between the death of Herod Agrippa I and the beginning of the regency of Herod Agrippa II, 44–53 CE', or in the 'phase of the First Jewish War, when it was important to show that one was a city loyal to Rome' (11). The fact that the 'Dekapolis' emerges in the second half of the first century CE as an entity which is taken for granted in such different sources as Mark, Josephus and Pliny the Elder means that it already had a long history. From the beginning their position between the aggressive Nabataean and Jewish states made an alliance of the cities a political necessity, especially as the seat of the governor was a long way off, in Antioch. The references to the 'ten cities' both in Josephus, *BJ* 3, 446; *Vita* 341f., 410 and in the NT (Mark 5.20; 7.31; Matt. 4.25) already presuppose a lengthy period of established and fixed terminology. This is not just a mere territory but also a politically motivated alliance of cities – presumably a loose one. Its roots lie in the dismemberment of the Hasmonaean kingdom; the expansion into the 'Dekapolis' could have taken place in the division of Herod's kingdom in 4 BCE (or 6 CE), or also in 37 CE.

284. *Nat. hist.* 5, 16, 74.

285. Eighteen cities: cf. Ptolemy, *Geogr.* 5, 14–17; five cities in Josephus, *Antt.* 14, 75: Gadara, Hippos, Scythopolis, Pella and Dium, cf. *BJ* 1, 155, where Dium is missing. Gadara could initially have been the capital. There is a Pentapolis in Cyrenaica and on the Black Sea; cf. also the five Philistine cities in Josephus, *Antt.* 6, 8.

286. Millar, *Roman Near East* (n.92), 310–19.

287. Josephus, *Antt.* 18, 153; A. H. M. Jones, *The Cities of the Eastern Roman Provinces*, Oxford ²1971, 269f., see also the index s. v., 582. Cf. also Mark 7.31: one could get to Lake Genessaret through Sidon through the territory of the Decapolis, as Damascus belonged to this (and Philip). Mark's knowledge of Palestinian geography is not so bad as some New Testament scholars claim.

288. See above, 85.

289. Cf. the clashes between Herod and Zenodoros, who supported the plundering forays against the Damascene, and Herod's trial before Augustus on the latter's visit to Syria *c.* 20 BCE with the citizens of Gadara, who had been under his supreme rule, Josephus, *Antt.* 14, 342–364. Cf. Grainger, *Hellenistic Phoenicia* (n.278), 175f., 178f.

290. Only in the east and south-east did it border on territory ruled by the Nabataeans; in the north-east it bordered on the territory of Palmyra, in the north on the temple state of Emesa and in the north-west on the Roman colony of Berytus/Heliopolis. Thus a good third of the frontiers adjoined territories administered by Jewish rulers.

291. Strabo 16, 2, 20, p. 756 reports that the Damascenes and the merchants from Southern Arabia suffered severly in the Trachonitis from Arabian and Ituraean robbers, cf. also Josephus, *Antt.* 15, 345ff., 389ff.; 16, 285 = *BJ* 1, 399f. See A.Schalit, *König Herodes. Der Mann und sein Werk*, SJ 4, Berlin 1969, 327f., 719; T. Bauzou, 'Les voies de communication dans le Hauran à l'époque romaine', in Dentzer, *Hauran* (n.276), 138–65: 138f., 140, 151–4, lists four roads which lead southwards from Damascus; id., 'Les voies romaines entre Damas et Amman', in *Géographie historique au Proche-Orient*, ed. P.-L. Gatier, B. Helly and J.-P. Rey-Coquais, Paris 1988, 292–7. For further information about the system of Roman roads and their predecessors see H. I. MacAdam, *Studies in the History of the Roman Province of Arabia. The Northern Sector*, BAR 295, Oxford 1986, 19–28, 68ff.

292. *Antt.* 14, 178, 295, see also Schalit, *Herodes* (n.291), 46, cf. 58.

293. Schalit, *Herodes* (n.291), 415f. This may also have been influenced by Nicolaus of Damascus.

294. Cf. Josephus, *Antt.* 18, 153f.

295. Cf. above n.250. The number 10,500 presumably relates primarily to men and not so much to women and children. Perhaps the variant 18,000 is meant to be the total. Josephus' figures here could be relatively reliable by comparison with other figures. By contrast Kasher, *Hellenistic Cities* (n.249), 285f., not only regards the figures in this case as tremendously exaggerated but also thinks the whole account historically untrustworthy, in our view wrongly. In his nationalistic approach to history he underestimates the *religious* influence emanating from the Jewish Diaspora communities.

296. See also Josephus, *Antt.* 8, 387: the Israelites were given the right 'to travel to Damascus'. For I Kings 20.34 ḥūṣōt see Köhler/Baumgartner, *Lexikon*, 286, and Schalit, *Herodes* (n.291), 289 n.502.

297. For the complicated history of the region of Ituraea and its later

division see Schürer I, 561–73; cf. also Schottroff, 'Ituräer' (n.277), 125–52.

298. Josephus, *Antt.* 13, 418.

299. *Antt.* 5, 35ff. = *BJ* 1, 400.

300. *Antt.* 17, 319 = *BJ* 1, 95.

301. *Antt.* 18, 237, cf. 19, 275 = *BJ* 2, 215.

302. *Antt.* 19, 275. For the territories of Agrippa I see D. R. Schwartz, *Agrippa I, The Last King of Judaea*, TSAJ 23, Tübingen 1990, 60f., 111f.

303. *Antt.* 19, 274f. = *BJ* 2, 215, see Schwartz, *Agrippa* I (n.302), 92. In detail G. Schmitt, 'Zum Königreich Chalkis', *ZDPV* 82, 1981, 110–24 with his alternative proposal.

304. In the 'synchronism' Luke 3.1, Luke with complete historical accuracy mentions before the appearance of John the Baptist Philip as tetrarch of the regions of Ituraea (i.e. the territory around Caesarea Philippi) and Trachonitis, and Lysanias as tetrarch of Abilene.

305. Schürer I, 568, 572.

306. Josephus, *Antt.* 20, 13 (his plea, along with his father, for the temple); under Vespasian he was promised the small kingdom of Chalkis, Chalkidene (*BJ* 2, 226), the location of which is disputed. After Philip's death he married Philip's widow Salome, the daughter of Herodias (*Antt.* 18, 137). These princes are descendants of Aristobulus, the son of Herod from his marriage with the Hasmonaean princess Mariamne. For a time the clan of his brother Alexander ruled in Greater Armenia (*BJ* 2, 221; cf. 1, 552; *Antt.* 18, 139f.), but Josephus emphasizes that from the beginning his children 'ceased to observe the customs accepted for Jewish territory and went over to those of the Greeks' (141). It is striking to what a degree Josephus, the Palestinian Jew and priest with inclinations towards the Pharisees, explicitly emphasizes this situation; cf. also on Tiberius Julius Alexander, Josephus, *Antt.* 20, 100, but cf. *BJ* 2, 220. See also Schmitt, 'Chalkis' (n.303).

307. Josephus, *Antt.* 20, 143ff.

308. But cf. Josephus, *Antt.* 19, 305–311.

309. A Jewish dynast was already residing in central Syria at the time of Pompey, Josephus, *Antt.* 14, 40, cf. Strabo 10, 2, 10, p.753. Herod was later given special authority over Syria by Augustus. The meeting of Agrippa I in Tiberias, to which he invited five client princes of Syria and eastern Asia Minor, thus arousing the mistrust of Marsus, the governor of Syria, shows that he wanted to exploit this political situation: *Antt.* 19, 338–342.

310. *BJ* 7, 367, see above n.251.

311. It is cheap and contrary to all historical reality for New Testa-

ment scholars, following a political fashion, to engage in unbridled polemic against this, thus K. Wengst, *Pax Romana and the Peace of Jesus Christ*, London 1987, see the review by the ancient historian U. Victor, *BThZ* 4, 1987, 96–106.

312. This is true despite, indeed because of, what is said in II Cor. 11, 26. For the exemplary cherishing of the law by Herod's son Philip cf. e.g. Josephus, *Antt.* 18, 106.

313. See A. Levanon, *EncJud* 5, 1239; for Kochaba see G. Reeg, *Die Ortsnamen Israels nach der rabbinischen Literatur*, BTAVO B 51, Wiesbaden 1989, 328; Riesner, *Frühzeit* (n.49), 211 n.24, 231. According to Julius Africanus, *Ep. ad Aristidem* = Eusebius, *HE* 1, 7, 14, 'kinsfolk of the Lord' are said to have lived in the Jewish villages of Nazara and Kochaba. However, this Kochaba may have been a Galilean village Kokab around ten miles north of Nazareth. The index in *BHHW* IV, 234, mentions several places of this name.

314. See M. Hengel, *Judaism and Hellenism*, London and Philadelphia 1974, I, 34, 43, 62ff., 90f., 293f.; B. Isaac, 'A Seleucid Inscription from Jamnia-on-the-Sea: Antiochus V Eupator and the Sidonians', *IEJ* 41, 1991, 132–44 (with bibliography).

315. II Cor. 11.32; see below 400 n.686.

316. Cf. Josephus *BJ* 7, 47, an ἄρχων of the Jews in Antioch whose son becomes an apostate, see below, n.1443; *Antt.* 14, 117 mentions an ἐθνάρχης; Philo, *Flacc.* 74 (cf. *Congress. erud.* 133 = Moses) a γενάρχης in Alexandria. For the constitution of Jewish Diaspora communities see Schürer II, 87–125. In Damascus it should be noted that the community was certainly old and rich in tradition. Another example is the alabarch Alexander in Alexandria, the brother of Philo, who, like Philo himself, played a leading role in the Jewish community there. Presumably the office of ethnarch had been in the possession of this family before its abolition. The epitaph of Abramos (Leontopolis, from the middle of the second century BCE) calls him 'garlanded' with ἀρχῇ πανδήμῳ ἐθνικῇ and a πολιταρχῶν of two cities, probably Leontopolis and another place nearby *(CPJ* III, No. 1530a; cf. W. Horbury and D. Noy, *Jewish Inscriptions of Graeco-Roman Egypt*, Cambridge 1992, 95, 100).

317. Josephus, *BJ* 2, 287, 292, cf. F. Herrenbrück, *Jesus und die Zöllner*, WUNT II/41, Tübingen 1990, 211–13. There was also a conflict between the Jews and the Syrians in Caesarea, though there the situation after the refounding of the city by Herod was far more tense than in Damascus.

318. Millar, *Roman Near East* (n.92), 310; one of the very few Aramaic inscriptions in Syria, from Nazala in the Lebanon, shows Palmyrene influence, see J. Starcky, 'Stèle d'Elahagabel', *MUSJ* 49, 1975/76, 501–

20.

319. See M. Hengel, 'Proseuche und Synagoge', in *Tradition und Glaube, FS K. G. Kuhn*, Göttingen 1971, 157–84; J. C. Salzmann, *Lehren und Ermahnen, Zur Geschichte des christlichen Wortgottesdienstes in den ersten drei Jahrhunderten*, WUNT II/59, Tübingen 1994, 450–4. The Christian liturgy of the word emerged directly from that of the synagogue without a break.

320. φοβούμενοι τὸν θεόν: Acts 10.2, 22, 35; 13.16, 26; σεβόμενοι (τὸν θεόν): 13.43, 50; 16.14; 17.4, 17; 18.7. See F. Siegert, 'Gottesfürchtige und Sympathisanten', *JSJ* 4, 1974, 109–64; id., 'Gottesfürchtige', *NBL* I, 1991, 931f. (with bibliography); M. Simon, 'Gottesfürchtiger', *RAC* 11, 1981, 1060–70; J. M. Reynolds and R. Tannenbaum, *Jews and Godfearers at Aphrodisias*, Cambridge 1987, 167–289; S. McKnight, *A Light Among the Gentiles. Jewish Missionary Activity in the Second Temple Period*, Minneapolis 1991 (110–13 on Luke); A. F. Segal, 'Conversion and Messianism. Outline of a New Approach', in *The Messiah. Developments in Earliest Judaism and Christianity, The First Princeton Symposium on Judaism and Christian Origins*, ed. J. H. Charlesworth, Minneapolis 1992, 296–340; M. Reiser, 'Hat Paulus Heiden bekehrt?', *BZ NF* 39, 1, 1995, 76–91. The most comprehensive treatment of the topic is by L. H. Feldman, *Jew and Gentile in the Ancient World: Attitudes and Interactions from Alexander to Justinian*, Princeton 1993. The discussion is still a very controversial one in which one extreme position is even the complete rejection of any pre-Christian Jewish recruitment to win Gentiles over to Judaism, thus A. T. Kraabel, 'Immigrants, Exiles, Expatriates, and Missionaries', in *Religious Propaganda and Missionary Competition in the New Testament World. Essays Honoring Dieter Georgi*, ed. L. Borman et al., Leiden, New York and Cologne 1994, 71–88; M. Goodman, 'Jewish Proselytizing in the First Century', in J. Lieu, J. Noth and T. Rajak (eds.), *The Jews among Pagans and Christians*, London and New York 1992, 53–78; E. Will and C. Orrieux, *'Proselytisme juif'? Histoire d'une erreur*, Paris 1992; M. Goodman, *Mission and Conversion. Proselytizing in the Religious History of the Roman Empire*, Oxford 1994; see the review by S. J. D. Cohen, *JSS* 46, 1995, 297–300; however see now also Feldman, *Jew and Gentile*, 292f. (on McKnight), 299, 342–82 etc. (on Goodman); J. M. Scott, *Paul and the Nations. The Old Testament and Jewish Background of Paul's Mission to the Nations with Special Reference to the Destination of Galatians*, WUNT 84, Tübingen 1995, 153 n.92 (earlier literature).

321. Kraabel, 'Immigrants' (n.320), 71–88. For the – revolutionary – inscription of Aphrodisias see Reynolds and Tannenbaum, *Jews* (n.320); P. W. van der Horst, 'Juden und Christen in Aphrodisias im Licht ihrer

Beziehungen in anderen Städten Kleinasiens', in *Juden und Christen in der Antike*, ed. J. van Amersfoort and J. van Oort, Kampen 1990, 125–43; id., 'Das Neue Testament und die jüdischen Grabinschriften aus hellenistisch-römischer Zeit', *BZ* 36, 1992, 169ff.; Feldman, *Jew and Gentile* (n.320).

322. Σεβόμενοι (τὸν θεόν), φοβούμενοι τὸν θεόν, θεοσεβεῖς, ἰουδαΐζοντες, *metuentes, yīr'e šāmāyim*, etc. Cf. Simon, 'Gottesfürchtiger', *RAC* 11, 1060–4; Siegert, 'Gottesfürchtige', *NBL* I, 931f.; Feldman, *Jew and Gentile* (n.320), 342–82.

323. Acts 10.35; cf. Luke 7.4f.; Acts 10.1f.; 16.14; 18.7.

324. Cf. Josephus, *c. Ap* 2, 282; Philo, *VitMos* 2, 21; Tertullian, Ad nat 1, 13; E. Lohse, σάββατον, *TDNT* 7, 17f.; Stern, *GLAJ* II, 106f.

325. For the repeated *metuere* see Stern, *GLAJ* II, 103–6 (with bibliography): 'Apparently it is not by chance that *metuere* occurs twice in this passage', referring to J. Bernays, who already emphasized the link with the 'godfearers' of the Talmudic and early Christian sources: *Gesammelte Abhandlungen*, Berlin 1885, 2, 71ff.; Siegert, 'Gottesfürchtige' (n.320), 153ff. For the epitaph from Pula (third to fifth century CE.), *CIJ* I, No. 642, see now D. Noy, *Jewish Inscriptions of Western Europe* I, Cambridge 1993, 16f. no. 9. As Noy rightly emphasizes, this is a godfearer, not a Jewish woman (*Soteriae matri pientissimae [sic] religioni Iudeicae metuenti*).

326. Juvenal, *Sat.* 14, 96–106. Cf. S. H. Braund, 'Juvenal and the East: Satire as an Historical Source', in *The Eastern Frontier of the Roman Empire. Proceedings of a Colloquium held at Ankara in September 1988*, ed. D. H. French and C. S. Lightfoot, British Institute of Archaeology at Ankara Monograph No. 11, BAR International Series 553(i), 1989, 45–52: 47; Feldman, *Jew and Gentile* (n.320), 345–8 refers for this to Plutarch, *Cicero* 7, 6, 5; Suetonius, *Tiberius* 32, 2 (on 36 see the next note); Petronius, frag. 37.

327. Dio Cassius 57, 18, 5a = Stern, *GLAJ* II, 365 no. 419; for this cf. already the Fulvia episode in Josephus *Antt.* 18, 81ff., but also Suetonius, *Tiberius* 36 = Stern, *GLAJ* II, 112f. no. 306 and Tacitus, *Ann* 2, 85, 4 with the commentary by Stern, *GLAJ* II, 68ff. = no. 284 on the measures against Jewish freedmen on the basis of a *senatus consultum* of the year 19 CE. The adherents of the Egyptian and Jewish cult were forcibly deported to Sardinia; 'the rest had to leave Italy if they did not give up their unreligious rites by a fixed date'. 'Tacitus may allude here to proselytes who were left with a choice of giving up Judaism or leaving Italy' – it must be added: as far as these were freedmen and *peregrini*. Possibly this also included zealous 'godfearers', especially as the Roman authorities did not draw the lines here in accordance with Jewish law.

Attendance at synagogue worship was probably the deciding factor.

328. Stern, *GLAJ* II, 71.

329. Schürer, I, 513, 528; II, 272f., etc.; Riesner, *Frühzeit* (n.49), 178f.; Botermann, *Judenedikt* (n.5), 66f., 163 n.526.

330. *Ep.mor* 108, 22; M. Stern, *GLAJ* I, 433f. (no. 181). Cf. also at the beginning of the first century Valerius Maximus 1, 3, 3; Stern, *GLAJ* I, 358 (no. 147a and b), who is not only describing an event of the year 139 BCE but is also alluding *to his own time*. A fear of the Jews in Rome which to some degree is blown up rhetorically already appears in Cicero's speech *Pro Flacco* 28, 67 (Stern, *GLAJ* I, 196 no. 68). In 59 BCE he already speaks of a *barbara superstitio* (28, 67). Cf. further Horace, *Serm.* 1, 9, 67ff.; see Feldman, *Jew and Gentile* (n.320), 299; Stern, *GLAJ* I, 324f. (no.129): the sabbath superstition of the Roman poet Fuscus Aristius and the grammarian Diogenes on Rhodes towards Tiberius (Suetonius, *Tiberius* 32, 2 = Stern, *GLAJ* II, 111f. no. 305). This evidence shows that even in Rome the Jewish presence and the propaganda associated with it caused considerable unrest. But see now the major investigation by P. Schäfer, *Judaeophobia*, Cambridge, Mass. 1997 (in preparation). Even more influential synagogue communities are to be assumed for Syria, with the densest Jewish Diaspora.

331. Augustine, *Civ. Dei* 6, 11 (= Stern, *GLAJ* I, 431f., no. 186).

332. *Antt.* 20, 34–48; cf. 3, 318f. (and n.344); GenR 46, 11 (Theodor/Albeck 2, 467f.). See L. H. Schiffman, 'The Conversion of the Royal House of Adiabene in Josephus and Rabbinic Sources', in L. H. Feldman and G. Hata (eds.), *Josephus, Judaism and Christianity*, Leiden 1987, 293–312.

333. 34: ἐδίδασκεν αὐτὰς τὸν θεὸν σέβειν, ὡς Ἰουδαίοις πάτριον ἦν.

334. 38: νομίζων τε μὴ ἂν εἶναι βεβαίως Ἰουδαῖος, εἰ μὴ περιτέμοιτο.

335. 43: πάνυ περὶ τὰ πάτρια νομῶν ἀκριβὴς εἶναι. The catchword ἀκριβής in connection with obedience to the law is typical of the Pharisees in Josephus (and Luke), see A. I. Baumgarten, 'The Name of the Pharisees', *JBL* 102, 1983, 411–28; Hengel and Deines, review of Sanders (n.62), 31.

336. 44: τὰ μέγιστα τοὺς νόμους καὶ δι' αὐτῶν τὸν θεὸν ἀδικῶν.

337. M. Simon, *Verus Israel. Études sur les relations entre chrétiens et juifs dans l'empire romain* (134–425), Paris ²1964, ch. X, 'Le prosélytism juif'; id., 'Gottesfürchtiger', *RAC* 11, 1064ff.

338. Cf. Ananias' argument in Josephus, *Antt.* 20, 41: the king 'could worship God without being circumcised provided that he had wholly decided to be zealous for the ancestral laws of the Jews. That counted more than being circumcised. God would forgive him if he had omitted

to do this for reason of an emergency and for fear of his subjects.'

339. Cf. Goodman, *Mission* (n.320), 131f.; he is opposed by Feldman, *Jew and Gentile* (n.320), 353–6.

340. The case of Titus Flavius Clemens and his wife Domitilla, the nephew and niece of Domitian who were accused of 'godlessness' along with many others 'who went astray into the Jewish way of life', is an enigmatic one. Here we could have Jewish or also already Christian tendencies, see Dio Cassius 67, 14, 2 and against him Eusebius, *HE* 3, 18, 4; see Hengel, Review of Schürer (n.257), 39f. It is significant that either is conceivable: Jews and Christians still stood very close to each other.

341. For the exclusion of the uncircumcised and aliens cf. the contributions of R. Deines, 'Die Abwehr der Fremden in den Texten aus Qumran', and H. Lichtenberger, ' "Im Lande Israel zu wohnen wiegt alle Gebote der Tora auf " ', in Feldmeier and Heckel (eds.), *Die Heiden*, WUNT 70, Tübingen 1994, 59–107. Alongside the rigorous accentuation of the law in Qumran we have the 'more moderate' ideas of the Pharisees as these can be recognized, say, in the Psalms of Solomon, thus 17.22ff., 30, 45: the Messiah will exterminate all uncleanness in the land and no alien (πάροικος) and foreigner (ἀλλογενής) will dwell in it any longer. Nevertheless, the expectation of the eschatological pilgrimage of the nations to Zion is not abandoned. But cf. Mark 11.17 par.: the unequivocally positive attitude towards the nations.

342. See Hengel, *Zealots* (n.122), 197–9.

343. See below, n.363.

344. Josephus, *Antt.* 3, 318f, ; cf. D. R. Schwartz, 'On Sacrifice by Gentiles in the Temple of Jerusalem', in id., *Studies in the Jewish Background of Christianity*, WUNT 60, 1992, 102–16: 108f.; Feldman, *Jew and Gentile* (n.320), 352. The text sheds light on the charges against Paul in Acts 21.28, see also Hengel, *Zealots* (n.122), 215. The notion of conscience here comes close to that in Paul. For the question of conscience and the law see I Cor. 8. For conscience in Josephus and Paul see H.-J.Eckstein, *Der Begriff Syneidesis bei Paulus*, WUNT II/10, Tübingen 1983, 132ff.

345. Cf. S. J. D. Cohen, 'Respect of Judaism by Gentiles According to Josephus', *HTR* 80, 1987, 409–30, and id., '"Proselyte Baptism" in the Mishnah? The Interpretation of M.Pesahim 8.8 (= M.Eduyot 5.2)', in *Pursuing the Text. Studies in Honor of Ben Zion Wacholder on the Occasion of His Seventieth Birthday*, ed. J.C.Reeves and J.Kampen, JSOT.S 184, Sheffield 1994, 278–92. It is not mentioned either in Josephus or in one of the earlier Jewish Hellenistic authors. The earliest testimony to it could be the controversy between the schools of Hillel and Shammai,

mPes 8, 8 and mEd 5, 2, cf. also mKer 2, 1; see Bill. I, 102ff., 110ff.; Schürer III, 173f., 642. However, in his most recent publication Cohen thinks this improbable. The starting point is probably the duty to offer sacrifice in the temple, which presupposed a bath by immersion. In other words, the problem of 'proselyte baptism' was initially limited to the pilgrimage to Jerusalem which was necessary for a complete conversion. After the destruction of the temple this then became a quite independent custom, presumably in opposition to Christian baptism. The earliest non-Jewish evidence is Epictetus in Arrian, *Diss.* 2, 9, 20; Stern *GLAJ* I, 542ff. no. 254. Sib. 4, 165 probably refers to a baptist sect. On this see H. Lichtenberger, 'Täufergemeinden und frühchristliche Täuferpolemik im letzten Drittel des 1. Jahrhunderts', *ZThK* 84, 1987, 38ff.

346. Schürer II, 162.

347. For Joseph and Asenath see now A. Standhartinger, *Zum Frauenbild im Judentum der hellenistischen Zeit. Ein Beitrag anhand von Joseph und Aseneth*, AGJU 26, 1995. The book of Ruth ist hardly to be put before the middle of the fourth century. It cultivates a deliberately archaizing style and like Jonah must be seen as a protest against the reforms of Ezra and Nehemiah.

348. 4, 4–5 and the subsequent reply of Joseph: οὐκ ἐν ἀκαθαρσία θέλει κύριος τοὺς σεβομένους αὐτόν; on this see Feldman, *Jew and Gentile* (n.320), 295.

349. Sib. 3, 827; cf. Schürer III, 618–54: 623, 628.

350. 3, 195; Sib.4, 35–48 expresses the disappointment that everyone does not follow the admonition of the Sibyl; judgment falls upon them, cf. 4, 152–161, 184ff. Feldman, *Jew and Gentile* (n.320), 314 cites Sib.3, 547–579 and 4, 162–167 as evidence that the Sibyl is addressing Gentiles and wants to gain *proselytes*. But Sib. 4, 162–167 can hardly be connected with proselyte baptism.

351. Above all Sib. 3, 583, 770, cf. 259f., 757, 768.

352. See J. M. Lieu, 'Circumcision, Women and Salvation', *NTS* 40, 1994, 358–70; B. J. Brooten, *Women Leaders in the Ancient Synagogue*, BJSt 36, Chico, Calif. 1982, 144–7: 'Women as Proselytes to Judaism'; for Fulvia see Josephus, *Antt.* 18, 82f. and on it A. A. Bell, 'Josephus the Satyrist? A Clue to the Original Form of the *Testimonium Flavianum*', *JQR* 67, 1976/77, 16–22; cf. also the enigmatic case of Pomponia Graecina, Tacitus, *Ann.* 13, 32, who was accused of *superstitio externa*. Even the blasphemous miller woman depicted in Apuleius, *Met.* 9, 14ff. who despises all gods in favour of 'a blasphemously invented notion of a God who proclaims himself to be the only one' (*quem praedicaret unicum*, 9, 14,

5) could be a caricature of a Jewish sympathizer or a Christian.

353. As a rule men assumed the name 'Judah'; cf. the ossuary inscription *SEG* 17, 1960, 207 no. 785: 'Ιούδα ν(εώτερος) προσήλυτ(ος) Τύρου; *CIJ* II, no. 1385, 1390 and that of the proselyte Aristo of Apamea, who bore the Hebrew second name Judah: ΑΡΙΣΤΩΝ *'rstwn 'pmy yhwdh hgywr,* see T. Ilan, 'New Ossuary Inscriptions from Jerusalem', *Scripta Classica Israelica* 11, 1991–1992, 149–59: 150, 154.

354. *CIJ* I, no. 523.

355. *Sat.* 6, 543ff, see Stern, *GLAJ* II, 100f. (no. 299).

356. Cf. Acts 13.50, the influential σεβόμεναι γυναῖκες in Pisidian Antioch, cf. 13.43; 16.13f.; 17.4, 12. For Paul see e.g. I Cor. 1.11; Rom. 16.1, 12; Phil. 4.2f., etc.

357. *Antt.* 20, 195: under Festus (c. 59–61), she held the high priest Ishmael and the treasurer Helkias hostage in her house. Cf. also Stern, *GLAJ* II, 202 n.6.

358. Martial 7, 82 mentions a Jewish actor and singer who wants to hide his circumcision: Stern, *GLAJ* I, 526f. (no. 243); see also the Jewish poet in Rom. 11.14 who plagiarizes his poems: Stern, *GLAJ* I, 527f. (no. 245).

359. *Vita* 16: under Albinus, c. 62–64.

360. Tacitus, *Ann.*16, 6; against this cf. Suetonius, *Tiberius* 36 (on Tiberius's contrary attitude): *Externas caeremoniis, Aegyptios, Iudaicosque ritus compescuit.* According to the apologetic correspondence between Paul and Seneca, *Ep.* 5, the empress is indignant about Paul's apostasy from the 'old religion', i.e. Judaism, *Ep.* 8. The correspondence comes from the beginning of the fourth century, but must have used older sources, see *Ep.* 11; see below, n.886.

361. See Stern, *GLAJ* II, 5f n.12; E. M. Smallwood, 'The Alleged Jewish Tendencies of Poppaea Sabina', *JTS* NS 10, 1959, 329–35. She probably shared the oriental enthusiasms of Nero, see Suetonius, *Nero* 40, 2; M. H. Williams, 'θεοσεβὴς γὰρ ἦν – The Jewish Tendencies of Poppaea Sabina', *JTS* 39, 1988, 97–111; Feldman, *Jew and Gentile* (n.320), 98, 351f.

362. See P. Trebilco, *Jewish Communities in Asia Minor,* SNTS.MS 69, Cambridge, etc. 1991, 58ff., 212; B. Levick, *Roman Colonies in Southern Asia Minor,* Oxford 1967, 106f. S. Mitchell, *Anatolia,* Oxford 1993, II, 9, 31 n.176; 35 fig. 15: 'a gentile woman from one of the city's leading families; related … to a Galatian dynasty which could trace its line back to the tetrarchs and kings of the Hellenistic period. She had close connections with the Turronii, an emigrant Italian family, one of whose members P. Turronius Cladus is named on the same inscription as *archisynagogus,* while another, Turronius Rapo, was priest of the imperial

cult, and appears alongside her on coins issued by the city.' We may presuppose similar conditions in Pisidian Antioch, where the family of
Sergius Paullus was influential. Cf. Mitchell, 8f.

363. Acts 13.6–12, and on this A. D. Nock, 'Paul and the Magus', in
Essays on Religion and the Ancient World, Oxford 1972, I, 308–30 (= F. J.
Foakes Jackson and K. Lake [eds.], *The Beginnings of Christianity*, Vol. 5,
1933, 164–8). For Sergius Paullus see F. Groag, *PW* 21, 1715–18;
H. Halfmann, 'Die Senatoren aus dem östlichen Teil des Imperium
Romanum bis zum Ende des 2. Jh.s', *Hypomnemata* 58, Göttingen 1979,
55f., 101, 105f.; Hemer, *Acts* (n.37), 109 with n.17; Mitchell, *Anatolia*
(n.362), 1, 151, 154, 157; 2, 6ff.; in detail Riesner, *Frühzeit* (n.49), 121–9,
245f. The procurator Felix, who perhaps claims the help of the same
magician (Josephus, *Antt.* 20, 141–144) to gain Drusilla, the pleasure-
loving sister of Agrippa II, belongs in a related milieu; cf. Acts 24.22–26:
Luke, who in our view is giving an eye-witness report here, is outstand-
ingly well informed about these events. However, Josephus sees this
second marriage, with a non-Jew in love with the beautiful Jewish
woman, as a transgression of the law. Cf. also nn.366 and 376.

364. *Legatio* 245, cf. 260–315; Josephus, *Antt.* 18, 261–288 (especially
in his confession of God and the temple, 280f.). P.Petronius was
governor in Asia for six years and legate in Syria from 39–42. See R.
Hanslik, 'P. Petronius', *PW* 19, 1937, 1199–201; Schürer I, 263, 394–8;
Feldman, *Jew and Gentile* (n.320), 295f. The Jewish petitioners in
Ptolemais and then in Tiberias must have had his sympathy, so that he
risked his life by deliberate delay.

365. We have a special early case in *CPJ* I, 236ff., no. 128, where a
Helladote daughter of Philonides complains in a petition to the king
that her Jewish husband Jonathas, whom she married κατὰ τὸν νόμον
π]ολίτικον τῶν ['Ιου]δαίων is doing her wrong (ἀδικεῖ). Contrary to the
editors, this suggests a pagan wife.

366. For Drusilla see n.363. Berenice's connection with Titus was at
least a relationship similar to marriage, see Dio Cassius 65, 15, 4;
Suetonius, *Titus* 7, 1, 2: *Berenicem statim ab urbe dimisit invitus invitam.*

367. Plutarch, *Cicero* 7, 6 = Stern, *GLAJ* I, 566 no. 263, tells of
Caecilius, a freedman and quaestor of Verres, who was suspected of
living in accordance with Jewish customs (ἔνοχος τῷ ἰουδαΐζειν) and is
mocked by Cicero. Possibly he is confusing this man with the orator
Caecilius of Caleacte, who was said to be of Jewish origin. However, this
could only be a proselyte or sympathizer. For the complicated historical
question see Stern, loc. cit. In Eusebius, *Praep. ev.* 9, 21, 5 in connection
with Theodotus' didactic poem about Shechem, ἰουδαΐζειν is used for

the circumcision of all the inhabitants of Shechem (GCS 43, 1, 514 Mras); for Josephus, *BJ* 2, 454, circumcision is the highest degree: μέχρι περιτομῆς ἰουδαΐζει. In Gal. 2.14 and Ignatius, Magn. 10.3 it simply means following precepts of the Jewish law, which are not defined. In the Acts of Pilate (Tischendorf, *Evang. Apoc.* 222) Pilate says that his wife is θεοσεβής ... καὶ μᾶλλον ἰουδαΐζει σὺν ὑμῖν. There are further Christian examples in Lampe, *PGL* 674. The term clearly has a considerable breadth of meaning.

368. Josephus, *BJ.* 2, 463; Goodman, *Mission* (n.320), 77 rejects this understanding. The interpretation in terms of Christians seems to us to be the most probable.

369. Feldman, *Jew and Gentile* (n.320), 78f. investigates the evidence in Philo and cautiously refers (487 n.174) to Berlin Papyrus no. 11641 (quoted after W. Schubart, *Einführung in die Papyruskunde*, Berlin 1913, 330). At least one of the Jewish epitaphs from Leontopolis seems to attest an Egyptian-Jewish mixed marriage between a Jewish woman and a pagan Egyptian, see Horbury and Noy, *Jewish Inscriptions* (n.316), 72 no. 33. But Egyptian names also appear in other Jewish inscriptions (Horbury and Noy nos. 34, 66, 114). Mixed marriages fit the liberal, less pious milieu of the Jews in Leontopolis. The best example here was Joseph and Asenath.

370. Against Goodman, *Mission* (n.320), 78 n.44, who emphasizes that there is no evidence for such a distinction between the Diaspora and Judaea in the first century CE. For the problem in rabbinic law see Bill. II, 741 ad loc. This was more frequently the case than is generally assumed because of the possibility offered by pagan masters for Jewish slaves (male or female) or freedmen to marry.

371. Feldman, *Jew and Gentile* (n.320), 380 assumes too high a percentage: 'the number of items with no Jewish element at all is small'; cf. W. Fauth, *Helios Megistos, Zur synkretistischen Theologie der Spätantike*, RGRW 125, Leiden 1995, 10, speaks of 'Jewish elements to be encountered in the Greek magical texts all over the world'; cf. index, 264f. s.v. Iao, etc.

372. Acts 13.6, 8; 8.9ff.; the itinerant Jewish exorcists in Ephesus 19.13ff. and the burning of the magical papyri worth 50,000 denarii in 19.19; cf. Mark 9.38ff.; Josephus, *Antt.* 8, 45–49; *Antt.* 20, 142. It is no longer possible to tell how far the Jewish magician Atomos from Cyprus is identical with the Barjesus/Elymas of Acts 13.6. Cf. also Lucian, *Philopseudes* 16 (Stern, *GLAJ* II, 222 no. 372); *Tragodopodegra* 173 (Stern, *GLAJ* II, 223 no. 374). For Moses as a magician see Pliny the Elder, *Nat hist.* 30, 11 (Stern, *GLAJ* I, 498f. no. 221); Apuleius, *Apol.* (Stern, *GLAJ* II,

203f. no. 361); J. G. Gager, *Moses in Greco-Roman Paganism*, Nashville 1972, 135, 152f.; Morton Smith, *Jesus the Magician*, London 1978, 114, 198.

373. Cf. P. Marincovic, '"Geh in Frieden" (II Kön 5.19). Sonderformen legitimer JHWHverehrung durch "Heiden" in heidnischer Mitwelt', in Feldmeier and Heckel (eds.), *Heiden* (n.341), 3–22. It is perhaps no coincidence that the Jerusalem priest Josephus does not say a word about the story of Naaman. In the time of Domitian and because of the case of Titus Flavius Clemens it may have seemed inopportune, or he may have rejected it.

374. *Apol.* 1, 210; cf. *Antt.* 3, 318f. Cf. n.344 above.

375. Cf. S. R. Hoenig, 'Circumcision: The Covenant of Abraham', *JQR* 53, 1962–1963, 322–34, who derives the strong emphasis on circumcision in the rabbinate from the opposition to Christianity; Cohen, *Respects* (n.345); L. H. Feldman, *Josephus and Modern Scholarship*, Berlin and New York 1984, 732ff.; against Will and Orrieux, *Proselytisme* (n.320). Even the rabbis could not deny the existence of the 'godfearers', but they clearly distanced themselves from them. Their attitude to the proselytes is essentially more positive. The rabbinic texts relate only to part of post-Christian Judaism and in part contradict historical reality, above all in the Diaspora. I would simply recall the question of images and the numerous pictorial representations in the synagogues.

376. Thus the marriage plans of the Nabataean ruler Syllaios come to grief (Josephus, *Antt.* 16, 220–225): however, Syllaios refuses, allegedly for fear of being stoned by his Arab subjects. By contrast, in *Antt.* 20, 139 King Azizus of Emesa accepts circumcision in order to marry Drusilla, the sister of Agrippa II (cf. n.363 above), after Epiphanes, the son of Antiochus IV of Commagene, has broken off the betrothal for this reason, despite his previous consent (19, 355). When the Jewish princess then left Azizus with the help of the Jewish magician Atomus and married the procurator Felix, Josephus emphasizes in disapproval that 'they transgressed the ancestral laws' (20, 143). In her third marriage, Drusilla's older sister Berenice married King Polemon II of Pontus, who from 41 on also ruled over some parts of Cilicia. Probably by arrangement with her brother, she herself arranged the marriage in order to avoid rumours that she had an incestuous relationship with Agrippa II. Polemon accepted circumcision, but when Berenice left him again after a short period he no longer observed the Jewish way of life (Josephus, *Antt.* 20, 145f.). This insistence on the circumcision of Gentile males was above all because of the 'internal politics' in Jewish Palestine. Agrippa wanted to win the approval of the Jews, see above, 247ff. Berenice

appears in *BJ* 2, 313f. as a pious Jewish woman, who fulfils a vow in the temple and intercedes before Florus for her people; in 70 CE she becomes the beloved of Titus (see n.366 above). The rabbis later rejected both conversions to Judaism motivated by marriage and the compulsory circumcision practised by the Zealots (bGer 1, 7).

377. Cf. I Macc. 1.15f., 60f.; 2.46; II Macc. 6.10; Josephus, *Antt.* 12, 241; Bill. 4, 33f.; see also K. G. Kuhn and H. Stegemann, 'Proselyten', *PW* Suppl. 9, 1962, 1247–57; further P. Schäfer, *Der Bar Kokhba-Aufstand*, TSAJ 1, 1981, 38–50, esp. 43ff. on mAb 3, 11 and tShab 15 (16), 9.

378. Acts 16.3 gives the precise reason, cf. I Cor. 9.19ff.: he does it for the sake of the πλείονας κερδαίνειν.

379. *De migr. Abr.* 80f. Cf. Hengel, *Judaism and Hellenism* (n.314), II, 202 n.285; 379f.

380. QGen 3, 45–52.

381. QEx 2, 2, Fragmenta Graeca, ed. F. Petit, *Les Oeuvres de Philon d'Alexandrie* 33, 1978, 239. Cf. Paul, Rom. 2.28f. (; Col. 2.11).

382. Rom. 2.25–29; Acts 7.51 cf. Deut. 30.6; Jer. 4.4; 9.24f.; cf. the circumcision of the ears in Jer. 6.10. For Barnabas 9.1–8; 10.12 cf. J. Carleton Paget, *The Epistle of Barnabas*, WUNT II/64, 1994, 143–9, 211f.

383. On this see J. Nolland, 'Uncircumcised Proselytes', *JSS*, 1981, 173–94, against N. J. McEleney, 'Conversion, Circumcision and the Law', *NTS* 20, 1974, 328–33. Against Nolland, Izates' conflict does not seem to us to be so special a case. This is the only explanation of the relatively large circle of sympathizers around the Jewish core communities in the Diaspora. The situation before 70 was even more complicated in the case of women, see n.352 above; cf. also Luke's terminological obscurity in Acts 13.43: τῶν σεβομένων προσηλύτων. There may have been zealous 'godfearers' not least among the women who virtually felt themselves to be 'proselytes', except that they did not undertake the last step of the pilgrimage to Jerusalem, the baptismal immersion and the offering of sacrifice (or in the case of males also circumcision). Perhaps before 70 conversion to Judaism was not yet so clearly marked for women as it was for men, so that the boundaries between sympathizers, 'godfearers' and proselytes were initially fluid.

384. For his sermon-like text preserved in Armenian (from an allegorical commentary?) *De Deo* see F. Siegert, *Philon von Alexandrien: Über die Gottesbezeichnung 'wohltätig verzehrendes Feuer' "De Deo". Rückübersetzung aus dem Armenischen*, German translation and commentary, WUNT 46, Tübingen 1988.

385. Acts 7; 13; cf. Heb. 11.

386. F. Siegert, 'Die Heiden in der pseudo-philonischen Predigt De

Jona', in Feldmeier and Heckel (eds.), *Heiden* (n.341), 53. As Siegert rightly emphasizes, the term 'Gentiles' does not appear at all in this sermon. The preacher always speaks of 'human beings', i.e. he addresses all his hearers in the same way.

387. § 216f. German translation in Siegert, 'Heiden' (n.386), 52f.; cf. id., *Drei hellenistisch-jüdische Predigten. Ps.-Philon, 'Über Jona', 'Über Simson' ... I, Übersetzung aus dem Armenischen und sprachliche Erläuterungen*, WUNT 20, Tübingen 1980; id., *Drei hellenistisch.-jüdische Predigten. Ps.-Philon, 'Über Jona', 'Über Jona' (Fragment) und 'Über Simson' II, Kommentar*, WUNT 61, Tübingen 1992.

388. See below, n.391.

389. For God's universal 'philanthropia' (a virtue of ancient rulers) see Titus 3.2; JosAs 13.1; Josephus, *Antt.* 1, 24; Philo, *Opif.* 81 etc.; Wisdom 1.6; 7.23 f.; U. Luck, *TDNT* 9, 107–12.

390. *De Jona* c. 46 §186; translation in Siegert, *Predigten* I (n.387), 42.

391. With this word-play the preacher takes up the ambiguity of the technical term for the destruction of Sodom and Gomorrah, used by the book of Jonah, *hpk* – in Greek probably καταστρέφω and ἐπιστρέφω, see Siegert, *Predigten* I (n.387), 43f.; commentary in id., *Predigten* II (n.387), 211f. ἐπιστρέφειν is also a basic term for Luke; cf. its use meaning 'convert' in Luke 1.16, 17; 1.74; Acts 3.19; 9.35; 11.21; 14.15; 15.19; 26.18, 20; 28.27 and ἐπιστροφή in Acts 15.3.

392. Cf. Paul, I Cor. 6.20; 7.23; Gal. 3.23; 4.5; and Rev. 5.9; 14.3f. The idea of 'ransom' may come from synagogue preaching.

393. Siegert, 'Heiden' (n.386), 57f.

394. *De Jona* § 118. Cf. Siegert, 'Heiden' (n.386), 56ff. By contrast, the anti-Jewish polemic of antiquity stereotypically emphasized the *misanthropy* of the Jews. Cf. Stern, *GLAJ* III, 136, index s. v. This may have motivated our preacher towards his unusual emphasis on God as a friend of humankind. This charge was incomprehensible to Jews, particularly in the Diaspora. See Philo, *SpecLeg* II, 163–167; cf. also Siegert, *Predigten* II (n.387), 106ff. In *c.Apionem* Josephus often emphasizes the philanthropy of Jewish legislation: 1, 283; 2, 146, 213, 261.

395. *Antt.* 1, 22, 24.

396. *Antt.* 1, 25; here Josephus is probably dependent on ideas like those in Philo's *De opificio mundi.*

397. The arguments for the Jewish sense of presenting the true 'philosophy' have been collected in O. Michel (Peter Schmidt), φιλοσοφία, *TDNT* 9, 177–80. By contrast, in the Talmudic literature the *pyloswpyn* are Gentiles; at least there is no indication anywhere that they are Jews. The superiority of the rabbis over the 'philosophers' is demonstrated in

fictitious dialogues. It is significant that in the NT and in the Apostolic Fathers the term appears only once, with negative connotations, in Col. 2.8. In Acts 17.18 the 'Epicurean and Stoic philosophers' are also opponents of the Christian message. The term occurs first with a positive sense in the Apologists and in Christian Gnosis, ibid., 181–5.

398. This was 'possessed' in the holy scriptures, the 'law of Moses', the translation of which into the world language of Greek was celebrated in Pharos with a popular festival in which many non-Jews also took part. See Philo, *Vita Mosis* 2, 41ff.: 'therefore to the present day, every year a festival and a popular assembly is celebrated on the island of Pharos, to which not only the Jews but also a mass of other people voyage by ship to venerate the place whence first the translation (of the LXX) emanated, and to thank God for the old *act of benevolence* (εὐεργεσία), which always remains young ... Normally the advantages of those who are not (at the climax of their) blossoming fade into the shadows. But if (for this people) the beginning of a more brilliant destiny were to dawn, how great then would the increase probably be (cf. Rom. 11.12!)? I believe that the other peoples will leave their own (customs) and in many ways bid farewell to their (own) ancestral (laws), and each will turn only to these laws to venerate them. For if things go well with the people, the laws will shine out and put the others in the shade, as happens with the rising sun and the other stars.' Cf. *Vit Mos* 2, 25f.; *Praem* 116f., 152; M. Hengel, 'Die Septuaginta als "christliche Schriftensammlung"', in M. Hengel and A. M. Schwemer (eds.), *Die Septuaginta*, WUNT 72, 1994, 182–284: 184f.; Feldman, *Jew and Gentile* (n.320), 311–14; A. M. Schwemer, 'Zum Verhältnis von Diatheke und Nomos in den Schriften der jüdischen Diaspora Ägyptens in hellenistisch-römischer Zeit', in *Bund und Tora*, ed. F. Avemarie and H. Lichtenberger, WUNT 92, Tübingen 1996, 67ff., 101–6.

399. 'Theocrasy' from the Jewish side can only be established by way of exception in the early inscriptions, i.e. those dating from the first and second centuries BCE; thus in the temple of Pan in El-Kanais: *CIJ*, II no. 1537, 'Praise be to God, Theodotus (son of) Dorion, a Jew, saved from the sea'; or *CIJ* II no. 1538, 'Ptolemaios (son of) Dionysius, a Jew, thanks God'; cf. Horbury and Noy, *Jewish Inscriptions* (n.316), 207–12 (nos. 121–3). The last inscription (no. 123, cf. no. 124) runs: 'I, Lazarus, came for the third time.' For the identification of the Jewish God with the highest God, whom the Gentiles also worship, cf. Letter of Aristeas 16.2; for the derivation of Egyptian (animal) worship from Moses see Artapanus, frag. 3, 4 (Eusebius, P*raep.ev.* 9, 27, 3–5); for the high estimation of the 'holy word' of Orpheus see Aristobulos, frag. 4, 4 (Eusebius,

Praep.ev. 13, 12, 5f.), see Feldman, *Jew and Gentile*, 66, etc. C. Colpe, 'Hypsistos', *RAC* 16, 1994, 1035–6: 1054 appropriately speaks in connection with the Jewish and pagan worship of the θεὸς ὕψιστος of the '*absorption*' of pagan notions of God by Jews.

400. For the ancient hostility to the Jews and the sharp reaction in the apocalyptic underground literature cf. Sib. 3, 545–549, 601–7; on this see Goodman, *Mission* (n.320), 56f. and Schäfer, *Judaeophobia* (in preparation).

401. Rom. 5.5; 8.35, 38; John 3.16; I John 3.1; 4.7–10.

402. Cf. McKnight, *Light* (n.320), 113. By contrast Feldman, *Jew and Gentile* (n.320), passim, deliberately uses the term 'mission' for Jewish recruitment, in order to refute sharply the attempts by McKnight and Goodman to deny that Judaism was involved in any activity to recruit sympathizers and proselyes. The truth probably lies between the extremes.

403. See Hengel, 'Mission' (n.116).

404. I Kings 19.15, cf. Josephus, *Antt.* 8, 352; 9, 208–214 on Jonah. In the *Vitae Prophetarum* Jonah is connected with the former Philistine coastal region (his place of birth is Kariathmaous near Ashdod, the city of the Greeks) and with Seir (he was buried in the tomb of Kenaz, probably the Idumaean 'tomb of the patriarchs'). This information reflects the Hasmonaean conquests, see Schwemer, *Vitae Prophetarum* II (n.134), 76ff. For the changes in the understanding of Jonah's preaching in Nineveh in the rabbinic literature see B. Ego, '"Denn die Heiden sind der Umkehr nahe"'. Rabbinische Interpretationen zur Busse der Leute von Ninive', in Feldmeier and Heckel (eds.), *Heiden* (n.341), 158–76.

405. See Hengel, *Judaism and Hellenism* (n.314), 24ff., 307f., etc. Cf. above n.320 for a bibliography on the more recent discussion.

406. After 70 and even more after 135 and then again after Theodosius the situation for Jewish 'propaganda' became more difficult. For the prohibition against the circumcision of 'proselytes' by Antoninus Pius see M. Hengel, 'Hadrians Politik gegenüber Juden und Christen', *JANES* 16/17, 1987, 153–82: 172ff.; cf. below, n.616; Goodman, 'Mission' (n.320), 138f.

407. *C. Ap* 2, 165: this is the only occurrence of this word in ancient texts. However, it stands in a relationship to the Jewish notion of the *malkūt haš-šāmāyīm* (the kingdom of heaven). Cf. Josephus, *Antt.* 3, 322: the Jewish πολιτεία derives from God himself. In Phil 3.20 Paul uses the metaphor πολίτευμα in an eschatological-transcendent sense.

408. See Goodman, 'Proselytizing' (n.320), 53–78; id., *Mission*

(n.320), 86f.; Reiser, 'Paulus' (n.320), though with the expedient that 'the Gentiles came wholly of their own accord' (85). He, too, sees things too one-sidedly; against Will and Orrieux, *Proselytisme* (n.320). The grain of truth in this polemical history of research lies in the fact that the term 'mission' is inappropriate for Jewish religious 'propaganda'. By contrast, I do not understand their polemic against the modern term 'proselytism'. For we should not doubt that the Jews in the Diaspora had a lively interest in attracting sympathizers and if possible making them real 'additions', not only for social reasons but also in the awareness that they were advocating the *only* true religion, the only true God. The rabbinic material adduced from many sides is usually relatively late and tells us little about the situation of the Diaspora in the first century CE. The phenomenon of the 'sympathizers' is treated quite inadequately by both authors. Their book is a typical example of the way in which where there is a failure to understand its religious roots and its unique – in antiquity – *claim to truth,* Judaism is misunderstood. An understanding of the special character of Jewish history, particularly in antiquity, threatens to be a victim of that historical secularism which no longer allows genuinely religious phenomena and therefore minimizes them or denies them completely..

409. *Virt* 107, cf. 220ff., quoted above 66f.; see also *Spec Leg* 1, 309: 'They become authentic lovers of simplicity and *truth* and have turned to piety' as 'those who revere what truly is'. See also Philo's remarks on the proselytes in *Spec Leg* 1, 51–53, where he uses political terminology: προσηλυθέναι καινῇ καί φιλοθέῳ πολιτείᾳ and also 2, 118f. Cf. Feldman, *Jew and Gentile* (n.320), 295f.

410. We already find the εἷς θεός often in Paul: Rom. 3.10; I Cor. 8.4; Gal. 3.20, cf. Eph.4.6; I Tim. 2.5 and James 3.1; I Clem. 46.6; Herm. 26.1 (*Mand* IV. 1).

411. Cf. the grandiose summary of Pauline theology in Rom. 11.25–36.

412. Colpe, 'Hypsistos' (n.399). E. G. Kraeling already conjectured that as God of heaven YHWH 'absorbed' the title of Baal Shamin, *The Brooklyn Museum Aramaic Papyri*, New Haven 1953, 84. See also D. K. Andrews, 'Yahwe the God of the Heavens', *FS Meeks*, 1964, 45–57: 50.

413. For the Greek and Latin dedicatory inscriptions for Jupiter Heliopolitanus of Baalbek/Heliopolis in Lebanon, who was also worshipped in large parts of Syria and Palestine, see *IGLS* VI, nos. 2714–31 and as a typical example no. 2729:

$$Διὶ \ μεγ[ίσ]τῳ \ ʽΗλιοπολείτῃ$$
$$κυρίῳ$$

Ἀπολλώνος ὁ καὶ Ἄπο
[λ]ινάριος Σεγνα Ἀρά(δ)ιος
[εὐξάμ]ενος κατὰ χ[ρη
ματισ]μὸν τὸν ἀνδριά[ντα]
[σὺν τοῖς] τέκνοις ἀνέθηκεν.

To Zeus, the supreme (God) of Heliopolis,
the Lord,
Apollo, who also (is called) Apo
l(l)inaros Segna Aradios (from Arados),
promised and according to an O(ra-
cl)e erected this statu(e
with his) children.

The epithet 'Lord', κύριος, for the deity is characteristic. δεσπότης appears in *IGLS* no. 2730, see n.629. The Latin dedications regularly use the abbreviation *'I(ovi) O(ptimo) M(aximo) H(eliopolitano)'*. Iuppiter Optimus Maximus is the official designation of the god of the Capitol. See F. Thulin, *PW* 10, 1, 1918, 1126–47: 1140; F. F. F. Cumont, 'Jupiter summus exsuperantissimus', *ARW* 9, 1906, 323–36; id., 'Deux autels de Phénice', *Syria* 8, 1927, 164; M. P. Nilsson, *Opuscula Selecta*, Lund 1952, 487, 493. Cf. H.Gese, 'Die Religionen Altsyriens', in H. Gese, M. Höfner and K. Rudolph, *Die Religionen Altsyriens, Altarabiens und der Mandäer*, RM 10/2, Stuttgart 1970, 184ff., cf. 212f. For the pre-Hellenistic period see H. Niehr, *Der höchste Gott. Alttestamentlicher JHWH-Glaube im Kontext syrisch-kanaanäischer Religion des 1. Jahrtausends v. Chr.*, BZAW 190, Berlin and New York 1990, 45–68; cf. also B. Janowski, 'JHWH und der Sonnengott. Aspekte der Solarisierung JHWHs in vorexilischer Zeit', in *Pluralismus und Identität*, ed. J. Mehlhausen, Gütersloh 1990, 214–41. For the crisis under Antiochus IV Epiphanes cf. E. Bickermann, *Der Gott der Makkabäer*, Berlin 1937; Hengel, *Judaism and Hellenism* (n.314), I, 267–309; Schürer I, 148–68; Colpe, 'Hypsistos' (n.399); for the later development up to the 'solarization of Christ' see Tubach, *Sonnengott* (n.90), passim; Fauth, *Helios* (n.371), discusses solar syncretism in the second to fifth centuries CE.

414. For ὕψιστος as a designation of God see M. P. Nilsson, *Geschichte der griechischen Religion*, II, Munich 1961, 572–8, 662–5; cf. further the pagan inscriptions: *IGLS* VII, no.4027 from Sahin, dated 260/1 CE: θε]ῷ ὑψίστῳ οὐρανίῳ, which does not refer to Mithras, as Cumont and Vermaseren had assumed; cf. now also C. Breytenbach, 'Hypsistos', *DDD*, 822–30 (with bibliography).

415. The core area of the Bar Kochba revolt around Hebron was

originally Idumaean; cf. already the role of the Idumaeans in the Jewish
War, Josephus, *BJ* 1, 63 = *Antt.* 13, 328, 353; 17, 254; *BJ* 2, 228–232; 3,
300–313. For the temple of Beer-Sheba built on an ancient site in the
Hasmonaean period see Z.Herzog, 'Israelite Sanctuaries at Arad and
Beer-Sheba', in *Temples and High Places in Biblical Times. Proceedings of the
Colloquium in Honor of the Centennial of Hebrew Union College – Jewish Insti-
tute of Religion*, ed. A.Biran, Jerusalem 1981, 120ff.

416. Cf. Philo of Byblos (Eusebius, *Praep.ev.* 1, 10, 7): 'For they
regarded this God ... as the sole Lord of heaven, calling him Beelsamen,
which among the Phoenicians means "Lord of heaven", among the
Greeks Zeus.'

417. See Fauth, *Helios Megistos* (n.371), index 266 s. v. 'Sol Invictus'.

418. For Daniel see Hengel, *Judaism and Hellenism* (n.314), I, 296ff.;
for Beelzebul see O. Böcher, *EWNT* 1, 501; Bill. I, 631ff.: '"Lord of the
dwelling" then means the sphere of heaven in which the demons dwell.'
For the rabbis z^ebul, etc. meant the heavenly sanctuary, see bChag 12b.
This designation could on occasion be satirized, thus probably already in
II Kings 1.2–16, where ba'al z^ebūl becomes ba'al z^ebūb, i.e. the god of the
flies. The fact that the designation does not appear in rabbinic texts
shows that it had a popular character and became insignificant in the
fourth century with the advance of Christianity. For this see also A.
Feldtkeller, *Identitätssuche* (n.88), 104–9, 119, though the conclusions he
draws from it are too fantastic. The charge against Jesus has nothing to
do with the 'Gentile mission without the law', nor should it be termed
the 'charge of syncretism'. That is to introduce a modern term which is
historically quite mistaken. The expression 'in league with the devil'
would be appropriate. Nor should the official designation for the
'anonymous' Jewish God as θεὸς ὕψιστος on the lips of Gentiles (Mark
5.7 and Acts 16.17) be confused with the Beelzebul slander. We have no
indication whatsoever that θεὸς ὕφιστος was a provocative title for Jews
and Christians orientated on Judaism, 'which signalized commandeer-
ing and narrowing to them'. How else were pagans adequately to denote
the 'unnameable' God in his all-surpassing universality? Philo's ὁ ὤν on
the basis of Ex. 3.14 sounded too philosophically abstract.

419. Feldtkeller, *Identitätssuche* (n.88), 107.

420. See Excursus III below on Tarsus and 8.3.1 on Antioch. At best
the Egyptian Isis cult had already taken on the character of a mystery at
that time.

421. W. Heitmüller, 'Zum Problem Paulus und Jesus', *ZNW* 13, 1912;
cited from the reprint in *Das Paulusbild in der neueren Forschung*, ed. K.H.
Rengstorf, WdF 24, Darmstadt 1964, 124–43; Bousset, *Kyrios Christos*

(n.150), 48f., 113ff., 164ff; cf. R. Bultmann, *Primitive Christianity*, London 1956, 156–61; id., *Theology of the New Testament* 1, London and New York 1952, 133–44.

422. Schmithals, *Theologiegeschichte* (n.97), 70ff., 90ff., assumes the massive influence of a 'Jewish gnosis' (or a gnosticizing Judaism) on Paul, which is said to have its origin in Samaria (85) and will already have influenced him in Damascus. We owe the pre-existence christology and the 'pre-Pauline hymn to Christ', Phil. 2.6f., 9–11, and even the Logos hymn, John 1, in its original form to the 'profound thinkers' of Damascene Christianity.

423. Cf. R. Turcan, *Les cultes orientaux dans le monde romain*, Paris 1989, 332; Tubach, *Sonnengott* (n.90), 59; Millar, *Roman Near East* (n.92); also the review by Seth Schwartz (n.91).

424. Cf. Josephus, *Antt.* 3, 214–218: the Urim und Tummim had ceased 200 years before his time, i.e. with the death of John Hyrcanus. Previously God had revealed his presence at the sacrifice by the shining of the stones on the shoulders of the high priest and announced victory in the coming battle through the radiance of the twelve stones of the high-priestly ephod. That this miracle no longer happened was divine punishment for transgressing the law. Cf. 4Q 375; 376 and 1Q 22; 29. The pious in Qumran handed down reports not only of the oracular function of the high-priestly ephod but also of mantic practices and astrology. Horoscopes, brontologies and exorcistic psalms have been found, and in *LibAnt* 53.3ff. – perhaps dependent on a Samuel apocryphon which could also have been in Qumran – Samuel receives from Eli the priestly tradition that in sleep one hears God's voice with the right ear and that of the demons with the left. There is dispute as to how far the Essenes themselves engaged in such practices. At all events, the inspired interpretation of scripture was more important to them than manticism. The Life of Zechariah in the *Vitae Prophetarum* connects the disappearance of the power of divination among the priesthood with the murder of this prophet (II Chron. 24); cf. mSot 9, 12; tSot 13, 2; see Schwemer, *Vitae Prophetarum* II (n.134), 307–20.

425. Cf. Y. Hajjar, 'Divinités oraculaires et rites divinatoires en Syrie et en Phénicie à l'époque gréco-romaine', *ANRW II*, 18, 4, 2236–320 enumerates 44 local gods and goddesses who give oracles. Speaking statues (2290ff.), the interpretation of dreams and incubation (2290ff.), prediction with the help of water (2296ff.), astrology (2298ff.), ornithoscopy and animal omens (2300ff.), decisions by lot (2302f.), oracles by letters (2304), the interpretation of meteorological phenomena, prodigies, and also prophetic ecstasy play a role. The cult personnel of

local sanctuaries, their priests and prophets, made enquiries of the particular deity in ritual purity and received the oracles (2313–20).

426. H. Gunkel, *Zum religionsgeschichtlichen Verständnis des Neuen Testaments*, Göttingen 1903, 35f., 88, 85.

427. M. Hengel, ' "Schriftauslegung" als "Schriftwerdung" ', in *Schriftauslegung im antiken Judentum und im Urchristentum*, ed. M. Hengel and H. Löhr, WUNT 73, Tübingen 1994, 1–71.

428. *BJ* 7, 43–62.

429. 7, 45. Goodman, *Mission* (n.320), 87f., measures these sympathizers too quickly by the criterion of later clear separation and differentiation and the regulations in the rabbinic literature. He does not discuss texts like the sermons of Pseudo-Philo (on which see Excursus I above). The historical picture of this time is distorted if Luke with his information about the godfearers and sympathizers is not taken seriously as a historical source (166 n.27). Luke, presumably himself a former sympathizer, knew this milieu from his own experience. This question had long ceased to be an acute one for Palestinian or even Babylonian Amoraeans of the third to fifth centuries.

430. Acts 8.5; Hengel, 'The Historian Luke' (n.36), 110–9, 124–6.

431. Acts 22.12.

432. Acts 9.11. In a version of the Acts of Paul in a so far unpublished Coptic papyrus this Judas is identified with Judas the brother of the Lord, *NT Apoc* 2, ²1992, 264, and Paul is introduced into the church through him. The text could come from the lost beginning of the Acts of Paul which supplement Luke's fragmentary account. See also below, n.453.

433. Berger, *Theologiegeschichte* (n.188), 234, who puts great trust in Luke's account here, conjectures that Luke is working over 'local traditions about an old Christian group in Damascus'. But did Luke ever visit the city? The source may well above all be Paul himself.

434. Cf. 11.22; 12.1.5; 15.4, 22; 18.22.

435. 15.3 Antioch; 15.41 for the first time in the plural: the communities in Syria and Cilicia; cf.also 16.5; 20.17, 28.

436. Bauer and Aland, *Lexicon*, 1125.

437. Used in the absolute, Acts 19.2, 23; 22.4; 24.14, 22; the use with the genitive is to be distinguished from this, see 18.25f.; II Peter 2.2, 15 in the sense of 'way of salvation'. On this see E. Repo, *Der 'Weg' als Selbstbezeichnung des Christentums*, AASF Ser. B, 132, 2, 1964, 84ff.; his remarks on Damascus are too speculative. See my review in *ThLZ* 92, 1967, 361–4. It is impossible to demonstrate more than a Jewish-Palestinian origin for the metaphor, cf. Jub. 23.20; IV Ezra 14.22 and some Essene examples

(1QS 9.17f.; 10.20f.; CD 1.13; 2.6).

438. Cf. already 9.10: Ananias is μαθητής.

439. Acts 9.20.

440. Acts 9.22.

441. Acts 22.3; cf. 23.6; 5.34 Gamaliel, the νομοδιδάσκαλος τίμιος. In that case his pupil Paul must have been on the best way towards being such a one, cf. Gal. 1.4.

442. Acts 17.34; however, McKnight, *Light* (n.320), 55 concludes from Philo, *SpecLeg* 1, 320ff. that for Philo the Agora '(would be) a specific place of proselytizing ... not the synagogue'. Here false alternatives are set up and Philo's rhetoric is completely misunderstood.

443. See above, 85.

444. Acts 22.12: for a Jewish audience in Jerusalem.

445. In Acts 26.11 the περισσῶς τε ἐμμαινόμενος αὐτοῖς ἐδίωκον ἕως καὶ εἰς τὰς ἔξω πόλεις is to be understood in the sense of a conative imperfect, *Grammatik*, [14]1976, 268 §326.

446. Only in 13.1 does an individual community appear outside Judaea, in Antioch. In 23 instances he only uses the plural twice (15.41; 16.5). The Pauline formula ἐκκλησία θεοῦ appears in the Miletus speech, 20.28. Probably for Luke, too, there was fundamentally only the one ἐκκλησία.

447. I Cor. 15.9; Gal. 1.13; cf. Phil. 3.6.

448. Cf. I Thess. 2.14, etc; cf. below nn.926, 1148, 1541; see also Gal. 1.22, against Berger, *Theologiegeschichte* (n.188), 351, cf.334ff., etc.

449. Against Feldtkeller, *Identitätssuche* (n.88), 168–71, who completely fails to grasp the chronological problem and therefore makes unfounded speculations.

450. Acts 9.9, cf. 19. In 22.12ff. nothing more is said about this. Berger, *Theologiegeschichte* (n.188), 234, wants to see this as 'a reminiscence of fasting before baptism, elsewhere completely unknown to Luke, indeed to the NT as a whole', but all his evidence belongs in the second or third centuries and is only partially relevant. Didache 7.4; Justin, *Apol.* 61, 2; Tertullian, *De bapt.* 20 do not speak about the duration of the fasts; Ps-Clementine *Recognitions* 7, 34, 1, 7 = *Homilies* 13, 9, 3 speaks of only a one-day fast. Acts 9.9, 19 and the prayer in 9.11 are meant to illustrate the intensity of the penitence of the persecutor in narrative form. According to 9.9 Saul cannot even know that he will be baptized. Thus Luke hardly means to refer here to a fixed liturgical custom. The Acts of Paul, which presuppose Acts, know both a community fast and frequently a fast by the hero and others for several days, see C. Schmidt, *Acta Pauli* (Heidelberg Coptic Papyrus), Leipzig [2]1905,

78, index s.v. νηστεύειν, νηστεία and *NT Apocrypha* 2, ²1992, 214f., 220 (Acts of Paul and Thecla, chs. 22, 25). Nowhere here is there any mention of baptism. By contrast Luke mentions fasting only in 13.2f., but mentions baptism often. At best this could be an old custom with John the Baptist and preparation for his baptism of repentance in the Jordan.

451. Matt. 9.18; Mark 5.23; 6.5; 8.23, 25; Luke 4.40; 13.13; Acts 8.17(19); 28.8.

452. Acts 6.6; 13.3; 19.6; I Tim. 5.22, cf. Acts 13.3; 14.23. There was no rabbinic ordination before 70. Cf. Hengel, *The Pre-Christian Paul* (n.51), 224 n.159 [119 n.159] (with bibliography).

453. C. Schmidt, *Gespräche Jesu mit seinen Jüngern nach der Auferstehung*, 1919, reprinted Hildesheim 1967, 100 [= c. 33(44)]: 'That man will come from the land of Cylicia to Damascus in Syria in order to root out the church (community) which it has been granted you to create ..., and he will come quickly.' See also the translation variant by A. Guerrier in the text. C. D. G. Müller in *NT Apocrypha* 1, ²1991, 268: 'which you must create'. For the dating see Hengel, *Johannine Question* (n.33), 59ff. For Jude in the 'street called straight', who in the Coptic Acts of Paulus is identified with a brother of the Lord, see above, n.432.

454. According to the Pseudo-Clementine *Recognitions* 1, 71, 4f. the *inimicus ille homo* (Paul) receives a letter of authority from Caiaphas, to persecute all believers, and rushes first to Damascus because he believes that Peter has fled there. In the Coptic Acts of Matthias. Matthias is given Damascus as mission territory and preaches there: R. A. Lipsius, *Die apokryphen Apostelgeschichten und Apostellegenden* II, 2, 1884 reprinted 1976, 260.

455. In Matt. 4.24 the author may be giving an indication of the origin of his Gospel. The εἰς ὅλην τὴν Συρίαν which follows immediately after the activity in Galilee is an exaggeration. A more realistic area would be: Decapolis, Jerusalem, Judaea and the region beyond the Jordan, 4.25; cf. Mark 3.7f., where Idumaea and the region of the cities of Tyre and Sidon are added; see also Luke 6.17, though the Decapolis is missing. By contrast it appears in Mark in 5.20: the Gerasene who has been healed proclaims in the Decapolis what Jesus has done for him. According to the note in 7.31 – which is geographically quite comprehensible – Jesus himself is active in the Decapolis, see Jones, *Cities* (n.287), 270; Hengel, 'The Historian Luke' (n.36), 193 n.19.

456. Cf. Matt. 10.6; 15.24; cf. 9.36; Mark 2.17. On this see Hengel, 'The Historian Luke' (n.36), 113; id., *Earliest Christianity* (n.25), 78f. With the ἀνὴρ Αἰθίοψ (Acts 8.27) the earliest Christian mission reaches

the south, the former kingdom of the Queen of Sheba (Luke 11.31), who once visited Solomon. Cf. Scott, *Paul* (n.320), 171f., 111f.

457. See Hengel, 'Vorchristlicher Paulus' (n.51), 279 [76]; Riesner, *Frühzeit* (n.49), 209ff.: what is said of Paul there could apply even more to the Hellenists who were expelled from Jerusalem and, according to my hypothesis, fled to Damascus. By contrast I regard the Essene motive as insignificant.

458. The catchword Syria appears in his writing only in Acts 15.23 and 41 along with Cilicia, which recalls Gal. 1.21. We then find Syria first only in 18.18; 20.3; 21.3. Evidently this province was not at the centre of Luke's interest (nor, any longer, that of Paul). This tells against the frequent conjecture that the author came from Antioch. On this cf. n.1052.

459. See Riesner, *Frühzeit* (n.49), 214–27, cf. index 464 ad loc.; Hengel, 'Vorchristlicher Paulus' (n.51), 182f., 201, 219 n.143, 277, 291 [1f., 10, 75f., 117 n.143].

460. Acts 21.8–14.

461. Acts 27.3.

462. PsClem *Hom* 4, 1, 1; 11, 36, 1ff.

463. The most easterly of the three main roads from Palestina to northern Syria (Emesa) went through Damascus. In addition there was also the coastal road and the road through the Biqa'. But the eastern road was almost as important as the coastal road. Another important caravan route led through Palmyra to the Euphrates.

464. Acts 8.5, 26f., see Hengel, 'The Historian Luke' (n.36), 110ff.; id., *Earliest Christianity* (n.25), 78; Scott, *Paul* (n.320), 163f.

465. I myself have used this adjective in earlier publications, but now I would not think it sufficiently precise.

466. For the law of God and the law of Christ cf. Gal. 6.2; 5.13–25; Rom. 12.1–3; 13.8–10.

467. I Cor. 5 and 6; 7.10; 10.1–22; II Cor. 6.14–16; 13.1ff.

468. Acts 6.13f., cf. 6.11; 7.48f.; Mark 15.38; Rom. 3.25; I Cor. 5.7; II Cor. 5.21, on which see Hengel, 'Between Jesus and Paul' (n.50); W. Kraus, *Der Tod Jesu als Heiligtumsweihe*, WMANT 66, 1991, 195ff., 232ff.; P. Stuhlmacher, *Biblische Theologie des Neuen Testaments I. Grundlegung. Von Jesus zu Paulus*, Göttingen 1992, 193f., 196, 233, 335.

469. The third Sibylline oracle, for example, nowhere requires circumcision 'of the Greeks' in so many words. Rather, 'the Greeks' will escape the eschatological catastrophic judgment if they observe the ethical monotheism for which the Gentile primal prophetess praises the people of the Jews, see Sib 3, 711–766 etc.

470. Cf. the sermon *De Jona* cited above, 73.

471. Intervention was necessary only if such arrivals caused unrest and threatened to split the communities; that was the problem in Paul's mission because of his heightened understanding of the law: Acts 13; 16; 18; in Rome cf. Suetonius, *Claudius* 25, 4 and Riesner, *Frühzeit* (n.49), 172–80; cf. also *BJ* 7, 407–421, 437–441, the unrest caused by the Palestinian Sicarii in Alexandria and Cyrene which were fatally dangerous for the Jewish communities.

472. II Cor. 11.24; Acts 9.23–25.

473. Gal 1.23; cf. Acts 9.13, 21. See E. Bammel, 'Gal 1, 23', *ZNW* 59, 1968, 108–12: Paul 'is giving not only in content but also in form a view which is not his, but which is of benefit to him and his cause' (108).

474. Καὶ ἔσται πᾶς, ὅς ἄν ἐπικαλέσεται τὸ ὄνομα κυρίου σωθήσεται· ὅτι ἐν τῷ ὄρει Σιων καὶ ἐν Ιερουσαλημ ἔσται ἀνασῳζόμενος, καθότι εἶπεν ὁ κύριος καὶ εὐαγγελιζόμενοι οὓς κύριος προκέκληται. Cf. Isa. 40.9; 52.7; 60.6; 61.1; cf. Nahum 1.15 (MT 2.1); Ps. 39 (40).9; 67 (68).11; 95 (96).2; PsSol. 11.1; ParJer. 3.11; 5.21 and on this J. Herzer, *Die Paralipomena Jeremiae*, TSAJ 43, 1994, 53f., 61f.; also the use of *biśśar* in the Qumran writings: 1QS viii 14 and the exegesis of Isa. 61.1 and 52.7 in 11QMelch ii 4ff., 16; Matt. 11.5 = Luke 7.22 Q, cf. Luke 4.18 = Isa. 61.1. Luke uses it 25 times, cf. especially Acts 8.4, 12, 25, 35, 40; 11.20; cf. Heb. 4.2, 6; I Peter 1.12, 25; 4.6; Rev. 10.7; 14.6.

475. For the absolute use of πίστις see also Gal. 3.23, 25; 6.10; Acts 6.7; 14.22.

476. Hengel, 'Between Jesus and Paul' (n.50), 24ff.

477. Gal. 1.11; cf. the accumulation in 1.8, 9, 16, 23 and I Cor. 15.1f.; II Cor 11.7; Rom. 1.15.

478. See e.g. still G. Strecker, 'Das Evangelium Jesu Christi', in id., *Eschaton und Historie, Aufsätze*, Göttingen 1979, 183–228: 189ff., 225f.: 'So it may be that the primary basis of the New Testament εὐαγγέλιον is to be sought in the context of Hellenistic ruler worship, which was also shaped by the language of the emperor cult' (191f.). Schnelle, *Einleitung* (n.76), 184. The scarcity of instances and the singular form tell against this. How could a Jewish Christian in Syria, where we have no corresponding imperial inscriptions at all (see the indices of *IGLS* III–VIII), and the word does not appear in connection with the emperor cult, take precisely this as a model and make it the central term of his messsage?

479. See P. Stuhlmacher, *Das paulinische Evangelium* I, FRLANT 95, Göttingen 1968, 63–108; id., *Theologie* I (n.468), 315; against Strecker, 'Evangelium' (n.478).

480. Klaus Berger's statement (*Theologiegeschichte*, n.188), 236, 'Paul

need not have understood himself as apostle to the Gentiles immediately after his Damascus experience. Rather, here Christianity is first of all visible as a crisis within Judaism', rests on a false alternative beloved of New Testament scholars. As a preacher addressing the sympathizers, i.e. the ἔθνη in the synagogues, Paul *accentuated* the 'crisis within Judaism' caused by the new messianic message of the death and resurrection of Jesus the Christ because he broke more strongly than the Hellenists with the Torah as the presupposition for salvation and grounded this on Christ alone. This grounding had to lead him to the 'Gentiles'.

481. Cf. even I Cor. 7.29 and Phil. 4.5.

482. I Cor. 1.1; II Cor. 1.1; cf. Rom 1.1 and Gal. 1.1.

483. Rom. 1.5. According to Gal. 1.15–17 this certainty was there from the beginning; by contrast the geographical framework of the 'nations' expanded gradually. For the relationship of the Pauline mission to the list of nations and its Jewish interpretation see Scott, *Paul* (n.320).

484. Rom. 1.1: ἀφωρισμένος εἰς εὐαγγέλιον θεοῦ.

485. See now 4Q MMT C 7 (= 4Q397 14–21), ed. E. Qimron and J. Strugnell, *Qumran Cave 4. V Miqṣat Ma'aśe ha-Torah*, DJD X, Oxford 1994, 58, the 'separation' (*pārašnu mᵉrob ha'am*: we have separated from the multitude of the people) of the Qumran Essenes from the people for reasons of obedience to the Torah.

486. εἰς τὸ εἶναί με λειτουργὸν Χριστοῦ Ἰησοῦ εἰς τὰ ἔθνη, ἱερουργοῦντα τὸ εὐαγγέλιον τοῦ θεοῦ.

487. Jer. 1.5; Isa. 49.1, 5; cf. Rom. 10.16 = Isa. 53.1 LXX.

488. For the creative linguistic power of the first Greek-speaking community already in Jerusalem itself see above, 92.

489. See the verb ἀποστέλλειν or ἐξαποστέλλειν = *šālaḥ*: Isa. 6.8; 48.16; 61.1; Jer. 1.7; Ezek. 2.3 etc.; but see also Moses, Ex. 3.10 and 3.1–4.17 generally and Jonah, who on being sent to pagan Nineveh wants to flee.

490. II Cor. 6.2 = Isa. 49.8; Rom. 8.1; 10.15; 11.31f.; cf. I Cor. 10.11; Rom. 13.4.

491. I Cor. 9.5; 7.7, 40; cf. Jer. 16.1–3.

492. Cf. Jer. 4.19; 16.1–4; 20.7–9 and for the 'Confessions' of Jeremiah the Pauline catalogue of sufferings, for which see H. Rengstorf, *TDNT* 1, 439–41; against this, however, cf. J. Munck, *Paul and the Salvation of Mankind*, London 1959, 29f. and now K. O. Sandnes, *Paul – One of the Prophets*, WUNT II/43, Tübingen 1991, 5f., 117–19, who among other passages also refers to Sib. 3, 295, cf. 162ff. and 490.

493. I Cor. 9, 16f. Cf. W. Schrage, *Der erste Brief an die Korinther*, EKK VII/2, 322–6. For the difference on Jonah see 73f., 176 above.

494. Rom. 1.1; cf. II Cor. 4.5; Gal. 1.10; Phil. 1.10.

495. I Cor. 4, 1f.: ὑπηρέτας Χριστοῦ καὶ οἰκονόμους μυστηρίων θεοῦ. In Paul ὑπηρέτης appears only here; elsewhere he has διάκονος, cf. II Cor. 11.23, διάκονοι Χριστοῦ; I Cor. 3.5; II Cor. 3.6; Eph.3.7; Col. 1.23, 25. For Paul as ὑπηρέτης, however, cf. Acts 26.16. Cf. also Luke 16.1ff.

496. II Cor. 11.2, 29; cf. Gal 1.14; II Cor. 7.7; Phil. 3.6.

497. Rom. 4.5; 5.10: ἐχθροὶ ὄντες; 5.6 ὑπὲρ ἀσεβῶν; 5.10: ἔτι ἁμαρταλῶν ὄντων; I Cor. 5.16; 4.4.

498. Rom. 4.5; I Thess. 5.4f.; II Cor. 4.4f.; Rom. 6.1–19; 4.5; 5.20; cf. Col.1.13; I Tim. 1.15; Luke 18.9–14; 15.1ff. See also W. Nestle, 'Legenden vom Tod der Gottesverächter', *ARW* 33, 1936, 246–69.

499. I Cor. 15.9; cf. I Cor. 9.1f.

500. F. Lang, *Die Briefe an die Korinther*, NTD 7, Göttingen, etc. 1986, 118, rightly emphasizes on I Cor. 9.16 that 'Paul's understanding of the apostolate is fundamentally shaped by his call'.

501. Rom. 5.9; 6.19; 7.6; 8.1; 11.30; II Cor. 5.16; Gal. 1.13; 4.9 etc.

502. Rom. 1.14f.; I Cor. 9.19ff.

503. See 4.2 above.

504. 1 Macc. 1.11 is the closest parallel to καὶ κύκλῳ (the nations around); cf. also nn.553, 678, 903 below.

505. I Cor. 15.1–11. I Cor. 15.3b–5 probably comprised the 'gospel' in the form of a 'confession' with a catechetical formulation which narrated the events very briefly and interpreted them. However, at that time he also communicated to the Corinthians what is reported in vv.6–8. For its significance cf. v.11. Against H. Conzelmann, *I Corinthians*, Hermeneia, Philadelphia 1975, *ad loc.*; id, 'Zur Analyse der Bekenntnisformel 1 Kor 15, 3–5', in id., *Theologie als Schriftauslegung*, BEvTh 65, Munich 1974, 138. We do not know where and how Paul gave it its present form; however, in our view this was relatively early.

506. M. Hengel, 'Erwägungen zum Sprachgebrauch von Χριστός bei Paulus und in der "vorpaulinischen" Überlieferung', in *Paul and Paulinism, FS C. K. Barrett*, ed. M.D. Hooker and S.G. Wilson, London 1982, 135–59; id., 'Jesus, der Messias Israels', in *Messiah and Christos, FS Flusser*, ed. I. Gruenwald et al., TSAJ 32, Tübingen 1992, 155ff.; id., *Studies in Early Christology* (n.117), 1–7.

507. Deut. 21.23; 27.26; cf. I Cor. 1.23; 2.2; Gal. 3.1; 3.13; I Cor. 1.17f.; II Cor. 5.20; Gal. 5.11; 6.12, 14; Phil. 2.8; 3.18: Hengel, 'Crucifixion' (n.72).

508. A saying like Mark 10.45 could also have played a role here, see M. Hengel, *The Atonement. The Origins of the Doctrine in the New Testament*, London 1981, 34ff., 42, 49, 53, 71, 73; reprinted in id., *The Cross of the Son of God*, London 1986, 222ff., 230, 237, 241, 259, 261; Stuhlmacher, *Theologie* I (n.468), 120ff., 127–30, etc.; O. Hofius, 'Herrenmahl und

Herrenmahlparadosis', in id., *Paulusstudien*, WUNT 51, Tübingen 1989, 225f., 339, on the relationship between words of interpretation and the eucharistic prayers which have been preserved in the epicleses and anaphoras of the early church (335f.).

509. See the composite volume edited by B. Janowski and P. Stuhlmacher, *Der leidende Gottesknecht. Jes 53 und seine Wirkungsgeschichte, mit einer Bibliographie zu Jes 53*, FAT 14, Tübingen 1996.

510. Cf. Hengel, 'Between Jesus and Paul' (n.50), 21–4.

511. Cf. also Luke's references to the 'hanging on the tree' of Deut. 21.23 in the preaching of Peter and Paul, Acts 5.30; 10.39; 13.29, though they have been very much toned down in keeping with his theology.

512. Gal. 3.13; cf. I Cor. 12.3 and the reversal of this curse in I Cor. 16.22. For the charge against Jesus of leading people astray see A. Strobel, *Die Stunde der Wahrheit*, WUNT 21, Tübingen 1980, and his references to Deut. 13 and 17.54–61. Cf. also the Baraitha bSanh 43a.

513. Cf. the charge against Stephen in Acts 6.11: λαλοῦντος ῥήματα βλάσφημα εἰς Μωϋσῆν καὶ τὸν θεόν. For the reaction see Acts 26.11. Indeed Jesus himself had been accused of blasphemy, Mark 14.64.

514. Gal. 1.14; Phil. 3.6; Acts 22.3; cf. also II Cor. 11.2; on this see Hengel, 'Vorchristlicher Paulus' (n.51), 200, 236, 240, 253, 268f., 283–92 [9, 36, 41, 50, 65, 79–86].

515. See the characterization in I Tim. 1.13: τὸ πρότερον ὄντα βλάσφημον καὶ διώκτην καὶ ὑβριστήν, which though late, is apt.

516. See the question of the risen Christ in the audible vision which is repeated three times by Luke: ... τί με διώκεις and the stereotyped answer: ἐγώ εἰμι Ἰησοῦς ὃν σὺ διώκεις: 9.4; cf. 22.7; 26.14. In my view this kernel of the Damascus vision ultimately goes back to Paul's own account of it.

517. See Acts 5.39 and the addition 23.9 in the majority text μὴ θεομαχῶμεν; on this see O. Bauernfeind, *TDNT* 4, 528. In II Macc. 7.19 the verb is used in connection with Antiochus IV Epiphanes. See also A. Schalit, *ANRW* II 2, 268ff., nn.124–6 and Nestle, 'Gottesverächter' (n.498), 250, 264ff. Like Josephus (*Antt.* 14, 310; *c. Ap* 1, 246, 263), Luke deliberately uses this motif, which comes from Euripides' *Bacchae* (45, 325, 1255, cf. 635). For the proverbial πρὸς κέντρα λακτίζειν (Acts 26.14) see *Bacchae* 795.

518. Cf. I Cor. 15.9.

519. Acts 9.8f.; 22.11.

520. Rom. 4.25: the antithetical parallelism points to an old formula, knowledge of which Paul presupposes in Rome, similarly Rom. 1.3f.; behind it stands Isa. 53.12 LXX; cf. 5.8–11; 8.31f.

521. Rom. 3.25; 5.8–12; 8.3ff; II Cor. 5.14f., 18–20.

522. Against E. P. Sanders, *Paul and Palestinian Judaism*, London and Philadelphia 1977, 446f. Bultmann's concept of 'decision' is also misleading here: everything depends on the decision of God in Christ which has already taken place.

523. Gal. 1.15: καὶ καλέσας διὰ τῆς χάριτος αὐτοῦ.

524. Hengel, 'Vorchristlicher Paulus' (n.51), 253f. [50f.]; for further parallels see H. Braun, *Qumran und das Neue Testament* I, Tübingen 1966, 169–240; for the parallel to ἔργα νόμου cf. especially 1QS 6, 18; 4QMMT C 27 and B 2: מעשי התורה or מעשי בתירה or simply מעשים, see E. Qimron and J. Strugnell, DJD X, 62 and the commentary on p.139 (with earlier literature). The term מעשים has the same meaning as מעשי התורה; they are interchangable in the manuscripts of the rule of the sect; for the frequency cf. J. H. Charlesworth, *Graphic Concordance to the Dead Sea Scrolls*, Tübingen and Louisville 1991, 407f. etc.; in 4Qflor I, 7 perhaps מעשי התורה is to be read; Avemarie, *Tora* (n.9), 584–8.

525. See Hengel, 'Erwägungen' (n.506), 135–59; D. Zeller, 'Zur Transformation des χριστός bei Paulus', *JBTh* 8, 1993, 155–67.

526. Gal. 3.13; 4.4; cf. I Cor. 6.20; 7.23. The terminology is not specifically Pauline, cf. Rev. 5.9; 14.3f. See also above 367 n.392f. on the Jewish sermon *de Jona*.

527. Luke 10.21f. = Matt. 11.26f.; cf. Mark 1.11; 9.7; 14.36; see also Hengel, 'Son of God' (n.117). The Aramaic son of God text 4Q 246 makes it more likely that 'son of God' was a Jewish messianic honorific title, cf. already the messianic interpretation of the quotation from II Sam. 7.11–14 in 4Qflor I. 10–12, followed in 18f. by the quotation of Ps. 2, which unfortunately breaks off. For the unity of messiah and son of God see Ps. 2.2, 7 and 39.52; 89.28. For 4Q 246 see E. Puech, 'Fragment d'une apocalypse en araméen (4Q246 = pseudo-Dan^d) et le "Royaume de Dieu"', *RB* 99, 1992, 98–131, and the detailed analysis by J. Zimmermann in his 1997 Tübingen dissertation on messianic figures in Qumran.

528. Hengel, 'Son of God' (n.117), 10, 86–90; Stuhlmacher, *Theologie* I (n.468), 305ff., 313ff.

529. I Cor. 16.22; cf. Rev. 22.21, see H.-P. Rüger, 'Zum Problem der Sprache Jesu', *ZNW* 59, 1968, 113–22: 120f. See also above 120–6 and below nn.632–50 on contemporary parallels.

530. Hengel, '"Sit at My Right Hand!"' (n.117), 119–225.

531. I Cor. 9, 1.

532. Acts 9.14, 21; 22.16, cf. 2.21; 15.27; Rom. 10.13; I Cor. 1.2. Feldtkeller, *Identitätssuche* (n.88), 168–71, wants to see this invocation of

the Kyrios as a specific feature of the 'sympathizers' scene' in Damascus, so it would then become a criterion for Paul 'acquired in Damascus'. However, this invocation goes back to the earliest community in Jerusalem and in its Greek form to the 'Hellenists', who also used it in Damascus from the beginning as a matter of course. It has nothing to do with itinerant Galilean radicals, about whom one can only speculate. It is significant that Joel 3.5 plays no role in the Synoptic tradition.

533. In the NT only in quotations: Heb. 2.6 = Ps. 8.5; Rev. 1.13; 4.14 = Dan. 7.13. Cf. also LXX Num. 24.17b: ἀναστήσεται ἄνθρωπος ἐξ Ισραηλ.

534. In Acts 7.55f. Luke indicates that it was used in the earliest community and by the Hellenists. This reference is typical of the historically thought-out way in which he deals with christological titles and formulae. Cf. Hengel, 'Between Jesus and Paul' (n.50), 27f.; id., *Earliest Christianity* (n.25), 104.

535. Phil. 2.6–11; I Cor. 8.6; 10.4; Rom. 8.3; Gal. 4.4; II Cor. 8.9; cf. Col. 1.15–18. See my contribution to the volume *Die Mitte der Schrift* dedicated to O. Hofius.

536. Luke 7.35 = Matt. 11.19; Luke 11.49, cf. Matt. 23.34; cf. Luke 13.34f. = Matt. 23.37f.; Luke 11.31 = Matt. 12.42. On this see M. Hengel, 'Jesus als messianischer Lehrer der Weisheit und die Anfänge der Christologie', in *Sagesse et Religion, Colloque de Strasbourg (octobre 1976)*, Paris 1979, 147–88 = *Early Christology* (n.117), 73–117; see also R. Riesner, *Jesus als Lehrer*, WUNT II/7, Tübingen ³1988, 330–43; H. Gese, 'Die Weisheit, der Menschensohn und die Ursprünge der Christologie als konsequente Entfaltung der biblischen Theologie', in id., *Alttestamentliche Studien*, Tübingen 1991, 218–48.

537. G. Schimanowski, *Weisheit und Messias*, WUNT II/17, Tübingen 1985; on this N. Walter, *ThLZ* 112, 1987, 896–8.

538. On this J. Schaper, *Eschatology in the Greek Psalter*, WUNT II/76, 1995, 101–7, 141f.; see also id., 'Der Septuagintapsalter als Dokument jüdischer Eschatologie', in M. Hengel and A. M. Schwemer (eds.), *Die Septuaginta zwischen Judentum und Christentum*, WUNT 72, Tübingen 1994, 53ff.

539. For Justin see Hengel, ' "Sit at My Right Hand!" ' (n.117), 126f. Hos. 6.2 is first of all quoted in Tertullian (*Marc* 4, 23, 1; A*dv. Iudaeos* 13, 23), but the whole of 'critical scholarship' believes that the 'on the third day' in I Cor. 15.4 is to be derived from there! Ps. 80 (LXX 79).15–18, which is not cited in the NT at all, would certainly have been interpreted christologically.

540. Rom. 6.14f.; I Cor. 9.20; Gal. 4.4f., 21.

541. Rom. 7.12, 14. The apostle is thinking here above all of the

Decalogue (especially the first) or the commandment to love, which cannot be restricted by casuistry, see Rom. 13.8ff.; Gal. 5.14; cf. also Rom. 7: οὐκ ἐπιθυμήσεις, Rom. 7.7 = Ex. 20.17; Deut. 5.21 LXX. Rom. 1.18ff. begins by mentioning sins against the first commandment.

542. Rom. 6.23; 4.15; 7.7–24; II Cor. 3.6b.

543. Cf. Phil. 3.6ff, cf. Rom. 5.10.

544. Sir 24; mAb 3.14; cf. Hengel, *Judaism and Hellenism* (n.314), I, 98, 128, 153f., 159f., 169ff.; Schimanowski, *Weisheit* (n.537), 217ff.

545. We find formulations with a relatively archaic ring in an apocalyptic context in Rev. 3.14 and 10.38.

546. See M.Hengel, 'Hymnus und Christologie', in *Wort in der Zeit, Festgabe für Karl Heinrich Rengstorf zum 75. Geburtstag*, ed.W.Haubeck and M.Bachmann, Leiden 1980, 1–23 = id., *Between Jesus and Paul* (n.50), 78–96; id., 'Das Christuslied im frühesten Gottesdienst', in *Weisheit Gottes – Weisheit der Welt, Festschrift für Joseph Kardinal Ratzinger zum 60. Geburtstag*, St Ottilien 1987, 1, 357–404 = id., *Studies in Early Christology* (n.117), 227–91.

547. On this see the Tübingen dissertation by U. Mittmann-Richert, *Magnifikat und Benediktus* (n.230).

548. Gal. 3.24.

549. Rom. 3.2; 1.4f.; cf. 15.8.

550. Gal 3.23; cf. Rom. 3.2.

551. Rom. 3.19f.; 4.5; cf. 5.1–11, 20f. and Rom. 7.7–25, which is not written autobiographically but from the perspective of believing self-knowledge. Cf. already Luke 18.9–14; Mark 2.17.

552. *The Mysticism of Paul the Apostle*, London ²1953, 225: "The doctrine of righteousness by faith is therefore a subsidiary crater, which has formed within the rim of the main crater – the mystical doctrine of redemption through the being-in-Christ. That it is an unnatural construction of thought is clear from the fact that by means of it Paul arrives at the idea of a faith which rejects not only works of the law but works in general. Thus he has shut off the road to ethics.' The Neo-Kantian and liberal Neo-Protestant Schweitzer did not understand the inner consistency with which the Pharisaic scribe took up the 'revelation of Jesus Christ'. Paul can lay the foundations for an 'ethic of grace' which alone merits the designation *Christian* only on his doctrine of justification: the works of the flesh stand over against the fruit of the Spirit: Gal. 5.22f. against 5.18ff. All boasting is excluded (Rom. 3, 27), for every good and necessary work is God's work in us (Phil. 2.13). Is there a more liberating form of ethics than this?

553. Becker, *Paulus* (n.61), 37, cf. 87, keeps quiet about the stay in

Arabia and emphasizes that alongside 'Mesopotamia, Arabia ... (is) not in the apostle's perspective ... As a Jew he does not think further south than Jerusalem.' This contradicts the apostle's own testimony who at this point (Gal. 1.17) speaks of his stay in Arabia, of which, according to Gal. 4.24f., he has geographical knowledge, and sums up Damascus and Arabia in Rom. 15.19 (on this see below, n.903) in the phrase 'Jerusalem καὶ κύκλῳ'.

554. I recently had to write the obituary of the distinguished classical scholar Günther Zuntz (1902–1992) (*Proceedings of the British Academy*, 87, 1994, 493–522). At that time Zuntz's daughter wrote how much information there was in it about the earlier days of her father which she had not known. I myself only got to know Zuntz in 1976, but after that was often with him. Here too the fortuitousness of the biographical information and the gaps in it, along with the sources of error bound up with this, caused me great difficulty, although I had information from the family and from older friends.This helped me to understand Luke's way of working better. He had to write his 'Life of Paul', related to mission in a readable continuous narrative which was at the same time 'edifying theology' in the best sense of the term. I had a similar experience in 1995 with the obituary of Kurt Aland. My own work on biographies makes me lenient towards the New Testament narrators.

555. Tertullian, *De bapt.*17.5.

556. Cf. 1, 8; 26, 20; see Burchard, *Zeuge* (n.5), 161: 'As the only preacher in Acts Paul works in Jerusalem and to the ends of the earth.'

557. It is the decisive event with which the information about the 'new time' begins. The ἔπειτα and the 'three years' are to be related to the ὅτε of 1.16 and not to later interim events. The εἰς Ἀραβίαν is not a mere 'alibi', thus O. Linton, 'The Third Aspect', *StTh* 3, 1949, 79–95: 84. For criticism of Linton's thesis see Burchard, *Zeuge* (n.5), 159f. 'But I remained in Damascus' would have been enough as an 'alibi' for Jerusalem. Rather, the reference to the (missionary) journey in 'Arabia' is meant among other things to demonstrate his independence from the Christians in Damascus, although this is problematical.

558. For the chronology see H. Lietzmann, *An die Galater*, HNT 10, ³1953, 8, on Gal. 1.18, taking up E. Schwartz, *NGWG.PH* 1907, 274 = *Gesammelte Schriften* 5, 1963, 138. Riesner, *Frühzeit* (n.49), 78f., 227–31, gives only the year of Aretas IV's death as a '*terminus ante quem*'and is very sceptical about the mission in Arabia, because he does not want to reckon with a 'Gentile mission' at such an early date.

559. H. Schlier, *Der Brief an die Galater*, KEK [12]1962, 56: 'the formula-tion ἐν τοῖς ἔθνεσιν means the *region* ... which Paul is assigned for

mission'; J. Murphy-O'Connor, 'Paul in Arabia', *CBQ* 55, 1993, 732–7. Gnilka, *Paulus* (n.198), 49f., conjectures: 'If Paul engaged in mission, he turned to Jews and proselytes. A direct mission to the Gentiles would have to be ruled out.' Gnilka sees the reason why Paul went to 'inhospitable Arabia' (50) as being resistance to his fellow believers. All this contradicts both Paul's information in Gal. 1 and that in Acts.

560. Acts 26.17f.; 9.15, cf. 22.15: πρὸς πάντας ἀνθρώπους, cf. 22.21: εἰς ἔθνη μακράν.

561. The starting point is the 'prophecy' in Deut. 32.21 LXX, see R. H. Bell, *Provoked to Jealousy. The Origin and Purpose of the Jealousy Motif in Romans 9–11*, WUNT II/63, Tübingen 1994, see index 430 ad loc. He too emphasizes the fundamental role of the godfearers. Paul, he argues, presupposes above all Christian former 'godfearers' from the synagogue as readers of Romans, 70f., 77f., taking up Schmithals and Lampe. See also 312ff. on Acts 13, 45; 327f. (excursus): 'The success of the Pauline mission among this synagogue fringe would inevitably provoke Israel to jealousy.'

562. Israel is already called God's son or sons in many ways in the Old Testament, see Fohrer and Schweizer, υἱός κτλ, *TDNT* 8, 347–57. Cf. Gal. 6.16; 3.7; Rom. 4.16; 9.6, 8.

563. See Jeremias in *Abba* (n.77), 132–8. As an exception to the rule, Luke also describes Philip's mission in Samaria, his being sent by the angel along the road to Gaza, his transportation to Ashdod and finally his settling in Caesarea Maritima (Acts 8) according to the model of the Old Testament prophets. Cf. above, n.259; for Paul and Philip see below, 411 n.784.

564. Cf. Sandnes, *Paul* (n.492), 59–64, etc.

565. This becomes vividly clear in the account of the voyage in Acts 27.21–25, 31, 33–38, 42f.; cf. Meyer, *Ursprung* (n.25), 27–36. For his relationship to Barnabas see above, 205–9.

566. Mark 1.12 = Matt. 4.1 cf. Luke 4.1 ἐν τῷ ἐρήμῳ and Mark 1.4 par.

567. Meyer, *Ursprung* (n.25), 345, see also below, n.743 and above, n.188.

568. Rom. 15.20; cf. I Cor. 3.10; 10.15ff. See also 7.1 above on Tarsus.

569. Ed. H. I. Vogels, CSEL 81, 3, 1969, 15.

570. Schlier, *Galater* (n.559), 57, speaks of the 'lonely way of the extraordinary apostle'.

571. For the Nabataeans see A. Negev, 'The Nabateans and the Provincia Arabia', *ANRW* II 8, 520–686; for the extension of the area of settlement see the map, ibid., 530 fig. 3; Schürer I, 574–86; Wenning, *Nabatäer* (n.278); Paul is using a piece of geographical information which

could not have been understood otherwise at that time. Cf. Diodorus Siculus 19, 94, 1; 94, 4: the Nabataeans surpass all the other Arabian tribes in wealth. See also 40, 4, 4, 1: Pompey subdues 'Aristobulus, king of the Jews, Aretas, of the Nabataean Arabs ... Judaea, Arabia'. Cf. Strabo 16, 4, 2 for the situation of 'Arabia' bordering on Palestine. However, he wrongly identifies the Nabataeans with the Idumaeans; he says that they voluntarily joined forces with the Jews as the result of a rebellion! See also the description of Syria in Pliny the Elder, *Nat. hist.* 5, 66: *namque Palestine vocabatur qua contigit Arabas, et Iudaea et Coele* ... and 74 on the Decapolis. Appian, *Bellum civile* 2, 71 (Stern, *GLAJ* II, 187): Pompey subdues τὸ Ἑβραίων γένος καὶ Ἄραβες οἱ τούτων ἐχόμενοι. See also C. Ptolemaeus, *Geogr.* 5, 16: the frontiers of the 'Arabia of Petra' are bordered in the East by Egypt, and in the north by Palestine/Judaea or Syria; cf. also n.607 below on Josephus, for whom 'Arabia' denotes the Nabataean kingdom and 'Arabs' the Nabataeans. For the Decapolis and Arabia see Bietenhard, 'Dekapolis' (n.283), 227–30, who rightly emphasized that the geographical details are somewhat blurred. Authors like Polybius and Strabo who base themselves on the older Hellenistic sources and do not know the area still like to regard Transjordan as part of Arabia, in contrast to Josephus, who reckons it with Coele Syria and distinguishes the Decapolis from Arabia. Here we have an expression of the difference between the Hellenistic period and Roman rule. Wenning, *Nabatäer* (n.278) and 'Dekapolis' (n.278), emphasizes on the basis of the archaeological evidence that the Nabataean influence in the cities of the Decapolis should not be overestimated; indeed in parts it was astonishingly small. Paul, who knew the area better, would have made a distinction here, as does Josephus (see below, n.576); so too do Mark and Matthew, who with historical correctness speak only of the Decapolis. The conjecture of Bietenhard, 'Dekapolis' (225f.), that in Paul 'Arabia' means only the Decapolis, is quite unfounded. That would not correspond to the terminology of the first century CE, for which 'Arabia' is clearly the Nabataean kingdom. The reference to the *Provincia Arabia* in Haenchen, *Acts* (n.5), 334 and Betz, *Galatians* (n.152), 73, is wrong, since this was established only after the annexation of the Nabataean kingdom by Trajan in 106 CE, including places of the Decapolis like Kanatha, Gerasa and Philadelphia.

572. This misunderstanding is close in Linton, 'Aspect' (n.557), 84; he is followed by Munck, *Paul* (n.492), 93 n.1.

573. Ambrosiaster (n.569) anachronistically thinks that he wanted to forestall the false apostles, who were preaching Judaism there.

574. For the Nabataeans and their relationship to the Jews, see the account by A. Kasher, *Jews, Idumaeans and Arabs*, TSAJ 18, Tübingen

1988, though this has a strongly nationalistic colouring, see index 263 s.v. 'Nabataeans'; Schürer I, 574–86, and index 3, 966f.

575. See Bill. IV, 1, 379–81(c+e). However, with regard to Ruth this prohibition was limited to men and probably was only theoretical, see the controversy mJad 4, 4 between R. Gamaliel II and R. Jehoshua over an Ammonite proselyte. The later argued that the Ammonites and Moabites had disappeared as a result of Sennacherib's mixing of the peoples. According to Judith 14.10, Achior, the leader of the Ammonites, becomes a proselyte, despite Deut. 23.4.

576. *BJ* 5, 159f.; cf. *Antt.* 5, 82: the region determined by lot by Joshua for the tribe of Simeon comprises Idumaea and borders on Arabia and Egypt. For Josephus' terminology see e.g. *Antt.* 13, 375; in 15, 111 the Nabataean king Malichus I is called Ἄραψ 110–11, Ἀραβία is said to be a Nabataean realm and the Nabataeans are described as Ἄραβες.

577. Targ Isa 60.6, 7 twice 'ᵃrābāʿē; 60, 7: nᵉbāyōt, cf. Ps. 70.2 (LXX).

578. *Dial.* 34, 4 = Ps. 72.10: βασιλεῖς Ἀρράβων; 77, 4; 78, 1f., 7, 8; 88, 1; 102; 103, 3; 106.4; here he connects Damascus with Arabia, though it is now part of Syro-Phoenicia, 78, 10.

579. *Antt.* 18, 109–115, 120–126. According to Josephus some of the Jews regarded this defeat as a punishment for the execution of John the Baptist by Antipas. See Schürer I, 344–50; H. W. Hoehner, *Herod Antipas*, SNTS.MS 17, 1972, 255; A. Kasher, *Idumaeans* (n.574), 176–83; G. W. Bowersock, *Roman Arabia*, London 1983, 65–8 with information about the chronology and the political situation.

580. *Antt.* 18.113: Γαμαλικη Ms A; Γαμαλίτιδι MWE; *Gamalica*, Lat. For the various conjectures see the information in Niese and Feldman, ad loc. See also Bowersock, *Arabia* (n.579), 65f.; Kasher, *Idumaeans* (n.574), 181f. According to *Antt.* 18, 114, fugitives from the tetrarchy of Philip who were fighting on Antipas' side betrayed him: these were probably troops who had joined his army after Philip's death. Cf. already Herod's difficulties (Josephus, *Antt.* 15, 345–48, 351–53).

581. Murphy-O'Connor, 'Paul' (n.559), 733, thinks that Paul had immediately had to withdraw from the mission in the Nabataean region and that three years after his stay in Arabia the Nabataeans had tracked him down in Damascus. Ambrosiaster (n.569) is probably too edifying: *reversus est Damascum, ut visitaret quibus rudis praedicaverat evangelium dei.*

582. See Schürer I, 581ff.; Bowersock, *Arabia* (n.579), 57–65.

583. Bowersock, *Arabia* (n.579), 61.

584. 16, 4, 21 C 779, see Bowersock, *Arabia* (n.579), n.10. For Athenodoras see also below, 425 n.887.

585. In Hegra (Mada'in Ṣāliḥ) there is a series of Jewish tombs, cf.

Negev, 'Nabateans' (n.571), 581; cf. already Ps. 120.5. A stone sundial
from Māda'in Ṣaliḥ bore the name of the Jewish owner, *mnš' br ntn*,
i.e. Manasseh bar Natan. It comes from the first century CE, see J.F.
Healey, 'A Nabatean Sundial from Mada'in Salih', *Syria* 66, 1989, 331–6,
see 334 nn.18–21 on the Jews in this region. The collection of inscriptions by S. Noja, 'Testimoni anche epigrafiche di Giudei nell'Arabia
settentrionale', *Bibbia e Oriente* 21, 1979, 283–316, is particularly important here.

586. Negev, 'Nabateans' (n.571), 581; Schürer III, 1, 16f.; *The
Documents from the Bar Kokhba Period in the Cave of Letters. Greek Papyri*, ed.
N. Lewis et al., Jerusalem 1989. Nabataean is basically an Aramaic
dialect, cf. K. Beyer, *Die aramäischen Texte vom Toten Meer*, Göttingen
1984, 40ff.

587. See H.M. Cotton, 'The Archive of Salome Komaise Daughter of
Levi: Another Archive from the "Cave of Letters"', *ZPE* 105, 1995, 171–
207. There are also references to the earlier publications there. For the
later dissemination of Greek in this area cf. the Greek names cited by A.
Negev, 'Personal Names in the Nabatean Realm', *Qedem* 32, 1991, 204–7;
the frequency of the name ΑΒΡΑΑΜΙΟΣ is particularly striking (ibid.,
208); it appears above all in later Christian inscriptions.

588. Millar, *Roman Near East* (n.92), 19f., 95–8, 404f., 414–17. For the
later Hellenization of the towns and villages of the Hauran cf. M. Sartre,
'Le peuplement et le développement du Hawran antique à la lumière
des inscriptions grecques et latines', in Dentzer, *Hauran* I (n.276), 194f.,
198–202.

589. The Jewish settlement at Petra, i.e. Jewish 'Petra', was probably
called Reqem. In rabbinic literature, Reqem is identified both with Petra
and with the biblical Kadesh, see Reeg, *Ortsnamen* (n.313), 592ff. (on the
different proposals for identification and localization); cf. G. Schmitt,
Siedlungen Palästinas in griechisch-römischer Zeit, BTAVO B 93, Wiesbaden
1995, 276. Josephus, *Antt.* 4, 161 shows that this tradition is older.
He identifies Petra, Reqem and Kadesh, for it was there that Aaron
ascended Mount Hor, on which he lies buried (*Antt.* 4, 82f.). According
to Num. 20.22, Mount Hor lay near Kadesh. It is also presupposed that
Aaron lies buried on Hor near Petra in the first-century CE Life of
Jeremiah in the *Vitae Prophetarum* (*VP*), cf. Schwemer, *Vitae Prophetarum* I,
TSAJ 49, Tübingen 1995, 230f. The Targums also identify Kadesh with
Petra/Reqem. This localization is similarly attested in Eusebius,
Onomastikon (Klostermann 176, 7f.) and has come down to the present
day in the name Jebel Harun (= Mount Aaron).

590. Hengel, 'Vorchristlicher Paulus' (n.51), 209ff. [15ff.]; Riesner,

Frühzeit (n.49), 130f., inclines more towards Lampe's suggestion that Paul 'made tents for private individuals out of linen and precious material', and that his training in the craft lies in his Christian period (131); cf. Haacker, 'Werdegang' (n.140), 920.

591. Τὸ δὲ Ἁγὰρ Σινᾶ ὄρος ἐστὶν ἐν τῇ Ἀραβίᾳ. For this see H. Gese in *Vom Sinai zum Zion*, BevTh 64, Munich 1974, 49–62.The text of Nestle/ Aland²⁶ is clearly the *lectio difficilior*.

592. H. Gese, Ἁγάρ (n.591), 59f.

593. For the significance of the descent of Abraham, Hagar and Ishmael for the self-understanding of early Islam see P. Crone and M. Cook, *Hagarism. The Making of the Islamic World*, Cambridge 1977, 12–15.

594 . Cf. the instances cited by Gese, Ἁγάρ (n.591), 59–61; see also Strabo 16, 4, 24 and above all Negev, 'Nabateans' (n.571), 577–84, with numerous illustrations of the tombs. Greek language and elements of style can still be demonstrated even here. In addition there is the Life of Jeremiah in the *VP* (2, 14), according to which Sinai lies between the mountains on which Moses (Nebo) and Aaron (Hor) are buried; for Hor near Petra, cf. above, n.589. As a later text, Targ. Neofiti has *ḥalūṣa*, the Nabataean capital in the Negeb, instead of *ḥagra* throughout, see Josephus, *Antt.* 14, 18, identical with the Elusa (Khalasa) of the Madaba map; on this see C. Möller and G. Schmitt, *Siedlungen Palästinas nach Flavius Josephus*, BTAVO.B 14, 1976, 144f. This identification is clearly secondary and was made when *ḥagra* had lost its significance after the end of the Nabataean kingdom in 106 CE. For Hegra (Madā'in Ṣaliḥ) and its role under Aretas IV see also Bowersock, *Arabia* (n.579), 48f., 57, 60–2, 70f., 88; for Jewish settlement in 'Arabia' and especially the Babatha archive see Bowersock, 74, 77–9, 88f.

595. *rqm*, M: *negeb*.

596. *ḥgr*, M: *šūr*.

597. He was identified with the Edomite king Jobab from Bozrah, Gen. 36.33. See also the historiographer Aristeas according to Alexander Polyhistor in Eusebius, P*raep.ev.* 9, 25, 1–4.

598. For a reconstruction of the text see F. M. Cross, 'Fragments of the Prayer of Nabonidus', *Israel Exploration Journal* 34, 1984, 260–4.

599. The Prayer of Nabonidus belongs in the prehistory of Dan. 4. It is dated to the Persian or early Hellenistic period. Cf. R. Meyer, 'Das Gebet des Nabonid ...' (reprinted in id., *Zur Geschichte und Theologie des Judentums in hellenistisch-römischer Zeit. Ausgewählte Abhandlungen*, ed. W. Bernhardt, Neukirchen/Vluyn 1989, 71–129); for the text see Cross, 'Fragments' (n.598), 260–4; further K. Koch, 'Gottes Herrschaft über

das Reich des Menschen. Daniel 4 im Licht neuer Funde', in *The Book of Daniel in the Light of New Findings*, ed. A. S. van der Woude, BETL 106, Leuven 1993, 77–119; Schwemer, *Vitae Prophetarum* I (n.589), excursus 7 (on the Life of Daniel in the *VP*, which has kindred features to 4QOrNab).

600. Meyer, 'Nabonid' (n.599), 101; cf. I.Ben-Zvi, 'The Origins of the Settlement of Jewish Tribes in Arabia', *ErIs* 6, 1960, 130–48: 133–8; 35f.* (summary); id., 'Les origines de l'établissement des tribus d'Israel en Arabie', *Le Muséon* 74, 1984, 143–90.

601. Koch, 'Gottes Herrschaft' (n.599) 98 (with bibliography), but he does not completely rule out Teman.

602. 1QGenAp 21, 15–19; cf. Scott, *Paul* (n.320), 29–33.

603. Cf. Josephus, *BJ* 1, 3, though he divides the world into the Greek-speaking peoples under Roman rule and the Aramaic-speaking peoples. For the tomb of the prophet Ezekiel in Babylonia in the cave of Shem and Arphachsad, the ancestors of Abraham, see Schwemer, *Vitae Prophetarum* I (Anm. 589), 259–68.

604. *VP* 21, 1: 'Elijah, (the) Tishbite, (was) from the land of the Arabians, (from) the tribe of Aaron; he lived in Gilead, for Tishbe was a gift for the priests.'

605. Rom. 11.2ff.; I Kings 19.10, 14; for a further relationship between Paul's mission plans and the early Jewish haggadah about prophets see 176.

606. Cf. E. Käsemann, *Commentary on Romans*, Grand Rapids and London ²1982 , 299.

607. *Antt.* 1, 220f. Here Josephus seems to have made a word play ('notarikon'). Cf. E. C. Broome, 'Nabaiati, Nabaioth and the Nabateans: The Linguistic Problem', *JSS* 18, 1973, 1–16.

608. *Antt.* 2, 213. Pompeius Trogus (Justin, *Epit.* 2, 10 = Stern, *GLAJ* I, 335), who has the Jews deriving from the Damascene and therefore makes Moses and the people simultaneously reach the Damascene and Sinai after a seven-day fast in the wilderness of Arabia.

609. Artapanus (F 2 = Eusebius, *Praep.ev.* 9, 23, 1) claims that on being threatened by his brothers, Joseph asked the neighbouring Arabs to take him to Egypt; they fulfilled his request since the kings of the Arabs are descendants of Israel, sons of Abraham and brothers of Isaac. Alexander Polyhistor, who wrote out Artapanus' work 'On the Jews', is probably confusing Israel and Ishmael; see N. Walter, *JSHRZ* I, 2, 127.

610. Rom. 4.1; cf. also the beginning of Stephen's speech, which is coloured by the Hellenist milieu, Acts 7.2; cf. 13.26, and James 2.21 – used against Paul.

611. Rom. 4.1–12; the completely different understanding of Abraham in James 2.21f. is directed against this.

612. Rom. 4.11; cf. 4.16–18.

613. Cf. Gal. 3.7, 29.

614. Matt. 3.9 = Luke 3.8 Q; Matt. 8.11 = Luke 13.28f. Q; Luke 13.16; 16.22ff.; John 8.33–58; II Cor. 11.22. Cf. also Matt. 1.1; Luke 1.55, 73; Mark 12.26; Acts 3.15; 7.2, 16f; 13.26.

615. *Antt.* 1, 214.

616. See already Herodotus 2, 104, which quotes Josephus, *Antt.* 8, 262 and *c. Ap.* 1, 169–71: Colchians (who are interpreted as Egyptians), Ethiopians, Egyptians, Phoenicians and Syrians in Palestine, who learned it from the Egyptians, are 'the only ones of all peoples to practise circumcision'. Cf. also the addition in Jer. 9.25: the Egyptians, Jews, Edomites, Ammonites, Moabites and 'all those that cut the corners of their hair, who dwell in the desert'. Barnabas 9.6: 'Every Syrian and Arabian and all the idolatrous priests' have themselves circumcised. This is confirmed by Epiphanius, *Haer.* 30, 33, 3 (GCS I, 379f. Holl): in addition to the idolaters and Egyptian priests the Saracenes, Ishmaelites, Samaritans, Idumaeans and Homerites (? in south Arabia) have circumcision. However, the majority of these do not do this 'because of the law, but because of a foolish custom'. See also Jerome, *in Hieremiam* 2, 84 on Jer. 9.25f. (CCSL 74, 101 Reiter): apart from the Jews, Egyptians, Idumaeans, Ammonites, Moabites *'et omnis regio Saracenorum'*. Circumcision was forbidden by Hadrian but allowed again by Antoninus Pius for Jews (not for proselytes); see Hengel, 'Hadrians Politik' (n.406), 172ff. In our view this was a reaction to reports of unrest in Judaea which led to the Bar Kochba revolt, c.131/132 CE. There are bibliographies in Meyer *TDNT* 6, 72f.; Schürer I, 537–40; O. Betz and F. Dexinger, *TRE* 5, 1980, 716–22.

617. For example the Nabataean regent Syllaeus refused to be circumcised, which meant the failure of his plan to marry Salome, Herod's sister: Josephus, *Antt.* 16, 225.

618. Gen. 17.1–14, 23–27; Gen. 15.1–6; 16.16; cf. Rom. 4.9–12.

619. Gal. 3.6–22.

620. Rom. 15.28.

621. Raymond A. Martin, *Studies in the Life and Ministry of the Early Paul*, 1993.

622. See Hengel, 'Vorchristlicher Paulus' (n.51), 220–4, 239–65: 248 [25–8, 40–53:46]; Haacker, 'Werdegang' (n.140), 875f. follows this somewhat half-heartedly, but would nevertheless like to keep the 'Shammaite' Paul. However, it is very questionable whether the young scribe from

Tarsus clearly took sides in the dispute between Pharisaic schools.

623. H. Maccoby, *Paul and the Invention of Christianity*, London 1986; id., *Paul and Hellenism*, London and Philadelphia 1991.

624. *Antt.* 11, 133.

625. See above, 171–7.

626. See the famous study by A. Alt, 'The God of the Fathers', in *Essays on Old Testament History and Religion*, Oxford 1966, 1–78, who cites 55 analogies completely from Nabataean and southern Syrian inscriptions which come from the late Hellenistic and Roman periods.

627. J. Teixidor, *The Pagan God. Popular Religion in the Greco-Roman Near East*, Princeton 1977, 161f. This tendency did not exclude a continuation of the worship of family and tribal gods. Thus the 'Gott of Aumos' (θεὸς Αὔμου), who is frequently attested, turns into the δεσπότην [Δία] Ἀνίκητον Ἥλιον Θεὸν Αὔμου (Alt, 'God of the Fathers' [n.626], 72–4, nos. 33–45), especially nos. 41–44, and also, 39ff: Ζεὺς Ἀνίκητος Ἥλιος Θεὸς Αὔμου – the solar henotheism, which was the final point reached by pagan religion ... in Syria, is here seen depriving the lesser god of his individual personality by seemingly exalting him to undreamt-of heights' (40). Cf. H. I. MacAdam, 'Epigraphy and Village Life in Southern Syria during the Roman and early Byzantine periods', *Berytus* 31, 1983, 109. See further the inscriptions in the temple of Baal Shamin in Si' in the Hauran, D. Sourdel, *Les cultes du Hauran à l'époque romaine*, Paris 1952, 21; Wenning, *Nabatäer* (n.278), 35f. and index 356 s.v. 'Götter', 'Ba'al Schamin'. Cf. Teixidor, *The Pagan God* (n.627), 13–17: 'Pagan Monotheism': 'Monotheism had always been latent among the Semites' (13). 'The epigraphical material reveals that the worship of a supreme God coexisted with that of other minor Gods' (17), who could be understood as messengers or sons (14f.), i.e. close to the Jewish (guardian) angels. 'The belief that one god is able to control all other Gods, or is supreme in that he has created and looks after the world does not constitute monotheism. But the increasing emphasis on such beliefs is evidence of a trend toward monotheism, namely to the exclusion of other Gods' existence' (17).

628. Teixidor, *The Pagan God* (n.627), 84f., on Qumran: 1QapGen ar (1Q20) Frg. 2, 5; xx 12f.; xxi 2 (cf. Beyer, *Texte* [n.586], 175, 178; F. García Martínez, *The Dead Sea Scrolls Translated*, Leiden 1994, 230, 233f.) alongside 'Lord of heaven' (1Q 20 vii 7; xii 17), etc.; 4QEn[b] iii 14 (Beyer, *Texte* [n.586], 237; García Martínez, *Scrolls*, 249); cf. J. T. Milik, *The Book of Enoch*, Oxford 1976, 171, 173 and also the examples from Palmyra and Hegra there. 'Lord of the world', *ribbon(o) šel 'olam*, becomes the most widespread Jewish form of address in the Talmud alongside 'King of the

world'.

629. Cf. from Bostra *IGLS* XIII, no. 9002 (Διὶ [Κ]υρίῳ) Κυρία Πατρίς: 9006–9; from Heliopolis/Baalbek *IGLS* VI, no. 2729 (quoted above, 370f. n.413); nos. 2730; 2978 from Angarr in Chalkis for Kore; cf. later inscriptions in Y. Hajjar, 'Baalbek, Centre Religieux sous l'empire', *ANRW* II, 18, 4, 2504f. No. 365: [Τ]ῇ Κυρίᾳ Ἀφ[ρ]οδίτῃ ...; ibid., no. 368; id., 'Dieux et cultes non héliopolitains de la Béqa'', *ANRW* II, 18, 4, 2533ff., on the dedicatory inscriptions to the Κυρία Ἀταρχάτη, many of which have been preserved (one from Kefr Havar [Waddington 1890; complete in Hajjar, 'Dieux et cultes', 2534] is mentioned by Bousset, *Kyrios Christos* [n.150], 96f.); see the index of *ANRW* II, 18, 4, 2791; cf. Starcky, 'Stèle' (n.318), 511, on *maran Našrā*; Tubach, *Sonnengott* (n.90), 533, index s. v. Mārā Samyā, etc. and 532 s. v. Barmārēn.

630. The wife also addresses her husband in this way; cf. 1QapGen (20) ii 9.13 (Beyer, *Texte* [n.586], 168), or the son his father, 1QapGen (20) ii 24 (Beyer, *Texte*, 169). The proper name 'Maran' appears on a Jewish epitaph from Rome (third-fourth century CE), see Noy, *Jewish Inscriptions* II (n.243), 406 no. 516. For the form of address 'Lord' to angels in the early Jewish writings (cf. e.g. 4QAmram[b] Frag. 2, 2: מרא; ET in García Martínez, *Scrolls* [n.628], 273), see L. T. Stuckenbruck, *Angel Veneration and Christology*, WUNT II/70, 1996, 97f.; ibid., 95f. on repudiating the title.

631. Teixidor, *The Pagan God* (n.627), 97f.; G. Mussies, 'Marnas God of Gaza', *ANRW* II, 18, 4, 1990, 2412–57, investigates the various derivations of the name in late antiquity and argues for a Philistine, not an Aramaic origin, though he cannot exclude the latter (2438f., 2443). Any Semite will have understood Marnas in the sense of 'our lord'.

632 *RÉS* no. 2117, *mrn' plpws*; cf. Millar, *Roman Near East* (n.92), 62; Kasher, *Idumaeans* (n.574), 176.

633. Philo, *Flacc.* 39.

634. *OGIS* 418 = Schürer I, 445 n.19; cf. Schwartz, *Agrippa* I (n.302), 56. Cf. the altar inscription (dated by the editor to 209–212 CE) from Gerasa HCI-1: Ἀγαθῇ Τύχῃ/ʻΥπὲρ σωτηρίας τῶ/ν κυρίων ἡ [/] Ἰουλίας Δόμνας Σεβ(αστῆς)/Διὶ Οὐρανίῳ/ Δ[/]ιων Νεικομαχ[ου] κατʼ εὐχ[ήν]; see Z. Borkowski, 'Inscriptions on Altars from the Hippodrome of Gerasa', *Syria* 66, 1989, 81f.

635. *OGIS* 426 = *IGR* III, 1127 presumably from the year 92 CE.: Διὶ κυρίῳ; cf. *OGIS* 425, the inscription from Sur dedicated to the same ruler: βασιλεῖ μεγάλῳ Ἀγρίππᾳ κυρίῳ Ἀγρίππας υἱός.

636. Waddington 2364 = *OGIS* 415 = *IGR* III, 1243. Cf. R. Dussaud, *Les Arabes en Syrie avant l'Islam*, Paris 1907, 162; Millar, *Roman Near East*

(n.92), 62.

637. J. Starcky, 'Pétra et la Nabatène', *DBS* VII, Paris 1966, 988: *CIS* II, 208, 209, cf. 211 and *RÉS*, 83. Alt, 'God of the Fathers' (n.626), 68 nos. 5–8 (8 from Petra); further inscriptions from the Hauran refer to Rabael/Rabilos II (70/71–106) and mention Dušara : Dušara *'lh mr'n'*. Cf. Alt, 'God of the Fathers', 69, nos. 10 and 11. In addition there is an inscription reported by J. Starcky, 'Inscriptions nabatéennes et l'histoire de la Syrie méridionale', in Dentzer, *Hauran* I (n.276), 167–81 (180f.): a sanctuary for Dusara *'lh mr'n' rb'l mlk'* (the god of our lord Rabbel the king), *c.*100/101 CE. Further examples, 178.

638. L. Y. Rahmani, *A Catalogue of Jewish Ossuaries*, Jerusalem 1994, 197f. no.560: κυρε τυς τουπου = κύριοι τοῦ τόπου; Aramaic: *mry qbr*; cf. p. 152 no. 327: Master Joseph, son of Behaja *(yhwsp mrh ...)* and p. 76 no. 8: *mry ḥwsh*, 'my lord Chosa', as a possible reading.

639. See the numerous epigraphic evidence for *'dn* (mostly Phoenician) and above all for *mar'* (in the Aramaic dialects) and *rab* (as a substantive, alongside *rbn*) in J. Hoftijzer and K. Jongeling, *Dictionary of the North-West Semitic Inscriptions*, 1995, I, 15ff.; II, 682–9, 1048–51, 1056.

640. I Cor. 16.21; cf. Rev. 22.20; Did. 10.5f.; 15.1, 46f.; I Cor. 9.5; Gal. 1.14; Luke 1.43.

641. Rom. 1.7; I Cor. 1.3; II Cor. 1.2; Gal. 1.3; Phil. 1.2; Philemon 1.3. See the Nabataean inscription from Hegra, above n.628. The distinction introduced by S. Schulz between a Palestinian Jewish-apocalyptic Mareh-Kyrios and the Hellenistic 'acclamations Kyrios', which is said to have first arisen in Antioch, is nonsensical; see *ZNW* 53, 1962, 125–44. This thesis was echoed in a number of places, e.g in W. Kramer, *Christ, Lord, Son of God*, SBT I 50, 1963, 94ff., 99ff., and on this see Hengel, 'Son of God' (n.117), 75ff. (bibliography).

642. Cf. A. Biran, 'The God who is in Dan', in id. (ed.), *Temples and High Places* (n.415), 146f., on the votive inscription 'the God in Dan' from the second century BCE; cf. V.Tzaferis, 'The "God who is in Dan" and the Cult of Pan at Banias in the Hellenistic and Roman Periods', in *ErIs* 23, Jerusalem 1992, 128*–135*. See also the inscription from Bosra in *IGLS* XIII, no. 9004, and on it the commentary by M. Sartre, ibid. A relief from Syria inscribed in Greek and Aramaic is dedicated anonymously to the gods (τοὺς θεούς); it depicts the priest Philotas sacrificing to the naked figure of a god which probably depicts Heracles; see P. Bordreuil and P.-L. Gatier, 'Le relief du prêtre Philōtas', *Syria* 67, 1990, 329–38. In the case of the triad of gods Maran, Mārtan, Barmārēn, 'our Lord, our Lady, Son of our Lord', worshipped in Ḥaṭrā, these names are basically epithets 'which suppressed or replaced the real gods'

names. The anonymity has been preserved in almost all the inscriptions, Tubach, *Sonnengott* (n.90), 258. The rulers of the city also bear the title *marya* or *malka* on inscriptions, see Tubach, *Sonnengott*, 245–51.

643. Starcky, *DBS* (n.637), 996 = A. Janssen and R. Savignac, *Mission archéologique en Arabie*, Paris 1909, I, 142 no. 2; cf. Teixidor, *The Pagan God* (n.627), 85, see also above n.628 on 'Lord of the world'. The formula 'who divides between light and darkness' (Gen. 1.4; 11QPsApa i 12f) appears among other places in the Havdala benediction, see W. Staerk, *Altjüdische liturgische Gebete*, KlT 58, Berlin ²1930, 26, see mBer 5, 2 and 8, 5a. Might there be Jewish influence here?

644. M. Gawlikowski, 'Inscriptions de Palmyre', *Syria* 48, 1971, 407–26: 408f.; id., 'Les Dieux de Palmyre', *ANRW* II 18, 4, 1990, 2632–4, 2626f., 2653 (bibliography); J. T. Milik, *Dédicaces faites par des dieux*, Paris 1972, 180–4, 293f.; the hypothesis of Teixidor, *The Pagan God* (n.627), 122–30, is dubious; cf. id., *The Pantheon of Palmyra*, EPRO 79, Leiden 1979, 115–19.

645. ἑνὶ μόνῳ ἐλεήμονι θεῷ, see Milik, *Dédicaces* (n.644), 293 = H. Seyrig, *Syria* 14, 1933, 269–75 under 5 (= *Antiquités Syriennes* 1, 118–24), *c.* 200 CE.

646. *qrh lh w'nyh* or similarly εὐξάμενος καὶ ἐπακουσθείς, Milik, *Dédicaces* (n.644), 180.

647. *bkwl 'tr'*, Milik, *Dédicaces* (n.644), 180: *CIS* II, 4011, cf. I Cor. 1.2.

648. *dy qr 'lh bybšwbym.' (w) 'nyh wšwzph w'ḥh*, Milik, '*Dédicaces*' (n.644), 294.

649. *mwd' kwl ywm u. a.*, Milik, *Dédicaces* (n.644), 180.

650. *'bd 'mhwn gbwrwt* or *gbwrt'*, see Milik, *Dédicaces* (n.644), 180f., 294: 'The term *gbwrt'* is not ... "the power" but a religious term corresponding to the Greek δυνάμεις in the sense of "miracles".'

651. Seyrig, *Syria* 14 (n.645), 270ff. See C. H. Roberts, T. S. Skeat and A. D. Nock, 'The Gild of Zeus Hypsistos', *HTR* 29, 1936, 37–88: 62–9; J. G. Ferrier and A. B. Cook, *Zeus*, I, 2, 1925, 876–9.

652. See now e.g. the new Greek inscription discovered at Halusa in the Negeb, θεῷ ὑψίστῳ, with an additional text in Palmyrene script, Y. Ustinova and J. Naveh, *Atiqot* 22, 1993, 91–6. For the sanctuary of Zeus Hypsistos in Dmeir see Hajjar, *Divinités oraculaires* (n.425), 2266f. There are further examples with the equivalent μέγιστος in inscriptions for the Baal of Hermon in ibid., 2252, and id., 'Dieux et cultes non Hélipolitains de la Béqa'', *ANRW* II 18, 4, 2538: κατὰ κέλευσιν θεοῦ κ[αὶ] ἁγίου ὗ (for οἱ) ὀμνύοντες ἐντεῦθεν; cf. ibid., 2540ff.: Διὶ μεγίστῳ or Θ]εῷ πατρῴῳ alongside Διὶ πατρῴῳ for the same God.

653. Thus in correct style Mark 5.7 = Luke 8.28; Acts 16.17. See

Hengel, *Judaism and Hellenism* (n.314), 297–9.

654. Stern, *GLAJ* I, 26, 22f. (no. 11, 4): τὸν περιέχοντα τὴν γῆν οὐρανὸν μόνον εἶναι τὸν θεὸν καὶ ὅλων κύριον. In Sib. 3, 174, 247, 261, 286 (cf. 3, 1, 19) the Jewish author puts the divine predicate οὐράνιος into the Sibyl's mouth to denote the only true God

655. *Anabasis* 7, 20, 1 and with it Dionysus. Strabo 16, 1, 11 Zeus and Dionysos, cf. also the Greek inscriptions in the temple of Baal Shamin in Si' (Secia), above 393 n.627 and the Θεὸς Ἀραβικός in Gerasa, Wenning, 'Dekapolis' (n.278), 27–9, cf. 13f.; there we also have a Hera as Thea Urania and *parhedros* of Parkeidas, a 'Semitic manifestation of Zeus Olympios'. A new inscription is dedicated to Zeus Uranios and another one from Pella to the 'Theos Uranios Arabikos' (ibid., 27f. nn.187–8). 'The motif of an eagle in one of the six inscriptions also suggests that the Theos Arabikos was a God of heaven.' Cf. the dispute over the golden eagle in the temple in Jerusalem, Hengel, *Zealots* (n.122), 103, 192, 207, 323f. For the problem see also Teixidor, *The Pagan God* (n.627), 82; also Celsus (Origen, *c.Celsum* 1, 23): the 'shepherds' who followed Moses believed it was a god, εἴτε Ὕψιστον εἴτ' Οὐράνιον εἴτε Σαβαὼθ εἴτε καὶ ὅπῃ καὶ ὅπως χαίρουσιν ὀνομάζοντες τόνδε τὸν κόσμον, cf. 5, 41. According to Strabo 14, 4, 26 they worshipped the sun, cf. Josephus, *BJ* 2, 128, 148; see M. Smith, 'Helios in Palestine', *ErIs* 16, 1982, 199–214; id., 'The Near Eastern Background of Solar Language for Jahweh', *JBL* 109, 1990, 29–39; Tacitus, *Hist.* 3, 24, 3; see also TestHiob 52, 8; ParJer 4, 4; GrBar 6, 2.

656. P.-L. Gatier and A.-M. Vérilhac, 'Les colombes de Déméter à Philadelphie-Amman', *Syria* 66, 1989, 337–48. For Baal Shamin in the area see U. Hübner, *Ammoniter*, ADPV 16, Wiesbaden 1992, 259 (n.62). For the Jews in Palmyra cf. J. G. Février, *La Religion des Palmyréniens*, Paris 1931, 219–26.

657. mJom 3, 8; 4, 1–3; 6, 2; tTaan 1, 11–13; see M. Hengel and A. M. Schwemer (eds.), *Königsherrschaft Gottes und himmlischer Kult*, WUNT 55, Tübingen 1991, 2–4 (Preface) and 290f.: T. Lehnardt, 'Königsherrschaft Gottes im synagogalen Gebet'; cf. also Ps. 72, 19.

658. *Tempel und Kulte syrischer Städte in hellenistisch-römischer Zeit*, AO 40, Leipzig 1941, 91f.

659. Gawlikowski, 'Les dieux de Palmyre' (n.644), 2633f.

660. Cf. the well-known malicious picture which Celsus paints of the threatening eschatological preacher and divine saviour in 'Phoenicia and Palestine' and which represents a polemical parody of Christ and the Christian preaching (Origen, *c.Celsum* 7, 9). See Hengel, 'Son of God' (n.117), 38f.

661. For Palmyra cf. Niehr, *Gott* (n.413), 35f.; H. Seyrig, 'Bêl de Palmyre', *Syria* 48, 1971, 85–114; id., 'Culte du Soleil en Syrie', *Syria* 48, 1971, 349f.; J. Starcky and M. Gawlikowski, *Palmyre, Édition revue et augmentée des nouvelles découvertes*, Paris 1985, 89–111; Tubach, *Sonnengott* (n.90), see index s.v.; Feldtkeller, *Reich* (n.88), 113f.

662. Hoftijzer, 51–61; Drijvers, *Inscriptions*, 377–800; for the inscriptions from Hatra, on which *mrn* 'our Lord', *mrtn* 'our Lady' and *brmrn*, 'son of our Lord' appear as a triad see Niehr, *Gott* (n.413), 39ff.; Hoftijzer and de Jongeling, *Dictionary of the Northern-West Semitic Inscriptions* II, Leiden 1995, 684ff., s. v. *mrn*.

663. Cf. the inscriptions from Heliopolis/Baalbek: *IGLS* VI, nos. 2711–13.

664. SeeY. Hajjar, 'Dieux et cultes non héliopolitains de la Béqa', de l'Hermon et de l'Abilène à l'époque romaine', *ANRW* II, 18, 4, 2509–604: 2529–32.

665. Instances in Aland, *Synopsis Quattuor Evangeliorum*, 34; *NT Apoc* I ²1991, 136 no. 3.

666. Jerome, *in Is IV* on 11.3 (CCSL 73, 1, 2 p. 148, M. Adriaen); Aland, *Synopsis*, 77; *NTApoc* I ²1991, 177 no. 2.

667. Prov. 8.30 MT *'amōn*; LXX: ἁρμόζουσα; Vulg *cuncta componens*; Wisdom 7.21f ... πάντων τεχνῖτις and as such πνεῦμα νοερόν, ἅγιον cf. 8.5f.; 8.3, συμβίωσις θεοῦ; 9.4 ἡ τῶν σῶν θρόνων πάρεδρος, see Hengel, *Judaism and Hellenism* (n.314), I, 153ff., 167.

668. Acts 17.8: ξένων δαιμονίων δοκεῖ καταγγελεὺς εἶναι, ὅτι τὸν Ἰησοῦν καί τὴν ἀνάστασιν εὐαγγελίζετο. D gig omits the last offensive sentence.

669. Against Feldtkeller, *Reich* (n.88), 240, who e.g. in Matt. 19.11f. concludes that self-castration has been taken over from the cult of the Syrian goddess.

670. See also the coin collections of the British Museum, G. F. Hill, *Catalogue of the Greek Coins of Palestine*, Bologna 1965, 323f., index s. v. 'City-goddess'; W. Wroth, *Catalogue of the Greek Coins of Galatia, Cappadocia, and Syria*, Bologna 1964, 322ff., index s. v. 'Tyche'; for the Tyche of Antioch on the Orontes as a statue and on coins see G. Downey, *A History of Antioch in Syria from Seleucus to the Arab Conquest*, Princeton 1961, 73ff.; also Y. Meshorer, *City Coins of Eretz Israel and the Decapolis in the Roman Period*, Jerusalem 1985, index 122 s. v. 'Tyche, the city goddess'. For Philo, Jerusalem with its sanctuary is the 'metropolis' of all Jews throughout the oikumene, see *in Flacc*.46 and frequently in the *Legatio ad Caium* 203, 281: all the regions in which Jews dwell; 294, 305, 334.

671. For κυρία as an epithet of the Syrian goddess see above, n.629. Cf. Hengel, *Johanneische Frage* (n.33), 136f. [39].

672. Cf. the address 'Lady' to the church in the visions of the Shepherd of Hermas. Cf. I Peter 5.13 ἡ συνεκλεκτή in Babylon = Rome.

673. Eph. 1.22f.; 3.10f. (cf. 1.11); 5.25f.

674. Rev. 21.2, cf. 3.12; Heb. 11.16; 12.22; cf. also the persecuted community of God and the child, i.e. the 'martyrs' in Rev. 12; also the metaphor of Christ as bridegroom and the community as bride in Rev. 21.2, 9; 23.17 cf. Paul in II Cor. 11.2.

675. Irenaeus, *Haer.* 1, 1 after Sige, Aletheia and Zoe, cf. 2, 2; 5, 6 etc. Twelve further aeons then emerge from this pair. Cf. C. Markschies, *Valentinus Gnosticus?*, WUNT 65, 1992, 45, etc.

676. Here one could perhaps also include cities of the Decapolis like Gerasa or Philadelphia bordering on Nabataean territory, although the designation 'Arabia' is not completely correct for them before the founding of the province of Arabia in 106 CE. A synagogue has later been identified in Gerasa, but this could go back to an earlier building from the first century, see F. Hüttenmeister and G. Reeg, *Die antiken Synagogen in Israel*, BTAVO B 12, 1, Wiesbaden 1977, 126–30 (bibliography). The direct Nabataean influence in these cities which were proud of their own 'Graeco-Macedonian' tradition was remarkably small.

677. Suetonius, *Claudius* 25, 4, see Riesner, *Frühzeit* (n.49), 139–80; see also the role of the synagogues in persecutions in the Synoptic Gospels (Mark 13.9; Luke 12.11; 21.12; Matt. 10.17; 23.34).

678. Haenchen, *Acts* (n.5), 334, knows precisely: 'However, this activity bore no fruit – at least Paul nowhere mentions having founded any communities in these regions' – but he does not speak at all of his mission successes in Syria, Cilicia and Arabia apart from hinting at them in Rom. 15.19 in the καὶ κύκλῳ; cf. I Cor. 15.10; II Cor. 11.5, 23. Cf. also Isa. 60.7, where Arabia is immediately followed by *Taršīš*, LXX Θάρσις, which in Paul's time could be identified with Tarsus.

679. Acts 9.30. One almost gets the impression that Paul does not know where to turn.

680. II Cor. 11.24, 26; cf. Gal. 4.29; I Thess. 2.16; see also n.472 above and n.710 below.

681. For dating see the thorough investigation by Riesner, *Frühzeit* (n.49), 66–79: Aretas IV ruled from 9 BCE to 40 CE, so at all events the flight must have been before 40 and on the basis of internal chronology presumably between 34 and 36. See also J. Starcky, *DBS* VII (n.637), 915.

682. See Nestle and Aland²⁷ ad loc. and Barrett, *Acts* I (n.77), 466f.

683. In the immediate context 9.10, 19, 26, 38, cf. 9.1 μαθητὰς τοῦ

κυρίου (only here).

684. Riesner, *Frühzeit* (n.49), 72ff.; cf. Starcky, *DBS* VII (n.637), 907f.; against Bowersock, *Arabia* (n.579), 24–7.

685. Riesner, *Frühzeit* (n.49), 77; cf. T. Zahn, 'Zur Lebensgeschichte des Apostels Paulus', *NKZ* 15, 1904, 40.

686. A. Knauf, 'Zum Ethnarchen des Aretas 2. Kor 11, 32', *ZNW* 74, 1983, 145–7; he is followed, with a lengthy discussion of views, by Riesner, *Frühzeit* (n.49), 74–6; cf. already Starcky, *DBS* VII (n.637), 915, who refers to the Jewish 'ethnarch' in Alexandria as a parallel (*Antt.* 14, 117f., see above, 61, with n.316); J.-P. Rey-Coquais, 'Syrie Romaine, de Pompée à Dioclétian', *JRS* 68, 1978, 50f. For Wenning, 'Dekapolis' (n.278), 16f., the comparison with a 'consul or trade attaché' is too little and he prefers a comparison with 'the Arabian Šeḥ'. However, this is a dispute over words. There are also 'consuls general' with considerable powers. On the trade routes to the east and the south-east the Damascenes were dependent on the good will of the Nabataean king (see above, 112). J. M. C. Bowsher, 'The Nabataean Army', in *The Eastern Frontier of the Roman Empire. Proceedings of a Colloquium held at Ankara in September 1988*, ed. D. H. French and C. S. Lightfoot, British Institute of Archaeology at Ankara Monograph No. 11, BAR International Series 553(i) 1989, 21, sees this ethnarch as 'the highest authority of Nabataean Damascus' with the command of a garrison. In my view this is wrong, but perhaps Nabataean cavalry provided protection for Damascene caravans to the east and south-east for appropriate payments of money.

687. Schürer III, 1, 92f. Cf. also the archon of the Jews in Antioch and in Leontopolis, see above, n.316.

688. Riesner, *Frühzeit* (n.49), 75f.; Knauf, 'Ethnarch' (n.686), 146f.; Starcky, *DBS* VII (n.637), 915f.: *CIS* II, 160, 188.

689. *Frühzeit* (n.49), 77.

690. Gal. 5.11.

691. Gal. 1.18–20.

692. Gal. 1.20; in my view the condemnation of swearing oaths in James 5.12 and also many other warnings in the letter are directed against Paul, who uses oath formulae with surprising frequency, see Hengel, 'Jakobusbrief' (n.12), 260f., 275 n.76.

693. See above, 128ff.; 134. This is immediately preceded by an oath formula similar to Gal. 1.20: one might almost assume that Paul's accounts of his early period were sometimes generally doubted.

694. As usual, Conzelmann, *Acts* (n.230), 75 decrees on 9.28f.: 'The entire description contains no concrete material.'

695. The best remarks on this disputed text are to be found in

Burchard, *Zeuge* (n.5), 145–50, 153–5; see also Barrett, *Acts* I (n.77), 468–71; Klein, *Apostel* (n.33), 162–6 completely misses Luke's intention. Haenchen, *Acts* (n.5), 333ff. also reads out of Luke things that he does not say.

696. For the translation of κολλᾶσθαι see Burchard, *ZNW* 61, 1970, 159f.; cf. 5.13; 10.28; 17.34; cf. id., *Zeuge* (n.5), 145f., and Barrett, *Acts* 1 (n.77), 274f.

697. Luke likes using this term as an exaggeration in Luke and Acts. It means all those who hear of this attempt. That creates a certain tension and a contrast with Barnabas' behaviour.

698. For the translation of ἐπιλαβόμενος see again Burchard, *ZNW* 61, 1970, 165, and id., *Zeuge* (n.5), 146f. It does not mean 'he looked after him' like the translation 'in all the German commentaries', but only 'take' or 'take with', see Acts 17.19 etc. 'Luke does not say a word about a close relationship between Barnabas and Paulus, or about any intermediary in making contact.' See already de Wette and Overbeck, *Kurze Erklärung der Apostelgeschichte*, 1870, 144.

699. Here at any rate we should presuppose a change of subject from Barnabas to Paul, either in the narrative or in the following sentence with the seeing of the Lord. The former is more probable. Such a change occurs relatively frequently in the narrative texts of the OT and especially in the early Jewish literature; by contrast, in Luke such 'carelessness' is rare (cf. e.g. Acts 2.24). We find it at every step in the *VP*. Cf. already A. Loisy, *Les Actes des Apôtres*, 1920, 423, but also Barrett, *Acts* I (n.77), 423 and Burchard, *Zeuge* (n.5), 147f.: 'moreover it is true to style that a person involved in a supernatural event narrates this himself'. Schneider, *Apostelgeschichte* (n.77), 38, points out that where Luke uses διηγέομαι elsewhere (Luke 8.39; 9.10), and above all in the parallel Acts 12.17 which follows the same course, there is a narrative of 'personal experience' (the scriptural quotation Acts 8.33 is the exception). As later, Luke presupposes that people wanted to hear what Paul experienced from his own mouth.

700. In 9.5 and 26.15 Saul puts only the stylized question 'Who are you, Lord?'; in 22.8, 10 also 'What shall I do, Lord?'. Jesus is the real speaker. Loisy, *Actes* (n.699), 423, sees here a 'hagiographical *faux pas*' of Luke's: 'In the letters, Paul himself does not pride himself on having spoken with Christ.' However, in v.27 the preceding object appears as the subject of the next verb: αὐτόν (= Paul) and διηγήσατο, τὸν κύριον and ἐλάλησεν. Then up to v. 29 Paul is again the active subject in the narrative.

701. 9.23 cf. 9.43; 18.18; 27.27 cf. 20.10. Peshitto: *sgyw lh tmn ywmt'*;

Vulgate: *dies multi*; cf. also P45 and h on 19.19b, where the other witnesses read ἡμέρας τινάς; see Barrett, *Acts I* (n.77), 463: 'Luke seems to use both expressions when he has no precise length of time in mind, but ἱκαναί suggests a longer time.' The only exact piece of information in the early period is in 11.26, see above, 8.22. For the later period cf. 18.11 (18.18bc means a part of these 18 months); 19.10 and 20.31 (which differ from one another; cf. also I Cor. 16.8); 25.5, 27; 25.1 etc. It is precisely these differentiations in the various details of time (see also Luke 2.1 and 3.1f.) which mark Luke out as a historian and distinguish him from the producers of apostolic romances. Here we must either recognize the seriousness of his writing, for all its defects, or generally reject it. Even radical criticism of Luke, however, does not venture to do the latter.

702. Klein, *Apostel* (n.33), 164 produces this caricature. Luke never speaks of Paul's 'ministry' but only of his 'sending' or 'task', and that comes only from the Lord himself. According to Haenchen, *Acts* (n.5), 335, Luke has Paul travel to Jerusalem 'very shortly after his call', so people there had not been informed of the happenings in Damascus. He concludes from this: 'the ground on which this entire Lucan edifice is erected will bear no weight, and all must come toppling down'. Haenchen is reading this into the text.

703. Cf. I Cor. 15.5, 7 and 9.5. James is evidently also counted among the apostles in Gal. 1.19 despite the distinction made in I Cor. 9.5. In our view, at first the twelve belonged to them, but the circle must have been wider. See also Rom. 16.7 and II Cor. 11.5, 13: the basic presupposition was an appearance of the risen Christ and the sending by him. We do not know how many people took part in this (which is generally recognized). However, in Gal. 1.19 Paul is possibly thinking primarily of the circle of twelve – in Jerusalem – with Cephas/ Peter at their head. It is possible that by way of exception Paul means the twelve, i.e. the 'apostles' as understood by Jerusalem.

704. *Die Apostelgeschichte*, KEK 1913, 175.

705. Cf. Acts 12.17, on which see 8.2.6 and Hengel, 'Jakobus der Herrenbruder – der erste "Papst"', in *Glaube und Eschatologie, FS W. G. Kümmel*, ed. E. Grässer and O. Merk, Tübingen 1985, 71–104: 98–103; W. Pratscher, *Der Herrenbruder Jakobus und die Jakobustradition*, FRLANT 139, 1987, 55ff., 57, following F. F. Bruce, *The Epistle of Paul to the Galatians*, NIGTC, Exeter 1979, 99: 'James was perhaps already the leader of one group in the Jerusalem church.' Pratscher rightly adds that this could have been only 'an open circle of members of the community' and refers to the 'rivalry formula' in I Cor. 15.7. Nor should one further

insinuate *a priori* that in general he had an 'anti-Pauline attitude'. Such an attitude is not reported 'for this time either of the leading representatives of the earliest community or in general of a group of the Aramaic-speaking, Jewish community; rather there was delight that Paul had been transformed from a persecutor into a preacher (Gal. 1.22ff.), even if some will have been restrained.'

706. Matt. 10.17–25; Mark 13.9–13; Luke 12.11f.; 21.12–19; John 9.22; 16.2ff.; the last two texts need not refer only to the time after 70, since after this fateful year Jewish communities and Jewish Christians were largely separated. See Hengel, *Johanneische Frage* (n.33), 288f. [114f.].

707. Acts 6.1, on which see Hengel, 'Between Jesus and Paul' (n.50); id., 'Vorchristliche Paulus' (n.51), 220f. n.146 [117f. n.146]; Ps.-Clement, *Hom* 11, 35, 4 later calls the Jewish-Christian community in Jerusalem ἡ τῶν Ἑβραίων ἐκκλησία, which is led by James. This would also explain the energetic protest by the 'apostles and brethren', i.e. 'those of the circumcision' against Peter over the baptism of the Gentile Cornelius and his 'house' in Jerusalem as described by Luke in Acts 11.1–3.

708. Cf. Jason, Acts 21.16; further 12.12f.; 11.22ff., 28; 15.22. It was not always easy to draw a clear line between the Jewish Christians who came from Eretz Israel and spoke Aramaic as their mother tongue and the Greek-speaking Jewish Christians in Jerusalem who looked towards the Diaspora.

709. Lietzmann, *Galaterbrief* (n.558), 9: 'If Paulus did not see any other apostle apart from Peter and James, that will hardly have been because all the apostles were on journeys, but rather that Paul had to remain in hiding from the Jews; that may also glimmer through 9.29.'

710. Acts 21.27–36. In our view Luke himself was in Jerusalem at that time. Because of earlier experiences, Paul foresaw this danger, Rom. 15, 30f., cf. also II Cor. 11.24, 26. First of all he always mentions danger from his fellow-countrymen: this is not one of Luke's quirks or an invention of his. The dangers depicted here existed from the beginning of his mission preaching.

711. Calvin already criticized this πάντες as an exaggeration (cf. also the πάντες in 9.26). On this cf. Barrett, *Acts I* (n.77), 391f. Luke has this abundant exaggerating πάντες more frequently than the other New Testament authors; cf. Luke 4.22 cf. 28; 8.40, 52; 9.43; 13.27; 14.18; 20.38; 22.70; 23.48, 49; in the special material 1.63, 66; 2.3, 18, 47; 6.26; 13.3, 5, 17; 14.29; 15.1; 19.7.

712. Cf. 11.19.

713. Luke wants to see the 'pious men' of 8.2 as 'good Jews', cf.

Barrett, *Acts* I (n.77), 392. However, I doubt whether Luke invented this reference himself.

714. Acts 6.2, cf. the 'eleven' in Luke 24.9, 33; Acts 1.13, 26; 2.24 Peter and the eleven. The reference to 'the twelve' in 6.2 could be the remains of an old source and at the same time contrasts to some degree with the 'seven' in 6.3; cf. 21.8; see Hengel, 'Between Jesus and Paul' (n.50), 15.

715. We meet the elders alone for the first time already as the recipients of the collection brought by Barnabas and Paul from Antioch, 11.30; cf. also 15.4, 6, 22f.; 16.4.

716. T. Zahn, *Die Apostelgeschichte des Lucas*, KNT V, 1, Leipzig ³1922, 331f.: 'So one should not speak of a serious contradiction between Acts and Galatians' (332). At any rate he also concedes that Luke's information is inaccurate; cf. de Wette and Overbeck, *Apostelgeschichte* (n.698), ad loc.

717. Not Barnabas, see n.699 above.

718. This reaction appears in Luke only during Paul's first visit to Jerusalem in Acts 21.20. For the formula see also 11.18 and II Cor. 9.13.

719. *Acts* I (n.77), 469f.

720. *Zeuge* (n.5), 148f., see also H. von Campenhausen on Luke's account: 'Again and again there is nothing for [the apostles] to do but to recognize what the Spirit has already done, and to confirm it with praise and thanksgiving, while the newly won Christians gratefully join the community. Then Paul moves the mission into completely new areas and situations. Whatever the piety which he displays in his dealings with the primitive community, he is not subject to it. The later, historically untenable conception of the central government of the whole Church by the Apostles is thus not supported by Luke' (*Ecclesiastical Authority and Spiritual Power in the Church of the First Three Centuries* [1953], London 1969, 153).

721. *Zeuge* (n.5), 154.

722. Cf. also Gal. 1.15f. and Matt. 16.16–19; I Cor. 15.5 and 8–10; 9.5f.; 3.11, 22; Gal. 2.7f., 11, 14. In our view, for Paul he is the exponent of the ὑπερλίαν ἀπόστολοι in II Cor. 11.5.

723. He withholds the title 'brother of the Lord' from him (Acts 12.17; 15.13 and 21.18), does not mention his name in 1.14 and is generally silent about his relation to Jesus. In the Gospel the brothers of Jesus are mentioned only in a negative connection in 8.19–21. See Hengel, 'Jakobus' (n.705), 72; Pratscher, *Herrenbruder* (n.705), 22ff.

724. Acts 15.13–21; 21.18–26.

725. Cf. I Cor. 15.11; Gal. 2.9.

726. That Luke knew of tensions but keeps quiet about some for the

edification of Theophilus is shown by the protest in 11.2; 13.13; 15.5, 39; the enigmatically brief reference in 18.22; the warnings in 21.4, 10ff. and the admonition by James in 21.20–25, following which puts Paul's life in danger and gets him imprisoned in 21.26ff.; and the bringing of the collection through the back door in 24.17. In chs. 22–26 the Jerusalem community leaves Paul in the lurch. He receives support in 24.23 from the ἴδιοι, i.e. probably through the community in Caesarea or his mission communities (e.g. perhaps Philippi, see also 27.3, Sidon).

727. The encomium of the monk Alexander on Barnabas which was composed on Cyprus in the second half of the sixth century or a little later relates that Barnabas had sought in vain to convert the persecutor Saul. That explains everything else. How could such an edifying reason have escaped Luke?! See *ActaSS Junii Tom* II, pp. 431ff. (c.1 end), ed. Papebroeck and on this R. A. Lipsius, *Die apokryphen Apostelgeschichten und Apostellegenden* II, 1, 1884 (reprinted 1976), 299.

728. No fictitious persons appear in his work.

729. See Burchard, *Zeuge* (n.5), 154 on 'Barnabas and his function' as an 'indication of the tradition'.

730. Cf. Gal. 1.10–12; I Thess. 2.4, but against this I Cor. 10.33.

731. 9.28: καὶ ἦν μετ' αὐτῶν.

732. 9.29: ἐλάλει τε καὶ συνεζήτει πρὸς τοὺς Ἑλληνιστάς.

Cf. 6.8: members from the various Diaspora synagogues engaged in disputations (συζητοῦντες) with Stephen. Luke uses the verb in Acts only in these two passages. Cf. I. Cor. 1.20.

733. Burchard, *Zeuge* (n.5), 154: 'I do not see … why Luke should have invented a controversy with the Hellenists.'

734. Significantly, Luke now no longer speaks of disciples. Those who first refused to recognize him as a disciple of Jesus have now become 'brothers'. The change of term seems to me to have been made deliberately here.

735. The ἐξαπέστειλαν, in itself a favourite word of Luke's, is striking, but cf. the sending of Barnabas to Antioch by the community in Jerusalem with quite a different motive in 11.22 and the sending to the peoples by the Kyrios in the report of the vision in 22.21. In this context it sounds like mild compulsion: he was helped to get away as quickly as possible (and as far as possible).

736. *Zeuge* (n.5), 154, cf. 161–8.

737. πορεύου, ὅτι ἐγὼ εἰς ἔθνη μακρὰν ἐξαποστελῶ σε. Cf. 9.15; 22.15; 26.17: τῶν ἐθνῶν εἰς οὓς ἐγὼ ἀποστέλλω σε. In respect of his sending by Christ to the nations, for Luke, too, Paul is ἀπόστολος, hence 14.4 and 14. The ἀποστέλλω σε could come from the LXX calls of the prophets in

Isa. 6.7 and Ezek. 2.3, see Sandnes, *Paul* (n.492), 76.

738. See already E. Zeller, *Die Apostelgeschichte nach ihrem Inhalt und Ursprung kritisch untersucht,* Stuttgart 1854, 209: 'The two accounts are ... not compatible; rather, each of them is concerned to give a single reason for Paul's departure, without needing to be supplemented by the other or even leaving room for it.' However, Zeller's reason for this is questionable. He argues that their common tendency is to make Paul's separation from the original apostles and the limitation of his activity to the Gentile world appear something that he did not want. This is to overlook the fact that Paul himself understands his whole activity since his conversion as obedience compelled by the Kyrios, I Cor. 9.16ff., 27. Thus in Luke too, Paul's way is firmly prescribed by his call.

739. Cf. Acts 13.46: 28.28.

740. See above, n.737 and below, n.791.

741. Burchard, *Zeuge* (n.5), 168: 'The conversion of Cornelius leads to nothing other than the fact that the Jerusalem community learns something new (11.18); the conversion of the Hellenists leads to Cyprus, Phoenicia and Antioch and ends there.'

742. Cf. II Cor. 12.1. See II Cor. 5.13; I Cor. 13.1ff.; 14.18f.; for Acts see also 16.9; 18.9; 23.11; 27.23–26. See also Heckel, *Kraft* (n.14), 54–6, 74–77, 307–11, etc.

743. O. Betz, 'Die Vision des Paulus im Tempel von Jerusalem, Apg 22, 17–21, als Beitrag zur Deutung des Damaskuserlebnisses', in *Verborum Veritas FS für Gustav Stählin*, ed. O. Böcher and K. Haacker, Wuppertal 1970, 113–14 = id., *Jesus der Herr der Kirche. Aufsätze zur biblischen Theologie* II, Tübingen 1990, 91–102, rightly refers to the vision at Isaiah's call in 6.1–13, above all the motif of hardening in 6.9ff. (cf. also Acts 28.26ff. and the motif of sending in Isa. 6.8).

744. For ἐπιμένειν with a note of time meaning 'stay as a guest with', see Acts 10.48: Peter with Cornelius; 21.4.10: Paul with the brethren in Tyre and with Philip; 28.14 cf. also I Cor. 16.7f.; μένειν Acts 21.7, cf. 16.15; 18.3. See also J. A. Cramer, *Catenae Graecorum Patrum NT,* VI, 1842 (reprinted 1967), ad loc.: τὸ δὲ ἐπιμεῖναι τοσαύτας ἡμέρας, φιλίας καὶ σφοδροτάτης ἀγάπης. Similarly Theophylact, PG 124, 965 ad loc.

745. Mark 6.10f.; Matt. 10.12–14; Luke 9.4f.; 10.5–12; Acts 9.43; 10.48; 16.15; 17.5, 7; 18.3; 21.4, 7, 10f., 16; Rom. 16.23; III John 5ff., see O. Hiltbrunner, *RAC* 8, 1972, 1103ff.; M. Puzicha, *Die Fremdenaufnahme (Mt 25, 35) als Werk der privaten Wohltätigkeit im Urteil der Alten Kirche,* MBTh 47, 1980; H.-J. Klauck, *Hausgemeinde und Hauskirche im frühen Christentum,* SBS 103, Stuttgart 1981, 59, cf. 34, 43, 89, 101; M. Hengel, *Johanneische Frage* (n.33), 132ff.[38ff.].

746. Codex Dd and sy[hmg] assume an interim stay with Mnason 'in a certain village' to tone down the report. From there they are said to have set out for Jerusalem. Cf. the critical comment on this by Ropes, *Beginnings* (n.363), III, 204 on v.16: 'The Western text is inherently highly improbable. Its indefinite reference to the "village" is futile and over-emphasized.'

747. 21.18 cf. Rom. 15.31b. It follows from the reference in 24.17 that Luke knew of the collection. Probably the diplomatic James advised Paul to use the collection to pay for the vows of the four Jewish-Christian Nazirites. In that way the community did not have to take them on and Paul could show that he was not an apostate. See Hengel, *Earliest Christianity* (n.25), 118; id., 'Jakobus' (n.705), 95f.

748. 11.12–13.3.

749. For the conflict in II and III John see Hengel, *Johanneische Frage* (n.33), 127–32, 145f. [35–8, 42f.].

750. What tells against the conjecture that contact was already made between Cephas/Peter and Saul/Paul or there was an exchange between them from Damascus is that the personal contact also broke off in the long years afterwards leading up to the 'Apostolic Council'. The letters, too, indicate tensions more than a personal link. The difference in the assessment of Apollos (I Cor 1.12; 3.4–12, where the θεμέλιος in our view refers to the claims associated with the name *Kepha/Petros* in Matt. 16.18; 4.6; 16.12) and Cephas (1.12; 3.22; 9.22) is striking, although the theological difficulties in I Cor. 1–3 are connected more with the preaching of Apollos and its Alexandrian colouring than with that of Cephas/Peter; in our view the latter's emissaries appear against Paul in II Cor. 10–12. Cf. also Gal. 1.12.16; Matt. 16.17.

751. Thus Mussner, *Galaterbrief* (n.200), 95. See also O. Hofius, 'Gal 1, 18: ἱστορῆσαι Κηφᾶν', in id., *Paulusstudien* (n.508), 262, who rejects the widespread translation 'visit' and says that the 'only possible' translation is 'to get to know Cephas (personally)'. But if I want to get to know someone personally, then of course that applies above all to his views and his knowledge.

752. Conzelmann, *History of Primitive Christianity* (n.163), 81. But nowhere in his letters does Paul report 'conversations', not even in Gal. 2.1–10; he speaks of valid agreements. In terms of 'theological substance', Conzelmann started more from present-day professorial small talk. One should not project one's own dogmatic rigidity on the two greatest figures of earliest Christianity from 2000 years ago – around six years after the death of Jesus.

753. Cf. Matt. 18.16; II Cor. 13.1; I Tim. 5.19; cf. Heb. 10.28. L.

Schenke, *Die Urgemeinde*, Stuttgart, etc. 1990, 321, thinks it 'conceivable
... that a basic clarification and agreement about the task of mission
among the Gentiles was reached at this meeting'.

754. Thus G. D. Kilpatrick, 'Galatians 1:18 'ΙΣΤΟΡΗΣΑΙ ΚΗΦΑΝ', in
A. J. B. Higgins (ed.), *New Testament Essays. Studies in Memory of T. W.
Manson*, Manchester 1959, 144–9: 149, following *LSJ*, 842 I.2.a: 'visit a
person for the purpose of inquiry'. For the Jesus tradition see ibid., 148
and above all J. D. G. Dunn, 'The Relationship between Paul and
Jerusalem according to Galatians 1 and 2', *NTS* 28, 1987, 461–78; 463ff.;
against this Hofius, 'Gal 1, 18' (n.751), 255–67. See also G. Klein,
Rekonstruktion und Interpretation, BEvTh 50, 1969, 112 n.71, who also cites
older views of this kind.

755. This personal and by no means short visit recalls the form of the
effect of the *Evangelium contra peccatum* according to Luther's Schmal-
kald Articles IV (BSELK 1, 449: '... *atque etiam per mutuum colloquium et
consolationem fratrum, Matthei 18: Ubi duo aut tres fuerint congregati* ...').

756. Rom. 1.1f.; 3.21; 15.7–12, etc.

757. That is even more true in the earliest period than later, see I Cor.
7.29; Phil. 4.5; I Thess. 5.2.

758. I Cor. 15.11. This is one of the most important theological statements made by the apostle!

759. Gal. 2.11–16. The role played by Cephas/Peter in the Corinthian
community presupposes that the question of the law was not basically a
matter of controversy beween him and Paul: I Cor. 1.12; 3.22; 9.5. In II
Cor. also, other questions are the issue. F. C. Baur and the Tübingen
school interpreted Peter's attitude falsely and thus depicted the history
of earliest Christianity in a one-sided and distorted way.

760. Gal. 2.7f.; I Cor. 15.9, cf. 7f. I have conjectured elsewhere in connection with the Gospel of Mark that the term εὐαγγέλιον plays a role
not only in Paul but also in Peter, see Hengel, 'Problems' (n.48), 54ff.

761. Burchard, *Zeuge* (n.5), 168; cf. Acts 15.7.

762. This may on the one hand go back to Jesus' own activity (where it
may be a custom which is taken for granted, but which then became
meaningless again). But it then seems to have become intensified and to
have continued in the Petrine communities up to Mark and Matthew.

763. Mark 2.17; cf. also Mark 14.72 and Luke 5.8; 22.31f., which relate
to Peter.

764. Hengel, 'Problems' (n.48); E. Schweizer, 'Markus als Begleiter
des Petrus?', in *The Four Gospels, Festschrift for Frans Neirynck*, BEThL,
1992, 751–73.

765. Tobit 8.20: 'You may not depart from here for fourteen days.

Remain where you are, with me, and eat and drink. You shall bring joy to my daughter again after all her suffering.' Cf. Tobit 10.7.

766. On this see Strecker, 'Befreiung' (n.54), 230. Gal. 5.11 (if it is to be understood in temporal terms at all) refers to the pre-Christian period. Paul was persecuted from the moment when he emerged as the preacher of a gospel radically critical of the law which was revealed to him before Damascus, i.e. from the beginning, see above, 91. On this cf. H. J. Schoeps, *Paul. The Theology of the Apostle in the Light of Jewish Religious History*, London 1961, 168, taking up E. Barnikol and Mussner, *Galaterbrief* (n.200), 358ff. Paul was certainly not a 'Jewish Diaspora missionary' (thus Barnikol, *Die vorchristliche und frühchristliche Zeit des Paulus*, FEUC 1, Kiel 1929, 21ff.), since Judaism knew no 'missionaries'.

767. *Schwäbisches Tagblatt*, 26 August 1995, 33. See J. W. Goethe, *Briefwechsel mit Friedrich Schiller. Gedenkausgabe der Werke, Briefe und Gespräche*, Vol. 20, ed. E. Beutler, Zürich ²1964, 419f.

768. Acts 22.3: born in Cilician Tarsus; 9.11; 21.39: Ταρσεύς, citizen of Tarsus, on which see Hengel, 'Vorchristliche Paulus' (n.51), 180–90 [1–6].

769. Which Paul reports in Gal 1.21.

770. De Wette and Overbeck, *Apostelgeschichte* (n.698), 147 n.**.

771. Zeller, *Apostelgeschichte* (n.738), 381.

772. Acts 9.15; 22.15, 21; 26.17f.

773. 11.26: ἐγένετο δὲ αὐτοῖς καὶ ἐνιαυτὸν ὅλον συναχθῆναι ἐν τῇ ἐκκλησίᾳ καὶ διδάξαι ὄχλον ἱκανόν, χρηματίσαι τε πρώτως ἐν Ἀντιοχείᾳ τοὺς μαθητὰς Χριστιανούς.

774. Cod. D⁽²⁾ gig p, sy^hmg emend here because this is too little for them: οἵτινες παραγενόμενοι ἐνιαυτὸν ὅλον συνεχύθησαν ὄχλον ἱκανόν 'when they had arrived (in Antioch) they stirred up a great mass of people for a whole year', without mentioning the worship of the community. That is the style of the later acts of apostles, which Luke does not adopt here.

775. In our view Ἕλληνας (p⁷⁴ Sin² A D* pauci) is quite certainly to be read rather than Ἑλληνιστάς. Only that makes sense. In our view it is no coincidence that Luke speaks here of Greeks and not simply of ἔθνη.

776. Acts 13.5.

777. 13.42–52. The turning point 13.46: ἰδοὺ στρεφόμεθα εἰς τὰ ἔθνη (cf. 28.28 ἀπεστάλη). Previously the key word appears with reference to Paul only with the call in 9.15; there it is still relatively unspecific, but cf. 22.21; 26.20, 23, and 22.15.

778. Luke 5.1–10; Matt. 8.29; 14.27f.; 15.15; 18.21; Mark 9.5; Luke 12.41 etc.

779. Becker, *Paulus* (n.61), 105 asks himself 'whether Acts 10 was not first put before the apostles' meeting' – contrary to historical reality – 'out of Lukan interest'. That is unfounded. And Peter certainly did not move 'to Caesarea' after his imprisonment, Acts 12.15. There similarly he was in the persecutor's sphere of power.

780. See Barrett, *Acts I* (n.77), 490–540; M. Hengel, 'The Historian Luke' (n.36), 171ff. Cornelius need not have had all his unit in Caesarea. He could also have carried out special duties in the most important port of Judaea with a small detachment of troops. Thus we know of a customs official and a ἑκατονάρχης with a troop in the Nabataean harbour of Leukekome on the Red Sea *c.*75 CE, see L. Casson, *The Periplus Maris Erythraei*, Princeton 1989, *c.*19, pp. 6f., 145; see also Bowersock, *Arabia* (n.579), 70f. Presumably this was a Nabataean officer. According to Pliny the Younger, *Ep.* 10, 77.78, the centurion of a legion was posted to Byzantium with a small troop because of the 'influx of travellers' *(confluente in eam commeantium turba,* cf. *Ep.* 21.1). Trajan turned down Pliny's request for the same thing to be done in the relatively insignificant (Gordiucome-)Juliopolis on the frontier between Bithynia and Galatia because he did not want to create a precedent. See A. N. Sherwin-White, *The Letters of Pliny. A Historical and Social Commentary*, Oxford ³1985, 665–8: 'Other centurions are known later in the territory of Prusias, Claudiopolis, Sinope, and a stationarius in Tium' (666), all places in northern Asia Minor. In Acts 10.1 it is only said that Cornelius belonged to a *cohors Italica* , not that this was itself stationed in Caesarea. There is evidence of a *cohors II Italica* in the Syrian army in 69 CE which Mucianus led against Vitellius in the West, see Schürer I, 365 n.54 (CIL III 13483a = ILS 9169 on a tombstone of Cornutus in Pannonia). There are further instances from second-century Syria here. Nor can we rule out the possibility that Cornelius had already retired from active service and was undertaking a special commission in Caesarea. See also A. N. Sherwin-White, *Roman Society and Roman Law in the New Testament*, Oxford ²1969, 160f. on the very widespread gentilic name Cornelius.

781. Acts 15.6. The term εὐαγγέλιον, which is rare in Luke, appears only here and in Paul's speech in Miletus (20.24: εὐαγγέλιον τῆς χάριτος). Luke deliberately puts this 'Paulinism' on the lips of Peter.

782. Luke can refer the term αἵρεσις even to the Christians: 24.5, 14 (to Paul himself); 28.22 and also to Sadducees (5.17) and Pharisees (15.5; 26.5). They are all Jewish 'sects'.

783. The 'apostles and brethen in Judaea' who hear of the conversion of the Gentiles (11.1) and 'those of the circumcision' who criticize Peter are identical: they are the Jewish Christians from the mother country.

After they had heard Peter 'they became calm and praised God ...', i.e. they were convinced. That this was then not completely the case is shown by the τίνες in 15.1 and the Pharisees who came to the faith 15.5. Even in Luke, for whom in his apologia to Theophilus harmonizing is a concern close to his heart, not everything goes so harmoniously, above all if, in accordance with his wishes, one notes hints and reads between the lines. Cod. D p w mae do away with the offence in a long quotation. They intensify Peter's missionary activity in Caesarea and have 'the brothers from the circumcision'(!) in Jerusalem criticizing Peter (11.2).

784. For Philip's activity see Barrett, *Acts* I (n.77), 393–436; Hengel, 'Mission' (n.116); id., 'The Historian Luke' (n.36), 110–16.

785. That Luke knows the geographical conditions follows from the fact that he makes Peter visit Lydda and Joppa, cities which since the Maccabaean period had been almost purely Jewish. He has to be called to Caesarea by the godfearing centurion, whereas previously he had Philip appearing in semi-Gentile Ashdod – through a miracle of transportation by the Spirit – and then of his own free will in Caesarea. See Hengel, 'The Historian Luke' (n.36), 110–21.

786. Acts 6.5. cf. already 2.11 and the vague mode of expression in 13.43 by comparison with 13.50.

787. Cf. 10.28 and the charge in 11.3, which in turn matches what happens in Gal. 2.11ff. The issue was loss of ritual cleanness by dealing with the uncircumcised – a specific problem for Palestinian Jews who observed the law strictly. Luke assumes that initially this was true of Peter and the Christians in Jerusalem.

788. Cf. also 15.14, where James with the πρῶτον stressed this priority in Acts.

789. 11.19: μηδενὶ λαλοῦντες τὸν λόγον εἰ μὴ μόνον Ἰουδαίοις.

790. Rom. 1.16, cf. Acts 2.9f.; 3.26; 13.46; I Cor. 1.23f.; 10.32; 12.13; Gal. 3.28. Paul always mentioned the Jews before the Greeks, as does Luke: Acts 14.1; 18.4; 19.10, 17; 20.21 cf. Barrett, *Acts* I (n.77), 549: '"to the Jews first, and also to the Greek" was a principle not discovered for the first time by Paul.'

791. Acts 22.21: Πορεύου, ὅτι ἐγὼ εἰς ἔθνη μακρὰν ἐξαποστελῶ σε. But cf. 9.15, which is already enigmatic and restrained; 22.15 is clearer and 26.17–20 is quite plain.

792. 9.30: καὶ ἐξαπέστειλαν αὐτὸν εἰς Ταρσόν. Perhaps Luke wants to use the sending by the brothers discreetly to indicate that they paid for the voyage of their penniless guest to Tarsus, cf. 20.37ff. The scene is unique. On later journeys the sending is done by the Spirit, 13.4; cf. 16.6f., 10 and above all 19.21; 20.22; or Paul decides himself, 15.36–40;

18.21–23. The only other mention of direct sending is on the journeys to Jerusalem in 11, 30: ἀποστείλαντες ... διὰ χειρός B ΚΣ and 15.2: ἔταξαν ἀναβαίνειν.

793. For him it denotes more the outward event and the inner motivation, while similarly in the three accounts of the conversion we see above all the oppositions. His logic was not necessarily the same as ours.

794. Schneider, *Apostelgeschichte* 1 (n.77), 40.

795. 9.22: ἐνεδυναμοῦτο. Luke's favourite word παρρησιάζεσθαι appears twice in 27.28, cf. 13.46; 14.3; 18.26; 19.8, usually in synagogues; 26.26 before Agrippa II, cf. 9.15: he bears the name of Christ 'before the nations and the kings of the children of Israel'.

796. That is now also conjectured by Haacker, 'Werdegang' (n.140), 919–21, who speaks of a 'retreat to Tarsus' and thinks that Paul now learned the craft of tentmaking.

797. One takes offence only where criticism of Luke is engaged in for its own sake. Thus Loisy, *Actes* (n.699), 425: 'For the moment he condemns ... Saul to inaction'; Haenchen, *Acts* (n.5), 333: 'The writer assumes that Paul now remains quietly for a while in his home town of Tarsus'; Conzelmann, *Acts* (n.230), 67: 'The time spent in Tarsus serves as a pause. In fact, Paul carried on missionary activity there for more than a dozen (sic!) years (Gal 2, 1).' G. Schille, *Die Apostelgeschichte des Lukas*, ThHK 5, Berlin (East), 229, is grotesque, as usual: 'Luke thinks of Saul there in a state of waiting, on a kind of holiday before the great work.' Luke does not say (or think) anything like that!

798. Cf. 14.22; 18.23; cf. R. E. Osborne, 'St. Paul's Silent Years', *JBL* 84, 1965, 59–65: 60.

799. Thus already de Wette and Overbeck, *Apostelgeschichte* (n.698), 147 n.: 'However, in 15.23, 41 the presupposition seems to emerge that Paul was active here as an apostle', cf. 243f. However, here the mention of Syria and Cilicia certainly cannot be explained by Gal. 1.21, but simply presupposes the geographical facts and thus indirectly and belatedly indicates that Paul had carried on a mission to the Gentiles in (Tarsus and therefore in) Cilicia. Cf. e.g. also the later reference to the collection in Acts 24.17.

800. Eusebius, HE 6, 46, 3; cf. 7, 5, 1, 4; 7, 28, 1: he stands in first place among the bishops assembled against Paul of Samosata, i.e. he must have had a prominent position and have been a kind of metropolitan bishop of Cilicia, see A. von Harnack, *Die Mission und Ausbreitung des Christentums*, Leipzig ⁴1924, 664, 730. [The English translation, *The Expansion of Christianity in the First Three Centuries*, 2 vols., London 1904, does not contain many passages which appear in the later German

edition and is not very helpful here; see only III, 324f.]. From now on Tarsus appears regularly in the synodical lists.

801. Thus Wendt, *Apostelgeschichte* (n.704), 174: but according to Gal. 1.21 Paul at that time came first to Syria and only then to Cilicia; cf. E. Preuschen, *Die Apostelgeschichte*, HNT IV, 1, Tübingen 1912, 61; Weiss, *Earliest Christianity* (n.89), 203.

802. According to de Wette and Overbeck, *Apostelgeschichte* (n.698), 147, early exegetes (Calov, Olshausen) had thought of Caesarea Philippi to achieve a harmony with Gal. 1.21. But even if the travel route should have led 'through Syria', a voyage from Caesarea by the Sea was also possible: 'he took ship to Seleucia and travelled on from there by land'. However, this, too, is an unnecessary supposition. See even Haenchen, *Acts* (n.5), 325. Tarsus was reached most easily from Caesarea (and via Caesarea from Jerusalem) directly by ship.

803. Cf. II Cor. 11.10: the 'whole extent of' the province of Achaea, Bauer and Aland, *Lexicon*, 887; Rom. 15.23; Philo, *Aet. mundi* 147; *Legatio* 89, etc.

804. E. Bickerman, 'The Date of Fourth Maccabees', in *Louis Ginzberg Jubilee Volume*, New York 1945 (= id., *Studies in Jewish and Christian History* I, AGJU 9, Leiden 1976, 275–81); J. Deininger, *Die Provinziallandtage der römischen Kaiserzeit*, Munich and Berlin 1965, 83, 87 refers to a united Agon of κοινὸν Συρίας Κιλικίας Φοινείκης, which is mentioned in an inscription from the second half of the first century (published in L. Moretti, *Inscrizioni agonistiche greche*, Studi pubblicati dall'Istituto italiano per la storia antica 12, Rome 1953); Riesner, *Frühzeit* (n.49), 236; G. Lüdemann, *Paul, Apostle to the Gentiles I. Studies in Chronology*, Philadelphia and London 1989, 20. We find the use of a similar formula in Luke, Acts 15.23, 41. See already Diodore 16, 42, 9. Cf. also Judith 1.12: πάντα τὰ ὅρια τῆς Κιλικίας καὶ Δαμασκηνῆς καὶ Συρίας; 1.7 τοὺς κατοικοῦντας τὴν Κιλικίαν καὶ Δαμασκόν. Here the perspective is from north to south, and as the capital of pre-Seleucid Syria, Damascus stands basically as the capital of all Syria. Cf. 2.25, Cilicia and Arabia as frontier points. See also IV Macc. 4.2: Apollonius the *strategos* in "Syria and Phoenicia" and Cilicia', i.e. the area west of the Euphrates ruled by the Seleucids.

805. See R. Syme, 'Observations on the Province of Cilicia', in *Anatolian Studies presented to W. H. Buckler*, ed. W. M. Calder and J. Keil, Manchester 1939, 299–332. From the time of Caesar until 72 CE it was then combined with Syria to form one province.

806. Against Lüdemann, *Paul* (n.804); with Riesner, *Frühzeit* (n.49), 242f. Individual scholars like Conzelmann wrongly regard this journey as

a Lukan construction.

807. Acts 13 and 14, see J. Roloff, *Die Apostelgeschichte*, NTD 5, Göttingen 1981, 194f.; Barrett, *Acts* (n.77), 598–693: 600, 608ff.

808. *Frühzeit* (n.49), 237f., cf. 223f. LXX Deut. 2.23; Amos 9.7 (LXX and Symmachus); Jer. 47 (29), 4 (Aquila and Theodotion). For the client kingdom and the province of Cilicia (after Tiberius) see D. Magie, *Roman Rule in Asia Minor*, I, 1950, 1966, 491–6; II, 1349–59.

809. Weiss, *Earliest Christianity* (n.89), 203. The events in 11.25 must have taken place before the third journey. But Paul already travelled by ship on the first and second journeys. For Cyrene and Syria see Schmidt, *Acta Pauli*, Leipzig ²1905, 65. However, it is questionable whether this is a journey of Paul at all. The Acts of Paul around 180 CE largely follow Acts in the routes of journeys, but they put them together in a very free way. They illustrate what Luke could have made of all his scanty reports from Paul's early period had he been writing a romance. The editor C. Schmidt thinks of other missionaries who go from Jerusalem into the Diaspora mission, Acts 11.19.

810. Cf. on Josephus n.1170 below, cf. 186 above; further the mention of the Taurus in the description of Abraham's circular journey in 1QGenAp (see above, 391 n.602 and below, 427 n.903).

811. For the expression cf. I Cor. 13.5 οὐ παροξύνεται and Acts 17.16; Bauer and Aland, *Lexicon*, 1271. It appears in LXX as a translation of *kesep*, Deut. 29.28 (M 27); Jer. 39 (M 32). 37; 10.10 Theodotion and L' s. *Sept. Gott.* ed. Ziegler, XV, 201, appendix on God's wrath. For the verb see PsSol. 4.21; Greek Baruch 1.6.

812. Acts 13.13; 15.39.

813. Κιλίκια τραχεῖα (or Τραχειῶτις) comprised the west part of the Taurus and the hilly Mediterranean coast between Pamphylia and the Cilician plain near Soloi. Strabo 12, 1, 4; 12, 2, 11; 14, 5, 1–7: the frontier city of Cilicia Pedias was Soli, a colony of Rhodes and the home city of the Stoic Chrysippus: Dio Cassius 59, 8, 2; 68, 8, 2. See Jones, *Cities* (n.287), 191–201. This region, notorious for pirates, which extended northwards to north of Derbe, came under Roman rule in 20 BCE and for a time belonged to Archelaus of Cappadocia (36 BCE – 17 CE), the father-in-law of Herod's son Alexander; later the region was given by Caligula and then again by Claudius to Antiochus IV Epiphanes of Commagene until he was deposed by Vespasian in 72 CE, who combined 'rough' and 'level' Cilicia into one province. Cf. Syme, 'Observations on the Province of Cilicia' (n.805), 327; T. B. Mitford, 'Roman Rough Cilicia', *ANRW* II, 7.2, 1980, 1230–61: 1239, 1241, 1246ff.

814. For bibliography see the account by W. M. Ramsay, *The Cities of*

St. Paul, London 1907, 55–244, which has still not been surpassed; also H. Böhlig, *Die Geisteskultur von Tarsus*, FRLANT 19, 1913; W. Ruge, 'Tarsos', *PW* 2. R. 4, 1932, 2413–39, esp. 2430ff.; id., 'Kilikien', *PW* 11, 1921, 385–9; E. Olshausen, *KP* 5, 529f.; K. Ziegler, *KP* 3, 208f.; Jones, *Cities* (n.287), 192–207; Hengel, 'Vorchristliche Paulus' (n.51), 180–93 [1–6]; Riesner, *Frühzeit* (n.49), 236f. For the excavations at Tarsus cf. H. Goldman et al., *Excavations at Gözlü Kule, Tarsus*, 3 vols, Princeton 1950–1963; M. V. Seton-Williams, 'Cilician Survey', *Anatolian Studies* 4, 1954, 125, 139, 169f. There is an urgent need for a thorough monograph on ancient Cilicia and its cities.

815. Kornemann, Κοινόν, *PW* Suppl. 4, 933. Deininger, *Provinziallandtage* (n.804), 83f.

816. For the roads see Magie, *Roman Rule in Asia Minor*, I, 276, 375, 397, 410; II, 788, 1144ff., 1152ff. Cf. above, 174f., on Abraham's journey in 1QGenAp 21.

817. See Ramsay, *Cities* (n.814), 169–86 (concentrates above all on the pre-Roman period); Böhlig, *Tarsus* (n.814), 128–57.

818. *Legatio* 281: they appear as colonies of the metropolis Jerusalem.

819. Despite Luke's imprecise terminology, here we have different communities, including that of the Jews from Cilicia, cf. Acts 24.12; 26.11 and above, n.233; see Hengel, 'Between Jesus and Paul' (n.50), 12ff.; id., 'Vorchristliche Paulus' (n.51), 205, 259, 271f. [13, 56, 69f.]; Barrett, *Acts* I (n.77), 323: 'Some if not all of the persons concerned are associated with a synagogue.' Where would these groups from particular areas have met for discussions if not in synagogues?

820. bMeg 26a Bar (*twrsyyn*); tMeg 3, 6 (Zuckermandel 224) = jMeg 3, 1 73d line 40: the Alexandrians. It was sold for profane purposes. According to bNazir 52 it was desecrated by dead bones, but the physician Theodos declared it to be clean. jSheq 2, 7 47a lines 20ff. mentions a synagogue of the Tarsians, presumably in Tiberias; according to LevR 35, 12 there was also one in Lydda. However, S. Krauss, *MGWJ* 39, 1895, 54f.; cf. id., *Talmudische Altertümer*, Leipzig 1910–1912, reprinted Hildesheim 1966, II, 625, and *Synagogale Altertümer*, Berlin 1922, reprinted Hildesheim 1966, 206f., sees this as a synagogue of weavers, who make precious fabric in the manner of Tarsus: *tarsî* can mean both, see Jastrow, *Dictionary* 1, 555b. We can by no means rule out a synagogue of people from that region. In Rome and in Sepphoris we have side by side synagogues relating to trades and synagogues named geographically according to the origin of their members.

821. *CIJ* II, no. 925. For the problem of Tarsian citizenship see Hengel, 'Vorchristliche Paulus' (n.51), 188–93 [4–6]; Riesner, *Frühzeit*

(n.49), 130f.; for other cities of Asia Minor see Trebilco, *Jewish Communities* (n.362), 171, 257f. nn.16–19.

822. *CIJ* II, no. 931: Ἐνθάδε κ[ῖ]τε Ἰσάκις πρεσβύτερος τῆς Καππαδόκων Τάρσου λινοπώλου. Krauss, *Synagogale Altertümer* (n.820), 237, conjectures that Τάρσος does not refer to a home city but rather means Tarsian linen; however, in that case one would really have expected the term to be put afterwards in the form Ταρσικοῦ/ῶν, see *LSJ*, 1759: λίνου Ταρσικοῦ or λίνα θάρσικα. A weaver of such fabrics can be called Ταρσικάριος or Ταρσικούφικος. Why should not someone from Tarsus trading in linen have belonged to the community of the Cappadocians, since Cappadocia was directly north of the Cilician Gate and adjoined the city territory of Tarsus? For the 'linen workers' in Tarsus see Ruge, 'Tarsos' (n.814), 2432; Dio Chrysostom, *Or.* 34, 16, 21, still emphasizes the large number of λινουργοί in Tarsus, who did not have full civic rights and caused unrest: 'The proletarian population of Tarsus.' Cf. also Philostratus, *Vit. Apoll.* 1, 7: the Tarsians 'value fine linen garments more highly than the Athenians value wisdom.'

823. On the other hand in Joppa/Jaffa we find even more tombs of Jews from Alexandria (or Egypt), see Horbury and D. Noy, *Inscriptions* (n.316), nos. 145–51.

824. *CIJ* II, 39ff. has only inscriptions from western Rough Cilicia, but see G. Dagron and D. Feissels, *Inscriptions de Cilicie*, Paris 1987: no. 36 from Tarsus (*c.* sixth century CE), no. 14 from Diocaesarea.

825. *CIJ* II, nos. 782–794; Schürer III, 33f.; cf. further H. Bloedhorn, *JJS* 35, 1990, 68; cf. M. H. Williams, 'The Jewish Community of Corycos – Two More Inscriptions', *ZPE* 92, 1992, 249ff.

826. I follow the text of J. Keil and A. Wilhelm, *Denkmäler aus dem rauhen Kilikien*, MAMA III, 1931, 140 no. 262, see H. Lietzmann, 'Notizen', *ZNW* 31, 1932, 313f. The text is relatively late: fourth–fifth century. The Jewish and the numerous Christian sarcophagi are not separated. For the formula οὐδείς ἀθάνατος which is frequent in Jewish epitaphs see also *CIJ* II No. 782 from Marash/Germanicia and above all P. W. van der Horst, *Ancient Jewish Epitaphs*, Contributions to Biblical Exegesis and Theology 2, Kampen 1991, 121f. and for 'astral immortality', 123f.: the notion was probably of an assumption into the heavenly spheres immediately after death. We also have numerous Hellenistic parallels to this; in addition to the literature cited by van der Horst see W. Peek, *Griechische Grabgedichte*, Darmstadt 1960, 40f., no. 12, 5; 74; 218, 3; 250; 351, 8; 391, 4ff.: the assumption of the soul into the ether or into the heavenly dwellings, cf. also 296; 345, 9. The dead person is transported to the Pleiades: 334, 5; he becomes a star: 304, 5f.; 310, 8–11; 317,

13; 343, 5ff. Possibly a Hellenistic form of Dan. 12.2 underlies this notion, see Hengel, *Judaism and Hellenism* (n.314), I, 124, 196–202, 232ff.

827. *CIJ* II 790; we also find this name for a presbyter from Hyllarima in Cara from the third century and a Eusabbatis in Rome, *CIJ* I 379.

828. For similar variants above all in Egypt see Horbury and Noy, *Inscriptions* (n.316), 127f. no. 58 (bibliography) and index, 262; in Italy: Noy, *Jewish Inscriptions* I (n.325), 165f. no. 126; id., *Jewish Inscriptions* II (n.243), index 524; further the indices of *CIJ* I and *CPJ.*

829. Williams, 'Corycos' (n.825), 248. Here he convincingly corrects the reading of MAMA III, 751.

830. See Lietzmann, *Notizen* (n.826) = Keil and Wilhelm, *Denkmäler* (n.826), 114 no. 166; 118 no. 177 and nos. 493b, 678, 686, 737.

831. OGIS II no. 573; F. Sokolowski, *Lois Sacrées de l'Asie mineure*, Paris 1955, no. 80, bibliography (I am following Sokolowski's text); cf. Gressmann, *RE* 2.R. 1, 1920, 1560–5; E. Lohse, σάββατον, *TDNT* 7, 8 n.44x; V. A. Tcherikower, A. Fuks and M. Stern, *CPJ* III, 1964, 41–87, 'The Sambathions' (46f.); Schürer III, 1, 622–6 (625 n.183); J. T. Milik, *Dédicaces* (n.644), 69–72.

832. θεοῦ [προν]οίαι (OGIS: [εὐν]όαι) Σαββατίστου συνηγμένοις.

833. See Gressmann, *RE* (n.831), 1562.

834. Heberdey and Wilhelm, *Reisen in Kilikien*, DAWW.PH 44, 1896, 67: ἡ ἑταιρήα τῶν Σαμβατιστῶν Αἰθειβήλῳ θεῷ ..., see Gressmann, *RE* (n.831), 1561.

835. By contrast, a link with the Thracian-Phrygian god Sabbazios, who was confused e.g. in Rome with the Jewish Sabaoth, is improbable. See E. N. Lane, 'Sabazius and the Jews in Valerius Maximus', *JRS* 69, 1979, 35–8; S. E. Johnson, 'The present state of Sabazios-Research', *ANRW* II, 17, 3, 1984, 1583–1613 (on Sabbazios and the Jews, 1602–7); Turcan, *Les cultes orientaux* (n.423), 314; Feldman, *Jew and Gentile* (n.320), 301.

836. Tcherikover and Fuks, *CPJ* III, 43–87: 47, 50ff.

837. Milik, *Dédicaces* (n.644), 67–72: 68; J. Keil and K. v. Premerstein, *Bericht über eine zweite Reise in Lydien*, DAWW.PH 54, 2, 1911, no. 224 and p.117; Naukratis: SGUÄ I, no. 12: [Ἀ]μμωνίου συναγωγός [ἀνέθηκεν τῇ σ]υνόδῳ Σαββατικῇ (time of Augustus); Sambathis: H. C. Youtie, *HTR* 37, 1944, 209–18. The most detailed discussion of the problem is in *CPJ* III, 1964, 43–87, with examples of names from Egypt. The Jewish Sibyl Sambathe/Sabbe (see below, n.845) possibly also encouraged the worship of the 'Sabbath goddess' among Judaizing pagans. For Sambathe/Sabbe see also Stern, *GLAJ* II, 198–299, no. 360; Schürer III,

1, 622–6.

838. *CIJ* 752, cf. Josephus, *Antt.* 16, 164 from Augustus' decree for the Jews in Asia: the theft of sacred scriptures or vessels ἐκ τε σαββατείου (vl σαββαθίου) is punished in the same way as the plundering of a temple, see *CPJ* III, 46; Schürer III, 1, 624f.; Trebilco, *Jewish Communities* (n.362), 198f. n.17.

839. *De Superst.* 3, p. 166 A = Stern, *GLAJ* I, 549. Quotation from Euripides, *Troiades* 764. For the term see Heb. 4.9 and Justin, *Dial* 23, 3: before Moses there was no σαββατισμός. Cf. also the *metuentem sabbata patrem* in Juvenal, above, 63, and Stern, *GLAJ* II, 106f., who refers to Josephus, *c. Apionem* 2, 282; Philo, *Vita Mosis* 2, 21, and Tertullian, *Ad nat.* 1, 13. Cf. also Augustus' letter to Tiberius, which confuses the Sabbath and Yom Kippur, in Suetonius, *Augustus* 76.2 and the grammarian Diogenes on Rhodes, who only lectured on the Sabbath and Tiberius, who wanted to hear him, referred through a slave to the seventh day, Suetonius, *Tiberius* 32, 5 = *GLAJ* II, 110f. nos. 303, 305.

840. It goes back to the Persian period: Sepharad in Obadiah 20 is Sardes, see Hengel, 'Schürer' (n.247), 34ff.; Schürer III, 1, 17–36, and H. Bloedhorn, *JSS* 35, 1990, 66–9. Trebilco, *Jewish Communities* (n.362), 5ff., 192f. begins his study with Antiochus III's letter to Zeuxis about the settling of Jews from Babylonia in the hinterland of Asia Minor, Josephus, *Antt.* 12, 148–153. For the number see Philo, *Legatio* 245.

841. For the Theos Hypsistos see 70, 76f. above and Trebilco, *Jewish Communities* (n.362), 127–44, 238; cf. T. Drew-Bear and C. Naour, 'Divinités de Phrygie', *ANRW* II 18, 3, 1907–2044: 2032–43: in Phrygia only θεὸς ὕψιστος is attested, and never Ζεὺς ὕψιστος. Cf. the illustrations, ibid., pls. XIIIf., nos. 31–35b. This was an easy point of contact for Jewish influence, and also for direct propaganda.

842. See M. Mach, *Entwicklungsstadien des jüdischen Engelglaubens in vorrabbinischer Zeit*, TSAJ 34, 1992, 70f. n.10; the essential literature is given there. A. R. R. Sheppard, 'Pagan Cults of Angels in Roman Asia Minor', *Talanta* 12/13, 1980/1, 77–101 is most important for the state of the discussion; see also Nilsson, *Geschichte* (n.414), II², 540 n.7 and 577 n.1; L. Robert, *Hellenica* 11/12, 1960, 430–5; id., *Anatolica* 3, 1958, 115–20; J. Michel, 'Engel' I, *RAC* 5, 1962, cols. 53–60; see now also L. T. Stuckenbruck, *Angel Veneration and Christology*, WUNT II/70, 1995, 103ff. (on Gal. 4.3, 8f. and Col. 2.18) and 181–200 (for the inscriptions in Asia Minor and the magical texts).

843. Trebilco, *Jewish Communities* (n.362), 86–99, 222–7. The Noah tradition was rooted on Ararat in the widest sense. According to Josephus, *Antt.* 1, 90, the ark landed on a mountain in Armenia. Even if

the coins minted in Apamea which depict Noah with the ark (in the form of a Torah shrine) and the Sibyl (thus Geffcken, Collins) or his wife (thus Stichel, Scott) appear only from the end of the second century CE, this goes back to earlier Jewish, not Christian, influence, see Schürer III, 1, 28ff.; Scott, *Paul* (n.320), 35f.

844. Trebilco, *Jewish Communities* (n.362), 88f., 223; Schürer III, 1, 30. An earlier Phrygian saga could have influenced the Jewish Enoch tradition here. The tradition in Stephen of Byzantium (FGrH 800 F 3) certainly has a Jewish stamp.

845. The figure of the Sibyl probably derives originally from Asia Minor and goes back to priestesses and seers there; she was taken over into the classical Greek world from there. The Jewish Sibyl explicitly rejects this origin in her 'genealogy', Sib 3, 813–827 (Circe in 8, 814f.). Books 3; 5; 11–14 of the Jewish Sibyls come from Egypt, and the Jewish substratum of books 1–2 probably from Phrygia, see J. J. Collins, 'Sibylline Oracles', in *OTP* I, 1983, 322, 332. In addition to being dependent on Hesiod and the list of nations in Gen. 10, the euhemeristic enumeration of the theogony (cf. Hesiod, *Theog* 453–512) in Sib 3, 110–155 shows points of contact with Cilicia: the Jewish Sibyl identifies Japetos (cf. Hesiod, *Theog* 18, 134, 507, 746), the father of Prometheus and ancestor of Deucalion, with 'Japhet', the son of Noah. There seems to be little evidence of cult places of Japetos, but Japetos is also regarded as the father of Anchiale, the goddess worshipped in the place of the same name, near Tarsus. Cf. E. Simon, 'Japetos', *LIMC* V, 1, 1990, 523f.; Scott, *Paul* (n.320), 36–40.

846. This tradition is first attested in Pausanias X, 12, 9 (Sabbe), in the prologue by the Byzantine editor (Geffcken, *Oracula Sibyllina*, GCS 7, 1902, 2, 33), and in the Suda, s.v., but it certainly reflects old tradition. It is conjectured that this name stood in the gap after Sib 3, 811. Thus Geffcken, *ad loc.*; cf. A. Kurfess, *Sibyllinische Weissagungen*, Munich 1951, 16.

847. J. Robert and L. Robert, *Bulletin Épigraphique* 4 (1959–63), 1961, 244f. no. 750 and 5 (1964–1967), 1965, 169, no. 412; cf. PsSol 5.2; 15.1. R. Feldmeier, 'Hypsistos', *DDD*, 829, argues for a Jewish origin, but that does not fit because of the altar and a pillar, and in terms of content it seems much better in the milieu of (pagan) 'sympathizers'.

848. For καταφυγή as a technical term for the godfearers and proselytes see Joseph and Asenath 12.13; 15.7; 17.6; 19.5, 8.

849. See Hengel, 'Proseuche' (n.319), 179. The term προσευχή appears only in Jewish texts.

850. Macrobius, *Sat* 1, 18, 18–21 = Stern, *GLAJ* II, 411f. no. 45. There

is argument over the dating of Cornelius Labeo, see Nilsson, *Geschichte der griechischen Religion*, ²1961, II, 477 n.8.

851. τὸν πάντων ὕπατον θεὸν ἔμμεν 'Ιαώ.

852. μετοπώρου δ' ἁβρὸν 'Ιαώ.

853. For knowledge of this Jewish divine name, in addition to its frequent occurrence in the magical papyri (cf. on these also Fauth, *Helios* [n.371], index 264 s. v. Iao) see Diodorus Siculus 1, 94, 2 = *GLAJ* I, 171 no. 59; Varro in Augustine, *Civ. Dei* 6, 31; *Cons. Evang.* 1, 22, 30 and 23, 31 = *GLAJ* I, 209f. no. 72a–c. The Jewish God = Jovis, Caligula in Philo, *Legatio* 353; see also D. E. Aune, 'Iao', *RAC* 17, 1–12; for the identification with Dionysus see above all Plutarch, *Quaest Conviv* 4, 6, 2 = *GLAJ* I, 553f. no. 258; Tacitus, *Hist* 5, 5 = *GLAJ* II, 19.43 no. 281, is dismissive.

854. H. Erbse, *Fragmente griechischer Theosophie*, Hamburg 1941, 167-80, cf. e.g. §§ 12, 13, 21, 27 (after Porphyry: lines 13f.: … παντόκρατορ, βασιλέστατε, καί μόνε θνητῶν ἀθανάτων τε πάτερ μακάρων), 31, 35, 38, 39.

855. Specifically on Asia Minor see Trebilco, *Jewish Communities* (n.362), 145–66; Mitchell, *Anatolia* (n.362), 8f., 31f., 35ff., 43–51.

856. For Aphrodisias see Reynolds and Tannenbaum, *Jews* (n.320), 167–289; Hengel, 'Schürer' (n.257), 35f.; van der Horst, 'Juden' (n.321); for the controversy with Kraabel cf. also McKnight, *Light* (n.320), 158 n.66–70. For the Hypsistarians or Hypsistani see Trebilco, *Jewish Communities* (n.362), 163ff., 255 nn.85, 86 (inadequate); see Mitchell, *Anatolia* (n.362), II, 50f., 68 for the father of Gregory of Nazianzus. They worship the 'highest God' and 'pantocrator', i.e. the God of the LXX.

857. By contrast in Syria, where the number of inscriptions is very much fewer, we are dependent above all on the testimony of Josephus. In Egypt the reports break off quite suddenly with the fearful rebellion of the Jews in 115–117 CE.

858. P. W. van der Horst, 'New Altar of a Godfearer', in *Hellenism – Judaism – Christianity*, Kampen 1994, 65–72. We may also presuppose that a certain Zopyros named on a small altar in Pergamon with the inscription θεὸς κύριος ὁ ὢν εἰς ἀεί who also dedicates a lampholder with a lamp, is a 'godfearer'; here similarly we cannot rule out the possibility that a pagan identified the God of the Jews with Sarapis as early as the first century. Trebilco, *Jewish Communities* (n.362), 163, 254f. nn.79–84 (bibliography) conjectures a Jew. However, once again the altar and the form of the inscription tell against this, see E. Bickerman, 'The Altars of Gentiles', *RIDA* 5, 1958, 137–64 = *Studies in Jewish and Christian History* II,

AGJU IX, Leiden 1980, 324–46. van der Horst, 'Das Neue Testament und die jüdischen Grabinschriften' (n.321), 187–90, cf. 170 reckons with the possibility (*inter alia*) that the inscription on the altar in Acts 17.23 could similarly go back to a 'godfearer'.

859. See above, 159f. and nn.813–16.

860. *BJ* 1, 88 = *Antt.* 13, 374. According to *BJ* 1, 93, 9,000 mercenaries (1,000 cavalry and 8,000 infantry) and 10,000 Jews fought on Jannaeus's side in the battle against Demetrius III Eukairos; according to *Antt.* 13, 377, 6,200 mercenaries and 20,000 Jews. According to *BJ* 1, 93f. = *Antt.* 13, 378 the mercenaries were not lured over to the side of the Seleucid king, although they were Greeks, and fell bravely in battle.

861. For Hyrcanus see *Antt.* 13, 249; on this see I. Shatzman, *The Armies of the Hasmonaeans and Herod*, TSAJ 25, 1991, 26, 30–5: 'It may be conferred that foreign gentile mercenaries became a constant element of the Hasmonaean standing army from the time of John Hyrkanus onwards.' See also the complaint of the Pharisaic (?) party to Pompey in Damascus about the 'mass of mercenaries' in Diodore 40, 2 (F 36 R), see Stern, *GLAJ* I, 185 and the commentary, 187.

862. They preferred to serve in the Roman army and from the time of the Flavians made up almost half of the 'legionary recruits' in the East, see D. L. Kennedy, 'The Military Contribution of Syria to the Roman Imperial Army', in *The Eastern Frontier of the Roman Empire. Proceedings of a Colloquium held at Ankara in September 1988*, ed. D. H. French and C. S. Lightfoot, Part 1, British Institute of Archaeology at Ankara Monograph No. 11, BAR International Series 553(i), 1989, 235–46.

863. 'Pisidian' probably indicates the hilly south of Asia Minor generally. Between 125 and 65 BCE we should probably think principally of those areas in which the pirates of Asia Minor were at home. For the Herodian mercenaries see Shatzman, *Armies* (n.861), 140–3, 150, 156, 164, 205, 215. Their origin is not so clear, but soldiers from Asia Minor certainly continued to play an important role. For the Galatians see Shatzman, *Armies* (n.861), 183–5.

864. See above, 160.

865. Phil. 3.5; Acts 23.6; see Hengel, 'Vorchristlicher Paulus' (n.51), 220ff. [25ff.].

866. Acts 22.3; 26.4f.; 5.34. See Hengel, 'Vorchristlicher Paulus' (n.51), 206f. [14f.]. There is also discussion there of the tradition handed down by Jerome that his family came from Gischala in Galilee; despite the author's inaccuracies this is hardly sheer invention.

867. PesR 15, 24. R. Nahum b. Simlai lived in the middle of the third century. In the parallel PesK 5, 17 (Mandelbaum 1, 106, line 10, v.l.

bṭrsys).

868. *Haer.*30, 11, 1–6. See now M. Jacobs, *Die Institution des jüdischen Patriarchen*, TSAJ 52, 1995, 308–12.

869. A.-M. Malingrey, *Palladios. Dialogue sur la vie de Jean Chrystome* I, SC 341, 1988, 404 (XX 126f.).

870. *Tarsos* (n.814), 8–107: 'Die Religion von Tarsos'. But cf. 4: 'The main difficulty is the state of the source material. This is so scanty that it is often hard to get a clear picture and indeed sometimes impossible to get even an approximate picture.' Nothing has changed in this respect even now. Ramsay, *Cities* (n.814), 137–53, cf. also 198–205, gives a more balanced picture.

871. C. Augé, 'Sandas', *LIMC* VII, 1, 1994, 662–5: 664 (bibliography); H. Seyrig, *Syria* 36, 1959, 43–8 = *AntSyr* VI, 1966, 16–21; cf. also H. Goldman, 'The Sandon Monument of Tarsus', *JAOS* 40, 1940, 544–53; id., 'Sandon and Herakles', *Hesperia Suppl.* VIII = *Com. Studies T. L. Shear*, 1949, 164–74; P. Chuvin, 'Apollon au trident et les dieux de Tarse', *JS*, 1981, 305–26: 319–26; E. Laroche, 'Un syncrétisme greco-anatolien: Sandas = Hérakles', in *Les syncrétismes dans les religions grecques et romaines, Coll. de Strasbourg, 9–11 Juin 1971*, 1973, 103–14. For the earlier literature see Höfer in *Roschers Lexikon* 4, 1909ff., 319–33; Philipp, 'Sandon', *PW* 2. R., 1, 2, 1925, 2264–8; Böhlig, 'Tarsos' (n.814), 23–41 with all the evidence then known. Dio Chrysostom 33, 47 mentions a pyre (πυρά) in honour of the ἀρχηγὸς ὑμῶν Ἡράκλης at a festival; for Perseus, Heracles and Apollo (and Poseidon?) as 'founders', see 33, 1; in 33, 45 Heracles, Apollo, Athene and other gods are mentioned. According to Strabo 14, 5, 12 (674) Triptolemos founded the city with an army of Argives. The supreme God was once Baal Tarz, later depicted as Zeus; in our view in the Roman period – contrary to H. Böhlig – he could be identified with Heracles-Sandon, especially as in depictions on coins the latter shows a similarity with the Zeus of Doliche and comparable Semitic gods. Cf. M.J. Price and B.L. Trell, *Coins and their Cities. Architecture on the Ancient Coins of Greece, Rome, and Palestine*, London 1971, 53: 'The deity stands on the back of a horned beast, in the typical pose of an eastern god … A pyramidal structure, or canopy, supports a lantern surmounted by an eagle. Without doubt this is the cult image of the great god of Tarsus'; and the illustration there, 55 fig. 97, 'Tarsus, Cilicia: Shrine of Sandan (Demetrius II of Syria 129–125 B.C.) BM.'

872. Böhlig, *Tarsos* (n.814), 44–7: 44f.

873. W. Burkert, *Antike Mysterien*, Munich ³1994, 64: 'Nor were there Heracles mysteries, either, though everyone knew of his "labours", his death, his ascent into Olympus, a life-story which kept offering itself as a

model for a personal career. But it was the mysteries of Eleusis which laid claim to Heracles as a proto-mystic. There were no mysteries in the Graeco-Roman style either in Egypt or in Babylon, although there were myths of suffering gods like Osiris or Marduk.' The same is also true of Adonis, 'in the myth almost ... a ... *Doppelgänger* of Attis'. See 9–11, 53–5 on Christianity; 57 on Gnosis; further A. J. M. Wedderburn, *Baptism and Resurrection*, WUNT 44, Tübingen 1987, 90–163. The widespread 'mystery language' which is to be found e.g. in Hellenistic-Jewish texts like Wisdom, Joseph and Asenath, the Testament of Orpheus and above all in Philo 'is a purely literary metaphor, of a kind which established itself from Plato to Philo', Burkert, *Mysterien*, 57, 116 n.6 with reference to E. des Places, 'Platon et la langue des mystères', in *Études Platoniciennes*, Leiden 1981, 83–98; C. Riedweg, *Mysterienterminologie bei Platon, Philon und Klemens von Alexandrien*, UALG 26, Berlin 1987 and id., *Jüdisch-hellenistische Imitation eines orphischen Hieros Logos*, Classica Monacessia 7, Tübingen 1993 on the so-called Testament of Orpheus. This mystery terminology was part of the religious language of the educated. Paul and the NT are strikingly free from it. In other words, no direct 'influence from the mysteries' can be indicated in Paul or anywhere else in the NT which would not have been mediated through Hellenistic Judaism, and even this is *very* small. Research influenced – in a scholastic way – by the old history-of-religions school should gradually have other thoughts here. As so often, H. Conzelmann and A. Lindemann, *Arbeitsbuch*, ⁹1988, see index 474 s.v. 'Mysterienreligionen' (and 473 s.v. 'Gnosis', which is mentioned as often as apocalyptic), is a typical example of this refusal to learn. The remarks on 185ff. are also misleading, as no distinction is made between oriental *cults* and real *mysteries*. Among other things, Isis is not a dying deity and Dio Cassius 53, 2, 4 does not say that 'under Augustus laws were enacted against the mysteries', but rather that he did not allow 'any Egyptian (!) sanctuaries within the Pomerium'. The sweeping verdict on 435, 'Elements of the form and content of the sacramental celebration of earliest Christianity were influenced by the Hellenistic mystery religions, i.e. the interpretation of baptism as "dying with Christ" as the cultic deity (Rom. 6). And the eucharist as a sacramental meal of the assembled community was also influenced by Hellenistic ideas [what is that meant to mean? M. H.]', reproduces the state of scholarship a century ago. Where and how is this 'influence' meant to have come about? On this see Burkert, *Mysterien*, 11, 86: 'There is so far no philological or historical proof that the New Testament conception is directly dependent on the teaching of pagan mysteries; far less should it be made the real key to the ritual and preaching of the older mysteries. It needs to be maintained that there is hardly any evidence of baptism in the pre-Christian mysteries, however often scholars may say so. See already Hengel, 'Son of God' (n.117), 75ff., above, 121–4, on the title Kyrios and below, 275 f., on Antioch.

874. Pompey 24, 5 (631).

875. *Mithras*, Königstein im Taunus 1984, 45; cf. also id., *Weihegrade und Seelenlehre der Mithrasmysterien*, Vortr. d. Rhein.-Westf. Akad. d. Wiss. (G 257), 1982; and on this W. Fauth, 'Plato Mithriacus oder Mithras Platonicus. Art and Umfang platonischer Einflüsse auf die Mithras-Mysterien', *GGA* 236, 1984, 36–50 (with bibliography); see also 37 n.6 on the relationship to Christianity. The discussion on whether the mysteries arose in the imperial period is in full flood. This process is increasingly shifted westwards. See now the fundamental investigation by M. Clauss, *Cultores Mithrae. Die Anhängerschaft des Mithras-Kultes*, HABES 10, 1990, who shows how little the cult had spread in the Greek East, Asia Minor, Cilicia, Syria and Egypt by comparison with the Danube and Rhine provinces, Gaul, Spain and Rome with Italy. Here Sarapis, who was not a mystery god, had quite a different significance. See also id., *Mithras Kult und Mysterien*, Munich 1990.

876. Merkelbach, *Mithras* (n.875), 75–7: the Roman Mithras mysteries are related to Iranian religion as Christianity is to Judaism.

877. Merkelbach, *Mithras* (n.875), 186 n.118.

878. Cf. L. Vidman, 'Isis und Sarapis', in M. J. Vermaseren (ed.), *Die orientalischen Religionen im Römerreich*, EPRO 93, 1981, 121–56: 121–4.

879. Rom. 2.22; cf. Acts 14.11–18; 17.16, 29; 19.23ff.

880. I Cor. 8.4–13; 10.14, 19–22, 28; cf. 5.10f.; 6.9; 10.7; 12.1–2; II Cor. 6.16; Gal. 5.20; I Thess 1.9.

881. 14, 5, 13f. (673f.) = Athenaios 215bc s. Ruge, *PW* 2.R., 4, 1, 2423f.; Böhlig, *Tarsos* (n.814) 107–28, who points out that the Stoa was founded and shaped above all by philosophers from Cyprus, Cilicia and Syria.

882. Philostratus, *Vit.Apoll.* 1, 3, cf. 1, 12, and the reference to Maximus of Aigai there.

883. See e.g. the literary dialogues between Philo and his nephew Tiberius Julius Alexander, who became an apostate for the sake of his career in Roman state service, in the two books *De providentia*, where Philo's opponent takes the role of the sceptic, and *De animalibus*. Both works have survived only in Armenian, see Schürer III, 864–6; the latter contains no direct references to Judaism.

884. B. Z. Wacholder, *Nicolaus of Damascus*, UCPH 75, Berkeley 1962, 29f.; Schürer I, 28–32; cf. Jacoby, FGrH 90 F 135: καὶ κοινῇ ἐρρητόρευον and on the journey to Rome καὶ κοινῇ ἐφιλοσόφουν.

885. Cf. Stern, *GLAJ* II, 206–16, Numenius; 224–305, Celsus, who refers to a Jewish confidant in connection with the Christians; 306–26, Galen, who travelled intensively in Palestina in search of asphalt and other healing materials. For him see also R. Walzer, *Galen on Jews and Christians*, Oxford 1949. Feldman, *Jew and Gentile* (n.320), 152, 14f., etc. reckons literary dependence on the LXX above all for Ps.-Longinus, *De sublimitate*, and Numenius.

886. For the Stoic elements in Paul cf. M. Pohlenz, 'Paulus und die Stoa', *ZNW* 42, 1949, 64–104; H. Hübner, 'Das ganze Gesetz und das eine Gesetz. Zum Problem Paulus und die Stoa', *KuD* 21, 1975, 239–56; M. L. Colish, 'Pauline Theology and Stoic Philosophy. An Historical Study', *JAAR* 47, 1949, 1–21; R. G. Tanner, 'S. Paul and Stoic Physics', *StEv* VII, 1982 = TU 126, 481–90; the articles by A. J. Malherbe, *Paul and the Popular Philosophers*, Minneapolis 1989; J. W. Masters, 'R 2, 14–16: A Stoic Reading', *NTS* 40, 1994, 55–67; for Paul and Seneca see the basic investigation by J. N. Sevenster, *Paul and Seneca*, NT.S 4, 1961 and now H.-J. Klauck, '"Der Gott in dir" (Ep 41, 1). Autonomie des Gewissens bei Seneca und Paulus', in id., *Alte Welt und neuer Glaube*, NTOA 29, Fribourg CH and Göttingen 1994, 11–31. This relationship still continues, with scanty content, in the correspondence between Paulus and Seneca from the fourth century CE; see C. Dömer in *NTApoc* 2, [2]1992, 46–53; text, translation and commentary in L. Bocciolini Palagi, *Epistolario apocrifo di Seneca e San Paolo*, Florence 1985.

887. *Tarsos* (n.814), 115–28; 127f. For Athenodorus son of Sandon, called Calvas, see further Ramsay, *Cities* (n.814), 216–27. Historical evidence in Jakoby, *FGrH* 746; for philosophical activity see Cicero, *Attic* 16, 11, 4 and 14, 4; Seneca, *Tranq. animae* 3, 1–8; 7, 2; Strabo 14, 4, 21 and 5, 13f.; Diogenes Laert. 7, 147, etc. The earlier Anthenodoros Kordylion in the first century CE was in charge of the library in Pergamon and later domestic philosopher to the younger Cato, see Plutarch, *Cato min* 10, 16; Strabo 14, 5, 14. R. Goulet, *Dictionnaire des Philosophes* I, Paris 1989, no. 497 and 498.

888. H. Böhlig, *Tarsos* (n.814), 127 n.2; P. Wendland, *Die hellenistisch-römische Kultur / Die urchristlichen Literaturformen*, Tübingen [2,3]1912, 354; E. Norden, *Antike Kunstprosa*, reprinted Darmstadt 1958, II, 474–6, 492–510 is still a basic work.

889. Hengel, 'Vorchristlicher Paulus' (n.51), 212–56 [18–53] (180–93 [1–6] on Tarsus); for synagogue preaching see Siegert, *Predigten* II (n.387), 407 Index s.v. 'Predigt'.

890. Hengel, *Judaism and Hellenism* (n.314), I, 109–53; id., *The 'Hellenization' of Judaea in the First Century after Christ*, London 1989, 21,

27.

891. See Norden, *Kunstprosa* (n.888), 513–16; Meyer, *Ursprung* (n.25), 8–12; Classen, *Bemerkungen* (n.14).

892. I am thinking of cities like Soloi/Pompeiopolis, Mopsuestia, Anazarbus, Mallus and its harbour Magarsus. Jewish communities are also to be presupposed in these *poleis* which were flourishing in the great Diaspora in Syria and in southern Asia Minor.

893. The Greeks knew that they received writing from there. The sagas of Europa and Cadmus, etc. showed them how much they owed to Phoenicia. Sidon is already mentioned in Homer *(Iliad* 6, 290f.; 23, 743; *Odyssey* 4, 84, 618; 6, 285; 15, 425). Menelaus is said to have visited Tyre, among other places, on his journey back from Troy, see Hengel, *Judaism and Hellenism* (n.314), I, 129.

894. Acts 11.19; cf. 13.4ff. This says nothing about the existence of Christians, but that is typical of Luke. We learn by chance from 28.15 that there are Christians in Rome.

895. See also Riesner, *Frühzeit* (n.49), 96–101, 286.

896. Thus rightly in respect of Paul H. Conzelmann, 'Paulus und die Weisheit', *NTS* 12, 1965, 233 = *Theologie* (n.505), 179. This applies even more for the early period up to the persecution by Agrippa I.

897. Mark 13.10; 14.9 par Matt. 28.19; Luke 24.47; Acts 1.8; 13.47 = Isa. 49.4 etc. See already Hengel, 'Mission' (n.116).

898. For the adoption of Isa. 2.1–4 (par. Micah 4.1–3); 11.11ff.; 55.9; 60.11–14; 66.18–20; Zeph. 3.9ff.; Zech. 8.20–23; 14.16–21, cf. Sib. 3, 710–724, 772ff.; PsSol. 17, 31, 34; Philo, *De praem et poen* 170f., cf. 152 (the praise of the proselyte); IV Ezra 13.12f.; SyrBar 71f.; R. D. Aus, 'Paul's Travel Plains to Spain', *NT* 21, 1979, 239ff., 246–60; Scott, *Paul* (n.320), 133; even the rigorist pious in Qumran maintained this expectation, cf. Deines, *Abwehr* (n.341), 66.

899. In part perhaps only a two-man collegial mission, see above, 109; Philip works only as an individual.

900. For John as later a very influential theologian see Hengel, *Johanneische Frage* (n.33), index 469 s.v. 'johanneische Schule'; 475 s.v. 'Lehrautorität'.

901. In *Geschichte der christlichen Religion, Die Kultur der Gegenwart,* Teil I, Abt. IV, 1, 1909, 96; cf. J. Wellhausen, *Das Evangelium Johannis,* 121 (= *Evangelienkommentare,* 1987, 721): 'John bases himself on Paul', see Hengel, *Johanneische Frage* (n.33), 299, cf. 160, 254 [129, cf. 51, 95f.].

902. See above, 158–61.

903. Here it is remarkable that Paul moves from the middle of the world (Jerusalem, his ideal and actual starting point, Rom. 15.19)

through Damascus as an intermediate stopping place to Arabia, a southern region diametrically opposed to the description of the journey in 1QGenAp, and then, when his mission becomes impossible for him here, goes to the northern frontier of the land promised to Abraham. The description of the journey in 1QGenAp is dependent on the list of nations in Gen. 10 and its interpretation in Jub. 8–9; for this see Scott, *Paul* (n.320), 29–33, who has shown how determinative this picture of the world is for early Jewish literature and also for Paul. Although right from his call Paul understands himself as 'apostle to the Gentiles', evidently it is only years later that he thinks of a 'strategic' mission in the sphere of Japhet, see Scott, *Paul* (n.320), 149f. First of all his mission is for particular Gentiles, and not for 'the Gentiles/nations' generally.

904. See above 399 n.602. Cf. Scott, *Paul* (n.320), 32.

905. That is the only possibility because there is a road, see 415 n.816.

906. *Antt.* 9, 208 cf. 214. Josephus is writing this in Rome and here he has in view the ending of Roman rule through the messianic kingdom; cf. on Dan. 2.36 *Antt.* 10, 209f. and on the Balaam prophecy *Antt.* 4, 114–17 and the closing remarks in 125.

907. *Antt.* 9, 208: εἰς Ταρσὸν ἔπλει τῆς Κιλικίας. The *taršiš* of Jonah 1.3, in LXX θαρσις, is here interpreted in terms of the metropolis in Cilicia. Here the Jewish priest from Jerusalem is probably giving a Jewish interpretation which was widespread in the first century.

908. *Antt.* 8, 181, Solomon's seafaring trade with the 'Tarsian sea' (ταρσικῇ … θαλαττῇ), the sea which the coast of Cilicia and southern Asia Minor faces with its important harbours. From there the trade led εἰς τὰ ἐνδοτέρω τῶν ἐθνῶν. Does not this tradition go back to the time of the mercenary link with Cilicia and Pamphylia? For *taršiš* see Köhler/Baumgartner/Stamm, *Hebräisches-Aramäisches Lexikon*, Lieferung IV, 1990 *ad loc.*

909. M. L. Klein, *The Fragment-Targums of the Pentateuch*, Vol. I, AnBib 76, 1980, 49; R. le Déaut, *Targum du Pentateuque*, SC 245, 1978, 134f.; on this see n.11. Cf. also the Targums on Ps 48.8; 72.10; II Chron. 19.36f. and Job 3.5; GenR 37.1.

910. *Antt.* 1, 127. For the explanation of the list of nations in Gen. 10 in Josephus cf. J. M. Scott, 'Luke's Geographical Horizon', in *The Book of Acts in Its First Century Setting II, The Book of Acts in Its Graeco-Roman Setting*, ed. D.W.J. Gill and C.Gempf, Grand Rapids, etc. 1994, 483–544: 517f.; id., *Paul* (n.320), 40–9.

911. Brit.Mus add. 27031; see le Déaut (n.909), 133 and M. Ginsburger, *Pseudo Jonathan*, Berlin 1903, 16: ויתגיירו בני וישרון בפמדרשא דשם. Cf. jMeg 1, 71c; bMeg 9b; GenR 26, 8; Bill. 2, 488; 4, 413: the later interpre-

tation relates this to the use of the Greek language in the synagogue and Aquila's translation. However, initially the 'missionary' significance must have been central.

912. *Haer* 3, 5; *Dem* 21.42.

913. *Antt.* 7, 30.

914. I Cor. 9.16f.

915. Cf. I Cor. 10.11; Rom. 4.1–24; 9.4–18; 11.1–5, 33f.; 15.4; Gal. 3.6–22.

916. It is to the credit of Munck, *Paul and the Salvation of Mankind* (n.492), that he pointed to this narrowing. Cf. also U. Luz, *Das Geschichtsverständnis des Paulus*, BEvTh 49, 1968, 387–402: 'Primarily Paul interprets the mission in the light of the Old Testament as the fulfilment of the promise of God' (392).

917. I Cor. 16; II Cor. 8.9; Rom. 1.13ff.; 15.19, 22–32; for the Old Testament/early-Jewish geographical background to the apostle's 'mission strategy' see now Scott, *Paul* (n.320).

918. I Cor. 15.1–11; 9.1ff.; 1.10–17; 2.1ff.; II Cor. 1; 10–12; Rom. 1.9ff. etc. Cf. already Mark 14, 25, which has a 'chiliastic' background.

919. See above, 136.

920. I Cor. 12.12f., cf. 4ff.

921. E. Delebecque, *Les Actes des Apôtres*, Paris 1982, 57; C. K. Barrett, *Acts* I (n.77), 554. Cf. Acts 10, the problem skilfully elaborated in narrative by Luke, that Cornelius' messengers find Peter in Joppa.

922. Barrett, *Acts* I (n.77), 555. However, according to 9.30 Paul's stay in Tarsus was said to be known in Jerusalem.

923. D mae (gig p* syhmg).

924. Rom. 15.19–23; cf. II Cor. 10.14–16.

925. Thus perhaps references to the Samaritan mission in John 4 and certainly the references to the gift of the Spirit in John 8.39; 14–16; also the persecution in 16.1–4 and the ἀποσυναγωγός in 9.22; 12.42 and 16.2 which prompts speculation; furthermore the whole broad complex of the failure of the disciples to understand before Easter and its correction by Easter in Mark and John.

926. Acts 4–7; 9.1; I Thess. 2.14; Mark 13; Matt. 10; 24; Luke 12.11f.; 21.12.

927. Josephus, *Antt.* 18.116f.; Mark 6.14–20 = Matt. 14.1–12; Matt. 11.2 = Luke 3.19f.; John was probably killed in 27/28, cf. Riesner, *Frühzeit* (n.49), 38ff.

928. Josephus, *Antt.* 18, 85–89; end 36 to beginning 37. Pilate arrived in Rome only after the death of Tiberius on 16 March 37.

929. Josephus, *Antt.* 18, 90–95.

930. Josephus, *Antt.* 18, 237.

931. Josephus, *Antt.* 18, 247–256.

932. I Cor. 2.8; cf. Luke 4.6. They are subject to 'the God of this age', II Cor. 4.4, and yet are ordained by God, Rom. 13.1. The two perspectives apparently stand side by side without any connection between them.

933. Acts 12.1: 'Herod' was to some degree the 'Caesar' of Judaea; the name took on the character of a title, at least for the people. Thus already with Antipas. Cf. Josephus on Pharaoh, *Antt.* 8, 155–7. See above, 229, and below nn.1184f. on the 'Herodianoi'.

934. Josephus, *Antt.* 19, 274.

935. Acts 12; cf. Riesner, *Frühzeit* (n.49), 104–10; Schwartz, *Agrippa I* (n.302), 119–24.

936. See Schürer I, 384–98; Smallwood, *The Jews under Roman Rule*, SJLA 20, ²1981, 235–80, 174–80; Schwartz, *Agrippa I* (n.302), 77–89.

937. Mark 15.38; Hengel, *Atonement* (n.508), 42, 45; cf. R. Feldmeier, 'Der Gekreuzigte im "Gnadenstuhl"', in *Le trône de Dieu*, ed. M. Philonenko, WUNT 69, Tübingen 1993, 213–32.

938. Cf. Josephus, *Antt.* 19, 1.

939. Mark 13.14: τὸ βδέλυγμα τῆς ἐρημώσεως ἑστηκότα ὅπου οὐ δεῖ. In Mark the masculine perfect accusative (cf. the emendation in Matt. 24.15 ἑστὸς ἐν τόπῳ ἁγίῳ, which alludes to the destruction of the temple) refers to a person; see Hengel, 'Gospel of Mark' (n.48), 20.

940. Cf. esp. II Thess. 2.4.

941. I incline to regard it as non-Pauline, though this too is not without its problems. In terms of content and partially also language the letter is completely dependent on I Thess., but on the other hand it shows considerable differences. Here it presupposes only I Thess. In other words, the pseudepigraphon must have been composed before the collection of the letters of Paul was made *c.* 100 CE, and like Eph. and Col. was already contained in this collection. Its historical context and the occasion for it are difficult to define. Perhaps like Mark 13 it is connected with the heightened expectation of an imminent end after the murder of Nero on 9 September 68. If the letter is authentic, it would have to have been composed soon after I Thess. in order to correct the enthusiastic expectation of an imminent end in Thessalonica with its social consequences. In that case one could connect the enigmatic κατέχων (2.7) with the Pauline expectation of an imminent end. But that too comes up against great difficulties. W. Trilling has rightly termed the letter 'in many respects enigmatic', *Der zweite Brief an die Thessalonicher*, EKK 14, 1980, 22. For the Antichrist and κατέχων see

ibid., 83–94; for the history of exegesis 94–105. In my view the destruction of the temple is not yet presupposed in 2.4, against Trilling 86f., who also underestimates the significance of the Caligula episode, 87 n.331, and dates it wrongly. Neither the interpretation in terms of God (the formulation in 2.7b tells against this), nor the later one in terms of the Roman empire, nor that in terms of the apostle and his missionary activity, are satisfactory. For us with our present knowledge the κατέχων motif remains a riddle.

942. Thus above all in Rev. 12; 13, where by gematria in 13.18 the second beast is indentified as Nero redivivus; cf. Mark 13.12f. (par) and Hengel, 'Gospel of Mark' (n.48), 14–28; further I Clem. 5.2ff.; AscIsa 4.2–8 and also Sib 4, 121, 138; 5, 29f., 142, 363 and 3, 63ff.

943. In Philo, *Flacc* 26, 181 the mockery of the king shows remarkable parallels to the mockery of Jesus by the soldiers hostile to the Jews in the passion narrative; for a discussion see Schwartz, *Agrippa* I. (n.302), 55f., cf. 67–70, 74–7. The unrest came to a climax in August 38. Agrippa's return journey also took him through Jerusalem, where he offered a thank-offering in the temple just as nineteen years later Paul redeemed the vows of Nazirites, and presumably also appointed a new high priest, who no longer came from the excessively powerful clan of Annas but from that of Boethus, which was friendly to the Herodians (*Antt.* 19, 297). The people seems to have welcomed him enthusiastically as the grandson of the Hasmonaean Mariamne. In the letter attributed to him in Philo, *Legatio*, 278, he emphatically emphasizes his high-priestly descent and calls himself a Jew and a worshipper of 'the most high God' (τοῦ ὑψίστου θεοῦ) who has obligations to the temple.

944. Philo, *Legatio* 200–203; Josephus, *Antt.* 18, 257–260; see Schwartz, *Agrippa I.* (n.302), 80ff.

945. Schwartz, *Agrippa I.* (n.302), 86 n.68: at around the same time as the deposition of Herod Antipas resulting from a denunciation by Agrippa I.

946. This is emphasized by Tacitus, *Hist* 5, 9, 1: *Sub Tiberio quies; dein iussi a C. Caesare effigiem eius in templum locare arma potius sumpsere, quem motus Caesaris mors diremit*, Stern, *GLAJ* II, 21 no. 281 with commentary, p.51 and P. Cornelius Tacitus, *Die Historien, Kommentar Bd. V*, by H. Heubner and W. Fauth, Heidelberg 1982, 131f.; cf. Josephus, *BJ* 2, 184; *Antt.* 18, 305–9.

947. *Legatio* 346 = Eusebius, *HE* 2, 6, 2; further examples in M. Smallwood, *Philonis Alexandrini Legatio ad Caium*, Leiden 1961, 315f.

948. Acts 11.20.

949. The standard work is still Downey, *Antioch* (n.670); cf. also the

shorter popular version, *Ancient Antioch,* Princeton 1963. See also G. Hadad, *Aspects of Social Life in Antioch in the Hellenistic-Roman Period,* New York 1949; Jones, *Cities* (n.287), 578, index s.v. Antioch by Daphne; J. Lassus, 'La ville Antioch à l'époque romaine d'après l'archéologie', *ANRW* II 8, 1977, 54–102: for Christianity 88, 100f. (with bibliography); F. W. Norris, 'Antioch on-the-Orontes as a Religious Center I, Paganism before Constantine', *ANRW* II 18, 4, 1990, 2322–79; Millar, *Roman Near East* (n.92), 54f., 79, 86–90, 259f.; on the sources: 'the silting-up of the site of Antioch during the intervening centuries means that we have hardly any epigraphic record on the functioning of this major city as it was in the first few centuries AD'. The literary evidence is also very fragmentary. For the fourth century, which we know best, see A. J. Festugière, *Antioch païenne et chrétienne. Libanius, Chrysostome et les moines de Syrie,* BEFAR 194, Paris 1959; J. H. W. G. Liebeschuetz, *Antioch. City and Imperial Administration in the Later Roman Empire,* Oxford 1972. There is an urgent need for a new monograph investigating Roman Antioch and the cities which are its immediate neighbours between the first century BCE and the third century CE.

950. *Antioch* (n.670), 190.

951. Tacitus, *Ann.* 2, 72, 2; 73, 4. For the murder charge against Piso and the trial, on which the inscriptions from Spain with a *senatus consultum* shed new light, see W. Eck, 'Das s. c. de Cn. Pisone patre und seine Publikation in der Baetica', *Cahiers du Centre G. Glotz* 4, 1993, 194–7.

952. Malalas, *Chron.* 10, 315, p. 244, 15ff., ed. Dindorf 1831; A. Schenk Graf von Stauffenberg, *Die römische Kaisergeschichte bei Malalas. Griechischer Text der Bücher IX–XII und Untersuchungen,* Stuttgart 1931, 23f. cf. the Old Slavonic Version in an English translation by M. Spinka and G. Downey, 1940, 54f.; E. and M. Jeffreys, R. Scott et al., *The Chronicle of John Malalas. A Translation,* Australian Association for Byzantine Studies. Byzantina Australiensia 4, Melbourne 1986, 129f. See further Downey, *Antioch* (n.670), 187, 190ff.; Smallwood, *The Jews* (n.936), 176 nn.110, 360f. Josephus may not report these events because they contradicted the peaceful attitude on the part of the Jews which he emphasized and because his attention is focussed wholly on Alexandria and then on the events in Judaea and Rome. See also A. A. Barrett, *Caligula,* New York, etc., 1990, 189, 300 n.27 and Schwartz, *Agrippa I.* (n.302), 93 n.15.

953. For the plural cf. above, 50f. on Damascus and Salamis on Cyprus.

954. Around 144 BCE; cf. Josephus, *Antt.* 13, 135–42. According to I Macc. 11.47ff. they set the city on fire, killed 10,000 and almost took possession of the city: these are certainly exaggerations – as with Malalas.

Probably the high priest Phineas referred to is the high priest Phanni (Stauffenberg, *Malalas* [n.952], 190, conjectures two high priests with this name). He was chosen by lot in 66 by the rebels, see Josephus, *BJ* 4, 155; *Antt.* 20, 227; cf. Hengel, *Zealots* (n.122), 224f. A great fire which was blamed on the Jews is reported for 70.

955. Stauffenberg, *Malalas* (n.952), 189–93: 'Although we do not have the full report ... as it is mutilated, it does seem to me that it is based on ... excellent material' (189).

956. Josephus, *Antt.* 19, 300–11; immediately after the arrival of Agrippa I in his kingdom, which had been extended by a grateful Claudius to all Judaea.

957. The city was on the very frontier of his kingdom, but was within the sphere of power of the Syrian governor.

958. Josephus, *Antt.* 19, 309.

959. *Antt.* 19, 278–85: ὅπως μηδεμία ταραχὴ γένηται. This edict for Syria contains an allusion to a letter of Petronius (19, 304) and among other things emphasizes the inviolability of the synagogues. Furthermore Claudius is said to have issued an edict 'to the rest of the ecumene' in favour of the Jews. How far these edicts were really issued in the form handed down by Josephus is a matter of dispute, see Smallwood, *Jews* (n.936), 195f., 246f., 360; Schürer I, 398. The edict for Alexandria will correspond more to Claudius' letter to the Alexandrians *CPJ* I, 36–53 no. 153, which speaks of 'the unrest and revolt, indeed "to tell the truth, of the war"' against the Jews (41 lines 74f.), but at the same time the Jews are warned 'to enter the games which are organized by the gymnasiarchs and kosmetes and to lend support from Syria and the Egyptian Chora' (lines 88–100). See Riesner, *Frühzeit* (n.49), 88f.

960. See Schürer II, 44–8, 54f. and index III, 993 s.v. 'Games' and 1001 s.v. 'Theatres'; cf. also the well-known inscription in the theatre in Miletus, *CPJ* II, 14 no. 748 = *SEG* 4, 1930, 75 no. 441; on which see H. Hommel, 'Juden und Christen im kaiserzeitlichen Milet', in *Sebasmata*, WUNT 32, 1984, II, 200–30; Trebilco, *Jewish Communities* (n.362), 159–62: 'Two groups – Jews and God-worshippers – were probably grouped together by the theatre management and allocated the privilege of special seats' (161f.); cf. further the Jews in the amphitheatre in Berenice, Cyrenaica, in G. Lüderitz, *Corpus jüdischer Zeugnisse aus der Cyrenaika*, BTAVO B 53, Wiesbaden 1983, 148ff. no. 70. Philo takes visiting the theatre for granted, see his polemic in *Agricultura* 35; cf. 11 and 113–19 about the athletic contests in the theatres which attract the masses; cf. also the advice of Aristeas, 284f. By contrast, the attitude of Palestinian Judaism was negative, see Bill. IV, 401ff.; this did not exclude

specific knowledge: S. Lieberman, *Greek in Jewish Palestine*, New York 1942, 31f.

961. In Seneca, *Apocal* 14, 2 he appears as a trusted former table companion and defender of Claudius. According to Malalas, pp. 244–5, Gaius sent two senators, Pontius and Varius, to Antioch; they were later punished by him because they had not prevented the unrest, see Stauffenberg, *Malalas* (n.952), 23; Downey, *Antioch* (n.670), 191, 193. Perhaps here they are delegates of Caligula, who are to be distinguished from Petronius. Petronius appears in Malalas (244, 21) under the name Pronoios, thus also Stauffenberg, *Malalas*, 189.

962. See above, 152ff.

963. Strabo 16, 2, 5.

964. Diodore 17, 52, 6. The very fragmentary PGiess (P.Bibl.Giess. 46 = H. A. Musurillo, *The Acts of the Pagan Martyrs*, Oxford 1954, III Col 1, 15 and 2, 5 pp. 12f., 106, 114) perhaps speaks of 180,000 male citizens. According to the well-known census inscription of Apamea, ILS 2683 = V. Ehrenberg and A. H. M. Jones, *Documents illustrating the Reigns of Augustus and Tiberius*, Oxford 1949, no. 231, a census in this Syrian city produced a figure of 118, 000 citizens. Antioch must have been bigger, see R. Duncan-Jones, *The Economy of the Roman Empire*, Cambridge 1974, 260f. n.4. Even in the fourth century Antioch was still the rival of Alexandria.

965. Perhaps the 30,000 in the fantastic report by Malalas originally referred to the number of Jews in the city. The Old Slavonic translation makes this 230,000, see Downey, *Antioch* (n.670), 193. For the number of Jews in Antioch see below, nn.1039f.

966. It is mentioned by Josephus, *BJ* 7, 44f., who gives the most detailed description of the Jewish community, see 7, 41–62; cf. 100–11 and *Antt.* 12, 119–24. For the main synagogue in Alexandria see Hengel, 'Proseuche' (n.319), 158ff., 168.

967. For its foundation cf. H. Seyrig, 'Séleucus I et la fondation de la monarchie syrienne', *Syria* 47, 1970, 290–307.

968. *Antt.* 12, 119; see Hengel, *Judaism and Hellenism* (n.314), I, 16.

969. For criticism see R. Marcus, *Josephus* VII, LCL, 1961, 731ff.; for a positive view the best expert is E. Bickerman, *The Jews in the Greek Age*, London 1988, 91f., with what in my view are convincing reasons; see also Schürer III, 1, 13f., 121, 126–9 on the discussion of his question which is a controversial one both for Antioch and for Alexandria.

970. *Antt.* 12, 12 for the refusal of the Jews to use pagan oil; for the advantage that John of Gischala derived from this see Josephus, *BJ* 2, 59–92, here related generally to 'all the Jews in Syria'; in *Vita* 74–76 this

event is limited to Caesarea Philippi. See Hengel, _Zealots_ (n.122), 200.

971. _BJ_ 7, 100–11; cf. Michel and Bauernfeind, _Josephus_, II, 2, 227f. n.44, 237 n.58.

972. In addition to _Antt._ 12, 119–28 see also _c. Ap_ 2, 38–42 and, with rather more restraint, _BJ_ 7, 44, where it is not Seleucus I but only the Seleucid successors of Antiochus IV who are said to have granted equal status with the Greek population.

973. Josephus, _BJ_ 2, 266–70, 284–92; _Antt._ 20, 173–8, 182–4: the Jews whose complaints were rejected by Nero 'took their dispute with the Syrians further until they finally ignited the flames of war'.

974. For the term see Josephus, _Antt._ 20, 173, 183 on Caesarea; 12, 8 (cf. _c. Ap_ 2, 35) on Alexandria; see also _BJ_ 7, 44 and _Antt._ 12, 119 on Antioch. Josephus' terminology is not completely consistent here. Perhaps he wants to conceal the fact that there was not really a situation of equal rights. See Michel and Bauernfeind, _Josephus_, II, 2, 228 n.27.

975. See I Cor. 15.25–28: Hengel, ' "Sit at my Right Hand!" ' (n.117), 163ff.

976. Rom. 13.11; cf. I Cor. 7.31.

977. Given the context, the reference is hardly to the sanctuary in Jerusalem, but to the leading synagogue which, like the five-aisle main synagogue in Alexandria, was particularly significant. See Krauss, _Synagogale Altertümer_ (n.820), 86f., 225f., and Michel and Bauernfeind, _Josephus_, II, 2, 228f. n.28.

978. _BJ_ 7, 45.

979. _BJ_ 7, 420–36.

980. Malalas, 260f.; Stauffenberg, _Malalas_ (n.952), 35, cf. 230f.; Downey, _Antioch_ (n.670), 206. We can understand why Josephus keeps quiet about this.

981. See J. Obermann, 'The Sepulchre of the Maccabean Martyrs', _JBL_ 50, 1931, 250–65; E. Bammel, 'Zum jüdischen Märtyrerkult', _ThLZ_ 78, 1953, 119–26 = _Judaica_, WUNT 37, Tübingen 1986, 79–85; E. Bickerman, 'Les Maccabées de Malalas', _Byzantion_ 21, 1951, 63–83 = _Studies in Jewish and Christian History_, II, AGJU 9, Leiden 1980, 192–209; J. Jeremias, _Heiligengräber in Jesu Umwelt_, Göttingen 1958, 21f.

982. Josephus, _BJ_ 7, 96.

983. See W. Eltester, 'Die Kirchen Antiochias im IV. Jh.', _ZNW_ 36, 1937, 251–86; Jeremias, _Heiligengräber_ (n.981), 18ff.

984. _Adv. Jud_ 7, PG 48, 904; S. Krauss, _Synagogale Altertümer_ (n.820), 225f.; L. Wilken, _John Chrysostom and the Jews_, The Transformation of the Classical Heritage 4, Berkeley u.a. 1983.

985. _BJ_ 7, 45: ἀεί τε προσαγόμενοι ταῖς θρησκείαις πολὺ πλῆθος

Ἑλλήνων κακείνους τρόπῳ τινὶ μοῖραν αὐτῶν πεποίηντο. I have already referred to this important text, above n.429.

986. Cf. Hengel, 'Between Jesus and Paul' (n.50), 12ff.; id., *Johanneische Frage* (n.33), 82, 167 n.47 [179 n.47].

987. C. H. Kraeling, 'The Jewish Community of Antioch', *JBL* 51, 1932, 130–60: 136. Cf. Riesner (n.49), *Frühzeit*, 98.

988. *BJ* 2, 429: similarly not in Apamea and Sidon, because in these cities the population believed strongly enough.

989. *BJ* 7, 47.

990. *BJ* 7, 50.

991. *BJ* 7, 47–53.

992. *BJ* 7, 54–62, 100–11; see also above, 51 ff.

993. *BJ* 7, 363, the old hatred of the citizens of Caesarea; 2, 478, the Syrian cities were dominated 'either by fear or by hatred', cf. 461; 2, 498, the excessive hatred of the Alexandrians; 2, 502, the auxiliary troops from the Syrian cities are urged on by hatred of the Jews, cf. 3, 133 and 5, 556. The hatred of the Jews on the part of the Arabians and Syrians led to indescribable atrocities about which Titus was furious. *Antt.* 18, 371, the Babylonians against the Jews.

994. Jos. *BJ* 7, 43.

995. Cf. T. Holtz, EKK XIII, Zurich etc. ²1990, 96–113.

996. However, Paul could no have had any inkling of the pernicious consequences of such a remark, lasting over two thousand years.

997. Cf. Riesner, *Frühzeit* (n.49), 311–18.

998. In my view the formulation is connected with the experiences of the Neronian persecution, see Hengel, 'Gospel of Mark' (n.48), 23. Cf. Luke 1.71; 6.22, 27; John 15.18; 17.14; Did 1.3; I Clem. 60.3; II Clem. 13.4; Ignatius, Rom. 3.3; Tacitus, Ann. 15, 44.4: *odio humanis generis convicti sunt.*

999. For a festive occasion which we can no longer identify more closely; I. Heinemann, 'IV. Makk', *PW* 14, 1, 1928, 802, thought of the feast of Hanukkah, opposed by H.-J. Klauck, *4. Makkabäerbuch*, JSHRZ III, 6, 1989, 663f.

1000. For Antioch see Klauck (n.999), 667. This is suggested by the tradition of Jewish martyrs there, see above 188, n.981. The difference from the milieu in Alexandria is considerable.

1001. The most significant attempt at dating is still that of E. Bickerman, 'The Date of Fourth Maccabees', *Louis Ginzberg Jubilee Volume*, New York 1945, 105–12 = *Studies in Jewish and Christian History*, I, AGJU 9, Leiden 1976, 275–81. An origin before 70, indeed before the events connected with Caligula in 39/41 CE, is suggested by the fact that the ruler cult still plays no part, though this might have been expected, and that the temple cult is still presupposed as a matter of course (3.19–4.10). The scribe Eleazar (II Macc. 6.18) is made a priest (IV Macc. 5.4; 7.6; 17.9). And after 70 a Jewish-Hellenistic author would hardly have praised Phinehas as ὁ ζηλωτής (14, 12). The argument emphasized by Bickerman of the unity of Syria, Phoenicia and Cilicia in IV Macc. 4.2 under a governor (II Macc. 3.5: of Coele Syria and Phoenicia) retains its validity. It is also striking that contrary to the later tradition of Jewish martyrs in Antioch, Eleazar, the seven sons and their mother were executed by Antiochus IV in Jerusalem, see Bickerman, 'Les Maccabées de Malalas' (n.981). This 'translation' of the martyrdom and the bones of the martyrs was probably first associated with the new synagogue in Antioch built after 70. See also, in detail, Klauck (n.999), 665–9.

1002. See also the Poseidonian definition of σοφία as γνῶσις θείων καὶ ἀνθρωπίνων πραγμάτων καὶ τῶν τούτων αἰτιῶν, though in 1.10 this has been identified with τοῦ νόμου παιδεία.

1003. IV Macc. 13.15; 16.24, cf. 9.1. By contrast, 4.6 and 6.4 speak of the orders of the king.

1004. 18.5. Perhaps the reading of Sin, τῶν πατρίων, is more original. For Paul, too, ὁ νόμος is the dominant term. We meet the ἐντολαὶ θεοῦ as a formula in I Cor. 7.19; nor does he use τὰ πάτρια ἔθη, but cf. Acts 6.14; 13.1; 21.21; 26.3; 28.17.

1005. 18.5; cf. Rom. 3.21; Matt. 5.17; 7.12; 11.13 = Luke 16.16; Acts 13.15; 24.14; 28.23; John 1.45.

1006. In the Jewish 'philosophical' writings the Pentateuch predominates. 3 Sib. is an exception. In her eschatological conclusion the 'pagan' prophetess quotes predominantly the prophets in her typical way, predominantly in fragments (3, 741–808).

1007. 6.28; 17.20–22; see Klauck (n.999), 671ff.; Hengel, *Atonement* (n.508), 60f. I regard a tradition of reading Euripides fairly improbable; the Daniel tradition is more important.

1008. 6.17, 22; 7.19; 9.21 Sin; 13.17; 14.20; 15.18; 16.20, 25; 17.6.

1009. 13.17 cf. 7.19; 16.25; 18.23; 5.37; 13.17.

1010. Cf. II Cor. 5.1ff.; I Thess. 4.17b, but also Acts 7.59; Luke 16.22; 23.43.

1011. Cf. II Macc. 6.9.

1012. Cf. 16.25 and 17.17, see again Dan. 7.13 LXX. Cf. Mark 12.26f.

1013. Phil. 3.20; cf. II Cor. 11.13–15.

1014. Cf. Phil. 3.21; II Cor. 11.13–15 negatively; I Cor. 15.50–54; Rom. 12.2. Cf. Mark 12.27 par and especially Luke 20.38: 'for in him all live'; Rom. 6.10; 14.7–9; Gal. 2.9; see Klauck (n.999), 721.

1015. Cf. Ex. 20.17 = Deut. 5.21, see Klauck (n.999), 695f., on which cf. James 1.14f. In IV Macc. 5.23 the law becomes the teacher of the four cardinal virtues. For the Decalogue in Paul as a summary of the law see Rom. 13.9.

1016. Rom. 5.20, cf. Gal. 3.10; 5.3 and positively Matt. 5.18; 7.12; Bill. I. 221–6. However, after Hadrian's persecution the rabbis limited obligations to obey the law where it might put life in danger.

1017. In 9.6, Eleazer himself, the teacher of the law, appears as such; cf. the brothers in 13.24 and the father in 18.10ff.; cf. the ironical description of the Jew and his self-consciousness about being a teacher of the law who boasts of being 'instructed by the law' and the 'educator of those who do not understand': Rom. 2.18–20.

1018. Gal. 3.23; cf. Rom. 3.1; 9.3ff.

1019. Menander, *Sententiae* no. 573; for the two terms see C. Spicq, *Notes de Lexicographie Néo-testamentaire*, II, OBO 22, 2, 1978, 639–41: in the Hellenistic period the two come closer together: 'Thus the pedagogue comes close to the imparter of instruction (παιδευτής), primarily because in the Bible the latter is envisaged as an educator who corrects and chastizes: Hos. 5.2; PsSol. 8.29; Heb. 12.9.'

1020. 5.33; cf. 4.24; 17.9; cf. Matt. 5.17; Acts 6.14.

1021. κατέλυσα, 2.18.

1022. I Thess. 4.13; IV Macc. 16.12.

1023. IV Macc. 16.13 cf. Gal. 4.19; cf. also I Cor. 4.14f.

1024. ὑπομονή appears 11 times in IV Macc. For ἐλπίς see also 11.7: ἐλπίδα ἔχεις παρὰ θεῷ σωτηρίου; πίστις: 15.24 and 16.22; πρὸς (τὸν) θεόν, cf. 7.19, 21.

1025. Cf. Luke 6.34; 16.25; 18.30; 23.41; II John 8.

1026. By contrast IV Macc. speaks only positively of the νοῦς and treasures above all the σώφρων νοῦς, 1.35; 2.16, 18; 3.17, cf. also 16.13. By contrast cf. Rom. 7.23, 25; 12.2; Phil. 4.7 and Col. 2.8. For δοκιμάζειν which is also a favourite word in Paul (Rom. 1.28; 2.18 = Phil. 1.10; Rom. 12.2 etc.), see IV Macc. 17.12.

1027. ἐπιθυμία appears 14 times in the work; cf. 1.3, 22, 31f.; 2.1, 4, 6 etc. For the prohibition against ἐπιθυμεῖν in the Decalogue see above, n.1015.

1028. It appears more than 60 times.

1029. This also applies to Ignatius, see O. Perler, 'Das vierte Makkabäerbuch, Ignatius von Antiochien und die ältesten Märtyrerberichte', *RivAC* 25, 1949, 47–72.

1030. Cf. B. M. Metzger, *A Textual Commentary on the Greek New Testament*, Stuttgart 1971, 563ff. κατακαυθήσομαι is a further development of καυθήσομαι.

1031. Cf. Col. 1.24; Rom. 15.16; II Cor. 12.15, but also Rom. 12.1–3.

1032. 6.29: καθάρσιον αὐτῶν ποίησον τὸ ἐμοῦ αἷμα ... cf. 17.22 καὶ διὰ τοῦ ἱλαστηρίου θανάτου αὐτῶν ... cf. 1.11: ὥστε καθαρισθῆναι δι' αὐτῶν τὴν πατρίδα.

1033. I Thess. 2.2; Phil. 1.30; Col. 2.1; I Tim. 6.12; II Tim. 4.7: here referring to the expected martyrdom.

1034. See W. Schrage, *Der erste Brief an die Korinther*, EKK VII, 1, 1991, 341f.

1035. *De Pud* 14, 7, see Schrage, ibid., ad loc.; *Ambrosiaster*, ed. H. I. Vogels, CSEL 81, 2, 1982 = Vetus Latina and similarly the Vulgate: *quasi morti destinatos*; John Chrysostom in. J. A. Cramer, *Catenae* V, 82: κατά-δικοι.

1036. Schrage, *Korinther* (n.1034), 342, and Lietzmann and Kümmel, *1. Korinther*, HNT 20, ad loc. There are references there to gladiator fighting and the Stoic battle metaphors.

1037. I Cor. 9.25; cf. I Tim 4.7f.

1038. *BJ* 7, 45; see above, 434 n.985.

1039. Cf. above 188f., further Michel and Bauernfeind, *Josephus* II, 2, 227 n.26; cf. also W. A. Meeks and R. L. Wilken, *Jews and Christians in Antioch*, 1978. For the multitudes of synagogues see Malalas (above, n.952) and John Chrysostom (above, n.987). There was a synagogue in Daphne (cf. below, n.1389). Cf. also Josephus, *Antt.* 17, 25, the settling of 500 Jewish cavalry from Babylonia in Hulatha near Antioch at the time of Herod, see Kraeling, 'Community' (n.987), 133–5.

1040. It can only be estimated very roughly, since even the total number of the population has not been established. Cf. above, n.987; Riesner, *Frühzeit* (n.49), 98 (with bibliography).

1041. Alexandria: Schürer III, 1, 49f.; Rome: Philo, *Legatio* 155: beyond the Tiber, see P. Lampe, *Die stadtrömischen Christen in den ersten beiden Jahrhunderten*, WUNT II/18, Tübingen ²1989, 26ff.

1042. See Lampe, *Christen* (n.1041), 28ff., 301ff. For the large number of house churches in Rome see Rom. 6.5, 10f., 14f. Cf. esp. Klauck, *Hausgemeinde* (n.745).

1043. See Hajjar, 'Divinités oraculaires' (n.425), and below, n.1233; Feldtkeller, *Reich* (n.88), 176 (on Lucian, *Dea Syria* 51) and 201. C. Forbes, *Prophecy and Inspired Speech in Early Christianity and its Hellenistic Environment*, WUNT II/75, 1995, 141ff. indeed mentions the prophet Eunus from Apameia in Syria, who staged the slave revolt in Sicily on the inspiration of the Syrian goddess, but otherwise does not go into Syria.

1044. Acts 16.13: 'because of the Jews' of that region, who all knew that he had a pagan father. Timothy should not be regarded as an apostate, cf. I Cor. 9.20; Acts 21.20–26.

1045. II Cor. 5.17; Rom. 13.8–10; Gal. 5.14, cf. 5.22f.; 6.2.

1046. Luke 6.43 = Matt. 7.17.

1047. Euthalios: Μωϋσέως ἀποκρύφου, see H. von Soden, *Die Schriften des Neuen Testaments* I, 1, 1911, 660; further A.-M. Denis, *Introduction aux pseudépigraphes grecques d'Ancien Testament*, SVTP 1, 1970, 160 n.36; Schürer III, 1, 285 following R. H. Charles, *The Assumption of Moses*, 1897, XVII for Christian origin.

1048. Riesner, *Frühzeit* (n.49), 144–8; Botermann, *Judenedikt* (n.5), 50–102.

1049. I Cor. 7.31; Rom. 12.2; 13.11ff.

1050. See above, 429 n.937; Hengel, 'Between Jesus and Paul' (n.50), 22ff.

1051. W. Schmithals, *Die Apostelgeschichte des Lukas*, ZB NT 3, 2, Zürich 1982, 119, 141; id., *Theologiegeschichte* (n.97), 85, 94, 177, would like to enlarge the inner group of five to seven by the addition of the 'Antiochenes' Judas Barsabbas and Silas/Silvanus. He argues that Luke has also deleted the title 'apostle' 13.2, cf. 14.4, 14 and I Cor. 12.28. But what do we know of the special 'understanding of apostle' in Antioch? See also 138 above and n.1072 below on Barnabas.

1052. The earliest Gospel prologue mentions Syrian Antioch as a home city; similarly some MSS of the 'Western' text make the 'we' narrative begin already in Acts 11.28 (D gig p Middle Egyptian translation). Origen, *Hom in Luc* 1, 6 identifies the 'brother' mentioned in II Cor. 8.18 with Luke. Ephraem's commentary speaks of Luke instead of Lucius of Cyrene, see Conybeare, *Beginnings* (n.363), III, 416. This tradition may go back into the second century. See Thornton, *Zeuge* (n.7), 268–71 etc.; against Riesner, *Frühzeit* (n.49), 35 (bibliography); see now also Barrett, *Acts* I (n.77), 564 ad loc. The Western text 'saw here a way of making history livelier and of giving it greater authority'.

1053. Heitmüller, 'Problem' (n.421), 124–43; Bousset, *Kyrios Christos* (n.150); Bultmann, Preface to Bousset (ibid.); cf. already Bultmann, 'The Significance of the Historical Jesus for the Theology of Paul' (1929), in *Faith and Understanding*, New York and London 1969, 220–46; and finally id., *Theology of the New Testament* 1, New York and London 1952, 63–184: 'The Kerygma of the Hellenistic Church Aside from Paul'; cf. the significant qualification 187: 'It remains uncertain, however, to what extent he had already appropriated in his pre-Christian period theological ideas of this syncretism (those of the mystery religions and of Gnosticism) which come out in his Christian theology.'

1054. Phil. 3.6; Rom. 11.1; II Cor. 11.22.

1055. Cf. the instances collected by Feldman, *Jew and Gentile* (n.320), 438–41, though he emphasizes that despite the restraint which is becoming evident in the controversies between rabbis over the status of proselytes, 'Jews continued to make converts in sizable numbers even after the advent of Christianity' (341).

1056. Gal. 3.28; I Cor. 12.13; Col. 3.11.

1057. Rom. 8.14; Gal 4.6.

1058. Justin, *Apol* I, 61–67; Salzmann, *Lehren* (n.319), 235–57.

1059. Cf. e.g. I Clem. 37.1–4, where the Roman army serves as a model for order in the community, or the constant admonition to ὁμόνοια; see Salzmann, *Lehren* (n.319), 150ff.

1060. Acts 20.7ff.; cf. I Cor. 16.2; cf. also W. Rordorf, *Sunday. The History of the Day of Rest and Worship in the Earliest Centuries of the Church*, London 1968; id., 'Ursprung und Bedeutung der Sonntagsfeier im frühen Christentum. Der gegenwärtige Stand der Forschung', *LJ* 31, 1981, 145–58.

1061. In Paul the λόγος τοῦ θεοῦ in the sense of the gospel still predominates: I Cor. 14.36; II Cor. 2.17; 4.2; Phil. 1.14; II Thess. 2.13, but see also 1.8; 4.15; Col. 1.25; 3.16.

1062. See C. H. Roberts and T. C. Skeat, *The Birth of the Codex*, London 1983, esp. 58ff. on Antioch. Possibly this is also connected with the fact that the Jesus tradition in the Greek languages was first collected in small codex-like notebooks, see Sato, *Q* (n.131), 62–5.

1063. Cf. Acts 2.41; 4.4; cf. 5.14; 6.7; 11.21, 24; 21.20: μυριάδες.

1064. Gregory of Nyssa, *De vita Gregorii Thaumaturgi* (PG 46, 909), *Opera* X, 1, 16, 2f. (ed. G. Heil). I owe this reference to C. Markschies. For the churches see Eusebius, *Vita Constantini* II, 1, 2–21, 1 (GCS I, 47f. ed. Winkelmann).

1065. Acts 19.1, τίνας μαθητάς and 19.7 ὡσεὶ δώδεκα.

1066. I Cor. 8.6; 12.3, 12; cf. Rom. 5.15, 17f.; II Cor. 5.13f.; 11.4 ; Eph. 4.5; I Tim. 2.5.

1067. I Cor. 12.9, 11, 13; Eph. 2.18; 4.4.

1068. Rom. 12.4f.; I Cor. 10.17; 12.12–14, 20; Col. 3.15; Eph. 2.16; 4.4.

1069. Rom. 15.31; Gal. 2.4ff., 11f.

1070. Eusebius, *HE* 3, 5, 3; cf. Rev. 12.6; AscIsa 4.13; further examples and discussion in F. Neirynck, *Evangelica*, BEThL 60, 1982, 566–71, 577–85, 57 n.98. There is no convincing reason to regard the report as unhistorical: it probably goes back to Ariston of Pella, whom Eusebius knows.

1071. Carleton Paget, *Barnabas* (n.382), though in my view he dates the letter too early. The period immediately before the Bar Kochba revolt *c.*130 CE still seems to me to be the most probable, 9–30. We should assume a Gentile-Christian, Alexandrian origin, 7–9, 30–42.

1072. It has the reference to the author as *inscriptio* and *subscriptio*, H only as *subscriptio*, V also the extended *subscriptio* Ἐπιστολὴ Βαρνάβα τοῦ ἀποστόλου συνεκδήμου Παύλου τοῦ ἁγίου ἀπόστολου. Clement of Alexandria already mentions Barnabas several times as author. The title seems to be original, as in the case of I Clement and Hebrews. See also Carleton Paget, *Barnabas* (n.382), 3ff. on the question of authorship. Tertullian, *De pud.* 20, knows of an attribution of Hebrews to Barnabas, cf. Jerome, *Vir. ill.* 5.

1073. *Die apokryphen Apostelgeschichten und Apostellegenden* II, 2 (reprinted 1976), 270.

1074. Lipsius (n.1073), 271.

1075. Clement of Alexandria, *Strom* 2, 20, 112, who moreover calls him μαρτὺς ἀποστολικός, i.e. witness to the apostolic age and 'fellow-worker with Paul', in connection with a quotation from Barnabas 16.7–9.

1076. 1.6–13.

1077. Ch. 4 (*Acta Apostolorum Apocrypha*, ed. Lipsius I, 49).

1078. Acts 15.6–7, 12.

1079. Acts 15.2, cf. Gal 2.1, 3: Titus was probably his special companion: ἀνέβην συμπαραλαβών. The other (possible) companions are not interesting, as they are Jewish Christians.

1080. The conjecture by Lüdemann, *Paul* (n.804), 20, 57–9, 75–7, that despite the chronologically continuous narrative in 1.13–2.10 the subsequent report about the incident in Antioch (2.11ff.) introduced by ὅτε δὲ ἦλθεν took place *before* the Apostolic Council is quite improbable. The reference to oratorical handbooks is not to the point, since Paul would hardly have read such books. He follows the rules of sound human understanding and presupposes this in his ancient readers (he could have had no inkling about his modern ones). The agreement in Jerusalem had not clarified the special problem of concrete table-fellowship at the eucharist; the primary issue was the fundamental question of *law and salvation*, whether the uncircumcised 'Gentile Christians' also should have a share in the salvation achieved by the Son of God. This was a question which had become problematical in Jerusalem at the end of the 40s, contrary to the earlier attitude. The result was a sudden threat to all Paul's mission work since Damascus (Gal. 2.2) and also that of the Christians in Antioch since the founding of the community, not to mention the position of many Gentile Christians in Syria and Phoenicia. The incident in Antioch is only understandable if it presupposes the agreement in Gal. 2.6–10. Moreover after the break Paul could never in any way have negotiated in Jerusalem in this way together with Barnabas, among other things also for the Antiochenes and the other Christians in Syria. See Hengel, *Earliest Christianity* (n.25), 99–110.

1081. In 2.1–2 he speaks in the first person singular, but mentions Barnabas as his usual travelling companion. Then in the decisive verses 4 and 5 he emphasizes their *shared* freedom in respect of circumcision and the other demands of the Torah and the firm resolve of both of them not to yield. The plural includes Paul, Titus and Barnabas. From 2.6–9a he again speaks in the singular, but in 9b and 10 the plural appears again in a significant context: 'And when they perceived the grace that was given to *me*, James and Cephas and John, who were reputed to be pillars, gave to *me and Barnabas* the hand of fellowship, that *we* should go to the Gentiles and they to the circumcised; only they would have us remember the poor, which very thing *I* was eager to do.' Here we can see clearly the partnership with Barnabas on an equal footing and the obligation which was on both of them.

1082. Galatians may have been written after I Corinthians and before II Corinthians *c.*54 in Ephesus or on the journey to Corinth. Against Schnelle, *Einleitung* (n.76), 118.

1083. Gal 2.9 ἡμεῖς εἰς τὰ ἔθνη.

1084. Acts 15.20f.: James's proposal; 28f.: the decree; 21.25: James's further reminder of it. Luke knows that James was behind this definition, which was presumably meant to resolve the problem of Gal. 2.11ff. by a compromise. Paul never officially recognized it, but his pastoral advice in Corinth in connection with eating meat offered to idols, I Cor. 8–10, and Rom. 14 in substance – with a quite different theological justification – go in the same direction. The decree was no longer a problem for the Pauline Gentile Christians, who were vegetarians and abstainers out of consideration for the weak. Table fellowship could not be hindered. It is striking that even according to Luke Paul reports the imposition of the Apostolic Decree only in the mission territory in Lycaonia which he shared with Barnabas and no longer in his own 'later' mission field. See Thornton, *Zeuge* (n.7), 342f.

1085. The πεπίστευμαι is a divine passive; it has been entrusted to him 'by the revelation of Jesus Christ' (Gal. 1.10, cf. I Cor. 9.1), just as Peter's has been entrusted to him by the protophany of the Risen Christ, I Cor. 15.5.

1086. 2.9: τὴν χάριν τὴν δοθεῖσάν μοι, cf. Rom. 1.5: δι' οὗ ἐλάβομεν χάριν καὶ ἀποστολὴν εἰς ὑπακοὴν πίστεως ἐν πᾶσιν τοῖς ἔθνεσιν, cf. 12.3, 6; 15.15; I Cor. 3.10; 15.10.

1087. We find this comparison with Peter indirectly also in the account of his call in Gal. 1.15f., and in I Cor. 15.5, 8ff. In substance it was not unfounded. Both were the most significant and historically the most effective figures in earliest Christianity.

1088. Compare the contrast between I Cor. 15.5 and 8ff. and the emphasis in 9.1 that he too has seen the Lord and therefore is just as much an apostle – at least for the many Gentile Christian communities which he has gained.

1089. Schmithals, *Theologiegeschichte* (n.97), 90f.; Becker, *Paulus* (n.61), 66–9, 89ff., 303.

1090. See above, 42, 62, 148, 153.

1091. On the formulation μή πως εἰς κενὸν τρέχω ἢ ἔδραμον: this is how he expresses his past as a preacher and his future plans; in fact he is writing six to seven years later, in Ephesus or on his way to Corinth; cf. also Phil. 2.16. The same would apply if the communities which he had founded lost their faith, see also I Cor. 15.10; II Thess. 3.5; cf. Isa. 49.4; 65.23 LXX.

1092. See above, 244–57.

1093. Acts 15.11: ἀλλὰ διὰ τῆς χάριτος τοῦ κυρίου Ἰησοῦ πιστεύομεν σωθῆναι καθ᾽ ὃν τρόπον κἀκεῖνοι (viz. the μαθηταί from the ἔθνη, vv.7, 10). Cf. Gal. 2.16 and on the χάρις Χριστοῦ 1.6, cf. 2.21; 5.4; Rom. 3.24; 4.16: ἐκ πίστεως ἵνα κατὰ χάριν, 6.14; 11.6 etc.

1094. See also Rom. 11, 13: ἐφ᾽ ὅσον μὲν οὖν εἰμι ἐγὼ ἐθνῶν ἀπόστολος; cf. Rom. 1.5, 13; 15.18; see further above, 8.2.8.

1095. Acts 14.12: to the inhabitants of Lystra Barnabas seems to be Zeus and Paul Hermes: ἐπειδὴ αὐτὸς ἦν ὁ ἡγούμενος τοῦ λόγου, cf. 13.9, 16; 14.9. In Cilicia and Lycaonia Hermes was the chief god. This is an old Luvian-Lycaonian legacy. It can still be read off inscriptions from the Hellenistic-Roman period, cf. Dagron and Feissel, *Inscriptions de Cilicie* (n.824), 44f. Luke cannot have invented this episode, since his explanation that Paul was the spokesman shows that he himself did not know the situation in Lycaonia so well. For him the identification of Paul with Hermes seems strange. Nor can Luke wholly have invented the fact that the priest of Zeus wants to offer sacrifices to them. This is a quite irreplacable authentic feature, since in this way the priest of Zeus wants to steal a march on the priest of Hermes, who represents the chief god and is of higher rank.

1096. See above, n.1080; but cf. the excellent account of Riesner, *Frühzeit* (n.49), passim.

1097. Ollrog, *Paulus* (n.27), perhaps involuntarily gives this impression, see the list on 61f., 94, where Barnabas is counted one of the 'pillars of the Pauline missions', 107: 'just as indeed Barnabas, Silvanus and Titus came to him from the community in Antioch'. This remains uncertain in the case of Titus; he may have been converted as a result of Paul's preaching, but we do not know where he comes from (against Ollrog, 34), and in the case of Barnabas and Silvanus (cf. 17–20) it is downright false: they both come from Jerusalem. That 'the sending of Silas from Jerusalem to Antioch is a Lukan construction' is an arbitrary assertion. It is only too understandable that after delegates from Jerusalem have caused unrest in Antioch (and probably also in other mission communities), on the journey back Barnabas and Paulus should be accompanied by delegates from Jerusalem who confirm the Jerusalem resolution there. The problem is only the content of the letter with the Apostolic Decree, which Luke has formulated himself in accordance with ancient historiography. 15.27: ... αὐτοὺς διὰ λόγου ἀπαγγέλλοντας τὰ αὐτά, indeed even 28a as far as βάρος here seem quite appropriate. The real decree presumably came about only some time later, to resolve the question which had become acute in Gal. 2.11ff. after the unpleasant interlude in Antioch.

1098. Cf. Paul and Prisca and Aquila, Acts 18.3; cf. 20.32f.

1099. F. Lang, *Die Briefe an die Korinther*, NTD 7, 1986, 115: 'Verses 4 and 5 are best interpreted in the light of v.6; the "we" which begins in v.4 envisages Paul and Barnabas.'

1100. Cf. Acts 14.4, 14; I Cor. 9.5f; Rom. 16.7.

1101. Cf. also Gal 1.19: ἕτερον ... τῶν ἀποστόλων.

1102. J. Roloff, *Apostolat, Verkündigung, Kirche*, Gütersloh 1965, 61: 'A large number of exegetes also include Barnabas among the apostles. However, Paul does not explicitly give him this designation.'

1103. I Cor. 9.2: εἰ ἄλλοις οὐκ εἰμὶ ἀπόστολος applies in the case of Paul certainly to Jerusalem and perhaps also for Antioch. There will similarly have been a dispute over this question in the case of Barnabas.

1104. See the survey by Barrett, *Acts* 1 (n.77), 257–60; S. Brock, *JTS* 25, 1974, 93–8, wants to derive it from the Aramaic root *by'*, 'console', formed from the verbal form of the third person masculine singular perfect, which could lead to the formation of the name *nbayya*. However, this only appears in Syriac from the third century. The Peshitta translates *bᵉrā' dᵉbūyātā*. But such a formation of a name would be unusual. It is also going too far to suppose that Luke is confusing the meaning with the name Μαναην, who in Acts 13.1 is named after Barnabas and corresponds to the Hebrew *mᵉnahem* = 'comforter', thus E. Schwartz, *NGWG.PH* 1907, 282 n.1 = *Gesammelte Schriften*, Berlin 1963, 5, 148 n.0; Conzelmann, *Acts* (n.230), 36; Haenchen, *Acts* (n.5), 231f.; Lake and Cadbury, *Beginnings* (n.363), IV, 49; Roloff, *Apostelgeschichte* (n.807), 93;

Schille, *Apostelgeschichte* (n.797), 146 et al. As a rule proper names (as opposed to surnames) were not translated. There are further earlier attempts at an interpretation in Deissmann, *Bibelstudien*, Marburg 1895, 175–8. In Babylonia, Hatra, Hierapolis-Bambyke and Palmyra we have the widespread theophoric name *brnbw,* after Nabū/Nebō, the god of the prophets and wisdom, in Greek inscriptions Βαρναβο[υ] (*IGLS* I, no. 126 from the neighbourhood of Zeugma) and in the accusative Βαρνεβουν τὸν καὶ Ἀπολλονάριον (*IGLS* I, no. 166 from Nicopolis), or in three further inscriptions from Syria Βαρνάβου (*SEG* 7, no. 381, 708 and 712), in which the form Barnabou and not Barnabas, as the editors over-hastily conjecture, is to be read, since the genitive of Barnabas is Βαρναβᾶ, see Col. 4.10; perhaps Βαρνᾶ (*IGLS* 1378) is an abbreviation of Barnebo. Cf. further *Dura Europos, Final Report V,* Part I, 1959, 67, 14, 100; VIII, 37. See also the instances of Nabu/Apollo in A. Bounnj, *LIMC* VI, 1, 1992, 608–701 (with bibliography), from Palmyra and Hierapolis, especially no.18: busts of the god with the inscription NBW and personal name BRNBW in H. Ingholt and H. Seyrig, *Recueil des tessères de Palmyre,* 1955, 41 no.296. Semitic names with the formation 'Bar-' in transcription appear more frequently in the Greek inscriptions from Syria, see e.g. Βαραδατος = 'son of Hadad' (*IGLS* no. 590; 778, 1; 2031) and Βαρναιος (*IGLS* 2372; 2510) or Βαραδονιος (*IGLS* no. 634 B 1), especially the Greek transcriptions of Bar-saumā = 'son (of the time) of youth' or 'son of the sun god (Šamaš)' as Βαρσουμης, Βαρσαμιος, Βαρσιμας. In general an Aramaic theophorous name with a Babylonian god as a sur-name seems to me to be improbable for a Levite born on Cyprus. The patronym of a Jew Βάρναβις (Πάμφιλος Βαρναβιος) on a tax receipt for the *fiscus Iudaicus* dated 31 October 105 from Edfu in Upper Egypt, *CPJ* III, no. 331, is interesting in this context. If Aramaic-speaking Jews used the name Barnabas, they did not of course think of the Babylonian and north Syrian god of prophets, oracles and scribes, but of the biblical *nābī'/ n'bī'īm/ n'bī'īn/ n'bīayya.* The tyrant of Sparta from 207 to 192 BCE is also called Ναβις, see V. Ehrenberg, *RE* 16, 2, 1471, as is a Carthaginian priest in Silius Italicus 15, 672, ibid., 1482.

1105. Hugonis Grotii, *Annotationes in Novum Testamentum denuo emend.,* ed. Zuigema, Groningen 1868–1828, Vol.V, *Acta Apostolorum,* 34: '*Apostoli ei hoc nomen dederant in omen doni prophetici ... Graeco sermone con-tracte* Βαρνάβας. *Nil mutandum: nam Hellenistis mos prophetiam vocare* παράκλησιν', cf. the λόγος παρακλήσεως in Acts 13.15; the παράκλησις του ἁγίου πνεύματος, 9.31; the παράκλησις brought about by the Spirit in 15.31; the παράκλησεις of Israel foretold by the prophets in Luke 2.25. Cf. also Heb. 13.22 and the Pauline terminology of the παράκλησις about through Christ, which goes far beyond the mere meaning of 'comfort', cf. I Cor. 14.3: προφητεύων ἀνθρώποις λαλεῖ οἰκοδόμην καὶ παράκλησιν καὶ παραμυθίαν; and Rom. 15.4: ἵνα διὰ τῆς ὑπομονῆς καὶ διὰ τῆς παρακλήσεως τῶν γραφῶν τὴν ἐλπίδα ἔχωμεν. Earliest Christian prophecy produces faith and hope through promise and admonition. The Lukan translation may sound like a 'popular etymology'; according to the earliest Christian understanding it is not 'false' (against Conzelmann, *Acts*, ad loc.). De Wette and Overbeck, *Apostelgeschichte* (n.698), 67, agree with Grotius. For the atypical use of *ben/bar* as a characterization of a professional group see H. Haag, *TWAT* 1, 674ff.

1106. Schille, *Apostelgeschichte* (n.797), 146f.; Haenchen, *Acts* (n.5), 231–3. Haenchen takes over this argument from Preuschen, *Apostelgeschichte* (n.801), 28 on Acts 4.36. It is totally groundless, especially as it is improbable that the surname was understood 'theophorically'. It has nothing to do with 'son of Nebu'. In the meantime we know through more recent discoveries that *surnames* to distinguish persons with very usual names were more the norm in ancient Palestine; cf. e.g. according to a new papyrus text from the death cave of the Bar Kochba rebellion Salome Grapte and her daughter Salome Komaïze (ed. Cotton; see n.587). Here 'Grapte' is a usual name, whereas Komaïze does not seem to be attested elsewhere and is probably derived from the lady's hairstyle. Nor were 'nicknames' rare in ancient Judaea. Cf. e.g. the 'Goliath' family; see R. Hachili, 'The Goliath Family in Jericho', *BASOR* 235, 1979, 31–6. See also the surnames on the ossuaries, and on them Rahmani, *Catalogue* (n.638), 14: 'Nicknames, often alluding to a physical characteristic of a deceased, occur frequently, usually in Status emphaticus ... Some of these names seem to have originated as terms of abuse or mockery ... but may have been accepted family names ... Double names, similar to classical signa [see Kubitschek, *PW* 2A, 2448–52] occur mainly in Hebrew-Greek ...' See also G. H. R. Horsley, 'The use of a double name', *New Doc* 1984, 89–96. In my view Barnabas is neither theophoric nor a patronym. A derivation from Jewish Palestine is most probable.

1107. Loisy, *Actes* (n.699), 262–5.

1108. Schmithals, *Apostelgeschichte* (n.1051), 109f., cf. 54 on Acts 4.36: 'He was active in the region of Antioch and we have no reliable indication that he comes from Jerusalem.'

1109. Schmithals, *Apostelgeschichte* (n.1051), 54.

1110. Haenchen, *Acts* (n.5), 332; cf. his article 'Barnabas', *RGG*³ 1, 880: 'Critical scholarship conjectures that B. (= son of Nebo) was a Hellenistic member of the earliest community ... and as one of the ἄνδρες Κύπριοι of Acts 11.20 founded the Gentile Christian community of Antioch'; Conzelmann, *Acts* (n.230), 75 on 9.27; 75x on 11.21, 25; id., *History of Primitive Christianity*, ²1971, 52, 140f.; Ollrog (n.27), 14–17, 296–315.

1111. See above, n.1104. In Egypt among the around 900 names of Greek prosopography here we have only the Barnabis already mentioned above (n.1104) and, in an epitaph from the late Roman period which perhaps comes from Alexandria, Βορζοχο[ρίας = Bar Zacharias (*CIJ* II, no. 1435; Horbury and Noy, *Jewish Inscriptions* [n.316], no. 127); cf. *CPJ* III, 171. In Rome among around 1,000 names we meet only a Barzaharona (= Bar Zacharias), *CIJ* I, no. 497 = Noy, *Jewish Inscriptions* II (n.243), no. 539; the reading 'Barvalentin' in *CIJ* I, no. 528 is improbable, see Noy no. 617 and enigmatically Barsheoda (?) as the surname of a girl who died at the age of eight months (*CIJ* no. 108; Noy no. 551). In Jerusalem, among around 150 Aramaic and Hebrew names, the ossuary catalogue of Rahmani (n.638), 292–6 contains only one *br yhwd* and one *br nhwm* and nothing resembling the name in the around 100 Greek names. We have four examples in Greek script in the later inscriptions of Beth Shearim (second to fourth centuries BCE) in Galilee, where the Greek names are by far the most predominant, see M. Schwabe and B. Lifshitz, *Beth Shearim, Vol. II, The Greek Inscriptions*, 1967, 108: no. 89, 97, 107, 160 (pure patronyms) and 23: Ιωσηφ Βαρ Μοκιμ. Cf. also the family Βαρβαβι in Joppa, *CIJ* II, no. 943 and 986 near Tiberias and the enigmatic 'false prophet' Bar Jesus on Cyprus in Acts 13.6. This patronym is clearly of Palestinian origin. Elymas may have been his exotic-magical surname (13, 8). As far as I can see there are virtually no examples in the whole of the rest of the Diaspora in the Eastern Mediterranean.

1112. Cf. also Acts 1.23 Ἰωσὴφ τὸν καλούμενον Βαρσαββᾶν and 15.22 Ἰούδας with the same surname, also Matt. 16.17; Ἰησοῦς Βαραββᾶς, Matt. 27.16f.; Βαρθολομαῖος, Mark 3.18 par. and Βαρτιμαῖος in Mark 10.46. But these are normal surnames coming mostly from patronyms.

1113. Acts 12.12–17: the description of the portico (πυλών) before the dwelling proper and the mention of a slave girl with the Greek name Rhode gives a historically apt picture of the milieu. Luke has no occasion to elaborate these features, as they contradict his ideal picture of the sharing of goods in 2.45 and 4.32–35. For the affinity with Mark see Col. 4.10 ὁ ἀνέψιος Βαρναβᾶ.

1114. Ἀγρός denotes a piece of land in the country which is used agriculturally but is not a garden. As a rule such property, which could also be a small estate or farmstead, was leased out and provided for the existence of city dwellers. Here property in the Holy Land was thought of as being essentially more important to Jews than in the Diaspora. As a rule they were not readily separated from it.

1115. Acts 6.7; cf. Luke 1.5; 10.31f.: Luke knows the difference in rank well.

1116. See above, n.1104.

1117. Acts 21.16; cf. 15.22.

1118. Hengel, 'Between Jesus and Paul' (n.50).

1119. Codex D; minuscule 6 suppl., pauci, it, vg mss: the change must have crept in as early as the second century.

1120. Byzantine majority text, majuscule 4 (044), minuscule 33 and Syr Harklensis. The short form Ἰώση for Ἰωσήφ is a typically Palestinian form of the name and is considerably more frequent there than the biblical form. Outside Palestine it appears very rarely, thus in Egypt only once as opposed to Ἰωσήπ(ος) or -φος 21 times. The rabbinic index in Billerbeck VI, 91–7 mentions 47 Joses to 8 Josephs! Luke himself has Joseph 8 times in the Gospel and Acts. We find this name elsewhere only in Mark 6.3; 15.40, 47, each time as the genitive Ἰωσῆτος and Matt. 27.56 as the genitive Ἰώση (v. l. on Ἰωσήφ). However, possibly this form, which sounds more original, has found its way into the text through the work of recension done in the library in Caesarea, where people knew the everyday Jewish names.

1121. ὥστε καὶ Βαρναβᾶς συναπήχθη αὐτῶν τῇ ὑποκρίσει.

1122. 18.22: καὶ κατελθὼν εἰς Καισάρειαν, ἀναβὰς καὶ ἀσπασάμενος τὴν ἐκκλησίαν, κατέβη εἰς Ἀντιόχειαν. Perhaps Paul learned that Peter was in Antioch.

1123. 18.23: καὶ ποιήσας χρόνον τινὰ ἐξῆλθεν.

1124. Philemon 24; cf. Col. 4.10. The Deutero-Pauline letter to the Colossians, probably written soon after the death of Paul (62 or 64 CE), presupposes the imprisonment of Paul and Aristarchus in Rome, cf. Acts 19.29; 20.4 and above all 27.2. See Ollrog, *Paulus* (n.27), 45f. For what seems the almost pathological tendency to remove John Mark from Jerusalem and transfer him to Antioch see Ollrog, loc. cit.: 'In this way a member of the Antiochene community is again anchored in the earliest Jerusalem community.' In *this* way, really everything can be twisted. Nowhere in the sources is Mark described as a 'member of the Antiochene community'. According to Acts 12.25 Barnabas and Paul take him with them to Antioch. He then accompanies them as a 'missionary assistant' (ὑπηρέτης) to Cyprus (13, 5), and according to 13.13 he returns to Jerusalem. In 15.37, where Barnabas wants to have him as a missionary assistant again and Paul objects, it is not said where he had been beforehand, but it seems likely that he followed Barnabas, Paul, Judas Barsabbas, Silas etc. from Jerusalem to Antioch.

1125. The fact that this report in Acts 4.36f. contradicts the idealized sharing of goods (4.32–35; cf. 2.45) shows its originality. For the problem see M. Hengel, *Earliest Christianity* (n.25), 179–82.

1126. Acts 15.27, 30f.; Rom. 16.2f. It is significant that the relationship between letter and messenger is not specifically discussed by Ollrog, *Paulus* (n.27), whose work is too schematic.

1127. II Cor. 11.16; Gal. 2.4; cf. II Cor. 2.17; II Tim. 3.6. II Cor. 3.1 is negative on letters of commendation for Paul, see also Spicq, *Notes* (n.1019), 2, 864f.; Hengel, 'The Titles of the Gospels', in *Studies in the Gospel of Mark* (n.30), 73, 80.

1128. Cf. Acts 15.23 and 41.

1129. Luke gives a positive report of his young nephew in Jerusalem only in Acts 23.16ff., to some extent as a counterpart to John Mark with Barnabas.

1130. 11.30; 12.25; 13.2, 7.

1131. 13.43, 46, 50.

1132. Barnabas/Paul 14.14; 15.12, 25; Paul/Barnabas 15.2, 22, 35.

1133. See above, 210.

1134. Acts 15.14. Luke has Symeon for Peter only at this point, but cf. Luke 2.25, 34 and the genealogy, 3.30. By contrast we find Simon for Peter 15 times in Luke-Acts. In other words, Luke makes the 'Hebrew' James call Peter by the biblical, non-Graecized form of his name.

1135. Acts 13.10f.; cf. 13.16; 14.12.

1136. In *CPJ* III, 191–3 we find 28 Simons for Egypt but only one Symeon. In Rome we find 6 Simons, but no Symeon, *CIJ* I, 616, 625; Noy, *Jewish Inscriptions* II (n.243), nos. 52, 305 (?), 310. Only in the case of the inscription from the year 521 CE from Venosa (Noy, *Jewish Inscriptions* I [n.325], no. 107) is there a possibility of deriving the genitive *Symonatis patris* both from Simon and from Symeon. The form Symeon also does not appear in the Diaspora of the East, Greece, Asia Minor, Syria. Even Josephus uses it only twice, *Antt.* 12, 265 and partially in the case of Simon son of Gamaliel (*BJ* 4, 159, the *Vita* has 'Simon' 7 times for him). By contrast, 29 different Simons appear in his work. Simon, the most frequent name in contemporary Judaism, as the Greek name was very close to the Hebrew *šimʿōn*, see Hengel, *Judaism and Hellenism* (n.314), II, 46 n.53, had also largely established itself in Palestine, but had become quite unusual in the Diaspora; here it should be noted that Josephus is writing in Rome. Cf. above n.1134 on Acts 15.14, where Luke deliberately puts the Hebraizing version 'Symeon' on the lips of James; cf. Luke 2.25 and later the archaism II Peter 1.1.

1137. Acts 11.20; cf. 6.9, the synagogue of the Cyrenians in Jerusalem,

2.10; Mark 15.21 par; see Hengel, 'Between Jesus and Paul' (n.50), 12ff. At a very early stage he was – wrongly – identified with Luke; cf. already Acts 11.28 Codex D (p w mae), the removal of the first person plural, see above, n.1052. For the tradition of an Antiochene origin for Luke cf. above, n.1052.

1138. For Manaen see H. W. Hoehner, *Herod Antipas*, SNTS.MS 17, 1972, 14, n.1 on the term σύντροφος; 121, 132, 184 n.3, 231, 305f. Among other things he conjectures that Manaen had possibly been 'an actual eyewitness of the banquet' (Mark 6.21ff.). That is probably going too far, but perhaps this Menahem knew Jesus. Antipas was banished by Caligula to Gaul in 38 on the urging of Agrippa I. Papias, according to Philip of Side, mentions the resurrection of the mother of a Μαναῖμος, see Funk and Bihlmeyer, *Apostolische Väter*, 1924, 138f fr. XI = J. Kürzinger, *Papias von Hierapolis ...*, Regensburg 1983, 116f. fr. 16.

1139. Clement of Alexandria, *Strom.* 2, 118, 3; 3, 25, 5–26, 3; Rev. 2.6, 15; cf. later Irenaeus, *Haer.* 1, 26, 2; Tertullian, *De pud.* 19, 4; Hippolytus, *Ref.* 7, 36, 3; *De resurr.*, GCS 1, 251 (Achelis); Epiphanius, *Haer.* 25, who makes him a preliminary stage of Gnostic libertinism with his unbridled sexual appetite; see also Jerome, *Ep.* (123) *ad Ctesiphontem* 4, who puts him, the one who as *omnium inmunditiarum repertor choros duxit femineos*, between Simon Magus with his Helen and Marcion with his woman messenger and Apelles with Philomene. Nicolaus and the Nicolaitans have also become a sphere of conjecture again in modern times, see T. Zahn, *FGNK* 6, 1900, 221–3; A. von Harnack, *JR* 3, 1923, 413–22; M. Goguel, *RHR* 1937, 1–37; N. Brox, 'Nikolaos und Nikolaiten', *VigChr* 19, 1965, 23–30; more recently see R. Heiligenthal, *ZNW* 82, 1992, 133–7, who sees in the 'Nicolaitans ... representatives of an enlightened sceptical trend ... which can be traced down to the position of the strong in the Pauline communities' and who resolutely reject the Apostolic Decree. The connection with Nicolaus is said to be very questionable. Brox already conjectured that the reference to him of the Nicolaitans was secondary. However, Feldtkeller, *Identitätsuche* (n.88), 185–7, cf. 144, wants once again to make a link between Rev. 2.14ff. and Acts 6.5 and arrives at fantastic conclusions: 'The activity of this group in or around Antioch would explain how Paul could already answer the challenge of Nicolaitans or those of like mind with a piece of Antiochene tradition when their influence had reached the community of Corinth' (185). He also knows that 'the Nicolaitans (were) certainly ... known to' Luke 'as a group which disputed the Apostolic Decree'. In reality we know nothing of Nicolaus apart from what is said in Acts 6.5. How the 'Nicolaitans' of Rev. 2 are connected with him is also unclear. They have even less to do with the later Gnostic formations than Simon Magus.

1140. ἐγένετο δὲ αὐτοῖς καὶ ἐνιαυτὸν ὅλον συναχθῆναι ἐν τῇ ἐκκλησίᾳ καὶ διδάξαι ὄχλον ἱκανόν D mae (gig p* sy^hmg): οἵτινες παραγενόμενοι ἐνιαυτὸν ὅλον συνεχύθησαν ὄχλον ἱκανόν. For the changes see Barrett, *Acts I* (n.77), 555 ad loc.: the statement is simplified, the community disappears and the success of the teachers is intensified by the συνεχύθησαν, here used positively (συγχύννω only in Acts 2.6; 9.22; 19.32; 21.31): 'they were shattered'. D² combines both readings, see Nestle and Aland NTG²⁷, 736. The reinforcing καὶ here before ἐνιαυτὸν, 'even a whole year', is missing in the majority text. The variant should be adopted in Nestle and Aland.

1141. Lake and Cadbury, *Beginnings* (n.363), IV, 130, see *LSJ*, 1691 συνάγω no. 7 with reference to Matt. 25.35, 38, cf. LXX Deut. 22.2; II Kingdoms 11.17 etc., see also Barrett, *Acts* 1 (n.77), 544, 555: 'met'.

1142. Luke 22.66; Acts 4.5, 26; 13.44; 14.27; 5.6, 30; 20.7f.

1143. Cf. Luke 10.1; 17.8; 18.4; Acts 5.37; 7.7: 13.20; 18.1.

1144. Barrett, *Acts* I (n.77), 559.

1145. Acts 18.11: 18 months in Corinth; 19.10: 2 years in Ephesus; 20.31: 3 years; cf. also Gal. 1.18; 2.1; II Cor 12.2.

1146. *PW* 2. R., 5, 1088, Tetrapolis nos. 4 and 2, 1206f. Seleucis 2.

1147. Cf. Acts 11.19; 13.4.

1148. I Thess. 1.9f; 5.9; Acts 17.31.

1149. I Thess. 2.14; Gal. 1.22; cf. I Cor. 7.17; 11.16; 16.19; II Cor. 11.28.

1150. At any rate he stands at the end of the list of the Antiochene five in 13.1. What is said in Gal. 1.14 in respect of his years of teaching as *talmid hakam* in Jerusalem must also apply in another form to the later apostles.

1151. Hengel, *Zealots* (n.122), 313–57.

1152. Josephus, *Antt.* 18, 88–89. After his ten years in office, Pilate arrived in Rome only after the death of Tiberius (16 March 37). Vitellius sent one of his friends, Marcellus, to Judaea to take over the administration. Perhaps he is identical with the Marullus appointed by Caligula in Josephus, *Antt.* 18, 237, who was replaced by Agrippa I in 41 CE, see Schürer I, 283.

1153. See above, 112.

1154. See Pliny the Younger, *Ep.* 10, 96, 2; and on it A. N. Sherwin-White, *The Letters of Pliny*, Oxford ³1985, 696f. and the apt comments by R. Feldmeier, *Die Christen als Fremde. Die Metapher der Fremde in der antiken Welt, im Urchristentum und im 1. Petrusbrief*, WUNT 64, 1992, 106–8, cf. also 144 with the reference to Acta Joannis 3, which in my view is in turn dependent on Esther 3.8. For the name *Christianoi* see Barrett, *Acts I* (n.77), 544f., *ad loc.*, who cites the important more recent literature.

1155. Ignatius, Rom. 2.2. He speaks at the same time for the 'community in Syria', Eph. 21.2; Magn. 14.1; Trall. 13.1; Rom. 9.1, and mentions 'Syria' 16 times but Antioch only 3 times, always as Ἀντιόχεια τῆς Συρίας.

1156. Around 8 times, once as an adjective in Trall. 6.1; cf. esp. Rom. 3.2f. In addition, Χριστιανισμός in contrast to Ἰουδαϊσμός appears for the first time in his writings, see H. Kraft, *Clavis Patrum Apostolicorum*, 1963, 458.

1157. See E. J. Goodspeed, *Index Apologeticus*, 1912, 293; Kerygma Petri according to Clement of Alexandria, *Strom.* 6, 5, 41: the Christians as the third race.

1158. Here mention should also be made of Theophilus of Antioch, see the index in von Otto, *CorpAp* VIII, 1861, 1961, 340; ActThom 22.23; PsClem., *Rec.* 4,20,4; Hegesippus in Eusebius, *HE* 3,32,3. The usage then only becomes established among Christians also as a self-designation in the second half of the second century and becomes very significant in the acts of martyrs as a confession: for the first time in MartPolyc. 10, 1: χριστιανός εἰμι cf. 12.2; see also the letter from the communities in Gaul (Eusebius, *HE* 5, 1, 10), etc. However, the Christians in Vienne and Lyons call themselves δοῦλοι Χριστοῦ or ἅγιοι, 5, 1, 3f.; i.e. they follow New Testament terminology.

1159. *Chron.*, ed. Dindorf, 246f (PG 97, 377) = Stauffenberg, *Malalas* (n.952), 25. See E. Peterson, *Frühkirche, Judentum und Gnosis, Rom etc.*, 1959, 64f. According to *Const. apost.* 7, 66, 4 Euodios was consecrated by Peter. The dating comes from Eusebius: according to the Armenian Chronicle, ed. J. Karst, GCS 20, 1911, 214, Peter arrived in Antioch in the third year of Gaius and went from there to Rome; Euodius was appointed bishop in Antioch in the second/third year of Claudius, see also *HE* 3, 22; according to the *Chronicle of Jerome*, ed. R. Helm, GCS 47, 1956, 178, 402, the foundation by Peter took place only in the second year of Claudius. Cf. Riesner, *Frühzeit* (n.49), 107f. n.86.

1160. Jesus was already given this title, cf. Matt. 2.23; 26.71; Luke 18.37; John 18.5, 7; 19.19; Acts 2.22; 3.6; 4.10; 6.14; 22.8; 24.5: in Tertullus' prosecution speech before Felix; 26.9. In Luke 4.34 and 24.19 by contrast the evangelist uses Ναζαρηνός, thus also in Mark 1.24; 10.47; 14.67; 16.6. This twofold formation of the name has a parallel in the designations Ἐσσαῖοι and Ἐσσῆνοι; for the groups, see H. H. Schaeder, *TDNT* 4, 879–84; cf. also Tertullian, *Adv. Marc.* 4, 8, 1: *unde et ipso nomine nos Iudaei Nazarenos appellant* (CCSL 1, p. 556 Kroymann). Jerome, *in Is*

5, 18 (CCSL 73), pars 1, 2, p. 76: *ter per singulos dies in omnibus synagogis sub nomine Nazarenorum anathemisant vocabulum Christianum.*
1161. Acts 1.11; 2.7; cf. Matt. 26.69 and Hengel, *Zealots* (n.122), 56ff.; B. Lifshitz, 'L'origine du nom des chrétiens', *VigChr* 16, 1962, 70.
1162. For the following see E. Bickerman, 'The Name of the Christians', in id., *Studies in Jewish and Christian History* III, AGJU IX, Leiden 1986, 139–51: 143f. = *HTR* 42, 1949, 109–24.
1163. Instances: Bickerman (n.1162), 143 n.30; cf. also J. A. Cramer, *Catenae Graecorum patrum in Novum Testamentum*, III, Oxford 1840 reprinted Hildesheim 1967, 198 ad loc. = Theophylact, PG 125, 677: Παύλου καὶ τοῦτο κατόρθωμα.
1164. Bickerman (n.1162), 143 n.28: Vigilius, *c. Arian.* I, 138 (PL 62, 194).
1165. *Pan* 42, 12, 3: *Refut.* 2 and 26 (GCS II, 174, ed. Holl).
1166. Bickerman (n.1162) with numerous examples.
1167. See B. Reicke, *TDNT* 9, 480f., cf. Rom. 7.3 and *LSJ*, 2005, in later terminology χρηματίζειν III, 2 'generally to be called'. See also Barrett, *Acts* I (n.77), 555f., and Bickerman, *Studies* (n.1162), 142 n.32 as a possibility, 'to bear a name'. Against this C. Spicq, *StTh* 15, 1961, 68, 78 and id., *Theologie Morale du Nouveau Testament*, Paris 1965, I, 406–16: 'an ingressive aorist: "The disciples began to call themselves".'
1168. Bickerman, *Studies* (n.1162), 145 n.37; Epiph., *Haer.* 29, 1, 1 and 4, 9–5, 5 (GCS I, 321, 325f. ed. Holl). Epiphanius confuses these obscure Ἰησσαῖοι with the Ἐσσαῖοι in Philo's *Vita contemplativa*. His report merely refers to a Jewish-Christian group of his time.
1169. Cf. Rom. 8.1; 1.1; 7.22; I Cor. 1.12ff.; 3.4, 22f.; Gal. 1.10; Phil. 1.1.
1170. Hengel, 'Erwägungen' (n.506); see also D. Zeller, 'Zur Transformation des Χριστός bei Paulus', *JBTh* 8, 1993, 155–67.
1171. See H. Schnorr v. Carolsfeld, 'Das lateinische Suffix *ânus*', *ALLG* 1, 1884, 177–94; Spicq (n.1167), 411 n.4: for the Greek sphere 'one would expect χρίστειοι or χριστικοί, i.e. a suffix in -ειος, -αιος, or -ιικος.
1172. For instances see *Oxford Latin Dictionary*, 1968ff., s. v. *Augustiani*; Tacitus, *Ann* 14, 15; Suetonius, *Nero* 25, 1: Nero's claque consisting of Praetorians. We also find the term as a rabbinic loanword to denote a soldier, S. Krauss, *Griechische und Lateinische Lehnwörter*, 1899, 2, 9; see also id., *Monumenta Talmudica* V, Leipzig 1914, 148 nos. 345/6. H. B. Mattingly, 'The Origin of the Name *Christiani*', *JTS*.NS 9, 1958, 26–37, saw Nero's *Augustiani* as the direct model for the *Christiani*, but that is historically improbable.

1173. Usually as an adjective, see *Oxford Latin Dictionary* s. v., but cf. Jerome, *Ep.*22.30: '"*mentiris*", ait, "*Ciceronianus es, non Christianus; ubi thesaurus tuus, ibi et cor tuum*".'

1174. Mark 3.6; 12.13 = Matt. 22.16; cf. Josephus, *Antt.* 14, 450: the Galileans rebel against their aristocracy (δυνατοί) and drown τοὺς τὰ Ἡρώδου φρονοῦντες in Lake Genessaret = *BJ* 1, 326; cf. *Antt.* 15, 2. By contrast, in *BJ* 1, 319 the supporters of Herod are called Ἡρώδειοι and those of Antigonus Ἀντιγόνειοι. The formulations derive from Nicolaos of Damascus and still come from the early period. Ἡρωδίανοι is a later formation.

1175. Bickerman, 'Hérodiens', *Studies* III (n.1162), 22–33, see especially 29ff., wants to follow Erasmus, Loisy, Lagrange and Goguel in having only the meaning 'the people following Herod Antipas' or 'the servants of Herod Antipas' for the three passages in the Gospels, but this meaning seems to be too narrow, see Schalit, *Herodes* (n.291), 479f., with reference to A. Momigliano and above all W. Otto, *PW* Suppl 2, 1913, 200–2: among other things they thought 'to restore the old kingdom of the king' and at the same time were firm 'friends of Rome' (ibid., 201). The development of Agrippa I's rule from 37 CE on and the restoration of the old Herodian kingdom in 41 CE shows how acute this question was.

1176. Persius 5, 179 speaks of Jews in Rome who celebrate the 'day of Herod'; the scholiast says that the 'Herodiani' celebrate Herod's birthday and also the Sabbath. However, the late interpretation by the scholiast is uncertain, see Stern, *GLAJ* I, 436 no. 190. The inscription *CIJ* 173, in which Frey conjectured a synagogue of the Herodians, is also disputed; see H. J. Leon, *The Jews in Ancient Rome*, 1960, 159ff., though his proposal for supplementing it is now questionable; see now Noy, *Jewish Inscriptions* II (n.243), 252ff. no. 292, who reads the name Ἡροδίων in the synagogue inscription; this is also attested as a Jewish name in Rome in the greeting in Rom. 16.11 and its connection with the house of Herod is manifest. Herod's clan had a whole series of members in Rome – both in the closer family and also among the slaves and freedmen of his palaces and their households – and certainly also by no means a few Jewish sympathizers. See the thorough description of the Jewish and Roman sources by W. Horbury, 'Herod's Temple and "Herod's Days"', in *Templum amicitiae, FS Bammel*, ed. id., Sheffield 1991, 103–49 (esp. 123–49 with bibliography).

1177. Antioch owed the building of a section of the triumphal street to King Herod I. See below, n.1434.

1178. See R. D. Sullivan, 'The Dynasty of Judaea in the First Century', *ANRW* II 8, 1977, 296–354. See especially 299 on the varied relations of the descendants of Herod and Mariamne 'to the dynasties of Armenia, Pontus, Commagene, Emesa, Galatia and Parthia – as well as to smaller aristocratic houses in Arabia and west to Pergamon and Ephesus', see the genealogy, 300. Cf. Josephus, *Antt.* 19, 305–11, the meeting of the client kings in Tiberias on the invitation of Agrippa I, which aroused the suspicion of anti-Roman ambitions on the part of Marsus the governor of Syria, who broke off this – family and political – 'summit meeting' by abruptly sending home kings Antiochus of Commagene, Sampsigeramus of Emesa, Cotys of Lesser Armenia, Polemo II of Pontus and Rough Cilicia and Herod of Chalkis; see Sullivan, ibid., 324; id., 'The Dynasty of Commagene', *ANRW* II 8, 1977, 787f.; Schwartz, *Agrippa I.* (n.302), 137–44.

1179. Peterson, *Frühkirche* (n.1159), 64–87: 74–7.

1180. For the first time in Justin, *Dial* 35, 6.

1181. Bickerman, 'Hérodiens', *Studies* III (n.1162), 31. The designation Ἑλληνιανοί in Justin's catalogue of Jewish sects, *Dial.* 80.4, is unexplained. Is it connected with the 'Hellenists' (Acts 6.1; 9.29)?

1182. *Antt.* 18, 64: εἰς ἔτι νῦν τῶν Χριστιανῶν ἀπὸ τοῦδε ὠνομασμένον οὐκ ἐπέλιπε τὸ φῦλον, cf. also 20, 200: the *Testimonium Flavianum* has only slight interpolations. This closing sentence completely in the style of Josephus is not a forgery, see also Peterson (n.1159), 82f. Josephus, who is writing *c.*93/94, knows (like I Peter) 'that to use the name as such is an offence'.

1183. Pliny, *Ep.*10, 96.97; Tacitus, *Ann.*15, 44, 2, originally ironical: *quos per flagitia invisos vulgus* Christianos *appellabat*, cf. Tertullian, *Ad nat* 1, 3, 9: *corrupte a nobis Chrestiani pronuntiamur; Apologeticum* 3, 5, 3; Suetonius, *Nero* 16, 3; cf. *Claudius* 25, 3: *impulsore Chresto*; Marcus Aurelius 11, 3, 2; Lucian, *Peregrinus* 11–13, 16; *Alexander*, 25, 33.

1184. Had Claudius appointed Agrippa I's son Agrippa II as his successor in 44 after the former's death, the Jewish War would have been avoided. The later church fathers conjectured that the Herodians made messianic claims for their rulers, see Bickerman, 'Hérodiens', in *Studies* III (n.1162), 22–5. Schalit, *Herodes* (n.291), 473–9, but also Riesner, *Frühzeit* (n.49), 109 ('aspirations ... to be recognized as messiah-like rulers') assume that this really was the case. However, this view certainly goes much too far, cf. Horbury, 'Herod' (n.1176), 111ff., 128. As Jews, Herod and his descendants held the view that their rule and also that of Rome rested on God's will, just as Josephus too regarded the Roman power as God-given and argued this view against the Zealots.

1185. Specifically in the Greek-speaking realm the ending -ιανός in conjunction with a ruler's name took on political significance; see

Appian, *Bell. civ* 3, 91: Octavian and his followers and troops: οἱ Καισαρίανοι, P. Gnomon 241 = *Der Gnomon des Idios Logos*, ed. W. Schubart, BGUV 1, 1210, along with the typically Greek Καισάρειοι in Dio Cassius 69, 7; 78, 16; cf. Appian, *Bell. civ* 3, 82: Πομπηιανοί, Epictetus, Diss 1, 19, 19: Καισαριανοί for members of the imperial house, 3, 24, 117: imperial officials; 4, 13, 22: dignitaries of the imperial court; Plutarch, *Galba* 171: κολάσεις τῶν Νερωνιανῶν: the punishment of the followers of Nero; for the adjective see Epictetus, *Diss* 4, 5, 18; Pliny the Younger, *Ep.*3, 7, 10: *ultimus ex Neronianis consularibus*. See also *Oxford Latin Dictionary*. s. v. on Galbianus, Othonianus, Vitellianus and Flavianus, which could be used both as adjectives, above all as an expression of belonging, and also as substantives for supporters. There are further examples in Bickerman (n.1162) and Spicq (n.1167). Against this manifold background the conjecture that the designation Ἡρωδιανοί in Mark 3.6, 12 is 'a redactional formation of Mark's', thus W. J. Bennet Jr, 'The Herodians in Mark's Gospel', *NT* 17, 1979, 9–14, and K. Müller, *NBL* 2, 122–4, is absurd.

1186. Cf. Mark 14.61; 15.21–26–32: the change from 'Christ' and 'king of the Jews'.

1187. In Sib.5, 68 all Israel is called θεόχριστοι. But this remains a unique exception in the sources at our disposal; against M. Karrer, *Der Gesalbte. Die Grundlagen des Christustitels*, FRLANT 151, Göttingen 1991, 231, who regards it as a 'stereotyped phrase, firmly rooted in the consciousness of authors and their audiences'. Through the Son Christians have become 'sons of God' (Rom. 8.17, 19, 23) and are 'anointed' with the Spirit (II Cor. 1.21, cf. Acts 10.38, 44ff.; I John 2.20, 27), but they never become 'Christoi', only 'Christianoi', those who belong to Christ. See J. M. Scott, *Adoption as Sons of God*, WUNT II/48, Tübingen 1992. For the believer bearing the name of Christ see then Hermas, *Sim* 9, 13–17 (90, 7; 91, 5; 92, 2; 94, 4), though he avoids the term Χριστιανοί.

1188. See LSJ, 2007 s. v.; cf. 1170 νεόχριστος, 'newly plastered'; W. Grundmann, *TDNT* 10, 495: 'spreadable, smeared, anointed, as noun τὸ χριστόν, ointment … Never related to persons outside the LXX and the NT.'

1189. See above nn.959, 1183 on the edict of Claudius and Riesner, *Frühzeit* (n.49), 87ff.; further Tacitus, *Ann.*15, 44, 1. The view of Karrer, *Der Gesalbte* (n.1187), 175ff.; 222ff.; 227f.; 363–76; 406 etc. is misguided. The masculine title Χριστός was incomprehensible to Greeks . It cannot be derived from the process of anointing in the temple, nor is Dan. 9.26 LXX (μετὰ τοῦ Χριστοῦ) neuter, but as in Theodotion Dan. 9.25f.

denotes the anointed high priest; nor could pagan listeners take a step towards understanding this most important title of Jesus which facilitated mission on the basis of the use of oil in the cult or the anointing with ambrosia in myth. The messianic texts from Qumran also show that his theses about the pre-Christian Jewish messianic expectation are untenable. By contrast, the title χριστός was known to the godfearers from the synagogue through the LXX. Here texts like Pss. 2; 18 (LXX 17); 89 (88); 132 (131) were essential. The work is a typical example of the way in which, starting from false presuppositions and using misleading interpretations of the text and arguments, one can so spin oneself into a cocoon that it is impossible to get out of it.

1190. Ἐν ταύταις δὲ ἡμέραις, cf. Luke 6.12; 23.7; Acts 1.15; 6.1 etc., see Preuschen, *Apostelgeschichte* (n.801), 27.

1191. In Acts 2.17 in the Joel quotation Luke has replaced the μετὰ ταῦτα of the LXX by an ἐν ταῖς ἐσχάταις ἡμέραις and added καὶ προφητεύσουσιν at the end of v.18 summarizing the preceding description. Cf. J. Jervell, 'Sons of the Prophets: The Holy Spirit in the Acts of the Apostles', in id., *The Unknown Paul. Essays on Luke-Acts and Early Christian History*, Minneapolis 1984, 96–121: 112.

1192. See also in 13.2 the five προφῆται καὶ διδάσκαλοι in Antioch; in 15.28 Judas Barsabbas and Silas from Jerusalem in Antioch; in 21.10 Agabus in Caesarea; cf. also Luke 11.49.

1193. Here the verb appears only after the baptism of the disciples of John and the laying on of hands by Paul as a sign of the bestowal of the Spirit, Acts 19.6.

1194. I Thess. 5.20, cf. also Rom. 12.6, a critical admonition which is probably similarly influenced by the Corinthian experiences. There is no investigation of Palestine-Syria in Forbes, *Prophecy* (n.1043); his study is above all orientated on the classical Greek sources and Egypt of the Hellenistic period. Nor is justice done to early Judaism.

1195. Eph. 4.11, cf. 2.20 'apostles and prophets' as the 'basic offices', similarly 3.5. For the evangelists cf. Acts 21.8: Philip. Later the εὐαγγελιστής was regarded as a non-apostolic missionary. I Tim. 1.18 and 4.14 around 110–120 CE later seek a balance between monarchical office and prophecy, by giving the latter some effect in the choice of the minister. By contrast, Ephesians could stand nearer to Luke in time, though it presents a resolutely 'Pauline' standpoint. Cf. 1.1 on Paul's apostolate.

1196. Matt. 7.22f.; cf. the false prophets in Mark 13.22 who are doubled in 24.11 and 24. In Matt. 28.20 there is no reference to an outpouring of the Spirit; instead, keeping the commandment is inculcated;

cf. also the unique emphasis on Christian scribes, 13.52. Christian prophets are mentioned only in 23.24 in the descriptive climax 'prophets, wise men, scribes' and 10.41 'prophet, righteous'. Cf. Luke 11.49 Q more originally 'prophets, apostles'. I Clement mentions only the Old Testament prophets, in 17.1 and 43.1. Thus the apostles and the presbyers appointed by them play all the greater a role, see below, n.1223.

1197. K. Niederwimmer, *Die Didache*, Göttingen 1989, 79.

1198. Ibid., 80. In Ignatius the Old Testament prophets are always meant, also Philad. 5.2, cf. 9.2. One might also assume that the great significance of the prophets in Syria and Palestine towards the end of the first century had provoked a counter-movement.

1199. Did. 11.3: the apostle who remains three days is a false prophet, cf. also Luke 11.49 Q 'prophets and apostles' (= messengers) as hendiadys; Eph. 2.20; 3.5 differs.

1200. Did. 13.1–3.

1201. Cf. Phil. 1.1. In *Apost.Const.* 7, 31, 1 the presbyters are added, see Niederwimmer, *Didache* (n.1197), 241.

1202. Did. 15.1.

1203. Niederwimmer, *Didache* (n.1197), 242.

1204. Cf. Acts 8.18f.; I Tim. 4.14; II Tim. 1.6: both texts point to an earlier usage.

1205. Cf. I Cor. 14.29; I Thess. 5.21. For laying on of hands by the apostles as a means of bestowing charismatic gifts of the Spirit see Acts 6.6, 8; 8.15–19; cf. also the institutionalized form in I Tim. 4.14; II Tim. 1.6. In Heb. 6.2 there is already a fixed διδαχή about this.

1206. For this metaphor for the ecstatic-visionary opening of the separation between earthly and heavenly worlds cf. Rev 4.1. Isaiah is transported in a vision from the earthly to the heavenly worship (cf. 9.27–10.6) and after that sees the coming of Christ on earth, the earthly life, crucifixion and exaltation of Christ. Cf. also Mark 1.10 par; Isa. 63.19 LXX.

1207. Cf. Isa. 57.15 (LXX): κύριος ὁ ὕψιστος ὁ ἐν ὑψηλοῖς κατοικῶν τὸν αἰῶνα, ἅγιος ἐν ἁγίοις ὄνομα αὐτῷ, κύριος ὕψιστος ἐν ἁγίοις ἀναπαυόμενος. Cf. I Clem. 54.3; *Const. apost.* 8, 11, 2.

1208. For a translation cf. E. Norelli, *Ascension d'Isaïe, Apocryphes. Collection de proche de L'AELAC*, Brepols 1993, 121f.; M. A. Knibb, in *OTP* II, 164f. Cf. Norelli's commentary, 66f.: 'the account certainly pre-supposes a practice common to the author and to the readers envisaged. They know real liturgies ... in the course of which ecstatic phenomena occur' (66). Now also Norelli, *Ascensio Isaiae*, CC.SA 7, 76ff.; CC.SA 8,

325ff.

1209. Cf. Heckel, *Kraft* (n.14), 56–66.

1210. Acts 10f.; 12.7–10 cf. I Cor. 15.4 and the colourful elaboration in the later legends of Peter. See R. A. Lipsius, *Die apokryphen Apostelgeschichten und Apostellegenden* II, 1 (1884, reprinted 1976), 176f., 218.

1211. We still need a really satisfactory in-depth account of early Christian prophecy. For the subject see E. Fascher, ΠΡΟΦΗΤΗΣ, Giessen 1927, though he neglects the specifically Jewish background too much in favour of a very general history-of-religions approach; Rendtorff, R. Meyer and G. Friedrich, Προφήτης, *TDNT* 6, 783–861, is still basic; G. Dautzenberg, *Urchristliche Prophetie*, BWANT 104, 1975, largely limits himself to I Cor. 12–14; D. A. Aune, *Prophecy in Early Christianity*, Grand Rapids 1983, there 263–6 on Acts 11.28; 21.11 and 13.2, gives a voluminous description from predominantly formal perspectives; Sandnes, 'Paul' (n.492), limits himself to prophetic motives in the letters of Paul. M. Frenschkowski, *Offenbarung und Epiphanie I. Grundlagen des spätantiken und frühchristlichen Offenbarungsglaubens*, WUNT II/79, 1995, 166–76, goes only marginally into early Christian prophecy; Forbes, *Prophecy* (n.1043), mainly investigates Acts and I Cor. 12–14. For the period before Constantine in Egypt cf. D. Frankfurter, *Elijah in Upper Egypt. The Apocalypse of Elijah and Early Egyptian Christianity ...*, Minneapolis 1993; id., 'The Cult of Martyrs in Egypt before Constantine: The Evidence of the Coptic Apocalypse of Elijah', *VigChr* 48, 1994, 25–45; also C. M. Robeck Jr, *Prophecy in Carthage, Perpetua, Tertullian, and Cyprian*, Cleveland 1992.

1212. Acts 4.8ff; 5.1–11; 10.9ff.

1213. Acts 6.8; 7.55f.

1214. Acts 8.26, 39, cf. Ezek. 11.24 and I Cor. 18.12; also his four prophetic daughters in Acts 21.9 and Papias and Polycrates of Ephesus, Eusebius, *HE* 3, 39, 9; 3, 31, 3 and 5, 24, 2.

1215. διδάσκαλος appears here only in Acts.

1216. 13.2, 3; cf. also 14.23; I Cor. 7.1f. Moreover fasting before receiving revelation is very frequent in the early Jewish apocalypses, cf. Dan. 9.3; 10.2ff.; IV Ezra 5.13, 20; 6.31, 35; 9.23; 12.51; SyrBar 9.2; 12.5; 21.1; also before healings, see the old v.l. Mark 9.29 with the addition μετὰ νηστείας and Matt. 17.21; cf. *VP* 4.2f. (Life of Daniel).

1217. See above, n.1104.

1218. The combination of 'prophet and teacher' is a Jewish legacy. According to the Life of Nathan in the *VP*, in a typical anachronism Nathan is 'David's teacher in the law'; see Schwemer, *Vitae Prophetarum II* (n.134), 196ff.

1219. It remains unclear how much he has to do with Joseph named Barsabbas with the surname Justus, who is mentioned in 1.23 as a candidate for election to the twelve. This Joseph is mentioned by Papias according to Philip of Side, see frag. 11 Funk-Bihlmeyer = frag. 11 Kürzinger. Presumably Papias knew Acts.

1220. Καὶ αὐτοὶ προφῆται ὄντες. In I Thess. 1.1 and II Cor. 1.19 Silas/ Silvanus (the best parallel to his Aramaic and Latin name is Ša'ūl/Paul) appears alongside Paul as a partner with equal status. Timothy, like John Mark a missionary assistant to Paul and Barnabas (13.5; 16.3; 17.14; 18.5), appears in third place.

1221. I Cor. 14.1, 6, 26ff.; cf. 11.4f.

1222. G. Theissen, *Studien zur Soziologie des Urchristentums*, WUNT 19, Tübingen ²1983, 79–141 (on the Gospels); 201–30 (on Paul); Feldt- keller, *Identitätssuche* (n.88), 261, index s.v. 'Wanderradikale', 'Wander- radikalismus'.

1223. In Acts 11.29 they appear first alone, in 15.2, 4, 6, 22f.; 16.4 together with the apostles; in 21.18 as a group around the monarchical James 'the brother of the Lord'. According to 14.23; cf. 20.17 Barnabas and Paul appointed 'elders' in the communities of Lycaonia. That corre- sponds to I Clem. 44, 47, 57, but has no support in the letters of Paul.

1224. Gal. 3.4; 4.5f.; Rom. 8.9ff., 14ff.; I Cor. 2.12f.; 3.16; 6.11; 12.7ff. etc.

1225. I Cor. 14.25, quotation from Isa. 45.14.

1226. Cf. Hengel, 'Schriftauslegung' (n.427), 20–8.

1227. II Cor. 4.13; cf. Gal. 5.3; I Cor. 2.4; 12.3 etc.

1228. II Cor. 2.6–16 and above all v.10: ἡμῖν δὲ ἀπεκάλυψεν ὁ θεὸς διὰ τοῦ πνεύματος. Paul's remarks here have nothing to do with a 'gnosis in Corinth'; they are to be understood against the background of Pauline christology (Gal. 1.12) and its apocalyptic presuppositions. See also II Cor. 3.12–19. See already Jesus himself in Luke 10.23 = Matt. 13.16f.; Luke 16.16 Q; cf. John 8.56; 11.13; I Peter 1.10.

1229. I Thess. 1.3; 5.8; I Cor. 13.13.

1230. See the thorough investigation by Sandnes, *Paul* (n.492), and the positive review of this book by Hans Hübner, *ThLZ* 118, 1993, 745–7.

1231. Gal. 1.10f., 16; Rom. 11.13 cf. 1.1–3.

1232. Eph. 2.20 cf. 3.5 and at the climax of a series 4.11.

1233. Cf. already Wenamun's account of his journey to Byblos *c.*1100 BCE, see J. B. Pritchard, *ANET* ²1955, p. 26: the young man with the ruler of Byblos seized by the prophetic spirit. See further H. Gese, M. Höfner and K. Rudolph, *Die Religionen Altsyriens, Altarabiens und der Mandäer*, RM

10, 2, 1970, 178f. on the cultic prophets and oracle priests at the Syrian and Phoenician sanctuaries: 'The activity of every sanctuary included a certain degree of manticism.' For the two Syrian seers Leios and Debborios in Antioch see below. For the Dea Syria cf. also Lucian, *De Dea Syria* 36; Feldtkeller, *Reich* (n.88), 150f.; cf. the Latin-Greek sarcophagus inscription of a prophetess from Niha, *IGLS* VI, no. 2929: *virgini vati Deae Syr(iae) Nihat(enae);* in no. 2928 it is said that the she ate no bread for twenty years. See also fig.164 in D. Krencker and W. Zschietzschmann, *Römische Tempel in Syrien*, Denkmäler antiker Architektur 5, Berlin and Leipzig 1938, 120. Also e.g the epitaph from Kanatha reported by J.-P. Rey-Coquais, 'Syrie Romaine', *JRS* 68, 1978, 49 n.59: τιβ(έριον) Κλ(αύδιον) Βαλσαμιον εὐσεβῆ προφήτην καὶ Ἀγριπεῖαν σύνβιον Βαλσσαμιος υἱὸς μετὰ ἀδελφῶν. Finally Lucian, *Dea Syria* 28f., reports that twice a year a priest spent a whole week without sleep on one of the two high pillars before the temple of the goddess in Hierapolis; the simple people believed that there he was closer to the gods with his prayers and prayed for the good of all Syria. The later Christian ascetics and pillar saints in Syria with their ostentatious and rigorous piety took over this heritage. We also find a similar interest in oracles and cultic prophets in Asia Minor. No wonder that alongside Syria this was the place where Christianity expanded most strongly in the first and second centuries. See R. L. Fox, *The Unauthorized Version*, Harmondsworth 1992, 168–264: 'The Language of the Gods'. In particular he goes into the oracles of Oinoanda, Klaros, Didyma and the cult of the snake and oracle god Glykon founded by Alexander of Abounoteuchos. Oracles blossomed again in Asia Minor in particular in the second century.

1234. Cf. Rev. 4.1; Mark 1.10f. and the 'door' in AscIsa 6.6, 9, see above, 233.

1235. I Cor. 12.3; 16.21, cf. Rev. 22.30; Rom. 8.15; Gal. 4.5. Cf. also the ὑπερεντυγχάνειν στεναγμοῖς ἀλαλήτοις in Rom. 8.26, which represents the earthly pendant of the Spirit to the priestly ἐντυγχάνειν of the Christ exalted to the right hand of God in Rom. 8.34.

1236. Against Bousset, *Kyrios Christos* (n.150), 84, cf. 90, 99–104, etc.

1237. Acts 2.46, see 462 n.1240 below.

1238. Acts 2.1–13. The mockery in 2.13 is probably directed against opponents in Luke's time. Cf. Barrett, *Acts I* (n.77), 125; O. Betz, 'Zungenrede und süßer Wein', in id., *Jesus. Der Herr der Kirche, Aufsätze zur biblischen Theologie* II, WUNT 52, Tübingen 1990, 49–65; cf. now Forbes, *Prophecy* (n.1043), who minimizes the enthusiastic phenomena.

1239. Acts 5.1–11; cf. I Cor. 5.4f.

1240. d: *erat autem magna exultatio* cf. the Old Latin p and w and the

Middle Egyptian Coptic tradition. Ἀγαλλίασις appears 18 times in the LXX Psalter for the praise brought about by the Spirit, but apart from 2.46 does not appear again in Acts, though it does in the Lukan infancy narrative Luke 1.14 and above all in 1.44. The verb ἀγαλλιᾶσθαι, which appears about 42 times in the Psalms, occurs twice in the Gospel (1.47; 10.21), of Jesus himself, ἠγαλλιάσατο τῷ πνεύματι τῷ ἁγίῳ, Acts 2.26 = Ps. 16.9; 16.34.

1241. Schille, *Apostelgeschichte* (n.797), 266.

1242. Haenchen, *Acts* (n.5), 376, cf. already Loisy, *Actes* (n.699), 472.

1243. Revelation offers a good example, cf. 22.6, 9, 18. The prophecy of the destruction of Jerusalem embraces a further complex, see Hengel, 'Gospel of Mark' (n.48). The prophecy about the flight to Pella and the primitive Christian 'miracle' as the working of the Spirit is also to be understood in this framework.

1244. For Paul, too, this is a part of his apostolate which he takes for granted: Rom. 15.19; II Cor. 12.12, cf. Gal. 3.5; I Cor. 2.4. Cf. J. Jervell, 'The Signs of an Apostle: Paul's Miracles', in id., *The Unknown Paul* (n.1191), 77–95.

1245. Lev. 11.22; Num. 13.33; Isa. 40.22; II Chron. 7.13; mShab 9.7; tShab 12 (13).5 etc.

.1246. TgO on Lev. 11.22: *ḥāgābā*; LXX Αγαβα and Αγαβ; Peshitta *ḥāgāb*. There are other explanations in Bauer and Aland, *Lexicon*, 4, the woman's name *agabā* from Palmyra = *RES* 2, 1914, no. 1086, perhaps derived from the Syriac *'gb*, 'lame'. Biblical Hebrew knows the verb *'āgāb*, 'sensual longing' and corresponds to the noun *'agābā*; the later Talmudic literature has *'agabāh* = rump, behind. Or could this be the Greek women's name Ἀγαύε in Semitic form? E. Bammel, *BHHW* 1, 30, conjectures for Ἀγαβος a derivation from the male form Ἀγαύος, 'the famous', following A. Klostermann, *Probleme*, 1883, 10. But this form of the name is very rare, nor does it fit the milieu. H. Wuthnow, *Die semitischen Menschennamen in griechischen Inschriften und Papyri des vorderen Orients*, Studien zur Epigraphik und Papyruskunde I, 4, Leipzig 1930, lists nothing comparable.

1247. Cf. above nn.1106 and 1112.

1248. Acts 21.10–14. For the significance of the prophetic symbolic action see H. Patsch, 'Die Prophetie des Agabus', *ThZ* 28, 1972, 228–32. According to Rom. 15.31 but also Acts 20.13, cf. 21.4, Paul already knew that his life was in danger in Jerusalem even before the beginning of his journey there. In both passages in Acts this foreknowledge rests on a communication 'of the Spirit'. The anonymity of the prophecy, which is demonstrated with Paul's girdle, is interesting, as is the fact that the prophecy and the narrative of Paul's arrest in Paul 21.27–36 do not correspond completely. Paul is not 'handed over' to the Romans but rescued, arrested and fettered by them (21.33).

1249. Riesner, *Frühzeit* (n.49), 111–21; see now also H. P. Kohns, 'Hungersnot', *RAC* 16, 1994, 828–93: 861–71 and H. Braunert, *Die Binnenwanderung*, Bonner hist. Forschungen 26, Bonn 1964, 201–3.

1250. Riesner, *Frühzeit* (n.49), 112. Cf. Rev. 6.6.

1251. Cf. Tacitus, *Ann.* 12, 43, 1. Something similar already happened under Tiberius.

1252. *Antt.* 20, 101, 51–53; Eusebius according to *Chronicle of Jerome*, ed. Helm, GCS 24, 181.

1253. *Antt.* 3, 20, the famine under Claudius; see Schwartz, *Studies* (n.344), 237ff.

1254. B. Z. Wacholder, 'The Calendar of Sabbatical Cycles ...' , *HUCA* 44, 1973, 153–96: 191, see Riesner, *Frühzeit* (n.49), 119.

1255. *Antt.* 18, 272, 274, 284. According to Philo, *Legatio* 249, Petronius was afraid that the Jews would destroy the ripe harvest. See the commentary by Smallwood, *Legatio* (n.947), 281f.; for the dating see Schürer I, 397.

1256. Acts 6.1ff. already indicates difficulties. As Acts 4 and 5 show, this 'sharing of goods' was only a voluntary one, with an eschatological motivation, though bound up with a certain pressure of expectation; it was not a legally fixed compulsory sharing as with the Essenes, and presumably it also soon came to grief. Acts 12.12ff. and 21.16 again presuppose prosperous members of the community who put their houses at its disposal and practised hospitality. See Hengel, *Property and Riches* (n.25), 179–82.

1257. Gal. 2.10; cf. I Cor. 16.1; II Cor. 8.3–6; Rom. 15.25–28, 31 and also Acts 24.17. It seems to me probable that the later Jewish Christians retained the designation *'ebyōnīm*/'Εβιωναῖοι (Irenaeus, *Haer.* 1, 26, 1f.; Origen, *Princ.* 4, 3, 8; *c. Celsum* 1; Eusebius, *HE* 3, 27, 1, 6) because of this economic decline of the community and then transformed it into an honorific title under James. See Hengel, *Earliest Christianity* (n.25), 179–82 against Strecker, *TRE* 17, 1988, 312, who completely misunderstands the historical context. With this designation the Jerusalem community then gave a theologically positive interpretation of the social reality which oppressed it.

1258. Cf. Mark 13.8: ἔσονται σεισμοὶ κατὰ τόπους, ἔσονται λιμοί· ἀρχὴ ὠδίνων ταῦτα = Matt. 24.7 = Luke 21.11; Jer. 15.2 cf. Rev. 6.8; 18.6; Eth.Enoch 80.2ff.; Sib. 2.6–27, 153ff.; IV Ezra 6.22; SyrBar 27.6; Hekhalot Rabbati §122; Sifre Num on 15.41b; §115 on Ezek. 20.32f.: the three plagues of pestilence, sword and hunger before the dawn of the kingdom of God; rabbinic instances in Bill. 4, 981ff.: e.g. bSanh 97a Bar on Amos 4.7: drought in the first year, pangs of hunger in the second and famine with mass death in the third.

1259. See Riesner, *Frühzeit* (n.49), 333.

1260. He does not say in so many words that he was not in Jerusalem during the fourteen years, but the trend of the argument makes this very probable. Nevertheless it would remain possible that he passes over this visit – unimportant in retrospect – because he had nothing to do with Peter and other authorities on it, as they had left Jerusalem because of the persecution by Agrippa, so that only the 'elders' received the gift from Antioch and the messengers had to leave the city again quickly because of the danger.

1261. Cf. Rom. 15.31 cf. Acts 20.23; 21.4, 11; see also 20.3, 19 and above nn.472, 680; see II Cor. 11.24. Paul will have suffered this fivefold synagogue punishment above all in his early time in Syria and Cilicia, that period about which Luke is silent. This is all too easily overlooked in accounts of Paul.

1262. Its date is uncertain. Schwartz, *Agrippa* I. (n.302), 107–11, 203–7, puts it early (late autumn 43, at the latest January/February 44), but see Schürer I, 452 n.43 on the basis of Josephus, *Antt.* 19, 343 and Acts 12.3–5 in early summer 44. Presumably he hardly died later than the beginning of 44, as Josephus gives him only three years as ruler over all Judaea.

1263. Loisy, *Actes* (n.699), 475, cf. Schille, *Apostelgeschichte* (n.797), 267f.

1264. Barrett, *Acts* I (n.77), 566, remarks that they are 'apparently ... the officials who deal with financial (and doubtless also other) matters'. However, Luke does not limit the term πρεσβύτεροι to a specific function. Here for the first time he indicates a major change.

1265. Acts 4.5, 8, 23: οἱ ἀρχιερεῖς καὶ οἱ πρεσβύτεροι; 6.12. The Joel quotation in 2.17 mentions the 'elders' in antithetical parallelism to the 'youths' and needs no explanation.

1266. 14.23 (Pisidian Antioch); 15.2, 4, 6, 22f.; 16.4 (the apostles and elders in Jerusalem); 20.17 (the elders in Ephesus); 21.18 (James and the elders); 23.14 (high priests and – Jewish – elders in Jerusalem); 24.1 (the high priest Ananias and his elders); 25.15 (the high priests and 'elders of the Jews').

1267. Gal. 1.17, cf. 19.

1268. Cf. already Gal. 2.4 and Acts 15.1, 3: the party in favour of strict observance of the law must have had growing influence in Jerusalem. It was certainly represented in the group of elders, but did not yet have a majority.

1269. See above, 244f.

1270. For the literary stylistic form of 'catching up with' in the Old Testament narrative works, especially the book of Jonah, cf. H. Gese, 'Jona ben Amittai und das Jonabuch', in id., *Alttestamentliche Studien*, 128, 131.

1271. Thus Haenchen, *Acts* (n.5), 378f.; G. Strecker, 'Die sogenannte zweite Jerusalemreise des Paulus', *ZNW* 53, 1962, 76f.; Schmithals, *Apostelgeschichte* (n.1051), 119; Schille, *Apostelgeschichte* (n.797), 268.

1272. Acts 9.26–30.

1273. Against Hemer, *Acts* (n.37), 183, 266f., who again identifies this visit to Jerusalem with the 'Apostolic Council', see Riesner, *Frühzeit* (n.49), 284f.: an 'evidently minority view put forward since Calvin' (with bibliography). If this journey is identified with the Apostolic Council, then the contradiction between Acts and Gal. 2 becomes insuperable. Cf. Hengel, *Earliest Christianity* (n.25), 94. But it is not improbable that Paul was occupied with the preparation of this collection in Antioch, on the basis of a feeling that the kind of support offered in previous years could also be useful in the future. Cf. U. Borse, *Der Standort des Galaterbriefs*, BBB 41, Cologne 1972, 36 n.169.

1274. Schneider, *Apostelgeschichte* 2 (n.77), 102, says only that Luke 'does not explicitly claim that the collection in Antioch ... and the persecution ... were contemporaneous'. The assumption that in 12.1–24 Luke is reporting events which must have taken place before Paul and Barnabas's stay in the city is much older. Overbeck, *Apostelgeschichte* (n.698), 181, rejects it as 'quite arbitrary'; cf. 188: 'it is unclear when and in what circumstances, whether during the persecution of the Christians or after they arrived in Jerusalem.'

1275. Of course that does not exclude the possibility that Luke has used several 'sources' here. For the problem of sources in Acts see above, 18–21. Haenchen in particular has referred – in an exaggerated way – to the language which diverges from Luke's normal style. J. Dupont, *Études sur les Actes des Apotres*, LectDiv 45, Paris 1967, 224: the narrrative style recalls Mark; it is not Luke's style. Cf. Barrett, *Acts* 1 (n.77), 568, who qualifies this judgment somewhat. Indications of dependence on a source would be e.g. that Agrippa I is called 'King Herod' or that though the death of James the brother of John was reported right at the beginning, immediately afterwards in v.17 there is mention of 'James and the brethren', where we would have expected 'James, the brother of the Lord, and the elders' in Luke. This 'source' could, for example be an oral narrative noted down by Luke.

1276. For example the delay between 8.2, 4 and 11.29 is striking. This does not mean that everything reported in the meantime in 8.5–11.18 also took place in the interim period, so that Paul arrived in Tarsus essentially earlier than the Hellenists who had been driven out to Phoenicia, Cyprus and Antioch. The activity of Philip from Samaria through Ashdod to Caesarea (8.4–40) also need not have taken place before the conversion of Paul (ch. 9). It interrupts the sequence between 8.3 and 9.1.

1277. Overbeck (n.698), ad loc.; Schneider, *Apostelgeschichte* 2 (n.77), 102; Barrett, *Acts* 1 (n.77), 575 rightly points out that the indication of time, κατ᾽ ἐκεῖνον τὸν καιρόν is quite indefinite (cf. Acts 19.23), like the preceding ἐκείναις ταῖς ἡμέραις, 11.27.

1278. Schille, *Apostelgeschichte* (n.797), 269, anachronistically feels the lack of a 'martyrology' for James son of Zebedee. Luke would have had such a document for Stephen. He can leave this out because he was interested only in Peter.

1279. Only Barrett, *Acts* (n.77), 577, rightly observes that ἀνάγεσθαι is a technical term for 'leading out' to execution and that this is not 'leading out' to legal proceedings. Cf. II Macc. 6.10.

1280. Even in Clement of Alexandria he is particularly emphasized after Peter, John and Paul as the recipient of 'Gnosis' from Jesus, see the index to *Clem. Alex.* IV, 1, p.119. According to *Hypotyposes* B. VII = Eusebius, *HE* 2.9.2f. James converts the person who denounces him and is beheaded with him. The scanty report of Acts was 'enriched' with such legends in the second century.

1281. When Luke mentions Peter, James and John as a group of three in the Gospel, he puts John in front of James. That is sometimes corrected at a very early stage in the manuscript tradition.

1282. Cf. Hengel, *Earliest Christianity* (n.25), 112: 'a sign that John continued his activity and was not killed along with his brother'. See also Gal. 2.9 and Hengel, *Johanneische Frage* (n.33), 91, 317f. [22, 129]. Here Luke is writing from the perspective of a later time.

1283. 'Lay hands upon' and 'mistreat' are rather different from an execution. Cf. the case of the prophet Ananias in Josephus, *BJ* 6, 302–5. But it is also wrong to suppress the τίνες and to claim that Luke knew of only two arrests; against Schille, *Apostelgeschichte* (n.797), 268. Cf. also Acts 15.2 on the delegation to Jerusalem and Josephus, *Antt.* 20, 200.

1284. E. Schwartz, *AGWG.PH* VII/5, 1904, 63–284; id., *ZNW* 11, 1912, 89–104; F. Hahn, *Mission in the New Testament*, SBT I 47, 1965, 88ff.; by contrast Riesner, *Frühzeit* (n.49), 108; Barrett, *Acts* (n.77), 575. For the death of John the son of Zebedee see Hengel, *Johanneische Frage* (n.33), 88–92 [21–3]. R. Eisler, *The Enigma of the Fourth Gospel*, London 1939, 69–77, refers to a late version of the *Toledot Jeshu* according to which Johanan was killed, but here there is a confusion with John the Baptist. By contrast Eisler conjectures that the reference to John was eliminated in the original text. That remains sheer speculation.

1285. Deut. 13.13–16; Temple Scroll lv 3–8; cf. mSan 9, 1 applies to a whole city and originally referred to destruction in war. Individual persons are to be stoned in accordance with the law, cf. Deut. 13.11; Temple Scroll lv 15–21. Thus Stephen (Acts 7.58) and James the brother of the Lord (Jos., *Antt.* 20, 200; Eusebius, *HE* 2, 23, 16) are dealt with according to the law. Against Haenchen, *Acts* (n.5), 382; Schille, *Apostelgeschichte* (n.797), 268 and with Riesner, *Frühzeit* (n.49), 105 cf. n.75.

1286. Schwartz, *Agrippa I.* (n.302), 123: 'Such an assumption ... would explain, moreover, Luke's silence about the reason for the persecution.'

1287. Cf. Hengel, *Zealots* (n.122), 55f., 69f., 338.

1288. See the description of the great-nephew of Jesus brought before Domitian according to Hegesippus in Eusebius, *HE* 18, 20, 4; cf. M. Hengel, 'Reich Christi, Reich Gottes und Weltreich im Johannes- evangelium', in M. Hengel and A. M. Schwemer (eds.), *Gottes Königsherr- schaft und himmlischer Kult*, WUNT 55, 1991, 163f.

1289. Paul, too, is first of all attacked by Jews in the temple precincts. The Roman soldiers intervene only to prevent a riot. The Jewish authori- ties are extremely concerned to do away with Paul as quickly as possible or have him executed by the Romans, while the Roman prefects seek to distinguish between unpolitical-religious disputes within Judaism and political-religious actions against Rome. That changed later. Whereas Domitian let the kinsman of the Lord summoned before his judgment seat go as a harmless 'peasant' (Hegesippus in Eusebius, *HE* 3, 19–20, 6), later Simeon, son of Cleopas, a nephew of Jesus, was crucified by Titus Claudius Atticus, who was governor of Judaea from 99/100 to 102/103 (also handed down as a quotation from Hegesippus in Eusebius, *HE* 3, 32, 6).

1290. Riesner, *Frühzeit* (n.49), 104–10; 110 n.96 against Schwartz.

1291. Riesner, *Frühzeit* (n.49), 109 with reference to Horbury; cf. above n.1184.

1292. Josephus, *Vita* 12f. Cf. Hengel, 'Jakobus' (n.705), 73ff.

1293. Cf. Schwartz, *Agrippa I* (n.302), 8–37 etc.

1294. Josephus, *Antt.* 19, 328–331: Agrippa I is εὐεργετικός, πραΰς etc.

1295. Josephus, *Antt.* 19, 331. It has also been inferred from this passage that the king was loyal to the Torah and that his sympathy was with the Pharisees, and this view runs through the commentaries. Agrippa certainly had no interest at all in the Pharisaic regulations about purity, but he fulfilled his duties towards the temple in Jerusalem and intervened against its profanation and that of the synagogue of Dora by a picture of the emperor. He knew that here the limits of the tolerance of the Jewish people were easily passed. He personally liked to live it up in every respect; he loved great banquets, luxury and splendour. He eventually died after a truly ostentatious appearance, which does not exactly indicate strict orthodoxy. His sisters also combined ostentatious forms of piety with a loose way of life. Whereas his Jewish subjects thanked him for his reign with the rumour that he had had himself worshipped as God and had died as an enemy of God, his pagan subjects rewarded his 'beneficence' after his death by erecting statues of his daughters in brothels. He was truly not filled with Pharisaic piety, but in accordance with the political and religious circumstances was a patron of the aristocratic party of the Sadducees. These were regarded as being particularly strict in their legal judgments. By contrast, rabbinic tradition transformed his portrait, cf. mSot 7, 8: Agrippa I reading the Torah in the temple and his weeping at the reading aloud of Deut. 17.15 along with the acclamation of the people; in mBikk 3, 4 he carries the basket with the firstfruits into the temple. Perhaps we can see here the picture of Agrippa painted by the 'patriarch' Jehuda han-Nasi, who was the redactor of the Mishnah and was well disposed towards the Romans. All this can also be applied to Agrippa II.

1296. Cf. Josephus, *Antt.* 20, 200: the accusation against James the brother of the Lord, see below, n.1310.

1297. Cf. Schwartz, *Agrippa* I (n.302), 124–30 (bibliography).Thus he was a ruler who cunningly sat between two stools. One could see it as a sign of his 'diplomatic gentleness' that he wanted to execute only one of the two leaders of the group of disciples and not a larger number of Jewish Christians, see above n.1294.

1298. Probably 38 rather than 41; in that case Simon Kantheras is identical with the 'Simon the Just' who is mentioned in tSot 13, 6; jSot 9, 14 24b etc. as the high priest who heard from the Holy of Holies a Bat Qol announcing to him the death of Caligula. Cf. Schwartz, *Agrippa* I. (n.302), 12 (bibliography).

1299. Johanan, the son of Theophilus, appears on an ossuary inscription from Jerusalem, see Rahmani (n.638), 259 no. 871; cf. below, n.1307.

1300. See Schwartz, *Agrippa I.* (n.302), 69f.

1301. Cf. Hengel and Deines, review of Sanders (n.62), 60, 63.

1302. See Riesner, *Frühzeit* (n.49), 105.

1303. Josephus, *Antt.* 20, 198; Jonathan held office from 36 to 37. He was appointed by Vitellius, see Schürer II, 230.

1304. Josephus, *Antt.* 19, 312–16 and on it Schwartz, *Agrippa I.* (n.302), 71, 115.

1305. Against Schwartz, *Agrippa I.* (n.302), 71ff, who conjectures – taking up in our view what is the completely unfounded thesis of Dockx – that Simon Kantheras had had to go because he had had Stephen stoned in Agrippa's absence in 40. Schwartz also depicts the good relations between Jonathan and Rome. The later murder of Jonathan, brought about by Felix, is another matter. See Dockx, 'Date de la mort d'Étienne le Protomartyr', *Bib* 55, 1974, 65–75; for critical comments see Hengel, 'Between Jesus and Paul' (n.50), 150 n.131.

1306. Thus R. Brody in an appendix to Schwartz, *Agrippa I.* (n.302), 190–5 (this is based on the assumption that Kantheras is the more strongly Graecized form of the name Caiaphas). Cf. also the dream wedding of Martha, daughter of Boethus, with the high priest Jesus son of Gamala, the leading Sadducee alongside Annas II, who was in office from 63 to 64. See Hengel, *Zealots* (n.122), 370 n.281.

1307. Josephus, *Antt.* 19.342; for the complicated family relationships see Schwartz, *Agrippa I.* (n.302), 185–9 and the appendix by R. Brody, ibid., 190–5.

1308. Cf. the list of high priests in Schürer II, 229–332, 332–6.

1309. The high priest John mentioned in Acts 4.6 probably appears on an ossuary inscription as John son of the high priest Theophilus (after 37) and thus as grandson of Annas and nephew of Caiaphas. See D. Flusser, *IEJ* 36, 1986, 39–44.

1310. Josephus, *Antt.* 20, 200ff.; Annas II therefore lost his office after only three months. Pharisees had complained about his unjust conduct to Agrippa II and to the procurator Albinus. Agrippa II deposed Annas.

1311. The reasons given by Riesner, *Frühzeit* (n.49), 105, for dating it to the year 41 or 42 are insufficient. We may assume that the description of Agrippa's return in Josephus, *Antt.* 19, 292–9 does not depict events in 41, but those of the year 38. After Caligula's attempt to erect his statue in the temple, Agrippa could hardly have hung up this chain given 'on the occasion of his release' from prison in 38 as a dedicatory gift in the temple; it will have been a gift of honour received from Caligula, his former drinking companion before the death of Tiberius. Here Josephus has made a mistake and put a section from his source in the wrong place. See Schwartz, *Agrippa I.* (n.302), 12–14 and passim.

1312. The death of the persecutor could be understood as a direct punishment for his crime even after an interval. Cf. Josephus, *Antt.* 18, 116: the defeat of Herod Antipas was regarded nine years later as divine punishment for his judicial murder of John the Baptist. At the end of Hegesippus' report of the martyrdom of James the brother of the Lord we read 'and immediately Vespasian laid siege to them' (Eusebius, *HE* 2, 23, 18). The church fathers regarded it as settled that the destruction of the temple and of Jerusalem was the just punishment for the crucifixion of Jesus. By contrast, there was less than a year between Agrippa's persecution and his death.

1313. Josephus, *BJ* 2, 219; *Antt.* 19, 343, cf. 351: he reigned four years under Caligula and three over all Judaea under Claudius.

1314. Cf. Schwartz, *Agrippa I.* (n.302), 107–11: 'In summary, it appears that Agrippa died between September/October ... 43 and January/February 44' (111); Riesner, *Frühzeit* (n.49), 104f., argues for the later date.

1315. Could an action by the anti-Herodian and anti-Sadducean opposition, say from Pharisaic circles, underlie this 'liberation' (quite apart from the narrative elaboration)? The 'angel' who freed Peter appears in the narrative as a young man whom Peter did not know and did not introduce himself to him, but disappeared again quickly into the darkness of the night. At that time – and later, at the time of the execution of James – there were evidently Pharisees who were well disposed towards the Christians (cf. Acts 15.5) and who wanted to put an end to this demonstration of power by Agrippa I and the clientele of the high-priestly nobility for religious and political reasons. The whole narrative has very earthly features, like the powerful blow with which Peter is awoken and the precise orders that he has to get ready to travel quickly. In this case all the typological echoes and Old Testament allusions that the commentators introduce lead in the wrong direction. Was this 'liberation' perhaps a successful action on the part of the (Pharisaic?) opponents of the high-priestly and Herodian party, which wanted to prevent a further spectacular 'judicial murder' of a Christian? Later these Pharisaic sympathizers could only protest after the event, as is shown by the accusations after the execution of James the brother of the Lord. Be this as it may, this protest cost the high priest Annas II his office. Cf. Hengel and Deines, review of Sanders (n.62), 8f.

1316. For the motif of the opening of the doors see at length O. Weinreich, *Religionsgeschichtliche Studien*, Darmstadt 1968, 118–298 (for Acts 12.3–19 see 153–8). This is an originally independent narrative within a collection of legends about Peter, which ended with εἰς ἕτερον τόπον. Furthermore it falls outside the framework of the 'liberation miracle'.

1317. C. Grappe, *D'un temple à l'autre. Pierre et l'Eglise primitive de Jérusalem*, EHPhR 71, Paris 1992, 242–51, takes too little note of the historical circumstances. He too sees above all the Passover typology and regards the tradition of the *EpApost* as a Jewish-Christian legend which is independent of Acts. But the author of the *EpApost* knew Acts well. Here we have the typical example of a legendary 'heightening' of the miracle.

1318. I Cor. 9.5 (it is interesting that the Corinthian community knows such details!); for the family, apart from the historical note in Mark 1.29–31 see also the Petrine family legends. Thus in Clement of Alexandria, *Strom.* 3, 52, 5: like Philip, he had children; the martyrdom of his wife, 7, 63, 3 = Eusebius *HE* 3, 30, 2; see also the fragment about his incurably paralysed daughter, presumably from the Acts of Peter, see *NT Apoc* 2 ²1992, 2, 285f.

1319. Cf. R. Pesch, *Die Apostelgeschichte (Apg 1–12)*, EKK V/1, ²1995, 368f. with a wrong dating; C. P. Thiede, 'Petrus', *NBL* 3, 1167, 1169 (bibliography); Botermann, *Judenedikt* (n.5), 76ff., 137–40; Barrett, *Acts* I (n.77), 587, rightly says that there is no indication that he went to Rome. S. Dockx, *Chronologies néotestamentaires et Vie de de l'Eglise primitive*, Leuven 1984, 166f., discusses the problem at length but all too fantastically. He also provides a survey of the sources: Eusebius, according to *Chronicle of Jerome*, GCS 44, ed. R. Helm, 1956, 179: *Petrus Apostolus cum primus Antiochenam ecclesiam fundasset, Romam mittitur, ubi evangelium praedicans XXV annis eiusdem urbis episcopus perseverat* for the year 42; according to Jerome, *Vir.ill.* 1, Peter came to Rome in the second year of Claudius, having previously been active in the provinces of Asia Minor mentioned in I Peter 1.1. According to ch.11 he is said to have disputed with Philo at that time, to have become friends with him, and consequently to have sent Mark to Alexandria. Here the author is elaborating a note in Eusebius, *HE* 2, 16, 17, 1, who regards the Therapeutae in Egypt as Christians. These late learned observations are not sufficient basis for an earlier stay of Peter in Rome. We cannot get beyond interesting conjectures.

1320. Just as his submission in Antioch was meant to further peace. Only Paul was not of this opinion – for the sake of the gospel (Gal. 2.11–21).

1321. The detached attitude of the Synoptic Gospels – based on Petrine tradition – towards the brothers of Jesus (cf. also John 7.2ff.), which mention James only in Mark 6.3 along with the other brothers, suggests such a tension. However, excessive emphasis should not be placed on this. Clement of Alexandria reports how the man who denounced James son of Zebedee became a convert and martyr. See above, n.1279. Cf. Hengel, 'Jakobus' (n.705), 98–102.

1322. Barrett, *Acts* I (n.77), 569 points out that this cannot be a matter of making a distinction between betrayal and death and martyrdom.

1323. Schmithals, *Apostelgeschichte* (n.1051), 118 makes this rebuke: 'Thus historically speaking he (Luke) has kept this circle of the twelve apostles, which is so important to him, unduly intact.' In reality Luke speaks of the twelve specifically only in 6.1; cf also 1.13–26. The number of the apostles is no longer given in 9.27; 11.1 and ch. 15. So it can have been smaller. Moreover it is probable that the majority of the twelve were still alive at the beginning of the 40s, see I Cor. 15.5f.

1324. Gal. 1.19.

1325. Thus Schmithals, *Apostelgeschichte* (n.1051), 118: 'Peter definitively … hands over leadership of the community to him.'

1326. Cf. Acts 21.20. His martyrdom in 62 (cf. above, n.1309) is testimony to this, as are the later hagiographical traditions about this exemplary 'just' man and 'intercessor' for the city which can still be gained from the scattered reports about him. See Hengel, 'Jakobus' (n.705), 75–88.

1327. Acts 15.2, 4, 6, 22f.; 16.4.

1328. Against G. Bornkamm, πρέσβυς, *TDNT* 6, 662–4, who has taken too little notice of the Jewish epigraphic evidence.

1329. *CIJ* II, 1404 ends ἦν ἐθεμελί[ω]σαν οἱ πατέρες [α]ὐτοῦ καὶ οἱ πρεσ[β]ύτεροι καὶ Σιμων[ί]δης. Cf. Hengel, 'Between Jesus and Paul' (n.50), 16, 18f., 150 n.132. See now in detail and convincingly, against Kee, R. Riesner, 'Synagogues in Jerusalem', in *The Book of Acts in its First Century Setting* IV, ed. R. Bauckham, Grand Rapids 1995, 192–200.

1330. Cf. Judith 6.16, 21; 7.23; 10.6; 13.12; II Macc. 1.8 and especially Susanna 5.41 etc. In the Letter of Aristeas the seventy-two 'elders' who translate the Torah into Greek all come from Judaea. This is the only Greek writing from the Diaspora in which the term is used as a designation of office and moreover occurs very frequently (32.3; 39.2; 46.2; 184.7; 275.3; 310.2). Cf. also Schürer II, 202ff., 427–33.

1331. We first have an example from the Diaspora from the synagogue in Syrian Dura Europos (middle of the third century), i.e. geographically close to Palestine; later from the church fathers, see Schürer III, 102. The inscriptions from Egypt do not mention any πρεσβύτερος; among those from Cyrenaica there is one from the year 3/4 CE, see

Horbury and Noy, *Inscriptions* (n.316), 339, cf. 319; this designation of office does not appear in the Jewish inscriptions from Rome, see Noy, *Jewish Inscriptions* II (n.243), 538f.; it emerges only later in the west of the empire: Noy, *Jewish Inscriptions* I (n.325), no. 75 (Hebrew from Venosa, fifth century CE); all the others are Greek: 148; 149 (both from Catania, fourth/fifth century); 157 (Sofiana); 181 (from Spain: presbyters are mentioned alongside the archons); for women nos. 59; 62; 71; 163. Possibly in the West the older and more widespread Christian office of presbyter prompted the Jewish communities to take over this title.

1332. For bodies of seven cf. e.g. Josephus, *BJ* 2, 570f.; *Antt.* 4, 214, 287 after Deut. 16.18; cf. also Billerbeck II, 641; Hengel, 'Between Jesus and Paul' (n.50), 13; for groups of ten see the Dekaprotoi in *Die Inschriften von Klaudion Polis*, Inschriften griechischer Städte aus Kleinasien 31, Bonn 1986, 45; cf. also Schürer II, 180 n.518.

1333. See Schürer II, 431f.

1334. For community discipline cf. Matt. 18.15–18; then especially on the presbyters, I Tim 4.14; 5.22.

1335. Hengel, 'Jakobus' (n.705), 81–5; Pratscher, *Herrenbruder* (n.705), 75f. doubts whether there was a body of presbyters alongside James in the early period.

1336. In Clement of Alexandria, *Strom.* 6, 43, 3, GCS ed. Stählin 2, 453.

1337. Eusebius, *HE* 5, 18, 14, on which see v. Harnack, *Chronologie* I (n.5), 370f., 724.

1338. *Acta Apostolorum Apocrypha*, ed. Lipsius, I, 49; see R. A. Lipsius, *Die apokryphen Apostelgeschichten und Apostellegenden*, I, 1883 (reprinted 1976), 13f.; Riesner, *Frühzeit* (n.49), 106f. For Peter's journey to Rome in the second year of Claudius see above, n.1319. The Pseudo-Clementine *Recognitions* shorten the period to seven years (1, 43, 3 [GCS ed. B. Rehm p. 33]; 9, 29, 1 [p. 312]).

1339. See Harnack, *Chronologie* I (n.5), 243f. with reference to Acts 12.17, cf. 244 n.2: 'It seems questionable to me whether the old tradition which brings Peter to Rome already under Claudius is totally unusable. Of course it can only have been a visit. In my view it is no longer possible to come to a decision on this question'; cf. id., *Mission* (n.800), 1, 49f. n.2; Riesner, *Frühzeit* (n.49), 106f.

1340. See Eusebius according to the *Chronicle of Jerome*, see Lipsius, *Apostelgeschichten* (n.1338), II, 5.9.21.

1341. *Epist.* 102 (*ad Deograt, sex quaestiones contra paganos expositus continens*) §2 (*de tempore christianae religionis*): '*longo post tempore lex Iudaeorum apparuit ac viguit angusta Syriae regione, postea vero prorepsit etiam fines Italos, sed post Caesarem Gaium aut certe ipso imperante'*. See also A. v. Harnack, *Porphyrius 'Gegen die Christen'*, 15 Bücher, APAW.PH, 1916, no. 1, 94f. no. 81.

1342. See v. Harnack, *Porphyrius* (n.1341), 95: 'here (unless something has dropped out ...) Judaism and Christianity are confused. Not the good chronologist Porphyrius but only the excerptor can have been guilty of that. There is also evidence elsewhere that Christian preaching came to Rome under Gaius.' See also T. Zahn, *Der Brief des Paulus an die Römer,* ²1910, 8f. n.16; Riesner, *Frühzeit* (n.49), 152f. Augustine goes into Porphyry several more times in *Ep*.102, see v. Harnack, *Porphyrius*, no. 46 = 102, 30; 79 = 102, 16; 85 = 102, 28; 91 = 102, 22; 92 = 102, 2.

1343. Rom. 1.13: ὅτι πολλάκις προεθέμην ἐλθεῖν πρὸς ὑμᾶς. For the expulsion see in detail and convincingly Riesner, *Frühzeit* (n.49), 139–80. His plans to travel to Rome were probably connected with the so-called second journey in 49/50.

1344. See especially Philo, *Legatio*, 155, 157 and Hengel, 'Vorchristlicher Paulus' (n.51), 203ff. [11f.].

1345. Hengel, 'Between Jesus and Paul' (n.50), 184f. n.121; Riesner, 'Synagogues', in *The Book of Acts*, 4 (n.34), 148. C. Clermont-Ganneau, *Syria* 1, 1920, 196f., refers to Vettienus, a financial agent of Cicero's (*ad AH* 10, 5, 2; 11, 5; 15, 13, 5), whom Cicero treasured, though he occasionally got furious with him, and sees him as a freeman of the Gens Vettia. However, his identification with the Jew Vettenus is speculative. For the name see also H. Gundel, *PW* 8A, 1958, 1841f.

1346. Four inscriptions (D. Noy, *Jewish Inscriptions* II [n.243], nos.2; 33; 578; 579) relate to the synagogue of the 'Hebrews'; they come from catacombs and belong in the third/fourth century CE, but there is nothing against applying them to earlier circumstances.

1347. For the early community in Rome see Lampe, *Die stadtrömischen Christen* (n.1041), but unfortunately he does not go into the Augustine note. For the note in Suetonius see now the thorough treatment by Riesner, *Frühzeit* (n.49), 39–180: by comparison with the numerous and sometimes unspeakable speculations this is a masterpiece of 'historical-critical' work which finally puts this much-disputed text in the overall framework of Claudius's religious policy.

1348. Cf. Lampe, *Die stadtrömischen Christen* (n.1041); P. Stuhlmacher, *Der Brief an die Römer*, NTD 6, 1989, 12f., 218–21.

1349. Cf. the very much later rabbinic legend on the hiddenness of the Messiah (bSan 98a; ShemR 1, 31 etc.): he is remaining hidden among the poor outside the gates of Rome and there is binding his wounds until his accession to rule. See Vermes, *Scripture and Tradition* (n.272), 217.

1350. Botermann, *Judenedikt* (n.5), 76ff., 81f., 137–40, 188 pleads cautiously for an early stay in Rome on the part of Peter, between 41 and 48 CE.

1351. D: ὃς ἦν κατηχημένος ἐν τῇ πατρίδι τὸν λόγον τοῦ κυρίου; similarly gig.

1352. Eusebius, *HE* 2.16; Jerome, *Vir. ill.* 1; the fragment of a letter of Clement of Alexandria published by M. Smith, 'Clement of Alexandria and a Secret Gospel of Mark', is allegedly older, but in my view it is a forgery.

1353. Cf. Matt. 2; mAv 1, 11; cf. Hengel, 'Vorchristlicher Paulus' (n.51), 230f. [32].

1354. Ex. 14.13; Deut. 17.16; 28.68; Jer. 42.7–22.

1355. Heitmüller, 'Problem' (n.421); Bousset, *Kyrios Christos* (n.150), 75–104: 'The primitive Gentile Christian community', thus Bultmann, Conzelmann and also still Becker, *Paulus* (n.61), 107–19.

1356. Cf. II Cor. 11.10 and Bauer and Aland, *Lexicon*, 887 s. v. κλίμα. Probably frontier regions like Nabataean Arabia, the Decapolis, Commagene and southern Cappadocia, Cyprus and Lycaonia can be included in τὰ κλίματα.

1357. Cf. also Rom. 15.26: the collections in Macedonia and Achaea.

1358. There has been much puzzling over this information. For a detailed discussion see A. Suhl, *Paulus und seine Briefe. Ein Beitrag zur paulinischen Chronologie*, StNT 11, Gütersloh 1975, 93–5; Thornton, *Zeuge* (n.7), 251f.

1359. Cf. M. Hengel's preface to T. Zahn, *Der Brief des Paulus an die Galater*, reprint of the third edition, KNT 9, 1922, Wuppertal and Zurich 1990, VI–VII; Hemer, *Acts* [n.37], 277–307; Riesner, *Frühzeit* (n.49), 254–9; Scott, *Paul* (n.320), 181–215; C. Breytenbach, *Paulus und Barnabas in der Provinz Galatien. Studien zu Apostelgeschichte 13f.; 16, 6; 18, 23 und den Addressaten des Galaterbriefes*, AGJU 38, Leiden 1966. The old disputed question should really finally have been settled with these thorough investigations. Gnilka, *Paulus* (n.98), 62, 72ff., completely fails to consider the state of scholarship and the weighty new arguments which tell against the countryside hypothesis; the 'south Galatian theory' (62) plays a role only in the earlier literature.

1360. Lüdemann, *Paul* (n.804), 238; but see Riesner, *Frühzeit* (n.49), 19ff., 239ff.

1361. See e.g. the scissors-and-paste method with which violence is done to Acts 18.1–23, Lüdemann, *Paul* (n.804), 141–94; or also the discussion of the chronological sequence in Gal. 1.10–2.24, pp. 50–64. The author himself does not observe his claim to arrive at a chronological framework solely on the basis of the letters of Paul. I can only regard his attempt at criticism of Luke as a failure all down the line and add that deep insights into other disputed areas of earliest Christian history are hardly to be expected from an author who deals so violently with clear statements in the sources.

1362. Pliny the Younger, *Ep.* 10, 96, 9f.; Tacitus, *Ann.*15, 44, 4 = Livy 39, 13, 14.

1363. Mark 6.7–12; Matt. 10.5–42; Luke 9 and 10; Did.11–13 (11.3ff.).

1364. *Mission* (n.800) 2, 672–6 [II, 376f.].

1365. Philad. 10, 2.

1366. Rom. 2.2; 9.1.

1367. Hengel, *Johanneische Frage* (n.33}, 70, 129, 159 n.25.

1368. Eusebius, *HE* 6, 12, 2ff.

1369. Mission (n.800), 2, 673 [II, 377]; on Cilicia see 730f. [II, 359f.].

1370. Rom. 1.1; I Cor. 1.1.

1371. Cf. Gal. 2.1; Acts 16.6–10; 19.21; 20.23; 22.18ff.

1372. Gal. 2.5: ἵνα ἡ ἀλήθεια τοῦ εὐαγγελίου (cf. 2.14) διαμείνῃ πρὸς ὑμᾶς: the ὑμᾶς is addressed directly to the South Galatian communities which had been founded at that very time, but also applies to the whole of the apostle's Syrian mission field.

1373. For the journey to Spain see Rom. 15.24; I Clem. 5.7; Can. Mur. 2.35–37; *Actus Vercellenses* 1 (Lipsius, *Acta Apostolorum apocrypha* I, 45); cf. H. Lietzmann, *Petrus und Paulus in Rom,* ²1927, 242–5. Whether Paul was freed after a two-year imprisonment in Rome (*c.*60–62), travelled on to Spain and was then killed in the Neronian persecution of 64 can be answered only with a *non liquet.*

1374. See now Scott, *Paul* (n.320), 185–215.

1375. Cf. above, n.1039f. There is no absolute figure for the total population of Antioch in antiquity. The fluctuating figures make it comparable with Seleucia on the Tigris and Alexandria. Josephus gives the city the predicate μεγάλη. Presumably the number of inhabitants of greater Antioch with its suburbs first numbered around 300,000 towards the end of the first century CE. The figures in F. W. Norris, 'Antiochien', *TRE* I, 99, and Riesner, *Frühzeit* (n.49), 98, are too high. In the first half of the first century CE Antioch was not as densely built with *insulae,* apartment blocks, as it was later. We owe this reference to Prof. F. Kolb.

1376. A good half of the population was not Christian before the time of Chrysostom, cf. *Johannes Chrysostomus. Acht Reden gegen die Juden,* with an introduction and commentary by R. Brändle, translated by V. Jeher-Bucher, Bibliothek der griechischen Literatur 41, Stuttgart 1995, 51: at that time there were 15% Jews and 40% Christians in Antioch. See

Harnack, *Mission* (n.800), 669.

1377. Isaac of Antioch, *Carm.* 15 (1, 294, ed. Bickell) in the middle of the fifth century; cf. Harnack, *Mission* (n.800), 670.

1378. Cf. e.g. Cicero, *Arch.* 4: 'a once heavily populated and prosperous city, which as the centre of a high intellectual culture attracted many educated men.' He exaggerates in favour of his client. The city did not attract great intellectuals. The Seleucids were not able to make their capital a cultural centre, as the Ptolemies did. However, it did have a library (a private foundation), though this was destroyed when the city was burned down in 23/24 CE. Cicero rightly emphasizes that the city was *once* more strongly populated and prosperous. It suffered severely during the downfall of the Seleucid empire. Tigranes I of Armenia (95–55) ruled Syria I in the period from 89–63 BCE and depopulated the city, cf. below, n.1394. Cicero's speech comes from the year 62 BCE (see M. Fuhrmann, *Marcus Tullius Cicero. Sämtliche Reden* V, Zurich and Munich 1978, 61), before the city took on new significance as a result of Roman promotion of it and the expansion of the city after Caesar.

1379. Strabo 16, 2, 4: Antioch consists of four districts; two were founded by Seleucus I Nicator, the third by Seleucus II Kallinikos, and the fourth by Antiochus IV; cf. Norris, 'Antioch' (n.949), 2327. For the foundation of the tetrapolis of Seleucia Pieria, Antioch, Apamea and Laodicea by Seleucus Nicator see Strabo, 16, 2, 4.

1380. Excavation reports: *Antioch on-the-Orontes* (5 vols), ed. G. Elderkin, J. Lassus, R. Stillwell, F. and D. Waagé, Princeton 1934–1972; cf. J. Lassus, 'La ville d'Antioch à l'époque romaine d'après l'archéologie', *ANRW* II, 8, 1977, 54–102; for the mosaics see D. Levi, *Antioch Mosaic Pavements*, Princeton 1947; S. Campell, *The Mosaics of Antioch*, Subsidia Mediaevalia 15, Luiseville 1988.

1381. For the few pieces of evidence for Syrian religion in the city see above, 273f.

1382. The next earthquake already came under Claudius, but that was not so serious.

1383. Malalas, 242 (PG 97, 372A/B); it must have lain within the Seleucid city, as Caesar had it restored (Malalas 217 [PG 97, 336 C]). Cf. Downey, *Antioch* (n.670), 275. The results of excavation in Antioch are very unsatisfactory; we do not even know where the Pantheon was, whether it was round, or whether as usual it was dedicated to the twelve gods of Olympus and the ruler.

1384. Cf. the divine honours for Demetrius Poliorketes in Athens, who is praised by the hymn performed in 290 BCE: 'We see you here in bodily form, not of wood and not of stone', in contrast to the Olympian gods, who are not concerned about human beings. See now C. Habicht, *'Athen'. Die Geschichte der Stadt in hellenistischer Zeit,* Munich 1995, 99.

1385. For sacrifice to 'Zeus Keraunios' (= Hadad, Baal) and Athene in Antioch see Malalas 212, 2–4 and on it Downey, *Antioch* (n.670), 75. For Seleucia and Mons Casius see Arrian, *Syr.* 58; Strabo, 16, 2, 5; Malalas, 199 (PG 97, 312C); cf. Hadrian's sacrifice, *Hist.Aug., Hadrian* 14, 3. The cult is attested down to the time of Julian the Apostate in 363 CE; cf. H. Niehr, 'Zaphon', *DDD,* 1746–50: 1749. Strabo and *Hist. Aug.* connect the cult on Casius with Antioch. For Antioch itself see Libanius, *Or.* 11, 85f.; Malalas 199–202 (PG 97, 313A–317A). Cf. Y. Hajjar, *Divinités oraculaires* (n.425), 2265.

1386. Malalas 200 (PG 97 213C/D); Libanius, *Or.* 11, 76 ascribes the first temple of Zeus to Alexander the Great himself. Cf. Norris, 'Antioch' (n.949), 2331.

1387. Malalas 204 (PG 97 320A). Cf. a document relating to the nomination of the chief priest by Antiochus III which has been preserved on an inscription, *IGLS* III no. 992.

1388. Strabo 16, 2, 6: ἄσυλον τέμενος.

1389. II Macc. 4.33ff. His memory was probably treasured in the synagogue in Daphne; for his piety see II Macc. 15.12ff.; further Dan. 9.26 and Isa. 53 LXX, see M. Hengel, 'Zur Wirkungsgeschichte von Jes 53 in vorchristlicher Zeit', in Janowski and Stuhlmacher (eds.), *Gottesknecht* (n.509), 49–91. The oracle 'fell silent' only in the middle of the fourth century CE when a martyr shrine was built next to it and the bones of the martyr bishop Babylas were transferred there; cf. Downey, *Antioch* (n.670), 364. Julian the Apostate restored the oracle for a short period and had the martyr removed. But Apollonius of Tyana is said already to have criticized the quality of the oracle, see Philostratus, *Vit. Apoll.*, 1, 16, cf. Norris, 'Antioch' (n.949), 2338f.

1390. Cf. above, n.980. With one exception the mosaics in Antioch all come from the period after 115 CE, i.e. after the great earthquake in which Trajan is said almost to have been killed.

1391. Apollo standing with the cithara and sitting on the omphalos, see A. Forni, *A Catalogue of Greek Coins in the British Museum. The Seleucid Kings of Syria,* Bologna 1963, 114 index s. v. 'Apollo'.

1392. Cf. the (later) lists of priests on the inscriptions from Seleucia Pieria, *IGLS* III, 1184, 1185; on them see Hengel, *Judaism and Hellenism* (n.314), I, 286f.

1393. Norris, 'Antioch' (n.949), 2342f.: 'Few artists had the chance to help to create the character of a city that would become one of the three most important in the Mediterranean basin. Eutyches fashioned a beautiful ... statue of Tyche.' Cf. P. Gardner, *New Chapters in Greek Art*, Oxford 1926, 260–6. The programme of the picture, which emphasizes Silpion so strongly, will perhaps have paid heed to the old Semitic mountain goddess, to whom the legends in Malalas still give the name 'Io'. The 'Tyche' became the model for the Calliope which then stood in the theatre completed by Trajan. The portable shrine with this type of goddess also appears on a coin from the time of Trebonianus Gallus (251–253 CE), see M. J. Price and B. L. Trell, *Coins and their Cities*, London 1971, 34f. (fig. 42). For the personification of Hellenistic cities in the form of Tyche see above, 125.

1394. Cf. Forni, *Catalogue* (n.1391), 45f.; plate XIV: seated Tyche with a cornucopia on the silver drachmae of Demetrius I Soter (162–150 BCE); cf. the Tyche on the coins of Tigranes of Armenia, king of Syria (83–69 BCE), see Downey, *Ancient Antioch* (n.949), figs. 14, 16 cf. 18. Tigranes was lord of the city for a while: he began its decline and transplanted parts of the population into the new imperial capital of Tigranokerta in Armenia which he had founded. By contrast, J. D. Grainger, *Cities of Seleucid Syria*, Oxford 1990, 175f., 188ff., follows the source favourable to Tigranes, the historian Justin, who emphasizes that Tigranes came peacefully at the invitation of the city, which voluntarily put itself under his protection.

1395. Ramsay, *The Cities of St. Paul* (n.814), 138 rightly emphasizes: 'In the growth of an ancient city no religious fact was ever wholly lost. When immigrants or colonists settled there, they brought their own religion with them, but they did not destroy the previously existing religion any more than they exterminated the older population. An amalgamation took place between the religions of the old and the new people.' Only the Jews did not join in this process of assimilation, so that their full civil rights were disputed.

1396. Polybius 30, 25, 13. It would be interesting to know whether and how a symbol of the Jewish God was brought here from Zion. Unfortunately the later description of the two Alexandrian delegations to Trajan, one of Jews and one of 'Greeks', is fragmentary. The 'Greeks' are carrying a statue of Sarapis, but are the Jews carrying their Torah scrolls (*Acta Hermaisci*, POxy 1242, ed. Musurillo, *Acta Alexandrinorum ...*, BSGRT, Leipzig 1961, 32ff.)? For the lack of balance in Antiochus IV's religious policy see Hengel, *Judaism and Hellenism* (n.314), I, 284–7. The best survey of the gods of the Greek pantheon worshipped in Antioch and the gods from the East, the temples and the festivals, and also the superstition, is given by Norris, 'Antioch' (n.949), 2322–79.

1397. *Or.* 11, 115.

1398. Cf. his writing in defence of the temple, *Or.* 30; in *Or.* 11 Libanius speaks on the *beginning* of Olympic contests in the city.

1399. The port of Seleucia Pieria had been in the possession of the Ptolemies between 246 and 219, see Ruge, *PW* 2. R. 2, 1187f. For Antioch, which became more significant as a result of this conquest by Ptolemy III, see Grainger, *Cities* (n.1394), 84, 122–6, 142, 150f.; id. *Hellenistic Phoenicia* (n.278), 123f.

1400. *Or.* 11, 114, 116.

1401. Malalas 318, 16–21: during the building of a basilica and a church under Constantine a bronze statue of the god was found which had been toppled in an earthquake and not re-erected. The governor had the statue melted down and used for a statue of Constantine. Malalas emphasizes that the statue of the Christian emperor was still standing in his day; cf. Norris, 'Antioch' (n.949), 2354.

1402. Cf. Norris, 'Antioch' (n.949), 2330 (with bibliography). For the early trade relationships, the discoveries in Al Mina, Knossos and Lefkandi in Euboea, which illustrate the influence of the Assyrian empire westwards and Greek sea trade eastwards, especially with Syria and Phoenicia, and its cultural significance for Greece, see W. Burkert, 'Homerstudien und Orient', in *Zweihundert Jahre Homer-Forschung. Colloquium Rauricum* 2, ed. J. Latacz, Stuttgart and Leipzig 1991, 168f.; for the first mention of 'Ionians' in Syria cf. id., *Die orientalisierende Epoche in der griechischen Religion und Literatur*, SHAW 1984/1, Heidelberg 1984, 17; Hengel, *Judaism and Hellenism* (n.314), I, 31f.

1403. Cf. Schwemer, *Vitae Prophetarum* I (n.589), 180–99; on Alexander and Antioch cf. Malalas, 234 (PG 97, 361A).

1404. For identification of Io with Isis see below n.1409.

1405. Strabo 16, 2, 5. Triptolemos was also regarded as a founder in Gaza and *Tarsus* (cf. above, n.871); cf. also Ramsay, *The Cities of St. Paul* (n.814), 168f.

1406. C. Habicht, *'Athen'* (n.1384), 25, 30, mentions only those born Athenians who were on the Persian side.

1407. *Or.* 11, 44–58: 'Inachos had a search made for his daughter Io, who had fled from Hera's jealousy by taking the form of a cow. He charged the Argives under the leadership of Triptolemus to seek his vanished daughter. They looked for her everywhere, on all the ways, in all the harbours, on all the islands and on all the coasts, ready to die rather than give up the search. Now when they came to this mountain, *Silpion* near Antioch, they knocked on the doors of the houses and asked the inhabitants about Io, but got no answer. The Argives remained when they saw the fertility of the area, and settled there.'

1408. Malalas 29 (PG 97, 97A): Ἐνταῦθα ἐιμι εἰγὼ ἡ Ἰώ. Cf. R. Merkelbach, *Isis regina – Zeus Sarapis. Die Religion um Isis und Sarapis in griechisch-römischer Zeit*, Stuttgart and Leipzig 1995, 67ff. on the Io myth.

1409. Herodotus already identifies Io with Isis (2, 41, cf. Diod. 1, 24, 8) and her son Apaphos with Apis. In the great Isis aretalogy POxy 11, no. 1380, 143f., as πρῶτον ὄνομα Isis bears the name Io Sothis (Ἰοῖ Σῶθι); for the Palestinian and Phoenician cities mentioned here see Hengel, *Judaism and Hellenism* (n.314), I, 158ff.; cf. *LIMC* V, 1, 782 on Isis-Io. The identification of Io with Isis has probably similarly found its way into Malalas' version. Iconographically Demeter and Isis are already hardly distinguishable in the first century CE. See F. Norris, 'Isis, Sarapis and Demeter in Antioch of Syria', *HTR* 75, 1982, 196–204; cf. below, n.1449 and nn.1514f. on Apuleius, *Met.* 11.

1410. For the 'harvest of Kronos' see Burkert, *Mysterien* (n.873), 123 n.117. For Isis as daugher of Kronos see the revelation speech of the goddess, the so-called Isis aretalogy, which was attached to temples in inscriptions and was presented by the priestess in the guise of the goddess; see now Merkelbach, *Isis* (n.1408), 113–19: 115; cf. 4.5 etc.

1411. Philo of Byblos F 3b; Serv., *Aen.* 1, 729; Diodore 2, 30: El; Alexander Polyhistor, fr. 3: Bel; Sophocles, *Andromeda* FrGT IV F 126; Plato, *Minos* 315c: in Carthage Moloch. In the Roman pantheon he is identified with Saturn. In Athens the festival Kronia was celebrated in the temple of Kronos and Rhea. Cf. E. D. Serbeti, 'Kronos', *LIMC* VI, 1, 146 no. 30: Kronos with Tyche and Helios with Selene are depicted on a 'golden bracelet' from Syria.

1412. For Dagan see J. F. Healley, 'Dagan', *DDD*, 407–13. Cf. also the unique *yehud* coins, *BMC Palestine*, 181 no. 29 verso, from the Persian period. Iconographically it is most closely related to depictions of the sending out of Triptolemus. H. Kienle, *Der Gott auf dem Flügelrad. Zu den ungelösten Fragen der 'synkretistischen' Münze BMC Palestine S.181 no.29*, GOF.G Y, Wiesbaden 1975, has gathered together the various iconographic sources and interpreted the coins as a syncretistic depiction of YHWH. However, the details indicate that this is to be seen as 'Elijah on the winged wheel', see Schwemer, *Vitae Prophetarum* II (n.134), 255f. Cf. below, n.1446 on the birth legend of Elijah.

1413. For oriental triads of gods see above, 123f.

1414. Normally something can be inferred from the names of mountains. The 'mountains of the gods' in northern Syria had no temples on them; offerings were made to the god of the mountain on an altar. Cf. O. Eissfeldt, *Der Gott Karmel*, SDAWB 1, 1953 (reprinted Berlin 1954); id.,

Baal Zaphon, Zeus Kasios und der Durchzug der Israeliten durchs Meer, BRA 1, Halle 1932; also the cautious reflections in Norris, 'Antioch' (n.949), 2355, on the 'temple of Zeus Kasios' on Silpion (Malalas 28–30). However, Norris does not go into 'Kronos'.

1415. Lucian, *Dea Syria* 13–27, reports only Greek stories about the founding of the temple in Hierapolis, but these do have oriental parallels. However, the cult which he describes is primally Semitic.

1416. Malalas 30, 3: 'Since the time the Argives came looking for Io, the Syrians of Antioch have commemorated this by shouting it every year into the houses of the Greeks to the present day.' Cf. the satire about the begging procession of the dissolute devotees of the Syrian goddess in Apuleius, *Met.* 8, 27ff.; or is this an allusion to Isis' surname 'Ιοῖ Σῶθι, 'Io Sothis' (POxy 1380, 143f.)? For Isis' epithet 'Sothis' (= Sirius, dog star) and the Sothis period see Merkelbach, *Isis* (n.1408), 110ff.

1417. Cf. Elderkin, in *Antioch-on-the-Orontes* I, 83f; Downey, *Antioch* (n.670), 103f. Feldtkeller, *Reich* (n.88), does not go into this.

1418. Malalas 205; he calls the seer Λήιός τις τελεστής. He is said to have written a couple of words on the bust, and then the pestilence ceased. The name seems to be Greek; *LSJ* s. v. λήιτον refers to Hesychius, *Lexicon*, 'λήίτη = ἱέρεια, a public priestess'; cf. Wuthnow, *Menschennamen* (n.1246), who does not list any corresponding form of the name in the transcriptions of 'Levi'.

1419. Cf. Hebrew Deborah (Gen. 35.8; Judg. 4.4ff; 5.1); Wuthnow, *Menschennamen* (n.1246), 43.

1420. Malalas, 265: with the inscription ἄσειστα, ἄπτωπα. A bolt of lightning is said to have struck it under Domitian, and Apollonius of Tyana is said to have refused to make similar protection against earthquakes.

1421. She was regarded as the daughter of the Syrian goddess Dekerto; cf. Herodotus 1, 184; 3, 154; Diodorus Siculus 2, 4–20; cf. W. Röllig, 'Semiramis', *KP* 5, 94f.

1422. Syrian names are not lacking in the inscriptions from Antioch, but are rare by comparison with Greek names (cf. *IGLS* III, iii–xi index for Vols I–III); a plate with menora and four consonants was found in the eastern part of the city (*IGLS* III, 1 no. 789); an inscription in Beth-Shearim, *SEG* XIV, 1957, 835 mentions Aidesios, the gerousiarch of Antioch, as founder; two in Apamea mention the archisynagogos of the Antiochenes, Ilsasios, as founder (*CIJ* II, 803–18).

1423. Oriental influence can also be established later, thus e.g. the Sassanid borders in the phoenix mosaic from Daphne, fifth century CE; see also J. Lassus, 'Antioche à l'époque romaine', *ANRW* II, 8,

1978, pl.VII, fig.12. The tradition in Malalas that Perseus (probably reinterpreted from Perses) introduced the cult of fire on Silpion (*Chron.* 37–38; 199) is probably older.

1424. Isis was already worshipped in Athens in the fourth century. The inscription *IG* II 2, 337 from the year 333/2 attests the cult, which was first introduced by Egyptian traders and then encouraged under Ptolemaic rule; finally, after the end of Ptolemaic rule over the Aegean, when it 'no longer had any political components', it became even more popular. Cf. now Merkelbach, *Isis* (n.1407), 122f. For her worship in Phoenicia cf. Hengel, *Judaism and Hellenism* (n.314), I, 158ff.

1425. Cf. Lucian, *Dea Syria*, 49, 59. The names of the children were inscribed in the sanctuary of the goddess in Hierapolis; locks of their hair were dedicated and they were tattooed.

1426. Malalas, 284f. (PG 97, 429B–C), cf. Downey, *Antioch* (n.670), 234; Norris, 'Antioch' (n.949), 2356; also the depiction of a water festival on the Nile in the mosaic of Palestrina (Praeneste); on this see now Merkelbach, *Isis* (n.1407), 646 fig. 178; the bishops raged against this festival, see F. R. Trombley, *Hellenic Religion and Christianization c. 370–529*, II, (EPRO) RGRW 115/2, Leiden, etc. 1994, 55; cf. id., RGRW 115/1, 73. But those taking part in the festival are also censured in Julian, *Misopag.* 362D; Cod. Theod. 15, 6, 2 forbids it: *procax licentia … foedum adque indecorum spectaculum.*

1427. See above, 183–6.

1428. For the numerous theatres in the city cf. Downey, *Antioch* (n.670), index s. v. Mucianus, the legate of Syria, was fond of going to the theatre and there among other things encouraged the populace to support Vespasian; cf. Millar, *Roman Near East* (n.92), 259f. For Josephus, *BJ* 7, 43–62, 110f., cf. above, n.428.

1429. *Chron.* 283f. (PG 97, 428C–429B); Libanios gave *Or.* 11 on the occasion of such a contest.

1430. Cf. Hengel, *Judaism and Hellenism* (n.314), I, 73. For the giving of oil see above, 187.

1431. For the date of his arrival and his buildings see Malalas, *Chron.* 216f.

1432. It was above all important to prevent the winter inundations by the streams flowing down from Silpion; cf. Downey, *Antioch* (n.670), 181. The Antiochenes explained the reliability of the Roman canal system by the fact that Tiberius had used a talisman made by a seer and priest which the Antiochenes called ὠνεωκά (= ὠνεακά) τῆς πόλεως (see Malalas 233 [PG 97, 359B/C]). An inscription on a building which attests the digging of a canal in 73/74 CE finally sheds light on names of the associations and the *insulae* and on the taxation, see F. Feissel, 'Deux listes de quartiers d'Antioche astreints au creusement d'un canal (73–74 J.C.)', *Syria* 62, 1985, 77–103; cf. also Millar, *RNE*, 86ff., on the military and civil significance of the Orontes canal.

1433. Cf. Downey, *Antioch* (n.670), 154f. For the numerous buildings of Tiberius see Malalas 234f. (PG 97, 360D–361C), who also mentions the burning of the city of which the library was a victim.

1434. See the city plan in Norris, 'Antioch' (n.949), 2324. It was driven through a slum area of the Seleucid city, and was one of the first such colonnaded streets, indeed the largest at that time. For the attribution of the buildings to the different rulers in Malalas see Downey, *Antioch* (n.670), 169–84. It could be that the final construction is to be dated only after 115 CE.

1435. Ignatius, Eph. 9.1, extends the comparison with the building of the temple for the saving event with the 'crane' (μηχανή) for the cross of Christ and the 'rope' for the Holy Spirit, through which the believers are raised to God on high. The buildings of the city did not yet impress Paul.

1436. *Kyrios Christos* (n.150), 99.

1437. Bousset's collection of material is exemplary. It primarily goes back to the use of the title Lord in the 'ruler cult' but he rightly does not attach any great significance to that for the origin of the Christian title (93f.); he refers (94f.) to Drexler, 'Kyrios', *Roscher Lexikon*, s. v. for κύριος as a divine epithet and gives as further examples the London magical papyrus CXXI 706 (Asklepios), 934, 937 (Selene) and the great Paris magical papyrus 1432 (Hecate), cf. 2499, 2502. He can 'pass over briefly' examples in Asia Minor (95) with reference to Cumont, *Les Mystères de Sabazius et le Judaisme*, 63ff. He lists in more detail the examples from Egypt for κυρία Ἴσις. Similarly, the male gods in Egypt are called κύριος. Sarapis is given the title first on later inscriptions and in private documents from Egypt; Bousset also mentions Plutarch, *IsOs*. The instances come from the period between the third century BCE and the third century CE. It seems to Bousset more difficult to 'determine an age' for the examples from Syria. He refers to the old Semitic divine epithets Baal, Adon, Mar, etc. In addition to the inscription of Lukios in honour of 'the Lady Atarcharte (sic!)' mentioned above, n.629, he can point to the examples reported by Dittenberger, Deissmann, Waddington, etc., but does not attach any importance to the epigraphic material from Syria; he now immediately goes on to the reports of the church fathers about the Gnostics and the Hermetic literature, finally reaching his goal, Syrian syncretism. But what have the Hermetica and the Alexandrian and Roman Gnostics to do with Syria? He then also inserts the LXX translation of the name of God into this picture as the 'most universal designation of God' (98). However, here he has forgotten that his earliest examples from Egypt were not divine epithets but were titles of rulers. The LXX translation of the Pentateuch which was the model for all the later instances was made as early as the third century BCE. Here κύριος was chosen as the *Q^ere* for the Tetragrammaton, precisely because it was *not* used by the Greeks as a divine title. None of this is clear in Bousset. Bousset had already attempted to demonstrate that the title κύριος for Jesus cannot go back to an Aramaic 'Mar' (77–84). For criticism of Bousset see already Wernle (see below, n.1462) and W. Foerster, *Herr ist Jesus*, NTF 2. R. 1, Gütersloh 1924; id., κύριος, *TDNT* 3, 1086–91; for Bultmann and Hahn cf. e.g. G. Vermes, *Jesus the Jew*, London ²1983, 103–28. For all too long, none of these critics has been taken really seriously. But cf. now D. Zeller, 'Kyrios', *DDD*, 918–28.

1438. Cf. e.g. R. Bultmann, *Primitive Christianity* (n.421), 177: 'It was, however, the title "Kyrios" which became the most popular … It characterizes Jesus as the cult deity who works supernaturally in the worship of the church as a cultic body. Hellenistic pneumatology, with ecstasy and glossolalia … find their way into the churches. The *Kyrios Jesus Christos* is conceived as a mystery deity in whose death and resurrection the faithful participate through the sacraments' (his emphasis). For Bultmann, the opposite to this is Old Testament-Jewish and popular-philosophical ethics mediated through the 'gospel tradition' and the Hellenistic synagogues: 'In fact, syncretism at first sight!' (165, his emphasis). Taken over by Conzelmann, 'Christ in the Worship of the New Testament Period', in id, *Theologie* (n.505), 125.

1439. Feldtkeller, *Identitätssuche* (n.88), 88. The fashionable worsening 'free from the Torah' is no more correct than 'free from the law'.

1440. I Cor. 8.6:

> εἷς θεὸς ὁ πατὴρ
> ἐξ οὗ τὰ πάντα καὶ ἡμεῖς εἰς αὐτόν.
> καὶ εἷς κύριος Ἰησοῦς Χριστός
> δι' οὗ τὰ πάντα καὶ ἡμεῖς δι' αὐτοῦ.

I Cor. 8.6 combines the traditional Jewish prayer formula from the *sh^ema* with the confession of the one Lord as mediator in creation and is perhaps set over against the monotheizing pagan cults (cf. I Cor. 8.10). Cf. Hengel, *Studies in Early Christology* (n.546), 280f.

1441. Statements like I Cor. 8.4b, οἴδαμεν ὅτι οὐδὲν εἴδωλον ἐν κόσμῳ καὶ οὐδεὶς θεὸς εἰ μὴ εἷς; 8.5, ὥσπερ εἰσὶν θεοὶ πολλοὶ καὶ κύριοι πολλοί and also 10.19 and 20 ἀλλ' ἃ θύουσιν δαιμονίοις καὶ οὐ θεῷ θύουσιν, are explicit 'Jewish-monotheistic' statements, cf. Lev. 17.7ff. (τοῖς ματαίοις = *lasᵉᶜ̔ĩrīm* = goat demons; Deut. 32.17; Ps. 106.37; Bar. 4.7: δαιμονίοις.

1442. For the 'oriental mystery religions' see Burkert, *Mysterien* (n.873), 9. Feldtkeller, *Reich* (n.88), 120ff., emphasizes sharply that there is no evidence of any kind of mysteries in Syria at this time. That is certainly true of Mithras.

1443. Cf. already the LXX: Num. 25.3, 5; Deut. 23.18; III Kingdoms 15.12; Amos 7.6; Hos. 4.14; Ps. 105.28; Wisdom 12.4f.; 14.23 see Hengel, *Judaism and Hellenism* (n.314), I, 68. According to III Macc. 2.30f. King Ptolemy IV made full civil rights for Jews in Egypt dependent on initiation into the mysteries of Dionysus. That is certainly a polemical Jewish distortion of the mysteries, but it is evidence for a controversy over Jewish participation in mysteries in the first century CE, which was regarded as apostasy. It goes back to a historical nucleus, cf. Ptolemy IV's decree on the registration of the heads of the Dionysus associations, G. Zuntz, *Opuscula Selecta*, 1972, 88–101. We have no such reports from Antioch. The apostate Antiochos himself sacrifices in the *Greek* way, i.e. he eats pork, brands the one who is faithful to the law but not the ivy-leaf of Dionysus (cf. III Macc. 2.29); rather, he compels them to offer pagan sacrifice and to work on the Sabbath (Josephus, *BJ* 7, 49–53).

1444. *IGLS*, 769 (mosaic: Hermes with the boy Dionysus [second to fourth century CE]); cf. further Dionysus mosaics in Levi, *Mosaics* (n. 1380); Dionysios as a proper name: *IGLS*, 898: tombstone from the end of the first or the second century; 1071Ad: on a coin of Antiochus Philopator *c.* 95 BCE; 1204: stamp on a roof tile; for the coins see P. Gardner, ed. R. S. Poole, *A Catalogue of the Greek Coins in the British Museum. The Seleucid Kings of Syria*, Bologna 1963, 115, index s. v. 'Dionysus'.

1445. Undated epitaph (*IGLS* III, 946: Κυρι χερε Δομητρι υγιενε); also the honorific form of address 'lord' for prominent persons, which often appears in late Palestinian inscriptions, see above 121 and n.638; *qiri* still appears in the Talmud.

1446. See Schwemer, *Vitae Prophetarum* II (n.134), 235f. n.68. Cf. also above, n.1412 on Triptolemos and Elijah.

1447. Cf. Klauck, *Hausgemeinde* (n.745), 92–7.

1448. I Cor. 8.10; cf. 10.14, 19ff., 26ff.

1449. We have impressive evidence for Isis mysteries outside Egypt at this period from Pompeii, Palestrina and Rome. For the frescoes from Pompeii see N. Yalouris, 'Io', *LIMC* V, 1, 670 nos. 65, 66 cf. V, 2 figs. 65, 66, where Isis is identified with Io (see above, n.1409). But even in Rome the Isis cult could only establish itself relatively late, under Caligula. Before that there was a scandal in Rome under Tiberius when a young man in love tricked a chaste but extremely naive married woman (a splendid example of the δεισιδαιμονία of women) with the help of the priests of Isis so that she received him by night in the temple of Isis as 'Anubis' and went round proudly telling of her night of love with the deity, see Josephus, *Antt.* 18, 65–80. However, this was as yet no mystery; it was a national Egyptian cult (*superstitio externa*). Moreover, this incident was an exception, since the Isis mysteries were intrinsically 'chaste'. In Book 11 of Apuleius' *Metamorphoses*, Lucius is converted from the unbridled libertinism for which he has been punished by being given the form of an ass. See Vidman (n.878), 144. Norris understands the mosaic from Daphne Harbiye near Antioch (second century CE), which Levi, *Antioch* (n.1380), I, 27, 49f., 163ff.; II, pls. Vb, VIIb, XXXIIIa–c XXXIV a–b has interpreted as initiation into the Isis mysteries, as an initiation into the Demeter mysteries, see F. W. Norris, 'Isis, Sarapis and Demeter in Antioch of Syria', *HTR* 75, 1982, 196–204.

1450. Cf. the previous note. For Triptolemos cf. above, 272; Libanius, *Or.* 11, 110: Ἐλευσινία. Ptolemy, the father-in-law of Antiochus II (261–247 BCE), liked her statue so much that he took it with him to Egypt. However, he had to give it back again because his wife became ill. The Eleusinian mysteries even continued to be firmly attached to this place; there were no 'offshoots'. Cf. L. J. Alderink, 'The Eleusinian Mysteries in Roman Imperial Times', *ANRW* II 18, 2, 1457–98. Young men of Antiochene origin are also mentioned in the ephebe lists from Athens. Prosperous Antiochenes received higher Greek education there. See Habicht, *Athen* (n.1384), 290.

1451. We also find depictions of the intoxicated Dionysus on the mosaics from Antioch, see Norris, 'Antioch' (n.949), 2348ff.

1452. Irenaeus, *Haer.* I, 24, 1. Cf. below, 285.

1453. Feldtkeller, *Reich* (n.88), 69, 77f., 80, 107, 178, 225 (no index). In Feldtkeller, *Identitätssuche* (n.88), the key word 'Antioch' appears frequently, see index s. v.

1454. Feldtkeller, *Reich* (n.88), 294.

1455. Berger now differs and puts everything under 'Antioch'. See below, n.1476. For the 'pan-Syrianism' of Vouga, Feldtkeller et al. see already above, 21f.

1456. Feldtkeller, *Identitätssuche* (n.88), 202.

1457. Cf. Tacitus, *Ann.*2, 69, 3: on his deathbed, Germanicus accused Piso, governor of Syria, of having poisoned him: 'The cruel virulence of the disease was intensified by the patient's belief that Piso had given him poison; and it is a fact that exploration in the floor and walls brought to light remains of human bodies, spells, curses, leaden tablets engraved with the name Germanicus, charred and blood-smeared ashes, and other of the implements of witchcraft by which it is believed the living soul can be devoted to the powers of the grave.' In the *senatus consultum* which marked the end of the trial of Piso, in contrast to the literary sources there is no mention of poison or injurious magic; see Eck, 'Baetica' (n.951), 195; for injurious magic cf. H.-J. Klauck, *Die religiöse Umwelt des Urchristentums. Stadt- und Hausreligion, Mysterienkulte, Volksglaube*, Kohlhammer-Studienbücher-Theologie 9, Stuttgart etc. 1995, 169–84.

1458. Lucian, *Philopseudes* 16; for superstition in Antioch see Norris, *Antioch* (n.949), 236–69; see there also the illustrations of the mosaics. Cf. also the prophets 'in Phoenicia or Palestine' in Celsus (Origen, c.*Celsum* 7, 9): the content of their preaching is simply 'Celsus' parody of perfectly good ante-Nicene Christian preaching of a rather enthusiastic type', W. L. Knox, *Hellenistic Elements in Primitive Christianity*, 1944, 83 n.3, quoted in H. Chadwick, *Origen* Contra Celsum, Cambridge 1953, reissued 1980, 403 n.6; see also Hengel, *The Son of God*, (n.117), 30.

1459. Becker, *Paulus* (n.61), 107f.

1460. Ibid., 108.

1461. *Kyrios Christos* (n.150), 75. Bousset for his part refers to his agreement with Heitmüller, *Problem* (n.421).

1462. The fact that Paul has the closest collaboration from two Jerusalem men, Barnabas and Silas/Silvanus, fades right into the background here, as does the fact that Jerusalem plays a far larger part in Paul's letters than Antioch. It is also significant that Bousset, *Kyrios Christos* (n.150), 112 n.2 and 276 n.4, indeed quotes Rom. 15.19, but only goes into the apostle's 'signs and wonders' and keeps quiet about the decisive ἀπὸ Ἰερουσαλήμ, although on p. 75 n.2 he takes back the doubt expressed in the first edition on the basis of Gal. 1.22 'that Paul ever appeared as a persecutor of the earliest Palestinian community' and was not rather only 'an opponent of the Christian movement in Damascus'. For a critical discussion of Bousset and Heitmüller see already P. Wernle, 'Jesus und Paulus. Antithesen zu Boussets Kyrios Christos', *ZThK* 25, 1918, 1–92, who rightly criticizes the neglect of the 'theology of late Judaism'. The response of W. Heitmüller, *ZThK* 25, 1918, 156–74, and Bousset in *Jesus der Herr, Nachträge und Auseinandersetzungen zu Kyrios Christos*, FRLANT 25, 1918, could not dispel his objections.

1463. Hengel, *Judaism and Hellenism* (n.314), index, II, 313 s.v. 'Jerusalem: Hellenism'; id., *Hellenization* (n.180), 22–6; further, id., 'Jerusalem als jüdische *und* hellenistische Stadt', in *Hellenismus*, ed. B.

Funck, Tübingen 1997.

1464. *Kyrios Christos* (n.150), v (our italics). Bultmann also added below: 'Bousset sought to gain an understanding of the *nature of Hellenistic Christianity* (his italics) by investigating the interweaving of Christian ideas ... with the thought world ... of pagan Hellenism. If here he emphasized above all the significance of the mystery religions and Kyrios worship, he already had Gnosticism in view, and this gave a powerful impulse to the present-day discussion of the problem of a pre-Christian Gnosis.' It is significant that Judaism can be completely passed over here. In terms of the history of religion Bultmann was wrong all along the line, especially as he developed the beginnings made by Bousset in a one-sided way. That same year, 1964, I began work on *Judaism and Hellenism* and at the time wrote in the margin: 'If a historical view has become generally accepted and is not constantly re-examined critically on the basis of the sources, it becomes sterile scholasticism.' For Gnosticism see now my sketch, M. Hengel, 'Die Gnosis und das Urchristentum', in the *Festschrift für Peter Stuhlmacher zum 65. Geburtstag,* which will appear in 1997.

1465. Described thus in the *Theology of the New Testament*, 1 (n.421), 130, cf. 132f., on the 'son divinity in the Gnostic myth'; 140 on the understanding of baptism 'on analogy with initiation sacraments of the mystery religions. The meaning of the latter is to impart to the initiates a share in the fate of the cult-deity, who has suffered death and reawakened to life – such as Attis, Adonis or Osiris'. For the waywardness of this alleged analogy see G. Wagner, *Das religionsgeschichtliche Problem von Römer 6, 1–11,* AThANT 39, 1962, and Wedderburn, *Baptism* (n.873), see the indices 481 on Adonis and Attis and 488 on Osiris, with the summaries. In part he points to the observation of A. D. Nock that the NT as a whole, and above all Paul himself, avoids typical mystery language and also largely avoids the vocabulary of 'Hellenistic' religion, see A. D. Nock, 'The Vocabulary of the New Testament', *JBL* 52, 1933, 131–9: 132–4 = *Essays* I, 341–7: 342f.; see also id., 'Hellenistic Mysteries and Christian Sacraments', in *Mnemosyne,* 4th Series 5, 1982, 177–213 = *Essays* II, 791–820; further Burkert, above n.873. According to Bultmann, *Theology* 1, 147, the mysteries interpretation has additionally been supplemented by the 'Gnostic thought of incorporation into the σῶμα Χριστοῦ'. His conjectures become completely fantastic when, following the confusions of R. Reitzenstein (*Die hellenistischen Mysterienreligionen,* ³1927, 108f., 145f.), he claims that 'the Gnostic movement also' – *before Christianity* – 'drew certain Jewish circles into its orbit' and 'attached itself to local cults in the ancient Near East, and in a syncretistic process melted together with them in the form of mystery-congregations; this happened, e.g., when the Redeemer was identified with the Phrygian mystery god Attis. The movement also penetrated the Christian communities in this way.' Ibid., 167 (cf. 292f., especially 293 on Phil. 2.6–11): 'It is plausible to assume that that mystery-conception [of the death of a mystery divinity] readily combined with the Gnostic myth in certain Gnostic groups organized as mystery cults. In one such group, for example, the mystery god Attis had coalesced with the Gnostic Redeemer figure. *At any rate such a combination is present in Paul'* (our italics).

1466. *Kyrios Christos* (n.150), 76, our italics.

1467. We know nothing of the intermediate period between 50 and 100. Cf. Ignatius' polemic against Ἰουδαϊσμός in favour of Χριστιανισμός, Magn. 8.1; 10.3; Philad. 6.1, which has a completely different character from that of Paul in Gal. 2.11ff. But Jewish-Christian tradition continues in Antioch even in the second century CE. That is true of rising Gnostics like the Samaritan Menander around 100 and Satornilus around 120, indeed still for the apologist Theophilus at the end of the second century, see R. Grant, 'Jewish Christianity at Antioch in the Second Century' (1932), in id., *Christian Beginnings: Apocalypse to History. Various Reprints*, London 1983, XVIII: 97–108; for Theophilus see his edition, *Theophilus of Antioch Ad Autolycum. Text and Translation*, OECT 1970, XVII and id., 'The Problem of Theophilus', *HTR* 43, 1950, 179–96; 188ff. = *Christian Beginnings* ... XXI: 'It is surprising to find in the See of Antioch towards the end of the second century a man who represents so much of what Ignatius had attacked seventy years earlier' (193).

1468. *Kyrios Christos* (n.150), 77 (our emphasis).

1469. *Kyrios Christos* (n.150), 78 n.7.

1470. See Hengel, ' "Sit at My Right Hand!" ' (n.117), 118–225, 135ff.; on the Qere 'Kyrios', 156 n.81.

1471. See Schimanowski, *Weisheit* (n.537). Cf. Ps 110.3 (LXX 109.3) and on it Schaper, *Eschatology* (n.538), 101–7, 129, 140f., 162f.; cf. 93–6 on Ps. 72 (LXX 71.17); on church history, 169–73. See also Dan. 7.13 in the LXX version and Hengel, ' "Sit at My Right Hand!" ' (n.117), 183; W. Bousset and H. Gressmann, *Die Religion des Judentums im späthellenistischen Zeitalter*, ³1926, 264.

1472. Phil. 2.6–11; Rom. 8.3; Gal. 4.4; I Cor. 8.6; 10.1ff.; cf. Col. 1.15–20.

1473. See above, n.1459.

1474. For the first time *Kerygma Petri* frag. 2d in Clement of Alexandria, *Strom.* 6, 5, 41; see W. Kinzig, *Novitas Christiana*, FKDG 58,

1994, 142–86.
    1475. Gal. 6.16, cf. 4.21–31; Rom. 2.25–3.3; 9–11; II Cor. 3.12–17.
    1476. K. Berger offers a deterrent example of 'pan-Antiochenism' in his *Theologiegeschichte des Urchristentums*, Tübingen and Basel 1994, in which more than half the work, namely Parts V–XI (178–422) and XV–XVI (580–693), is under the heading 'Antioch'. According to Berger the Paulines and Deutero-Paulines, the Johannine corpus and the Synoptics are governed by 'Antioch'. Even James and his letter, Simon Magus and Samaritan Christianity, and the Roman Christians before Paul's letter (including the Shepherd of Hermas), are put under the heading 'Away from Antioch'. There is hardly any basis for this striking collection (which is at the same time chaotic – and not just in chronology). We note how the learned work has been stitched together with a red-hot needle. I can only explain the laudatory review by Kurt Flasch, 'Klaus Bergers wahre Geschichte des urchristlichen Denkens', in the literary supplement to the *Frankfurter Allgemeine Zeitung* L. 24, no. 230 of 4 October 1994 – 'a great venture which stands alongside Harnack and Bultmann in conception and execution' – on the presupposition that the reviewer did not really read the book, but simply skipped through it and in addition has forgotten what and how Harnack and Bultmann wrote. The investigation by E. Rau, *Von Jesus zu Paulus. Entwicklung und Rezeption der antiochenischen Theologie im Urchristentum*, Stuttgart, etc. 1994, is concentrated on the Hellenists and then above all on Antioch. But what do we really know about 'Antiochene theology'? Schmithals, *Theologiegeschichte* (n.97), see index 331 s.v. 'Antiochien; antiochenische Theologie', conjectures (76f.) an 'Antiochene *theologia passionis*' which Paul will have taken over (80). On 94ff. he then describes the 'Antiochene christology of adoption' (Rom. 1.3f.) and in conjunction with that on 96–105 the ' "Antiochene" soteriology orientated on the death of Jesus' (the influence of Isa. 53, though this goes back to the 'Palestinian sphere'). In contrast to II Cor. 5.21, with the 'Damascene' formula orientated on the incarnation, the Antiochene soteriology was 'orientated on the death of Jesus', cf. Rom. 4.24b, 25; 3.25; I Cor. 15.3–5; I Cor. 11.23–25. Coming first of all from a strictly antinomian universalistic 'Damascene' Christianity which was itself in turn influenced by Gnosticism, later he developed 'the view of Hellenistic Jewish Christianity with an "Antiochene" stamp' into his 'soteriology of the cross' (116f., cf. 90ff., 139, 146). A distinction is also made between an originally Damascene 'understanding of baptism' and an Antiochene version dependent on it; the latter is said to be visible in I Cor. 6.11 (189f.). In *Paulus und Jakobus* (n.132), 23f., he also wants to

transfer the stoning of Stephen to Antioch, 'the home of freedom from the law'. Later he is rather more restrained here, see *Die Apostelgeschichte* (n.1051), 66; *Theologiegeschichte* (n.97), 85: in no way, however, did it take place in Judaea, and it was transported by Luke to Jerusalem. In ibid., 94, he finally conjectures that 'the prophets Judas and Silas', whom Luke similarly transfers to Jerusalem, have 'their home in Antioch' and with the five prophets and teachers in 13.2 will have formed a 'leading group in Antioch of seven members', analogous to the 'seven "deacons" of Stephen'. Thus 'the Antiochene community' is 'the mother community of that Hellenistic Christianity', which up to 70 CE 'organized itself in an association of synagogues' and accordingly the 'Hellenistic Jewish Christianity' dependent on it, as 'by far the strongest part in Christianity', is 'to be termed Antiochene'. Here we have a fine example of the way in which radical criticism of Luke gives free play to the completely unbridled fantastic 'reconstruction' of scholars.

1477. Becker, *Paulus* (n.61), 119.

1478. Rom. 1.9–13; 15.22ff.; cf. Acts 19.21; 23.11.

1479. Suhl, *Paulus und seine Briefe*, 1975, 95f., 326f.; Riesner, *Frühzeit* (n.49), 262f., cf. Acts 18.2; Rom. 15.22; 1.13.

1480. See M. Hengel, ' "Sit at My Right Hand!" ' (n.117), 138, 144f., 151f., 158ff.: elsewhere in the letters Paul no longer speaks of sitting at the right hand of God, but cf. Luke, the Gospel of Mark, which was composed in Rome, and Hebrews, I Peter and I Clement 36.5, which have connections with Rome.

1481. *The Eucharistic Words of Jesus*, London 1966; see also Stuhlmacher, *Theologie* I (n.468), 130–43; Hofius, *Herrenmahl* (n.508), 202–40, esp. 230ff.

1482. Hofius, *Herrenmahl* (n.508), 230–3.

1483. The καταγγέλλετε is indicative and not imperative: in the prayers at the meal they publicly proclaim the saving event in a way which all can hear. There is no trace of an 'arcane discipline'.

1484. Cf. 10.15: τὸ ποτήριον τῆς εὐλογίας ὃ εὐλογοῦμεν, cf. Hofius, *Herrenmahl* (n.508), 234f.

1485. Hengel, *Studies in Early Christology* (n.117), 238f., 269ff.

1486. 1, 66, 3.

1487. *Theology of the New Testament 1* (n.421), 146. Bultmann completely fails to see that the form of the apology allows only a very brief and extremely abbreviated description (that also applies to the following description of the liturgy of the word of God, 1, 67), and that it is in no way a matter of 'liturgical correctness'. For the influence of the Fourth Gospel on Justin see Hengel, *Johanneische Frage* (n.33), 65 [12].

1488. I Cor. 12.12ff. Cf. I Cor. 8.6 and the μία πίστις, Eph. 4.5.

1489. Eph. 4.5; I Cor. 12.13.

1490. Cf. J. Becker, *Galater*, NTD 8, ³1990, 45f.; id., *Paulus* (n.61), 110ff., 260, etc.; Schnelle, *Gerechtigkeit* (n.54), 58f.; U. Mell, *Neue Schöpfung. Eine traditionsgeschichtliche und exegetische Studie zu einem soteriologischen Grundsatz paulinischer Theologie*, BZNW 56, Berlin 1989, 308; Stuhlmacher, *Theologie* I (n.468), 220, 353f. (with a question mark).

1491. I Cor. 10.16.

1492. Cf. the discussion of the contribution of J. McHugh, 'Galatians 2:11–14: Was Peter Right?', in *Paulus und das antike Judentum*, ed. M. Hengel and U. Heckel, WUNT 58, 1991, 328ff.

1493. Against Schnelle, *Gerechtigkeit* (n.54), 54f., who makes the controversy with Peter end in v. 14 and Paul begin something quite new in vv.15–21. Cf. now H.-J. Eckstein, *Verheissung und Gesetz. Eine exegetische Untersuchung zu Galater 2, 15 – 4, 7*, WUNT 86, Tübingen 1996, 4f., though he assumes a longer interval between the conflict in Antioch and the composition of Galatians than we do.

1494. 3.26 For you are all sons of God through faith in Christ Jesus
         27. For as many of you as were baptized into Christ have put on Christ
         28. There is neither Jew nor Greek,
            there is neither slave nor free,
            there is neither male nor female;
    for you are all one in Christ Jesus.

Cf. I Cor. 12.13, where because of the situation in the community (11.3ff.) 'man and woman' is missing; also the expansion in the (early) Deutero-Pauline letter to the Colossians (3.9–12), which not only reverses the sequence of 'Jew and Greek' and adds 'barbarian' and 'Scythian' but also speaks of putting off the old man and putting on the new. Here we have an early explanation of the Pauline baptismal terminology. For the formation of series cf. I Cor. 3.22f.; Rom. 14.6ff. For the antithetical style and formation of series with the sons of God motif, here in the context of the bestowing of the Spirit which belongs inseparably with baptism, see also Rom. 8.12–16, esp. v.13: ὅσοι γὰρ πνεύματι θεοῦ ἄγονται, οὗτοι υἱοὶ θεοῦ ....

1495. In Gal. 2.2 Paul is thinking of his whole missionary activity and not just of his activity in Antioch. Fond as Pauline exegetes are of rejecting the information in Acts as completely unreliable, they do not bother much about this principle when information in Luke fits their own schemes.

1496. Schnelle, *Gerechtigkeit* (n.54), 59; cited with assent by Mell, *Neue*

Schöpfung (n.1490), 308 n.102; Stuhlmacher, *Theologie* I (n.468), 220, 353f. I Thess. 5.5; I Cor. 11.6bc; Gal. 4.6f; Rom. 8.14f. are regarded as further 'baptismal cries', thus Schnelle, *Gerechtigkeit*, 39.

1497. Cf. Acts 16.34: joyful meal after baptism; similarly ActPetr 5. Didache 7.1–4 only deals with the question whether running water must be used and whether there can be baptism when immersion in the water, etc., is impossible; Hippolytus, *Trad. Apost.* 21 (text and German translation in W. Geerlings, *Traditio Apostolica*, Fontes Christiani 1, Freiburg etc. 1991, 256–71). In the *Apostolic Tradition* baptism with the baptismal confession is followed by the post-baptismal anointing, and then the prayer of the bishop for the Holy Spirit and the first celebration of the eucharist in church with the assembled community. H. v. Campenhausen has righly criticized the inflationary conjectures of New Testament scholars about liturgical credal-type formulations at baptism in earliest Christianity, see 'Das Bekenntnis im Urchristentum', in *Urchristliches und Altkirchliches*, Tübingen 1979, 217–72: 239ff.

1498. Cf. Acts 10.34f.; Rom. 2.10f., 25–29; 3.29ff., etc.

1499. Cf. O. Hofius, 'Rechtfertigung des Gottlosen als Thema biblischer Theologie', in id., *Paulusstudien* (n.508), 128; Mell, *Neue Schöpfung* (n.1490), 316f.

1500. Becker, *Paulus* (n.61), 111: 'the new creation' is of Jewish-apocalyptic origin, whereas 'in Christ' is a 'creative linguistic innovation', cf. id., *Galater* (n.1490), 45f.

1501. Mell, *Neue Schöpfung* (n.1490), 308, following Oepke, δύω, *TDNT* 2, 318, emphasizes that the middle here has a passive sense. That corresponds better to the 'Pauline antinomy of the indicative and imperative of salvation' (n.98). Normally the middle tends more to be an active, but there are example in the NT of the middle with a passive meaning, see *Grammatik*, 262f § 317, 'allow ... oneself'.

1502. A. Kehl, 'Gewand (der Seele)', *RAC* 10, 1978, 1008ff., 1019ff., emphasizes the ethical meaning rather too one-sidedly, since what comes nearest is Dionysus of Halicarnassus, *Ant. Rom.* 11, 5, 2, 'put on Tarquinius', i.e. act as an evil tyrant (1008). The image is also used in TestAbr 17, 13: death puts on the mantle of a tyrant and shows himself in his terrible form. The exegesis of the early church almost unanimously put forward the ethical interpretation, as do Zahn and Oepke. Here the eschatological-soteriological motif – which was not understood later – is undervalued: it is about real participation in the 'new creation' brought about by Christ.

1503. Cf. Schnelle, *Gerechtigkeit* (n.54), 193 n.242. The older 'ontological' interpretation appears e.g. in H. Schlier, *Der Brief an die Galater*,

KEK VII, [12]1962, 173ff., who speaks of 'Christ as a heavenly garment prepared for all' (173).

1504. Cf. I Thess. 5.8; Rom. 13.12; Col. 3.10, 12; Eph. 4.24; 6.11, 14.

1505. Cf. *LSJ* s.v.; Kehl, 'Gewand (der Seele)' (n.1502), 945–1025.

1506. II Chron. 5.12: ἱερεῖς σου ... ἐνδύσαιντο σωτηρίαν; Ps. (LXX) 131.9, οἱ ἱερεῖς σου ἐνδύσονται δικαιοσύνην; cf. Isa. 59.17; Job 29.14; Wisdom 5.18: ἐνδύσεται θώρακα δικαιοσύνην; Job 8.22; I. Macc. 1.28: αἰσχύνη. For the further Old Testament examples see Mussner, *Der Galaterbrief* (n.200), 263.

1507. 20.1f. (text: A. M. Denis, *Concordance Grecque des pseudépigraphes d'Ancien Testament*, Louvain-la-Neuve 1987, 816). For being clothed with glory cf. Isa. 52.1; I Macc. 14.9 or Bar. 5.1: ἔνδυσαι τὴν εὐπρέπειαν τῆς παρὰ τοῦ θεοῦ τῆς δόξης.

1508. 29.10 (text: Denis, *Concordance Grecque* [n.15–7], 816). But it is also possible that Eve is to go 'clothed' into the water. Adam goes into the Jordan and God commands him, as soon as he is in the water, to flatten his hair, pray, and remain standing. The miracle at the Jordan (Josh. 3.14–17) repeats itself in a different form; water and angels surround Adam like a wall. Eve's inferiority and proneness to the tempter could be expressed with the command that she is to go into the river clothed. In the Latin *VitAd*, as she emerges from the river her hair has become like *'herba'*, i.e. the Satan does not see her 'naked'.

1509. *VitAd* (Latin) 16.

1510. W. A. Meeks, *The First Urban Christians. The Social World of the Apostle Paul*, New Haven 1983, 155, cf. below, n.1518. For the exegesis of the 'clothes of skin' (Gen. 3.21) in terms of the human body see Markschies, *Valentinus* (n.675), 284–9.

1511. II Chron. 24.20 cf. Judg. 6.34; I Chron. 12.18.

1512. Wagner, *Problem* (n.1465); Wedderburn, 'Baptism' (n.873).

1513. Apuleius, *Met.* 11, 24, 1–5; cf. 11, 24, 3f.: *hanc Olympiacam stolam sacrati nuncupant ... sic instar Solis exornato me et in vicem simulacri constituto.* In 11, 29, 5 Lucius is taught that he needs a new initiation in Rome, because the garments of the goddess *(exuvias deae)* in which he was dressed on his first initiation are deposited in her temple in the province. The Isis cult was organized locally. Cf. also Klauck, *Umwelt* (n.1457), 116ff.

1514. Apuleius, *Met.*11, 6, 5.

1515. Alexander the Great is already said to have put on garments of gods appropriate to each particular situation, cf. Athenaios, *Deipn.* 12, 537e and the numerous instances in F. Taeger, *Charisma* I, Stuttgart 1957, 216 n.40. As depicted on coins, the Hellenistic rulers after

Alexander the Great appear with the attributes of the gods. The twelfth Ptolemy bore the surname Neos Dionysos. Augustus and later emperors held Olympian meals in groups of twelve, dressed in the costumes of gods, cf. F. Kolb, *Rom. Die Geschichte der Stadt in der Antike*, Munich 1995, 283f.; Cleopatra VII, 'in the holy robe of Isis', had herself called 'new Isis', see Plutarch, *Antonius* 54, 6; for Caligula, Nero and Commodus see Taeger, *Charisma* II, 1960, 285f. (referring to Philo, *Leg.* 75–113), 307ff., 396ff.

1516. Wedderburn, 'Baptism' (n.873), 332–42: 339: 'It seems to me undoubtedly true that the widespread convention of attiring priests and worshippers in the manner of their deities would have made this particular New Testament usage a great deal more intelligible in the Graeco-Roman world, and may indeed have suggested to early Christians this step beyond the language of the Septuagint which speaks of a metaphorical wearing or putting on of moral or religious qualities like righteousness. For all around them they saw the adherents of the various pagan cults "putting on" their deities, dressing up as them and imitating their actions.' Cf. Riesner, *Frühzeit* (n.49), 332f., on the question whether in I Thess. Paul is warning against participation in the Dionysius mysteries.

1517. Cf. Ps. 132, 9; TestLev 8.2: τον στέφανον τῆς δικαιοσύνης.

1518. Against Wedderburn, 'Baptism' (n.873), 339; Meeks, *The First Urban Christians* (n.1510), 155.

1519. Rom. 6.6; cf. Eph. 4.22ff.; Col. 3.9ff.

1520. The garment may not be pledged, and if the cloak is pledged it must be returned in the evening, Ex. 22.25f.; Deut. 24.10ff., 17; Matt. 5.40. In the rite of self-diminution in mourning one rends one's garments. Ahijah of Shiloh annonces the division of the kingdom in a prophetic symbolic action by rending his garment into twelve pieces (I Kings 11.30ff.). Christ's robe is 'seamless', like the garment of the high priest (John 19.23f.). Eckstein, *Verheissung* (n.1492), 222: 'With the metaphorical talk of "putting on Christ", Paul reminds the Galatians that their belonging to Christ which is attested in baptism has important consequences for their being: now Christ is the permanent reality which surrounds them.' Here 'putting on Christ' denotes a 'being clothed' with the saving power of Christ in a way which comes from outside *(extra nos)*, completely and utterly as a gift. It corresponds to life 'in Christ' and to 'being baptized into the body of Christ' (I Cor. 12.13).

1521. For Rom. 6 see above, 299.

1522. I Cor. 8.6. The 'unified person' is an unhappy formulation of Mussner, *Galaterbrief* (n.200), 265. In Galatians Paul is not concerned with an ideal unified person but rather with reminding the former (god-fearing) Gentiles in Galatia that with the eschatological initation rite of baptism they have to some degree legally become fully-born Christians, Abraham's seed and sons of God.

1523. Cf. Rom. 6, 13; similarly and more easily understandable in the eschatological context I Cor. 15.53f.; II Cor. 5.2ff.

1524. *Comm. in Rom.* 9.34 (PG 14, 1234 A–B); cf. the further instances in Kehl, 'Gewand (der Seele)', *RAC* 10, 1012f.

1525. Cf. W. Schrage, *Der erste Brief an die Korinther*, EKK VII/1, 426f.

1526. By contrast, in I Cor. 16.17 Stephanas is praised as 'the first fruit of Achaea'; Crispus is a born Jew and president of the synagogue (Acts 18.8); Gaius is the ξένος mentioned in Rom. 16.23 who welcomes Paul and the ἐκκλησία. Paul writes his letter to the Romans as Gaius' guest.

1527. I Cor. 4.15; 9.1f.; 19.22. Cf. Hofius, 'Wort Gottes und Glaube bei Paulus', in: id., *Paulusstudien* (n.508), 148–74: 149, 151, 154, 163.

1528. I Cor. 3.10; 1.14–17; 2.2; Gal. 3.1ff.

1529. Gal. 6.25; Rom. 6.1–11; 8.1–17 etc. This term should not be understood too narrowly.

1530. I Cor. 10.1–13. Cf. K.-G. Sandelin, 'Does Paul Argue Against Sacramentalism and Over-Confidence in 1 Cor 10.1–14?', in *The New Testament and Hellenistic Judaism*, ed. P. Borgen and S. Giversen, Aarhus 1995, 165–82.

1531. Cf. I Cor. 1.30; 6.11; cf. Acts 2.38; cf. 3.19; 16.31–34.

1532. Cf. Hofius, 'Wort Gottes' (n.1527), 169f. Opposing the way in which it is taken for granted that for Paul 'the Spirit is bestowed through baptism', he comes to the convincing conclusion: 'According to Paul, baptism takes place in the power of the Holy Spirit, but it in no way first of all gives the Spirit' (170). The faith through which the believer strives for baptism and makes a confession before baptism is already a result of the Spirit which is at work through the word of the gospel. Cf. also Luke, who similarly knows of an outpouring of the Spirit before baptism (Acts 10.44f.; 11.15).

1533. I Cor. 15.29.

1534. Cf. above, n.88 on I Cor. 15.11. Becker, *Paulus* (n.61), 301, mistakenly derives all baptismal traditions from Antioch.

1535. H. Gese, 'Der Johannesprolog', in id., *Zur biblischen Theologie*, Munich 1977, 200.

1536. Ibid., 201.

1537. This is already visible in individual sayings of Jesus, where – following the language of John the Baptist – βαπτισθῆναι corresponds with dying. Cf. Mark 10.38f.; Luke 12.50; but also in a Christian transformation, John 3.5 and 12.24.

1538. Käsemann, *Commentary on Romans* (n.606), 165, following Eichholz.

1539. Cf. the miracle at Pentecost, Acts 2. When the pious (v.5) Jewish onlookers at the Pentecost miracle who hear Peter's sermon ask what they are to do now, in v.38 Peter replies: 'Repent and be baptized every one in the name of Jesus Christ for the forgiveness of your sins and *you will receive the gift of the Holy Spirit.*' The transition from the notion of the 'baptism' of a fiery judgment to 'baptism' in an atoning and saving fire can already be read out of 4Q541 (Aaron A); cf. Schwemer, *Vitae Prophetarum* II (n.134), 242f.

1540. Eckstein, *Verheissung* (n.1492), 20, on Gal. 2.16. Cf. the remarks on δικαιοσύνη in Rom. 6.12–23.

1541. Acts 17.11; cf. I Thess. 2.14 and also 1.6; 3.4; also in 2.17 the ἀπορφανισθέντες ἀφ' ὑμῶν and the hope for seeing him again very soon could indicate the violent interruption.

1542. I Thess. 2.2; cf. II Cor. 11.25: Philippi (Acts 16.22, 37) is already included here. We must also conjecture a flogging for Ephesus (II Cor. 1) and perhaps in connection with Acts 18.12–17. In that case Paul would have received the synagogue punishment above all in Syria, Cilicia or Arabia, and the flogging from city or Roman authorities on his journeys in Greece and Asia Minor. Here the basic features of what Paul and Luke say about persecution correspond.

1543. Rom. 1.13 cf. 15.22: Διὸ καὶ ἐνεκοπτόμην τὰ πολλὰ τοῦ ἐλθεῖν πρὸς ὑμᾶς, P46, B, D, F, G improve stylistically: πολλάκις.

1544. I Cor. 16.1. Paul had presumably arranged this in Galatia on his journey through there to Ephesus. After the clash in Antioch he wanted to keep his promise for Jerusalem even more. The unity of the community had to be preserved.

1545. I Clem. 47.1ff. presupposes I Corinthians as a letter.

1546. Cf. Gal. 2.12; cf. 1.7; 4.16f.; 5.1–10; 6.12f.

1547. Rom. 15.31; cf. II Cor. 8 and 9 and Acts 21.24; 24.17.

1548. Gal. 3.1–4, cf. Hofius, 'Wort Gottes', in id., *Paulusstudien* (n.508), 168ff.

1549. Cf. the very personal lines Gal. 6.11–17.

1550. The term appears six times: 1.5; 2.2, 4, 8, 9; 3.2, more frequently than in Galatians (four times) and almost as often as in II Corinthians (seven times).

1551. Cf. also I Cor. 1.18; 2.4f.; 4.20; Rom. 1.16.

1552. 2.13 ἐδέξασθε, cf. 1.6. The term is typical of the Pauline (II Cor. 6.1; 11.4; cf. I Cor. 2.14; Gal. 4.14) and Lukan (Acts 8.14; 11.1; 17.11, cf.

Luke 8.11; 18.17, etc.) mission strategy.

1553. 2.2f.: ἐπαρρησιασάμεθα ἐν τῷ θεῷ ἡμῶν λαλῆσαι πρὸς ὑμᾶς τὸ εὐαγγέλιον.

1554. The word appears only in 2.7 and not in the prescript. The apostle's authority is not doubted in Thessalonica, so the preachers did not have to bring it to bear. Here we have a very gentle echo of the problem of I Cor. 9, cf. 2.9.

1555. 2.13: ὃς καὶ ἐνεργεῖται ἐν ὑμῖν τοῖς πιστεύουσιν.

1556. I Thess. 1.6–9.

1557. 1.4 εἰδότες, ἀδελφοὶ ἠγαπημένοι ὑπὸ τοῦ θεοῦ <u>τὴν ἐκλογὴν</u> ὑμῶν. God's love comes before faith. Because they are loved by God, they come to faith. Cf. Rom. 8.6–11; 9.16.

1558. Cf. also Rom. 9.11; 11.7, 28; also Rom. 8.33 and I Cor. 1.27f.

1559. καλεῖν, I Thess. 2.12; 4.7; 5.24.

1560. I Thess. 5.24, cf. 23.

1561. We find a very similar wish expressed as a prayer in the opening of the letter, I Cor. 1, 9: πιστὸς ὁ θεός, δι’ οὗ ἐκλήθητε εἰς κοινωνίαν τοῦ υἱοῦ αὐτοῦ Ἰησοῦ Χριστοῦ τοῦ κυρίου ἡμῶν. Cf. 10.13; II Cor. 1.18; cf. also Rom. 3.4, γινέσθω δὲ ὁ θεὸς ἀληθής, which has been formulated in another confrontation. II Thess. 3.3 is dependent on I Thess. 5.24, but speaks of the faithfulness of the Kyrios, perhaps one of the numerous small indications of the Deutero-Pauline origin of the letter, which is largely dependent on I Thess. The πιστὸς ὁ λόγος in the Pastoral Epistles, I Tim. 1.15; 3.1; 4.9; II Tim. 2.11; Titus 3.8, which is frequently now related to the doctrinal tradition, is clearly set apart from Paul; Heb. 10.23 and 11.11 are closer. See B. Rigaux, *Saint Paul. Les épîtres aux Thessaloniciens*, Paris 1956, 601f. The formula may go back to statements like Isa. 49.7b, where election is similarly mentioned, and Deut. 7.9, cf. PsSol. 14.1. For a discussion of the Pauline prayer formulae see P. von der Osten-Sacken, 'Gottes Treue bis zur Parusie', *ZNW* 68, 1977, 176–99, who conjectures that in I Cor. 1.7b–9 Paul 'has worked over already formed tradition'. Could this not simply be a typically Pauline formula, since there are no really comparable Jewish parallels? Cf. Rigaux, ibid., on I Thess. 5.24: 'This is the final point of Pauline writing. It sums up the whole of Paul's letter, the whole of his apostolate, the whole of his life ... God, who is faithful, calls him and chooses him ... he will hold fast to what he has begun (Phil. 2.6), since he keeps every promise (Rom. 4.21 ...).'

1562. εἰ γὰρ πιστεύομεν ὅτι Ἰησοῦς ἀπέθανεν καὶ ἀνέστη, οὕτως καὶ ὁ θεὸς τοὺς κοιμηθέντας διὰ τοῦ Ἰησοῦ ἄξει σὺν αὐτῷ.

1563. For the passages see M. Lautenschlager, 'Verhältnis von

Heiligung und Heil', *ZNW* 81, 1990, 39–59.

1564. Cf. Acts 17.31; for the Old Testament Jewish linguistic form of the formula I Thess. 1.10 see T. Holtz, *Der erste Brief an die Thessalonicher*, EKK XIII, 1986, 59f.

1565. Cf. Isa. 54.5, 8; 44.6; 47.4; 48.17; 49.7 related to God's own work of redemption with the root *g'l;* 49.26 *yš'.*

1566. Cf. Rom. 2.5: θησαυρίζεις σεαυτῷ ὀργὴν ἐν ἡμέρᾳ ὀργῆς καὶ ἀποκαλύψεως δικαιοκρισίας τοῦ θεοῦ, cf. 2.8; 3.5; 4.15; 5.9; 9.22.

1567. Rom. 5.1–11 (9): δικαιωθέντες νῦν ἐν τῷ αἵματι αὐτοῦ σωθησόμεθα δι' αὐτοῦ ἀπὸ τῆς ὀργῆς.

1568. This is how M. Dibelius, HNT 11, 31937, translates ἔργον τῆς πίστεως. Here Paul in no way understands faith as a 'work'.

1569. I Thess. 1.3; cf. 5.8; 3.6 πίστις and ἀγάπη.

1570. I Cor. 13.13; cf. Col. 1.4f.

1571. I Thess. 4.3f., 7, cf. 5.23 as God's work; II Thess. rightly interprets ἐν ἁγιασμῷ πνεύματος. Cf. I Cor. 1.30; Rom. 6.19. Therefore in all the letters of Paul the believers are ἅγιοι: I Thess. 5.27, cf. 3.13, which is to be understood from 4.14 and 17.

1572. 3.13 ἀμέμπτους ἐν ἁγιωσύνῃ cf. II Cor. 7.1.

1573. I Thess. 2.4: καθὼς δεδοκιμάσμεθα ὑπὸ τοῦ θεοῦ πιστευθῆναι τὸ εὐαγγέλιον ...; cf. Gal. 1.10; 2.4.7f. As a formula in I Tim. 1.11; Titus 1.3.

1574. J. Becker, *Paulus* (n.61), 119.

1575. G. Ebeling, *Luther. An Introduction to His Thought*, London 1964, 48: 'I know of no parallel in the whole of history, in which a spiritual upheaval of such proportions can be studied with anything approaching the same fullness of original sources.'

1576. For Paul's age cf. Acts 7.58: νεανίας (cf. 23.16–18, 22) and Philemon 9: πρεσβύτης.

1577. Through his lengthy lifetime he had time to deepen these insights in old age. These fruits can be read from his last lectures on Genesis, which extend over the years 1535–1545.

1578. H. A. Oberman, *Luther*, Berlin 1981, 166f.

1579. The seven penitential psalms with a German exegesis. Cf. Ebeling, *Luther* (n.1575), 50ff.

1580. Cf. e.g. towards the end of the *Resolutiones disputationum de indulgentiarum virtute* (Bonner Ausgabe I, 15–147): *Ecclesia indiget reformatione, quod est unius hominis Pontificis nec multorum ... sed totius orbis, immo solius dei. Tempus autem huius reformationis nouit solus ille, qui condidit tempora* (146f.).

1581. Ebeling, *Luther* (n.1575), 62: 'which is the very essence of the Reformation'.

1582. 1520 March to May: *Sermon on Good Works;* August: *To the Nobility of the German Nation;* 6 October: appearance of *De captivitate ecclesiae;* November: *On the Freedom of a Christian.* On 15 June he received the bull *Exsurge Domine,* threatening excommunication.

1583. The year 1521, stamped by the papal excommunication and the edict of Worms, left Luther little time for publications: on 3 January he was invited to the Reichstag for 6 April; the hearing before the Reichstag was on 17/18 April; the Edict of Worms on 8 May; and from 4 May to 1 March 1522 he was in protective custody on the Wartburg. December 1521 – February 1522 saw his translation of the New Testament; March, *Invocavit* sermons in Wittenberg; the translation of the New Testament appeared in print in September 1522. In 1523 Luther resumed his lectures and worked out an order of worship. The most important works to appear in 1524 were: *That Jesus Christ was born a Jew; Of Worldly Authority; Letter to the Princes of Saxony against the Rebellious Spirit; To the Councillors of all Cities ...;* 1525: three further writings on the Peasants' War and in November/December *De servo arbitrio.*

1584. Bonner Ausgabe 4, 427f. (translation in Ebeling, *Luther* [n.1575], 39–41).

Index of Biblical References

OLD TESTAMENT

NEW TESTAMENT

Index of Modern Scholars